ALSO BY GRANTLEE KIEZA

Banjo

The Hornet (with Jeff Horn)

Boxing in Australia

Mrs Kelly: The Astonishing Life of Ned Kelly's Mother

Monash: The Soldier Who Shaped Australia

Sons of the Southern Cross

Bert Hinkler: The Most Daring Man in the World

The Retriever (with Keith Schafferius)

A Year to Remember (with Mark Waugh)

Stopping the Clock: Health and Fitness the George Daldry Way
(with George Daldry)

Fast and Furious: A Celebration of Cricket's Pace Bowlers

Mark My Words: The Mark Graham Story
(with Alan Clarkson and Brian Mossop)

Australian Boxing: The Illustrated History

Fenech: The Official Biography (with Peter Muszkat)

MACQUARIE

GRANTLEE KIEZA

ABC
BOOKS

The ABC 'Wave' device is a trademark of the
Australian Broadcasting Corporation and is used
under licence by HarperCollins*Publishers* Australia.

First published in Australia in 2019
by HarperCollins*Publishers* Australia Pty Limited
ABN 36 009 913 517
harpercollins.com.au

HarperCollins*Publishers*
Level 13, 201 Elizabeth Street, Sydney NSW 2000, Australia
Unit D1, 63 Apollo Drive, Rosedale, Auckland 0632, New Zealand
A 53, Sector 57, Noida, UP, India
1 London Bridge Street, London, SE1 9GF, United Kingdom
Bay Adelaide Centre, East Tower, 22 Adelaide Street West, 41st floor, Toronto,
  Ontario M5H 4E3, Canada
195 Broadway, New York NY 10007, USA

A catalogue record for this book is available
from the National Library of Australia

ISBN 978 0 7333 3590 7 (hardback)
ISBN 978 1 4607 0758 6 (ebook)

Index by Kerryn Burgess
Cover design by HarperCollins Design Studio
Jacket images: Macquarie portrait, ca.1805–1824 courtesy Mitchell Library, State Library of
New South Wales [a128471h]; Panoramic views of Port Jackson, ca. 1821 / drawn by Major
James Taylor, engraved by R. Havell & Sons courtesy State Library of New South Wales
[Album ID:839732]
Endpapers: Plan of the town and suburbs of Sydney, August, 1822 courtesy National Library of
Australia [nla.obj-229911701]
Author photo by Milen Boubbov
Typeset in Bembo Std by Kelli Lonergan
Printed and bound in Australia by McPherson's Printing Group The papers used by
HarperCollins in the manufacture of this book are a natural, recyclable product made from
wood grown in sustainable plantation forests. The fibre source and manufacturing processes
meet recognised international environmental standards, and carry certification.

For Gloria Kieza (1931–2019)

Your love and kindness will always be an inspiration.

Prologue

My most fervent prayers will accordingly be offered for the welfare and prosperity of this country, and for the happiness of its inhabitants.

LACHLAN MACQUARIE IN HIS FAREWELL SPEECH TO
THE COLONY OF NEW SOUTH WALES[1]

THE MORNING SUN turned the water a golden hue and cast an aura over the khaki-coloured forests as artillerymen packed black powder and wadding into nineteen cannons that guarded the most magnificent harbour in the world. Whaling vessels were being refitted before sailing off to the hunt. Convicts were unloading Madeira wines, Persian rugs and English vinegar[2] from wooden ships that had sailed way beyond the horizons of London to bring civilisation to the wild frontiers of New South Wales.

Drums were beating outside the two-storey whitewashed mansion that served as Sydney's first government house, sited on the most prominent point of Sydney Cove. Inside this comfortable but perpetually damp home, Major-General Lachlan Macquarie[3] looked up from his desk and gazed out at the stunning vista of a vibrant city that had mushroomed to include 12,000 people[4] since he and Elizabeth,[5] his beautiful young wife, had arrived to take charge.

He had once described himself as an 'awkward, rusticated Jungle-Wallah',[6] back when he was an obscure army officer whose career was fizzling into anonymity after almost two decades in India.

Now, after eleven-and-a-bit years as the fifth governor of New South Wales, Macquarie had transformed the dumping ground for British refuse that he had inherited into a thriving settlement that was on the way to becoming a prosperous nation. Further south, in Van Diemen's Land, he had also overseen enormous change and progress.

Just as his rambling mansion towered over the landscape, the sixty-year-old governor had a formidable bearing, standing more than 180 centimetres tall, 'a clean-shaved, lusty looking man … and very broad-shouldered',[7] as one early resident would recall. His skin was darkened by decades of military service in India, Egypt and New South Wales, his once-sandy hair was now a wiry grey, and his dark, penetrating eyes shone with both kindness and strength. He regarded himself as a liberal thinker, but when his brows knitted, he meant business.[8]

His commanding presence and booming voice had demanded respect ever since he and Elizabeth had sailed through the Heads just after Christmas 1809, to become king and queen of all they surveyed. With them had been their most loyal subject, George Jarvis, whom Macquarie had bought as a slave in India, but who was now a free man, married to a convict Macquarie had pardoned.

In his vast kingdom, Macquarie's seat of power was a newly constructed ornamental chair, which two of his convicts[9] had fashioned from rose mahogany and lined with kangaroo fur. The two prisoners had included the Macquarie family crest in their work, and protruding from the chair's top rail was a carved arm clutching a dagger, the symbol of the Macquarie family's fighting spirit.

Macquarie himself had always been ready for a scrap – from his days as a poor barefoot boy on a remote Scottish island, to his decades as a British officer fighting against the pirates of George Washington in North America, and the hordes of Tipu Sultan in India. In Egypt, Macquarie had waged war against the forces of Napoleon, and a more personal campaign against syphilis.

As a young military officer he had presided over the execution of a deserter and, in Sydney, where he regarded himself as a benevolent dictator offering an olive branch to its native people, he still sanctioned terror and cruel death for any Indigenous person who would not recognise his absolute authority.[10] He was always in conflict with powerful opponents. He had despised Captain William Bligh and relentlessly battled the 'flogging parson' Samuel Marsden.

Now, Macquarie dipped his quill into an ink pot and cradled the writing instrument in his large hand, preparing to put the finishing touches to the farewell speech he would deliver later that day, at a special ceremony marking the installation of his replacement, Thomas Brisbane,[11] as governor.

Macquarie's brow furrowed a lot in these times. As a soldier he had travelled the world, from Denmark to Persia and Jamaica to Russia, yet after all these years, his position of prestige had been usurped not by a warring army but by the power of the pen.

While he had been fortunate to survive the cases of fraud he had committed as a British officer on the take, he now believed he had been dealt a cruel hand, despite the work he had done on the Crown's behalf. There had been many times in his life when his stoic façade had cracked and given way to tears. But this latest blow was almost crippling.

Needing a distraction from such thoughts, Macquarie threw himself into his speech. He wanted to remind his subjects of just what he had achieved, for he had never been shy about his accomplishments, nor slow about self-recommendation. He had named the main street of Sydney and the town square after himself, had overseen the route of Mrs Macquarie's Road to her carved stone seat overlooking the harbour, and told everyone he met of his pride that his first-born son[12] – also named after himself – had been born in this new land of wonder and potential.[13] The little fair-haired lad had been such a welcome arrival for the Macquaries after the death of their daughter Jane – named for Macquarie's ill-fated first wife – and six subsequent miscarriages.

Now Macquarie climbed from his wooden throne and stretched out his large, regal frame. A manservant helped him put on the red ceremonial jacket, with its gold brocade and epaulets, that indicated his status as a British colonial ruler. His fingers fastened the gold buttons as he glanced down to admire his black patent-leather dress boots, imported from Mr Hobby's store in London.[14] Finally, he donned his black bicorne hat, and he and Elizabeth made their way to the vehicle that would carry them 800 metres south to Hyde Park, the area that Macquarie had set aside as Sydney's first public recreation ground.

It was where the colony's first official horse-race meeting had been organised, with much hoopla, by the officers of his 73rd Regiment in October 1810. The carnival had lasted five days, and it had seemed as if all of Sydney and its surrounds had come out to gamble, drink and fight. Macquarie liked a drink, loved a punt and adored women. To admirers he was 'generous-hearted', and he was always 'very liberal to those who befriended him or did him a slight service'.[15]

He climbed into his carriage with ease, despite his advancing years and the aches that came from a lifetime in the saddle. Sydney's residents were well accustomed to seeing him and Elizabeth driving through town, and he would often stop and talk kindly to youngsters.[16]

As he and Elizabeth left Government House, Macquarie took in the view along Bridge Street, named after the stone bridge that crossed the freshwater rivulet known as the Tank Stream. Behind him, the gardens and orchards of his home led down to the government wharf that jutted over the mud flats at the southern edge of Sydney Cove, and across the expanse of the harbour. The green hills dotted with windmills, the rocky cliffs and the bare, sandstone outcrops reminded him of the wild country he had been born into, half a world away.

To his left was the rolling green expanse of the park known as the Domain, and behind him to his right, in the centre of the city, was Macquarie Place, the cornerstone of Sydney's commercial, civic and domestic activity. Its six-metre-high sandstone obelisk had been designed by Francis Greenway,[17] a convicted forger who, under Macquarie's patronage, had become one of Sydney's most prominent architects.

Macquarie's belief in a second chance for criminals with potential had made him enemies among both the London bureaucracy and the growing ranks of Sydney's free settlers. But his own childhood had taught him of the pain and desperation of the poor, and he was proud to see New South Wales earning a reputation as a place where men and women could flourish through their ambition, rather than rot because of their past.

Near Macquarie Place, former convict Simeon Lord[18] had established his three-storey sandstone mansion adjacent to his lucrative warehouse. Sydney had also been a fertile field for emancipist Mary Reibey,[19] and D'Arcy Wentworth[20] who had been the colony's principal surgeon, a magistrate, commissioner of police and commissioner for toll roads, after having been acquitted of four armed robberies in England.

How different this city had been when Macquarie had arrived to take control after the Rum Rebellion, and the overthrow of Governor Bligh! Then, he had found New South Wales in a state of anarchy.

He had immediately reduced the number of public houses and, after introducing a new currency, opened the colony's first bank to house it. He had begun a widespread construction program that would characterise his administration, resulting in an astonishing 265 public works. Streets had been straightened, houses had been numbered, traffic had been ordered to travel on the left and a new barracks had been built for his regiment. He had used money made from the importation of rum to build a magnificently porticoed hospital, even if its bloodletting had earned it the nickname 'The Sidney Slaughter House'.[21]

His improvement program had extended to his own residence, where he had installed the colony's first flush toilet for his wife. His enemies decried such extravagances as 'expensive trifles' and 'fugacious toys',[22] yet they could not deny that he had boosted commerce to unprecedented levels.

New towns had been established to the north and south of Sydney, and agriculture and stock numbers had improved. Exploration to the west had led to the crossing of the Blue Mountains, which had been an economic bonanza for the fledgling colony, though it had meant displacement and sometimes murder for the Indigenous inhabitants already there.

Above all, he had tried to administer law fairly, without regard to rank or class, insisting that men and women should be promoted on their merits rather than through their connections; that a judge had to pay a road toll the same as a convict; that the privileged should not be allowed to flout the law. He had mandated marriage over cohabitation as a way of protecting women's rights over property and inheritance.

While many of his contemporaries saw this land at the end of the known world as one vast outdoor jail, Macquarie saw instead the seeds of a rich and majestic nation. He wanted to remind everyone who would soon hear his goodbye speech that their land was one of limitless potential, and that they had the ability to realise that potential for themselves.

The new continent was still being referred to as New Holland in official documents, yet Macquarie had been the first to use a different name for it in his government reports. He had included this name in the opening sentence of his farewell to the people and the land he had grown to love.

As the carriage arrived at Hyde Park and the large gathering stood to hear his address, the governor alighted and looked around at the community of people he had helped create.

He stepped forward, puffed out his chest, cleared his throat, and in his booming Scottish burr, first heard on a tiny outcrop of the Inner Hebrides, welcomed his people with the greeting:

'Fellow citizens of Australia!'[23]

Chapter 1

*My dear uncle and worthy friend ... I reflect upon the many happy
days I have spent under your kind patronage and parental
care and protection.*

MACQUARIE WRITING TO HIS UNCLE, MURDOCH MACLAINE,
WHILE PREPARING TO LEAVE FOR WAR IN INDIA[1]

THE ARCTIC SOUTH WIND roared and wailed across the
freezing grey-green water of the North Atlantic to batter the
old, weathered face of the Scottish Highlands. The driving rain
that came with it swept and shrieked across the island of Mull,
off Scotland's west coast. It rolled violently over the snow and ice
on the peak of Ben More[2] and continued further west, howling
above the dark and icy waters of the narrow Loch na Keal strait. It
then echoed through the crags and caves of the tiny, far-flung islet
of Ulva, shaking the very foundations of the foreboding place,
which the seagoing Norsemen had called the Island of Wolves.[3] It
was an eerie setting of 'double, double toil and trouble',[4] as bleak
as anything William Shakespeare ever wrote about that dark
Scottish king Macbeth.

This rocky, barren, oval-shaped speck in the Inner Hebrides
was barely eight kilometres long and less than half as wide.[5]

In the summer, warmed by the Gulf Stream, the outcrop of fir trees, nettles and heather was a place of grand beauty, topped at its highest point by Rocky Mountain – Beinn Chreagach – towering majestically 313 metres above the ocean that crashed onto Ulva's coastline. More than 100 different species of birds nested in the azure beauty of the place, including heron and white-tailed sea eagles.[6] Red deer dug up the rocky ground, and minke whales, sea otters, dolphins and porpoises used the sea as their playground.

But in winter, Ulva's stark moors, wedged between the steep hills and cliffs, became lonely, godforsaken, windswept places, their miserable, sodden vegetation cowering for cover against nature's fury. The islet's impoverished inhabitants would be held to ransom by a landscape and climate as fierce as the red-kilted warriors it had spawned.

It was here, in a small worker's croft on the last day of January 1761,[7] that thirty-three year old Margaret Macquarie[8] gave birth to a baby who would one day become known as the Father of Australia. At the time, no Europeans had ever inhabited the fabled Great South Land, Terra Australis Incognita, but Margaret Macquarie's wrinkled, crying child would rule over it for longer than any European before him.

However, on this day – on a mountainous chunk of volcanic rock in a bleak season, among a volatile population of 600 who had known nothing but hardship and war for millennia – such grand ambitions seemed entirely out of place.

Ulva had been inhabited since the Stone Age, bearing shell middens dating back thousands of years.[9] The Norse Vikings settled there about 800 AD[10] as the Scandinavian seafarers conquered new lands all the way to North America and Russia. Ulva became a small part of the Norse Kingdom of the Isles.

In the thirteenth century, the Norsemen reported that Scotland was full of dangerous natives who spoke an incomprehensible language and endured awful weather.[11] Medieval Icelandic sagas, written down on yellowed calf vellum, described Scotland – or Skotland, as it was then known – as an inhospitable country offering rewards only to the bold. One saga warned that anyone wanting to practise robbery should go there, though 'it may cost them their life'.[12]

As the Norsemen began to concentrate on trading rather than pillaging, they were especially nervous about sailing up the west-coast sea lochs around Mull and Ulva, which they referred to as the 'Scottish fjords'. For Norse leaders Ketill Flatnose[13] and Magnus Barefoot,[14] the Hebrides were difficult to control from a distance, and the Vikings eventually lost their hold over the region. But by that time they had intermarried with the local Celts, and the result was a hardy Gaelic-speaking people who for centuries survived whatever nature and mankind threw at them.

In the fifteenth century, Ulva came under control of a clan that called itself the Sons of Guaire – or MacGuaire. Over time the name took various forms, including MacGorrie, MacGurr, McGuire and MacQuarrie (though in later years the Governor of New South Wales would use the spelling 'Macquarie').[15] The clan could trace its ancestry to a ninth-century monarch[16] and the first public record of Clan MacQuarrie details that their chief, John Macquarrie of Ulva, died in 1473. Clan MacQuarrie eventually owned the islands of Ulva, Gometra and Staffa, with its remarkable basalt columns, as well as coastal tracts along a strip of Mull.[17]

The harsh life on Ulva encouraged survival of the fittest, and the MacQuarries earned a reputation as fierce fighters in the battles for Scottish independence in the thirteenth and fourteenth centuries alongside both William Wallace and Robert the Bruce. The MacQuarries' crest was an uplifted dagger, their badge the almost indestructible fir tree, and their war cry *'An t'arm breac dearg'*, 'Here comes the red-tartaned army'.[18]

The bloody wars with the English would later become even more grisly.

On the morning of 8 February 1587, in the Great Hall of Fotheringhay Castle in Northamptonshire, Mary Stuart, the Catholic queen of Scots, knelt on a scaffold draped in coarse black linen. A crowd of about 500 looked on, some in tears.[19] Mary had been found guilty of plotting against her cousin, the Protestant queen Elizabeth I of England.

She stretched out her arms to signal to the axeman that she was ready. He raised the weapon high above his head and brought it crashing down.

The first mighty blow missed Mary's neck and hit her in the back of her head, knocking her unconscious. The second blow severed her neck, except for a small bit of sinew, which the executioner then cut with a third strike. Then he leaned down amid the gushing blood and raised Mary's head towards the crowd.

'God Save the Queen,'[20] he declared, holding the trophy aloft. As he did so, Mary's auburn wig came away in his hand and her head hit the floor, revealing that her own grey hair was cropped short to her scalp. Mary's little lapdog was found hiding under the dead queen's skirts, soaked in her blood and one onlooker[21] reported that 'Her lippes stirred up and downe a quarter of an hower after her head was cut off'.[22]

Mary triumphed in death, though. When Elizabeth died childless in 1603, it was Mary's son, James VI of Scotland, who became James I of England, the first ruler of a united British kingdom and the driving force behind the colonisation of America. His son Charles I, met the same fate as Mary, Queen of Scots, beheaded during the English Civil War that also saw savage fighting between royalists and rebels in Scotland. At the Battle of Inverkeithing against Oliver Cromwell's forces on 20 July 1651, Allan MacQuarrie of Ulva, chief of Clan MacQuarrie, died along with most of his followers.[23] Widowhood became common on Ulva and poverty was rife.

With poverty came crime. Some of the MacQuarries were implicated in illegally cutting down trees for survival in 1720.[24] Others were sent to court at Inveraray Castle in June 1722 for 'illegally disposing of whale oil belonging to the Admiral and his deputies' after a sperm whale was beached on Ulva.[25] They were each fined two shillings and sixpence for every pound of oil they had drained from the unfortunate creature, and were lucky to escape a worse punishment.

To understand the man that Lachlan Macquarie became is to understand the harsh world in which he grew up, where it was not uncommon for an offender to have an ear nailed to a post or an appendage cut off. The MacQuarries lived in an era when public hangings, drownings and burnings were regular entertainments, like the fairground frolics or vaudeville shows of a later age.

At the time of Lachlan's birth, memories remained vivid of how one sheriff had 'hanged two brothers on one tree near Abernethy [a village near Perth] and burned their bodies on the roadside; and how a chief hanged two notorious thieves, parboiled their heads, and set them on spikes'.[26] In Aberdeen, as many as 700 orphans and waifs had been sold as slaves to American planters.[27] Many court records of eighteenth-century executions stated 'concisely the name of the criminal, the offence, and the verdict, whether "clenzit" [acquitted] or "convict" to the latter being crisply appended the sentence, which is too often "hangit" or "drownit"'.[28]

More than 1500 women accused of witchcraft were said to have been executed in Scotland in the seventeenth century, and, as late as 1727, Janet Horne, a senile woman accused by her neighbours of meeting with the devil, was stripped, smeared with tar, paraded through the Highlands town of Dornoch on a pitch barrel then burned alive inside it.[29]

THE 1745 JACOBITE REBELLION, sixteen years before Macquarie's birth, devastated the Highland clans and made the MacQuarries of Ulva even poorer. The Jacobites took their name from Jacobus, the Latin form of James.[30] Charles Stuart, a Catholic descendant of Mary, Queen of Scots, known popularly as 'Bonnie Prince Charlie', tried to take the English throne for his father, 'The Old Pretender' James Stuart, son of King James II of England, a Catholic who had been deposed by his Protestant daughter Mary II and her Dutch husband and cousin William III in the 'Glorious Revolution' of 1688.

Charles launched his rebellion on 19 August 1745 at Glenfinnan, deep in the Scottish Highlands, but the Battle of Culloden, fought on moorland near Inverness on 16 April 1746, ended with the kilted clansmen cut to pieces by the swords, muskets and artillery of the much better equipped and trained English redcoats. The Jacobite Rebellion was over.

The English Government now viewed most Highlanders as barbarous and disloyal savages, and the old order of the Highlands was decimated as the British used the Highland Clearances to break up the clan system of self-rule.[31]

The British banned traditional Highland dress and the possession of arms and bagpipes, which were deemed to be an 'instrument of war'.[32] Some Highland landowners who had supported the Jacobites had their estates forfeited as punishment, or had to sell up because of growing debt. Soon, more than half of the Scottish Isles were controlled by absentee landlords. Small tenant farms were broken up and replaced with crofts on smaller allotments to increase profitability. The plight of the impoverished Scotsmen placed in this desperate predicament touched Lachlan Macquarie's heart all his life and, over the many years he spent working his way up through the British military ranks, he never forgot the plight of his kin.

From the 1500s, rural poverty had forced increasing numbers of Highlanders to enlist in foreign armies, such as the Dutch Scots Brigade, but after Culloden, foreign service was banned. Recruitment into the British Army accelerated as the English empire-builders exploited the natural aggression of what they saw as a warlike people.

The bayonet offered these men a meal ticket and the chance to share in prize money taken from the spoils of victory.

THIS WAS THE WORLD that welcomed Lachlan Macquarie in the bleak winter of 1761.

King George II had died from a ruptured heart three months earlier[33] but Britain was overshadowing the French, Dutch, Spanish and Portuguese to build the biggest empire in history. Its most valuable overseas treasurers were in India and North America. Two weeks before Macquarie's birth, the British had captured the Indian city of Pondicherry from the French and, later that year,[34] retired Virginia general George Washington advertised a reward for the capture of four fugitive slaves. Towards the end of 1761, British Army colonel Henry Bouquet issued the first proclamation against British settlement on Indian lands in America.[35]

There is argument as to the exact site of Macquarie's birth on Ulva. It was most likely in the village of Ormaig where his branch of the clan lived, but local tradition suggests that Margaret Macquarie gave birth near the inlet at Cùl a' Gheata, where his father may have been farming.[36]

The whole island shared the same poverty, though. Most of the inhabitants were tenant farmers. A visitor to the Inner Hebrides reported that their huts were no better than the 'wigwams of the American Indians',[37] and much more poorly constructed than the houses of even the most indigent farmers on the Scottish mainland:

They are generally built of round stones or pebbles, without any cement … The floor consists of the native ground, from which the grass has been trodden by the inhabitants: these floors are in general damp, and in wet weather quite miry. In the middle of the floor … they make a fire of peats, over which, by an iron hook that comes from the roof, they hang their iron pot. In many cottages there is a hole in the roof for the exit of the smoke, in others not; but in every one the apartment is filled with smoke … Round the sides of the room are ranged the little cribs for the beds, which are generally composed of heath, with the roots placed downwards and the tops upward. Above these beds are generally laid some poles, and upon these some turf, which forms a kind of shelf, where they can stow their lumber, and which likewise prevents the rain, which gets through the roof, from falling upon the beds. The cottages are generally thatched with fern or heath, and sometimes with straw … the whole inside of these huts, and particularly the roof, is lined with soot. It is not surprising that their cottages should be unhealthy, and particularly fatal to children … I was informed by some of the ministers, that not one more than one-third of the children born arrive at the age of 12 years.[38]

Lachlan Macquarie was one of seven children. Four of the six sons and a daughter survived. There is no record of how the future governor spent his boyhood on Ulva, but young Lachlan would quickly have become familiar with hand-me-down clothes, roaring gales, hard times and hunger.

His father, who shared his name, was a cousin of Lauchlan MacQuarrie,[39] the sixteenth and last chieftain of the clan. According to local tradition, the father of the future governor of New South Wales was either a miller or a carpenter, probably both. In that penurious environment he probably worked as a farm labourer too.

Macquarie's mother Margaret was the only sister of Murdoch Maclaine,[40] who would become a significant figure in young Lachlan's life. Intermarriage among the Macquarie and Maclaine clans was common.

Murdoch had been apprenticed to a linen manufacturer in Edinburgh at the age of fourteen,[41] and became a lieutenant in the 114th Royal Highland Volunteers[42] aged thirty-one, in the year Lachlan was born. Murdoch would be associated with the British military for the next thirty-six years, initially serving briefly in the Seven Years' War in North America. At the end of that war he became a general merchant in Edinburgh, patronised by most of the lairds and tacksmen – farm managers – from Mull and nearby Lorn and Morven.[43] He was a hard-living man who, along with a large legitimate family, would have at least one illegitimate daughter, whom he married off to a coppersmith. He knew all the bars of Edinburgh and he recorded the names and addresses of prostitutes.[44]

The family connection to the wealthier and more connected Maclaines was of huge assistance to Lachlan as he took his first baby steps into the world upon Ulva's rocky ground. From his earliest days he was aware of the dire straits in which Ulva lay and the decline of his family's fortunes. 'Our ancient clan and name are of late years reduced to great poverty, indeed,' Macquarie would write, 'and I assure you it would afford me the most heartfelt pleasure and gratification to raise a few of the most deserving of them from obscurity.'[45]

WHEN MACQUARIE was seven years old, the British Admiralty commissioned Yorkshireman James Cook to command a scientific voyage to the Pacific Ocean, to observe and record the 1769 transit of Venus. The voyage would help determine the distance of the Sun from the Earth and thus refine the accuracy of navigation as intrepid sea captains continued to make the world a smaller place.

Cook was promoted from master to lieutenant for the voyage, and he and his crew left England aboard the former collier HMS *Endeavour* on 26 August 1768. On board was the wealthy young botanist Joseph Banks, who had funded seven others to join him, including the Swedish naturalist Daniel Solander, two artists and two black servants from his estate.

The *Endeavour* arrived at Tahiti on 13 April 1769, where the observations of the Venus transit were made. Then Cook sailed on to pursue his second, more speculative mission: searching the South Pacific in an attempt to learn more of the rumoured continent known as Terra Australis Incognita.

The *Endeavour* crew mapped the coastline of New Zealand – discovered by Abel Tasman over 100 years earlier – and on 19 April 1770, they became the first recorded Europeans to reach the eastern coastline of Terra Australis when they sighted what Cook called Point Hicks, between the present-day towns of Orbost and Mallacoota in Victoria.

Ten days later, Cook and his crew came ashore on the continent for the first time, at what is now known as the Sydney suburb of Kurnell. They were confronted by two Gweagal warriors brandishing spears and fighting sticks. The invaders had tossed ashore some nails, beads and other trinkets, which were readily accepted and they tried to explain they wanted drinking water. Instead, one of the local men threw a stone at these pale-skinned foreigners who were wearing strange clothes and speaking gibberish. One of the warriors, named Cooman, was shot in the leg with light bird shot. The only effect it had was to make him grab a wooden shield to fend off further attacks. Cook's party pressed on and the locals threw two spears at them before another musket shot sent them running. Banks noted Aboriginal weapons he would later learn were called 'boomerangs'.

There was considerable caution and little interaction between the Europeans and Indigenous inhabitants for the eight days that the *Endeavour* remained at anchor but, by the time it sailed away, Banks had collected about fifty spears he said were abandoned on the water's edge. Cooman's descendants claim that he also took their ancestor's shield and that it is among the collection of Aboriginal artefacts held by the British Museum.

Cook originally called the area Stingray Bay, but later renamed it Botany Bay, after the new and exotic vegetation being found by Banks and Solander. Upon the *Endeavour's* return to England in 1771, Banks took much of the credit for the voyage and became famous throughout the British Empire.

There is no evidence that Lachlan Macquarie ever met the great naturalist, but when Banks and Solander came to stay at Drimnin[46] House on the Sound of Mull in 1772,[47] while exploring the Inner Hebrides, he heard all about the visit. Banks was astounded by the MacQuarrie Clan's enormous basalt cavern on the islet of Staffa, which he named Fingal's Cave. The breathtaking natural wonder would become internationally famous.[48]

A year after Banks visited the Scottish Islands, the venerated writer and lexicographer Dr Samuel Johnson came calling too, along with his travelling companion and biographer James Boswell. They brought along a copy of Martin Martin's book *A Description of the Western Isles of Scotland*[49] as a research guide.[50] Dr Johnson, whose English dictionary had become a landmark in literature,[51] found the islands 'a gloom of desolation',[52] a 'dolorous and malignant place' where the shallow earth grew little more than heath and there was no tree higher than a table. All that wasn't mountain was bog. The people were engrossed in a daily fight for mere survival. For transport, Johnson had to place his considerable bulk on the back of a little highland pony that buckled under the weight. He was glad none of his London friends could see their mutual discomfort.

The esteemed visitors spent a short time with the Maclean family on Mull, but missed their ferry in bad weather and were forced to lodge in the 'mean'[53] hut of Lauchlan MacQuarrie, the clan chief, on 16 October 1773.[54]

Boswell thought fifty-eight year old MacQuarrie a generous host, 'intelligent, polite, and much a man of the world',[55] but Dr Johnson saw an intemperate fool, whose ancestors had reigned on Ulva since 'beyond Memory', but whose 'negligence and folly'[56] had brought financial ruin to his clan and his heritage. He had sired eight daughters and seven sons with two wives, but his lands were far less fertile and the only thing growing for him was debts. His small farm on Ulva was soon to be lost to the rival Campbell family, along with a farm at Ormaig on Mull and the glorious island of Staffa. Over a very liberal supper, the laird told Johnson and Boswell that the ancient law of *Mercheta Mulierum* remained on Ulva, in theory if not in practice. While once the Highland laird was accorded the right to spend the first hours with his vassal's wives on their wedding night, Johnson noted that MacQuarrie had long sold that right for five shillings or a sheep as compensation.

Inside MacQuarrie's ramshackle home, the ornate furniture did not always suit the downsized accommodation.[57] After their meal, Dr Johnson and Boswell were conducted to the best bedroom, where they found elegant beds of Indian cotton spread with fine sheets. Johnson undressed himself but, in the dark, found he was standing in muddy water. The fine bed and linen stood upon the bare earth, which a heavy fall of rain through the broken windows and patchy roof had softened to a puddle.[58]

AROUND THE SAME TIME as Banks and Solander were visiting the isles, Lachlan Macquarie's family moved from Ulva to a small farm at Oskamull[59] on the Isle of Mull. They leased 30 hectares from John Campbell, the Fifth Duke of Argyll,[60] who had helped put down the Jacobites at Culloden and would one day be promoted to field marshal.[61] The family were too poor to stock the farm themselves, so they shared the property with two other tenants, and Lachlan's father worked their tiny parcel of land along with Lachlan and his three brothers, Hector,[62] Donald[63] and Charles,[64] as well as their brother-in-law Farquhar Maclaine, a tradesman, who had married Lachlan's sister Betty when Lachlan was ten.

Growing up in this hostile, unforgiving world in the closing years of the traditional clan system, Lachlan must have known that he would have to fight hard to make his own way through life. On Mull, he lived alongside widows and orphans, saw children and animals abused and mistreated, knew of thieves and rapists, and witnessed smallpox and influenza epidemics as well as plagues of vermin. He watched the herring fishermen toil for hours in the cold, wind and rain to make a shilling for every hundred fish they caught, and saw the forlorn kelp harvesters cut seaweed from rocks and lug it to furnaces to make fertiliser and soap for a few pennies a day. His home was nothing more than a hut but home was where his heart was.

Lachlan's father died of pleurisy when Lachlan was about fourteen and was buried at Kilvickewen in Ulva, alongside Lachlan's two brothers who had died in infancy.[65] Under the protection of her brother, Murdoch Maclaine, Lachlan's mother Margaret would carry on working the land on Mull with the help of whichever sons were on the island.

Macquarie would remember his hardy, resolute ma with great affection wherever his travels took him, referring to her as 'my amiable, good affectionate, mother'. In later years, he would use her brother Murdoch as an intermediary, sending him money to pass on to her and letters to read to her, because she was illiterate. In 1803, when Lachlan wrote to Margaret at her request, he asked Murdoch 'to cause some proper person to read to her',[66] and in one of his letters from India, he wrote: 'Send for my good mother, on receipt of this, and with my dutiful and affectionate good wishes, tell her all my good fortunes, and that she must now live for at least 20 years longer'.[67]

His dear old mother obeyed. From 1794, Lachlan provided her with £20 a year[68] and £30[69] from 1800 until her death, enough to make sure she did not starve or freeze. She would live long enough to hear of his appointment as Governor of New South Wales and die at Oskamull on 29 November 1810, aged eighty-two.

UPON THEIR FATHER'S DEATH, Lachlan and his younger brother Charles were welcomed into Murdoch Maclaine's protective arms, just like their widowed mother. Tradition has it that Lachlan learned to read and write on Ulva and Mull before Murdoch Maclaine sent him to Edinburgh to study at the Royal High School, under its eminent rector and headmaster Alexander Adam,[70] though no record of his ever having been there survives. Rather, the Gaelic-speaking boy was sent to live in the Edinburgh home of a poorly reimbursed teacher; Murdoch paid about 11 guineas a year for Lachlan's schooling, board and washing and a further £1 12s 3d for his clothes.[71]

Macquarie was no scholar. He once described himself 'as not able or inclined to attend much to study'.[72] But by 1776, aged fifteen, he could read and write English well, and his meticulous records of his life as a British officer provide a clear window into history on five continents over five decades.

He also knew enough arithmetic to realise that he could make no money by staying on Mull, so he decided to make the most of the opportunities Uncle Murdoch had provided.

Lachlan never forgot his uncle's generosity and, in later years, he sought to assist his own young relations wherever possible, even if meant defrauding the British Army. He would always have a special place in his heart for his 'dear uncle' Murdoch, who had helped him in 'getting through the world, from my earliest youth, with credit and honour'.[73] Lachlan was always his 'obliged and dutiful nephew and servant'.[74]

Yet Murdoch Maclaine was approaching the point where he could ill afford to be so generous. He had enjoyed success as a merchant for several years but about 1772, he had started to suffer as his customers struggled to pay their bills. The 'black winter' of 1771 to 1772 had killed many cattle in the Highlands, and these losses were compounded by the failure of the Ayr Bank about the same time. Trapped in a web of debt along with his customers, Murdoch struggled on for the next couple of years,[75] but what he needed was a new way to make some money.

The clan chief Lauchlan MacQuarrie found himself in very similar circumstances. Like Murdoch, Lauchlan would realise the only opportunity for him was to fall back on the kind of work his people knew best.

ACROSS THE ATLANTIC, years of simmering tensions between American settlers and the British Government were boiling as thirteen British colonies flexed their muscles and loaded their muskets. There were protests by the colonists against taxation without representation and then boycotts that led to the Boston Tea Party, the destruction of a shipment of the British East India Company's tea in Boston Harbor in 1773 by the underground group the Sons of Liberty, some of whom were disguised as native Americans. Britain responded by closing Boston Harbor. The local colonists of Massachusetts then formed a shadow government to take control of their land. Other American colonies followed and, in late 1774, a Continental Congress was formed to coordinate their resistance against Britain and the Americans who remained loyal to the crown.

Attempts by the British redcoats to disarm the Massachusetts militia in Concord led to a battle on 19 April 1775, resulting in a British withdrawal. The Americans then coaxed George Washington out of retirement and appointed him to command their Continental Army. On 4 July 1776, America's leaders signed their Declaration of Independence.

On the British side, Scottish-born Major John Small,[76] who had served in the war against the French in North America two decades earlier, began recruiting American loyalists and immigrants to fight for the king, along with Murdoch Maclaine's kinsman Colonel Allan Maclean[77] of Torloisk, an old Jacobite rebel.

Starting on 13 June 1775, Small had been building a force called the Young Royal Highlanders, which would become the Royal Highland Emigrants (84th Regiment of Foot). Four days later, Small fought in the celebrated Battle of Bunker Hill[78] and was immortalised in a series of paintings of him parrying the bayonet of a British grenadier, who was about to drive it through the wounded American, General Joseph Warren, the artist highlighting the misery of former comrades at war.[79]

With his financial difficulties growing, Murdoch Maclaine was happy to accept a commission as a captain in the regiment's 2nd battalion on 14 June 1775. Ninety-six men from twenty-six of the Lochbuie farms on Mull enlisted and accompanied Murdoch to America, including Lachlan Macquarie's older brother Hector, who was made a lieutenant.

The 84th Regiment would eventually number 2000 men in two battalions, divided further into twenty companies. Allan Maclean commanded the 1st Battalion and John Small the 2nd.

Murdoch had impressed his commanding officers and, in February 1776, he was ordered to travel to England to organise new uniforms and equipment.

His 2nd Battalion was desperate for clothing after a year spent wearing the worn-out civilian outfits that they had on their backs when they arrived. The previous Canadian winter had been particularly brutal. The men were supposed to be clothed, armed and accoutred as the Black Watch, with dark tartan kilts and red coats, but they did not have enough hats to protect their ears from frostbite, and their holey boots were always wet from deep snow.

Many of the officers had expressed amazement that the men did not mutiny, with Captain Alexander McDonald, who commanded companies in Nova Scotia and Newfoundland,[80] complaining to his superior officers that his bedraggled troops were being mocked at 'every moment' as 'ragged rascals' by the other, better dressed soldiers. The men, McDonald said, were 'horrid and scandalous in appearance'.[81] McDonald, based in Halifax, pleaded with Major Small at Fort Edward, Windsor, sixty kilometres, north-west: 'for god sake send down all the cloathing you have there in order to save the people from perishing the plaids in particular and be so good as to let me know, when you can expect the rest of our cloathing and camp equipage, whether they are ordered or not and what place to come to'.[82]

LACHLAN MACQUARIE was too young for a commission, but when Murdoch arrived in London to procure the uniforms and equipment for his regiment, his teenage nephew knew he had to be part of this great adventure. Life as a subsistence farmer on Mull had no future and Macquarie knew that the British Army offered more possibilities for advancement than any small flock of sheep on a remote corner of Scotland ever could. All his life, Macquarie had a desire to take up a tough challenge, to discover new horizons, to explore all possibilities of advancement. To his young mind, war with the Americans offered him a better life, so long as it didn't end it. His brothers Hector and Donald had decided the same thing, eager to wear the red coat.

The young farm boy sailed from Leith to join Murdoch in London and embark on the voyage back to America as a proud soldier of the 84th.

Lachlan Macquarie's boyhood was barely over, but the life of a poor subsistence farmer was behind him forever.

At fifteen, he had become a man of war.

Chapter 2

1775 TO 1782, THE WILD FORESTS OF NORTH AMERICA

Now I believe I shall remain a soldier for life.
LACHLAN MACQUARIE TO HIS BROTHER CHARLES, 26 JANUARY 1800[1]

ON 27 OCTOBER 1775, King George III had declared American soldiers traitors and refused them prisoner of war status. The 84th Regiment that Macquarie was about to join had been tasked with defending the British maritime provinces, including Nova Scotia, where captured American prisoners were being forced to labour in coal mines.[2]

George Washington had done everything in his power to strike back at the British. He authorised some of his ship's captains to engage in privateering raids, using converted merchant ships fitted with cannons, and often manned by tradesmen, farmers and fishermen rather than sailors. They received no pay unless they managed to capture 'prizes', in which case they received a share of the loot.[3]

Some had remarkable success. The pirate ships *Hancock* and *Franklin* made an unopposed landing at Charlottetown, Prince Edward Island, on 17 November 1775. Three days later, they sailed to Nova Scotia and raided the town of Canso, disrupting the British fisheries there.

As the war marched on, American privateers had devastated Britain's maritime economy with continued raids. Washington's

Scottish-born big gun John Paul Jones[4] became a feared opponent for British sea captains.

Around Christmas 1775, a handful[5] of men from the 84th under Captain John MacDonald[6], the eighth Laird of Glenaladale,[7] had boarded a privateer off Lunenburg, Nova Scotia, while some of her crew were on shore seeking plunder. MacDonald's men had captured those on board and sailed the American ship into Halifax.[8]

As Macquarie prepared for the ocean voyage from England that would take him to the war zone, George Washington was leading a mass evacuation of 10,000 rebel soldiers through the thick forests of Brooklyn and Manhattan. On 30 August 1776, his army suffered a catastrophic defeat at the Battle of Long Island. The British, rolling to victory to the tune of fife, trumpet and drum, now had control of the strategically important New York City. Britain's early expectations that this rebel uprising would be shortlived looked appropriate.

MACQUARIE and Uncle Murdoch, together with twenty-six other untested Highland recruits, sailed for the new world from St Helens Roads,[9] between the Isle of Wight and Portsmouth, on 9 September 1776.

They were bound for the British headquarters at Halifax, Nova Scotia, on board the *Newcastle Jane*, one of six transports in a convoy being guarded by the warships *Vulture* and *Hunter*[10] as they crossed the Atlantic. The *Newcastle Jane* was carrying £20,000 in payrolls for the British war effort, as well as guns, tents, 1164 swords[11] and 3000 sets of uniforms for the underequipped soldiers, many of them from the 84th,[12] garrisoned in Halifax. The Highland kit included 14,760 yards of tartan,[13] red short coats with dark blue facings, red and white or tartan hose, sporrans made from raccoon fur, black leather accoutrements, dark blue bonnets with a flash of black cocks' feathers, and thousands of pairs of white trousers.[14]

Macquarie and his comrades enjoyed relatively smooth sailing until 7 October, when a violent storm separated every ship in the fleet, blowing them all off course. The captain of the *Newcastle Jane*,

A soldier in The 84th Regiment of Foot (Royal Highland Emigrants) in traditional, kilted, uniform, drawn in 1778 by a prisoner of war, at Saratoga, Province of New York. New York Public Library

Edward Carey, managed to rejoin the *Hunter*, but on 19 October, a thick fog blanketed the east coast of the Americas for forty-eight hours, again depriving the transport vessel of her protector.

Murdoch Maclaine was the only man on board who had seen military action, and with the stories of Washington's privateers circulating, he knew he had to get the raw rookies, including his fifteen-year-old nephew, battle-ready. The normal action for sailors besieged by privateers was to give up the ship, row ashore and wait for another ship to rescue them. But Murdoch knew his recruits would obey his command to fight.[15] They were Highlanders, after all.

Murdoch told Captain Carey and his two junior officers that he was taking command of the vessel. His young recruits said they would fight to the death for him and Murdoch then called the eleven crewmen together and told them there was a good chance of encountering privateers in these waters. Murdoch gave a rousing speech, pumping his fist and beating his chest as he tried to animate the sailors, declaring that if they got into a fight with the rebels he expected the men of the *Newcastle Jane* to 'behave like British Seamen'.[16]

The response was tepid. The sailors shuffled their feet and one or two replied that they had not been hired to fight. Murdoch was livid, but out here on the high seas he knew his power was limited, so he quickly changed tack. To 'obviate these objections', he promised them money and 'that persuasive liquor called grog'.[17]

Grog? Well, that changed everything. The men gave him three cheers and 'swore they would not flinch whatever should happen'.[18]

The sailors did not have to wait long for their mettle to be stress-tested.

On the cold afternoon of 23 October 1776, the *Newcastle Jane* was travelling between Boston and Halifax, about 200 kilometres[19] off Cape Race, Newfoundland. Murdoch later recalled: '... at four o'clock in the afternoon we saw a sail to windward bearing down upon us. We soon discovered her to be a rebel privateer. I immediately ordered every man to his station and we stood our course. A little after five o'clock she came within 30 yards of us, on our larboard [left] quarter ...'[20]

The privateer's Yankee skipper ordered the *Newcastle Jane* to lower her colours and surrender.[21] When Murdoch refused, the pirate ship 'saluted us with a Broad-side of her Carriage Guns, Swivels, and Small Arms: But being prepared for her we returned the Compliment so briskly, that in less than an hour she thought proper to sheer off'.[22]

Murdoch and his comrades were vastly outclassed, outgunned and outnumbered. The 200-tonne American ship had a crew of more than eighty, operating ten carriage guns and twelve swivel guns that made the British ship's six three-pounders look impotent. But so many of His Majesty's transports had given themselves up to the rebel pirates that Murdoch and Carey were not about to let down the Highland troops or the ship's owners from Corke.[23]

With night falling, Murdoch wanted to get away from the privateer as quickly as possible in case of a return engagement. But, although the crew hoisted all the sail they could, they soon realised their Yankee rival was 'by much the fastest sailer, and only lagged astern to keep sight of us till morning'.[24] The Americans were staying within striking distance, ready for another assault.

Murdoch spent the night preparing the ship against being boarded, ordering his wild-eyed troops to make nets out of their hammocks and to use them in barricading the deck.[25] The men were on the watch with their muskets and three cannons all night, ready for a surprise attack.

It came at four o'clock the next morning. The pirates bore down on the *Newcastle Jane* again, and Murdoch ordered a cannon to be fired to signal that 'By God' the British were ready. Captain Carey quickly changed course and the Highlanders raked the pirates' deck with fire from their guns.

The onslaught disconcerted the Yankee skipper and again he backed away. But half an hour later, the black morning lit up with a barrage of cannon fire, as though chain lightning were flying across the water. At times, as the guns blazed, the ships were almost at touching distance, within 20 yards of each other.[26] Men on both ships fired at each other with muskets. Hot lead whizzed across the deck of the *Newcastle Jane*. Some of the Highlanders had their muskets shot out of their hands. Many of the lead balls hit the hammocks being used as rudimentary defences. Between decks, Macquarie loaded ammunition for the *Newcastle Jane*'s gunners.[27] He rushed about, his heart going faster than a gale on Ulva.

The warfare continued for five and a half hours, until both ships had all but exhausted their ammunition. Captain Carey 'observed the pirate was satisfied he had true Britons to encounter',[28] and the raiders withdrew again. Under instructions from Murdoch, Captain Carey took his speaking trumpet, and with his voice echoing across the sea, called out: 'All hands ready for boarding.' He then ordered the men to give chase, planning to make 'a prize of the rebel'.[29] But the pirates were even quicker in making their escape, and with just two cannon balls left to fire, Captain Carey gave up the hunt and continued on his voyage to Halifax.

For the first time, a merchant British vessel had defeated an American privateer. The *Newcastle Jane* had taken thirty-nine hits from the cannons, but the Americans had suffered eleven dead and thirteen wounded. Murdoch would write: 'It is very remarkable, that we had not a man killed or wounded, though the bedding, of which we made a breast-work was full of balls … considerable damage was done to our ship and rigging.'[30]

Battered and holey, the *Newcastle Jane* arrived in Halifax on 31 October 1776. Having saved a government cargo worth more than £20,000, and delivered the uniforms and guns so desperately needed, the young Highlanders and their commander were given a rapturous welcome,[31] and Macquarie was paid half a guinea as a reward for his courage under fire.[32]

Major-General Eyre Massey,[33] commander of the British forces in Nova Scotia, later observed that the *Newcastle Jane* had meted out 'what is due to all rebels'.[34]

NOT ALL OF THE YOUNG Scotsmen were so full of fight though. One of Macquarie's cousins, Farquhar MacQuarrie, of Captain Ranald McKinnon's 4th Company in the 2nd Battalion, was caught absconding. Captain Alexander McDonald wrote to Major John Small in January 1776 to explain:

> About McQuarrie the little fellow that deserted from the Yankys into Boston and which General Gage gave up to McKinnon as he was a Highlander the damned rascal deserted and stole a piece of silk and other things from his master Ranald McKinnon. I have catched him and all the deserters that went from me except two, this rascal cost me six pounds odd shillings. I beg to know whether you will have him hanged or Shott. I Lay any money that you will send me word to Let him at Liberty for a bear Reprimand because he is a highlander.[35]

Eyre Massey[36] sentenced young Farquhar and another deserter named Harris to 400 lashes. In the dead of winter, it would have been a death sentence as McDonald went on to explain:

> The whole Garrison has been under Arms to day to see the punishment inflicted on McQuarrie and Harris by a Garrison Court Martial. Each of them are ordered four hundred Lashes and General Massey is So very Genteel as to Leave it to me to remit what part of their punishment I think proper, but the weather was so Excessive Severe that we were Not Able to go through any part of it at all, for fifty Lashes would certainly made their backs Mortify And the Men Could not Stand out so Long so it was put off 'till another time.[37]

IN NOVA SCOTIA (Latin for 'New Scotland'), Major John Small took the young Lachlan under his wing, calling the teenager his 'pupil'.[38] Macquarie kept his nose clean and did as he was told.

He was initially assigned the job of keeping pay records for the regiment – from the foot soldiers earning sixpence a day, to the officers whose parents had bought them commissions. As he would continue to discover, being an officer had its rewards.

In a nod to the records he would keep later in his long run as a colonial governor, Macquarie also kept meticulous records of his own expenses on food, washing and clothing – shirts, shoes, handkerchiefs and a cape that cost 2 shillings and sixpence.[39] Macquarie never lost the habit of valuing every penny he earned and his lifelong practice of meticulous financial record-keeping was evidence of that. He was keen to make money for himself, yet soon he would share it generously with his kith and kin, and remain forever in debt to the more senior officers and bureaucrats who helped him climb the ladder of success. He gave Major Small three dozen bottles of port wine and borrowed money from Uncle Murdoch. By July 1777 Macquarie owed him £20 19s 6d.[40]

Lauchlan Macquarie, the clan chief, was in far greater debt. In 1777 his ancestral lands were sold from under him at a public auction for £9080 to Captain Dugald Campbell of Auchnaba. Dr Samuel Johnson lamented to James Boswell:

> It is scarcely to be imagined to what debts will swell, that are daily increasing by small additions, and how carelessly in a state of desperation debts are contracted. Poor Macquarry was far from thinking that when he sold his islands he should receive nothing ... Every eye must look with pain on a *Campbell* turning the *Macquarries* at will out of their *sedes avitæ*, their hereditary island.[41]

Still, Lauchlan was a tough rooster. In need of a job, he enlisted on 23 December 1777 as one of the oldest lieutenants in the British Army, at sixty-three, knowing that when he had finished marching in the tartan of the 74th Highland Regiment of Foot – the Argyll Highlanders – he could draw a half-pay pension for the rest of his days.

He survived the war in America and then cost the British military dearly, living to 103.[42]

ON 21 JANUARY 1778, the Muster Roll at Halifax of the 1st Company of the Young Royal Highland Regiment of Foot, 2nd Battalion, reported that among its ranks were 'one major command't, one capt.n lieutenant, one ensign, one adjutant, one qr. master, one surgeon, one surgeon's mate, two serjeants, three corporals, two drumm'rs, and twenty eight privates'.[43]

John Small was the major-commandant, the captain-lieutenant was John MacLean and the ensign was Lachlan Macquarie. He had received a commission to the lowest officer rank on 29 April 1777. Meanwhile, Uncle Murdoch was commander of the 6th Company of the same battalion.

The Highlanders spent their time patrolling the coastline and manning distant outposts in Nova Scotia, Newfoundland and New Brunswick. They were also used as marines in amphibious attacks on rebel-controlled territory,[44] though after the battle of the *Newcastle Jane*, Lachlan saw very little close-quarter fighting. His work was mostly confined to garrison work and record-keeping, but it paid better than scratching around in the cold of Mull.

Still, his world travels had only just begun and already he envisaged a very different future for himself.

By now he was right at home at Ford Edward, the 84th's headquarters in the Nova Scotian town of Windsor. Reminiscing with Uncle Murdoch later, he wrote that a soldier could not have been 'more agreeably situated as to a pleasant situation and an agreeable society'.[45] Many of the Highlanders thought Canada a place of much greater opportunity than their villages back in Scotland, and some, including Major Small, eyed homes for themselves for when the fighting was done.[46]

Macquarie's own liking for Canada stemmed more from the high proportion of females, with their 'kind looks and lovely charms'.[47] The dashing young officer was particularly smitten with the 'very pretty' Polly Gray. He was keen to get out of the war and settle down with her in Nova Scotia on some of her family land,[48] but he had many rivals for her affections and the war kept getting in the way.

Macquarie found the 84th Regiment full of corruption. With young officers posted to far-flung frontiers in the Canadian wilderness without supervision or guidance, mischief flourished.[49] Officers were pilfering funds and, in later years, their sleight of hand would give Macquarie ideas to try his own luck at the same game. The 84th had a disproportionate number of officers convicted over misconduct or forced to resign.[50]

One of them, Lieutenant John Maclean, was arrested for both misappropriating the payroll for a company of the 84th then taking goods from a merchant in Montreal and distributing them to his men, all the time ignoring pleas from the merchant and orders from his commanding officer to pay for them. Maclean was allowed to retire from the force on the condition that he eventually made good on the debt.[51]

Before he knew it, Macquarie was shipping out. On 18 January 1781, Macquarie was promoted to lieutenant and transferred to the 71st Highland Regiment. He was glad to miss the hanging of Private Samuel Grimes,[52] who was strung up as a spy in front of the regiment.

Macquarie had learned much about the British Army since sailing to America on the *Newcastle Jane* five years earlier. He had seen discipline administered with the rope and the cat-o'-nine-tails. He had seen the rank and file sleeping on straw outdoors while men in smarter uniforms reclined by fireplaces under solid roofs. He knew about brothels and bawdy barracks life. He had followed orders in the cold wilds of Canada and kept his eyes and ears open but his mouth shut.

Now that his military career was starting to progress, he could see the benefits of life as a British officer even amid the dangers of a war zone.

Life had not been quite so kind to his elder brothers, though.

Hector had been captured by the Americans on 21 July 1776 and died from pleurisy in South Carolina eighteen months later, while a prisoner of the rebels. Lachlan later wrote inside the cover of his brother's Bible, which he kept all his life as a treasured possession:

This Bible Belonged to Hector McQuarie lt. in the N. York Volunteer Regt. of Foot; – who died a prisoner with the rebels in America 7th. Jany. 1778. This Bible was then in his possession – and was carefully kept by a faithful friend of his Lt. John Stewart, till delivered to his brother the present owner [from?] Charlestown S. Carolina.[53]

Donald was captured by French forces, fighting alongside the Americans, in December 1778, but was finally repatriated to Britain in 1780. He went home to Mull to help his widowed mother on her farm, but war had left Donald a broken man and he lived the rest of his life in an 'infirm imbecile state of mind'[54] until his death in 1801 at the age of fifty.

AS BRITAIN faced the potential loss of its American colonies, it began to eye other parts of the world as replacements for the dumping of transported convicts. On 10 April 1779, Joseph Banks appeared before a House of Commons committee on convict transportation, organised by Sir Charles Bunbury, a horse-racing enthusiast whose flyer Diomed was about to win the first Derby, held in 1780.[55]

Banks was asked his preference for a site, 'in case it should be thought expedient to establish a colony of convicted felons in any distant part of the globe, from whence their escape might be difficult, and where, from the fertility of the soil, they might be enabled to maintain themselves, after the first year, with little or no aid from the Mother Country'.[56] The revered naturalist replied that, from his travels with James Cook, the place that appeared to him to be best adapted to such a purpose was Botany Bay, 'on the coast of New Holland, in the Indian Ocean, which was about seven months' voyage from England'.[57]

He said he 'apprehended there would be little probability of any opposition from natives, as, during his stay there, in the year 1770, he saw very few and did not think there was above 50 in all the neighbourhood, and had reason to believe the country was very thinly peopled ...':

He was in this bay in the end of April and beginning of May 1770 when the weather was mild and moderate; that the weather he apprehended was similar to that about Toulouse, in the south of France, having found the Southern Hemisphere colder than the Northern ... The proportion of rich soil was small in comparison to the barren but sufficient to support a large number of people.

Upon the same continent there were no beasts of prey, and he did not doubt but our oxen and sheep, if carried there, would thrive and increase. There were no tame animals and he saw no wild ones during his stay of ten days but he observed the dung of what were called kangaroos, which were the size of a middling sheep, but very swift and difficult to catch. Some of those animals he saw in another part of the bay. There was a great plenty of fish, he ... struck several stingrays, a kind of skate, all very large; one weighed 336 pounds [152 kilograms]. The grass was long and luxuriant, and there were some eatable vegetables, particularly a sort of wild spinage. The country was well supplied with water; There was abundance of timber and fuel, sufficient for any number of buildings, which might be found necessary ... He recommended sending a large number of persons, two or three hundred at least. Their escape would be very difficult, as the country was far distant from any part of the globe inhabited by Europeans.[58]

The Bunbury Committee resolved that it might be of public utility if the laws sending convicts to North America were made to authorise the same to 'any other part of the globe that may be found expedient'.[59]

MACQUARIE'S NEW REGIMENT, the 71st Regiment of Foot, was also known as Fraser's Highlanders, having been raised by Lieutenant-General Simon Fraser of Lovat, under the British system in which high-ranking commissions were awarded to aristocrats who could provide quotas of fighting men.[60] Fraser was the son of a leading Jacobite known as The Fox.

The 71st had arrived in New York City in July 1776 and been involved in the August victory over Washington's men in the Battle of Long Island. Two years later, they had headed south to Georgia to take part in the routing of Savannah and, in March 1780, in the great British triumph at the Siege of Charleston in South Carolina, where Macquarie was stationed after first being posted to New York. In Charleston, Tadeusz Kościuszko,[61] a Polish military engineer fighting for the Americans, was commanding two cavalry squadrons and an infantry unit.

Macquarie was again tasked with garrison duty and keeping the pay records of the 71st as the tide of the war turned. The French had entered the war in 1778 on the side of the Americans and, two years later, the British faced war in India as well, when attacked by the Kingdom of Mysore. The British forces were further divided by battles against the Dutch and, in the Carolinas, they suffered defeats at King's Mountain in 1780 and Cowpens a year later.

Macquarie was fortunate to miss the 71st's action at the Siege of Yorktown in Virginia in October 1781, being on garrison duty away from the fighting. A French fleet under Rear-Admiral François Joseph Paul, the Comte de Grasse, had sunk British hopes on the mouth of Chesapeake Bay in September, preventing reinforcements and supplies for Lord Cornwallis's[62] army at Yorktown.

Spain supplied silver and gold from private citizens in Havana, Cuba, to help the American war effort, and George Washington, backed by the enormous artillery power of American and French generals such as Benjamin Lincoln, Alexander Hamilton, the Marquis de Lafayette and the Comte de Rochambeau, forced Cornwallis to surrender.

On hearing of the American victory, the British Prime Minister, Lord North, is said to have exclaimed: 'Oh God, it's all over.'[63]

Indeed, the defeat all but ended England's hopes. Many of Macquarie's former comrades were among either the 800 casualties or the 8000 captured prisoners.

From the men left in the 71st, two new companies were formed. They stayed in South Carolina until the evacuation of Charleston on 14 December 1782,[64] then 189 of them set sail for Jamaica in the 319-tonne ship *Sally*.[65]

British loyalists left behind fell to the mercy of the rebels. Some were tarred and feathered, some paraded around town bearing placards featuring the word 'Tory' before being horsewhipped. Twenty-four were hanged on a gallows beside Charleston Harbour, with the fleeing British fleet and loyalist refugees in plain view.[66]

Chapter 3

*Your taste and mine coincide as P.G. was a very great favourite of
mine and is so now. I thought her indeed very pretty*
MACQUARIE DISCUSSING AN EARLY FLAME, POLLY GRAY,
WITH HIS UNCLE MURDOCH MACLAINE[1]

THE BRITISH had held the Caribbean island of Jamaica
since Sir William Penn's forces drove the Spanish away in
1655. For more than a century, black African slaves had been used
in the production of sugar, Britain's most lucrative import.[2] The
American War of Independence threatened all that as Britain's
old enemies, France and Spain, were supporting the Americans in
their revolution.

But trouble had begun brewing in the Caribbean long before
the start of the current war. Beneath the sublime beauty of its
turquoise seas, white sands and lush vegetation, there was a
heart of darkness. The unrest among the huge slave populations
on Jamaica and the surrounding British islands bubbled like hot
molasses.

As early as 1760, the slave leader Tacky[3] had led a murderous
uprising with hundreds of followers, only for it to end with
his head stuck on a pike in the marketplace at Spanish Town.

Twenty-five of his followers had committed suicide rather than surrender.[4] As many as 400 slaves and sixty whites had died in the fighting,[5] while about 600 rebels had been either executed or sold away from their families.[6] One captured slave had been chained to a stake and burned alive, and two more put on a 'dry diet' – hung in iron cages over the Kingston Parade until they died of thirst.[7] In 1769, slaves had hatched an unsuccessful plot to burn the Jamaican capital, Kingston, and kill all white inhabitants.[8]

British rule was threatened not just by a rebellion of this kind every four or five years,[9] but also by 'malingering, petty theft, sabotage, arson, poisoning, running away, suicide and armed resistance'.[10]

By 1775, Jamaica had 12,737 white settlers and 200,000 slaves, and the masters were getting restless.[11] American naval blockades were curtailing food imports to the islands and sugar exports to Britain. Thousands of slaves were starving,[12] and something had to give.

The following year, as stories of American victories against the British blew around the West Indies, slave leaders waited until white defences were down. On 3 July 1776, the day before fifty-six Americans – forty-one of them current or former slave owners[13] – signed their Declaration of Independence, asserting that all men were created equal, Britain's 50th Regiment sailed from Jamaica's Montego Bay to bolster General William Howe's army in New York. The removal of troops from Jamaica's Hanover parish was the signal for another mass revolt.[14]

The plot was uncovered, however, and martial law imposed. By October, seventeen ringleaders had been executed. Some were hanged by the neck, others burned alive and some hung in chains for days on public display until they were dead.[15]

MEANWHILE, seeing the British campaign in America tottering, France had decided to regain key territories that had been lost to Britain almost twenty years earlier. While the British plantation owners had been able to quickly quell the threatened slave rebellion of 1776, the local military could do little when

1800 French troops and 1000 volunteers[16] invaded the island of Dominica early on 7 September 1778.

Young British naval officer Horatio Nelson vowed to do his best to make sure the French captured no more. A day after passing his lieutenant's examination on 9 April 1777, Nelson had received his commission and an assignment on HMS *Lowestoffe*, sailing to Jamaica.

He distinguished himself in skirmishes with enemy vessels, and the commander-in-chief at Jamaica, Sir Peter Parker, appointed him as Master and Commander of the brig HMS *Badger* on 8 December.[17] Before long, he took command of the twenty-eight gun frigate HMS *Hinchinbrook*, newly captured from the French, and later of the forty-four gun *Janus*.[18]

THE CARIBBEAN AIR was thick with unrest and heavy with tension as Lachlan Macquarie and the rest of the 71st joined the British force trying to maintain order in the West Indies, the collection of picturesque islands south of those thirteen rebellious United States of America.

Macquarie's time in this grim, sweltering environment was spent doing garrison duty, but he was already winning friends and influencing people in high places. He would later recall that Jamaica's British governor, Major-General Sir Archibald Campbell, showed him 'very civil and friendly attention'.[19]

In Macquarie's opinion, the worst part of Jamaica was not the suffering of the slaves but the lack of suitable white women for him to court. Back at Windsor, Uncle Murdoch, newly widowed after the death of his first wife Anne,[20] was charmed by the beauty of Macquarie's old flame Polly Gray. None of the 'belles' in Windsor had such a powerful effect on Murdoch as the girl Macquarie called 'PG'. Macquarie considered leaving Jamaica for Nova Scotia when the war was over and entertained ideas of settling down with Polly, if she would have him as a husband. He had made many friends around Nova Scotia, and was right at home in Canada's 'New Scotland'. But Murdoch was circling Polly Gray, too. He was a benevolent uncle, and Macquarie wrote to him from his base at the Apostles Battery in Port Royal to say he was actually 'flattered' that his mentor shared his taste in women. The young lieutenant informed Murdoch he would 'willingly relinquish all my claims and pretensions' to the prize and be happy in calling PG his aunt rather than his wife.[21] It was not to be, however. Macquarie sent money home to help his brother Donald with expenses on the farm at Mull and to help younger brother Charles with his education in Edinburgh. He told Murdoch, that with the army about to go home, he still had hopes to retain a position on full pay but, if that was not possible, he had an idea to try his luck in the 'Eastern World', though he did not like a warm climate.[22]

LIKE THE BRITISH ARMY, Margaret Macquarie and the rest of the family back on Mull were suffering heavy defeat as famine and food riots gripped Scotland. The harvests of 1781, and 1782 were bleak. In 1781, the summer was cold and too dry for the grass or corn to grow, and in 1782, some areas saw the corn buried by snow. Then Scotland was blanketed by clouds of dust and sulphurous fog from great volcanic eruptions in Iceland in the summer of 1783. Falling ash shrouded the crops in Scotland's north.[23]

WITH THE WAR LOST, Macquarie was soon heading home – but not before he had fought a fierce battle against fever in Jamaica, where young Horatio Nelson had almost died from malaria three years earlier.

The Treaty of Paris was signed at the Hôtel d'York in the French capital on 3 September 1783, and Macquarie finally sailed out of Jamaica on board the *Martha* on 28 October with five other subalterns and forty enlisted men from the 71st.

It was hardly a relaxing journey. It took seventeen weeks and five days on rough seas. He caught a cold, and water was rationed before the *Martha* arrived in Greenock, Scotland, with her passengers and crew shaken and stirred, on 29 February 1784.

The men of the 71st marched to Perth, which Macquarie thought 'dull', and whose inhabitants he found of a 'very unsociable, uncommunicative disposition' and a 'jealous eye' when they looked at men in uniform.[24] The regiment was officially disbanded.

Lieutenant Macquarie was retired on half pay, but already he was planning to try his luck as a soldier in the British East Indies.[25] Now twenty-three, he had spent a third of his life in uniform, and he found that military life suited him.

In the meantime, he went home to Mull to live with his mother and, in August 1785, paid a sailor a pound from what remained of his officer's pay to buy a headstone for his father's bare grave.[26] Macquarie was young and restless, and while glad to see his family again, a return to Mull meant a return to dullness and routine. He was already planning new adventures but in the meantime took a job as an overseer of Uncle Murdoch's land on Mull, which expanded the following year when Murdoch unexpectedly became the 18th Laird of Lochbuie,[27] following a grisly murder.

The heir to that title, Archie Maclaine,[28] had received the estate from his father in 1775 but, burdened by debt, gave the lands over to trustees and headed to the war in America, where he served as a captain-lieutenant with Macquarie's 84th Regiment in Nova Scotia. He was a 'hot-headed, proud and stubborn man, and was in the habit of using his tongue too freely'.[29] He repeatedly clashed with his commanding officer, Lieutenant-Colonel Allan Maclean.

At a court martial in 1782, Archie was accused of causing every dispute in the 84th Regiment 'for the last three years and a half'.[30] He was called to account for 'conduct unbecoming of a gentleman and officer' – and was found guilty of 'fraudulent commissioning, lying to his commanding officer, perjury and false witness before a board of inquiry'.[31] The court ordered Archie suspended from pay and duty for six months and declared that he should be severely and publicly reprimanded. This sentence was confirmed by King George III, who went one step further and ordered Archie's dismissal from the service, meaning that he lost his commission, which he might otherwise have sold for £1500.

Archie left Canada to lay his case personally before the monarch. He had married loyalist Barbara Lowther in Boston, and took her with him, but it was no pleasure cruise across the Atlantic and he was in a foul mood from the very start. True to form, Archie got into a dispute with a fellow passenger, named Daniel Munro.[32] Although Munro tried to avoid him, Archie was determined to have the last word and kept up the quarrel day after day.

Finally, on 6 August 1784, Archie became so enraged that he marched off to his stateroom to find his sword, vowing to kill his rival.[33] Munro hid behind a door and, as the cocky young aristocrat returned to the fray with sword in hand and murder in his eye, Munro ran him through with his own blade. Archie was just thirty-five and had yet to be proclaimed laird. Munro was eventually acquitted of the crime.

Archie's new wife inherited £779, while Murdoch Maclaine, back from the war, inherited a castle on a yellowish hill in Mull and the grand Moy House nearby, but also the great debts surrounding them. In 1785, Murdoch also became the new clan chief of the Macleans.[34] Macquarie would come to regard his relative as 'a great Highland Laird whose grounds for game are the most extensive in Mull … the best shooting ground in all the Highlands for grouse, black game and the red deer'.[35]

In 1786, at the age of fifty-six, having long since abandoned Polly Gray in Nova Scotia, Murdoch married Jane Campbell, the daughter of Macquarie's second cousin Sir John Campbell of Airds and Ardnamurchan. Together, they eventually had eleven children.[36]

MACQUARIE'S NEW ROLE working for Murdoch involved acting as a 'birleyman', resolving such difficulties as tenant disputes over potato fields and Mrs Alex Maclaine's claims for three lots of cream from the one milking. He recorded his own expenditure in detail: money spent on postage, liquor and wages for his servant, even his one-sixteenth share in a State Lottery prize that put £1 5s into his pocket.[37]

He had come up in the world since his childhood in the smoky hovel on Mull. He bought a scarlet cloak for £1 4s 4½d, and paid another 5 shillings for a pair of black silk napkins. He went out on the town with his brother Charles and uncle Donald Maclaine, and spent £2 on clothing for Murdoch's illegitimate daughter.

Macquarie spent nine months of 1786 on the mainland, mostly working on Murdoch's business concerns in Edinburgh. And between July and September of that year, he was obliged to travel to London to represent Uncle Murdoch at a War Office inquiry into missing funds from the 84th Regiment in America.

Macquarie had kept the regimental records from December 1776 to April 1777, but they had remained in disarray for the rest of the war. There were three sums, each of more than £1000, that Murdoch couldn't account for, and some of his expense claims were knocked back. The 84th's paymaster also accused Macquarie's old commander Major Small of complicity in Murdoch's apparent forgetfulness.

Though suffering a bout of ill health, Macquarie sailed from Leith aboard the *Lovely Mary* on 14 July 1786 and took a room at 41 Whitcomb Street, Leicester Fields, for 6 shillings a week and later at 7 Young Street, Kensington. He gave evidence declaring the paymaster's accusations against Murdoch to be 'Billingsgate libel'[38] – as foul as the language heard at London's notorious Billingsgate Fish Market – and the paymaster himself to be a 'rascal'[39] and the 'greatest of villains'.[40] The War Office agreed and Murdoch and Small were cleared.

However, short sojourns in Edinburgh and London were not enough to satisfy the wanderlust that seven years in North America had created in Macquarie. All the while he was back in Scotland, he longed to see far horizons again.

In total, he would spend two and a half years – until December 1787 – working for Murdoch. For a while, he paid Murdoch's grounds officer John Maclaine to cover his work for him, before giving the job of birleyman to his brother Charles, who described himself as Murdoch's 'ever dutiful nephew'.[41]

His dreams were changing rapidly, mirroring developments around the globe as new lands were reached and conquered.

ON 6 DECEMBER 1785, the British Government finally decided to act on Joseph Banks's endorsement of Botany Bay. Eleven ships, under the command of Commodore Arthur Phillip[42] and the guard of the frigate *Hyena*, sailed from Portsmouth on 13 May 1787. On board were about 800 convicts, male and female, and a smattering of their children. To guard them was a total of about 600 crewmen, marines, British officials and their families.

The *Hyena* escorted the fleet until it left English waters for its eight-month journey to the Great South Land. A week after the fleet left Portsmouth, a convict revolt was quelled and the conspirators flogged; two weeks later, the fleet anchored in Tenerife. On 5 August, the ships reached Rio de Janeiro and on 13 October, they arrived at Cape Town's Table Bay.

MACQUARIE, now almost twenty-seven, and believing that his life and the events around it were worth recording, bought a white, vellum-bound book to use as a diary. He carefully numbered and dated each page, and drew lines down the left and across the top of each one.

On the cover of his new book, he wrote:

Journal – No. 1
Kept by L. Macquarie,
Commencing 15th Decr 1787.

On the first page, he added: 'The late bustle with France having obliged Government to make an augmentation to the Army, orders were issued to raise four regiments to serve in India.'[43]

Thus would begin a lifetime of meticulous record-keeping – characterised by copious underlining, capital letters and exclamation marks – of every detail from the cost of a bottle of wine, to his own follies and triumphs, and his innermost feelings about momentous events that would shape the modern world. Macquarie would wear his heart on his sleeve almost every time he picked up his quill, especially when writing of the women in his life or his family in Scotland, emotion flowing from him as though he were writing romance fiction rather than chronicling battles and bureaucracies. He wrote fully expecting his words to eventually be read by others and, therefore, he put on his best face for posterity. His innermost thoughts, particularly those regarding some of his nefarious dealings, he confined to his private letters.

AROUND THE SAME TIME, the threat of war simmered between England and her constant enemy, France. The French had given every indication of being ready to fight alongside the Dutch Patriots in their battle against the forces of the British ally William V, Prince of Orange. The prince and his wife, Wilhelmina of Prussia, had been forced to retreat from The Hague but, in June 1787, the princess was arrested by the Patriots while attempting to return there, which gave her brother Frederick William II of Prussia an excuse to invade.

On 19 September 1787, the British Cabinet decided to recommend an immediate preparation of the armed forces in case of war.[44] However, the Patriots were expecting French support against the Prussians, but it didn't come and the rebel forces were quickly forced to surrender. Though the immediate crisis was averted within six weeks, Prime Minister William Pitt (the Younger)[45] was only too well aware that his forces had been disastrously reduced by the war in North America.

One of the most difficult English territories to protect against possible takeovers was India. The French had claims over substantial parts of the subcontinent, while the precarious nature of the political situation in the Netherlands, combined with the vast holdings of the Dutch East India Company, presented a constant threat.

The English troops stationed in India were financed by the British East India Company, a trading business that ruled much of Asia. The 'Company', as it was known, was strengthening its position as the dominant military power in India at this time. It was also expanding its fleet, not only to supply England with tea, sugar, silk and calico carried on heavily armed merchant vessels called East Indiamen, but with warships to ensure that Britannia ruled the waves.

For more than two centuries, since the defeat of the Spanish Armada in 1588 gave Britain the control of captured Spanish and Portuguese ships and their treasures, England had aggressively expanded its empire. Back then London merchants had petitioned Queen Elizabeth I for permission to smash the Spanish and Portuguese monopoly of Far Eastern Trade in the Indian Ocean. The Company began importing pepper from Java and soon established a base in the Indian city of Machilipatnam on the Bay of Bengal. Before long, the Company's power eclipsed the Portuguese trading company, Estado da Índia, which had established bases in Goa, Chittagong and Bombay (now Mumbai). Portugal later gave Bombay to England upon the marriage of their Catherine of Braganza to England's King Charles II in 1661.

Officers of the Company became rich and, back in Britain, built vast estates, businesses and political power.

In the meantime, the Dutch United East India Company[46] had expanded their control of the spice trade and such valuable commodities as pepper, nutmeg, cinnamon, cloves and ginger from the Straits of Malacca by forcing out the Portuguese. In the early 1600s, it had become the wealthiest commercial operation in the world with a fleet of 200 ships and 50,000 employees. Its shareholders, who traded on the world's first stockmarket, received an annual dividend of 40 per cent. For more than a hundred years, the British and Dutch East India Companies were aggressive competitors whose battles often ended in bloodshed during the Anglo-Dutch Wars of the 17th and 18th centuries. There were battles with the local populations and with the French over the sub-continent, too.

With the decline of the Mughal Empire, which once ruled more than 150 million people in much of modern-day India, Afghanistan and Bangladesh, the French looked to strengthen their position on India's coastline. They had control of Mahé on the south-western Malabar Coast, Pondichéry, Karikal and Yanaon on the south-eastern Coromandel Coast, and Chandernagor in Bengal. From 1741 the French took an aggressive approach against both the Indians and the British until they were finally defeated by Robert Clive,[47] in a series of campaigns. Eventually, the Company seized control of Bengal and slowly the whole Indian subcontinent.

The Company also launched a joint attack with the Dutch United East India Company on Portuguese and Spanish ships off the coast of China, which helped secure its ports in China and it eventually created a monopoly on Bengal opium to be sold to the Chinese.

By the late 1780s, the Company was rapidly escalating recruitment in Britain to augment its huge private army, which was composed mostly of Indian 'sepoys'[48] trained with European methods and run by British officers. The Company's army soon numbered more than a quarter of a million soldiers,[49] double that of the British Army, and it had the potential to mushroom in strength with the support of as many as 400,000 Indian warriors supplied by local rulers friendly to their British conquerors.[50] The most powerful military force in the Indian subcontinent was divided into the Presidency Armies of Bengal, Madras and Bombay, each of which had its own infantry, cavalry, and artillery units.

Soon Macquarie would add to the swelling tide of troops on that distant shore. Macquarie's old commander, Allan Maclean, now a general, used his connections to appoint Macquarie the oldest lieutenant in Colonel James Marsh's[51] 77th Hindoostan Regiment, on the proviso that Macquarie rounded up fifteen recruits to follow him. Marsh had commanded the 43rd Regiment of Foot at Rhode Island in 1776 during the American Revolutionary War and was now raising the 77th for India.

Macquarie received his recruiting instructions at his mother's home in Oskamull on 16 November 1787,[52] and tramped for miles across Mull and Ulva, trying to gain support among his own clan. Many of his friends and relatives, including Murdoch Maclaine and Lachlan Maclean,[53] the Laird of Torloisk, tried to procure recruits for him, but the local people's appetite for war had waned.

Macquarie lamented that it seemed the aging clan chief Lauchlan MacQuarrie, back from the war in America, 'had lost his Power and influence over them, at the same moment he had lost the Estate of his Ancestors':

> Every fair and lawful means were used by their old Chief and Master, my relation the Laird of Macquarie, and myself; but, such is the aversion of these people to become soldiers or to go abroad, that notwithstanding all the entreaties of their old Chief and Master, not one of his ungrateful clan, (to whom he had been, in the days of his prosperity, a most kind and generous Master,) would enlist or follow me and his own son Murdoch Macquarie, (a lad about sixteen years of age) who voluntarily offered to follow my fortunes, and push his own in India – as a volunteer.[54]

After a month on his recruiting drive, plodding from village to village, croft to croft, Macquarie had just one unreliable sixteen-year-old relative to show for it. So he sailed across to the mainland and hammered the towns of Morven and Ardnamurchan.

Yet, 'notwithstanding all the aid and assistance' of his friends in these districts, too, his recruiting drive again met with no success. He would be forced to search further afield.

So at noon on Saturday, 15 December 1787, a dejected Macquarie said goodbye to his mother, not knowing when he would see her again. With malevolent storm clouds gathering above, he trudged away from her little soot-filled house at Oskamull, heading to another war.

He spent more than a week walking through the cold winter rain, journeying, soaked, for more than 160 kilometres, part of the way in company with his brother Charles and young Murdoch Macquarie, the clan chief's son. He passed through Moy, Lorn and Inverary, then took a ferry across the Clyde on a moonlit night to Greenock, where he slept at the White Hart Inn. With a guide carrying his portmanteau, he hiked through the thick snow and frost on the hills of Cowal and down their steep icy slopes, until he reached Glasgow at noon on Christmas Day.

By 31 December, he had five recruits. He used agents in Glasgow and Edinburgh to hunt down more – men desperate for food, money or a sense of self. At Edinburgh on New Year's Day 1788, he found a few good men and made the best of them a sergeant on the spot. He moved on to base himself at Glasgow's Black Bull Inn, and by 14 January, was able to send Colonel Marsh a list of ten recruits.

Next day he confided to his journal: 'I cannot help observing in this place, the constant and kind solicitude of my worthy and good friend General Maclean, concerning my success in recruiting – he corresponded closely and regularly with me, and sent me very useful and judicious instructions with regard to my conduct on the recruiting service'.[55]

By 7 February, Macquarie had twenty men[56] following him – more than his quota – including his friend and distant relative Sergeant Lachlan Maclean. Another Mull friend, Gillean Maclean, had taken 'particular pains' to procure for Macquarie 'a most valuable recruit, an excellent servant, in Donald Campbell; whom he had enlisted at Edinburgh, and whom he had sent to join me at Glasgow on the 18th. Inst. … to wait upon me as my servant, as such I received him and find him a very good one — he dresses hair remarkably well, waits table and plays very well upon the fiddle'.[57]

Macquarie's recruits were something of a ragtag bunch, but he was proud of the number of men he had gathered, and on 7 February he marched them 4 kilometres from Edinburgh to the port at Leith, with a hired piper providing the music to lift their feet.

TWENTY DAYS EARLIER, on 18 January 1788, the first of the eleven ships in Arthur Phillip's fleet had sailed into Botany Bay. Phillip found the place much less inviting than Joseph Banks had promised. The expansive waterway was open and unprotected against storms, and the water was too shallow for the ships to anchor close to shore. The soil was also poor and fresh water was scarce.

Phillip decided to sail on up the coast for a better site for his settlement, and on the night of 25 January 1788, aboard HMS *Supply*, he sailed into Port Jackson and what he thought the finest harbour in the world.[58]

The next morning, men came ashore and started clearing land to make a camp. That evening, they erected a flag pole and raised the Union Jack, and to volleys of musket fire from his marines, Phillip saluted the King's health and the future of this new colony. He found a freshwater spring in a cove that he named in honour of Lord Sydney, the British Home Secretary.

Before long, the new settlers were approached by the curious but suspicious Eora people. Phillip's official orders regarding the Indigenous tribes he would encounter were to 'conciliate their affections', to 'live in amity and kindness with them', and to punish anyone who should 'wantonly destroy them, or give

The First Fleet passes through Sydney Heads. As depicted on the centenary of that event, 1888. State Library of NSW

them any unnecessary interruption in the exercise of their several occupations'.[59] Phillip's plan was to cultivate friendship with the Indigenous people so they would provide help to the new arrivals and Phillip planned to impress them so as to 'give them a High Opinion of their New Guests'.[60] The early meetings between the two peoples were marked with 'friendliness, curiosity, gift giving and dancing together on the beaches'.[61]

The Eora wondered if these pale creatures were ghosts. They pondered over their gender because their clothing was so strange and they were clean shaven, though the question was answered when Phillip ordered one of the sailors to drop his pants to prove the new arrivals were men.[62] At other times, the Eora made overt displays of their physical strength and ferocity. Warriors stood on beaches and clifftops, brandishing weapons and shouting angry warnings not to come too close. At what became the suburb of Manly, warriors waded out to meet a British longboat in a show of strength. Phillip wanted a peaceful co-existence but he wanted the Eora to realise the new arrivals had much superior firepower. Marine officer Watkin Tench[63] wrote that the first object of the British was to 'win the affections' of the Indigenous people 'and our next was to convince them of the superiority we possessed: for without the latter, the former we knew would be of little importance'.[64] The British fired their muskets over the heads of the Eora and shot musket balls right through their wooden shields.[65]

While Arthur Phillip was overseeing the birth of European settlement in Australia, Lachlan Macquarie had booked a passage to India.

News of the First Fleet's successful landing in Britain's new colony was still months away when he made ready to ship out from Scotland with his twenty recruits.

Chapter 4

*Out of sixteen cabin passengers, there were only three that I could
with any satisfaction, either speak to or converse with ... all the rest,
were gentleman's footmen, boys, and whores, going to
hunt after their fortunes in London.*

A DISGRUNTLED LACHLAN MACQUARIE ON THE FIRST UNCOMFORTABLE
LEG OF HIS JOURNEY TO INDIA, 17 FEBRUARY 1788[1]

Off shore at Leith, Captain Mackie and his packet boat
Livingston were at anchor, preparing to set sail. Macquarie
had agreed to pay 1 guinea for each recruit and 2 guineas for his
own cabin, 'the captain engaging to give good usage and to land
myself and party at Gravesend'.[2]

The men were sent to the ship in small boats and a piper played
them on board. Having seen them safely onto the vessel, Macquarie
returned to shore and headed for Gibb's Coffee House, where his
Uncle Murdoch, debts or no debts, had gathered Macquarie's
brother Charles and some of the Highland chiefs, including Maclean
of Drimnin, who had once entertained Joseph Banks on Mull.[3]
The group of old friends enjoyed a 'most excellent farewell dinner'.[4]

Macquarie, Charles and Murdoch Macquarie then boarded the
Livingston, where Macquarie found his recruits in good spirits.

Their accommodation was 'pretty tolerable', and Macquarie procured some fine porter from Captain Mackie for them all to drink before they retired to rest.

It was going to be a rough voyage in more ways than one. Macquarie's own men were fair enough, but already he was finding the raucous company of the other ne'er-do-wells he was 'doomed for some time to live with ... not at all so agreeable'.[5] He preferred the society of a little terrier dog, Carnag, which he was delivering for the family of Murdoch Maclaine's wife to Lady Frederick Campbell in London.[6] He wrote some thank-you letters to General Maclean that he gave to Charles to forward, and the two brothers embraced 'tenderly' and said their goodbyes at about 8 p.m.

An ill wind was blowing off the North Sea, and it would be five days before the *Livingston* finally left Leith. Macquarie used this time to do some accounting, and realised the extent of Uncle Murdoch's 'uncommon generosity'. He noted that 'ever peculiar to himself whenever my interest was concerned', Murdoch had furnished him with whatever money he had required to raise his quota of men, as well as to fit himself up for an East India voyage. Macquarie now owed him £127 17s but Murdoch told him he was in no hurry for the money.

When the *Livingston* finally set sail on 12 February, the anticipated four-day journey stretched to four weeks because of 'tempestuous' winds and rough seas. Captain Mackie had to take refuge for ten days in the mouth of the River Tyne, near Newcastle.

The gales continued as the *Livingston* wobbled down the English coast, powerless against nature's fury. Captain Mackie again took refuge in the mouth of a river – this time, the Humber near Hull, where 100 other boats were likewise sheltering from the storm. Macquarie and his men watched in astonishment as 'an unfortunate brig, sailing very close to ours ... was drove on shore near the lighthouse, by the violence of the gale and surge, and in about half an hour was dashed all to pieces'.[7]

Finally, on 5 March 1788, they dropped anchor in the River Thames, a few miles from Gravesend. The next day, they disembarked. Macquarie lodged his men in an ale house, met the Mayor of Gravesend and, over dinner, settled his account for the voyage with Captain Mackie. The Mayor of Gravesend ordered a constable to provide a cart for transporting the baggage of the men to their first stop on the way to Dover Castle, the largest fortress in England,[8] where the rest of the regiment was assembling.

At 3 p.m. on 6 March, the men marched stoutly from Gravesend, with Macquarie leading by way of encouragement. They kept up the pace for five hours through the little towns and villages of Kent, 'without a man being knocked up or even being much fatigued'.[9]

On their arrival at Dover Castle, Macquarie found the regiment was nearly complete, with 600 men already there. The senior officer was another Scot, Captain James Dunlop,[10] late of the 82nd and an old American acquaintance of Macquarie's.

On the morning of 12 March, Macquarie's recruits were paraded very early and, after a strict examination by Lieutenant-Colonel James Balfour,[11] Macquarie was mortified when four of them were rejected.

Balfour told Macquarie that recruit McKenzie had a 'rupture', McInnes was too old and – wait for it – Waddle and Dick were too small.[12] Macquarie complained of the 'very great and cruel loss', having paid the men 'very high bounties' to join him as well as having 'subsisted them for some months and paid their passage from Scotland'.

But all these arguments achieved nothing when put to the stern-faced Balfour. Macquarie did some sums in his head and calculated that the rejection of his four recruits had cost him about 40 guineas. Times had been lean in the Highlands for a long time, and the loss gave Macquarie 'no small uneasiness, as I could not well afford it'.[13] He stewed over the situation.

While Macquarie had hoped for support from 'the old gentleman' Colonel Marsh, he was received with none of 'that civility and attention that I might naturally expect', nor 'with that politeness that I had always been accustomed to, from my former colonels, and commanding officers'.[14]

Marsh expressed great surprise that Macquarie had brought so few men under his command, 'without making the smallest allowance for the length and tediousness of my unavoidable long voyage from Scotland'. Apparently, he 'expected from what he was told, of the great interest and influence' that Macquarie's friends had in the Highlands, that the young lieutenant would be bringing at least 100 recruits for the regiment.[15]

There was some consolation, though. Balfour appointed Macquarie to command the 5th Company, 'one of the best battalion companies in the regiment'.[16] The men drilled and practised with sword and bayonet as Macquarie took five days' leave to visit London and fit himself out for the voyage to India.

He took the overnight mail coach from Dover with two friends and stayed at the Cecil Street Coffee House in the Strand, run by one of the Macleans. He dined with General Maclean and his wife and visited his old battalion commander, now Colonel Small, who was staying with other former officers of the 84th. Macquarie then collected his pay right up until 23 September 1788, 'order'd by His Majesty to be paid in advance to the four regiments going to India'. He sent £45 of it to Uncle Murdoch, 'in part payment of my debt to him'.[17]

Next day, General Maclean accompanied Macquarie to different shops, pointing out everything that was necessary for an Indian voyage, and Macquarie amused himself by dining at the Cecil, watching an enjoyable play at Covent Garden and taking a 'very droll ramble' with friends through 'many very curious places in the town'.[18] He left it to the imagination of future readers what young soldiers might get up to in the nights before deployment in a city that, from 1757, published an annual guide to the physical appearance and sexual specialities of almost 200 prostitutes operating around the Cecil.[19]

Macquarie had coffee with friends at the Blue Boar in Holborn,[20] regretting that he did not have time to make a social visit on his distant cousin Betsy Campbell, a girl who in future years would become one of the most important figures in his life. He then took the mail coach back to Dover.

His last restaurant meal in England for many years was breakfast at the City of Antwerp Inn on the morning of 27 March 1788.

The following day, Macquarie marched his remaining sixteen recruits 12 kilometres to the port of Deal, north of Dover, where four East Indiamen[21] waited to take the regiment to India. Macquarie's men were scheduled to be the first to leave, on the 720-tonne *Dublin*, commanded by Captain William Smith. The three companies of the 77th each consisted of sixty-three men, but taking into account the officers, women and children, the regiment's total strength was about 200.

The soldiers were supplied with hammocks and bedding, and directed to sleep on the orlop deck – or, as Macquarie called it, the 'hollop'[22] – which, despite being the lowest deck on the ship, was well lighted and aired. The officers – Lieutenant-Colonel Balfour, Macquarie, Lieutenant Charles Erskine, Ensign John Tait and surgeon Colin Anderson[23] – fixed upon their berths in the 'large, lofty and well lighted great cabin'. Only Balfour, a soldier for twenty-five years, would have any personal privacy, as he had a small area partitioned for himself. Anderson, who had been commissioned as a surgeon five years before, would become one of Macquarie's dearest friends.

Macquarie thought the *Dublin* 'a very fine ship' – well rigged with a crew of about 100 and with twenty-four nine-pounder guns to shoot at any troublesome Frenchmen. There was a quarterdeck that Macquarie thought big enough for walking or dancing, and there were several 'neat apartments' for the captain and the female passengers, whose names Macquarie was careful to record: '1 Miss Seccome – 2 Miss Blair – 3 Miss Hunter – 4 Miss Lofty – 5 Miss Charlote Lofty'. There was also '6 Revd. Mr. Lofty',[24] who 'favors us now and then with prayers and a sermon on a Sunday, upon which occasion the soldiers and the whole ship's company assemble on the quarterdeck'.[25]

It took a few days for the wind to grow in strength, but at 10 a.m. on 4 April, Captain Smith ordered that the *Dublin* weigh anchor and set sail in company with the *Northumberland* and several other Indiamen, 'a fine smart favourable breeze wafting us down the English Channel; the chalky cliffs of Dover on our right and the coast of France on our left'.[26]

Macquarie finished composing letters to friends in Scotland, to be delivered on shore by the pilot. He was not sure when or if he would ever see Uncle Murdoch Maclaine again but, with tender affection, he asked his uncle to take care of his dear old ma, and requested letters of recommendation to give to General William Medows,[27] who would soon be Governor of Bombay. He wished Murdoch a long life and every earthly blessing. He told him he would eventually send back all the money he owed him, but that he would forever be in debt for the kindness his uncle had always shown to the Macquarie family.[28]

THE FIRST EUROPEANS at Sydney Cove received far less hospitable treatment than the passengers on the *Dublin*. Thomas Barrett – who had created the first artwork in the new colony, the Charlotte Medal,[29] an ornate etching on a silver kidney dish commemorating the First Fleet's arrival – also became the first person executed in New South Wales.

Macquarie would find food plentiful in India, but it was scarce in the new colony, and Governor Phillip had warned the convicts that stealing food would be punished by death.[30] Barrett was hanged on 27 February 1788 and his body was left to hang for an hour as a warning to others.[31]

Phillip found conditions at Sydney dismal. Before long, all the settlement's cattle, brought from Cape Town, ran away.[32] The surrounding bushland had little vegetation to suit English tastes. The soil was sandy and poor, the big trees hard as granite. He feared there was not enough local game or fish to sustain so many people once their year's supply of beef, pork, rice, peas and butter ran out. There was an enormous amount of work to be done in clearing the land, building houses, making roads and guarding the convicts.

There was also an Indigenous population none too pleased with finding invaders on their hunting grounds and in their waters.

During March and April 1788, several straggling convicts went missing, presumed killed by local tribesmen and, before long, a pair of convict rush-cutters, twenty-year-old William Okey and eighteen-year-old Samuel Davis, were killed by Aboriginal men for stealing one of their canoes.[33] When found, Okey's body had been speared three times, his eyes were missing – perhaps picked away by birds – and his skull was so bashed in that 'his brains easily found a passage through'.[34]

While Arthur Phillip punished convicts for harming the Eora or stealing from them, some of his military men fired at Aboriginal warriors, usually with bird shot, to frighten them or prevent attacks with stones and spears. In September 1789 Henry Hacking,[35] the violent, heavy drinking quartermaster from the *Sirius*, who would eventually be sent to Van Diemen's Land for theft, may have been the first colonist to kill a local when he fired into a group of the Eora while hunting on the North Shore. He either killed or wounded two men,[36] who were carried off by their companions. By then, the Indigenous people around Port Jackson were being decimated by the arrival of smallpox.[37]

Despite their hardships, the convicts and settlers of the First Fleet were faring far better than the crews of two French ships sent to Australia by the King of France, the ill-fated Louis XVI.[38] The king had closely studied the accounts of Captain Cook's voyages and wanted more knowledge on the Great South Land and the South Pacific. He commissioned the Comte de La Pérouse,[39] a French hero who had tormented the British Navy during America's War of Independence, to circumnavigate the Pacific with 220 men aboard a pair of frigates.[40]

One of the young hopefuls who applied for the voyage was an ambitious fifteen-year-old Corsican named Napoleon Bonaparte,[41] a second lieutenant from Paris's military academy. He made the shortlist for the great adventure but not the final cut, though he would create some excitement for himself and France in years to come.

La Pérouse and his two ships had arrived in Botany Bay on 26 January 1788, after the First Fleet had decided to move from there to Port Jackson. However, Phillip had left Captain John Hunter at Botany Bay, in charge of the *Sirius* and the fleet's transport ships. Hunter and the French were cordial to each other and La Pérouse sent his journals and letters home to Europe on board the *Sirius,* with a note that he intended to be back in France by June 1789. After six weeks in Botany Bay, he and his ships set sail for New Caledonia on 10 March 1788 on their way to France. The ships and their 220 men never made it home.[42]

ON BOARD the *Dublin*, Macquarie found Captain Smith to be a gracious and generous host. There were sixteen cabin passengers and, with the ship's officers, this meant twenty-five 'genteel looking people'[43] at the captain's table every day for breakfast at nine, dinner at four and supper at ten.[44] Captain Smith was 'extremely civil' and 'attentive to everyone',[45] though the canny Scot in Macquarie observed that it would be hard for the skipper to make a quid from the voyage:

> We (the King's officers) in particular, have very great reason to be well pleased with our situation, as our passage cost us nothing at all – the East India Company paying the passage money of all the officers of the four regiments now going to India: ... The captain is only allowed by the honble. company one hundred pounds for the passage of a field officer and seventy pounds for the passage of every captain and subaltern; — I cannot help observing, that I by no means think these sums adequate to the expence of Captain Smith's table; and unless we have a very short passage, he can be no gainer by the allowances made him for our passage — The total number of souls on board the *Dublin* is about three hundred and fifty.[46]

On 6 April, those 350 souls watched the pilot sail away and the sunset fade over Lizard Point in Cornwall, the most southerly point of mainland Great Britain. There was a 'fine fair wind at north east' and Macquarie feasted his eyes on the land for as long as he could discern it, wondering if it would perhaps be his last sight of 'Old Britain'.[47]

As the *Dublin* sailed into the Bay of Biscay between France and Spain, there was 'fine weather and fair wind' with very little swell, and the 'greatest harmony' was forming between him and his 'very agreeable' fellow passengers, both male and female. They passed the island of Madeira on 15 April, and by the 20th, Macquarie was making his move on the ladies on the quarterdeck every moonlit night as the band played beautiful music. War might be looming in India, but for now, Macquarie was having a ball, playing cards and backgammon for 'triffles' by day and dancing the nights away.

But this was the eighteenth century, and there couldn't be a sea voyage without a flogging or two. To keep order among the men of the 77th, Macquarie presided over courts martial now and then, with John Tait and Charles Erskine sitting beside him in judgment, and they prescribed corporal punishment for the recruits 'according to the nature and degree of their offences'.[48] Captain Smith also ordered a dozen lashes for misbehaving crew, and the occasional tearing of skin from men's backs broke up the monotony of the long voyage.

The soldiers were on a tight rein, though it was mostly for their own benefit. Balfour safeguarded the men against scurvy with wholesome provisions, especially sauerkraut – or 'sour-croute',[49] as Macquarie spelled it. They also received a dram of rum a day and sometimes punch. Macquarie could not help but feel a sense of satisfaction that many of his Highland men were eating well for the first time in their lives.

'I must confess, that during all my travels,' Macquarie noted, 'I never saw soldiers live near so well, either on shore or on board of transports; – indeed, too much praise cannot be given to Capt. Smith for his extreme good and humane attention'.[50]

The *Dublin* crossed the Equator at about 11 a.m. on 6 May 1788. The weather was 'intolerably hot and sultry',[51] but Macquarie and the rest of the travellers forgot about that as the ship's company put on a ceremony for 'Neptune's Visit ... which is practised upon this occasion with great humour by the sailors, to extort money or grog from such passengers as have never crossed the line'.

THAT SAME MONTH, work commenced on the first government house building on land of the Gadigal Aboriginal people at Sydney Cove. Convicts would take a year to erect the first two-storey building on the Australian mainland, using 5000 bricks imported from England and others made locally from clay, shellfish and imported lime.

The finished government house would have six rooms, two cellars, a rear staircase and an orchard planted in the front. Out the back, there would be smaller buildings to house the kitchen, bakehouse, stables, offices and workrooms.

AS THE *DUBLIN* travelled south along the African coast towards the Cape of Good Hope, the weather seemed to become cooler every day. Macquarie noted that the men on board 'catched a number of very large sharks in these latitudes'[52] and that all on board were intrigued by the curious sea birds — especially the giant and plentiful 'albicross' with its 'immense long wings'.[53]

In time, the mighty, rugged peak of Koeëlberg[54] near Cape Town rose from the water. It grew bigger and bigger as the *Dublin* sailed into the 'very deep' and 'capacious'[55] False Bay.

Captain Smith came to anchor on 13 June in Simon's Bay, 'a very Romantick and beautiful situation at the foot of a very high mountain'. There were already Dutch East Indiamen in the harbour as well as some French ships and an English man-o'-war, the *Bounty*. It was commanded by Lieutenant William Bligh,[56] a brooding thirty-three year old with dark woolly hair and a permanent scowl.

Years later, Macquarie would describe Bligh as a 'most disagreeable person to have any dealings with … uncommonly brash and tyrannical in the extreme'.[57] In 1788, however, Bligh was a rising star in the British Navy. He had first come to prominence twelve years earlier as master of *Resolution*, under the

command of Captain James Cook on the great mariner's third,
fatal voyage through the Pacific. Now, he and HMS *Bounty* were
bound for 'Ottaheitta [Tahiti] in the South Sea ... particularly
sent to carry and transplant the bread fruit from Ottaheitta to the
West India Islands' as cheap food for slaves.[58]

Captain Smith and his crew spent ten days procuring fresh
provisions and water for the remainder of the *Dublin*'s voyage,
leaving the passengers free to explore Cape Town. Macquarie
made the most of the short holiday, starting with a delightful
'romantick' horseback ride round the bay at the foot of Table
Mountain, then visiting the vineyards of Constantia, which
produced an 'excellent fine flavoured' eponymous wine.
Boarding-house accommodation and entertainment for 1 Spanish
dollar a day, however, fell 'very far short indeed of the mighty fine
promises and elegant description' that Macquarie's host Mr Keiver
'was pleased to give us of them on the road from False Bay'.[59]

On Sunday, 15 June, Macquarie accompanied Balfour and Captain Smith to the residence of Cornelis Jacob van de Graaff,[60] the Governor of the Cape Colony. They strolled about his gardens, observing a 'great collection of birds and wild beasts ... these, in particular, that struck me most and that I had never seen before in any other country, were the wild African buffalo; the antelope; the zebra, or queen's ass; the casawara (a very strange bird); and an ostrich of an immense size. This bird cannot fly, but runs very swift when hunted.'[61]

In the evening, Macquarie and his brother officers strolled about Cape Town's gardens, watching the most fashionable South Africans enjoying their evening walk after coming out of church, especially 'the Dutch ladies', who were 'very finely and richly dressed up'. Macquarie thought some of them were 'very pretty women'[62] but, to his frustration, he only shared his bed that night with the bugs at Mr Keiver's.[63]

At the Beer Gardens, Macquarie watched the Dutchmen smoke and play bowls. He saw Black Africans dance and was shown some of the Hottentot people, 'the original inhabitants of the Cape of Good Hope'. He was told that 'they were once a very wild, fierce, savage, race of men' but were now 'tame and inoffensive'.[64]

Back on board the *Dublin*, Captain Smith hosted Colonel Robert Gordon,[65] commandant of the Dutch troops at the cape, as well as Lieutenant Bligh and Francis Masson,[66] whom Macquarie described as 'a famous botanist sent out by His Majesty to collect strange plants etc in Africa'.[67] The guests 'staid on board till very late at night' and a fine dinner was augmented by 'a great deal of dancing with the ladies' to 'fine moonlight on the quarterdeck'.[68]

If Macquarie had any inkling of the trouble Bligh would cause him in years to come, he didn't let on, but he found Colonel Gordon a 'very fine jovial fellow, and a most agreeable companion as can be'.[69] He lived in a manor house known as Schoonder Sight and had been on more expeditions through southern Africa than any other explorer. He had named the Orange River and he would soon introduce merino sheep to the Cape Colony, the same sheep that would give birth to a huge industry in Australia.[70]

Gordon not only spoke Dutch, English and French, but had also learned the indigenous languages Xhosa and Khoekhoe. He regaled Macquarie, Bligh and the other officers with his tales of journeying 'a thousand miles' into Africa's interior.

> His descriptions of the savage and wild inhabitants of the different nations he has visited are very entertaining – he sang a number of their songs to us in their own real manner and language; – this gentleman has so great a facility at learning languages, that, to my great astonishment he entertained us with a Galic song. Although not born in the Highlands or even Scotland, being born in Holland but of Scotch extraction; he is very communicative and extremely well informed – in short, as agreeable and facetious a companion as I ever met with. In figure, Colonel Gordon is a tall, stout soldierlike man; he spent the greatest part of two days with us, and we were not a little sorry when he went away from Simon's Bay.[71]

Macquarie spent the next five days taking pleasant walks on shore with the ladies and writing a long letter to Uncle Murdoch, which he put on board a ship bound for Port Lorient in France. Finally, at 3 p.m. on 23 June, the *Dublin* set off again alongside several Dutch East Indiamen.

After a patch of boisterous weather, the passengers enjoyed a serene cruise north, passing between Madagascar and Africa's east coast and drinking in the tranquil beauty. For a time, the *Dublin* sailed alongside the *Raymond,* which was carrying part of the 75th Regiment. Officers from each ship would travel between the vessels by row boat to dine with their comrades.

The *Dublin* reached the Equator again on 24 July and the return of turbulent winds meant heavy seas and 'a vast deal of very disagreeable rolling and unpleasant motion', but on the whole, the men felt they were 'well supplied with everything – and the whole of our society are chearful, pleased and happy in their situation'.[72]

They were not so cheerful a week later, when 'a very fine lad called Thorogood' fell overboard and was drowned before it was possible to give him any assistance, 'the ship going very fast through the water under full sail'. Macquarie's sadness was compounded by the fact that he supposed the *Dublin* was only a day's sail from 'our destined port'.[73]

He supposed correctly. After four months at sea, those aboard the *Dublin* saw India in the distance at 10 a.m. on 3 August 1788, and four hours later, a pilot came on board to steer the ship into the harbour of the island of Bombay, then under the control of the British East India Company.

At 4 p.m. the *Dublin* put down anchor and Macquarie sat down to a fine celebration dinner, the men eating and drinking heartily and congratulating one another upon their safe arrival. The harbour was 'commodious and capacious as well as secure' and full of ships.

Lieutenant-Colonel Balfour was rowed ashore to meet the governor, and cannons on the *Dublin* and in the harbour saluted his landing.

Macquarie and the other officers fitted the men with their clothing and accoutrements before disembarking. Sadly, one of the soldiers who had been ill for a long time died on the ship and was committed to the deep.[74]

It was a sombre end to a long voyage but, as twilight approached and the harbour glistened like a jewel in the last rays of the golden sun, the tiny Macquarie home on Mull seemed a world away.

The vast, mysterious land of opportunity before him presented 'a most beautiful prospect'.[75] Lachlan Macquarie was a go-getter, and he was making a new life for himself.

Chapter 5

*Went at 3 o'clock to the governors to dinner … walked afterwards to
see the castle of Bombay and other parts of the town until it was dark.
Returned at night to sup at the governors, and for the
first time smoked out of a Indian hooka.*

MACQUARIE ON HIS FIRST NIGHT IN BOMBAY[1]

T HE ANCIENT ISLAND CITY of Bombay was teeming and
overcrowded, its people perpetually hot and wet. Every degree
of abode from hovels to ornate palaces was nestled among luxurious
green vegetation and British colonial grandeur. There were beggars
and banquets; children starving in the streets, and men being carried
about on palanquins or doolies, small cabins borne on the shoulders
of up to eight labourers. In the harbour lay all manner of grand
and colourful ships from every corner of the world, while on the
boulevards, British officers in their red coats and gold braid mixed
with young pigtailed soldiers, and fashionable women looking for
rich husbands or military men with prospects. Union Jacks fluttered
against the rain, and brown, irregular buildings crowded around
the high, dark walls of Fort George.

Macquarie reckoned that the island of Bombay was no more than
15 kilometres long and 40 kilometres in circumference[2] – not much
bigger in area than old Ulva – but it was nothing like what the poor
boy from that Hebridean wasteland had ever seen. It was the gateway

to a subcontinent that stretched more than 3000 kilometres north to south and 2500 east to west, from the ice and snow of the Himalayas to the golden sand of tropical islands in the south. Bombay was a melting pot of humanity – rich and poor, old and young, Hindu, Muslim, Christian and Jew. The Mughal Empire had ceded Bombay to the Portuguese in 1534 and it then came to the British Crown when Charles II married a Portuguese wife.[3] Seven years later, the city was leased to the British East India Company.

India's promise stirred Macquarie's soul like nothing had before.

The city of Bombay was 'amazingly populous … especially in natives; a vast many of whom, live within the fort as merchants and mechanics'.[4] It was fortified all around with about 5 kilometres of thick walls. Entry came by three gates or ports – the Bazaar, Church and Apollo Gates – each of which featured a drawbridge over a moat.

Inside, the fort was 'crouded with old nasty dirty looking houses; excepting the Government House and a few others belonging to the [East India] Company and gentlemen of fortune, which are pretty neat and handsomely built'.[5] About 100,000 people lived inside the walls, and another 100,000 outside,[6] including 2000 British soldiers and 8000 Indian troops. The place was steaming hot, so that after meeting Governor Andrew Ramsay – the man keeping the seat warm for incoming governor General Medows – Macquarie was so knocked about by the sun fighting its way through the clouds that he could not walk about to take in the sights. It wasn't until sunset that he could stroll about, and after dark enjoyed supper with Ramsay and the experience of smoking an Indian hookah for the first time.[7]

Gradually, he became more reconciled to the place and climate[8] and began to savour the exotic sights and smells and the grandeur of colonial India, promenading along Bombay's esplanades and visiting its castle, which the British had built upon the old manor house of a Portuguese nobleman.[9] Before long, Macquarie was travelling regularly in a palanquin – 'a very easy and comfortable mode of travelling in this country',[10] and soon he hired a servant called 'Abdella (a Moor Man)'[11] at 5 rupees a month.

The stone elephant on Elephanta Island, 1786. Sarmaya Arts Foundation

After three months in Bombay, Macquarie was accompanying Colonel Balfour on voyages around the islands near Bombay – Butcher,[12] Karanja[13] and Elephanta,[14] with its extraordinary sixth-century cave temples carved into the rock. Elsewhere on the island, Macquarie was amazed[15] by an ancient life-sized elephant hewn from basalt.[16] He went to water parties, and explored a fort on the mainland called Bellapore belonging to the Marathas, the dominant power on the subcontinent. The local ruler would not permit Macquarie and his friends to go inside the fort, but was civil enough to allow him to take a short walk escorted by two of his sepoy privates, though only after taking away their fowling pieces.[17]

MUCH OF MACQUARIE'S WORK initially was the routine discipline of the young Scotsmen in his care, who had been transported to a world alien to their former way of life. He supervised their parades, and twice-daily drills at 5 a.m. and 4.30 p.m., and accompanied them to the frequent brigade field days.[18] He oversaw their washing, the repair of their weapons, the planting of vegetables to ward off scurvy, and their allowances of the local grog, arrack – 2 drams per day during the wet season and 1 dram per day for the rest of the year.[19]

He encouraged the wearing of trousers instead of kilts as a protection against the ubiquitous mosquitoes. Knowledge of infections was still rudimentary, and the camp hospital stood in close proximity to a cemetery.

Macquarie's friend, Ensign John Tait, succumbed to disease, and Lachlan Maclean, who had followed Macquarie as an early recruit, was another of the regiment's first casualties.

Walter Ewer, a director of the East India Company, estimated that 90 per cent of Bombay's inhabitants who claimed to have 'the liver complaint' were actually suffering venereal disease.[20] Syphilis was rampant among British troops,[21] and purging with mercury was the most common treatment. Its use was based on the theory that 'the less material there was in the body, the less progress a disease could make'.[22]

The heat and close quarters and the lack of European women kept tensions boiling, and there were frequently quarrels to settle among the men. There was even a duel between ensigns Robert Campbell and John Andrew Dick, 'both very young lads'; it saw Campbell 'severely wounded in the head' and both men 'sent to Coventry', ostracised by the regiment for a month.[23] Macquarie also made a fruitless search over several days for one of his soldiers, Dennis Fennon, who was said to have deserted from the Apollo Barracks and gone on board the *Admiral Hughes,* an East Indiaman heading to China. On the final day of his hunt, Macquarie had to row to and from the mouth of the harbour in an open boat in teeming rain and was soaked to the skin.[24]

Macquarie began to enjoy his social life, and was introduced 'to the most genteel and fashionable circle of acquaintance in Bombay'.[25] Soon he was a regular at the balls, suppers and garden parties held in the lush and manicured grounds of Bombay's most lavish homes. At 'a very Grand General Subscription Union Ball and Supper' at the St George's Gardens, with all guests in fancy dress, he came 'dressed and accoutred in the full and complete Highland garb', which he had procured from Lieutenant George McKenzie of the 75th Highland Regiment. Occasionally, there were dinners with senior officers, who he noted lived 'remarkably well'.[26]

MACQUARIE had hopes of joining their ranks one day and, early on, he realised that his best opportunities for advancement in the British Army were from patronage and connections rather than from individual merit or courage on the battlefield. Social engagements gave him not only the opportunity to meet a wife with aristocratic breeding but to impress the army's top brass. His family may not have had money, but he was descended from Scottish nobility which gave him something of a headstart in social circles. And while the British had forced his people into poverty, Macquarie believed that, if he couldn't beat those responsible, the next best thing was to join them and exploit every opportunity to lift himself, and the rest of his clan. If he bent some of the British rules along the way, so be it.

For the time being, however, his circumstances remained frustratingly meagre. On arrival in Bombay, Macquarie and surgeon Colin Anderson had moved into 'the Tavern or as it is called here The Punch House; being the only one in the town or fort that gentleman can be accommodated in'.[27] Macquarie had spent eight nights sleeping at The Punch House before moving to the Bunder, 'a large square of buildings originally built as quarters for the [British East India] Company's civil servants'.[28] Always cautious with his own money, Macquarie declared he was 'perfectly sick and tired of the enormous expense of living at a tavern in Bombay'.[29]

But Macquarie wasn't the only soldier in Bombay counting his pennies. Only a few weeks after he arrived, 'a strict system of economical reform in all departments' was enforced on the army, which meant cutbacks to living expenses. As a result, by Macquarie's calculations the soldiers at his base were on a 'far inferior' deal to their comrades in Bengal and Madras.[30]

Macquarie had no private income and had always needed Murdoch Maclaine's support. Now he was on the other side of the world, earning a mere £2 (about 16 rupees) a week as a lieutenant, and his living allowance had been cut from 48 to 28 rupees a month. He therefore had to borrow money from his sergeant's wife, and implement austerity measures unknown to many of the other officers. There was no military action on the horizon yet, and the prospect of sharing in the spoils of war – 'our golden dreams', as he called them – seemed agonisingly remote. 'So that, and the flattering prospects, we had formed to ourselves in Britain, of soon making our fortunes in the east, must now all vanish into smoke; and we must content ourselves, with merely being able to exist, without running into debt.'[31]

His financial situation might have been grim, but at least he was able to make a successful application to Colonel Balfour to promote the clan chief's son Murdoch to the rank of ensign. As Macquarie tried to climb the military ladder, he wanted his friends and relatives to do the same. His nature decreed that a blessing gained was always a blessing to be shared with those he loved.

As the oldest lieutenant in his regiment, at almost twenty-eight, he decided to put up his hand for promotion to captain. He wrote out a curriculum vitae declaring his 'services and pretensions to promotion'.[32] Lieutenant-Colonel Balfour took him to see Bombay's new governor and the Bombay army's commander, General Medows, who in turn said he would forward it to the army commander-in-chief, Earl Cornwallis, who was hoping for better luck on the subcontinent than he had had in those troublesome United States.

Macquarie was not going to have his application filed away in a drawer, however, and soon wrote a long letter to Major-General Sir Archibald Campbell, now Governor of Madras, reminding him of their association when Campbell was Governor of Jamaica and hoping Campbell would back his promotion.[33]

He was not put off when Sir Archibald told him that, while he 'would be very happy to oblige and serve me', he couldn't 'meddle'.[34] Instead, Macquarie persevered, writing to friends serving in Bengal, Major Skelly and Captain Madan, who 'spoke strongly' in his favour to Cornwallis, 'and were favourably heard by him'.[35]

Word of Macquarie's promotion to captain-lieutenant,[36] backdated to 9 November 1788, finally came through on 30 March 1789[37] and, while he had talked up his abilities on his CV, in the privacy of his own intimate journal, he admitted that it was help from his friends in the military – General Maclean as well as the others – that had pushed him over the line. He didn't mind that his immediate rise came from who he knew, rather than what he knew.

> I must here, for the sake of truth and justice, observe, that I have very great reason to be thankful, and to think myself extremely fortunate indeed, in succeeding to this rank on the present occasion: – there being at least 30 lieutenants now serving in India in His Majesty's different regiments who are older lieutenants in the army than I am by a great deal.[38]

The other lieutenants were clearly not as persistent.

Macquarie's pay was still a meagre £6 a month, but he had already climbed a couple of rungs on the army ladder and at last was looking at the sky. Soon after his promotion, the ambitious young officer was given duty as captain of the day in the garrison, and for the first time, had command of all 500 guards during the daily grand parade.[39]

ANOTHER LIEUTENANT, William Bligh, was having far less success. His men had fallen in love with the hedonistic pleasures of the South Pacific.

On 28 April 1789, ten months after he had left Macquarie in Cape Town and sailed off in search of breadfruit, Bligh became a prisoner of his own crew. Lieutenant Fletcher Christian, an old friend of Bligh's, led a rebellion to seize control of the *Bounty* and set the skipper and eighteen of his loyal crew adrift in the ship's open boat.

Bligh and his men then endured a voyage of nearly two months, across more than 6500 kilometres of sometimes mountainous seas that threatened to sink their tiny craft, before they sailed into Timor's Coupang Harbour, waving a makeshift Union Jack[40] and demanding justice be served on the mutineers.

AT ABOUT THE SAME TIME as Fletcher Christian was commandeering the *Bounty,* an East Indiaman, the *General Elliot,* arrived in Bombay, bringing news of the madness of King George III. Rumours of the monarch's erratic behaviour had been circulating among the troops for some time.[41]

Four months later the *Ponsborne* brought news of his 'happy recovery', and Macquarie noted that everyone looked upon the news as 'a most fortunate and happy circumstance for the British nation'.[42] While he was delighted to hear of the 'peace and quietness' this had caused at home, there were reports of uprisings against the royals in France, 'with the people wishing to enjoy more liberty'.[43] The American Revolution against the British monarchy had been aided by French troops and the success of the colonists was now inspiring a rebellion in France against the extravagances of King Louis XVI and his wife Marie Antoinette. The French lawyer, politician and revolutionary leader Maximilien Robespierre[44] advocated that the words 'The French People' and 'liberty, equality, fraternity' be written on uniforms and flags.[45]

Macquarie saw the uprising of peasants as a dangerous thing and there were also worrying reports from Anchuthengu,[46] in the kingdom of Travancore on India's southwest coast. On 28 December 1789, the Sultan of Mysore, Tipu Sultan,[47] and 14,000 of his men had attacked the kingdom, which Macquarie reckoned was Britain's best ally in India.[48]

A locally stationed battalion from the Madras Presidency, a British province in southern India, had fought back. One officer had been wounded and several soldiers killed before Tipu's army was repulsed by Travancore's six-pounder cannons.

Tippoo Sahib (better known as Tipu Sultan) at the lines of Travancore. Illustration from 1850s. Public Domain

Trouble would simmer in the area for months as Tipu, seen by the East India Company as a robber baron and its greatest threat, prepared another strike, precipitating the Third Anglo–Mysore War.

Tipu and his Muslim hordes were carrying on the work of Tipu's father Hyder Ali,[49] who had allied himself with the French and waged war against the British for thirty years. He had shown his enemies no mercy, once hanging one of them in a cage like a human parrot and feeding him only a little rice and milk until his inevitable, agonising death.[50]

Since Ali's own demise in 1782, Tipu had ruled as the Tiger of Mysore. By all reports, he was an arrogant, self-assured eccentric, full of feelings of invincibility.[51] He was inclined to pudginess, and had a luxurious moustache and 'small, delicate hands and feet … an aquiline nose, large lustrous eyes, the neck rather short and thick. He is described as having been so modest that no one ever saw any part of his person, save his feet, ankles and wrists; while in the bath he always covered himself from head to foot.'[52]

Tipu's army had developed iron-cased rockets as early weapons of mass destruction. According to the British propaganda of the time, and even some independent French reports, Tipu was a murderous monster, his cruelty to both Christians and Hindus nauseating. In his diary entry of 14 January 1799, Francois Fidele Ripaud de Montaudevert, a French soldier fighting for Tipu, wrote: 'I'm disturbed by Tipu Sultan's treatment of these most gentle souls, the Hindus. During the siege of Mangalore, Tipu's soldiers daily exposed the heads of many innocent Brahmins within sight from the fort for the Zamorin and his Hindu followers to see.'[53]

Macquarie had heard the stories of the East India Company's defeat in the Battle of Pollilur,[54] in which 7000 British soldiers had been held captive by Tipu and his father in the fortress of Seringapatam. Survivors claimed that more than 300 soldiers had been forcibly circumcised,[55] and young drummer boys made to wear female clothes and dance for their conquerors.

In 1784, when Tipu captured 50,000 Catholics in Mangalore, he was also said to have subjected them to forced circumcision.[56] He ordered the widespread destruction of churches and the seizure of money and properties belonging to Christians.[57]

Sometimes prisoners were executed by being dragged across rough ground by elephants. Tipu also used his father's 'parrot cage' to torture enemies to death, and would occasionally force his foes to climb onto saddles studded with lethal, sharp spikes.

Britain's Prime Minister William Pitt the Younger had forbidden the East India Company to make war unless its possessions were attacked,[58] but the British wanted Tipu under control, and at long last Macquarie and the 77th might see some action.

In April 1790, the 75th Regiment was deployed to bolster the forces under the Rajah of Travancore.[59] More troops followed: battalions of sepoys and a company of artillery.

However, Macquarie and the rest of the 77th were told to cool their heels. All Macquarie's comrades were 'mortified and much hurt'[60] when informed they would not be getting their marching orders, and Macquarie wondered if they would ever be 'employed during the present war at all'. He grumbled to his friends that they had all 'put ourselves to very great expense in providing camp equipage and necessaries for the field'; the 77th was the only King's Regiment in India that was 'not on actual service, or full batta [field service pay]'.

'While a war is carrying on under the fortunate auspices of … General Medows against Tippoo Saib [Tipu Sultan] we are made a Garrison Regt. in Bombay,' Macquarie complained. 'Hard and cruel fate!'[61]

Still, financially he wasn't doing too badly.

Mixing with the upper echelons of society and the military had proved profitable and Macquarie was making important connections. He made sure his family back in Scotland shared his good fortune. By November 1790 he was able to pay Uncle Murdoch the balance of the £127 loan and to provide money for his mother, brothers and sister. He sent his brother Charles an extra £30 'for his own sole use and behoof' and lodged 1000 rupees (about £125) with his bankers.[62] On 8 November, he spent 'a very pleasant and agreeable evening in the country at the house of lawyer White's, where the nuptials of Miss James and John Fell Esqr. (of the Bombay Civil Establishment) were celebrated with great festifity mirth and good humour'.[63]

The mood changed – quickly. Tipu was on the charge again after a monumental attack with 40,000 soldiers on the cavalry of Colonel John Floyd[64] and his 19th Light Dragoons. Finally, on 10 November 1790, the 77th was ordered to hold itself in readiness to embark for 'immediate and actual field service'. Macquarie underlined the words in his journal with a flourish, his excitement leaping from the page, and noted: 'What made this order the more agreeable, was, that we had almost despaired of being employed during the present war at all'.[65]

Now the 77th was on its way to Cannanore, where the local royals, Sultan Ali Rajah and his bibbee (queen), were said to have vast stores of gold and jewels in their fortress.

Macquarie wanted to get his hands on the treasure.

Chapter 6

*The two brass field eighteen pounders were brought up ... this evening
with immense labour; and which, could hardly have been effected
without the powerful assistance and exertions of these noble and
sagacious animals, the elephants. I went down ... to see them drag
up the guns and was much pleased by the sight.*

MACQUARIE, READY FOR BATTLE, WATCHING ELEPHANTS DRAG BRITISH
CANNONS UP A STEEP RAVINE IN MYSORE[1]

MACQUARIE AND THE 77TH marched from their
barracks on Old Woman's Island to board the ship *Hercules*
at 9 a.m. on 24 November 1790. The *Hercules* was a large vessel,
'but not sufficiently large to accommodate 650 soldiers and
twenty-four officers'.[2]

The anticipation of battle made up for the cramped quarters,
however, and the skipper, Captain Galloway, made sure the officers
lived 'extremely well'. They ate at his table throughout the eleven-
day voyage that would take them 1200 kilometres south to the tip
of India, with each officer digging into his own pocket to meet the
expense.[3] Macquarie's food and beverage tab would be 58 rupees.

On 4 December, the *Hercules* arrived at Tellicherry (now
called Thalassery) on the Malabar Coast in India's southwest.

Macquarie's regiment paraded and marched for 5 kilometres to their camp at Durmapatam – 'a very pretty hill formed into an island, by the confluence of two rivers'[4] – only to find that their tents had been left behind and they had to sleep on the bare ground in driving rain. They also spent the next few days without any shelter from the burning daytime sun.[5]

The British force of 4500 was bolstered by another 2500 Nair Hindu fighters provided by local rajahs, eager for revenge against Tipu for the brutal conquest of their lands.[6]

At daybreak on 10 December 1790, Macquarie marched with the rest of the British forces along a fine beach. On either side of the British troops rode Indian cavalry, spurs jingling as they stayed one step ahead of the teams of elephants towing the heavy cannons. It was a fine sight: the British army in their red coats, stiff-backed, the ceaseless blue and white foam of the Arabian Sea on their left, and on their right, the mountains and seemingly impenetrable jungles that they would soon traverse.

The troops crossed two rivers to take their place on a hill, where Major-General Robert Abercromby[7] was waiting. He was in command of the Bombay Army, of which Macquarie's 77th Regiment was part.

Tipu's ally Sultan Ali Rajah was positioned on the heights covering the town of Cannanore (now called Kannur), holding Avery and Carley Forts, which were separated by a deep valley. The sultan was said to be so strongly attached to Tipu that he never would allow the surrender of Cannanore to the British while he was alive.[8]

Macquarie noted that Cannanore stood at the head of a very fine bay, surrounded by rich countryside, dominated by the royal durbar or palace, a grand home that was 'something in the English stile'. The town was large, but the streets were all very narrow and lined with numerous mosques and temples.[9]

Early on 14 December, a day of extraordinary heat, the British advanced. Elephants were brought in to tow the three big eighteen-pounder cannons into place about 1350 metres from Fort Avery.

The artillerymen opened fire, but the distance was too great to do the enemy any harm. Two of Tipu's big guns at Fort Carley fired back, only to land 300 metres in front of the British line. Tipu's snipers fired at the British from jungle lairs, but while some of their shots kicked up dirt near British boots, the only success they really had was breaking a biscuit in the pocket of a soldier from the 77th. For the first time, Macquarie saw Tipu's vaunted rockets being launched, but they too landed short, or sailed over the British heads without doing harm.[10]

At 11 a.m., the enemy made a 'very spirited attack' with rockets and muskets on the British right flank, trying to destroy the cannons being used against Fort Avery. Both the enemy and local Indians fighting for the British suffered heavy casualties.

At 3 p.m., General Abercromby, realising the cannons were not having enough effect, ordered a ceasefire and told the men to rest in the shade.[11] He ordered Macquarie to take two subalterns – junior officers – and sixty men and establish an artillery battery 350 metres closer to Tipu's strongholds, where the cannons could do more damage.

Macquarie had the men filling sandbags at sunset. The enemy kept firing towards the sounds of the men digging, and one of Macquarie's workers was hit in the shoulder. As night fell, the soldiers started carrying the sandbags to the designated site, but the moon was as bright as a lighthouse and the enemy soldiers, having advanced so close that Macquarie could hear them speak, 'saw very plainly, what we were about, and kept up a very heavy fire of musquetry upon us during the whole night'.[12] One sepoy was mortally wounded just as he was laying down his sandbag, but even though the enemy commenced 'an unremitting heavy fire' until 3 a.m., to Macquarie's relief, the rest of the troops escaped injury.[13]

At 7 a.m. the next day, Macquarie's three British eighteen-pounders opened up from their new position towards Fort Avery and their fire was much more accurate. Although the enemy fired back, the fort was 'totally silenced' in an hour as the walls came crumbling down.[14] The fort at Carley was soon overrun as well.

On 17 December, the British took two of Tipu's 'head generals, vizt. Mier Mahomed, the commander in chief, and Seid Mahamood, the second in command; several officers and about 5000 fighting men, thirty-four stand of colours, two field pieces, and about 4000 muskets'. Macquarie estimated that the numbers killed and wounded among the enemy 'must have been considerable; but could not be exactly ascertained, as it is the custom among the Mahometans to bury their dead as soon as they are killed'.[15]

He thought the killed or wounded on the side of the British, the sepoys and nairs, tallied no more than ninety. None of Macquarie's brother officers was killed or wounded, 'excepting Mr. Cochrane, surgeon to the 2nd Battalion of Native Infantry, who was struck by a spent cannon shot on the breast slightly, which bruised and stunned him a good deal, but not dangerously'.[16]

General Abercromby's victory at Cannanore and a similar victory by Colonel James Hartley at Calicut (now Kozhikode), 90 kilometres south, gave the British control of the Malabar Coast. The prisoners at Cannanore were marched along the front of the British line in a 'humiliating ceremony … to a place allotted for them on the right, where a guard was placed over them and proper provisions supplied to them until they were sent away to their own country'.[17]

Victory was sweet, but there was a sour taste in the mouths of the money-hungry troops. Under the terms of the truce, the queen was allowed to keep all her private property. She had ensured there would be no public treasures for the British in the town or fort of Cannanore, 'having sent off all her valuables to the Lacadive [Laccadive] Islands'.[18]

Macquarie was amazed at the enemy's surrender, but later learned that the bibbee was inside Cannanore's triangular fort, in a 'not very elegant'[19] house, mourning the loss of her husband, who had died during the attack on Fort Avery. It was strongly suspected by the British that he had been poisoned under her orders, because of his staunch refusal to surrender, which posed a risk to so many thousands of lives.[20]

The dearth of prize money was a disappointment to Macquarie, but he put himself in a better mood by attending a public auction at which enemy horses went under the hammer. He treated himself to a 'very pretty chestnut coloured mare, between five and six years old and between fourteen and fifteen hands high, for ninety rupees'.[21] He borrowed a 'very elegant saddle and bridle' and hired a 'very good horse-keeper' from among the prisoners of war. He also paid 18 rupees for a pair of bullocks to carry his tent.[22]

On 24 December 1790, Macquarie became the regimental paymaster, and five days later he and the other troops received word that Cornwallis, now Indian Governor-General as well as army commander-in-chief, had arrived in the area from Calcutta, taking the reins from General Medows and ready to curtail Tipu once and for all. Cornwallis was assembling 22,300 combatants and 130,000[23] camp followers, with many more to come. There were 80,000 bullocks and 100 elephants carting the soldiers' big guns, food and equipment.

Cornwallis planned to attack Tipu's fortress capital Seringapatam,[24] situated on an island in the Cauvery River,[25] about 20 kilometres northeast of the city of Mysore.[26] The British forces made their camp 'on a very pleasant ground beside the Balyapattanam River',[27] about 10 kilometres north of Cannanore.

On 8 February 1791, the army was drawn out in a great semi-circle to see the execution of two deserters. With that unpleasantness over, an advance brigade under Colonel Hartley left at daybreak on 22 February, and Macquarie's 77th marched from their camp along with the 2nd Battalion of Native Infantry and the Corps of Artillery early the following morning. Energised by the scent of battle, they headed towards the steep, slippery, rain-washed ravines – called ghauts by the locals – that would characterise their long, arduous journey into the next war zone.

Macquarie had come up in the world since his early days in Bombay: he now had four bullocks to carry his tent and luggage, his chestnut mare, his horse handler, a cook, a head servant named Francis, his faithful Scottish servant Donald Campbell, a boy servant or *massaljee*, and four coolies (labourers) to carry his palanquin if he felt like being hoisted around on the shoulders of underlings. Some of the other officers had even more servants than he did.

The great columns of redcoats and Indian cavalrymen were joined by women and children in bullock-drawn wagons, and following behind, dogs, horses, camels and goats, as well as tradesmen and merchants, snake-oil salesmen, conjurers and harlots. Stressed, lonely men were always in need of comfort. It was like a travelling carnival, and circling in the distance were the bandits – the looties – waiting for the chance to rob the vulnerable.

The soldiers carried five days' bread, besides their arms, accoutrements and forty rounds of ammunition for their muzzle-loading muskets. The artillery and heavy stores were sent up river in boats and some bullocks were shot in the woods for beef.[28]

The troops made only 12 miles (20 kilometres) on the first day, but Macquarie noted that 'with this load, and in such a climate, twelve miles is a long enough march'.[29]

Two days later, the 77th crossed the Balyapattanam and marched through the village of Illiacour, but Macquarie had to leave Donald Campbell there, because he had a severe case of dysentery. Macquarie wished him a speedy recovery but Campbell died five days later, 'notwithstanding the aid and assistance of every medical skill being administered to him' by Dr Grant Clugstone, the surgeon-general.[30]

The soldiers climbed higher and higher, up steep, 1200-metre ravines on narrow, bad roads, 'the descents and ascents of which were in general exceedingly steep and rough'.[31] Macquarie passed the bloated carcasses of a number of dead bullocks, hoofs to the sky, driven to death from exhaustion.

At the village of Viator, the men had to camp in the woods because their tents had not arrived from their last stopover. A party was sent out to shoot more bullocks, but none could be found, so the troops had nothing to eat but biscuit.

Macquarie couldn't comprehend how the heavy cannons, which had arrived at Illiacour, could be carried over this terrain. From 10 March, he was tasked with taking two subalterns and

100 men of the 77th to build roads. Every morning, they would greet the sun and have a mile of road made within five hours.

On 21 March the weary, worn-out 77th reached the top of Poodicherrum Ghaut, but 'the ascent we found exceedingly steep indeed for four miles [seven kilometres], and consequently very fatiguing to the poor soldiers ... The first two cannons were finally dragged up the ghaut by elephants, hired from a black merchant in Tellicherry named Mooser.[32]

WHILE MACQUARIE cooled his heels amid India's mountain air, life remained brutal for the convicts at Sydney Cove. European settlement now stretched by the river to what would soon be known as Parramatta,[33] and exploration extended north to the Hawkesbury River and west to the Nepean.

In 1790, the Second Fleet arrived in Port Jackson with much-needed supplies, and with 759 new convicts guarded by the first detachment of the New South Wales Corps. Among them was an ambitious, pugnacious British lieutenant, John Macarthur,[34] who had soon been appointed the commandant of the Parramatta prison camp.

The new colony was a place of torment but Phillip tried to keep a peaceful relationship with the Eora people. He placed two of them, Colebee and Bennelong,[35] under his personal care, and built a hut for Bennelong on the point that is now the site for the Sydney Opera House. The Aboriginals did not try to drive out the new arrivals but, instead, had a reverence for their leader whose missing front tooth recalled their initiation ceremonies. Even when Phillip was speared in the shoulder at Manly Cove over a misunderstanding, he showed restraint. He would not always be so benevolent.

Watkin Tench recalled a hunting party, including a sergeant of marines and three convicts, encountering a pair of natives in the bush when without 'the least warning' one of them, believed to be the warrior Pemulway[36] of the Bidhigal clan, launched his spear at Governor Phillip's convict gamekeeper John McIntyre, lodging it in his left side.[37]

The Aboriginal group was pursued by the settlers with muskets, but they escaped. McIntyre was taken back to the settlement, mortally wounded. He had a reputation for ill-treating Aboriginal women and Tench suspected that he had previously killed Aboriginal people.

Even Bennelong had a fear and hatred of him.

Phillip was livid over the killing. He ordered that two of the Bidjigal people were to be captured and ten killed in retaliation, and that those ten were then to be beheaded. Tench managed to talk the Governor out of the killing spree but relations with the land's first people remained bitter. Pemulwuy persuaded some of the Eora, Dharug and Dharawal people to rise up against the settlers, leading raids that burned crops and killed livestock. Even escaped convicts joined his marauders in a 12-year guerrilla campaign until Pemulway was shot and killed by Henry Hacking. Pemulway's head was cut off, preserved in spirits and shipped to Joseph Banks in England.[38]

The harshness extended to convicts. On 3 May 1791, Lieutenant Ralph Clark of the Royal Marines recorded in his diary that he had ordered floggings for three female convicts who had been taken from Sydney Cove to work on Norfolk Island, an outpost of the settlement at Sydney. Catherine White fainted after the first fifteen lashes and Mary Teut after twenty-two. Under doctor's orders, Clark had them untied. Mary Higgins received twenty-six lashes from her sentence of fifty before Clark 'forgave her the remainder' because she was 'an old woman'. Clark said he hoped it would serve as a warning to other female prisoners who thought about misbehaving.[39]

In his diary, he often expressed his enjoyment of the floggings. On the voyage out with the First Fleet, he had repeatedly noted the bad behaviour of Elizabeth Dudgeon, whom he referred to as a 'great whore'. After she was accused of being impertinent to Captain Frederick Meredith, the captain had ordered one of the corporals to flog her with a rope. 'The Corporal did not play with her but laid it home which I was very glad to see,' Clark wrote, '… she has been long fishing for it which she has at last got until her hearts content.'[40]

MACQUARIE spent six weeks taking in the grand mountain vistas of southern India as he readied to go into battle again. There were reports that Cornwallis had taken the fort and garrison of Bangalore 250 kilometres away,[41] then Darwar.[42] The soldiers in camp were eager for action again, and hostilities boiled over, with Ensign Statham of the 73rd Regiment killing Lieutenant Hoy from the Artillery Corps in a duel.

On 12 May, Macquarie received his orders to move the men forward, but they made slow process, with frequent halts due to fatigue. Carriage wheels were smashed in the rough country, so that some of the eighteen-pounders were temporarily left behind on broken vehicles.

After travelling for five days, the whole army descended down the Pass of Seedasur into the Kingdom of Mysore and, as if by some prearranged signal, rain began bucketing down with 'great violence for at least two hours'.[43] Macquarie and his comrades in the 77th were soaked.

What made it 'doubly disagreeable' was that they were obliged to stand still under arms during the whole downpour while the advance guard took possession of the fort of Periapatam at noon, hoisting the Union Jack. Tipu's men had run away without firing a single shot and, although the enemy had planned to destroy the fort with explosives, they could only detonate two mines, which caused little harm.[44] There was hardly anything in spoils except some grain and cattle, and the disappointment was compounded by the 'violent' rain day after day.

On 15 May, Cornwallis routed Tipu's forces at Arakere, near the fortress of Seringapatam. He had hoped to march on to Seringapatam to finish the job but Tipu's slash–and–burn retreat left the British without provisions.[45]

Finally, the skies cleared and on 20 May the soldiers at Periapatam fired a twenty-one gun salute in honour of Earl Cornwallis.

The weather remained cold and miserable, so much so that the floors of the British tents were constantly wet despite the trenches that had been dug around them. Tipu's men were even more of a threat, with Mysore cavalrymen venturing into Periapatam and stealing one of the elephants and some bullocks belonging to the 14th Madras Battalion, and severely wounding some of the coolies tending the animals. General Abercromby was on horseback most of the day in the hard rain, observing enemy movements, but without proper cavalry he was unable to punish Tipu's raiders 'for their temerity'.[46]

At about 8 p.m. on 23 May, Macquarie and his men received orders to strike their tents immediately and send their baggage and all the sick to the rear of the British line. No one doubted that they were going out under cover of night to surprise the enemy, and 'the thoughts of giving them a handsome drubbing before or by daybreak' put the men 'in the highest of spirits'.[47] But, to their astonishment, instead of wheeling to the right and advancing towards the enemy, the corps in front wheeled to the left and began retreating as fast as the mad, bad, deeply rutted roads would let them.

Macquarie was gobsmacked. Mortified. All the 'laurels, fame, honour, riches and promotion' he had hoped for by laying siege to Tipu's 'great capital' at Seringapatam gave way 'to gloomy and desponding thoughts on our being obliged to retreat or fall back (as it is called)'.[48] Abercromby had wanted to attack with bayonets, but had received an express message from Cornwallis to fall back to the ghauts and then to Bangalore, because the army was running low on provisions and an expected early monsoon would swell the Kaveri River before Cornwallis's Grand Army arrived from Madras. The siege of Seringapatam would have to wait.

Macquarie wrote privately that he could not pay 'any great compliment' to Abercromby for the 'judgment and coolness he ought to have shewed'[49] in conducting the retreat. There was great confusion over the sick, who were left behind, and 100 men fell into Tipu's hands as a result, consigned to a grim fate. Much of the artillery and baggage was also lost in the confusion.

The steep downward journey back to the coast on muddy slippery roads was a nightmare, and the cattle 'were quite knocked up'.[50] Macquarie complained that 'the labour and fatigue of the troops in dragging the guns thro' these horrid roads and sloughs is beyond all description'.[51]

As night fell, such hard toil while soaked through to the skin in heavy rain had taken its toll. Macquarie now had the fever and bowel symptoms of dysentery.

For days he rode his chestnut mare on into the rain, slogging his way down the dangerous ravines, barely able to stay in the saddle because of the driving rain. He had a high fever and was battling to contain his diarrhoea. The muddy tracks that passed for mountain roads were now covered with water that, in many parts, was thigh-deep and almost impassable.

Macquarie spent two days in a jungle hut recovering slightly from his illness, only to get back in the saddle and come upon mountain tracks that were so precarious that he had to hobble down rather than ride, using a wooden pole to stop himself from 'falling and sliding down the steep part of the ghauts'.[52]

The labour of the soldiers, in dragging out cannons bogged in quagmires after marching 10 kilometres in heavy rain, 'was exceedingly severe indeed'.[53] The stress of having to sleep outdoors in pouring rain because tents were lost meant 'that the whole army became very sickly' and men were sent off in scores every day to the general hospital at Illiacour.[54]

Eight days after starting his march from Periapatam, Macquarie made it to the Balyapattanam River on 2 June 1791 and hitched a boat ride. But another boat carrying sick soldiers had recently overturned in high winds and as many as forty of Macquarie's comrades had drowned. The young captain could only look on in horror during the course of the day as their bloated bodies came floating alongside him.[55]

The next day, Macquarie tried to ignore his groaning bowels and walked 25 kilometres using a strong pole to Durmapatam, where the 77th was due to camp. It 'was rather too long a walk for a convalescent, especially, as there were a number of little rivers or rullas in the way, all of which I was obliged to ford'.[56]

He finally made it, 'much indisposed, greatly fatigued, and wet and dirty', hoping to find his servants waiting with his baggage.

Instead, he was rendered 'extremely uncomfortable indeed', with no clean clothes to change into and nothing to eat or drink. There were no houses where he could shelter from the foul weather so he stayed in an 'old ruinous bungaloe', bedding down on a hard wooden cot with his cloak for a mattress, and 'in this ruinous habitation' spent one of the most uncomfortable nights of his life.[57]

The situation improved, however. The next day, friends supplied Macquarie with good things to feast upon and his servant Francis and his coolies arrived with his chestnut mare and baggage.

On 7 June, General Abercromby arrived at Durmapatam, and journeyed on to Tellicherry with instructions that, for now, the fighting was done and it was time to regroup.

'Thus ended our campaign!' the weary, ailing Captain Macquarie wrote. 'Our next, it is hoped, and expected, will be a more prosperous, as well as, a more brilliant and successful one.'[58]

Chapter 7

JUNE 1791 TO SEPTEMBER 1792, THE KINGDOM
OF MYSORE AND BOMBAY, INDIA

*I could not ride and was therefore under the necessity [of] being carried
the whole of the way in my dooly ... a very disagreeable mode of
travelling being very uneasy to a weak person from the constant jolting
and so oppressively hot that I thought I should be roasted alive.*

MACQUARIE TO MURDOCH MACLAINE, EXPLAINING
ANOTHER SERIOUS ILLNESS IN INDIA[1]

GRADUALLY, Macquarie's strength returned, and the yellow of his skin darkened to a healthier hue under the golden sun of Tellicherry. The city was an important trading port for spices, especially pepper and cardamom, and was protected by an imposing fort with huge walls and an impenetrable gate. But Macquarie was more interested in the restorative goodness of the local pawpaw, mango and jackfruit.

He spent months recuperating beside the beach, amid swaying palms and the large colonial homes of the Malabar Coast, with their wide verandas and colonnades and their verdant gardens. He moved into the house of his 'generous warm-hearted friend'[2] William Shaw,[3] a Bombay merchant, who for some time had also been indisposed, and had moved to the balmy climes of Tellicherry to boost his condition.

Macquarie felt right at home in the comfortable home of Shaw, who demonstrated a warm heart, but he despaired for his seriously ill friend. Macquarie would be deeply saddened when Shaw 'departed this life'[4] in early October, four months after Macquarie's arrival.

While he continued to recuperate, Macquarie read letters from friends and family in Scotland, of weddings and inheritances and a match between a friend, Christopher Lundin, and an 'amiable, deserving girl'.[5]

His spirits soared when he received 'a very agreeable letter' from his brother Charles, giving 'good accounts of himself, and the rest of our family's being all well and doing well'.[6] Charles had not yet settled into a business and was keen to try his fortune abroad. Soon Macquarie would send his brother £179 12s 10d 'to enable him to pay for his passage'[7] to India, and 'took the liberty to solicit [the] patronage and interest' of Generals Abercromby and Maclean on Charles's behalf.[8]

Soldiering was the only occupation in which Macquarie could 'possibly be of assistance and service' to Charles, though he was torn over it. He knew that, if Charles stayed on Mull, he would never arrive at the 'comfortable and genteel livelihood' that Macquarie wanted for him.[9] Yet he felt a 'repugnancy'[10] in taking him from their 'worthy affectionate good Mother' when she so needed him as comfort in her old age.

Macquarie received a letter informing him that Lauchlan would receive the prize money owed to his son, 'the deceased Lieut. John Macquarie', from a campaign against the Rohilla people in Northern India. Macquarie regarded the payout – 'two hundred and sixty one pounds, ten shillings and three pence, three farthings, sterling money' – as a 'most fortunate godsend' for 'the old gentleman … which, to him and his numerous family, in their present necessitous situation, is quite a little fortune'.[11]

It was a different story, however, for the clan chief's other son Murdoch Macquarie, Lachlan's first follower on the march from Mull to India. Lachlan had managed to score him a position in the Bombay Marine[12] as an ensign, but the teenage troublemaker had been dismissed as 'a worthless drunkard'.[13]

ON 13 AUGUST 1791, the local population of Tellicherry celebrated 'a great Holyday ... it being what they call Cocoa-Nut-Day; which they celebrate always on the first-full-moon in August, by throwing a cocoa-nut into the sea'. Macquarie was told that, once the ceremony was performed, the worst part of the monsoon on the Malabar Coast was over, and it was safe for all vessels to venture out to sea.[14]

The drums of war were beating, though, and by 27 November, he was back inside a tent at Cannanore, ready to move against Tipu Sultan at any time.

For 20 rupees a month, he had bought another servant, 'a Moor man', on the promise that the man's salary would rise to 25 a month if they got on.[15] However, his new head servant, sent to him in December by employment agents in Bombay, 'turn'd out a great rascal', and deserted Macquarie's service 'although he was always well treated, and received previous to his leaving Bombay ... 60 rupees as three months wages in advance'.[16] So Macquarie hired a new head servant, Malcolm McInnes, to run his own small army of ten underlings, including his team of coolie labourers. 'I reckon myself very well equipped for taking the field this campaign,' he noted, documenting in his journal that, along with 'several other little equipments', his team was bringing for him:

> ... a horse to ride occasionally, six bullocks for carriage of my baggage, a dooly to sleep in or to be carried in case of sickness, four dozen of Madeira [wine], four doz. brandy, some gin, two maunds [about 30 kilograms] of fine biscuit, a cheese, spices, two thirds of a tub of sugar, eight pounds [3.8 kilograms] of fine tea, some fowls and a small quantity of salt beef ... two small light trunks contained my clothes, linens and books and shoes. I have a new tent, a table, a chair, lamps or lanthorns, and 10 pounds [4.5 kilograms] of wax candles.[17]

The army finally moved off on 6 December 1791, but Macquarie had so much gear that the bullocks baulked at carrying it all, often lying down in the road and refusing to budge, no matter how much the coolies tried to move them. Macquarie left men and beasts where they were and carried on to meet his regiment, sleeping the first night in Dr Anderson's tent and faring much better than most of the other troops, who again had to sleep out in the open during a violent downpour.[18]

The next morning, Macquarie rode back to the recalcitrant bullocks with soldiers to help march them on, but the beasts would dawdle for most of what was a miserable journey for them and the men.[19] Rains flooded waterways and turned the roads into quagmires, and again the ghauts proved treacherous and almost impassable. On the ascent back up Poodicherrum Ghaut, equipment and baggage did not arrive on time, so men were again forced to lay themselves out on the ground during the night, 'which was exceedingly cold indeed'.[20]

On 13 February, when the 77th was guarding the rear, a force of looties roared in trying to steal the army's supplies. The looties killed a few soldiers who were leading bullocks, before 'flanking parties were sent out to disperse them'.[21] The next day Colonel Floyd, sent by Cornwallis to aid the army's progress, arrived with a body of infantrymen and 4000 local cavalrymen just in the nick of time: 4000 of Tipu's best horsemen 'made their appearance at the same instant' on Macquarie's right flank. Macquarie rather drily noted that the enemy cavalry 'would have annoyed us very much, had it not been for this very seasonable relief'.[22]

Some of Floyd's officers told Macquarie about the attack that Cornwallis, General Medows and Lieutenant-Colonel Hamilton Maxwell had led on Seringapatam a week earlier.[23] They claimed that a 'great and dreadful slaughter was made of the enemy, who fought bold and desperately for a long time, but were at last obliged to quit all their out works'. Cornwallis had lost only '11 officers killed and 22 wounded, and between 500 and 600 rank & file kill'd and wounded'. By contrast,

Macquarie heard that 'while the loss of the enemy could not be ascertained ... vast numbers of them were killed in the pursuit and Tipu, on a muster of his troops next morning, found that there were 21,000 short'[24] from the night before.

The forces of Maxwell and Cornwallis, bayonets drawn and screaming their battle cries, had chased the fleeing Mysoreans as they fled back across the bridges over the Kaveri and onto their island stronghold at Seringapatam, seeking protection within the fort. Tipu had raised his drawbridge to halt the British troops, but this had left many of his troops trapped outside.

Macquarie would later learn that Medows's role in the battle had been a disaster. In the dark of night, his forces had strayed too far to the left and left a gap in his line, dangerously exposing the British flank. Tipu had attacked the weak point and very nearly recovered his position, with Cornwallis wounded in the process.[25] Medows sank into a deep depression as a result.

Cornwallis, however, now had the town of Seringapatam at his mercy and was preparing to take the fort.

Macquarie finally caught sight of Cornwallis's huge fighting force, the Grand Army, on 16 February, as his own Bombay Army marched in columns of half companies to meet their comrades. Cornwallis and his senior officers passed along Macquarie's line, inspecting the different corps, and Macquarie described it as 'one of the happiest days I ever experienced in all my life, as there is nothing I ever so much wished for, as being present at the Siege of Seringapatam and joining the Grand Army'.[26]

His brigade got busy digging trenches while he dined with General Medows who, despite battling the blues, welcomed Macquarie 'very politely'.[27]

On 22 February, Tipu's men attacked from their fort, but they were driven back and the next day, Tipu sent out envoys to discuss a ceasefire. Macquarie's 77th Regiment was ordered into the trenches that night, and at daybreak, even though the peace process had started, Tipu's men 'commenced a pretty smart fire of long shots on the trenches and working parties', killing and wounding a few.[28]

Macquarie predicted the 'total ruin'[29] of Tipu, but at noon on 24 February, the 'Preliminaries of Peace' were signed and the great anti-climax of victory was announced. Macquarie had missed out on a thrilling battle just as his blood had begun to boil in anticipation. He told Uncle Murdoch that, faced with such an immense 'Confederate' army – consisting of the British, as well as the State of Hyderabad and the Mahratta (Maratha) Empire to the north – Tipu had 'unexpectedly got out of this scrape better than anyone could have imagined'.[30]

It was a blow to all the soldiers, Macquarie included, who had expected to acquire a great deal of honour, and plunder, in the storming of Seringapatam.[31] News of a peace treaty 'damped the spirits of every one who wished the downfall of the tyrant, and who hoped to have the satisfaction, in a few days more, of storming his capital'.[32]

Still, all was not entirely lost. Macquarie noted that, under the Treaty of Seringapatam, Tipu was obliged to 'relinquish forever half of his present dominions', and to pay 'three crores and thirty lacks [33 million] of rupees towards defraying the expenses of the war'.[33] Cornwallis announced a handsome gratuity for the soldiers from that payday.

To make sure Tipu upheld his end of the bargain, Cornwallis demanded that the vanquished sultan hand over two of his sons as hostages so that, as Macquarie wrote, 'every article of the treaty' was fulfilled.[34] So it was that on 26 February – in a ceremony commemorated by the painter Robert Home,[35] who travelled with Cornwallis in the campaign – Tipu's sons, aged seven and eleven, arrived in the British camp 'in great state and splendour'.[36]

General Medows couldn't help but feel guilty over the near-disaster on 6 February, however, and retired to his tent in a deep funk. Taking his pistols and hoping to end his misery, he shot himself three times. The whole camp was startled by the gunshots, coming just as the peace was concluded. But Medows failed in his suicide attempt, too.[37] 'He was severely wounded,' Macquarie reported, 'but the balls were immediately extracted, and he is again in a fair way of recovering.'[38]

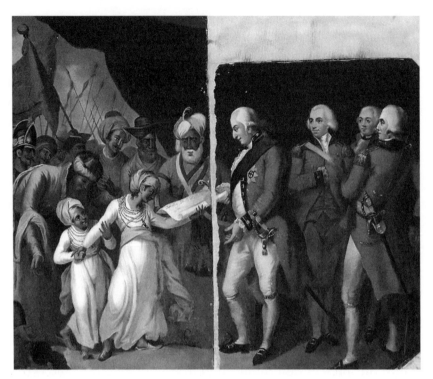

A 1792 painting by Mather Brown depicting British General Charles Cornwallis receiving as hostages two sons of Tipu Sultan at the end of the Third Anglo-Mysore War that year. The Bowes Museum

Medows spent days in great agony, and even greater embarrassment. When he was better, though, he distributed £5000 from his share of Tipu's settlement among the troops. He left for Great Britain six months later, only to be knighted at the end of the year.[39] The following year, he was promoted to lieutenant-general.[40]

The 77th had finished the siege without loss of life, and Macquarie had collected £308 as his prize money as well as some jewels, but he was again feeling like death warmed up as he began the arduous journey back to the coast. He had started to feel ill on his first night in the trench outside Seringapatam, and soon was sick again with what he said was 'the liver and dysentery (both peculiar to India and very dangerous complaints)'.[41]

For the next few weeks, he hovered close to death on the onerous return trek that began on 26 March 1792. He began ingesting tablets containing mercury,[42] intended to make him salivate and perspire. Macquarie's mouth was constantly sore and he had no strength in his legs.[43] He faced a severe trial trying to keep up with an army marching 25 kilometres a day through hard country. Not even the welcome news that General Abercromby had approved an ensigncy for Charles in the 77th could ease his burden.[44]

For much of the way across the barren desert and down the ghauts of Mysore, he was too weak to stay in the saddle. Instead, he was carried by eight men in his dooly while Dr Anderson rode by his side, offering 'friendly, tender and kind care'.[45]

At one point, the bearers dropped the dooly and broke it, and Macquarie was reluctant to get back in until proper repairs could be made, not trusting the patch-up work of the coolies.[46]

Abercromby took a keen interest in Macquarie's welfare, sending everything he could to ease his captain's distress, visiting him when he was able and dispatching aides to check on his welfare. Such concern from a man of Abercromby's standing and rank 'was very pleasing to a sick man'.[47]

Finally, on 6 April 1792, six weeks after Tipu's surrender, Macquarie was 'quite overjoyed' to fill his lungs again with the healing air of the sea at Cannanore. For a while, he stopped using mercury and began taking long morning rides on the beach, breathing in the sea air and growing stronger by the hour.[48]

On 13 April, he was rowed out to the *Hercules* and, with 500 men of the 77th, set sail for Bombay, the city he had left sixteen months earlier. Captain Galloway gave Macquarie his own cabin,[49] because he was still not over his sickness, and was back on the mercury tablets for a week.

The troops disembarked at Bombay on 21 April, and though Macquarie felt 'much better for the voyage',[50] it would take at least another month and the careful ministrations of the Surgeon-General of Bombay,[51] Dr Anthony Toomey, a 'humane good man',[52] before he felt on top of the disease.[53]

By September 1792, he could write to Uncle Murdoch and rejoice: 'Thank God I have got well over it … and I was never in better health than I am this moment … I look at least 10 years younger than when you last saw me in February 1788'.[54]

Macquarie hired a head servant, 'a Moor man named Bappoo', as well as a cook and a *massaljee*, and when the 77th marched from Bombay to the adjacent Colaba Island, Macquarie moved from his old rooms at the King's Barracks to a bungalow there. His new home was a little run down, but it had a fine view of the harbour and of the city beyond it.

Macquarie rented it for 60 rupees a month, 20 more than the army provided him in rent assistance.[55] He could only afford to stay there for five months before moving to a smaller house closer to town that cost 40 rupees a month,[56] but it was a happy home while it lasted.

It was there that Macquarie learned in September 1792, in a letter from home, that Uncle Murdoch and his wife Jane were celebrating the birth of a son and heir to continue the Lochbuie dynasty. Macquarie was gushing in his congratulations and in his fervent prayers for the family's happiness.[57]

It got him thinking about a wife and family of his own.

Chapter 8

Oh! what felicity – I actually thought for some minutes
I was in a dream! – Blessed adorable girl!
MACQUARIE ON HIS FIRST CARRIAGE RIDE WITH JANE JARVIS,
THE GIRL OF HIS DREAMS[1]

RETURNED TO VIGOUR, Macquarie resumed his former busy social life in the grand homes and ballrooms of Bombay. On 7 November 1792, at the home of banker John Forbes, Colonel Balfour introduced him to a wealthy merchant named James Morley[2] and his 'charming ... very kind and very attentive'[3] wife of three years, Dorothea.[4]

Morley was a member of the Bombay Council, and the most senior civil servant of the East India Company in Bombay. He had first arrived there as a teenager thirty-three years earlier, eager to make his way in the world. He was now fifty years old and his wife just twenty-four. Macquarie learned that Morley, who had been widowed three times, had married Dorothea in England, and returned to India in 1790 with assets of £25,000 to make an even larger fortune.

With the Morleys was Dorothea's younger sister, Jane Jarvis,[5] a twenty-year-old beauty with brown hair and blue eyes, cultivated, and with a personal fortune of £6000,[6] enough to buy a mansion of her own if she so chose. She also owned at least half a dozen slaves in the Caribbean, left to her by her father.

Dorothea and Jane had been born on the Caribbean island of Antigua, and Jane was the youngest daughter of Thomas Jarvis,[7] a sugar plantation owner who had been the chief justice there, and the sire of twenty-one children. Before his death in 1785, Jarvis had been growing 400 hectares of sugarcane on Antigua.[8]

He left a fortune to his widow and children. Macquarie noted that his widow, Jane and Dorothea's mother Rachel Jarvis,[9] now lived at 49 Welbeck Street in London in 'very genteel stile', and that a son, Thomas Jarvis III, ran the Antiguan plantations, which were worth £2000 a year.

Jane was with her sister merely as a companion and, unlike many young Englishwomen in Bombay, was not looking for a wealthy husband, because her own money put her 'far above such views'.[10]

Macquarie wrote in his journal that 'Mr. Morley's family' was 'seemingly a very pleasant one to be acquainted in; Mr. Morley is a sensible gentlemanlike man; Mrs. Morley, and her sister, Miss Jarvis, both appear to be well-bred elegant agreeable women'.[11]

Two weeks after meeting Jane, Macquarie danced a reel with her at the governor's ball,[12] and soon he was dining at the Morley home.[13] He found Jane 'young and handsome', with 'an excellent figure, rather above the middle size, with a most comely pleasing face and countenance (what I call pretty) ... but above all, a most amiable disposition and temper; with a good understanding, and a mind well cultivated and instructed by the best and finished education'.[14] He wondered how best to 'get possession of this jewel', because she seemed so far out of his league, and already many suitors of higher rank than his had proposed and been rejected. Poverty, he felt, had made him a 'coward lover', but he resolved to keep pursuing Jane, 'as amiable a good girl as ever lived'.[15]

Macquarie spent part of Christmas at the Morley home,[16] and danced the night away with Jane on New Year's Eve at a ball for Cornwallis's birthday. Two weeks later, he became a freemason, which meant more social connections, more invitations to more dinners and balls, and more chances to dance with Jane, who was on his arm at the Bombay Theatre for the knighthood investiture ceremony of General Robert Abercromby.[17]

Meanwhile, ships coming to Bombay brought news of 'the troubles in France … as violent and cruel as ever; – the Royal Family degraded and kept close prisoners without being allowed any attendants' by 'violent, infamous Republican leaders'.[18] The French Revolution meant trouble in Britain, too, 'where a great number of disaffected people to the present Government and Constitution' were 'endeavouring to foment a spirit of tumult and disorder amongst the lower classes' with 'acts of riot and insurrection'.[19] Before long, an American ship brought news that France had declared war against Great Britain and Holland, and that the French had put their king to death 'with many circumstances of horror and cruelty, after having gone through the form of a mock trial'.[20] The French had declared the First Republic[21] and ushered in a 'Reign of Terror' with a series of lynchings followed by the almost non-stop beheadings facilitated by the 'people's avenger', the guillotine. Between June 1793 and July 1794, there were 16,594 official death sentences in France, as those deemed enemies of the Republic were killed in macabre public displays.

General Abercromby appointed Macquarie as one of the managers of his farewell ball, held on 15 July 1793. The night was soured when a drunken civil servant brawled with another oddball, known as the Russian Bear, in the ballroom and had to be thrown out the door by a guard of sepoys. Moreover, Macquarie was to waltz there with Jane but she had 'a bad head–ach'.[22]

By now, he was 'sincerely and deeply in love'[23] with his 'Dulcinea',[24] though his natural reticence meant he had hid the truth even from himself for some time.

The next day at 10 a.m., James Morley called on Macquarie to talk about Jane.

> I thought at first that he only came to pay a complimentary
> visit – but to my very great surprise, after a few minutes

general discourse, he informed me, that the cause of his visit was to talk to me respecting my attentions to Miss Jarvis (his sister-in-law) to know what my views were, and if I was in a situation, with respect to fortune, to propose marriage to her – but that if my income did not admit of my making such proposals, that I should desist from paying his sister [in-law] such assiduous and pointed attentions.[25]

Morley looked Macquarie up and down. 'Macquarie,' the imperious businessman began, 'if you are really seriously attracted to Jane and if you have the fortune to marry her, Mrs Morley and I would both be very happy to forward your views. If that were the case, Macquarie, we would think ourselves much honoured in being connected with you.'[26]

Macquarie was so unprepared for such a delicate question, and 'so very much embarrassed and agitated' that he started talking gibberish, stumbling and stammering a reply:

… but in short, I confessed and avowed my partiality and love for Miss J. and that I should have made my sentiments known long ago had my situation in life with regard to fortune authorised me so to do, but that my circumscribed income precluded such a declaration at present; — however, that I was resolved, as soon as any change for the better in my circumstances warranted my so doing, to pay my addresses to Miss Jarvis as the woman of all others in the world I loved and adored most.

The conversation ended with a pledge from Macquarie 'not to be so particular in my attentions to Miss Jarvis untill I should be enabled to make proposals of marriage'. In return, Morley promised not to divulge the contents of their conversation to anyone except his wife, 'whom he would at the same time enjoin to secrecy'.[27]

The visit had drawn a truth from Macquarie that he had not wanted to make known to anyone for some time. He was now in the 'most perplexed, painful awkward situation that can possibly be conceived', 'extremely uneasy' in his mind and 'tortured between fear and hope'.[28]

> I have resolved to defer making any declaration of my sentiments to her, untill I know whether Sir Robert Abercromby will be kindly pleased to appoint me Major of Brigade to the King's Troops. If he does, I can and will then with propriety, and without departing from my promise to Mr. Morley propose marriage to my dearest and loveliest of women, Miss J.[29]

The favour Macquarie had curried with Abercromby, and his record in the campaigns he had fought in against Tipu, paid off. Two weeks after Morley asked Macquarie to show him the money if he wanted to marry Jane, Macquarie received the promotion he desired.[30] Being brigade-major meant a pay rise of £260 on top of the £500 per annum he was making, with expenses, as a captain.

Macquarie was 'now resolved' on quickly making Jane acquainted with his sentiments, and went to Morley's for supper that night.[31] But while he threw loving glances at Jane all evening, to his frustration, the opportunity to pour out his heart did not come.

He decided he could better express his feelings in a letter the next day. At eleven o'clock the next morning, he sent his servant Bappoo to the Morleys' house with 'strict orders' to deliver the letter into Jane's own hand, 'which he did, but got no answer only to make compliments'.[32]

Morley then left a note at Macquarie's house, making an appointment for 9 a.m. the following day.[33] Macquarie's 'anxiety between fear and hope'[34] was greater than he could describe.

His feelings were not eased the next morning, when Morley told him that Jane had read his letter but 'wished to take a little time to consider' the proposal 'before she would give a decisive answer'.[35]

Morley looked at Macquarie coolly. 'You know, Macquarie,' he said, 'it is very expensive to maintain a wife and family in a genteel way in this country. If you do not have a sufficient fortune you should not think of involving my sister-in-law in difficulties.'[36] Jane's fortune, Morley said, was hers and not to be shared.

Macquarie bristled. 'I never thought of Miss Jarvis's fortune,' he answered back. 'I, sir, am not guided or influenced by sordid or mercenary motives of that sort. My attachment to her proceeds alone from real love and admiration and the pleasing manners and qualifications she is endowed with.'

Macquarie got into his stride. 'I was so happy as to enjoy her good opinion,' he later confided in his journal, 'and that she could place her affections on me. I now feel myself in a situation to maintain her in a genteel moderate way without touching her private fortune, which I did not conceive I had any right to meddle with or use.'[37]

Macquarie promised Morley he would settle £1000 on Jane, which was all he had, but whenever fortune threw more in his way, he would top up the amount to convince her and her friends how dear she was to him and 'how sincerely and warmly' he was attached to her.[38]

He gave Morley a card on which he had noted his income and expenditure. Macquarie's plan was to stay in India for six years so that he could bank enough to earn £500 a year in interest.

Morley thanked him for his honesty and promised to immediately consult Jane and his wife.

He stood to leave. 'Macquarie, I should be exceedingly happy to see you and Jane united,' he said, 'but you know it is my duty to do all in my power to prevent Jane from connecting herself with one who cannot support her in a genteel comfortable style.'

Macquarie's heart was going faster than it had been climbing the ghauts.

'However, I will explain your circumstances to her,' Morley promised, 'and I will leave it entirely to her.'

Silence filled the void.

'Good day, Macquarie, you should hear from me in two or three days.'[39]

Only an hour later, Macquarie received a note saying Morley would call on him once more:

He came in about half an hour afterwards, and was pleased to announce to me the most delightful, acceptable and pleasing intelligence that I ever yet was made happy with – vizt. – that he had talked to Miss Jarvis and that she was resolved to accept of my offers, to which he added, that she had declared that she preferred me to all other men in the world. — What heavenly news this! Oh delightful glorious and generous girl! — It was not in my power to express to Mr Morley my unfeigned joy on this happy occasion – all I could say was to thank him and that I felt much more than I could say – but to assure Miss Jarvis that I thought myself most highly honoured in possessing her good opinion, and that I felt myself now the happiest man on earth.[40]

Morley invited Macquarie to come to his house at 7 p.m. the same day.

Macquarie was so full of joy he couldn't contain it. He had to rush out and tell someone the good news as quickly as possible, so he trotted over to Dr Anderson's digs to receive the heartiest of handshakes and backslaps from the man who had helped to save his life.

That afternoon, he took a short walk on the Bombay Esplanade to clear his mind and compose his thoughts, before arriving at the Morleys' house at 7 p.m. sharp. Mrs Morley and Jane made their appearance and Macquarie had some 'pleasing and interesting conversation' with the 'delight of [his] heart and soul':

… but some strangers coming oblig'd us to break off our discourse abruptly, tho' I never felt myself in the whole course of my life happier than at this delightful interview. I believe it was fortunate that we were interrupted for I was so agitated and overcome with joy, that I did not well know what I said to Miss Jarvis. I must have spoken very incoherently indeed, for I never felt myself so much discomposed … I spent the happiest evening of my life in company with my beloved and dearest of women.[41]

It was now the fifth anniversary of his departure for India aboard the *Dublin*, and he confided in his journal that he felt he had spent the greater part of his time engaged 'very improfitably and idly'. With marriage on the near horizon, he promised himself that he would alter his conduct. Weighing his present situation and pursuits, he was thoroughly convinced he should live 'more temperately and rationally', as it was 'absolutely necessary ... for the preservation of my life and health, as for my future happiness through life'. He had not read or studied 'near so much as I ought to have done'.[42]

He now 'very seriously resolved and determined' to live in the following manner:

First. Whether I am late out overnight or not, I am always to rise and get up at sunrise; or at farthest at six o'clock; and if not, for any duty or obliged to attend parades, I am to employ the morning from six till seven o'clock, in exercise of walking or riding; – to read from seven till eight o'clock; and breakfast precisely at eight o'clock.

Secondly. If I have any duty or business to transact, either as Major of Brigade or paymaster of the regiment, or capt. of the company I command, the hours between nine and twelve o'clock, always to be devoted entirely to such duties or occupations as my offices may require.

Thirdly. The time from twelve to two o'clock, to be always employed in improving my mind by serious reading and study – a part of this time is always to be devoted to reading such military books, as may tend to teach me my profession and instruct me in a further knowledge of it.

Fourthly. I am always to dress at two o'clock or at half past two o'clock at farthest.

Fifthly. When I dine abroad, I am never to drink more than equal to one bottle of wine – that is to say, twelve glasses; three of those only to be Madeira, and the rest hock or claret – to avoid drinking malt liquor as much as possible, but on no account to drink any at night, nor never to exceed one lumba [small bottle] of strong beer even at dinner.

Sixthly. While in Bombay to make it a rule, in order to keep up my acquaintance to visit the families I am acquainted with in Bombay, each once in the fortnight; – for this purpose, the evenings of Mondays and Fridays, are to be set apart for visiting those families that I am only slightly acquainted in; and to visit those I am more intimate in, on the other nights of the week or as it may suit my conveniency; but, to eat suppers as seldom as possible, and then, never exceed two glasses of wine.

Seventhly. When I spend the evenings at home, to amuse myself with music, or light reading untill bed-time; and if possible, always to go to bed before eleven o'clock. – There may be exceptions now and then to the foregoing rules or distribution of time, but care must be taken to make as few deviations as possible from them: – this I am resolved and determine to adhere strictly to, in testimony whereof I subscribe my name on this the fifth day of August, 1793.

L. Macquarie.

N.B. Punctuality with regard to time and appointments, to be particularly attended to, as well as the foregoing rules from this day henceforth.[43]

He began spending every day with Jane, who always 'looked charming and elegant',[44] and he went hunting for a suitable home for them. He started accompanying her to church on Sundays, and Mrs Morley arranged for them to ride together 'in the chariot'[45] with the Morleys' infant son Charles.[46] Macquarie couldn't wipe the smile from his face, 'for, in Bombay a gentleman and a lady in a carriage together, marries them immediately'.[47] Another suitor gave Macquarie evil 'Gorgon looks' as he and Jane walked with the Morleys through Bombay's cloying heat.[48]

In his first official duty as brigade-major, Macquarie supervised the execution by firing squad of a deserter named Private John Stevens, 'an awful and solemn occasion'.[49] But almost as soon as the dead man's bloodied, bullet-riddled corpse was being carried away, Macquarie was writing a note to his 'lovely dear, to enquire how her head–ach was' and sending her Boswell's *Journal of a Tour to the Hebrides* to read. After being indisposed for much of the evening, Jane made her appearance at the Morley dinner table, her countenance beaming 'benignity and love'.[50]

The next evening, Macquarie and Jane were guests at another officer's wedding, and Macquarie wished it was theirs instead, because it was painful to wait with 'so much bliss in view'.[51] He used his connections to help Jane's younger brother, George Jarvis,[52] a young ensign newly arrived in India, find a place in the army. Macquarie's 'loveliest and dearest Jane' gave him the 'elegant' dress watch and seals she had received from her mother, which she insisted he should wear for her sake. His 'angel' also cut off a lock of her hair so Macquarie could wear it on a chain around his neck. Dorothea Morley gave him a handsome steel corkscrew and he promised to keep it 'forever for her sake … what a happy fellow I am!'[53]

The wedding was set for Sunday, 8 September 1793, and Macquarie and Jane spent the weeks beforehand riding in the country and confessing their love for each other again and again. Macquarie's vows to concentrate solely on military matters from 9 a.m. to noon were quickly forgotten.

He bought Jane a wedding ring and found a house worthy of his beloved.[54] It had been lent to him by Bombay's Superintendent of the Marine, and was situated in a 'clean, airy, undisturbed' part of town. Although the rent was a steep 150 rupees a month, Macquarie was willing to spend anything to keep Jane in the style to which she was accustomed.[55]

On 2 September, the pair agreed to the marriage contract joining Jane's £6000 with Macquarie's £1000 being held in trust for subsequent children. The money was to be banked in England, where they felt it would be safer, and where it would attract 9 per cent interest. On 7 September, the acting governor of Bombay, George Dick, gave Macquarie his marriage licence.

Finally, the grand day arrived. Macquarie and Jane had arranged for the wedding to be held on the veranda of the Morleys' home in the company of 'numerous and very respectable' friends and acquaintances. The Reverend Arnold Burrowes, midway through a forty-year stint as the Anglican minister of Bombay,[56] would perform the ceremony at 7 p.m.

Macquarie had his last bachelor's dinner with Colin Anderson before heading home to dress in his officer's uniform with all his pomp and glory. He lingered a little too long over his appearance and arrived at the Morleys' house red-faced and late, only to run into Jane in the hall after she had just finished dressing. Jane was 'elegantly attired (her lovely countenance beaming full of beneficence, beauty and unaffected modesty)'.[57] She was on Morley's arm, and was followed by Mrs Morley and the ladies in her bridal party.

After Burrowes pronounced the Macquaries husband and wife, Macquarie kissed Jane passionately and then kissed all the other ladies in the bridal party, his fellow officers repeating the ritual close behind him.

Dorothea had prepared 'a most elegant supper' and twenty-eight guests sat down to enjoy it. 'All was mirth and good humour, tempered by strict decorum, politeness and temperance', though songs were sung until after midnight.[58] Macquarie reckoned that no Benedict[59] could be 'better pleased with his lot and good fortune, in the choice of a wife!'[60]

Dorothea accompanied the Macquaries to their new home and saw Jane to her matrimonial bed. Macquarie told her he would take it from there and ushered Mrs Morley away to her carriage as quickly as possible.

Dorothea's wheels had hardly started turning when Macquarie fairly flew 'on the wings of love' into the bedroom where Jane, his 'dearest of women', waited with bated breath.

At last, Macquarie could crown his 'measure of happiness and bliss'.[61]

He was not to know that the joy would be shortlived.

Chapter 9

SEPTEMBER 1793 TO JULY 1795,
BOMBAY AND CALICUT, INDIA

Lieut. Gray having been sent on duty to Cochin after deserters,
I commissioned him to procure and purchase two young
smart slave boys at that place.

MACQUARIE ON THE PURCHASE OF TWO HUMAN BEINGS, ONE OF WHOM
WOULD PLAY A HUGE PART IN HIS LIFE[1]

FOR THE NEXT FIVE DAYS, Mr and Mrs Macquarie put up the 'Do Not Disturb' notice at their new house, 'not wishing to have our own little interesting society and conversation interrupted'.[2] The groom wanted Jane all to himself, but the Morleys came calling every day and spent two or three evenings dining with the happy couple and listening to their excited plans for the future. Macquarie tried to restrict visitors to 'a very few select friends'[3] but, in all, thirty-eight people called in over those few days to inquire how married life was treating them both.

Eight days after being united in matrimony, the newlyweds borrowed the carriage of East India Company bigwig John Tasker[4] to take them to a ball and supper, and this was followed by three nights of 'sitting up in form',[5] in accordance with 'the old Bombay custom', 'to receive visits and compliments of such friends as should be disposed to call on us'.[6]

Macquarie could not wipe the smile off his face as he and Jane became A-listers in Bombay's high society, even though he was 'much displeased' when a letter arrived from his brother Charles telling him that, despite Macquarie's enticements, he would stay on Mull for another year to help Uncle Murdoch, 'whose affairs [were] a good deal deranged and embarrassed'. Murdoch needed Charles, who for some years had acted as his uncle's birleyman on the Lochbuie estate. Murdoch was in such dire financial straits that he had accepted a position as a half-pay major of the Argyleshire Fencible Regiment, 'lately raised by the Marquis of Lorn'.[7] Macquarie no longer saw his mentor as a powerful laird and benefactor, but rather as a 'pleasant old veteran' who, out of desperation, offered to sell Macquarie some of his mortgaged lands[8] to ease his own debt.

Meanwhile, Macquarie wasn't getting on so well with the abrasive and imperious James Morley, who still saw himself as Jane's guardian and, by default, Macquarie's boss. Macquarie, though, was enamoured with Morley's better half Dorothea, whom he repeatedly referred to as 'a most charming woman'. He reached out to their mother Mrs Rachel Jarvis, too, writing to her in England and referring to her as 'my dear Mother'.[9] He asked her to sit for a miniature portrait at his expense and to put some of her hair in the back of the picture and in a breast locket, in which Macquarie also planned to keep locks from Jane and her 'lovely sister'.[10]

He told his new mother-in-law it was unnecessary for him to give her a 'panegyrick' of such a charming daughter:

> … you already know her worth and excellencies, which are far beyond my praise; and therefore I shall only observe, that I reckon myself not only supremely happy, but also, the most fortunate and happiest of men, to be in possession of so great and valuable a blessing … my fortune is very small, but I believe, I may say without vanity, that my character and connexions are unexceptionable and will bear the strictest enquiry.[11]

Despite their wedded bliss, money was tight for the Macquaries even on a major's salary. Morley had been right to warn him how expensive it was to provide for a genteel Englishwoman in style, particularly given that they had now become 'constantly engaged' in a round of entertainments organised by their many friends in Bombay.[12] There were nights Macquarie spent smoking hookahs with fellow officers at the Sans Souci Club, and lavish balls and suppers at the governor's home, or at Tasker's Admiralty House, or at the mayoral mansion of P.C. Bruce the banker, or with the Balfours, or the Hallidays, or the Morrises, or the Sandifords, Simsons, Setons, Crokatts and Lewises,[13] or dozens more of Bombay's smart set. Then there was Jane's twenty-first birthday party, 'our first publick dinner'.[14] On another occasion, the Macquaries watched on in a gathering of crisp uniforms, flowing skirts, bright palanquins and ornate carriages as:

> ... a race was run over Back–Bay Sands, from the General Hospital to the Arbour, between Mr. Morley's arab horse *Sheik* and Lt. O'Donnell's arab horse *Sultan*; the latter horse won the race. The sport was highly pleasing, and a very numerous company of ladies and gentlemen attended – my dearest Mrs. M. rode on horseback, and I went thither in my palanquin.[15]

Six weeks after the wedding day, having settled his £1000 into a mutual fund with Jane, Macquarie was 5200 rupees in debt. At least his marital home was well supplied with 'plate, furniture, wines, liquors and stores',[16] and he planned to clear off his arrears within a short time 'by rigid and strict but genteel economy in our manner of living', even though 'in Bombay ... every family of any consequence must live as their neighbours do'.[17]

After hosting a few friends who had 'been so very polite and attentive in entertaining us after our marriage', he resolved that he and Jane would try to save in order to discharge some of their debts.[18] He reckoned it would be his fault and not Jane's if their living expenses exceeded their budget of 500 rupees per month.

And Jane's amiable nature proved a blessing in more ways than one. Just a few days after Macquarie was scratching his head over their costs, his bride received 4000 rupees in the will of a dead colonel who had admired her from afar:

> My dearest, generous wife has transferred this sum over to me to do what I like with it, and I have lodged it accordingly in the hands of my agents, Messrs Bruce, Fawcett & Co. to bear interest at nine per cent, for our mutual use and support. This by the bye comes in at the present moment as quite a godsend to us, as it clears me of debt entirely ...[19]

Before long, Macquarie was sharing his new wealth with his family in Scotland, sending home presents – shawls for his mother and sister and Murdoch Maclaine's wife, who sent a locket in return, containing some of her and Murdoch's hair.[20] He offered to pay the rent on his mother's farm at Oskamull at £22 a year 'to enable her and my brother Donald to live comfortably'. He also wanted to provide some money for his sister Betty and her young family, and a couple of years' schooling for his nephew Murdoch.[21] He gave Charles £300[22] to tide him over on Mull, as the good life continued in Bombay, with lavish banquets almost every second night. He dined with Rear-Admiral William Cornwallis, the general's wildly popular younger brother, affectionately known as Billy Blue. Macquarie thought him 'a plain honest blunt man, and quite the gallant brave sailor in his appearance',[23] and found his behaviour 'extremely polite, affable and attentive'.[24]

The dead colonel's largesse could not last forever, though. Macquarie was earning 500 rupees a month but was spending 800. He was paying rent of £200 a year and another £150 for servants, and from the rest had to find money for a fine carriage, 'for there is no doing without one in this country, when there is a lady in the question'.[25] Yet he told Murdoch that Jane was 'a great economist and manager' and they would be able to continue living 'comfortably and genteely' on his salary.[26]

The couple decided to save £65 a year by moving to a cheaper house owned by the businessman Daddy Nasserwanjee,[27] opposite the dockyard. They eventually gave up plans for a carriage from England that Dorothea Morley had promised to source[28] in favour of 'a new Bengal-built Gigham, from Mr Joseph Harding', which cost 500 rupees and would be drawn not by a team of chargers, but rather by a 'good, strong well-tempered white coloured horse' bought from Nasserwanjee Monachjee for 400 rupees.[29]

WHILE MACQUARIE was trying to stay ahead of his debts in India, John Macarthur was building a fortune in Parramatta. Major Francis Grose had taken control of New South Wales in 1792 after illness had forced Arthur Phillip to return home, accompanied by two Indigenous men from the new colony, Bennelong and the teenager Yemmerrawanne.[30] Grose had doubled Macarthur's salary, making him paymaster of the New South Wales Corps, and Inspector of Public Works, which gave Macarthur control of the colony's captive workforce, materials and machinery.

Macarthur and his wife had established Elizabeth Farm at Parramatta, on a 40-hectare grant of land that Elizabeth called 'some of the best ground that has been discovered'.[31] Convict labour helped Macarthur become the first man in the colony to clear and cultivate 20 hectares of virgin land and this earned him another 40-hectare grant.

By 1794 he was on his way to becoming a land baron.

THE MACQUARIES' WORLD was rocked in January 1794 when news arrived from London that Jane and Dorothea's mother was ailing. Dorothea prepared to visit her, not realising she would not get there in time to say goodbye.

On the day of Dorothea's departure, 16 January, Jane went to the Morleys' house immediately after breakfast and stayed there with Dorothea and her three children, Maria, Charles and Harriet, 'all with heavy aching heart', until the final minute came to embark. It was agony saying goodbye to the children, too, because Jane so desperately wanted to be a mother like Dorothea.

'The moment of their parting was a hard trial on them both,' Macquarie wrote, 'and proved extremely affecting – my lovely girl was quite overcome with grief and suffered exceedingly on the occasion; we were obliged to tear them from each other's embrace.'[32] A friend stayed with Jane until she regained her composure.

With a heavy heart, Dorothea left Jane and proceeded to the dock, accompanied by Macquarie, Morley and two friends. Privately, Dorothea implored Macquarie to try to get along with her mercurial husband in her absence.

Two weeks later, Macquarie received word that his promotion to major should have been sold as a 'purchase' under the British cash for ranking system and that, consequently, he owed the army £550.[33] It was bad news on his thirty-third birthday, but things were about to go from bad to worse.

Without Dorothea to smooth things out, his relationship with Morley was worsening every day, even though the ageing businessman dined with Macquarie and Jane every Sunday 'in a friendly way'.[34] Morley was one of the most successful businessmen in Bombay. He saw in Macquarie an opportunist who had married a woman far above his station and who was amassing a considerable fortune because of her and her family.

Meanwhile, Macquarie stayed busy with the vagaries of colonial life. George Jarvis, Jane's younger brother, was made a lieutenant in the 36th Regiment[35] and Macquarie's friend Major Henry Oakes[36] lost his infant son to smallpox. Macquarie and Jane used one of his bunder boats for some pleasant sailing around the harbour.[37]

Even though things were becoming frosty with Morley, Macquarie accepted his offer of a nine-day cruise on board his new square-rigged, two-masted yacht *Maria*,[38] named after his eldest daughter. The banker John Forbes was coming too. Morley had a skipper, two officers and about twenty lascars – Indian sailors – as crew.[39] In case of attack from pirates, his yacht was equipped with four six-pound cannons and some short-barrelled muskets.[40]

As they sailed south, the swell made the passengers seasick, but they got the better of it by dinner time and all displayed a 'tolerable good appetite'[41] at Morley's table as they talked about some sightseeing at 'the famous city of Goa'.[42] When they arrived there, after two days luxuriating on the high seas and feasting on mangoes and melons, they were entertained by the city's Portuguese governor, the esteemed military man Francisco da Cunha e Meneses,[43] who provided his own government barge and '12 oarsmen, all in rich uniform'[44] to transport the party up river. He also gave the English tourists an officer as a guide to all the grandeur, and a selection of palanquins so they did not have to get their feet wet or dirty.[45] The party took in the magnificent view of frigates in the harbour and the lush surrounding islands, before taking a closer look at the city's ornate churches and other buildings, as well as the black marble tomb of St Francis Xavier, topped by silver and gold.

Tension was high as the yacht sailed home to Bombay, staying as far in front as they could from nearby pirates. Morley and Macquarie had struggled to get on, even if the cruise had been a pleasurable one.

The first news that greeted them all when they moored was that Marie Antoinette, Queen of France, had been beheaded by revolutionaries.[46]

ON 14 JUNE 1794, Morley forwarded a letter he had received that morning from Jane's eldest brother, Thomas Jarvis. It informed them that Jane's mother had died on 14 January, two days before Dorothea had left for England, and before Macquarie's affectionate letter had reached her. Rachel Jarvis had left her London home to stay in Southampton, hoping the sea air would act as a tonic, but it had not proved to be the case.

Jane was a delicate, fragile creature, and 'was always doatingly fond'[47] of her mother. Macquarie was so concerned by what the news of the tragedy would do to his wife that he didn't have the heart to tell her. Instead, he waited a day until two of her friends,

Mrs Stirling and Mrs Dorothea Oakes, could break the news 'with the greatest delicacy, tenderness and friendship'.[48]

Though the two women tried to cushion the blow, Jane suffered 'the keenest anguish and most poignant grief' before Macquarie joined the three ladies, and with tender kisses 'endeavoured by every means' in his power to soothe her pain.[49] It worked for a while, but two days later Jane was still bursting into frequent tears, giving full vent to her sorrow, notwithstanding all Macquarie said or did to console her.[50]

Time helped to heal the wounds. Macquarie took Jane on carriage rides and out to suppers, and they watched the comedy *She Stoops to Conquer*,[51] which was performed to great applause.[52]

Money problems, however, continued to haunt him. In her will,[53] Rachel had left her oldest son Thomas £1000 a year and 'the rest part of the negroes which I had reserved in a deed during my natural life'.[54] Thomas was not so generous. He stalled when it came to handing over Jane's inheritance, and with money running short, Macquarie asked Tasker to fire up his London money men, the Goslings, 'should it be found necessary, to make immediate payment' of the money she was owed.[55]

Macquarie also put up his hand for the 'handsome and lucrative' position of Deputy Paymaster-General of Bombay, on a salary of 600 rupees a month plus allowances,[56] but was 'a good deal disappointed'[57] when it went to his friend Captain James Dunlop.[58]

Morley was more than disappointed in Macquarie when he found that, months earlier, he had asked Dorothea to source both a carriage and silverware in London and to have them engraved with the 'arms of Ulva'.[59] Macquarie had told Dorothea that Francis and Gosling, the London bankers who held the Macquaries' money, would provide payment from Jane's accrued interest. Morley – or 'Old Morley'[60] as Macquarie now referred to him in correspondence – was livid, pointing out that, as co-trustee (with John Tasker) of Jane's money, it was *he* who decided how the fortune should be spent.

Despite Macquarie's protest that it had been an innocent mistake, Old Morley flew into a rage and told him that his behaviour had been 'fraudulent'. He was suspicious about Macquarie's motives in chasing Jane from the start. He served him with notice 'in very harsh language, desiring to be discharged from their trust'.[61]

Macquarie's back was up. He described Old Morley's behaviour as 'imperious caprice and marked ill nature' and vowed to sever all ties with him. He hoped Dorothea might talk some sense into her husband and told her 'of the innocence and rectitude of my own conduct, which has yet been unsullied and no one has ever dared to impeach'.[62]

Morley got on his yacht and sailed home to London, though Macquarie secretly hoped he might 'fret himself to death' before he reached England.[63] Jane was more stressed than ever. She had lost her mother and knew now that she might not see her sister and the children for a long time.

It looked like Macquarie might soon be on the move too.

On 16 July 1794, his 77th Regiment was ordered to 'hold themselves in readiness to proceed to Madras'[64] (now Chennai), though Macquarie was instructed to remain in Bombay for now.[65] Still, it made Macquarie nervous – and not just because more fighting with Tipu seemed to be on the horizon.

Whatever happened, Macquarie faced a cut in pay. If he marched out of Bombay with his regiment he would no longer be the brigade-major there. If he stayed as part of the headquarters staff, he would lose his extra money as regimental paymaster. By now, his living expenses had him in the red again to the tune of another 5200 rupees.

More unsettling news followed. On 4 September a fleet of Indiamen arrived in Bombay, and Macquarie was 'much chagrined and disappointed' when his brother Charles did not arrive with it, having paid for Charles's passage on one of the ships.[66] Charles had drawn an ensign's salary for a year while actually thousands of miles from his regiment, and a lieutenancy had been on offer when he arrived in India.

'All these good prospects he has lost and sacrificed, by accepting of a lieutenancy in a new regiment, raising in Scotland by the Earl of Breadalbane'.[67] He poured out his frustrations in a letter to his sibling:

> Oh! Charles! Charles! You have indeed hurt my feelings very much. My word, which, as yet, has been held sacred, is forfeited. I pledged myself in the most solemn manner to Sir Robert Abercromby, that you certainly would come out this season. I once stood high in his esteem. I shall now be affronted and degraded in his opinion and never – never – shall I have the face to ask him for another favour, as long as I live.[68]

But his sour mood was brightened slightly on 24 September: as the rest of the 77th got ready to ship out to the Malabar Coast, James Dunlop offered to act as brigade-major while he was away, thus solving his earlier dilemma. The move would have other benefits too: 'it is much for my interest, for many reasons, to go down the coast and leave Bombay; where, I find my expences, far exceeds my present income; and, on the Malabar Coast, I hope, we shall be able to live within our income'.[69]

Things improved even further on 10 October, with news brought by the ship *Panther* that the British had sunk French ships off Ushant in Brittany. In Paris, the French Revolution's 'monster and Chief of Crimes Robespiere' had been executed, which Macquarie saw as 'due and just vengeance' on an 'unfeeling barbarian', who had caused so much misery and death among the French aristocracy.[70]

Two weeks later, Colonel Carr Howson, commander-in-chief of the British forces serving in the west of India, died suddenly in Bombay,[71] and Balfour was appointed his successor. Despite having resigned himself to leaving Bombay, Macquarie now saw an opportunity to stay and make even more money.

Macquarie wrote to Balfour asking him to make him 'one of his family'[72] by appointing him to his staff. He asked the colonel to move in with Jane and him while his own quarters in the Tank Barracks were made ready. Balfour accepted this invitation, but knocked him back for a staff post, and Macquarie seethed.

He had believed that Balfour 'had a sincere friendship for, and a wish to serve me, but I am now fully persuaded he has neither'. Bitterly, he wrote that Balfour was 'not capable of doing a friendly office to anyone but as far as it tends to his own advantage; in short I have done with him as a friend ... I consider him what he really is, a most selfish, sordid, avaricious unfeeling character; and as such, I withdraw my friendship entirely from him from this day henceforth'.[73] So there.

Things remained tense while Balfour stayed in the Macquarie home, and although they eventually became firm friends, Macquarie knew he now had no alternative but to pack up and head to a new base for the 77th's next campaign at Calicut.

ON 20 DECEMBER 1794, the Macquaries set sail on board the *Endeavour*,[74] and though 'poor dear Jane', who had been ill in the preceding days, was 'very much affected' at farewelling her friends, having a team of servants and all her baggage on board made the parting bearable.[75] The *Endeavour*'s skipper, Captain Bampton, did his best to make her comfortable during the voyage, and Colonel Bowles, the brigadier, 'sung every night for the ladies'.[76] But it was not a merry voyage.

Christmas Day was spent 'very sociably and merrily',[77] but two days later, Macquarie's clerk Harvey died an agonising death from dysentery.

On 30 December, after eight days at sea, the Macquaries arrived at Calicut and settled into a bungalow that Macquarie had bought from Dr Charles Ker, surgeon to the 75th Regiment. It was about 6 kilometres outside town, in a 'most delightfully situated [area] on high, airy beautiful hills, commanding a most charming view and prospect of the country round and of the sea at a distance'.[78] It was a 'sweet spot', a good distance from the road, as well as the bazaar, and had an excellent garden and large bedrooms. Dr Ker 'was so obliging' as to leave a large stock of bullocks, goats and pigeons.[79]

Macquarie named it 'Staffa Lodge'[80] after his clan's island territory in Scotland. He dreamed of one day having such a home in the place of his birth.[81]

He had paid Dr Ker 400 rupees for the property, and soon forked out another 700 for renovations,[82] with native labour plugging the holes in the bamboo walls and roof with a mud stucco for when the monsoon rains came in June[83] and they would be shut inside for an entire sodden month.

The Macquaries did not need a carriage, because they were well provided 'with cavalry'. Even though 'Mrs. M.' always had the use of a palanquin and bearers, Macquarie paid 300 rupees for a Bengal 'Turkai' horse, which was 'very quiet and gentle, but sufficiently lively for a lady'. He preferred to ride his old grey, because as everyone knew, he was 'not the best horseman in the world'.[84]

Living expenses were so moderate in their new home that Macquarie could splash his cash on luxuries. Two weeks after they had arrived in Calicut, on hearing that Lieutenant Gray was going 180 kilometres south to Cochin[85] chasing deserters, Macquarie asked him to buy two young Indian slave boys. He stipulated that they had to be smart.[86]

Ten days later, Macquarie was delighted to note:

Lieut. Gray returned from Cochin, and brought me two very fine, well-looking healthy black boys; both seemingly of the same age, and I should suppose from their size and appearance that they must be between six and seven year old. The stoutest of them Mrs Macquarie has called Hector after my brother: and the smallest I have called George after her brother … We had the boys immediately well washed, their hair cut and combed, and well clothed.[87]

Macquarie thought the boys were a bargain at 170 rupees a pair and he would grow fond of them both, in contrast to many slave owners of the time.

The happy couple did not scrimp on other purchases either. When comrade Lieutenant Shaw's wife had to leave for Bombay in April 1795, on account of her pregnancy, Jane was the only woman left at the military camp and she became the pivot of social activities. The Macquaries had to entertain in some style, and soon Macquarie was sending a grocery list to Nash, Grantham & Co in London for:

> 12 dozen of Madeira in bottles of the same kind I had from you in December last at eleven rupees per dozen.
> Two casks of good pale ale,
> 4 English hams of the smallest size,
> 6 good pineapple cheeses,
> 1 case of pickles,
> 2 bottles of pickled mushrooms,
> 6 bottles of ketchup,
> 1 box of fine raisins,
> 1 maund of fresh almonds in the shell,
> 1 keg or firkin of salt tongues,
> 1 kit of salt salmon,
> 10 pounds of coffee,
> 10 pounds of barley,
> 1 maund of wax candles.

Macquarie asked that the suppliers send him the goods 'per the first boat that comes down the coast', and that they 'be of the best quality and carefully packed up; directing them for me at Calicut, accompanied with an account of their amount'.[88]

Macquarie started working on his own little kingdom, fencing his 'estate' and planting trees for what he envisaged would become an English country garden, as Jane — or 'Lady Mull' as he liked to call her — followed him, 'charmed with the beauty of the countryside and the novelty of carrying the knapsack and roughing it as a soldier's wife'.[89] Macquarie was most at home in the country setting and his new rural home gave him endless possibilities to plan for life as a Sottish laird.

In July 1795, Jane's younger brother George Jarvis arrived for a visit to Staffa Lodge, drenched after an overland trip during the monsoon. Both the Macquaries were overjoyed to see him, especially 'Poor Jane', who 'was beyond measure happy at seeing her brother in her own house',[90] brushing the water off his back as she planted kisses on his cheek. Macquarie thought George to be 'a fine stout handsome young man', and very like his sister. 'I like his appearance and manner very much,' he wrote. Macquarie and Jane longed one day to have a son just like him.[91]

AS MACQUARIE planted trees around his home, he was also busy building another empire, through a clandestine scheme with Major (formerly Captain) Dunlop, the Deputy Paymaster-General of Bombay. Macquarie realised he could use Dunlop's situation, and his own position as paymaster of the 77th, to make money for himself.

In 1795 and 1796, he drew his regiment's pay from three to five months in advance and invested it with local shroffs – bankers – including the Arab moneylender Hadjee Eesooff.[92] He was able to pick up 3 to 6 per cent interest,[93] and in mid-July 1795, he transferred 7000 rupees into his personal account with John Forbes in Bombay.[94] Between 1790 and 1799, Macquarie would make no less than £9000 from his different stints as a paymaster, or about $A1.6 million in 2019 value.

But his banking activities were fraught with danger. He knew it was 'an advantageous thing' to be 'regimental paymaster on the coast',[95] but he did not want to face an inquiry as Murdoch Maclaine had after the war in America. On 24 July, after a period of silence from Dunlop, Macquarie assured his partner in the scheme that 'it never was my wish or intention to allow you to run the least risk on my account'.[96]

Macquarie was now making more money from investing regimental funds for himself than he was as an officer, and six months after he arrived in Calicut he was able to tell Forbes, somewhat mendaciously: 'from our economical mode of living since we came down the coast, I've nearly cleared off all my little debts'.[97]

Macquarie saw nothing wrong with what he was doing, and believed it was a perk of the job. He knew the way British redcoats had devastated the Highlands over countless generations, and he'd also seen the way army promotion was just a giant game that had more to do with hobnobbing among the right people than working hard or being fearless. He was prepared to milk the system to help his clan at every opportunity. One day, he planned to return to the Highlands and establish a great estate, financed by the very people who had sentenced his people to poverty.

Macquarie had a good lurk going with the soldiers' pay, but he began to despair at his 'sluggish, inactive' life, and the decline of the 77th, which from 'being one of the finest in India was going to the devil'. Colonel Bowles was forever fighting Major Bulstrode Whitelocke,[98] Commandant of the Regiment, over who should take the profits from the soldiers' bazaar[99] – their main market – and the troops had become so undisciplined that they were drinking heavily and even burning down their barracks.[100]

What Macquarie and the 77th needed was another war.

Chapter 10

*I am not quite so much of a patriot as to wish for a long peace
in this country. War is always the soldier's harvest.*
LACHLAN MACQUARIE ON THE FINANCIAL BENEFITS OF WAGING WAR[1]

WHILE MACQUARIE languished in Calicut, Europe was being besieged by what he called 'the infernal and destructive principles of democracy'.[2] In the Netherlands, there was a continuation of the Dutch Crisis of 1787 that had originally resulted in Macquarie joining the army bound for India. William V, Prince of Orange,[3] the Stadtholder of the Dutch Republic and Captain-General of the Dutch States Army, had been forced to flee to London in January 1795 by Dutch revolutionaries, who were supported by the French Army and inspired by the uprisings against monarchies that had taken place in France and America. It was a troubling time for colonial powers such as Britain, although the relative political stability in that country allowed the British to expand their rule while other nations lost territories.

The British had offered to protect the Dutch East India Company's interests at Cochin, which the Dutch had taken from the Portuguese a century before. As Macquarie observed, the redcoats would 'garrison and hold it for the Prince of Orange until he is restored again as stadtholder or a general peace is concluded'.[4] *In theory*, the British were in alliance with the stadtholder –

123

which meant wresting Dutch holdings in India away from the revolutionary forces – but in practice, it was pretty much just an opportunity to grab land for Britain.

There had been a military build-up for some time in Britain in response to the threat of the French Revolution, and new tactics learned from the hand-to-hand fighting of the North American Indians were being employed in Britain's first drill book,[5] drawn up by Sir David Dundas[6] in 1792.

The 77th practised the new drills twice a day 'in great stile'.[7] Macquarie declared: 'Our commandant is torturing his poor unfortunate brains in studying the new system, and in endeavour to make us perfect in it – but, all to very little purpose; for, he makes a most miserable hand of it, notwithstanding the fine subject he has to exercise his bright talents upon.'[8]

Only the cleanliness of the men deserved praise, because their movements were 'slovenly executed and their firing was neither close nor regular'.[9] The planned grand manoeuvres descended into farce, 'with a very confused impetuous charge, or rather race, each striving [to see] who could run fastest after poor Colonel Bowles, who with all his military ardour, narrowly escaped being run down in the charge'.

Macquarie had been hoping for another campaign against the 'restless dog' Tipu Sultan, and feared that, in a war to 'protect' the stadtholder's interests at Cochin, 'there is neither honour, glory or profit to be reaped'.[10] Nevertheless, two companies of the 77th and the Grenadier Battalion of Native Infantry marched the 180 kilometres south to Cochin on 23 July 1795, with their leader Lieutenant-Colonel Petrie ready to negotiate with governor Jan van Spall, now representing the Dutch Patriots and their Batavian Republic.

Macquarie, who stayed behind him, described the men as 'embassadors of piece'.[11] They carried no artillery, but if van Spall did not accept their 'amicable terms' they had orders to 'force the Dutch to a compliance in a hostile way'.[12]

Macquarie and the others left behind called themselves 'the precious remains', but in case they had to follow the first wave of troops, Macquarie took a house for Jane in town, where it was safer. It was with very great regret that he and Jane made this move, because they had put so much effort into improvements at Staffa Lodge, and it was 'an exceedingly pleasant place'.[13] They planned to return as soon as Macquarie's campaign was over.

Their new abode, however, was 'very well situated, and in a good neighbourhood, being close to Colonel Bowles's house and Mr Wensley's the Paymastr. General's',[14] both of whom 'promised to pay her every attention in their power during [Macquarie's] absence'.[15]

Macquarie soon got his orders and it was time to ride to Cochin with his servant, William Stewart. He had an awful realisation that, for the first time since they had been married almost two years earlier, he and Jane would be apart. It gave Jane 'inexpressible pain and made her very unhappy', even though Macquarie and her visiting brother George did all in their power to comfort her and 'to reconcile her to what was unavoidable'.[16]

On 19 August 1795, the day of Macquarie's departure, he and George stayed with Jane until 4 p.m., then with sorrowful hearts set out on horseback after the 77th, George having offered his services as a volunteer. They soon overtook the regiment and slept the night in a mosque near the Beypore River.[17] Macquarie wrote to Jane every day of the journey from his different camps, rebuffing her entreaties to join him on the battlefield by insisting 'she drop every idea of this kind'.[18]

The 77th reached Cochin after nine days. As Governor van Spall mulled over whether to let the British into his fort, Macquarie celebrated his second wedding anniversary on 8 September, drinking with his closest friends to the health of 'dearest Jane in many overflowing bumpers'.[19]

The following day, van Spall sent Lieutenant-Colonel Petrie 'a pretty clear and decisive answer to the proposals … that he is positively determined *not* to admit a British garrison into Cochin – but on the contrary to defend it to the last extremity'.[20]

This meant another bloody conflict. Before long, heavy artillery and stores for a planned siege arrived from Bombay.

Meanwhile, Macquarie wrote to Murdoch Maclaine to tell him that Abercromby would grant the commissions Macquarie had applied for on behalf of Murdoch Maclaine, his sister Betty's son, and Hector Macquarie, a younger son of the poor old clan chief. The commissions as ensigns were being held in readiness for the two boys to join their regiments in India post-haste. Before long, Macquarie was signing up young relatives across Mull so that they could receive half-pay with no intention of fighting. The scheme was fraught with danger.

While the 77th awaited their next move in the shadow of Fort Cochin, Macquarie took up residence in the house of the wealthy postmaster Francois Josef von Wredé in Muttoncherry.[21] Von Wredé was 'a man of considerable property in Cochin, and attached to the stadtholder and English Government' rather than the Dutch revolutionary forces.

For five weeks, Macquarie and his comrades waited and waited for their orders. On 1 October, Macquarie wrote in his journal 'Nothing extraordinary' and for five days after that 'Ditto'. On the evening of what was his 'beloved Jane's' twenty-third birthday, 16 October, he scrawled the news that 'a working party of 300 men broke ground on our side of the water within about six hundred yards of the walls of Cochin Fort, without being molested or even apparently perceived by the enemy'.[22]

Two days later, van Spall let loose, his men blasting away from their fort with 'a heavy fire of shot and shells on all our posts during the whole of this day; but fortunately with no effect'.[23] Instead, Macquarie watched like a spectator at a fireworks display: 'the noise of the cannonading, and beautiful sight of the shells in the air, was grand and awful … Our shells from Vypeen [an island off the coast now known as Vypin] appeared to be extremely well directed, all of them falling and bursting in the town of Cochin, where they must have done very considerable damage'.[24]

The next morning at daybreak, Macquarie and his detachment started firing on the fort with his own 'little six pounder' from behind an earthen barricade to divert the enemy from 'our grand breaching battery'. He was almost 500 metres away but 'had the

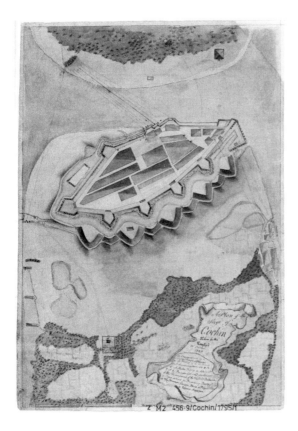

A plan of the Siege of Cochin undertaken by the British on 20 October 1795. The main Brirish battery is shown upper left. State Library of NSW

satisfaction to see that every shot I fired reached and fell into the town of Cochin'.[25]

He kept blasting away for two hours, but the Dutch were 'very much provoked' and 'so much enraged' that they kept up a 'most tremendous fire' on Macquarie's post the whole time, using what seemed like every available gun in the fort. Earth and dust exploded all around Macquarie's ears as he kept his head down and his cannon barrel up.

Somehow not a single man was killed in the onslaught, but the nearby houses in Muttoncherry were obliterated, so Macquarie stopped firing, hoping the Dutch would follow his lead. However, just as Captain William Grant came up to relieve Macquarie with a fresh detachment, Grant was hit in the shoulder by a splinter from a wooden house as another Dutch shell tore into yet another wooden wall.

Macquarie then rode over to Vypeen Point, where the British eighteen-pounders were raining down havoc 'dreadful indeed' on Fort Cochin. The front of the fort had almost been demolished, all its defences knocked off, and most of its guns silenced.[26]

At 4.30 p.m. Governor van Spall ordered the white flag to be hung on a bastion and had his men sound the *chamade* of surrender. At a very late hour that night, van Spall signed the terms of capitulation. Before going to bed, Macquarie wrote to Jane, 'giving her the good news', and directed von Wredé to send his letter by express mail to Calicut at daybreak.[27]

At noon the next day, the thousand-strong Dutch garrison – '200 Europeans and 300 Malay and regular sepoys; [with] five or six hundred irregular besides [extra troops outside the formal army]' – marched out 'in a most shameful noisy disorderly unsoldierlike manner, behaving most brutally and insolently to their officers':

> Most of the soldiers were very much intoxicated, and were most abusive to their poor fallen governor for so soon surrendering his fort to the English – telling him aloud that he ought to be hanged … It was with some difficulty we could restrain them from cutting down some of their officers – which they several times attempted to do with their swords.[28]

Macquarie and Major Whitelocke led four subalterns and 150 men into the fort through the Muttoncherry Gate, after what Macquarie said was 'an easy made conquest on our part, having only lost during the whole siege by the enemy shot, one European artilleryman and one native follower'.

The view of the countryside from the fort was magnificent, and before long Macquarie was meeting Governor van Spall and inspecting the fort's treasures, including its magnificent brass cannons.

'The ordnance, and military and naval stores found in Cochin Fort, are very considerable,' he wrote, 'and of great value; so that I hope we the captors, will share handsomely in prize–money'.[29]

MACQUARIE fairly raced to get home and into the arms of his beloved Jane, boarding a patamar sailing boat with George Jarvis and some officer friends for an overnight voyage on 27 October. To his boiling frustration, it turned out to be an exasperatingly slow journey of sixty hours because of light winds. Jane was waiting in the Calicut house with open arms, however, and their 'mutual joy and felicity' was, he wrote, 'easier conceived than described after such a separation'.[30]

All was not entirely well, however. Jane's skin was pallid and her eyes runny. She 'did not look near so well in health' as when they had parted two months before. She told Macquarie that she had caught a bad cold on her daily hour-long walk in the garden, and while 'her very troublesome cough' caused Macquarie 'great uneasiness', she assured him it was nothing to worry about.[31]

The next evening, by 'a most beautiful moonlight',[32] Macquarie and George Jarvis rode on horseback beside Jane's palanquin as the three moved back to Staffa Lodge, which had been kept in readiness by servants for their return, the stillness of the quiet country air broken only by Jane's coughing fits.

Slowly Macquarie's 'dear Mrs. M.' got better, and when they entertained, using the new plates Dorothea had sent them from England bearing the MacQuarrie Clan crest,[33] she was always 'in high spirits and the best good humour', traits that made her a 'very great favourite with all the officers of the regiment.'[34] By mid-November a little of her cough remained, but Macquarie hoped it would be cleared up by a 1200-kilometre voyage north aboard the *Helen* to Bombay, where he had to appear as a witness at a court martial.

The fair winds and sea air did her a world of good and her appetite returned, but soon her spirits were low again when Macquarie told her on 3 December that he would have to travel to the island of Ceylon[35] as the British prepared to repeat their efforts at Cochin on the Dutch fort of Columbo (modern Colombo). George rejoined his 36th Regiment on 19 December, also bound for the fort.

Jane's cough came back, she couldn't sleep and she lost her appetite once more. Doctors said she would benefit from a daily drink of 'warm milk from the cow or buffalo', so Macquarie would walk with her every morning at sunrise to Bombay's esplanade, where the buffaloes were milked; she would take a tumbler of milk straight from the udders into her empty stomach.[36] Macquarie placed an order for her own 'milch cow'[37] but his impending departure meant Jane's health was 'very far from being good'. He tried to be as jovial as possible, but she 'could not be comforted by any mirth'.[38]

Jane 'entreated and begged very hard' to accompany Macquarie on the expedition to Ceylon 'and to share the toils and hardships of a soldier's life during a campaign'. It was only with great difficulty that he persuaded her to abandon the plan. She wanted to return to Calicut, which was so much nearer Columbo, and remain there until his return, but, holding her in his strong arms, he told his darling that it would be a 'very lonely and awkward situation for her to be in – perhaps for several months'. The best place for her, given that her cough had still not dried up, was 'surrounded by numerous friends and acquaintances' in Bombay.[39]

As Macquarie's departure drew near, Jane was constantly crying and begging him to stay. She pleaded with him to do everything he could to remain with her, even using his position as Major of Brigade as an excuse.

Macquarie could only despair: 'It goes deep into my heart to see her thus miserable and unhappy. She is most earnest in her entreaties and solicitations … as, she says she cannot survive my absence a second time … however wretched it makes me to part and thus so soon leave her a second time – yet, honor – honor calls – and I must obey!'[40]

Chapter 11

JANUARY TO JULY 1796, INDIA, CEYLON AND CHINA

*I then took leave of all I held dearest in life. My poor dear Jane
was deeply affected at parting, and I was no less so myself tho'
I strove to hide it. Her distress however was very
great and went deep to my heart.*

MACQUARIE ON SAYING GOODBYE TO HIS YOUNG WIFE
AS HE SAILED OFF TO CEYLON[1]

THE DUTCH fired several blasts across the Mahaweli, Ceylon's great sandy river, and they had 700 men and seven cannons to stop the 77th from crossing the water. It was five weeks since Macquarie had made his tearful goodbye to Jane, and his heart still ached.

On 3 January 1796, after 'good dear Mrs Oakes' had served up an elegant 'tiffing' of light snacks, Macquarie had sailed aboard the *Helen*, which carried enough provisions for a four-month campaign. They had hardly set sail when the men aboard the *Exeter* coming the other way informed them that the British had taken Cape Town from the Dutch.[2]

By 31 January, Macquarie's thirty-fifth birthday, the 77th had swapped ships and were on board the *Epaminondas*, off Tuticorin (now known as Thoothukudi) on India's southeast coast. Four days later, they were at their final rendezvous point, Negombo on Ceylon's west coast, where they met the Madras Army under Colonel James Stuart.[3] They had then begun their march to Columbo, 40 kilometres south.

On 10 February at the Mahaweli River, the British prepared for a fierce battle with the Dutch. But at daybreak the next morning, Macquarie was astonished to learn that the enemy had abandoned their entrenchments during the night and run away in such a hurry that they had thrown their cannons into the water rather than dragging them along behind. At 1 p.m. the redcoats crossed the river, and 'without being in the least annoyed or molested by the enemy', advanced for about 1500 metres to camp about 5000 metres from the town and fortress of Columbo.

Things got hotter at dawn on 12 February when, with blood-curdling cries, the enemy charged 'in considerable force not being less than a thousand Europeans and Malays'.[4] The 'Malays' went into the firing line first, and made repeated, desperate efforts to stab the British artillerymen with their kris daggers.[5]

George Jarvis distinguished himself with 'handsome gallantry ...' in his first real military action, 'being warmly engaged during the whole time of the attack',[6] and Macquarie knew Jane would be proud. Before long, the enemy's commanding officer, Colonel de Lisle, was dead, and 150 of his troops were killed or wounded, while the British had only nineteen casualties. They advanced to a hill within 1800 metres of the fort.

Heavy siege guns arrived on 14 February, and it was all too much for the Dutch governor, Johan van Angelbeek,[7] who looked out from his fortress aghast. When British adjutant-general Major Patrick Agnew[8] trotted into the fort under a white flag of truce, he told the governor to 'surrender the fort to the British arms – or take the consequence'.[9] After two days of negotiations, most of Ceylon was in British hands, and even though the plan had been to hold it temporarily for the stadtholder, the island and all its earthly treasures would remain a British possession for the next 152 years.[10]

Three thousand Dutch soldiers – 1200 Europeans and 1800 Asians – were marched out of the fort on 16 February, but most had been drinking so heavily following the surrender that it was hard for many to walk straight or even stay upright. Like the captives at Cochin, they exited in 'a most disorderly tumultuous manner ... and [were] very abusive and insolent to their officers, who were very much ashamed of the noisy and very unruly conduct of their men'.[11] Under the terms of capitulation, the prisoners were being shipped out of the war and on to the Dutch possession of Batavia[12] on the island of Java.

For Macquarie, the victory at Columbo was sweet:

This is a most important and valuable capture and acquisition to not only the East India Company in a commercial point of view — but also to the British Nation at large in a political one, in as far as it contains the only good harbour for our navy on this side of India, and the French being prevented from possessing themselves of this valuable island. There are immense quantities of cinnamon, pepper, arrack, and various other goods and merchandise, belonging to the Dutch company, found in Columbo; the guns, ordnance and naval stores, are also of very great value; so that there is good reason to hope the captors will share very handsomely indeed in prize money in this occasion.[13]

MACQUARIE wanted to get home to Jane as soon as possible but there was still work to be done by the occupying forces. The best he could do was to write to her in Bombay with the grand news that Colonel Stuart had heard of Macquarie's 'very high character' from Lieutenant-Colonel Petrie and others, and wanted him to take a detachment to the Point de Galle, 130 kilometres south of Columbo. Petrie told him there was public property of great value in the stores and arsenals at Point de Galle, and because it was such an important assignment, he wanted to send 'an officer of capacity and experience'.[14] Macquarie may not have had a lot of real battle experience but he had twenty years of service and had maintained trusted administrative roles as paymaster and Major of Brigade. He also had learned the art of diplomacy, winning friends and influencing his superior officers from an early age.

On 19 February 1796, Macquarie moved out as commander of 700 Madras sepoys, thirty artillerymen and three junior officers, who were paraded for him at Columbo Fort's south gate. After three days of marching, the men were 7 kilometres from Galle.

Macquarie sent a letter to the local Dutch governor, Dietrich Fretz,[15] via an interpreter, Sergeant McKenzie. Macquarie explained that he was in command 'of a British detachment of troops for the purpose of taking possession of Galle in the name of His Britannic Majesty according to the articles of capitulation signed by the British and Dutch commanders at Columbo'.[16] He also sent an explanatory letter from the deposed Governor van Angelbeek, and told Fretz of his intention to march into Galle to take possession of the fort the following day at noon. He politely asked Fretz to please 'make the necessary arrangements for delivering it up at that time'.[17]

Fretz was no fighter, and he sent word back that Macquarie could have Galle even sooner than that if he so wished.

As the British marched towards the fortress the next day, two men came out in a carriage to see them, explaining that they were members of the government and that Governor Fretz had asked them to conduct Macquarie into the fort, where the governor and his council were ready to receive the British commander at Government House.[18]

This was a civilised invasion. Macquarie ordered one of his junior officers, Lieutenant Harris, to keep his troops 200 metres from the fort in a show of courtesy, and was escorted into the conquered territory like a head of State.

Fretz introduced Macquarie to all his council members and the commanding officer of the Galle troops, and presented him 'in a most solemn and formal manner, on a large silver salver, with the keys of the different gates of the garrison'. Fretz started to cry during a short speech, as did some of the Dutchmen around him.

Macquarie, too, 'was very much moved at this scene, and wished it over as soon as possible since its being farther prolonged would only add to their distress'. He therefore made a short reply, assuring them all that he 'was most sincerely disposed' to make their situation as 'easy and comfortable as possible'. Wine and cake were then carried round and they all drank to each other's good health.[19]

Macquarie took his leave and returned to his detachment, parked where he had left them at the fort's southeast gate, and he marched the men straight in, with drums beating and colours flying, to the grand parade in the middle of the fort. The 650 Dutch troops already assembled there presented arms then put down their weapons and surrendered as prisoners of war. The Dutch flag was struck, the Union Jack was hoisted in its place and a royal salute of twenty-one guns boomed out 'in honour of the occasion of the Town and Fortress of Point de Galle being taken possession of in the name of His Britannic Majesty'.[20]

Macquarie reported to Colonel Stuart that:

> ... the place was delivered up and surrendered to us in the most orderly, regular, and polite manner possible. The Dutch garrison paraded, presented their arms, and piled them afterwards with the utmost regularity and order, on the grand parade within the fort. Fronting the British detachment which was formed on the same parade opposite to them, I afterwards introduced the officers of the detachment to Mr Fretz, who politely invited them all to a very handsome entertainment at his own house at 2 o'clock, and when assembled received them with the utmost politeness and hospitality.[21]

Macquarie allowed the Dutch soldiers to remain in their barracks, but under guard, until there was an opportunity to send them to Madras and then on to Batavia like the troops in Columbo. The British, on the other hand, marched into the new barracks allotted to them and were given a double allowance of arrack to drink His Majesty's health.[22]

Macquarie appointed Lieutenant Harris to take charge of the fort and district of Matura a few kilometres south, then sat down with Fretz and about sixty other gentlemen at 4.30 p.m. for a 'most excellent and plentiful dinner', with 'plenty of wine' available and the tired and emotional Dutchmen 'hobber-nobbing very frequently'.[23]

After the meal, Macquarie took a short ride into the country with the deposed governor in his open carriage and, on their return, he took a walk along the fort's ramparts, and visited the guards and their prisoners. Fretz, a widower, invited him to supper at 9.30 p.m., when he introduced Macquarie to his son and four daughters. Fretz 'very politely' asked Macquarie if he would do him and his family the honour of staying with them while in Galle, and after supper, the 'good old gentleman' took a lamp and led Macquarie to his cosy bedroom, 'where a very elegant bed had been made up'.[24]

Fretz later told him that 'he and his family could never expect to experience so much kindness and polite attention from any succeeding commanding officer at Point de Galle'.[25] Macquarie felt real affection for Fretz and his family too, assuring him that 'I shall ever have particular pleasure and satisfaction in cultivating and maintaining a friendly correspondence with you',[26] and that he was grateful to have secured the friendship of so very 'respectable a character as yourself'.[27]

Fretz asked Macquarie to help his daughter Anna[28] in her problems with her husband Pieter van Spall,[29] the son of the former Cochin governor. Macquarie was later able to tell Fretz that he had checked with the top brass, and they would allow Fretz's 'own Civil Court of Justice to take cognisance of your daughter's present very unpleasant and unhappy situation ... and I trust an eternal separation will very shortly be the consequence'.[30]

The day after Point de Galle was taken, Macquarie wrote to tell his 'beloved Jane' all about his thrilling adventure: how he, the poor boy from Ulva, had been at the head of a triumphant military procession and was 'being now dubbed Governor of Galle!'[31] He wished Jane were with him to share the moment, but they would have plenty of time to celebrate when he went home.

Macquarie was so busy with administrative matters over the next four weeks – itemising all of the stores and weapons in Galle's arsenal, dining with Fretz and sometimes going to church with him – that there was no chance to get back to see her. He wrote to her every week, instead of every day.

On 7 March he learned that she had moved in with the family of his friend Colonel James Kerr, the Auditor-General of Bombay.[32] Then, eight days later, he was hit hard in the heart. Kerr sent him the startling news that Jane had 'for some time back been in very delicate health'.[33] She had been unwell when Macquarie sailed for Columbo and had never really recovered.

The news alarmed Macquarie so much that he wrote to Colonel Stuart, asking to be relieved from his command as soon as possible.[34] Fretz and his daughters offered up 'a thousand prayers'[35] for Macquarie, and were overcome as he raced away on a palanquin early on the morning of 19 March, telling his twelve bearers to run for their lives. And Jane's.

They did, going as fast as their legs could whirl. The runners covered the 130 kilometres to Columbo in just two days.[36]

MACQUARIE had to wait for what seemed like forever for the ship *Jane* to take him to his Jane, and while he anxiously waited to get sailing, constant praise and platitudes came his way. Macquarie handled the situation more sensitively than many other commanders might have done. He avoided bloodshed and befriended his captives in the ultimate display of diplomacy, something that the British Army wanted at every opportunity. Colonel Stuart thanked him 'in very handsome terms for what he was pleased to call my very able and officer-like conduct and judicious arrangements during my command at Point de Galle'. Stuart had reported his performance in 'the manner it deserved to the Commander in Chief in India, Sir Robert Abercromby – and also to Lord Hobart the Governor of Madras'.[37] With Jane so ill, however, this news and what was to then his greatest achievement in two decades as a soldier, did not lift Macquarie's spirits in the way it might have under different circumstances.

Meanwhile, he wrote letter after letter to his 'dear Mrs M' and, politely declining the role of town major in Ceylon, he boarded the *Jane* on 30 March.

Foul winds meant the ship took two weeks to reach Calicut for a day-long stopover, but when she did, Macquarie went to visit Colin Anderson, who promised to get Staffa Lodge re-daubed and waterproofed for their imminent return from Bombay, 'providing my dearest Jane's health will admit of it'.[38]

Despite his anxiety, Macquarie was optimistic that, when his 'good, amiable girl' was back in rude health, everything would be wonderful for them, given his success at Point de Galle and Colonel Stuart's accolade. He was building a promising military career and the money was pouring in. Before they knew it, they would be back in Britain and returned to a real English country garden, living off their interest.

While on the road back from Staffa, Macquarie met a man with letters for him from the Bombay mail boat. One of them was from Jane.

Opening the envelope excitedly, Macquarie stopped right where he was and sat down on the roadside to read it.

Jane had poured out her heart to him. His own heart was racing and his mouth dry as he read 'these dear letters with a joy and real delight that cannot possibly be expressed'.[39]

'For besides my Angel telling me that her health was lately much improved by her living in the country – she informed me – to my inexpressible joy – that she had every reason to believe she was pregnant! and that she would soon make me a happy, happy father!'[40]

Jane had longed for a child and her inability to conceive thus far must have been distressing for the couple, especially as her sister Dorothea and her three children had returned to England. Given Macquarie's long use of mercury medications, the leading treatment for syphilis, Jane's pregnancy after a long time of being unable to conceive, must have made Macquarie's heart leap with gladness.

Macquarie read and reread those words at least twenty times, 'almost, devouring them with kisses'. He would have sat there all day reading them again and again, but his housekeeper came along and reminded him that it was getting late. He had a boat to catch and a wife to congratulate.

So, mounting his horse, Macquarie rode on 'with a lighter heart than I had ever done before; being now more anxious than ever to get to Bombay to hold my darling Jane to my heart'.[41]

THE SHIP was delayed at Mahe, and it took twenty-one long, lonely days at sea before Macquarie finally bounced off the boat when it anchored at Bombay on 6 May 1796. He was so happy to be home that he raced off to hold Jane close and celebrate their joy.

Only there was no joy.

There was no baby.

The glorious young wife he had left behind was close to death.

Consumption had ravaged her body and her senses. In her fevered delusion, and in the mad desperation to have a child, she had believed that her illness had meant she was pregnant when, in truth, she was more dead than alive.

Macquarie had shown himself to be a brave and capable soldier, but he told Colin Anderson in a tear-stained note that:

> I confess to you I have not fortitude enough to sustain this dreadful shock with manly resignation. I sink under it and I'm actually at this moment as miserable a wretch as any that lives on the face of the earth. O my dear Anderson, if you saw her, how you would pity me! She cannot live! Alas! … she is in the last and worst stage of deep consumption, and probably will not be many days in this cruel world.[42]

MACQUARIE considered his 'Angel's' delusions about her pregnancy a blessing. Despite the pain he felt at not becoming a father, Jane's fantasies gave her great pleasure and made her 'insensible to the unhappy and cruel malady'.[43] He knew they would never be going back to sweet Staffa Lodge, where their hearts had been joined in the dream of a blessed future. He told Anderson to do as he liked with the house, the garden, the horses and the servants, providing he got rid of that lazy Andrew the cook, 'an idle, useless fellow, and also a drunkard'.[44]

The doctors treating Jane conferred and told Macquarie that some sea air and a rise in temperature might improve her condition. For some misguided reason, they thought the even hotter and more humid metropolis of Macao, China, all 8000 kilometres away, might help.

Yet her condition was so serious, and the disease so contagious, that, one after another, captains 'had the barbarity' to refuse them passage.[45] Finally, Captain Lestock Wilson[46] took pity on them and gave berths on the *Exeter*, refusing to take any money for their fare because he wanted to take the desperate pair to China for 'very different motives to that of gain'.[47]

They sailed on 18 May 1796,[48] and it was a pathetic voyage lasting six sad weeks. Macquarie ceased writing in his journal, because it was so agonising to watch, day after day, the rise and fall of the ship, and the fall and fall of the twenty-three year old girl he adored.

In her delirium, and with the vain prospect of motherhood somehow keeping her frail, wasted body alive, Jane would make lists of toys she wanted to buy for her friends' children in Bombay,[49] and the thought of their smiling faces at opening the presents lifted her spirits. Against all reason, Macquarie began to have some sense of hope.

They arrived in Macao on 2 July, sailing up the South China Sea and into the wide mouth of the Pearl River Delta[50] opposite the island of Hong Kong.

The voyage seemed to have helped Jane. Perhaps it was a cruel illusion, but she now seemed to have become 'so stout and hearty' again that she was able to sit up at dinner with some of the British expatriates, including the powerful merchant James Drummond,[51] who would become one of Macquarie's most trusted friends.

Jane still seemed so full of merriment, apparently blissfully unaware of what was happening inside her lungs. If she did know, she never once mentioned it.[52] She tried to maintain a regular domestic routine, rising for breakfast, making tea then resting on a couch or in an easy chair as Macquarie read to her or spoke to her about the beautiful life they would share together when she was well again. She drank the tonic of red wine and spices the doctors prescribed and consumed the tincture of yellow bark they gave her. She could still walk some way hand in hand with Macquarie on the terrace as they discussed names for their child.

But her outward display of good cheer was all a fatal deception.

Soon, she told her doting husband that her feet were not of any use to her. She could no longer stand without help.

The local English physician, Dr Alexander Duncan, mournfully told Macquarie that there was no hope, and that soon there would be an 'eternal separation'.

Jane died in Macquarie's arms at 5 a.m. on 15 July 1796. He went into shock.

He cradled Jane's coffin as though he were cuddling her and splashed it with salty tears. Marianne, Jane's Indian maid, would hear him sobbing in his bed, crying himself to sleep. He did not come out of his house for ten days.

He blamed himself for the whole horrible tragedy. He told everyone that he should have done more. Why hadn't he come home from Galle sooner? Why hadn't he sent the poor girl to England?[53]

But his self-recriminations were gibberish. He could barely speak. Paper and quill were the channels for his grief as he tried to make sense of the tragedy in a letter to his sister-in-law Dorothea:

> Yes! my heavenly darling Jane is gone!, she is gone and lost to me and you forever! – and with her all my earthly happiness is forever fled! … she died as she has always lived – like an angel and a saint – with perfect ease and tranquillity, resigning her soul to Heaven without pain or struggle or even a sigh, retaining the entire and perfect use of all her senses and faculties to the very last moment of her existence. Thus then died in the prime of her youth and beauty the best woman and the best of wives.[54]

Chapter 12

JULY 1796 TO APRIL 1801, MACAO, CHINA,
AND BOMBAY, INDIA

*As a small testimony of my love, affection and respect to the memory
of my dear and excellent wife, I have got a coffin constructed — after
the Chinese manner of preserving their dead — which preserves the
body sweet and incorruptible for many years.*

MACQUARIE TO GEORGE JARVIS, ON THE PREPARATIONS
TO BURY HIS BELOVED[1]

MACQUARIE was a broken man, inconsolable in his grief.
Attempts to comfort him were useless, because he was
'stupefied with horror and affliction'.[2]

He continued to express his guilt and sadness by pouring out
his heart and soul to Jane's loved ones. He wrote forty-eight sad
foolscap pages to Dorothea, at the grand home she shared with
Old Morley in Wimpole Street, London.[3]

He told George Jarvis about the Chinese coffin he had bought.[4]
Yet he did not want to leave Jane in the godforsaken hole where
she had died, but to take her home to Bombay, where she had had
so many friends.

The year 1796, which had seen Macquarie reach new heights
in his military career, ended with him reduced to a sad, forlorn
and lonely figure in Macao. He spent months there writing letters

to loved ones and sorting out the red tape with Chinese officials before escorting Jane's coffin as bearers carried her to the Macao docks. He and his wife's remains – his 'dear corpse' – sailed home together on Morley's Indiaman, the *Sarah* (named after Morley's daughter[5] from a previous marriage),[6] under skipper Charles Christopher McIntosh, who refused to take any money from the grief-stricken officer.

Macquarie was still in a semi-daze, but all the way to Bombay the crew were on the lookout for French cruisers 'into whose hands we were in hourly fear of falling, but whom we very fortunately never saw'.[7] The *Sarah*, though, like Jane, would later fall foul of cruel fate and be lost in a battle with the French off Point de Galle, when she encountered Napoleon's admiral Charles-Alexandre Durand.[8]

Macquarie arrived in Bombay on 13 January 1797 and was met at the dock by his friend John Forbes, who took him home to the house where he had first met his beloved. Three days later, on Monday 16 January at 5.30 p.m., as the orange Indian sun sank slowly into the golden spread of the Arabian Sea, Macquarie prepared to lower 'the dearest and loveliest of women!'[9] to her eternal rest. She was to be buried in a coconut garden[10] set aside as a burial ground for Europeans, on the western side of Bombay.[11]

The funeral procession marched along the Esplanade, in the shadow of Bombay's citadel. Macquarie wore a black crepe armband that would adorn his left arm for the next four years. The *Bombay Courier* reported that, after Macquarie, Forbes was the chief mourner, '(supported by Major Cameron, and Captain Mackenzie) — pall bearers, General Balfour, General Nicholson, Commodore Thistleton, Lieutenant-Colonel Kerr, Lieutenant-Colonel Gore, and Lieutenant-Colonel Oakes, besides a numerous train of gentlemen of the first rank and respectability in the settlement'.[12]

Even though the funeral took place six months after Jane's death, Macquarie lapsed back into an almost catatonic state. His friends waited for his strength and vitality to return, but it was a slow process. He did not leave Forbes's house for a fortnight, and was so incoherent when he spoke that he resorted to writing to Forbes even though they shared the same roof. Six days after the funeral, he told the banker in ink that, while 'it will doubtless appear extremely odd to you my addressing you by letter … I really find it easier in my present unhappy and agitated state of mind, to express my sentiments in writing than by word of mouth'.[13]

Macquarie's tongue might have been misfiring, but he could still think straight when it came to doing all he could to preserve the memory of his wife. In the midst of his great grief, he was unstinting with his generosity. With his Moor servant running his errands, Macquarie began distributing gifts Jane had bought in Macao for her Bombay friends, toys for the children, and fans and shawls for their mothers. Jane's doctors each received a china breakfast set. Macquarie sent 1000 rupees to Captain McIntosh for the ride home to Bombay on the *Sarah*, but McIntosh sent it back. Two weeks after Jane's burial, Macquarie wrote to the army agents in London, Cox and Greenwood, enclosing the *Bombay Courier's* report on Jane's funeral and asking that they circulate it to the 'principal papers in London'.[14]

Then he sat down to compose 475 words of undying love that detailed the dates of Jane's birth, marriage and death, and the travails of her journey to Macao and of her last trip home to her final resting spot. It was awfully long for a grave marker and, as he explained to George Jarvis, 'not elegantly or well written', but 'true and sincere', and it expressed the real feelings of a 'wounded and distracted heart'.[15]

It was full of Macquarie's constant capitalisations for emphasis, erratic punctuation and heartfelt emotion. In part, it read:

To those who knew her modest Worth no Panegyric can be necessary: and to those unacquainted with her suffice it to say, that she possessed in a most eminent degree all the Virtues that adorn the Female Character, and render it worthy of universal Admiration. As a Wife, Daughter and Sister, she was preeminently conspicuous, and an excellent Pattern for Others. In her Manners, she was mild, affable and polite; In her Disposition sweet and even. In her Opinions liberal. And in her Appearance elegant without extravagance – True Christianity gave a superior lustre to all her Virtues. She was an excellent Model of every Female Virtue: and those of her Sex who make her their Pattern, may with Confidence anticipate a glorious Immortality and look forward with Pleasure to Virtue's best Reward – the applauding Smile of HEAVEN. This is the least tribute of Praise and Gratitude that a fond affectionate and disconsolate Husband can pay to the beloved and honored Memory of the best of Wives and the best and most amiable of Women.[16]

Macquarie begged John Forbes to make his words everlasting by sending them back to London and organising their inscription onto 'one of the best and most elegant black marble slabs that can be procured', then organising transport of the huge piece of stone on the next available ship to Bombay so it could be placed over Jane's grave.[17] The final words on the marble were to say:

> This TOMB STONE is erected by him not only in honor of her Memory and in Testimony of his sincere Grief for her Loss but also as a lasting Monument of their mutual disinterested Love and Affection for One another. For he can safely and without Vanity affirm that never yet lived a happier or a more contented Couple in WEDLOCK.[18]

JANE'S DEATH made Macquarie an independently wealthy man, and he soon set about sharing some of the money and property with those he deemed most deserving.

Jane's will[19] awarded Macquarie £6000 and bequeathed another £1000 to her sister Rachel Wilkins, who had married a reprobate and was the only one of her family in dire circumstances. Jane left instructions to give one of her slaves, Cassius, to a brother living in Antigua, along with a cedar press and a looking glass. She awarded freedom to another five slaves in Antigua.

However, the will had not been signed by a witness, and since Jane was deemed to have died intestate, Macquarie was granted all her money and possessions. He still carried out her wishes though – and then some – making only one change to ensure that Mrs Wilkins's errant husband did not get a penny of Jane's money.

He gave guineas to some of the Antigua slaves and sent £10 for Jane's old 'mammy', an old slave named Dinah, saying that he was prepared to buy her freedom at any price so that 'the poor old woman should spend her declining years, in ease, freedom, and peace'. To Marianne, the little Indian maid who had tried to still Macquarie's tears immediately after Jane's death, he gave a certificate of freedom, as well as providing money for her schooling and care, 'not only for her own intrinsic worth, but also on account of her fidelity and strong attachment to my late beloved wife'.

George Jarvis refused to accept Jane's plates because they bore the Macquarie crest, but Macquarie gave him £300 instead, and sent him a hookah engraved with snakes that his 'heavenly angelic sister Jane' had bought for him.[20] He offered to send George to Bengal to see the sights there, if the young man was so inclined.

The relationship between Macquarie and Dorothea's husband had ended on a sour note in Bombay, but Macquarie knew that Jane would have wanted Dorothea's children – 'these little dears' – to have 'tokens of her affection and love for them', because she was 'doatingly fond of her godchildren, sweet Maria, Charles and Harriet'.[21] So, despite Dorothea's protests that the 'sums are too large', he gave each of the children £100. He gave smaller amounts to some of Jane's other nieces too, with instructions that they should buy some 'jewel or trinket to be worn in remembrance of their dear deceased aunt'. Locks of Jane's hair were sent home to be used in jewellery. Jewels from the Siege of Seringapatam in 1792 were packed up and sent off.

Over the next few years he would also lavish the Macquaries of Ulva and Mull with gifts, providing increases in the funds he already sent to his mother, sister and brother Donald, as well as a whole clan of island people in need of food and education.

Macquarie was a British soldier but his heart was always in the rugged islands on the west coast of Scotland. He explained to his brother Charles that, because he could no longer find happiness 'in this cruel world' he would do all he could to raise his impoverished kin from 'obscurity and want' and place them in 'respectable and eligible situations in life'.[22]

When he heard about the existence of a portrait of Jane painted before he met her, he asked that it be copied by the 'very best and most eminent artist in London'. He declared that to have her likeness close to his heart as a miniature would give him 'more real and heartfelt joy' than if he had an estate giving him £10,000 a year.[23]

He was an odd fellow, a soldier of fortune with a heart of gold, and as he told Uncle Murdoch, he now had more money than he could ever spend.[24] Yet just five weeks after Jane's funeral, on 4 March 1797, Macquarie joined the 77th back in Cochin. Although knocked around by the funeral, he was becoming sick of being idle. He knew also that, going forward, he had to capitalise – albeit belatedly – on the reputation he had earned from the capture of Galle. Leave it much longer, and superior officers would have forgotten all about his achievements there. He also feared that he would soon be sent home to Britain, as hostilities in the East Indies had abated, but he wanted desperately to remain in India because 'I am unfit in my present temper and disposition of mind to enjoy happiness or comfort *anywhere*'. India gave him the chance 'in the course of time, to dissipate and dispel melancholy and mournful impressions'.[25]

Meanwhile, he was making more money hand over fist. He was paymaster to the regiment at Cochin, the Major of Brigade at Bombay and Deputy Paymaster-General of Bombay, a lucrative position he had bought from James Dunlop (now a lieutenant-colonel), and for which he paid his friend £700 a year. Macquarie had long ago learned to milk the system by using Government money to create bank interest for himself.

Eventually, he journeyed back to Calicut, sold Staffa Lodge and gave the two horses he and Jane had ridden, his old grey and

Jane's Turkai, to friends.[26] When he set about gathering together the possessions from their 'days of delight and felicity', he was overcome with emotion, becoming 'perfectly unmanned', but finally he finished collecting Jane's 'cloathes and wearing apparel' – everything not spoiled by 'white ants and wet weather' – and sent them aboard the Indiaman *Sullivan* to Dorothea, saying that, if she didn't want them, perhaps Jane's other sisters or their daughters would. If they were no longer fashionable in London, they would no doubt gladden the hearts of old Mammy Dinah and her daughter in Antigua.[27] Everything of his own from Staffa Lodge that he could carry, he packed onto the brig *Active*, along with his head servant Bowmanjee, his staff and the two little slave boys, George and Hector.

The vessel set sail for Bombay, but on 25 April, while they were anchored at Mahé, Macquarie heard news of another military strike. Bombay's new governor, Jonathan Duncan,[28] and Lieutenant-General (previously Colonel) Stuart were in Tellicherry on the Malabar Coast, preparing to move against the renowned freedom fighter Pazhassi Raja,[29] the 'Lion of Kerala' and de facto head of the kingdom of Kottayam.

Pazhassi had previously fought against the Mysorean army of Hyder Ali and Tipu Sultan, but now Tipu had become his ally, and he was in revolt against the British for violating the terms of their alliance and imposing cruel taxes on his peasants.[30] On 18 March 1797, Macquarie's great pal Major Donald Cameron,[31] who had been one of Jane's chief mourners only a few weeks earlier, had been leading 1100 men down the narrow Periya Pass in the Wayanad district east of Tellicherry, when he realised that he had brought them into a fearful ambush. From both sides of the treacherous mountain pass, Pazhassi's bowmen and musketeers emerged from their camouflaged bunkers and cut down hundreds of the British. Cameron's seventeen-year-old bride Helen, who had travelled with him to India, was now a widow.

Macquarie immediately volunteered for active service. Apart from wanting to avenge his good friend's death, another battle seemed like the perfect antidote to the months of grief and inactivity he'd just been through. He was given command of an advance guard of 700 men, comprising four companies of the 77th Regiment and a battalion of the 3rd Native Infantry Regiment.[32]

For the first time in a year – since he had arrived in Bombay to find Jane dying – Macquarie began keeping a journal again.

AT THE SAME TIME as Macquarie was preparing to ship out to Tellicherry, New South Wales naval officers Captain Henry Waterhouse[33] and Lieutenant William Kent,[34] under orders from Governor Hunter, were bringing the first merino sheep to Australia. The sheep had come from a flock originally given by King Carlos III of Spain to Prince William V of Orange. In 1789, Prince William had sent two rams and four ewes to the warmer Dutch colony at the Cape of Good Hope, to be cared for by Colonel Robert Gordon, that tall, stout commander who had so impressed Macquarie when he had met him with William Bligh almost a decade before.[35]

Gordon had returned the original breeding animals to the Netherlands in 1791 but kept the offspring. Then, in 1795, the British had arrived at the cape, claiming – just as they had in India and Ceylon – that they were occupying the colony to keep it safe for when the Prince of Orange returned from exile. Gordon handed over control, but committed suicide[36] when vilified as a traitor by his men.

Two years later, Gordon's wife sold twenty-six merinos for £3 per head to Waterhouse and Kent,[37] who divided the flock between their two ships, *Reliance* and *Supply*, for the journey back to Australia. En route more than half the sheep perished.[38]

Captain John Macarthur, who had resigned from the army to concentrate on farming, offered Waterhouse 15 guineas a head for the surviving sheep, on the condition that he could buy them all. Waterhouse refused, and grazed them at the Vineyard, his 55-hectare property on the Parramatta River, but eventually distributed a few between Macarthur, the Reverend Samuel Marsden, Lieutenant Kent and Captain Thomas Rowley, formerly the senior British officer on Norfolk Island and now a prominent landowner at Bankstown, Petersham and Concord.

The merino wool industry in Australia was born.

MACQUARIE was ready to fight again, but was 'very far from being in good health ... having hardly sufficient strength to undergo the fatigues of the campaign'.[39] To overcome his depression, he was driving himself hard, 'going in to the field contrary to the advice of friends who wished to see his health restored'.[40]

The plan was to send a force of 7000 men – 3000 European and local soldiers, including Macquarie's advance guard, together with 4000 irregulars – under the command of Colonel Alexander Dow. Dunlop was appointed as his deputy, in charge of the field army. Pazhassi's wild territory had rarely been explored by Europeans, but Macquarie was all for Dow's plan to 'drive him up to the ghauts and burn and destroy all his houses, towns and villages' and 'seize the rebellious rajah's person if possible'.[41]

It was sure to be ferocious work, but the dark clouds of mourning were lifting and Macquarie's mojo was returning. He felt that he was back where he belonged, with Dow telling him on 3 May, after the march east from Tellicherry, that he 'was very glad to see' him, and expressing 'great satisfaction' that Macquarie was under his command.[42]

Dow's force was divided into two wings. The left, under his own command, would take the easier route inland into the Wayanad district, dragging the big guns behind them. Dunlop would command the right wing, with Macquarie under him. They would lead the left wing by about 500 metres, hacking their way through the jungle and cutting down any resistance. Behind them, burning and looting the villages, would be fearsome irregular soldiers: 'Nairds and Moplahs ... famous for the cruel work of destruction and devastation'.[43]

On 9 May, 10 kilometres into the jungle, the enemy made their first attack with a 'smart scattering fire' for half an hour from behind high banks and enclosures beside the narrow road. Macquarie's small flanking parties chased them off.

On and on Dunlop's men trudged through the dense foliage, until they reached a narrow pass through thick vegetation and 'rough broken ground full of ravines, rocks and [river] banks that afforded excellent cover for the enemy'.[44] Pazhassi's men had killed three British officers on the same spot in an earlier ambush.

The men had only marched another 800 metres before the jungle again erupted with gunfire from behind the rocks and banks. Macquarie ordered his men to drive the rebels from their cover, 'but [the enemy] were no sooner dislodged from one set of rocks and banks than they occupied others at a distance' and continued their fire. Sergeant Wilson, 'a fine active fellow', was gunned down close to Macquarie's position. Captain Browne, Dunlop's acting aide de camp, 'a brave and very deserving officer', also lost his life, and sixteen privates were killed or wounded before the enemy marksmen were driven off.[45]

Macquarie continued the march to Mananderry, 'a considerable Nair village, situated in a large beautiful valley, surrounded by pretty high hills'.[46] The local muskets again roared, raining lead down onto Macquarie's troops from the heights above. Some of the irregulars, not being trained like the British soldiers, huddled together in their panic and confusion, and the bullets tore through their massed flesh.

Macquarie's charging troops again chased the enemy away, and with Dunlop's permission, Macquarie had his men take scaling ladders to rout the village fort. Pazhassi's men took flight, setting fire to the few houses inside the stronghold before they could fall into British hands.

For the first time in his life, Macquarie was hit by a bullet – on the upper part of his left foot – but it did not even penetrate his boot and left only a slight blue bruise. He picked up the lead ball and kept it as a souvenir. Twenty other soldiers were killed or wounded, though, and the dead were buried in the village.

At 6 a.m. the next day, 10 May, they marched towards Pazhassi's stronghold at Todicullum, reaching his copper-covered pagoda and houses at noon. The 'rajah and his principal adherents' had 'fled up the ghauts'.[47] But the harassing fire continued from rebels concealed in the upper branches of distant trees, until grapeshot, fired from cannons like giant shotgun pellets, dislodged what Macquarie sarcastically called 'these intrepid warriors' from their 'lofty nests'.[48]

However, not all the enemy marksmen were scared off as the British marched across the Canote River to storm Pazhassi's pagoda. Brigade-Major Batchelor had ridden up to the head of the advance guard to deliver Macquarie orders from Colonel Dow when a piece of his head was blown away, and he fell dead at Macquarie's feet. Eight other men from the advance guard and some of the auxiliary troops were killed or wounded by bullets that burst out of the trees.

Once across the river, the British went on a rampage, destroying the pagoda, burning all the houses around it and stealing all the cattle to starve out any resistance.[49]

The army proceeded on its destructive wave to Cherwancherry, 'a large and populous well cultivated district' 8 kilometres southwest of Canote. Along the way, they set all the villages on fire, but within a few days, 'this short but successful little campaign in the jungle'[50] was over, with a monsoon on its way to extinguish the flames. The British were ordered back to their various garrisons until the rains passed. Macquarie believed that their achievements:

> … must have proved to the enemy that our troops can penetrate through every part of their country – however difficult of access – and their troops must now be fully sensible that they never can stand us in the field, even in their own extraordinary mode of warfare and monkey–like–way of fighting from the tops of trees! … if we may judge from the dreadful yells and screams of the enemy every time our troops fired at them into the jungle … there must have been a considerable number of them killed and wounded on this last service.[51]

Macquarie had distinguished himself in the campaign, the fighting a welcome distraction from grief, but the 'rebellious rajah'[52] would prove a constant irritation to the British for the next eight years, and a more difficult opponent of the young Colonel Arthur Wellesley, later the 1st Duke of Wellington,[53] than even Napoleon. Finally, Pazhassi was betrayed and brought down in 1805 in an ambush orchestrated by civil servant Thomas Baber, who had married the widow of Pazhassi's victim Major Cameron.

MACQUARIE eventually made it back to the coast, struggling through the horrific rain and dense jungle only to be laid up with a 'most severe bowel complaint and fever', a result of 'great fatigue' and long exposure to the sun.[54] He was so sick that part of him wished he'd been shot dead in the fighting.[55] It brought 'a terrible change' in his appearance, and he told Dorothea Morley that she would hardly recognise him now, yet he was not disappointed that nature was hastening him 'towards a dissolution'.[56]

He was bolstered by news that his brother Charles had fallen in love with Old Morley's 'delightful'[57] daughter Sarah, but he prophetically cautioned his younger brother not to get his hopes too high: the ruthless money man was not likely to let his daughter marry anyone without 'a very large fortune'.[58] Macquarie was right, and five years later, Sarah would marry William Ogilvy, later a rear-admiral and 8th Baronet of Inverquharity. Charles already had an illegitimate son, named Hector Macquarie, with a local girl from Mull, Janet Maclaine.

Charles, like his brother, wanted their poor relatives to benefit from their army connections and, while Lachlan was convalescing, they kept up an elaborate scheme of subterfuge. They continued signing up young relatives – including Murdoch Maclaine's six-year-old son of the same name, the boy's five-year-old brother John, and the sons of Macquarie's sister Betty – to receive payment as British army officers on half-pay as standby troops. Macquarie contributed all manner of know-how on how to beat the system, using fake names and changing identities.

At one point, he told Charles:

In respect to what you propose of giving the commission in the 73rd Regt (that was intended for our nephew Murdoch) to our cousin Lochbuy's eldest son Murdoch, I cannot possibly have the least objection, and most willingly and readily give my consent to it if it can possibly be done; providing the boy Hugh (our sister's second son) has not already assumed the name of Murdoch, and claimed the commission in the manner I directed and advised it to be done in my former letters … The commission was given at my solicitation, by Sir Robert Abercromby, to my relation Mr Murdoch Maclaine; – but neither he – nor the War-Office care one pin about who that Murdoch Maclaine is – if he is a gentleman and otherwise properly qualified for holding the commission … It was under this idea, and on the supposition that the Agents did not know what Murdoch Maclaine the commission was intended for, that I desired my nephew Hugh to assume the name of Murdoch so as to entitle him to take up the commission in question.[59]

Soon, he would write to Captain John Abercromby,[60] the general's nephew, who was in command of the 53rd Regiment, asking him to procure an ensigncy for his 'cousin John'. He didn't mention the fact that John was five years old.[61]

MACQUARIE finally arrived back at his house in Bombay on 9 January 1798, to be greeted by his head servant Bowmanjee and the two 'black boys Hector and George', of whom Macquarie had become very fond[62] and whom he treated as family members. For the next year, he lived a reclusive life, mixing only with friends such as Colin Anderson, telling him he would gladly lay down 'this miserable poor life of mine' on Anderson's behalf.[63]

He continued to pour out his grief over Jane in letter after letter to his relatives in England and Scotland. He was lonely and homesick – taking a keen interest in Uncle Murdoch's seven daughters and two sons, asking for particulars about 'all names, ages, size, general appearances, dispositions, talents and progresses in education', and telling their mother that Uncle Murdoch should spare no 'expence' on their schooling, even if he could not leave them fortunes. Macquarie himself would pay for a year's education at a good London school for them. No children of the Maclaines, he said, would ever need 'a friend and protector as long as I exist'.[64]

Although he admitted he was 'a very indifferent French scholar', he offered to correspond in the language with their daughter Jane ('a name that will ever sound sweet and dear to my ear'), who he guessed must be eleven or twelve. If they so desired, he would bring their older girls to India, and with 'brotherly care'[65] help them find husbands among the young men making their fortunes on the subcontinent.

He told his aunt, however, that his religious faith had been sorely tested by Jane's passing. 'However exalted and sublime our emotions may be of a Supreme Being; we must both feel and lament the crosses and calamities he pleas[es] to inflict upon us in this life; more especially when they deprive us of our greatest happiness and dearest interests in it!'[66]

AS MACQUARIE fought the blues, Rear-Admiral Sir Horatio Nelson was fighting the French on the Nile Delta, trapping Napoleon's forces in Egypt after three days of war on water from 1 to 3 August 1798. Macquarie was sure that Bonaparte, 'the Corsican monster', had designs on Bombay, where the British were 'ready to give him a warm reception'.[67]

Bonaparte was making a rapid rise to power with plans to take large slices of the world in the name of France. The little Frenchman was a descendant of minor Tuscan nobility and Macquarie believed he had pretensions to be a new Caesar. After failing to gain a place on La Pérouse's mission, which visited Botany Bay in 1788, Bonaparte had become an artillery officer in the French army when the Revolution exploded the following year. He rapidly seized the opportunities this created and was a general at age 24. He was given command of France's Army of Italy to crush a royalist revolt against the new government in Paris and, at 26, began his first military campaign of conquest against the Austrians and the Italian monarchs. He became a hero in France and, in 1798, led the military expedition to Egypt. He was also building on France's alliance with Macquarie's 'old enemy', Tipu Sultan, to overthrow the British in India.

Macquarie was acutely aware that Tipu was mustering his forces and that yet another 'campaign under canvas' loomed, in which the British would again try to strip their long-time foe 'of his rich valuable dominions'.[68] The 77th Regiment and the rest of the Bombay Army's 6420 men – 1617 European soldiers and 4803 native sepoys – were ready for what history would come to know as the Fourth Anglo–Mysore War.

When Richard Wellesley, Lord Mornington,[69] the new governor-general of Bengal, learned of the proposed alliance between Napoleon and Tipu Sultan, he decided to strike first.

On 14 February 1799, Macquarie, carrying the Bombay Army's money as paymaster, embarked from Bombay on the ship *Viper*, and after five days of travelling south, arrived at Cannanore to begin another slow, deliberate march up the ghauts.[70] He had almost died on previous journeys there, and this time had not made out a will, because he was still not in a fit state of mind to 'undertake a task of so serious a nature'.[71] His friend James Dunlop was with him, commanding the Centre European Brigade, comprising 1454 men.

Two British armies were boosted by 21,000 troops sent by the *nizam* (ruler) of Hyderabad, a British ally, so that Tipu's army of 30,000 warriors faced a combined force of more than 40,000 men. The *nizam*'s men were under the control of Lord Mornington's brother, the future Duke of Wellington.

The Bombay Army, under Lieutenant-General Stuart, would attack from the Malabar Coast in the west, while the Grand Army, now under the command of General George Harris,[72] would come from Madras in the east.

Eight years earlier, Lord Cornwallis's campaign against Tipu had been plagued by supply problems. This time the British were taking no chances. When the 21,000 men of the eastern army marched out of Vellore, inland from Madras, on 11 February, they had 200,000 camp followers, and more than 100,000 oxen, horses, donkeys and elephants carrying supplies, ammunition and ordnance.[73]

Again, Macquarie was forced to climb through 'wild jungly country'.[74] There was just one narrow track for much of the route, with no clearing alongside it large enough for a single battalion, much less an army, to camp in.

But on 5 March, as Macquarie looked out at the Mysore plains from the top of the Seedaseer Hill, he saw a huge encampment of enemy troops forming to the right of Periapatam, with a large green tent in the middle.

Tipu had 18,000 men with him.[75] The next morning, 6000 of them attacked the British from the front, while two other armies of similar strength attacked from left and right in a great circuit through the jungle, with rapid fire and blood-curdling screams. The column in front raged at the British 'from nine in the morning till two o'clock in the afternoon',[76] until it was finally repulsed by the Right Native Brigade under Lieutenant-Colonel John Montresor.[77] The two attacking columns in the rear were dispersed by the men under Dunlop.

Macquarie proudly announced later that no part of Tipu's plan had succeeded. Just 143 men on the British side had been reported dead or missing, whereas for 'two miles and a half in the rear of the post, [Tipu's] dead and wounded are to be seen scattered on the road and in the jungle in great numbers'.[78] Later reports claimed that 2000 of the enemy's troops, including twelve of his principal officers, were killed, wounded or missing.

Both forces licked their wounds, too weak to continue the fight and, on 11 March, with 'all his schemes now completely frustrated by the smart drubbing',[79] Tipu retreated 80 kilometres to his capital at Seringapatam.

The British followed. Macquarie, ailing still, was carried in a palanquin.

On 10 April 1799, the cavalry, under Major-General John Floyd, formed a junction with Stuart's Bombay Army at the fort of Periapatam, and six days later, they crossed the 'rough and stony'[80]

650-metre-wide bed of the Kaveri River's Great Ford. They approached Seringapatam from the north, while Harris's Grand Army stalked from the south.

Over the next few days, Tipu's men kept up a constant fire of both cannon and musketry, and on 18 April, 'two very valuable artillery officers died within half an hour of one another … both being killed by cannon shots when pointing their own six-pounders at the enemy in the bed of the river'.[81] Yet the Mysorean rocketmen were eventually driven off by grapeshot from the British cannons.

On 2 May, 'a most tremendous peal of fire' opened on the fort of Seringapatam from the surrounding batteries: 'no less than fifty-two pieces of ordnance – including eight howitzers'.[82] Piece by piece, the southwest wall of the fort was being blown down by artillery shells.

Two days later, at daybreak on 4 May, another 'most tremendous fire of shot and shells' was hurled at Tipu's fortress, and the breach in the wall appeared sufficiently wide 'to admit two grand divisions'.

Inside his palace, Tipu told his officers and servants he was unconcerned. He was a picture of haughtiness, arrayed in fine clothing, 'a jacket of fine white linen, loose drawers of flowered chintz, with a crimson cloth of silk and cotton round his waist: a handsome pouch with a red and green silk belt, hung across his shoulder'.[83]

As he ate his noon-day meal, Tipu was told that the British were coming. He refused to leave his food.

Then, at 1.30 p.m., Major-General David Baird[84] told his men it was time to settle old scores. Baird was cranky and ill-tempered at the best of times, but he had spent more than four years as Tipu's prisoner following the Battle of Polilur in 1780, carrying a bullet wound inside his body the whole time. Now, he wanted revenge. He stepped from the British trenches surrounding the fort and waved his sword to signal the charge.

Macquarie watched as 4000 redcoats crossed the river and waded through the waist-deep ditch in front of it. Then, with bayonets gleaming, they swarmed through the hole in the wall of the fort, slicing through any defenders brave enough to challenge them. Most of Tipu's guards ran for their lives in all directions.

James Dunlop was challenged by a *sirdar*, one of Tipu's noblemen, who made a desperate cut with his sword. Dunlop parried it and slashed the man across the breast but, as he was dying, he made a second strike at Dunlop that almost severed his right hand at the wrist.

With his hand hanging by a thread, Dunlop slashed on, charging into the fray, until blood loss caused him to collapse.

Inside his palace, Tipu finally called for his sword. Followed by four men who carried his muskets and a fifth who carried a blunderbuss, Tipu mounted the northern rampart and trotted toward the breach. He stood behind a transverse wall and fired at the advancing redcoats, while his servants loaded for him. He gunned down three or four Englishmen, but could do nothing to stop the tide of men pouring in, or the wash of his frightened troops rushing out.

He mounted his horse and began to ride east atop the fort's rampart. Near the Water Gate, a musket ball hit him in his right side. He tried to ride through the Water Gate into the palace to his family, but he was caught in the middle of a large crowd trying to escape. Bullets ripped through his fine clothing and, all around him, his followers were gunned down. His horse was shot from under him and both beast and rider fell among a heap of dead and dying.

Tipu still had enough fight in him, however, to slash open the knee of an Englishman who tried to take his adornments. The wounded soldier stepped back and killed the Tiger of Mysore with a shot to the head.

Major-General Baird had hoped to take Tipu alive, but he found his corpse among 300 bloodstained bodies massed together at the Water Gate archway.

'His eyes were open,' wrote Major Alexander Allan,[85] 'and the body was so warm that for a few moments Colonel Wellesley and myself were doubtful whether he was not alive … He had four wounds, three in the body, and one in the temple; the ball having entered a little above the right ear, and lodged in the cheek.'[86]

ON 24 MAY, Macquarie sent his journal from the campaign in Cannanore for safekeeping to his friend and banker Charles Forbes,[87] John Forbes's nephew, back in Bombay. He wrote:

> The final result of this glorious and memorable day, was, that our troops were in complete possession of Tippoo Sultaun's fortress and capital in less than an hour from the commencement of the assault; – the Sultaun himself, and a great many of his principal officers, killed in the storm; – his sons and all his family our prisoners; and all his immense riches and treasures in our possession.[88]

With Tipu's defeat, the British had eliminated their greatest enemy in southern India and were now able to secure control of the whole region.

Aggressive expansion by the 'Company' then led to Britain gaining control of almost all of India and part of Nepal. The 'Company's' armies were also used to seize colonial possessions of other European nations, including the islands of Réunion and Mauritius. Indian princes became Company vassals, and although British control was facilitated by hundreds of thousands of Indian troops, none could ever rise much above the level of major even with years of loyal service. They received no training in administration or leadership to make them independent of their British officers.

For more than half a century after the fall of Tipu, the Company ruled India and drove the smuggling of opium into China, but the cost of expansion and administration was prohibitive and only government support kept the business afloat.

Resentments festered over the British occupation, with tensions simmering for decades over religious differences, invasive social reforms, harsh land taxes, and the disrespect shown to local landowners and rulers.

In 1857 at the garrison town of Meerut, 70 kilometres northeast of Delhi, Company sepoys staged a mutiny that led to the Indian Rebellion of 1857, and the destruction of the cities of Delhi and Lucknow. There was devastation throughout the country. The British Government decided to nationalise the Company immediately with the Crown taking control of its Indian possessions and its armed forces. The new rule became the British Raj and it lasted until 1947, when the British territory was partitioned into two sovereign states: India and Pakistan.

MACQUARIE HAD HOPED to pocket as much as £3000 in prize money, but his loot, which included seventeen ruby rings, amounted to a disappointing £1300.[89] The campaign, though, had been something of a tonic for him, and he abandoned his once 'serious intention of quitting the army'[90] and moping around mourning Jane. He holidayed at Fort William in Calcutta, describing his first view of the city from the Ganges as:

> … magnificent and beautiful beyond anything I had ever seen in my life; the great City of Calcutta, and the superb elegant buildings at Chowringee … The elegant villas, houses and gardens, all along the banks of the river in Garden Reach, looked most beautiful from the water, as we sailed up the river past them. Fort William upon our nearer approach to it, made a very grand appearance.[91]

He rode around to parties and balls in his palanquin. He courted favours over the dinner table. He dined with Lord Mornington in Calcutta, and Sir Alured Clarke,[92] now the army commander-in-chief, gave ensigncies to his nephew Hector Maclaine and his cousin Lachlan MacQuarrie, son of the old clan chief. At least they weren't children.

On 2 October, however, Macquarie 'was greatly vexed and provoked':

… my boy Hector was absent and could not be found anywhere, notwithstanding I sent all over the town to look for him. The boy has always appeared so attached that I can hardly allow myself to believe that he has run away or deserted of his own accord as he has always every indulgence he could wish for. I therefore conclude he has actually been stolen or kidnapped in the course of last night by a set of villains who make a trade of carrying off boys of this description. I am however very sorry to lose him, and have left directions with my friend Captain Cameron if possible to find him out.[93]

Macquarie never saw Hector again. His heart had already been broken by Jane's passing but he was deeply saddened by the loss. Young George had lost his closest friend since they were sold together at the slave market but at least, in Macquarie, he had a kind and benevolent father figure, who cared about his welfare for the rest of his life.

Moving on to Madras, Macquarie dined with the Governor of India, Lord Edward Clive,[94] son of Robert, 'Clive of India', the 'Company's' most famous leader.

Back in Bombay in December 1799, Macquarie was still Deputy Paymaster-General and Major of Brigade, but Governor Duncan soon asked him to join his 'family' as his 'confidential military secretary'.[95] The new role did not add a single farthing to Macquarie's pay but he made a pact with the governor that his predecessor, 'being a married man and not rich', would not lose any money by forfeiting the role.[96] Macquarie's concern for others duly impressed Duncan, who had earned a great reputation from trying to stamp out infanticide when he ruled the Indian city of Benares under Lord Cornwallis.[97]

Macquarie moved almost 300 kilometres north to a new office in Surat, where Duncan had decided the people could benefit from a new government. Surat was a vital centre for maritime commerce, for shipbuilding, textile production and the export of gold and it had been a political football with the British and

The NABOB of SURAT.

The Nabob of Surat
Macquarie encountered
took the role after the
death of his brother
whose portrait was
engraved by the British
artist William Birch.

Dutch fighting for control. The British wanted the Nabob of
Surat to squeeze more taxes out of his subjects to pay for their
army to protect the city from attack. The nabob couldn't find
the money and the British decided to install a government that
could. Macquarie arrived there on 2 May 1800 as part of the
governor's suite, and was treated to days of ceremonial welcome
by the nabob.

The ruler and his 'great officers' appeared in procession, all
mounted on 'large beautiful elephants most elegantly dressed
and decorated, and attended by an immense retinue of horse and
foot'.[98] In his journal, Macquarie wrote that the nabob was 'a very
fine, handsome-looking man about forty-four years of age – and
was very richly dressed'. As the nabob passed along, he threw
handfuls of silver to the crowds.

Macquarie reckoned that the procession 'most probably is, the
happiest day the nabob will ever spend: – for alas! poor man, he
yet little thinks of the fate that is hanging over him, or that he is
about to be very soon stripped of all his power & consequence'.[99]

In case the nabob refused to hand over power to the British quietly, Macquarie carried out a scouting mission of his palace and other public buildings where guards were posted, and took notes on the ground available for siege works.

In the end, the nabob considered the fate of Tipu Sultan and handed over control, though only 'after much procrastination, and various objections to the measures proposed', and 'with infinite regret and reluctance'. In lieu of all the taxes, tolls and customs he had previously collected, the British offered him a pension.[100]

Their immediate business finished, the governor and Macquarie returned to Government House in the Parel district of Bombay, covering 183 miles (295 kilometres) in twelve days, most of the time protected in their palanquins from the driving rain that soaked their bearers.[101]

MACQUARIE was gradually finding himself in a better place psychologically, and realising that he needed to get on with life and make the most of his opportunities. Jane's tombstone had finally arrived in Bombay after an earlier version was damaged in transit. On 18 September, the day he became president of Bombay's Sans Souci Club, he ceased wearing the black crepe armband 'for my ever-to-be-lamented angelic wife … the least respect I was bound to pay to her beloved memory'.[102]

His improved spirits would benefit all those around him, financially. Not only did he continue to send gifts and money home to Scotland but, in November 1800, he rewarded the head clerk in the king's pay office, Jaganath Gunpetjee, with a gift of 1000 rupees and a pay rise of 30 rupees a month. The same month, he was a guest at the wedding of Jaganath's eldest daughter, a ceremony 'performed with great pomp and expence according to the Hindoo custom'.[103]

THE BRITISH WAR EFFORT against Napoleon rolled on, and on 21 March 1801, Macquarie looked out on Bombay Harbour at the large fleet of transports ready to take troops to fight the French in Egypt, where war had again erupted. Arthur Wellesley and the government of Bombay were 'indefatigable in their exertions in completing the fleet with all the necessary supplies for six months'. Bonaparte had left Cairo in August 1799 and handed command to General Jean-Baptiste Kléber, but not before attempting major cultural changes before he left. Bonaparte ensured his name and Mohammed's were mentioned together because he portrayed himself as Egypt's liberator from Ottoman oppressors, gifts were distributed to the people, and his officers were given kaftans. Bonaparte tried to reshape Egypt along French lines. Cairo began to look more like a European city with a local government chosen from the most capable men. He established Egypt's first scientific institute, the Institut d'Égypte and he set up a library, antiquities museum, chemistry laboratory, health service, botanical garden, observatory and menagerie.

Under his orders, scholars compiled a French–Arabic dictionary and calculated a triple Egyptian, Coptic and European calendar.

On 30 March, there came news from Lord Mornington that David Baird would command an expedition against the French in Egypt, and of all the 8000 troops were to be sent from India. Mornington's brother, Colonel Wellesley, would be second in command. This news, Macquarie said, was very unexpected, and Wellesley was 'very much hurt at this supercession'.[104]

But it was a different story for Macquarie himself. His reputation for diplomacy and for organisational skills preceded him. To his 'agreeable surprise',[105] as he and Baird were walking on the veranda of Government House, the general asked him if he would accept the posts of head of his staff and deputy adjutant-general of his army. It was an offer Macquarie was only too happy to accept, and it meant that Wellesley's pick for the job, Major Colman, missed out on a posting as well. Eventually, Wellesley himself had to withdraw from the campaign because of ill health.

Major-General Baird had a reputation for ferocity even against his own men. Two decades earlier, upon hearing that Tipu had chained him to another British soldier, Baird's mother reportedly exclaimed: 'The Lord help the puir chiel that's chained to our

Davie!'[106] Yet Macquarie had learned no end of diplomacy since first buttoning on his red tunic all those years ago, and he and Baird would become lifelong pals.

Arthur Wellesley told a brother officer that Baird 'was very candid, and told him that Macquarie had been recommended as a man of business, and he wanted a person having that qualification ... he is an excellent man.'[107]

On 6 April 1801, Macquarie sailed with Baird on the transport *William* for the Red Sea, and war on a new horizon.

Chapter 13

AUGUST 1801 TO DECEMBER 1803, EGYPT,
INDIA AND ENGLAND

*A musquet ball had entered a little below his left eye and came out at
the back of his neck ... poor dear, he had ... thank God
– a most miraculous escape indeed.*

<small>MACQUARIE, RELIEVED THAT HIS BROTHER CHARLES WAS STILL ALIVE
AFTER TAKING A FRENCH BULLET IN EGYPT[1]</small>

IT HAD BEEN thirteen years since Macquarie, bound for
India, had farewelled his brother Charles at Leith, tenderly
embracing him as though they might never meet again. Charles
had been a callow youth of seventeen when they said their
goodbyes in 1788, but he was now a captain in the Black Watch,
the 42nd Regiment of Foot, stationed at Gibraltar.

Macquarie's Indian army would be joining British troops
from England, Turkey and the Mediterranean in a three-pronged
campaign to flush the French out of Egypt. The 42nd was part
of the Mediterranean contingent, led by General Sir Ralph
Abercromby,[2] brother of Macquarie's mentor Sir Robert.

Macquarie was forty, and nowhere near as strong as he had
been when he traipsed across the Highlands trying to lure
recruits to follow him to India. His body had been ravaged by
illness, grief and fatigue, and though once broad-shouldered and
stout, he now weighed just over 70 kilograms. Yet as he sailed

for Egypt, he was buoyed by the prospect of being reunited with Charles, after a separation soothed only so much by paper and ink, and by their consorting in the enlistment of child officers. The death of their brother Donald in 1801 had made the bond between Charles and Lachlan even stronger.

The *William* sailed west into the Arabian Sea and then into the Gulf of Aden, stopping at Mocha, the coffee port of Yemen. At Jeddah on the Red Sea, the Shereef of Mecca, steward of the holy city, presented Major Macquarie with a shawl.

The expedition finally disembarked on the Red Sea coast at Cosseir (now called Al Qoseir), not far from the pyramids of Luxor. It would be the first Indian army to serve outside Asia.

Macquarie thought Cosseir 'the poorest and most wretched miserable looking place I have ever seen in any part of the world'.[3] The heat was intense – but Macquarie burned more from the news that there had been an administrative bungle and that, without consulting Baird, officials in London had appointed Lieutenant-Colonel Samuel Auchmuty as the Indian Army's adjutant-general and chief of staff. Macquarie was ropeable at the insult, and Baird had to cajole his young charge into not getting on the first boat back to Bombay.[4]

The Indian expeditionary force – now numbering 7886 European and Sepoy troops and ancillary staff – marched or rode west through a 'wild, dreary, arid desert' for 207 kilometres until they reached the green oasis of Kenné (now called Qena) on the Nile. Then there was a 700-kilometre voyage up the river to the island of Rhoda, where Baird had set up his headquarters.

Throughout the nine-day voyage, Macquarie marvelled at the landscape along the Nile, and the wonders that had stood there centuries before the Vikings arrived on Ulva. The canny Scot in him knew a bargain, too, when he paid 1 Spanish dollar for 1200 eggs for his men and stocked up on 'good, fat geese' at fourpence a head.

He had arrived in Egypt just as the fighting was ending and finally reached Alexandria in September 1801, shortly after the surrender of the French Army.

Just as Macquarie was preparing to leave Bombay with Baird, an Anglo-Ottoman land force under Ralph Abercromby defeated the French in the Battle of Alexandria on 21 March 1801.

In April, French troops were forced to surrender at Fort Julien, on the left bank of the Nile near Rosetta (Rashid) and, on 27 June, British commander John Hely-Hutchinson, backed by Ottoman troops, surrounded the 13,000 French soldiers garrisoned in Cairo and forced another surrender. The remaining French troops in Egypt retreated to Alexandria, which remained under siege, and finally gave up the fight on 2 September 1801. The French army was repatriated in British ships, but not before giving Britain priceless Egyptian antiquities such as the Rosetta Stone. The following year, Egypt was under Ottoman control.

In Alexandria, Macquarie gazed in astonishment at the 20-metre-high Pompey's Pillar, a 1500-year-old tribute to the Roman emperor Diocletian's suppression of an Alexandrian revolt. To Macquarie, it was 'truly the most magnificent and most beautiful object' he had ever seen. The Sphinx and Pyramids were 'wonderful and stupendous monuments too'.

Yet Macquarie's enjoyment of these sights was dampened when, to his shock, he learned that some months earlier, his brother had been shot in the face.

On 8 March 1801, at Abukir[5] near the Nile Delta, Ralph Abercromby had been trying to drive out 21,000 French troops and land 17,500 of his own. That day, 130 British troops were killed and 600 wounded. Charles Macquarie had been spurring on his company of Royal Highland Grenadiers when he was hit. He had since recovered sufficiently to be back in charge of a company in the 52nd Regiment under the command of John Moore,[6] an officer Macquarie had known in the American war.

Macquarie found his brother sitting alone in his tent at sundown, with a huge scar on his face but unable to mask a wide smile. Macquarie was not too proud to characterise their meeting, after so many years, as akin to a 'romance' that 'produced in both of us a variety of interesting and uncommon emotions'.

Macquarie had travelled 'over seas and deserts from so remote a quarter of the globe', and 'to attempt to describe the scene that took place at this most happy and most unexpected meeting' was impossible: 'hearts and sensibility and true affection can very readily conceive, what the feelings of two most affectionate, most loving brothers must have been at such a meeting, in such a country, under circumstances of such recent danger to him and his miraculous escape from death.'[7]

For the next few weeks, the two brothers caught up on old times – drinking and carousing, and dining with Moore and his second-in-command Hildebrand Oakes,[8] the older brother of Macquarie's friend Henry Oakes. Soon, though, the brothers were saying their goodbyes as Abercromby's forces returned to their Mediterranean bases and awaited Napoleon's next move. Charles left for the Spanish island of Menorca, carrying a gift from Macquarie of £2000 to buy a Scottish estate, and also toting with him Macquarie's twelve-year-old Indian slave boy George, so that the boy could gain an education in Scotland. In return, Charles gave his brother a pair of pistols, while Colonel Dickson of the Black Watch gave him 'a fine large camel', which Macquarie nicknamed 'the Laird of Kilbuckie'.

The weeks he had spent with Charles improved Macquarie's outlook on life no end, and he joked with Dorothea Morley about how her stepdaughter Sarah had given Chares the slip to marry William Ogilvy. Old Morley had died[9] and left £41,000 to be divided among his seven children. Macquarie told the widowed Dorothea that his friend John Forbes, the Bombay banker, was unattached and loaded.[10]

Macquarie tried vainly for a promotion to lieutenant-colonel but was rejected by the Duke of York,[11] the King's son, who oversaw promotions as army commander-in-chief.

Instead, he became a major in the 86th Regiment, which had been tasked with occupying the citadel in Cairo.

Still, he had his crosses to bear. In January 1802, he was kicked in the thigh by a horse. Soon after, he became gravely ill with similar symptoms to those that had made him so sick in India.

Dr James McGrigor[12] of the 88th Regiment began feeding him huge doses of mercury: '4 pills at night and 3 in the mornings', and more of it to be rubbed into his body twice a day. McGrigor noted there was 'an immense number of venereal cases'[13] in the 86th and that syphilis could lay dormant for years. He later wrote that, at the time of embarkation, there was hardly a sick man in the army except those with venereal diseases, who had resisted treatment with mercury.[14]

After seventeen days of treatment Macquarie was also taking a daily dose of nitric acid for mouth ulcers and required 'a chirurgical operation'. McGrigor often found that the application of mercury to the gums required blood to be drawn first.[15]

The treatment ravaged Macquarie's frail body. One morning his servant William Stewart found him unconscious in his blood-soaked bed after a rupture. If not for timely action, Macquarie would have died. Generally expansive about illnesses, Macquarie was unusually coy about his condition in letters home, telling Charles and Dorothea that he was in a 'weak state of health'[16] from his 'severe attack'.[17]

Three doctors, daily visits by Baird to his tent – which was twice the size of that occupied by most officers[18] – and a large slice of luck in fighting a disease that was often fatal helped Macquarie recover sufficiently to attend a dinner in a mosque on the anniversary of his brother's miraculous escape from death. There he read a moving letter of thanksgiving.[19]

On 25 March 1802, Joseph Bonaparte, Napoleon's older brother, and Charles Cornwallis signed a treaty in the French city of Amiens that brought about a temporary peace between the two world powers. By May, Macquarie was able to be carried by twenty porters in his palanquin back to the *William* for the return journey to India on 5 June.

By 5 July 1802, Macquarie was back living at Bombay's government house, setting up the old clan chief's son, Lachlan, as aide de camp to the governor.

For a while there was talk of going to Madras to prepare a report on the killing of the Persian ambassador, who had been caught in a crossfire between sepoys and his own men, but nothing came of it.[20]

He also chaperoned Jane's niece, Louisa Wilkins, who was in India to find a rich husband. He contacted his old friend Francis Wredé, the postmaster of Muttoncherry, to order for her 'a couple of smart little slave girls, each about twelve years of age ... the cheaper the better'.[21] But Macquarie was aimless in India and depressed.

BACK ON MULL, Uncle Murdoch Maclaine's financial position was sinking faster than ever, with pieces of his estate being sold from under him to cover debts. Macquarie gave him £10,600 for 4000 hectares. John Forbes guaranteed the money, preventing the Campbells and other mortgagees from stepping in.

The prospect of one day having heirs had been Macquarie's 'principal motive in wishing to become a landed proprietor in my own native country', and now he was keen to walk around his new estate. His various money-making schemes as paymaster had paid off. At the time of Jane's death in 1796, he had had a fortune of £7000 invested with Francis and Gosling in London, but he was now worth more than £20,000 in cash and property, and had earned half of that in the last two years.[22] He wanted to live the life he had always dreamed of as a poor boy on Mull.

On 6 August 1802, he dined with Governor Duncan at the country home of Sir William Syer, Bombay's chief justice. On the way out to the carriage after the meal, he told Duncan that he planned to return to Britain by the following January.

Macquarie had been in India for fourteen years. When he left Scotland, it had been with borrowed money and borrowed clothes. He had made his fortune in what had become 'this vile country', where the love of his life was now 'mouldering dust'.

He prepared his will and, on 30 December 1802, he visited Jane's grave. He stood, head bowed over the black marble, and remembered how they had flirted and danced, and how his heart had raced when Old Morley had told him he would put Macquarie's proposition to Jane. He remembered how they had made love and planned a family together. He read his words on her tombstone over and over as his tears fell onto the black marble.[23]

On 5 January, Duncan gave him a lavish farewell dinner at Government House, promising to sing his praises in London. The next day, Macquarie boarded the Indiaman *Sir Edward Hughes*, bound for home.

He felt 'extremely low and melancholy' looking back at Bombay, because it was where he had spent 'by far the happiest period of my whole life'.

All the way out through the harbour, past the lighthouse and into the Arabian Sea, his mind was wrapped up in mournful reflections. He was full of 'emotions that cannot be expressed but which I must now endeavour to suppress'.[24]

He could not stop thinking of the good times that had gone bad, of the great love he had enjoyed and the great love he had lost.

MACQUARIE'S £70 FARE to India back in 1788 had been provided by the British East India Company and had allowed him a humble cabin berth. Now, he handed over £400 to James Urmston, skipper of the *Sir Edward Hughes*, for quarters worthy of a wealthy gentleman.

The three-masted vessel of almost 1000 tons headed south with its twenty-eight passengers and its wounded and invalided soldiers, reaching Tellicherry a week later before sailing on to Calicut then Cochin, two cities where Macquarie had experienced both love and war. He took some of the female passengers under his wing – Mrs Carnac and her three daughters and 'the widow Gray and her young family'.[25]

By 5 March, Macquarie was in Cape Town, a very different man from the young officer who had dined there with Bligh and Robert Gordon. The cape had been returned to Dutch rule only two weeks earlier.[26]

Raw and unlearned when he first tasted Constantia wine fifteen years earlier, he was now a connoisseur and a fêted guest, who travelled to the vineyard in the 'best carriages that could be procured', and repaid the hospitality of Mr Cluyter, the owner, by handing over £52 for 60 gallons (273 litres) of his best produce.[27]

The *Sir Edward Hughes* sailed away from Table Mountain on 10 March and, two weeks later, arrived at the remote South Atlantic island of St Helena, which though just '9 miles long and 28 in circumference' was 'very high and rocky, and very wild and barren in appearance'.[28] Since dispensing with the black crepe armband, Macquarie was becoming more interested in sensual than geographic matters, and even more beautiful than the windswept St Helena coastline were the three unmarried daughters of the Scottish-born governor, Colonel Robert Patton.[29] A fourth daughter – the 'amiable and accomplished' Sarah Patton,[30] whom everyone called Sally – had just married Henry Torrens,[31] a young major in the 86th Regiment, who had served with Macquarie in India and Egypt.

Macquarie spent two nights on St Helena. He rode a horse around the island and took some of the ladies to a ball and a play. He eventually bade the Pattons farewell, but not before writing letters of recommendation for Torrens and Sally, and setting them up with friends and accommodation for their imminent return to Bombay.

Five weeks later, on 4 May 1803, Macquarie saw 'dear old England' again for the first time in fifteen years. He spied the Lizard, the island's southern-most point, 30 kilometres away during the brief and hazy interludes in a violent squall,[32] and he was chuffed that he had won 2 guineas in a bet over the time it would take to reach their destination.[33]

A pilot cutter called the *Stag of Dover* sliced through the fog of the English Channel to steer the *Sir Edward Hughes* home, but the ill winds blowing across the water were accompanied by news from the *Stag*'s captain 'that there is a great probability of our being at war again immediately with France'.[34]

It was not the news Macquarie wanted to hear, but three days later things were looking up when the ship arrived at Brighton.

He celebrated 'a prosperous and pleasant short voyage of 4 Kalendar months', in which only five passengers had died, by taking Mrs Carnac, Mrs Gray and their children to a Brighton inn called the Castle. For the first time in a decade and a half, he enjoyed a 'most excellent comfortable English dinner'.[35]

Macquarie hired four post-chaise carriages to ferry him and the women and children in his care the 100 kilometres to London. After stopping overnight 20 kilometres along the way at Cuckfield, they cantered on the next day through a glorious English spring, the birds and the bees and the green trees and hedges welcoming Macquarie home. After passing through Crawley, Sutton and Surrey, the carriages arrived in the great city at 5 p.m on 8 May.

Macquarie found lodgings in Jacquier's Hotel in Leicester Square, the former town house of the artist William Hogarth.[36] Charles Macquarie, now making his own way in the military, was staying nearby, at the fashionable Old Slaughter's Coffee House in St Martin's Lane, where Benjamin Franklin had once played chess. Their reunion was 'a most joyful and happy one', and Charles provided 'highly gratifying accounts' of the welfare of their 'dear good old mother, sister, and uncle & aunt Lochbuy'.[37]

Macquarie planned to move on to Scotland soon, proud to be returning as a wealthy man of the world, far removed from the awkward youngster who had relied so heavily on Uncle Murdoch's benevolence. He wrote to Murdoch, asking him to find room in his wine vault at 'Moy-Castle' for some 'excellent fine, old Madeira' that he had brought all the way from India and which had cost him £130, including customs duties. He asked Murdoch to pass on news of his safe arrival as quickly as possible to Macquarie's 'dear good mother … I hope in God she is alive and well'.[38]

He sent a distress signal, however, to Dorothea Morley, letting her know that he would see her the next morning but that he was out of practice in the ways of sophisticated London:

You know what an awkward, rusticated Jungle-Wallah I must appear at first among your friends. You must therefore prepare them for beholding a very uncouth and unpolished Indian … I must place myself entirely under your direction to be a little humanised and modernised … I shall prove at least a willing and obedient pupil – tho' I fear a very dull and stupid one.[39]

Macquarie spent many emotional hours the next day with Dorothea and her family at Wimpole Street, talking mostly about Jane and her last days. He would be a frequent visitor there over the following few weeks.

He had been falsely modest in declaring his rustic ways, however: even though he had not been in London for fifteen years, he was soon right at home, meeting with his bankers, dining with various officials of the East India Company, drinking with former comrades from India and ingratiating himself further with military bigwigs. It was the secret of his success.

On 16 May 1803, as had been feared, King George III declared war on France with an announcement to both Houses of Parliament. The British were fearful of Napoleon's military build-up after the peace treaty had been signed at Amiens a year earlier, and especially with his sending troops into Switzerland. Two days later, Macquarie accompanied his old commander General James Marsh to St James's Palace, where he was presented to the monarch, 'kissing His Majesty's Hand … the King was graciously pleased to speak to me, and asked me several questions'.[40] On 20 May, he was telling the Duke of York all about his fifteen years of continuous service in India. Six days on, he was at court along with General Balfour, kissing the hand of Queen Charlotte and 'seeing all the princesses looking most lovely, and dressed with great splendour … a grand most pleasing splendid sight of the finest women in all the world'.[41]

To curry further favour, he presented many of these important people with exotic gifts from the East Indies, after he had paid £215 in customs duty on his luggage from Bombay.

He gave an ivory and sandalwood inlaid box to the Duchess of York, and presented a similar gift to the queen, writing to ask that she 'graciously forgive' his presumption in offering the token 'for Her Majesty's benignant acceptance ... as a humble testimony of [my] high veneration and most respectful attachment for Her Royal Sacred Person, and for her innumerable, great, and exalted virtues'.[42]

WITH EXPERIENCED OFFICERS crucial to the war effort against France, the army hamstrung Macquarie's movements, stymying his plans to leave for Mull as soon as possible. Instead, he undertook a seemingly endless round of sightseeing tours and dinner parties.

Lord Hobart,[43] Secretary of State for War and the Colonies, wanted him to go to Portugal to report on the British ally's preparedness for war, but Macquarie begged off, saying he would be lost without the language. He also dodged another posting to the island of Guernsey, where he would have been in charge of recuperating Indian veterans.[44] Instead, he was made assistant adjutant-general on the staff of the London District under General Charles Stanhope,[45] the Earl of Harrington. Macquarie's war record and diplomatic skills were key to the promotion. The administrative role made Macquarie right-hand man to a powerful military and political figure. The Harringtons loved to entertain and, on accepting his first invitation to their home, Macquarie met 'a great number of very fine and beautiful women'.[46] He would meet many more over the next few months, once again spending more than he earned as his life became another social carousel.

He moved into a new home at 4 Bennet Street, St James's.[47] He admitted he was no great horseman, but he paid 145 guineas for two striking black chargers, one from a horse dealer in Oxford Street and one from the famous auction house of Richard Tattersall. Then he paid 3 shillings a night to keep each horse at Moore's Livery Stables near his new home.[48]

He was now so well off that he became flippant about monetary matters, writing to Charles Reeve Esquire, Collector of the

Income Tax: 'Being at a loss how to fill up the enclosed printed paper received by me on the 30th ultimo, I take the liberty of returning it to you, and requesting that you will be so obliging as to take the trouble of filling it up *yourself* in the proper manner from the following statement of my property.'

Macquarie then fudged the true nature of his assets to the taxman, telling Reeve that £3000 of his stock actually belonged to his brother Charles and that £1000 of it was the property of his servant Stewart.[49]

He had to write to Charles Forbes in Bombay for £1000 from his Indian account, but before long he was sitting for the Cornish portrait painter John Opie, 'one of the most eminent artists now in London', paying him 28 guineas for a 'half-length picture … which is reckoned by everyone who has seen it very like me'.[50] Macquarie had planned to give his mother the painting but presented it to Dorothea Morley instead, such was her fascination with it.

His near-death experiences with illness in India and Egypt still haunted him, and three days before Christmas 1803, 'Doctor Everard Home of Sackville Street – accompanied by his assistant Mr. Nicholson' came to Macquarie's lodgings and, for 12 guineas, 'performed a surgical operation on me of a very delicate nature; from which I hope to derive great relief and benefit in due time'.[51] It took him ten days of convalescence before he could venture out his front door to wish Harrington and his family a happy new year.[52]

It was to be anything but that for Macquarie.

His delicate surgery had been relatively painless compared with the trials – both professional and personal – that he was about to face.

Chapter 14

JUNE 1804 TO APRIL 1805, ENGLAND AND THE SCOTTISH HIGHLANDS

This girl is quite a heroine! —What a most excellent soldier's wife she would make! – and happy – in my mind – will that man be whose good fortune it may happen to be if he get her!

MACQUARIE, GOBSMACKED BY THE FISHING SKILLS OF HIS NEW
LOVE INTEREST, ELIZABETH CAMPBELL[1]

MACQUARIE had spent more than a year dreaming of returning to Scotland and seeing his ageing mother and Uncle Murdoch again, but he was constantly thwarted in his attempts to leave England.

By the middle of 1804, Macquarie had become desperate, his anxiety fuelled by letters from Murdoch's wife that the old man, now seventy-four, was 'most severely attacked' with the 'gravellish complaint' of kidney stones.[2] Murdoch suffered 'great torment', and soon his eldest daughter Jane was giving Macquarie 'such very bad accounts' of Murdoch's health that he began to be 'very much alarmed for my poor dear good uncle's life'.[3] Murdoch's physician, Dr Allan Maclean, also provided 'most alarming accounts' of his patient's condition, and asked Macquarie to seek out the advice of the most eminent medical men in London.[4] Macquarie went straight around to Sackville Street, where Dr Home scribbled down instructions for the doctors in Scotland, and had Macquarie send them north post-haste along with a 'flexible gum cathetor'.[5]

Six days later, Aunt Jane wrote to Macquarie to say that her husband's end was near, and urged him to rush north as quickly as possible to see his uncle one last time.[6]

After a brigade review at Hyde Park, Macquarie asked Harrington to plead with the Duke of York to grant him two months' leave. The duke obliged, saying it was a reasonable request given that Macquarie had endured 'an absence of near 17 years' from his loved ones.

Macquarie sent his servant William Stewart on ahead with his two black chargers; hired a roomy, clean post-chaise carriage; and set out on a six-day ride to Edinburgh in company with his dearly departed Jane's sister, Mrs Christiana Scott,[7] and her friend, Miss Carnegie, the sister of the Earl of Southesk.

All the way north, as Macquarie contemplated his uncle's grave illness, there was another dark cloud hanging over him. He tried not to think about the storm that was brewing, however; he had enough to worry about as it was.

At Dumbreck's Hotel in Edinburgh's New Town, Macquarie's distant cousin Major John Campbell[8] of Airds, Aunt Jane's brother, called around with 'melancholy tidings' that Macquarie's 'poor dear good uncle … was at the point of death, there being now not the least hope of his recovery'.[9] Jane's younger sister, Elizabeth Campbell,[10] had left Edinburgh for Mull ten days earlier with her two nephews, John[11] and Murdoch junior,[12] because 'poor Lochbuie' had 'expressed a strong desire to see his two boys before he died'.[13]

Macquarie and Campbell took off in the post-chaise across the western Highlands, galloping along as fast as the mountain roads would allow. They travelled north through Linlithgow, Falkirk, Stirling, Callender and Lochearnhead before spending the night at Luib House in Glen Dochart. The next day they rattled on, travelling until 11 p.m. before retiring at the Inn of Ballachuilish. Early next morning, they continued on beside Loch Lihnne before arriving at Airds House in Appin, where John Campbell showed Macquarie a beautiful garden that his sister Elizabeth had lovingly cared for, exhibiting good taste in her 'ornamental improvements'.[14]

Macquarie told himself that he would have to meet this girl, whom he had heard of as 'Betsy' when she was a schoolgirl in London. He had once regretted not having time to visit her then, but he would not make the same mistake again. Elizabeth had lived a pious life in a religious household, holding firmly to Anglican beliefs and Scottish patriotism, determined to support herself rather than live with friends in London. Her old school in Hammersmith had taught her well.

The next day, the two men took the barge to Mull, and Macquarie saw Lochbuie House for the first time in seventeen years. They arrived at 4 p.m. and 'were most cordially received by poor Mrs. Maclaine and her lovely and numerous young family, consisting of two sons and nine daughters!' Also present was Macquarie's Indian slave boy George, now in his mid-teens, who had been living with the Maclaines ever since he came home from Egypt with Charles. George had become a great favourite with poor Murdoch, especially since his illness had worsened.[15]

It was an occasion of great rejoicing and, at the same time, great sadness for Macquarie, meeting so many family members he had not seen for so long, but realising that he would soon farewell the man who had put him on the path to success. He went to his uncle's bedside immediately.

He knew me directly, and embraced me with the greatest ardour and affection, holding me in his arms for some moments, and testifying his joy and happiness at seeing me once more before he died ... Thus I had the consolation of finding ... my dear good uncle not only alive – but still in perfect possession of all his senses and faculties as much as ever. I felt however very deeply affected, at seeing so near a relation for whom I have naturally and justly so strong an affection, thus labouring under a mortal disease; and my sorrow is greatly increased by the deep distress of his amiable good wife and fine family of young children, at the near prospect of his dissolution – and their consequent irreparable loss of a kind husband, and tender affectionate parent and protector![16]

After fifteen minutes or so, Macquarie let his uncle rest. He wanted very much to travel on to see his mother that night, but his 'dear uncle and worthy friend'[17] was in such a poor state that Macquarie knew he must not leave him.

At the dinner table, his Aunt Jane finally introduced him to the remarkable Elizabeth Campbell. The forty-three year old Macquarie was immediately attracted to this lithe, athletic and confident twenty-six year old, with her reddish-brown curly hair, blue eyes, pale skin and easy, affable manner. He was even more impressed by her 'benevolent generous motive of affording all the consolation and assistance in her power to her Sister Mrs. Maclaine and her young family in their present great distress'.[18] Elizabeth and Aunt Jane were constantly by Murdoch's bed; when he was awake, he could not bear to be alone.[19]

Two doctors, Donald Maclaine and Allan Maclean, were attending to the dying man. The eighty-nine year old clan chief Lauchlan MacQuarrie also turned up to greet the conquering hero, back on Mull after so many years and battles. Macquarie would take turns with old Lauchlan, John Campbell and Maclean of Coll to hold Murdoch's cooling hand.

Over the next few days, for as long as Murdoch's failing strength allowed, he and Macquarie talked over old times, reflecting upon the many happy days Macquarie had spent under the old man's 'kind patronage and parental care and protection'.[20]

On 28 June, Macquarie sat with his uncle for two full hours, with both of his hands clasped around Murdoch's. His dying uncle 'very frequently repeated that he had the greatest confidence in the affection, friendship and attachment' of Macquarie and Charles, 'that he trusted everything' to them, 'that he was convinced that he left his young helpless family in good hands', and that the Macquarie brothers 'would take care of them'.[21]

By the time Charles finally arrived on 3 July, in a cutter from his new posting in Ireland, Murdoch could no longer speak, but he clutched Macquarie's younger brother 'in his arms and kissed him with the greatest ardour and affection'.[22]

Murdoch breathed his last 'without pain or struggle' at a quarter to three on the morning of 5 July 1804. His body was laid out and prepared for the funeral, to be held five days later.

The next morning, Macquarie and old Lauchlan rode away from the 'house of sorrow'[23] and Macquarie boarded a ferry and crossed over to Oskamull. He arrived at his mother's house at 7 p.m., to find the old lady and his sister Betty there alone and overjoyed at seeing their hero finally come home.

> The scene that passed on my first introducing myself to my dear good mother after nearly 17 years absence … is much easier conceived than expressed … both my mother and sister were supremely happy at seeing me once more under their own roof. My poor mother had not yet heard of her beloved brother Lochbuy's death, but knowing before that there were little hopes of his recovery, she was in some degree prepared for the fatal tidings which I now brought her of that most mournful event. She bore it therefore with great fortitude and resignation at first; but when her joy at so unexpectedly seeing me once more in her own house, had a little subsided, she gave way to the deepest and most poignant affliction on account of her greatly beloved brother's death, who had ever shewn her the tenderest and most kind affectionate brotherly attention in all her wants and distresses.[24]

It had been only a few short months since Macquarie had conveyed to Betty through Uncle Murdoch the 'most mournful and melancholy' news about her 'much beloved, amiable and good son' Lieutenant Hector Maclaine[25] of the 19th Regiment of Foot. He had been killed in a massacre at Watapulawa near Kandy in Ceylon,[26] after surrendering to 'merciless, ferocious, and cruel' local forces. Hector had been Macquarie's favourite nephew, 'a gallant and most promising youth',[27] and only nineteen. They pondered on that point for a while.

By degrees, Macquarie brought the conversation around to a more pleasing subject: the progress of Betty's son, Hugh Maclaine,[28] a lieutenant in the 77th. He then gave his sister and mother a 'brief sketch' of his 'own adventures in India, and the fortunate and unfortunate turns of my life in that country'.[29] Macquarie stayed up half the night, telling his mother and Betty all about Jane and Bombay, Napoleon and Egypt, Tipu Sultan and the Kingdom of Mysore. The teenager who had sailed away with his uncle to fight the American rebels was now a wealthy military officer living near a palace in London. But, he told them, he dreamed of finally coming home to become a Scottish laird himself.

ON THE AFTERNOON of 10 July 1804, all of Murdoch's friends and family from Lorne, Morven and different parts of Mull, as well as 300 tenants from his estate, gathered for his funeral at the 'ancient family seat of Moy', and he was interred in the 'family burying place of "Capelle-Fuhier"' at Laggan. Macquarie and twelve-year-old Murdoch junior walked ahead of the casket as chief mourners, with Charles Macquarie and eleven-year-old John Maclaine behind. The six pallbearers were all titled Scotsmen. For the tenants, there was hospitality in 'old Highland stile' in 'an open field adjoining to the castle with abundance of meat and drink', and in the evening, Macquarie and the gentry sat down to an elegant dinner in the great dining room of the mansion.[30]

Macquarie stayed with his Aunt Jane and her grieving brood for six more days, but with Elizabeth Campbell there to look after them all, he felt it would not be improper to take a ride around the 4000 hectares he had bought from his uncle while still in India.

He set out on horseback with Charles, their new factor (estate manager) Dugald McTavish and Charles's servant James Todd,[31] then walked across the rolling green hills of his farms at 'Callachilly and Kilbeg – including the Great Moss and Crofts of Salen'. He christened his new estate Jarvisfield, in memory of his 'late angelic excellent wife'.[32]

With the money Macquarie had given him in Egypt, Charles had also purchased an estate at Pennygown, overlooking the Sound of Mull. He had called his land Glenforsa.

That night, Macquarie sat down amid a group of nineteen relatives, including the clan chief, and a number of friends at the Callachilly Inn for a 'most excellent dinner prepared for the occasion and to celebrate this day of my brother and myself taking possession of our respective estates'.[33] They drank 'bumper toasts' to the success of Jarvisfield and Glenforsa.

While Macquarie planned to build his mansion at Callachilly and make it his 'family seat', his only regret was that the land was under a nineteen-year lease to Donald Maclaine, one of the doctors who had treated Murdoch. He had offered Maclaine £500 to vacate, but Maclaine wouldn't budge. So Macquarie settled for another site for his home by the fishing stream at Gruline.

There would be a lot of water under the bridge before that happened, though.

He spent the next two weeks with his mother and Aunt Jane, visiting old friends and family. He was getting to know Elizabeth Campbell well, but when he offered to give her a ride back to Edinburgh in his handsome post-chaise, she seemed 'disinclined to accept'.[34] He would have to try harder.

AS MACQUARIE SURVEYED his Highland kingdom, ships were slowly bringing reports to Britain of an insurrection in the new colony of New South Wales, perpetrated by what authorities called the 'dregs of the misguided Munster men'.[35]

The Castle Hill Rebellion, which had begun on Sunday, 4 March 1804, had been inspired by the 1798 Battle of Vinegar Hill at Enniscorthy in Ireland's County Wexford, an uprising that had claimed 30,000 lives. Local peasants, armed with steel-tipped pikes, had been mown down by well-drilled British redcoats armed with muskets. Many of the captured rebels had been burned alive,[36] but more than 400 others had been sent to New South Wales to brood and plot revenge.

Unrest among Irish convicts in the prison camps around Sydney had fomented as soon as they had begun hearing reports of the massacre back home. There were repeated small disturbances among prisoners that resulted in floggings and hangings. The Irishmen were stubborn, eager to break the Saxon yoke. They sensed the vulnerability of their captors in this remote colony, thousands of kilometres from reinforcements.

Finally, more serious unrest erupted. Just after sunset on 4 March, 200 convicts at the government farm at Castle Hill, 30 kilometres northwest of Sydney, made their move. They set fire to a convict hut as a signal that the revolution had begun. Most of the prisoners, guarded only by a few convict constables, joined the cause under Philip Cunningham, a stonemason and publican in his native Ireland, who had been transported for sedition. Cunningham had become overseer of government stonemasons but had really been working on bringing the system crumbling down.

Stirred on by Cunningham's mantra 'Death or Liberty', the convicts fled their compound like ants, fanning out and raiding local farmhouses for weapons. Cunningham assured them that the settlements at Sydney and Parramatta would soon fall, and that, by the time they reached the Hawkesbury River, 60 kilometres from Castle Hill, the escapees would be part of a convict force of 1100 men. The plan was to commandeer ships and sail back to Ireland.[37]

At his Parramatta home, the Reverend Samuel Marsden, known as the 'flogging parson' for his reported severity as a magistrate, was hosting a leisurely supper for Elizabeth Macarthur, another sheep farmer with ambition. Mrs Macarthur's husband, John, had been sent to England to face a court martial after wounding his superior officer Colonel William Paterson[38] in a duel.

Things were sedate at the Marsden residence until about 9 p.m., when the door was flung open and in burst another local settler, William Joyce, 'pale and in violent agitation'. He blurted out that the convicts had risen, were at the nearby Seven Hills Farm and 'that numbers were approaching Parramatta'.[39]

The convicts massed together on Constitution Hill at Toongabbie, where there was a panoramic view of approaching trouble, before moving north towards the Hawkesbury. The alarm was sounded at 11.30 p.m. in Sydney by the firing of cannons and the beating of drums.

The new governor, Philip Gidley King,[40] declared martial law in the early hours of 5 March. Soldiers from the New South Wales Corps, led by Major George Johnston[41] and supported by a posse of armed volunteers, rode out to put the rebels back in their place.

Johnston had known Macquarie in the North American war, where he had fought at the age of just eleven alongside his father, George Johnston Sr. He was said to have been a hero at the battle of Bunker Hill, grabbing the regimental colours from a dying ensign and carrying them into the fray.[42]

Johnston believed the convicts should be driven into the dust. He chased them to Rouse Hill,[43] where he spoke to them under a flag of truce before he and Trooper Thomas Anlezark[44] treacherously drew pistols and dragged Cunningham and another ringleader, William Johnston, away. Major Johnston then ordered his troops to open fire.

During fifteen minutes of shooting from both sides, fifteen rebels were killed. The rest were soon subdued by the soldiers. Philip Cunningham was cut down with a cutlass, but lived long enough to be hanged alongside seven other renegades. Seven more were sentenced to receive between 200 and 500 lashes, before they were pressed into a group of thirty unfortunates on the Coal River chain gang in Newcastle. William Johnston and another ringleader, Samuel Humes, were hung in chains from gibbets, their lifeless, tortured bodies dangling for days, serving as a warning to others.[45]

HANGING BODIES for days as a warning to others was a tactic Macquarie would employ during his own career in the fledgling colony of New South Wales. But there was nothing like that on his mind in the wilds of Scotland, as he and his manservant William Stewart took Macquarie's two black chargers for a 660-kilometre ride. It took them to Fort William, past the snowy clefts of 'the immense high mountain of Ben Nevis' and to 'a bad supper and a worse bed'[46] near Fort Augustus. He rode on past the engineering works of the Caledonian Canal to Loch Ness, Inverness and then Fort George, to see imposing military fortifications and meet with a former officer friend from America. Macquarie had friends and relatives all over the place, and was thrilled to be out in the fresh air on a magnificent horse, meeting as many of them as he could.

Passing Glamis Castle, he came to Lindertis House, the home of Sarah Morley and her new husband, William Ogilvy. Dorothea Morley and her sister Christiana Scott were visiting too, and they all had a 'charming sociable family party'.[47]

Macquarie wanted to see as much of Scotland as he could, because he knew his time there was short. It was now only a matter of time before his past would catch up with him.

BACK IN 1798, as part of the scheme he had been running with his brother Charles, Macquarie had procured a place for Murdoch's son John as a half-pay reservist in the army, even though John was only five years old. By ten, John had been promoted to lieutenant in the 9th Regiment, even though no one in command had actually laid eyes upon him.

Similarly, Charles's frail[48] illegitimate son Hector[49] had become a lieutenant in the 40th. Macquarie considered him a 'very fine handsome smart boy'[50] and a 'young hero',[51] but it was still a rather exalted military position for a nine-year-old.

Hardly anyone apart from Macquarie and Charles knew the true story of John and Hector's ages, but that had all changed in September 1803, when the two schoolboys were just getting started at Mr Taylor's academy in Musselburgh, east of Edinburgh. They had been called up for active service after a check of the records, and Macquarie despaired that 'they are both still much too young to join any Corps; and I have in vain endeavoured to save them their Commissions!'[52]

He then began a desperate battle to save his own. He had concocted a story, telling the Duke of York's military secretary, Colonel William Clinton,[53] that the pair of budding young military officers could not join the war against Napoleon because they had gone to the West Indies 'with a view to settle in that country as planters'.[54] He hoped 'His Royal Highness, the Commander-in-Chief' would 'be graciously pleased to dispense with their services for the present', adding that the two were 'the sons of old officers'.

The commander-in-chief didn't believe a word of it, and with an anonymous informant on the Isle of Mull revealing the truth, Macquarie finally had to admit that two schoolboys had been on officers' pay for five years. All his time in the army, however, had given him a thick skin and a resolute air, and he still had the gall to write to Clinton in March 1804, suggesting that it would be better if the two boys stayed at school rather than going to war.[55]

The duke was unmoved by Macquarie's attempts to minimise his deceit, even though he himself had been appointed the honorary bishop of Osnaburgh aged just six months, on a salary of £50,000 a year. Macquarie was finally forced to beg for forgiveness over the incident, writing to Clinton:

> I am beyond measure grieved to find that His Royal Highness should entertain so very unfavourable an opinion of me and to suppose me capable of such conduct; and I must therefore entreat, sir, that you will do me the favour to assure His Royal Highness that I have made no misrepresentation … that I am incapable of such conduct, and that I indulge a fond hope His Royal Highness will not entertain sentiments so prejudicial to my character.[56]

Nice try. Both young officers were decommissioned, and Macquarie was on the nose with the duke for a long time. It was such a humiliating blow to his prestige that the incident was completely ignored in his journal. He knew he'd been very lucky not to be dismissed from the army in disgrace.

AT LEAST, as he rode one of his black chargers back to Oban to take the ferry across to Mull, Macquarie had his thoughts about Miss Elizabeth Henrietta Campbell to take his mind off the great blunder of his military career. He arrived back at Lochbuie House on 12 August 1804, delighted to find Aunt Jane, his brother Charles and Elizabeth, especially Elizabeth, waiting to greet him and to hear his exciting travelogue by the fireside.

Macquarie's leave was almost over but, for the next eight days, he occupied himself with the Lochbuies, 'principally with reading, walking, and fishing', and he was greatly impressed that Elizabeth was as adept with a long line as any fisherman. She was proving to be a 'most amiable, agreeable, and very sensible girl', who would make 'a most excellent soldier's wife'.[57]

At last he was making headway with her, too. After much 'importunity', he finally convinced her to ride in the post-chaise with him, young John Maclaine and Murdoch Maclaine junior on a 180-kilometre journey east to Edinburgh: the first leg of his return trip to London. She agreed to meet him in Inveraray after she had gone off alone to visit friends. He was mightily impressed with her spunk, when she left Mull for Crinan on 20 August 1804 in an open boat, 'without any other company or society than the boat's crew!!!'[58]

The next day Macquarie, Charles and George, now more like a son to Macquarie than a servant, journeyed to Gribben on Mull to farewell the old clan chief, staying the night and enjoying his 'usual hearty hospitality!'[59] Then it was on to Oskamull for a tearful farewell to his mother, who 'felt poignantly the necessity of separation', though he promised the old lady that he would 'certainly come to reside permanently' at the Jarvisfield estate on Mull 'as soon as the present war with France should be over'. In the meantime, to make her life 'more comfortable as well as more respectable for her remaining days', Macquarie arranged for 'considerable improvements and additions' to her humble home and asked his Aunt Jane to supply her with 'whatever money she may have occasion for; and also, with such articles of wines & groceries as may be necessary'.[60] He would repay Aunt Jane whatever it cost.

As he left his mother's front door and waved goodbye, he could not know that he was seeing her for the last time.

Making his farewells at Lochbuie House, he promised Aunt Jane that he would oversee the schooling of her two boys and two-year-old daughter, Jane Jarvis Maclaine, named in honour of Macquarie's beloved. He took the promise seriously, and before long, was writing to Murdoch junior:

> It gives me a very sincere concern, my dear Murdoch, to hear from very good authority, that, you in particular had been very negligent careless and inattentive to your studies … surely you are old enough to know that it is very wrong to be thus idle and careless; and that nothing is more disgraceful and shameful to a gentleman than to be a bad scholar when a boy – and consequently ignorant and illiterate when grown up as a man … I must therefore call on you peremptorily to pay in future the strictest attention to your education and instruction you receive from your Master Mr. Taylor and his ushers or assistants; assuring you, that, if I ever hear any more complaints of this kind, I shall think it is my duty – as your near relation and guardian to desire Mr. Taylor to punish you most severely whenever you are careless, or refuse to apply properly and closely to your civil studies.[61]

After crossing to the mainland, with John and Murdoch in his post-chaise, and William Stewart and George riding beside on horseback, Macquarie arrived in Inveraray to rendezvous with Elizabeth, whom he now called 'our amiable relation and friend'.[62] He couldn't get enough of her. During intervals in their journey they strolled together, taking in the panorama of Loch Lomond and enjoying a 'pleasant romantick ride' beside Loch Long.[63] Elizabeth smiled easily, had an easy rapport with the children and, in all ways, was 'a most excellent traveller, ready to put up with any fare and fatigue, as well as a most pleasant cheerful and agreeable companion'.[64]

Macquarie farewelled her and his young cousins in Edinburgh on 3 September and headed for London, now with Dorothea Morley and Christiana Scott in his post-chaise, visiting Manchester and Cambridge University along the way. He resolved to renew his friendship with Elizabeth as soon as he could.

Three months later, on 2 December 1804, he had dinner with her at the London home of her aunt, Elizabeth Campbell of Corwhin, mother of the Earl of Breadalbane.[65] Elizabeth had moved into her aunt's house in Wigmore Street, only 1600 metres from Macquarie's lodgings in St James's.

On 8 January 1805, Macquarie was back at Wigmore Street again and he knew the budding romance was full of promise. Late that night, however he was knocked flat.

HE RETURNED TO ST JAMES'S to find an official letter on his table. He knew what it would be before opening it.

The orders were curt, direct and irreversible. The Duke of York, still fuming over Macquarie's rorts, had ordered him to join his 86th Regiment in India.[66] Since young Major Torrens, now the acting commandant in Bombay, had fallen ill and there were no other effective field officers, the duke had decided Macquarie could do with a stint back on the subcontinent to reconsider any other bright recruiting ideas he might have.[67] Lord Harrington did his best to make the duke change his mind and allow Macquarie to stay in England for six months longer, but all his pleadings 'proved fruitless'.[68]

Macquarie did not know what to do. He was falling in love with Elizabeth, but who knew how long he would have to remain in Bombay, and what might happen there or in any other trouble spots war might take him to?

He determined to make 'one more effort' to dodge a bullet, and decided to front the duke personally, 'making the strongest application' he could. On the regular levee-day at the horse guards, he waited for his chance.

While the commander-in-chief received his sheepish underling 'graciously enough', he still told Macquarie in no uncertain terms that 'it was absolutely necessary' for him to get himself back to India 'without a moment's delay'.[69]

But Macquarie had a hide thicker than the elephants he had watched towing artillery pieces up the ghauts. Even though he was lucky to have a job at all, he made a vain suggestion that Charles could take over his role as assistant adjutant-general in London. *And* he asked the duke for a pay rise.

> I took the liberty, however, of reminding H.R.H. that, I was still only an effective major in the 86th. — and after 28 years' service as an officer and that I thought I had some claim for an effective lieut. coloncy [lieutenant-colonelcy]. He replied in a very gracious manner, that ... he would not forget my claims and that he would avail himself of the first favourable opportunity of promoting me![70]

Afterwards Macquarie and Charles, who was on leave from duties in Ireland, dined quietly 'tete a tete' at a coffee house, and had 'a great deal of very serious discourse' on their next moves, particularly Macquarie's dilemma over Elizabeth, 'the die being now finally cast in respect to my returning once more to India'.[71]

Over the following days, Macquarie spent a lot of private time in contemplation. Then he made a momentous decision. On 26 March 1805, he began his daily journal entry by writing: '!!!' He was about to make his mark on Elizabeth with an exclamation.

'After very mature and deliberate consideration and reflection on all the consequences of so important a step, I took an opportunity this forenoon of waiting on Miss Elizabeth Henrietta Campbell at the house of her aunt Mrs. Campbell of Corwhin in Wigmore Street'.[72]

Finding Elizabeth alone in the grand home, and not having a minute to waste with the duke breathing down his neck, Macquarie cut to the chase. He made a 'full avowal to her of my sentiments, and of my sincere love and affection for her', asking her to become his wife. Elizabeth, young enough to be Macquarie's daughter, listened 'with the kindest and most good natured attention'.[73]

'But,' Macquarie went on — and it was *some* 'but' — way back in 1796, he had promised the spirit of the late Jane, 'his late angelic and beloved wife', that he would never marry again in India, or take a wife there. He explained to his prospective bride 'the utter impossibility of our immediate union, nor until after my return from India — which I promised should not, if possible be delayed beyond four years at farthest'.[74]

Four long years.

Elizabeth listened without saying a word. Macquarie wanted to marry her, but she'd have to wait because the promise he'd made to his dead first wife took priority. It was a lot to take in.

But Elizabeth liked the cut of Macquarie's jib. To his 'infinite joy and delight' and 'with a degree of noble candour, and delicate liberal frankness', she 'most kindly consented' to be his wife.[75]

She would wait as long as it took for her man to come home.

They embraced affectionately, and spoke for a long time about the 'very interesting and delicate subject' of their great love for each other. 'Her readiness in yielding to the unavoidable delay of that happy event, has endeared her to me more than ever,' Macquarie wrote, 'notwithstanding the high and exalted opinion I had already formed of her rigid virtue, refined delicacy, and most excellent judgment and sound understanding'.

Macquarie and Elizabeth agreed to meet as often as possible before his departure for India, which was approaching quickly, to their 'mutual sincere regret'.[76]

In the meantime, however Macquarie was still caught up in London's social whirl. He had been appointed one of the managers of the entertainment for the Highland Society's gathering at the Crown and Anchor Tavern on 9 March. Charles, the Duke of Sussex and most of the other titled guests had arrived in full Highland dress.[77] It had turned into such a 'debauch'[78] that Macquarie was forced to stay home and eat chicken broth the next day, cancelling a dinner engagement with Elizabeth's cousin, the Earl of Breadalbane, and his wife.

Instead, Breadalbane hosted a farewell for Macquarie on 14 April: 'an elegant entertainment … at his own house', with a guest list that included the Duke of Sussex, the Earl of Strathmore, Lord Montgomery, Sir Sidney Smith, Sir John McPherson, Macleod of McLeod and Major-General Robert Stewart.

On 20 April, Macquarie's last day in London, his servant William Stewart carried all of his master's excess baggage to Dorothea Morley's house, where a room had been set aside for its storage. He asked Dorothea to send the portrait of him by John Opie to his mother if he did not make it back. Stewart was recently married, and Macquarie thought it 'almost cruel' to take him to India because 'his young wife' was 'very averse to his going'. So he paid out Stewart's wages and gave 'this worthy good fellow'[79] a gift as well. George, just arrived from Edinburgh, would take Stewart's place in India.

Macquarie spent his final day with Elizabeth, and they enjoyed a farewell dinner with a small party of ladies at the home of her favourite friend, Miss Meredith. Then they passed the rest of the evening with their 'mutual good and sincere friends the Miss Stewarts of Albemarle Street'.

Macquarie and Elizabeth exchanged locks of hair and talked of their love for hours, before finally, reluctantly, tearfully, he 'took a tender, affectionate and most affecting leave of her – : our distress was mutually severe'.[80]

He left Elizabeth in the care of the two Miss Stewarts and went home at a late hour to his lodgings. He retired to bed immediately but tossed and turned, deeply affected. His mind was too 'full of future prospects', and he got no sleep that night.[81]

Macquarie was about to fight another war, and begin yet another great adventure that would take him right across Asia and Europe. He did not know it yet, but Elizabeth would soon join him on the greatest adventure of all.

Chapter 15

*I am equally incapable of duplicity as I am conscious of never having
swerved from those principles of rectitude and integrity, which ought
ever to guide and influence the conduct of a gentleman
and a man of honour.*

MACQUARIE BRUSHING ASIDE THE MILITARY RORTS SCANDAL TO GIVE
HIMSELF A SOLID RECOMMENDATION TO THE COUSIN OF
HIS INTENDED BRIDE[1]

MACQUARIE had learned enough from his occasional Sunday
Anglican services to know that the first book of the Bible
contains the story of God's creation of Adam and Eve in a
paradise called the Garden of Eden. He knew also that they had
committed the original sin by eating of the forbidden fruit from
the Tree of the Knowledge of Good and Evil.[2]

He himself had no such qualms, however, about sampling the
vegetation from the lush ground outside the small, walled town
of Chorna (now called Al-Qurnah) in Mesopotamia (what is
today southern Iraq). Folklore holds that the Garden of Eden once
existed near the town, on a tongue of land between the two great
rivers, the Tigris and Euphrates.

Macquarie arrived at Chorna on 29 April 1807, passing a
Turkish galley stationed nearby to pay customs. He and four
travelling companions, including his servant George, landed

on what he called 'these sacred grounds'[3] as the sun was going down across the wide waterway. He walked about on the site of the garden for half an hour, imagining where Eve and the serpent might have had their fateful meeting, before picking a fine ear of corn out of a field of excellent wheat that was almost ripe. He planned to preserve it as a holy relic to carry home to his fiancée.

She had now been waiting for him to come home for two years, and Macquarie was rushing to get there. He was in the middle of an odyssey that would take him to places few Scotsmen of the early nineteenth century had ever seen.

His travels had begun on 21 April 1805, when a post-chaise came to the door of his new London lodgings in Duke Street at 7 a.m. His servant William Stewart was 'bathed in tears'[4] as Macquarie drove off, accompanied by George and a young cadet friend, Henry Rivett-Carnac, also bound for Bombay.

Macquarie was forever thinking of the girl he had just left behind, considering himself 'as much her husband as if I were ten thousand times married to her', and telling himself that 'of all women living, I love her the most'.[5] If Elizabeth's family were worried about his odd behaviour – asking her to marry him then taking off post-haste in a post-chaise – he assured her cousin Lord Breadalbane that 'those who know me will, I trust, bear testimony to my character being yet unsullied by any unworthy action incompatible with true honour and honesty'.[6] Breadalbane liked Macquarie, but he had wanted to be sure.

There were so many soldiers joining the India fleet on that April day that the road to Portsmouth was gridlocked and, at one stage, Macquarie and his two sidekicks were forced to travel in a fish cart, before spending an uncomfortable night in a crowded inn 16 kilometres from the docks. The next morning, they found better digs at the George Inn, closer to the harbour, and Macquarie had breakfast with his old friend's brother, General Hildebrand Oakes, now the Lieutenant-Governor of Portsmouth.

Macquarie spent his last moments on English soil reading letters from Elizabeth, Charles and Dorothea. Then he boarded the *City of London* with the well-groomed, well-educated George, whose life now was so very different from the day he had been bought at a Cochin market.

Macquarie had paid Captain Landon £250 for his own fare and £14 for George's[7] but, to his delight, he was immediately upgraded. The small cabin he had paid for was not ready, so instead he was moved into the 'much more agreeable, commodious, and pleasant' larboard half of the ship's roundhouse, 'not only on account of my superior rank – but also on account of my having paid … a higher sum for my passage than anyone else on board'.[8]

At daybreak on 25 April 1805, 'with a fine fair gentle breeze' behind them, Rear-Admiral Sir Thomas Trowbridge, commanding the seventy-four gun HMS *Blenheim,* led out of Portsmouth a fleet consisting of the frigate *Greyhound* and twenty-two Indiaman transport ships, carrying the 53rd, 56th and 67th Regiments. They were 'destined for the three presidencies in India as a reinforcement' against the threat of Napoleon's advances.[9] The voyage would take fifteen weeks.

Two months in,[10] Macquarie took Captain Landon's cutter to visit friends on other vessels, and while on board the *Dorsetshire* he chatted with young Colonel Ralph Darling,[11] a rare man in the British Army, who had started life as a private and risen through the ranks. He would one day become Governor of New South Wales.[12]

When the *City of London* anchored in Bombay Harbour on 11 August, Macquarie wished that he were anywhere but there. He was in 'very indifferent health, and also in exceeding low spirits'.

Elizabeth was waiting at home for him but, right now, Jane dominated his thoughts. She was still in her everlasting grave beside the sea, beneath his long marble love letter, and the thought of it all filled him with 'the most painful and mournful emotions and reflections on a most calamitous and irreparable event that can never be erased from my heart'.

He did not feel like going ashore to mix with his old Bombay acquaintances. His great friend, Dr Colin Anderson, had drowned a year earlier, along with all others on board, when the brig *Candidate* sank during a voyage between Calcutta and Bombay.[13]

Most of his other old friends had likewise departed the city, or this life. So, even though he received word that an elegant room had been prepared for him at Government House, he slept that night on the ship.[14]

The next morning, he went ashore to be met by his sister Betty's son, Lieutenant Hugh Maclaine of the 77th, and his cousin Lieutenant Lachlan MacQuarrie of the 86th. They all walked together to Government House, where governor Jonathan Duncan welcomed his old friend 'in the kindest and most affectionate manner possible', conducting him to one of the most elegant rooms in his mansion and telling him it was his for as long as he wanted.[15]

He spent 'a jovial merry day' at the Bombay Tavern, where the passengers of the *City of London* gave Captain Landon and his principal officers an 'elegant entertainment' as a testimony to their high esteem. Macquarie stayed 'till a very late hour'. As president of the festivities, he felt he was 'under a necessity of drinking more wine than was agreeable to me, in order to shew a good example'.[16]

Two days later, however he was beside the grave of that 'most beloved and best of wives' and giving 'free vent to the sorrows and overflowings'[17] of his heart, unable to forget the magic they had made together.

NO MATTER how friendly the welcome or how luxurious the accommodation in Bombay, Macquarie felt haunted by the past. He immediately began planning to get away.

He sought the help of his English banker, Charles Greenwood, in appealing to the Duke of York for a move to the Foot Guards and a transfer home. But Governor Duncan quickly offered another solution: Macquarie could become his military secretary again and travel with him to England in January 1808 when Duncan's tenure ended. That was three years away, but Macquarie accepted.

Not that this was the end of the story. On 25 October, Macquarie sat down to read a Madras newspaper and stumbled by mere accident upon a piece of good news that left him 'most agreeably surprised'. He hadn't received any word on the matter from the military yet, but the news item said he had been 'lately promoted at home to the effective Lieut Colonelcy of the 73d. Regiment',[18] which was based in Dundee and had recently left India after twenty-seven years with the British East India Company. It seems the duke had promoted him knowing the regiment would be gone before Macquarie reached India, and the promotion was really a cruel joke designed to rub salt into the wounds for the recruitment scam. The 'effective lieutenant-colonelcy' was just what Macquarie cheekily asked the duke to grant him before being ordered back to India.

Macquarie wished he could go back to join the regiment but instead, as soon as the rains lifted, he would be fighting the warriors under 'that powerful Mahratta chieftain'[19] Maharaja Yashwantrao Holkar,[20] who was trying to unite other Indian rulers in a collective war against the British. The British had always refused to recognise the Maharaja as royalty and he had vowed to kick them out of his land. Macquarie was ordered to join the 86th Regiment in the field, and spent 5000 rupees on equipment.[21]

On 7 November 1805, Governor Duncan learned of the death from fever of his best friend, Marquis Charles Cornwallis, for more than thirty years one of Britain's major military figures and, more recently, the 'Governor-General and Commander in Chief of British India'.[22] Cornwallis had just been recalled to India, largely to deal with Holkar's threat, after a decade away. The Governor-General had 'breathed his last on the 5th of October at Ghazipore near Benares[23] on the banks of the River Ganges – an event that must ever be considered as a great and severe publick national calamity – as well as an irreparable private loss to his family and friends'.[24]

The flags of the garrison, and of all the ships in the harbour, were flown at half-mast, and sixty-six cannons were fired, corresponding with the general's age.

That afternoon, with Macquarie's servants, horses and baggage having gone ahead of him, he sailed for war again. He headed north on the armed schooner *Vigilant* for six days until it glided into the Nerbudda River, opposite the Fort of Baroach in the province of Guzerat.[25]

By 1 December, he had journeyed through Baroda[26] then another 160 kilometres to 'the frontier station of Dohud',[27] where he had command of 'nearly 1300 fighting men', consisting of 'a small detachment of European artillery & lascars; two companies of H.M. 65th. regt., and the entire of the 1st. Bn. of the 4th. Regt. of Native Infantry Commanded by Lt. Col: Drummond' as well as a detachment from Baroda'.[28] He worked the men hard[29] to ensure they would be battle-ready by the time he received orders to march them to Hindustan, through country 'infested and over-run with large bodies' of Holkar's 'predatory' cavalry. The Native Detachment Corps under Lieutenant-Colonel Drummond came in for special attention, after he found them 'in very bad order both in point of dress and discipline'. They received 'very strict and constant drill ... for two hours in the morning and the same in the evening'.[30]

Macquarie seconded shopkeepers to establish a bazaar for the troops, including a bakery and two butcher shops, and he turned avenger for local merchants in their fight against Dohud's town governor, the *kiladar*,[31] who had been accused of exploiting and extorting them. Macquarie 'remonstrated strongly with him on the impropriety and injustice of such conduct' and, as a result, the *kiladar* promised not to 'molest them in future'.[32]

While Macquarie was giving his men extra drills, the British High Command was working overtime, too, on a peace deal to stop Holkar's guerrilla warfare that threated the East India Company's trade. Hostilities ceased before Macquarie could sool his men into battle, and the only fighting he did was a minor skirmish in the aftermath, when he put in a claim for expenses, including 1558 rupees for wine and liquor. He maintained this was chickenfeed compared with the 'between three and four thousand rupees' he had saved the East India Company in bullock feed during his command.[33]

He got his way. But getting a ticket home was another matter.

Three 'severe attacks of the liver' he had suffered over the years on the subcontinent had ruined his health, making it impossible for him to bear the heat of India's 'vertical sun'. There was money to be made in India, though, and if he had to stay, he might as well swap his colonelcy in the 73rd for that of the King's Regiment in the north of India, known as Hindustan, where apparently the vertical sun was not as hot as in Bombay. He wanted to save as much money as he could for Elizabeth, telling her that if he stayed three years he could put together an extra £3000.[34] He wrote to her every time he saw a ship in the harbour ready to head home, including one saga of thirty pages.[35]

He asked for her approval of his plan to stay in India until he could accompany Governor Duncan home on the overland route to dodge Napoleon's ships. In response, there was a long and awkward silence. She felt unhappy that she was not in India with him. He apologised repeatedly for making her sad; sometimes, he needed her words of love to heal his bruised soul. His health was no longer robust, and sometimes he would become depressed, as he did at the news that his 'worthy and highly esteemed servant William Stewart' had died in England.[36]

He asked Elizabeth's friend Jane Stewart — without mentioning his name — to meet whatever 'pecuniary' needs 'Miss C' might have on the promise that he would reimburse her immediately.[37] Dreaming of their future together, he told Elizabeth to keep her eyes peeled for a 'snug pretty little cottage within fifteen or twenty miles of London' that they could use when the weather on Mull turned savage. He wrote to his old pal, the sea captain Charles McIntosh, asking him to collect 'bawbles' for 'a thousand female cousins'. He also asked for him to buy 'a fan of very handsome new pattern with the initials E.H.M.' and a lacquered sandalwood box to be marked on top with the name 'Mrs. Macquarie of Jarvisfield'.[38]

AS MACQUARIE TRIED to bridge the distance between himself and Elizabeth, Captain William Bligh was sailing into his new role as the fourth governor of New South Wales.[39] On the recommendation of Sir Joseph Banks,[40] now President of the Royal Society, Bligh had been offered the job on £2000, twice the salary of the outgoing governor, Philip Gidley King, who had been worn down by illness and the stresses of conflict with the military officers of the New South Wales Corps.

Two decades earlier, Bligh had been cast adrift by mutineers in the South Pacific, and he was steeled to ensure his subordinates never dictated terms again. After a court martial into the loss of his ship exonerated him, Bligh had remained in the Royal Navy and distinguished himself as a master mariner and firm disciplinarian. He had visited Tahiti again and the West Indies, and was Captain of *Director* at the Battle of Camperdown in the North Sea on 11 October 1797, capturing the Dutch ship *Vrijheid* and its commander, Vice-Admiral Jan de Winter. Bligh won praise from Admiral Horatio Nelson at the First Battle of Copenhagen four years later.[41]

When he arrived in Sydney on 6 August 1806, he was ready for another fight.

As with so many episodes in the life of William Bligh, though, his time at the top would not be smooth sailing.

DESPITE his career misstep, Macquarie continued to successfully push for promotions for relatives such as his nephews, Hugh Maclaine and Martin Wilkins, son of his wife's sister, and his cousin Lachlan MacQuarrie, now the governor's aide de camp.

His own position left him dissatisfied and anxious. Elizabeth was becoming increasingly impatient with his tardiness in returning to Britain, and made it clear that, if he really wanted to marry her, he should get home soon.

After the thwarted campaign against Holkar, Macquarie stayed at Dohud for several weeks, seeing off his troops and selling all the now unnecessary camp equipage. He arrived back in Bombay in late February and busied himself with administrative duties and writing letters home. On 18 October 1806, he wrote to his 'dear and beloved Miss Campbell' to inform her of his intention to return to England within months. Governor Duncan had 'kindly released' Macquarie from his commitment to remain in India until January 1808, after he had explained the nature of his 'matrimonial engagements'.[42] He wanted to hold his Elizabeth close to his heart as soon as possible.

Macquarie wrote to his friend Samuel Manesty, the East India Company's resident (manager) in the Mesopotamian city of Basra, and received 'very favourable and pleasing accounts of the safety and practicability of travelling by that route to England'.[43] He asked Manesty to arrange overland passage for George and himself, and to buy some shiraz wine that Macquarie could give friends in England.[44]

He planned to travel to Constantinople (now Istanbul) via Baghdad, then sail home through the Mediterranean. But he would be journeying through a political minefield, with war raging throughout the Ottoman Empire and much of Europe, and he already knew that the route might change.[45]

The exotic allure of Bombay was long gone. The Christmas and New Year celebrations contained no real joy for him. On Christmas Eve he attended the last review of his old 77th Regiment before it was sent home, eighteen years after its arrival in India and nineteen years after he had trudged the Highlands in the rain, trying to find fifteen recruits.

On 15 January 1807, he 'paid a mournful and most affecting visit … to my late beloved and angelic wife's tomb'. It was ten years less one day since Jane had been buried there, and Macquarie was still in pain. He ordered the iron railing around the tomb to be painted and the stonework whitewashed as his farewell gift to her.[46] A month later, he was back to check the work had been done. He gave his great friend Charles Forbes a parting gift of an 'elegant new saddle and bridle and military horse-furniture'.[47]

One of his last acts in Bombay, on 18 February, was to set matters right with some family members. Jane's niece Louisa Wilkins had come to Bombay five years earlier, looking for a husband with prospects, but had instead formed an 'impudent union'[48] with Macquarie's young and feckless namesake:

I this day had a most serious conversation with my relation and namesake Capt. Mc.Quarie of the 86th. Regt. on the subject of his late very improper conduct and intemperance, having for several weeks past neglected his duty at the Government House as aide de camp, and entirely abandoned himself to tippling and low drinking all-day-long. I have lectured and admonished him most severely and seriously on the shameful and disgraceful low-lived practice; pointing out the inevitable ruin, misery and ignominious fatal effects of it![49]

Young Lachlan felt severely chastened. In the presence of his stern-faced wife, he solemnly pledged 'his word and honor' that he would 'discontinue this vile practice, promising never to be intoxicated again before dinner!'[50]

Five days later, Macquarie received a letter from 'dear Miss Campbell' written four months earlier, 'the contents of which, I am grieved to say, were rather of an unpleasant nature'.[51] He knew he had to get moving fast.

He packed his belongings and sent most of them to England on board the *Northumberland* and, on 16 March 1807, he paid his 'final melancholy visit' to Jane's tomb. He was going home to marry for the second time, but he felt just as strongly in love with his first wife as he had been when they first met at John Forbes's house fifteen years earlier.

Even though he would never see Jane's grave again, she would be in his heart forever. He paused in front of the verbose tombstone for what seemed forever, 'giving it the tribute of ... tears!'[52]

MACQUARIE'S JOURNEY HOME from Bombay began three days later, when he and George boarded the cruiser *Benares*.[53] They were travelling with Assistant-Surgeon William Thomas[54] and Lieutenant George Brande,[55] who were technically prisoners of war of the French, their brig *Grappler* having been captured by a French warship. The two men were 'on parole' and were returning to England to be swapped for French prisoners.[56]

The four passengers reached the Persian city of Bushire[57] four weeks later, but the welcome was hostile:

> About halfway between the ship and the shore, just as we were crossing the bar, an immense heavy sea broke over us, half-filled the boat with water and tilted her over on her beam-ends! – we hung by her with some difficulty and in the most peril of our lives for about a minute until she again righted. – Our bodies were almost wholly in the water, we got a most complete soaking, and very narrowly escaped drowning; which most assuredly would have been our fate had not the boat providentially righted again at the very instant she did. – We landed at the town of Bushire about half past 5 o'clock in the evening in a very uncomfortable state, and like half drowned rats.[58]

By 21 April 1807, they were on the Shatt-al-Arab River and heading towards Basra, near the meeting point of the Tigris and Euphrates. Macquarie gazed on 'fine extensive plantations of date trees all along both banks' and saw 'immense herds and flocks of cattle and sheep, and also a great number of very beautiful Arabian horses'.[59]

Bad news awaited them, though, when they anchored near Haffar Creek, about 50 kilometres from Basra, at 11 p.m. that night:

> Here we found lying at anchor the *Prince of Wales* and *Princess Augusta* ... and also the *Euphrates* ... being obliged to remain here for the present in consequence of our having recently quarrelled with the Turkish Government.
>
> We found orders here from Mr. Manesty the British Resident at [Basra] for the *Benares* to proceed no farther up the river but to remain at Haffar with the other vessels until further orders.[60]

The next morning, Macquarie, George and the two prisoners were able to travel to Basra in the *Balloon*, Mr Manesty's pleasure boat. On the way, they passed a fleet of small Turkish warships, and Macquarie learned that the Turks were now at war with Britain's 'faithful allies the Russians'. There were reports of a naval battle between the British and Turkish fleets in the Dardanelles, and the East India Company's vessels travelling to and from England had all been detained for the past two months in Baghdad or Constantinople.[61]

Macquarie still hoped to proceed either through Turkey to Constantinople, or through Georgia and over the Russian steppes.

The local ruler had ordered Manesty to get out of Basra as soon as possible, but he managed to arrange permission for Macquarie to proceed as far as Baghdad. Manesty gave Macquarie 5000 rupees and asked him to carry vital letters with him to the East India Company's directors in London. Mrs Manesty, a beautiful Armenian who had borne thirteen children, entrusted Macquarie with a diamond ring as a present for her daughter, who was in England and soon to be married.[62]

Manesty had also arranged for a 'very large elegant' yacht flying the Turkish flag and with a crew of twenty-eight, including a cook, interpreter and two Turkish guards, to take Macquarie 500 kilometres to Baghdad.[63]

They left Basra on 28 April, and the next morning arrived at Chorna, 150 kilometres away. Macquarie walked for half an hour through lush vegetation upon the 'sacred grounds' of what was 'supposed to be the real Scite of the Garden of Eden!'[64] But there was not a moment to spare in returning to the increasingly impatient 'Miss Campbell', so they continued on their slow boat along parts of the Euphrates and Tigris to Baghdad, the marshy jungle confining them to just 3 kilometres an hour for days on end.[65] Macquarie saw lions beside the Tigris and had a close look at the ruins of the Persian capital of Ctesiphon and the palace of Taq Kasra,[66] which had 'the highest and finest arch I ever saw in my life'.[67]

They reached the grand 'mosques and minarets of Baghdad' on 9 May 1807, and there they were joined by Major Robert O'Neill of the 56th Regiment of Foot, who had been on the same fleet

Macquarie was fascinated by the ruins of Ctesiphon in Persia. public domain

that had carried Macquarie to India two years earlier,[68] and who was 'a valuable acquisition' to their 'little society – being a very pleasant well informed man'.[69]

In Baghdad, Macquarie and his companions farewelled Mr Manesty's yacht and exchanged their European clothes for Arab robes.[70] Mr Hine, the local East India Company representative, gave Macquarie more important documents to carry to London, as well as the use of an Armenian linguist[71] fluent in English, Turkish and Persian. He also arranged for a 'caravan of horses, mules, and asses'[72] to take Macquarie and George beyond Baghdad, along with Major O'Neill and the two English prisoners. Having realised that both the routes he had earlier decided on would be fraught with danger, Macquarie had decided to head through Persia to the Caspian Sea.

On 15 May, they trotted through Baghdad's Eastern Gate at sunset: a noisy, braying, clip-clopping cavalcade that travelled northeast all night over flat desert country, heading toward Rasht, almost 1000 kilometres away on the Caspian.[73] Over the next few days, they followed the Great Khorasan Road, the old silk route between the Mediterranean and China. They crossed the Hamareen Hills [Jebel Hamrin][74] and took a winding road through the steep, rough and stony hills of Kurdistan.[75] 'The Kurds, or inhabitants of this wild looking country,' Macquarie noted, 'are famous robbers, but none of them molested us.'[76] Not yet, anyway.

They reached the ancient city of Qasr-e Shirin, near the border of modern-day Iran and Iraq, and Macquarie bathed in the River Alwand.[77] After five days of trekking through the desert and climbing steep rocky hills, he found himself 'greatly refreshed'[78] by the fast-flowing waters streaming down from the thick snow in the Zagros Mountains.

The next evening when they ascended a mountainous pass, 'the immense high wild scenery of it, tho' terrific, was truly magnificent and sublime'. The caravan was detained for half an hour by toll collectors at 'the Tauk – or Arch – forming here the boundary between the Turkish and the Persian territories; and where the King of Persia has established a toll on every description of the human and brute creation entering his dominions by this wild pass'.[79] Eight days later, they made their way to Bisitun, past the massive ancient carvings of the Persian king Darius the Great, high up on the face of a mountain.[80]

After crossing the Zagros Mountains, Macquarie met emissaries from the Shah of Persia at Casbeen (modern-day Qazvin) and was entertained by the local governor, but he was more concerned about finding Major O'Neill, who had stayed behind in a village when the caravan moved on and had failed to reappear.[81]

For eight days, Macquarie sent out search parties looking for him, with no success until the evening of 13 June, when their caravan leader:

> ... delivered our poor friend from his vile captivity – slavery – and most probably death also! – The major's history since his straying from the caravan eight days ago

is most piteous and melancholy to a degree. – He fell in on the evening of the day he parted from us with a wild [Kurd] banditti in the hills, who robbed him of his horse and everything else he had about him, including his clothes, stripping him naked to the skin, and in that forlorn condition left him to his fate in the mountains ... He fell in the day following with some inhuman wretches who beat him most cruelly – and after having dragged him to their village, made him work there as a slave for 3 days, treating [him] all the time with the greatest cruelty and every mark of indignity and insult ...[82]

The shah had arrived in Casbeen the day before and, for days, his viziers had been prevailing upon Macquarie to wait for an audience with 'His Majesty'. But it never happened. Macquarie told his comrades that this delay was 'to avoid giving offence to or exciting the jealousy of the French Ambassador now at the Persian Court'.

Instead, the viziers themselves 'entered into a very confidential conversation on political subjects ... being extremely anxious to be at peace and form a close alliance' with the Russian Empire. The shah wanted Macquarie's help in gaining the support of 'the King of Great Britain',[83] and the viziers presented Macquarie with a Persian sword and a bag of money from the shah to 'defray my expences to England':

I accepted the first, but returned the latter as entirely incompatible with my honour and ideas of propriety. Several messages passed on this subject, and I was repeatedly importuned to accept the money – but which I persisted in positively refusing. — At length they gave up the point, and the king sent me a present of a very handsome Persian scymitar.[84]

MACQUARIE'S PARTY JOURNEYED ON through the vast mulberry plantations of Gilan province, where silk worms worked overtime.[85] A guard of honour welcomed them to Rasht, and at nearby Anseley (modern Bandar-e Anzali), a small, four-oared boat, navigated by a pilot and six other men, took them out to brave the fierce winds of the western shore of the Caspian beside wild, mountainous and woody country.[86] They had breakfast with the skipper of a Russian brig, the *Volga*,[87] and the next day passed a great sturgeon fishery at Salyan in present-day Azerbaijan.[88]

After three and a half days, the boat arrived in Baku, where 'very useful rich oil' that smelled of turpentine was being collected and where there were five great pits filled with the 'extraordinary phenomenon of "The Everlasting Fire"'.[89]

With the snow-capped Caucasus mountains providing a magnificent backdrop,[90] they left on their 1000-kilometre voyage toward Astrakhan, only to be detained at Solyanka, near the mouth of the Volga River, by the 'cruel detention'[91] of a strict medical quarantine against an epidemic of fever. As a result, they were delayed for twenty-five days.

As soon as they received a 'clean bill of health', Macquarie and George left the others and each travelled day and night in a kibitka carriage, towed by three horses, to cover the 1400 kilometres to Moscow. They drove past Tartar villages containing mobs of horses and numerous herds of black cattle, past the great flocks of game beside the Volga, then into the wild Cossack country beside the Don River, past countless peasants reaping their harvests of corn and hay. In the village of Cheremushka, Macquarie met Robert McKenzie, 'all the way from Edinburgh', who was the overseer on the estate of a Russian general.[92]

The kibitkas were 'vile, horrid uneasy things',[93] but Macquarie did not spare the horses and they made good time until reaching the province of Kolomna. There, even though Macquarie 'did not fail to exclaim most bitterly and remonstrate in the strongest manner',[94] they were detained for six more days of quarantine. Then there were further delays over Macquarie's passport and when he finally crashed into his bed in a Moscow inn at midnight on 30 August 1807, he was 'heartily tired of Russian police'.[95]

Moscow was 'a most elegant city, and one of the largest in the world'[96] but, with Elizabeth still waiting at home, there was hardly time to see 'a twentieth part of it'.[97] He and George were reunited with Major O'Neill, Lieutenant Brande and Dr Thomas, and Macquarie paid 75 roubles for a more comfortable kibitka for the next leg of their journey to St Petersburg, 700 kilometres northwest on the 'Gulph of Finland'.[98] There, in early September, he checked into the 'Dhaimond' Hotel and hired an English-speaking valet for 2 roubles a day.

While Macquarie waited for the Royal Navy 'sloop of war'[99] HMS *Calypso* to take him, George and the two prisoners home, he took in the city sights aboard a carriage with four horses that he had hired for 12 roubles a day.[100]

Macquarie had seen many great sights in his travels, from dense jungles and impenetrable mountains to opulent Indian palaces. But St Petersburg was breathtaking.

He was astonished by 'that part of the emperor's Winter Palace called the Hermitage fronting the River Neva', with its 'magnificent galleries, fine paintings, and beautiful spacious apartments'.[101] There were 'three beautiful branches of the Neva' running through what Macquarie declared was 'this most magnificent elegant city which is certainly by far the finest and most beautiful I have ever yet seen … the finest city in the whole world'.[102]

He didn't know it yet, but soon he would see a very different landscape, in a wild frontier on the other side of the world.

Chapter 16

Mrs Macquarie of course goes out with me, and we must endeavour to make ourselves as happy as we can in our exile for 3 or 4 years, at the end of which I suppose they will allow me to return home again to my native country.

MACQUARIE ON BEING ORDERED TO AUSTRALIA WITH HIS 73RD REGIMENT, THOUGH NOT LONG BACK FROM INDIA[1]

THE FIFE AND DRUMS of the British Grenadiers' marching song erupted as 400 redcoats, their muskets loaded with ball cartridges and their bayonets gleaming in the hot summer sun, prepared to bring down the government.

William Bligh had done it again.

He had been in Sydney for less than eighteen months, but his rare knack for losing friends and irritating people had already turned much of the populace against him – at least the ones with money, power and guns. As Macquarie was still strolling about, gazing with an admiring eye upon the opulence of the Hermitage, Captain Bligh was facing yet another mutiny.

Trouble had followed the incoming governor of New South Wales even before he set foot on the *terra firma* of Terra Australis. He had been reluctant to accept the governorship of Britain's most

213

far-flung colony and only the assurance from Sir Joseph Banks, that it would not affect his future promotion to admiral, had convinced Bligh to set sail.

Bligh's beloved wife Betsy had not been up for the long journey south, and five of their six daughters had stayed in England with her. The First Lady at Government House in Sydney would be Bligh's married daughter Mary,[2] said to have a temper 'as violent as that of her father'.[3]

A fleet of five convict transports had left Portsmouth on 28 January 1806 for the seven-month voyage to Sydney. Bligh was skipper of the *Lady Madeleine Sinclair*, with Mary on board, while her husband Lieutenant John Putland was on the ten-gun HMS *Porpoise*, the fleet's escort, under the command of Captain Joseph Short.[4]

The six ships had hardly felt the first puff of wind in their sails before Bligh and Short were at war. Orders from the Admiralty were ambiguous regarding who was actually in charge of the voyage. Short, who was travelling with his wife and six children, believed he was the boss until they reached New South Wales; Bligh maintained that, as the incoming governor, he was also in charge of the six vessels.

The two jockeyed for control of the fleet from the outset. Bligh found Short irritating and insulting, 'a wicked and most violent man', 'a specious and low character'[5] with a 'brutal temper and bad heart'.[6] Short regarded the stocky, red-faced and pompous Bligh as the worst kind of crusty old sea dog, with a foul mouth and a tongue salted by years at sea.

Even before they had reached the Cape of Good Hope, Bligh had steered his ship into the lead as a symbol of his authority. Short signalled to Bligh to change course, a signal Bligh ignored. Short then ordered Putland and the rest of his men to fire a cannon blast over Bligh's bow. Though the blast sent shivers down the spines of the *Lady Madeleine Sinclair*'s crew, Bligh ignored it.

Short, now clenching his fists in rage, bellowed for his men to fire the cannons across Bligh's stern. The new governor felt it was as though Fletcher Christian himself were shooting at him. Yet he ordered his men not to change course.

Finally, Short ordered Putland to load the cannons and fire right into the middle of Bligh's ship, even though Putland's own wife was on board. Common sense prevailed and a calamity was averted, but already Bligh was plotting his revenge.

Bligh set foot in Sydney in August 1806 and started treading on toes immediately. He refused to give Short the land grant of 240 hectares his rival had been expecting, and instead, sent him straight back to England to face a court martial. Short's pregnant wife and one of his children died on the return voyage; it was said that Mrs Short was carved up and preserved for burial in a cask of pickle. Her husband, however, was eventually exonerated.

Bligh found Sydney mired in corruption and sloshed by rum, which was being used as a currency for barter at enormous profits. Farmers who could not afford the inflated prices left their land uncultivated and ripe for confiscation from cashed-up predators. On 4 October 1806, Bligh issued new laws governing the ports, tightening the government's control of ships and their cargoes, especially spirits.

In February 1807, writing to William Windham,[7] the British Secretary of State for War and the Colonies, Bligh called rum the great 'evil in this country',[8] sometimes sold at a more than 1000 per cent mark-up:

> A sawyer will cut one hundred feet of timber for a bottle of spirits—value two shillings and sixpence—which he drinks in a few hours; when for the same labour he would charge two bushels of wheat, which would furnish bread for him for two months; hence those who have got no liquor to pay their labourers with are ruined by paying more than they can possibly afford for any kind of labour which they are compelled to hire men to execute, while those who have liquor gain an immense advantage.[9]

The rum trade was controlled by the New South Wales Corps, as well as by wealthy landowners such as John Macarthur, whom Philip Gidley King had called a 'perturbator' with a 'diabolical spirit'.[10]

Bligh was quickly at loggerheads with Macarthur and senior officers of the New South Wales Corps, including its commander, Major George Johnston, the man who had brought down the 1804 convict rebellion.

He also clashed with the colony's principal surgeon, Irish-born Thomas Jamison,[11] who was defying government regulations by engaging in private trading ventures. Bligh sacked him from the magistracy he held, claiming that he was 'not an upright man, and inimical to government'.[12] In addition, he complained to Windham that Judge-Advocate 'Mr [Richard] Atkins has been accustomed to inebriety; he has been the ridicule of the community', and that 'sentences of death have been pronounced in moments of intoxication'.[13]

Still, Bligh was not immune to feathering his own nest. As soon as he arrived, he received from the outgoing governor, Philip Gidley King, grants of 97 hectares at Camperdown, 42 hectares near Parramatta and 400 hectares near Rouse Hill. He did not mention them in dispatches home, though regulations required it, nor did he refer to the 320 hectares he gifted to King's wife. Bligh's daughter Mary also received a sizeable land grant, and both made personal use of government stores and flocks.

On 31 October 1807, as Bligh's list of enemies mounted and powerful forces under John Macarthur began conspiring against him, he told Windham that the governor 'must be determined and firm in his measures and not subject to any control here'.[14] This attitude would bring him into conflict with the *other* man in the colony who wouldn't take no for an answer from anyone …

MACQUARIE spent five days in St Petersburg and met British and Russian bureaucrats. The British ambassador gave this well-travelled mailman yet more letters for London. Finally, on 13 September 1807, Macquarie and his companions sailed from the Russian naval base at Kronstadt, after Macquarie had inspected the defences of the port and its '700 pieces of cannon'.[15]

They sailed up the Baltic Sea for eleven days, until they sighted the church spires of Copenhagen – or at least what was left of them after the British had bombarded the city with phosphorous Congreve rockets developed from Tipu Sultan's weapons in a ferocious firestorm two weeks earlier.[16] From a force of 30,000, just 200 British soldiers had been killed or wounded in taking the city. One of the few casualties had been Macquarie's old commander, David Baird, who had 'been wounded twice during the siege – first in the left breast, and afterwards in the forefinger of his left hand – both by musket balls; but, I am happy to hear not dangerously'.[17]

The *Calypso* anchored close to the British fleet, which included twenty-four of the biggest warships, 'besides smaller vessels of war, and at least 300 transports'.[18] Macquarie disembarked to pay his respects over a cup of tea to Admiral James Gambier,[19] the Commander in Chief of the British Squadron, on board his ninety-eight gun flagship *Prince of Wales*.[20] The admiral had rained down fire on the Danish city, and would soon give his name to an extinct volcano in Australia. He received Macquarie in a 'very polite kind manner', his good cheer heightened by the fact that he and Lord Cathcart, the British military commander at Copenhagen, were about to split £300,000 in prize money from the spoils of war.[21] Gambier gave Macquarie yet more top-secret letters for London.

Macquarie noted: 'It appears we [have] taken possession of the whole of the Danish Navy lying at Copenhagen, consisting of 24 ships of the line, and upwards of Forty Smaller Vessels of War; together with the whole of the naval stores in the Danish arsenals and dock yards, which are to be carried away with the whole of their fleet.'[22]

Macquarie was weary from months of travel, but the next day, Cathcart lifted his spirits by telling him he had been promoted *in absentia* to First Lieutenant-Colonel in the 73rd Regiment. The 'effective lieutenant coloncy' Macquarie had previously held gave him the rank as an honour but without the payrise. Now he had the money and the power. Cathcart also provided a carriage for Macquarie to ride out into the countryside to meet the wounded General Baird, 'who was astonished' to see him and, completely out of character, threw his arms around him in a 'most friendly and affectionate manner'. Macquarie wrote in his journal: 'I staid with him for half an hour in close confab – and was rejoiced to find my dear good friend in such good health and spirits.'

Back at Lord Cathcart's, Macquarie met Lieutenant-Colonel Lord Blantyre, and was heartened to hear from him that Charles now commanded the 2nd Battalion of the Black Watch. Later, Lord Blantyre introduced Macquarie to his friend the Earl of Rosslyn, and Cathcart placed him on his right hand and 'was extremely attentive and kindly communicative during dinner'. Macquarie left the table not just with some powerful friends, but also another armful of dispatches.[23]

Three days later, at Elsinore (or Helsingør), Macquarie looked upon a vast harbour filled with an immense number of ships from many nations, and behind them 'the town of [Elsinore], the ancient Castle of [Kronborg] on the Danish shore and the opposite town of [Helsingborg] on the Swedish shore'. He called it one of the 'grandest and finest' sights he had experienced anywhere in the world. He had the pleasure of seeing the King and Queen of Sweden and their little princess riding in their carriage, and was chuffed when they returned his bow as they passed by.[24] He was able to 'take a good view of the old and gothic castle' of Kronborg and walk in 'Hamlet's Gardens'.[25]

It would be nearly two weeks before favourable weather finally allowed Macquarie to make out the coast of 'dear old England', 40 kilometres away at Sunderland.[26] He estimated that he had covered 10,300 kilometres by sea and land from Bombay in six months and twenty-four days. He finally set foot on English soil on 16 October 1807, for the first time in two and a half years.

Almost the moment they anchored in Yarmouth Roads, Norfolk, Macquarie and George were leaping into a post-chaise and racing to London. After an overnight stay at Colchester, Macquarie arrived at Leadenhall Street at 2 p.m. the next day and delivered weighty dispatches into the hands of Mr Parry and Mr Grant, the Chairman and Deputy Chairman of the East India

Company, respectively.[27] An hour later, he was at Downing Street, delivering the other dispatches for the king and government to George Canning,[28] the thirty-seven year old Secretary of Foreign Affairs, and a future prime minister. Canning, a man with penetrating eyes and a protruding lower lip, invited Macquarie to dine with him.

Eighteen months later, Macquarie would invoice the British Government for £500 for carrying the precious dispatches across Asia and Europe, even though Samuel Manesty had given him 5000 rupees for the job when he left Basra. Just as he had not been averse to other money-making ventures, Macquarie was not averse to double-dipping. He duly received not £500, but £750, and an apology from Canning for not paying him sooner.[29]

YET MACQUARIE'S most important mission remained unfulfilled.

Elizabeth had not wanted to wait in London as Macquarie had journeyed through Persia, Russia and the Baltic lands. She had been determined to support herself rather than living with friends. She was now in Holsworthy, Devon, working as a governess to the grandchildren of the Reverend Owen Meyrick,[30] a distant relative who had been the local vicar for forty-one years.

Her independence and strength of character only made Macquarie more determined to make her his wife. So, after more than a half a year of travelling, he was soon on the move again. He received an episcopal licence from the Archbishop of Canterbury and wasted no time in reaching her.

Although Macquarie had wanted his family and friends to attend their wedding, Elizabeth insisted on a small private ceremony straightaway. So, eighteen days after setting foot back in England, Lieutenant-Colonel Lachlan Macquarie – forty-six year old widower of St James's – married Elizabeth Henrietta Campbell – twenty-nine year old spinster of Holsworthy – on 3 November 1807.[31] The venue was Holsworthy's small Norman church of Saint Peter and Saint Paul, which had stood since the 1200s. Owen Meyrick performed the ceremony.

After the simple wedding, Lieutenant-Colonel and Mrs Macquarie stepped through the church cemetery and into the rectory, where Elizabeth had worked and lived while waiting for her man to return. Lachlan shook hands with the few guests and Meyrick presented Elizabeth with a wedding gift, Boswell's *Life of Samuel Johnson* in three volumes, which she would carry with her for the rest of her life.

The couple inscribed their books, including their shared Bible, with a combined 'L. E. Macquarie',[32] and followed the instructions in its first chapters to become 'one flesh'.[33] Elizabeth entered family details on the flyleaves and marked passages of Scripture that struck a chord with her, including 'Jesus answered and said unto him, "Verily, verily, I say unto thee, except a man be born again, he cannot see the kingdom of God."'[34]

Their first marital home was Mrs Grove's private hotel near Jane Stewart's house in Albemarle Street, London, where they paid 3 guineas a week for rooms.[35] Macquarie, true to his generous nature, set about fulfilling long-standing promises. He chased down a share of the prize money from the 1795 siege at Cochin for the widow of his faithful servant, William Stewart, and he arranged with Elizabeth's aunt Mrs Campbell for Bombay governor Jonathan Duncan's illegitimate son[36] to be sent to a public school as a boarder. He had already drawn a lieutenant-colonel's back pay through Duncan from March but, in another instance of double-dipping, he wrote to the army agents in Britain asking for back pay from them from the same period.[37]

Yet here was no chance for a long honeymoon for Elizabeth: in early 1808, the soldier's wife had to pack up and ship off to Perth in Scotland with the 73rd.

It was a bleak time in Perth. Napoleon's armies were in Spain and Portugal, but morale among the British troops was low and the 73rd was nowhere near ready for a fight. Macquarie's regiment had been so brutally stripped of men, it was skeletal. Out of 1000 or so, 512 had been transferred back to India.

To win the loyalty of the junior officers, Macquarie wined and dined them, paying out of his own pocket. He was so liberal in his entertainment that his wine tab with Messrs Maclaine and Gilchrist of Leith was soon £271 7s 11d. He also waged a campaign for some officers, who had not been paid in two years, to receive back pay and protested to senior officers that two of his soldiers had been owed twenty-three months' pay since 1800.

In early 1808, in the depths of Perth's winter, Elizabeth discovered she was pregnant. It was a blessing to her and a tonic for her husband, who was forty-seven but looked much older, his skin yellowed by several fevers in the tropics, his body racked by syphilis and the mercurial 'remedy'. There were years of high life and hard living, the booze, the late nights. And then the stress of all the years of lonely grief following Jane's death.

Elizabeth's pregnancy left Macquarie overjoyed. He wanted to share the good fortune with his extended family. Having heard nothing about his attempts to have his young relatives receive commissions in India, he wrote to the Duke of York again, hoping he had forgotten about Macquarie's previous recruiting indiscretions. With not a hint of shame, he told His Royal Highness that a 'young relation' was desirous of going into the army, and that sixteen-year-old 'Murdoch Maclaine Lochbuy' [Uncle Murdoch's son] was now 'the head and representative of one of the most respectable families in the County of Argyle – being Chieftain of the Clan Maclaine'.[38] He sought a commission for Murdoch's younger brother John too, then looked for a place for fourteen-year-old former lieutenant Hector, Charles's illegitimate son, as a cadet 'in the Junior department of the Royal Military College' at Great Marlow in Buckinghamshire. While Hector had been dismissed from the army aged ten, Macquarie insisted he was now 'well-grounded in the knowledge of Grammar, in the first four rules of Arithmetic, and writes a good hand'.[39]

In August 1808, he and Elizabeth visited Airds and Mull to share the good news of her pregnancy. Macquarie surveyed the work of his factor Dugald McTavish, who was on £20 a year – £13 from Macquarie and £7 from Charles – to administer the brothers' estates, Jarvisfield and Glenforsa.

Macquarie insisted that McTavish collect rents promptly and from the money send £10 every year to his mother and £10 to his sister Betty. He also wanted him to send £10 6s to his relative Flora Macquarie on his property at Salen 'to defray the expence of bringing manure to her croft there', and another £10 to local schoolmaster Archibald Macquarie, 'to enable him to go to attend some good school in the Low Country ... in order to qualify himself the better for keeping the school at Salen'.[40] Macquarie had planned out his own little town at Salen, with 'sixteen separate distinct crofts, exclusive of that at present occupied by Flora Macquarie'. He planned for the settlement to include a blacksmith, carpenter, shoemaker, tailor and woodkeeper.[41]

He was 'very anxious ... that all the crofters should have good comfortable houses built on their own respective crofts – close to and facing the High Road', and he offered to subsidise the building of them all, provided they met his guidelines, with lime-pointed joints, in which the mortar was less likely to crack, and each 'having two glass windows' and 'high stone gables'.[42] Macquarie also made provision for one 'poor old man' and 'two poor women' to be accommodated on his Kilbeg farm.[43] Macquarie had a dream to be a Scottish laird but he would also take his ideas of benevolence for his people to another land far away soon enough, in the hopes that they would become self-sufficient and prosper.

A month after the grand tour of Jarvisfield, on 15 September 1808, Macquarie became a father for the first time. Given Macquarie's age and poor health, and the fact Jane had not been able to conceive, Macquarie was both overjoyed and relieved that his wife had given birth. Whether Elizabeth liked it or not, he named his tiny wrinkled daughter Jane Jarvis Macquarie in honour of his first wife, believing the child would perpetuate Jane's memory. The little girl was baptised on 7 October.[44]

Even with Napoleon – now Emperor of France, King of Italy and Protector of the Confederation of the Rhine – continuing to create havoc across Europe, Macquarie contemplated a placid future for himself with his young family in the Highlands. He had spent thirty years in the army, and while he had achieved a rank of some importance, it had not been an astonishingly successful military career. Yet he was content to retire gracefully, having made a modest fortune to support his vibrant young wife and beautiful little daughter.

But his world was about to be turned upside down.

WHILE MACQUARIE was doing his best to make friends with the young officers in his regiment and the crofters on his land, Captain Bligh continued to make enemies across the spectrum of Sydney society.

The merchant John Blaxland[45] later alleged that Bligh never tempered justice with mercy, and that one of his greatest pleasures was 'signing a death warrant'.[46] The governor was said to order that houses be pulled down, 'gratified' by the distress it caused:

> If any person dared to object or remonstrate against the unlawful conduct of the Governor, his rage became unbounded; he lost his senses and his speech; his features became distorted; he foamed at the mouth, stamped on the ground and shook his fist ... On the recovery of speech, he offered a torrent of abuse in language disgraceful to him as a Governor, an officer, and a man.[47]

But Bligh's most vehement wrath was reserved for the wily John Macarthur. He not only stopped Macarthur from distributing large quantities of rum throughout the New South Wales Corps, but also claimed to have prevented him from importing illegal stills. Bligh described Macarthur as an 'arch fiend' who 'inflamed the minds' of 'wicked monopolising persons', and whom he had 'checked in the enormous practice of bartering spirits'.[48]

They clashed again over a piece of land that Governor King had granted to Macarthur because it did not fit Bligh's town-planning interests. The final straw was a breach of the Port Regulations, arising from the escape of a convict on Macarthur's ship *Parramatta*.[49]

In December 1807, Bligh ordered Macarthur's arrest over this incident. According to Bligh, Macarthur responded that, if anyone tried to take him, 'blood would be spilt'.[50]

Nevertheless, one of the few men who could match Bligh's arrogance was arrested and bailed. His trial was set down for 25 January 1808. Six of the judges who were presiding over the case alongside Judge-Advocate Richard Atkins dined with Macarthur, his son and nephew at the new officers' mess the night before the trial, after receiving a permit from Bligh for a 'pipe [570 litres] of wine from Edinburgh'.

The next day in court, Macarthur objected to having Atkins sit in judgment over him, claiming that Atkins was his sworn enemy and had owed Macarthur money for fifteen years.[51] The other six members of the court – all soldiers of the New South Wales Corps – took Macarthur's side and the court was dissolved.

Bligh feared that the 'Civil power' was in a 'precarious state'. He accused the six judges of sedition,[52] and summoned the corps commander Major George Johnston to leave his 'country house ... about four miles from town' at Annandale, which he had named after his birthplace of Annan in Scotland.[53]

Johnston sent word back that he was too ill to meet Bligh, having fallen out of his chaise after a good sampling of the pipe of wine at the officers' mess. Bligh had Macarthur re-arrested on the morning of 26 January 1808, but Johnston, apparently recovered from his chaise spill, went to the jail and released Macarthur on a warrant he signed as 'Lieutenant-Governor' (the position of governor's deputy that he had illegally assumed).[54]

Macarthur then called on Johnston to arrest Bligh and take charge of the colony. He wrote a petition, declaring:

> The present alarming state of this colony, in which every man's property, liberty and life is endangered induces us most earnestly to implore you instantly to place Governor Bligh under arrest and to assume the command of the colony. We pledge ourselves at a moment of less agitation to come forward to support the measure with our fortunes and our lives.[55]

Lt. Col. George Johnston.
Watercolour portrait by
R. Dighton, 1810.
State Library of NSW

Macarthur and Johnston gathered support on a hot summer's day when contraband rum was flowing freely. At 6 p.m., 400 redcoats marched to Government House to the marching song of the British Grenadiers and with their colours flying.[56]

Bligh would later recount the incident to Viscount Castlereagh, Secretary of State for War and the Colonies.[57] He wrote that they broke into all parts of the house without ceremony, even into the ladies' room. There the invaders progress' was halted momentarily when Bligh's fiery daughter Mary Putland charged at them with her parasol.[58] Her husband John had died of tuberculosis just three weeks earlier.

Soldiers, thrusting bayonets in his direction, would later claim that they found Bligh cowering under a bed, which he denied, but Australia's first political cartoon would depict the master mariner as a gutless wonder, being dragged out of his hiding place by the heroic military men. According to his own account, Bligh was arrested 'for crimes that render you unfit to exercise the supreme authority for another moment'.[59] He and Mary were confined to Government House, under house arrest. George Johnston took over as lieutenant-governor, and John Macarthur became colonial secretary, effectively running the colony.

Now that New South Wales was in the hands of the military, Bligh knew that 'nothing but calamity upon calamity was to be expected, even massacre and secret murder'.[60] The new rulers set about burning any records of previous crimes as the colony descended into chaos.

The asthmatic and beefy Lieutenant-Colonel Joseph Foveaux,[61] Governor of Norfolk Island, returned from a period of recuperation in England on 28 July, six months after Bligh's overthrow. As the colony's senior officer, he assumed command.

MACQUARIE had thought there was no grief worse than when Jane had died in Macao but, in Perth on 5 December 1808, her namesake, his angelic little daughter Jane Jarvis Macquarie, coughed and spluttered for the last time. She had not been alive even three months.

The stresses on Macquarie's marriage were monumental, but rather than tear it apart, the collective sorrow of husband and wife drew Macquarie and Elizabeth ever closer. Macquarie was lost for a short time, but the army quickly found him and took his mind off the agonising loss.

On 22 December, just two weeks after they had buried their beloved child in Perth, Macquarie received secret orders to prepare the 73rd for a march to Edinburgh Castle, in preparation for a voyage from Leith to Portsmouth. The final destination would be Botany Bay.[62]

REPORTS OF THE REVOLUTION in New South Wales had first reached England on 12 September 1808, eight months after the uprising, when Macarthur's son Edward[63] arrived with the first bale of merino wool to be exported from the colony and presented his family's version of Bligh's overthrow. Meanwhile, Bligh had written to Lord Castlereagh on 30 April, giving his own side of the story.

But London was far more interested in the threat of Napoleon on its doorstep than the overthrow of a cantankerous old naval officer thousands of kilometres away. Before long, Edward Macarthur was fighting the French in Spain and Italy rather than fighting his father's cause.[64] The press ran a few paragraphs on the uprising here and there, but Sydney was no bigger than a small English town, its importance diminished even more by its great remoteness.

It was, however, decided to recall the New South Wales Corps, now known as the 102nd Regiment, to Britain, and to send out a military man as the new governor, after four naval commanders had been tried in the role.

A new regiment, untainted by the intrigue of the 'Rum Corps', would go with him.

Sir Joseph Banks was fighting hard to have Bligh retained in office, but Arthur Wellesley, now a lieutenant-general and soon to become a duke for his triumphs against Napoleon, was consulted over taking the role. Then in November 1808, Bligh's successor was announced as forty-year-old Miles Nightingall,[65] the son-in-law of the East India Company Chairman Sir Lionel Darell[66] and rumoured to be the son of the late Marquess Cornwallis. He would be backed by the 1st Battalion of Macquarie's 73rd Regiment. (The 2nd Battalion would be staying in England to fight in the war with France.)

The £2000 governor's salary was not a lot for Nightingall. He asked Lord Castlereagh to award him an annual £1000 pension when he returned from New South Wales, but the guarantee was not forthcoming.

BY 20 JANUARY 1809, Mr and Mrs Macquarie, together with Charles's son Hector, were back staying with Mrs Grove in Albemarle Street.[67] With them were their coachman, Joseph Bigge,[68] their cook, Mrs Ovens, and the servant-cum-son who now went by the name George Jarvis, and whom Macquarie referred to as his 'smart Portuguese boy'. A week later, Macquarie escorted Hector to the military college at Great Marlow,[69] and on 21 February, he welcomed Charles back from his service with the 42nd on the Iberian Peninsula. The pair then hurried south to inspect the 73rd, now garrisoned at Colwell on the Isle of Wight.[70]

Macquarie was still hoping he and Elizabeth could avoid their 'exile to the Land of Convicts',[71] telling his 'dear friend' Charles Forbes in Bombay that, while the Government of New South Wales was 'to be entirely new modelled and made a military one', the posting was not fair on him after his regiment had spent twenty-four years in India and only the last three at home.[72] Elizabeth was still fragile after losing their firstborn, and Macquarie's own nerves weren't too flash either.

Nightingall meanwhile began assembling new staff to accompany him on his journey to the other side of the world. He appointed a tall, beefy young barrister named Ellis Bent as a judge, and accepted Macquarie's choice for aide de camp in thirty-year-old Captain Henry Colden Antill,[73] who had been born in New York to a British loyalist before being exiled to Canada as a child, after his father's land was confiscated in the revolution.[74] Macquarie knew Antill was a stout fellow: he had been shot in the shoulder while carrying the 73rd's colours at Seringapatam ten years earlier.

Yet already, Nightingall was wavering. He had a reputation for taking huge amounts of sick leave that bordered on hypochondria[75] and, by March 1809, he claimed that rheumatism in his right arm and wrist was preventing him from using a pen, let alone sailing to Sydney. By April, he had pulled out of the venture, though his arm had seemed fine when he was fighting Napoleon in Spain the previous year and when he took him on again in Portugal in January 1811.

Captain Antill complained bitterly that he had wasted his money buying a new staff uniform, but Macquarie told him not to despair. He himself had received word that he was to be the Lieutenant-Governor until Lord Castlereagh could decide on a suitable man for the top job.

Francis Grose,[76] who had run the colony for two years after Arthur Phillip became ill in 1792, had applied to be governor but that was never going to fly because, in his stint at the top, he had effectively let John Macarthur run the whole show and word of that had filtered back to London. Macquarie was never backward in coming forward, and he wrote to Castlereagh, offering himself for the role and reminding His Lordship that both the Duke of York and Wellesley had given him their endorsement.[77] Macquarie could stretch the truth when it suited. He hadn't seen the future Duke of Wellington since 1801 and the king's son had resigned command of the army over a scandal in which his mistress, Mrs Mary Anne Clarke, testified before the House of Commons that she had sold army commissions with the Duke of York's knowledge.

Macquarie told Charles Forbes that he was wary of going to Sydney:

> ... I am appointed Lieut. Governor of New South Wales (– alias Botany Bay!) with the rank of Colonel in that colony, and shall have the chief charge of it until such time as a Governor is sent out from this country ... Genl. Nightingall, who had been nominated Govr., having lately been obliged to resign it in consequence of bad health. — I was at first in some hopes that they would appoint myself Governor, but I find there is no chance of their doing me that honour; so that I shall probably have all the trouble, plague, responsibility, and odium of new modelling the Government of New South Wales, and restoring order and tranquillity there; and most likely be immediately afterwards superseded by a Governor sent out from England – which, I must confess, I shall think rather hard; but, I must however be contented – and do my duty.[78]

At least he now had a proper fighting force at his disposal. The 73rd had been boosted by more recruits but it was still only about 600 strong when Macquarie brought it from Scotland in January. It had now increased to 800 men by drafts and volunteers from the militia regiments, so that it would go to Sydney as 'a very respectable battalion, and complete in a very good and genteel corps of officers'. Two 'very fine ships', the *Hindostan* and *Dromedary*, both 'large and commodious', had been readied for their departure. The Macquaries would travel on the *Dromedary*, because it was 'by far the finest ship of the two'.[79]

On 23 April 1809, Macquarie and Elizabeth took Communion at St James's Anglican Church in Piccadilly, and three days later, Macquarie was presented to King George III as the new lieutenant-governor of New South Wales, during the same ceremony at which David Baird was knighted.

Perhaps Baird had a word to the king, because the next day, Castlereagh stopped Macquarie as he was walking at Berkeley Square and told him that he would be the new governor of New South Wales, on £2000 a year. Candidates were in short supply, and Castlereagh wanted a man of conviction, determination and doggedness. If Macquarie stayed in Sydney for eight years, Castlereagh promised he would have a sizeable pension.[80]

This was a position offered to no less a luminary than the future Duke of Wellington. Castlereagh was no fool and he saw something in Macquarie, despite the recruitment scandal. Just when he thought his career was over, Macquarie was receiving the accolade of his lifetime. The poor boy made good was being given the opportunity to write his name into the history books and to create his own masterpiece, on what was essentially a blank canvas. He would do so in a way that surpassed all who went before and after him.

At long, long last, the poor boy from Ulva had risen to become laird of not just a highland estate, but a vast untamed kingdom.

Chapter 17

MAY TO DECEMBER 1809, LONDON, ENGLAND,
TO SYDNEY, NEW SOUTH WALES

*... they had resorted to a precaution at which humanity shudders,
namely, that of throwing the unfortunate slaves overboard
as soon as they were taken ill*

ELIZABETH MACQUARIE ON ENCOUNTERING A SLAVE SHIP RIDDLED
WITH YELLOW FEVER ON HER VOYAGE TO AUSTRALIA[1]

ON THE AFTERNOON of 15 May 1809, Macquarie collected his directions from Lord Castlereagh's office in Downing Street. The orders across four dispatches from the Secretary of State for War and the Colonies were clear-cut:

If Captain Bligh was still in the settlement, to liberate him immediately and order him to return to England, as his continued presence in New South Wales 'might tend to keep alive dissatisfaction'.

To arrest George Johnston (recently promoted to colonel) and send him back to England so that he could face trial, and arrest John Macarthur and have him tried in the 'settlement'.

To restore all those who had been deposed following the revolt against Bligh to their places of authority.

To revoke all land grants made by Johnston and Foveaux.

To improve the morals of the colonists, encourage marriage, provide for education, prohibit spiritous liquors from being used for barter and increase agriculture and stock.

To abolish the 'extraordinary and disgraceful' situation whereby 'unfortunate' female convicts were handed out 'indiscriminately' to anyone who wanted them, and for any use.[2]

The work of John Macarthur and George Johnston had cleared the way for Macquarie's appointment, but he wished them nothing but harm, telling Castlereagh's deputy Edward Cooke that he hoped there would be 'sufficient evidence' to convict them both once Bligh returned to England.[3]

Macquarie was with Lord Castlereagh between 4 and 5 p.m. then, before he knew it, he and Elizabeth were cantering south in a carriage with Charles, heading for Portsmouth and the long voyage south.

Elizabeth had been in a 'very weakly low state of health' for some time, and at the start of May had become 'seriously ill', perhaps because of nervousness. She had never travelled beyond the British Isles before, and her only previous experiences on water had been short day trips from Airds across the Firth of Lorn, the Sound of Mull and Loch Linnhe to visit her elder sister Jane and the other Maclaines on the Isle of Mull. Now she was facing a seven-month voyage to the other end of the world.

The *Dromedary* and *Hindostan* would be sailing in four days' time, however, no matter how nervous she might be.

The Macquaries slept overnight at Kingston and spent a second night at Liphook before putting up at Portsmouth's George Inn,[4] where Macquarie dealt with the deluge of requests that had arrived concerning his departure.

Gout-riddled Sir Joseph Banks reminded Macquarie of his old chieftain's hospitality on Ulva, when the botanist visited there back in 1772 and he asked Macquarie to keep paying Banks's protégé, the botanist George Caley, a guinea a week as

Governors King and Bligh had done.[5] Army officer and politician Lord Uxbridge[6] asked Macquarie to grant 400 hectares to his nephew Nicholas Bayly,[7] one of the plotters who had brought down Bligh.

At 10 a.m. on 19 May, Macquarie and Elizabeth boarded the *Dromedary*, commanded by Captain Samuel Pritchard,[8] who was travelling with his wife, two-year-old son and his servant Black Tom. The *Dromedary* had a crew of 102, and there were 592 souls on board. The Macquaries had brought with them George Jarvis, coachman Joseph Bigge, cook Mrs Ovens, Robert Fopp the butler, and Mrs Jones, a lady-in-waiting for Elizabeth. Deputy Judge-Advocate Ellis Bent, his wife Eliza and seven-month old son Ellis junior were fellow passengers on the *Dromedary*, along with Henry Colden Antill, Ensign Alexander Huey, Ensign John Maclaine (Murdoch's son, now an ensign at last), and more than 350 officers and soldiers of the 1st Battalion of the 73rd Regiment, as well as about 100 women and children.

The fifty-gun man o' war *Hindostan*[9] was under the command of Captain John Pasco,[10] who had been Horatio Nelson's signal officer on board HMS *Victory* at the Battle of Trafalgar in 1805, and advised on the wording of his commander's famous signal, 'England expects that every man will do his duty'.[11] The *Hindostan* carried the remainder of the 1st Battalion – more than 400 officers and soldiers – under the command of dashing Irishman Lieutenant-Colonel Maurice O'Connell,[12] and at least 100 women and children. O'Connell had been appointed lieutenant-governor after an impressive military career that included battles with the French in the West Indies.

There was a false start to the great voyage, because the wind was too westerly for the ships to make any progress, but three days later they set sail again, and at 4 p.m. on 24 May, Mr and Mrs Macquarie said goodbye to 'good old England'.[13]

They would not see her again for thirteen years.

There were numerous detours that slowed their progress because Captain Pasco chased just about every sail he saw in the hope of securing the lucrative 'prize' of a captured enemy ship.

Pasco was travelling with his pregnant wife Rebecca[14] and two young children, and needed the extra cash for his growing family. On 29 May, the day when a little boy was born on board, he fired three cannon blasts and chased down the American ship *Gustuvas,* which had been sailing from Charleston, South Carolina, to Liverpool with £45,000 in cargo before falling into the hands of French privateers. Pasco dispatched a skeleton crew to sail her to Plymouth.[15] The sight of another huge ship showing no colours caused palpitations until they learned it was an American cargo vessel bound for Canton. The Americans and British were in the midst of a brief period of peace.

Elizabeth began keeping a lively record of her experiences on the day they left London. Seasickness plagued her during violent storms in the Bay of Biscay, off the coast of France and Spain. Furniture was thrown about, plates were smashed, and three men drowned on 4 June when a small boat travelling between the two ships overturned. Elizabeth's 'bad state of health' prevented her from seeing much of the island of Madeira, and prevented her husband from accepting many 'agreeable' invitations,[16] but at the Church of the Lady of the Mount, she was carried up the mountain in a hammock:

> … the appearance of which seem'd to shock Colonel M. not a little; this did not altogether displease me, as he said I look'd exactly like a corpse, so I flatter'd myself as he did not like my resemblance; that he had no wish to see me in that state, & to tell the truth I never dreaded that he had, as he is not of a nature to wish ill to any one, much less his own wife.[17]

Seasickness rocked many other inexperienced travellers too, and for days on end, Elizabeth's maid was confined to the sick bay.[18] There were also more serious cases of illness on board. When they were just off Parma, one of the Canary Islands, Robert Watt from Captain Antill's company died from a lung complaint and was committed to the deep with all solemnity.[19] Two infants and a woman succumbed to disease as well, and a boy whose leg was crushed by a falling cask died despite stoically undergoing amputation, biting on a bullet to stifle his screams.

On the whole, however, Elizabeth found being at sea was 'a very agreeable life'.[20] There were few troublesome incidents; Macquarie and Pritchard enforced strict discipline, with the occasional flogging for fighting, drunkenness or insolence. Macquarie spent much of his time reading and writing while Elizabeth plied her needle.[21] Every Sunday, when the weather was moderate, Ellis Bent performed Divine Service 'in the most agreeable manner'.[22] Sometimes the Macquaries played whist with Captain Pritchard, but he played for keeps, severely reprimanding his partners any time they made a mistake.

On 29 June, the ships stopped at the Cape Verde Islands for twenty-four hours as fresh bananas, pineapples, pumpkins, lemons and bullocks were taken on board. Ellis Bent, who was keeping a shipboard diary as well as writing letters home, confided that he couldn't wait to get away from this hotbed of immorality, where the Portuguese governor slept with a Cornish mistress under an image of the crucifixion.

On 3 August, the ships met a Portuguese brig sailing from the coast of Guinea to Rio de Janeiro, laden with 436 female slaves[23] chained and locked in the dark below deck. The ship was full of yellow fever and, to put a stop to it, Elizabeth recalled in her journal, the 'monster'[24] who commanded the ship 'had resorted to a precaution at which humanity shudders, namely, that of throwing the unfortunate slaves overboard as soon as they were taken ill'. Fifty slaves had been drowned to stop the fever from spreading.[25] When the Macquaries heard about this, their thoughts immediately turned to anti-slavery campaigner, William Wilberforce.[26] Macquarie had pause to think about the fate of his own slave boy George, who was now like his son. In Britain, slavery was now outlawed, after Wilberforce's long crusade resulted in the passing of the *Slave Trade Act* in 1807.

At one point, Elizabeth saw something fall past her cabin window. She had no idea it was a man until she ran out onto the deck to see Macquarie encouraging a drowning sailor 'by every means in his power to keep a hold which he had fortunately caught of a fishing line'. Eventually, the man was saved.[27]

A few weeks later, Charles Tomkin, one of the carpenter's mates, was not so lucky, and drowned before any assistance could be afforded him.[28] Among Tomkin's possessions were 'a great many letters from a young woman who was engaged to him' and, to Mrs Macquarie, they contained 'more pure affection, expressed in a more natural and affecting manner' than anything she had ever read. She knew that the sufferings of that poor girl when she heard of this event would be 'dreadful to think on'.[29]

An outbreak of dysentery on the *Hindostan* forced the ships to stop at Rio on 7 August, and Elizabeth was astounded by the 'wonderful beauty and grandeur of it', with the sun setting behind the Sugarloaf Mountain. She found the harbour 'one of the most magnificent scenes in nature [that] bursts upon the eye ... everywhere studded with innumerable little islands'.[30]

THE MACQUARIES had thought often of the reasons they were 'being sent on this unexpected service and the probable state of the colony' when they arrived, but they had no real information on the latest developments there. To their amazement, when they came ashore in Rio, they found that George Johnston and John Macarthur had left the city only four days earlier. Lieutenant-Governor Foveaux had been succeeded on 1 January by Colonel William Paterson – the man Macarthur had once injured in a duel – and Paterson had sent Macarthur and Johnston back to England in March to answer for their deeds. Macarthur would arrive in London in October with a gift of emus for Castlereagh's wife but, due to ill health, would have to contend with a diet of water, bread, milk, fruit and vegetables as he waited for Johnston's trial.[31]

Meanwhile, New South Wales Surgeon-General Thomas Jamison and magistrate Dr John Harris[32] – both on their way to give evidence in Johnston's favour – were still in Rio when the Macquaries arrived, having left Sydney slightly later.

They told the Macquaries that Bligh had been released from prison, and:

> … with the permission of those persons in power embarked on board the *Porpoise*, the ship that fired on him during his voyage to Australia. He was under the promise of sailing for England; but no sooner did he find himself out of their power, than he issued a proclamation pronouncing the New South Wales Corps to be in a state of mutiny, and rebellion, … and prohibiting all masters of vessels at their peril taking any persons out of the colony, who had been connected in the rebellion', specifically Macarthur, Jamison and others.[33]

Lieutenant-Governor Paterson had published a counter-proclamation, declaring Bligh to have acted in direct violation of his promise, as a gentleman, to proceed immediately to England. Paterson prohibited all persons in the colony from having any communication with Bligh, or anyone connected to him who was on board of the *Porpoise*.

Elizabeth noted in her journal:

> We had a good deal of conversation with Dr. Jamison regarding the extraordinary events which had taken place in New South Wales, and it appeared to us that even by their own account the conduct of those persons who had acted against the governor was not to be justified, or even excused; we felt sorry that a man such as Colonel Johnston … should have committed himself as he has done, by an act of the most open and daring rebellion, by which in as far as it appears to us, he will probably forfeit a life, which has till this unfortunate period, been spent in the service of his king and country.[34]

Privately, Macquarie was relieved that Johnston had left before their own arrival in the colony, because he did not relish the thought of arresting a man of 'amiable character and in their early years an intimate companion of his own'.[35]

Jamison and Harris showed the Macquaries a number of drawings that displayed Sydney's great natural beauty, including one of Mr Harris's house, Ultimo, situated in a park stocked with deer about a mile from Sydney.

The Macquaries were startled to find Harris later 'in a shabby little shop making merchandise of some precious stones he had brought for sale from New Holland'.[36] They also found Jamison, the deposed surgeon-general, selling shoes and stockings. It seemed everyone in Sydney was trying to make a quid any way they could.

THE DAY AFTER the *Hindostan* and the *Dromedary* arrived in Rio, Macquarie went on board the eighty-gun *Foudroyant* to meet Rear Admiral de Courcy, and together they went ashore to see Lord Strangford,[37] the British ambassador. The Prince Regent of Portugal took them to the opera, but the princess was in a foul temper towards Strangford, because, as he explained to Macquarie, he had prevented her from being proclaimed Queen of Mexico. She had to endure the fat prince asleep against her throughout the performance.[38]

British consul Sir James Gambier, the cousin of Admiral James Gambier, considered it his duty to keep an open table for any British visitors. Colonel and Mrs Macquarie dined with him and his wife Lady Jemima, 'one of the most elegant and pleasing women we had ever seen, and very handsome'.[39] Their manner of living was 'quite magnificent', in a grand home 'paper'd & furnished in the newest English style'. Later, Gambier hosted a ball for the 73rd.

Captain Pritchard accompanied the Macquaries on an excursion around Rio, after taking 'the greatest pains to assure us that he was a first rate horseman'. The burly Pritchard procured a horse, and Elizabeth could not help but laugh as he set off:

> ... with his ponderous load on a weak half famish'd beast, at full speed ... by his account the poor horse got sick when he was not much above a mile out of the town, here the order

of things became completely reversed, for he was obliged after treating his horse to wine, & everything that he could think of to recover his exhausted strength, to support & almost carry him back to the town.[40]

The two ships left Rio on 23 August and by late September they were in Cape Town, with a great swell running. Lieutenant-Colonel O'Connell was 'much amused' at seeing Elizabeth forced to climb the pier steps on all fours, remarking that she had not been brought up in the Highlands for nothing. They breakfasted with the local East India Company agent, John Pringle, an old friend whom Macquarie had first met at Jeddah, on his way to Egypt in 1801. Elizabeth stretched her sea legs in an elegant, large room, 'where all was stillness and quiet … such a change from the noise, continual motion, and confinement of the ship'.[41]

They took carriage rides along the shore, with the strong wind driving foam over the sand. The sight of a wrecked ship dashed to pieces on the rocks did little for Elizabeth's morale, but the scenery was magnificent: wild heather everywhere, 'the most luxuriant shrubs' on the grand mountains, the quaint cottages and the inspiring vistas from the high places.[42] Elizabeth quickly made friends, even though she was normally reticent around people until she knew them well.[43]

Pringle took the Macquaries and a few others horseback riding, trotting through a small valley known to be inhabited by hyenas and many other 'tremendous animals', and Elizabeth surprised herself with her composure as she sat on her little horse 'in the immediate neighbourhood of ungentle folks … before I left England, I should not have thought myself capable of going willingly into such a place, but such is the force of example'.[44]

When Macquarie was last in Cape Town, in 1803, it had just returned to Dutch hands. Three years later, however, the war resumed and the British returned their garrison to the Cape after defeating Dutch forces. Now Lord Caledon,[45] the Governor of the Cape Colony, hosted a ball for his visitors. He was a handsome, charming young man, but surprisingly diffident, and none of the ladies could get him onto the dance floor. By contrast, the ageing Admiral Bertie,[46] who commanded the British fleet at the cape, waltzed the night away 'with great industry'.

The Macquaries also met Colonel William Sorell,[47] the deputy adjutant-general of the forces at the cape, and one of the stewards at the ball. Elizabeth liked him 'by far the best' of anyone she met on her visit, and 'thought him the most gentlemanly looking man I saw at the cape, which is saying a great deal, as there were several very pleasant persons there'.[48] Elizabeth was unaware that Sorell had left his wife, the mother of his seven children, and was now conducting a scandalous affair with the wife of a colleague. He would eventually make his way to Van Diemen's Land.

The Macquaries had a ball at the cape, even when there was no dancing. Elizabeth could not help but laugh at the sight of Captain Pasco and his wife on horseback, breaking from a canter into a gallop in their rush to dine with the governor, 'Mrs. P being desirous of enjoying as much of his Lordships company as she could'.

At a regimental feast 'in the true Highland style', a piper played constantly, marching round the table, to Pringle's great annoyance. The sound was driving the East India agent to despair, and while there were calls for quiet, Elizabeth noted that 'Colonel M. most wickedly said that Mr. P. liked [the bagpipes] above all things, & begged it might go on. [T]he time bestow'd on this entertainment was far beyond all reasonable limits.'[49]

BY 7 A.M. ON 13 OCTOBER, the *Dromedary* was off again, and the Macquaries were glad to be on their way to their final destination. They had an extra passenger with them, J.T. Campbell,[50] a trim, fiery Ulsterman who had managed the Bank of the Cape of Good Hope and enjoyed Lord Caledon's patronage.[51] Macquarie promised to give him a position of authority in New South Wales; Henry Antill described him in his journal as having 'the appearance of being a gentlemanly well informed man'.[52]

Elizabeth felt the ship to be a happy home, because she had the 'great comfort of my husbands company uninterrupted all the morning when we read or write in a social manner, which I shall never enjoy on shore, as when he has it in his power he shuts himself up alone all the morning to business'. Many times Elizabeth thought of 'the advantage a poor cottagers wife has over persons as she may think in a far happier line of life – she has the satisfaction of inhabiting the same room with her husband and children, she has the objects nearest her heart in her sight at once; a luxury of enjoyment seldom experienced by those she considers above her.'[53]

The bitterly cold conditions in the Indian Ocean meant that Macquarie and Elizabeth became even closer in their quarters at night-time. The weather was murder on Ellis Bent's pleurisy, and a doctor bled him three times in the hope of relieving his suffering. But it only made things worse, as his wife cried buckets over his bed. Captain Pritchard suffered terribly with rheumatism. The Macquaries lent him their more comfortable quarters for a night, and called Joseph Bigge and Mrs Ovens to help haul the inert captain's considerable bulk into bed amid great hilarity.[54]

Macquarie did his best to protect the men and women on board from illness and accident. According to Elizabeth, nothing could exceed 'the minute care and attention paid by Colonel M. to his men at all times'. The voyage had been remarkably free of illness, 'the number of soldiers on the sick list seldom exceeding five or six', and at no time had there been a 'contagious disorder'.[55]

Still, more accidents happened: on 31 October, as Macquarie and Elizabeth were walking on deck, a young man named Thomas Jackson, who had a fondness for strong drink, fell from the top of a mast and suffered a fatal skull fracture. The sailors were much affected by the accident, and some shed tears the next morning as Ellis Bent conducted his funeral service and committed his body to the deep.[56]

ON THE MORNING of 10 December, some land birds came to the *Dromedary*, welcoming the ship to the new world. Macquarie felt the sight of a seal frolicking nearby was a sure sign that land was nearby and all aboard the two ships rejoiced that they would soon step foot on the Great South Land, this world of tantalizing mystery and potential.

Pasco proposed sailing to the colony at Port Phillip, but Macquarie wanted to meet with the deposed Governor Bligh, and requested that they sail to Port Dalrymple (near Launceston), believing from rumours he had heard in the Cape that the HMS *Porpoise* might be moored in the Derwent River at Hobart Town.

Macquarie's hunch proved only partially correct. Bligh and his widowed daughter Mary Putland had indeed sailed into Hobart on the *Porpoise* on 30 March 1809, trying to drum up support from Colonel David Collins[57] to retake New South Wales. The devilishly handsome Collins had served with Macquarie in Nova Scotia, and had been Arthur Phillip's deputy on the First Fleet. He had since become the founding lieutenant-governor of Van Diemen's Land. No European had been in Australia longer.

Collins had received Bligh graciously and vacated Government House in deference to the man who, according to the Crown, was still the rightful Governor of New South Wales and Collins's boss. But in the end, Bligh did not stay there long. He promised Collins that he would not interfere with his administration, but he did. He complained to Castlereagh of Collins's low morals: though a married man, Collins walked about Hobart Town with Margaret Eddington, 'his kept woman (a poor, low creature) arm-in-arm',[58] and brought her daily to his office adjoining Government House, in full view of Bligh and Mary.

Bligh had sailed the *Porpoise* into midstream and later to Storm Bay at the mouth of the Derwent, where he imposed tolls on incoming ships and fired on boats that refused to pay.

ON 13 DECEMBER, Captain Pasco changed course and headed for the southern coast of Van Diemen's Land. The next day, Elizabeth saw whales and big bonito fish. Then, at 10.30 a.m. on 15 December, her husband had his first sight of his kingdom. Despite hazy weather and a sharp gale, he was able to make out the Mewstone, 'a high peaked rocky island' off the southern shore of Van Diemen's Land[59] that had been named after a similar outcrop in Cornwall. Macquarie had the band play 'God Save the King'.

Bad weather prevented them from looking for Bligh but, the next day, they sailed past the spectacular rock formations of Cape Pillar, on Van Diemen's Land's southeast tip, which reminded Elizabeth of Macquarie's home on Mull. She immediately thought back to some of the happy times she had spent with Macquarie's mother at Oskamull.[60]

By Christmas Eve, Macquarie was ailing, and the relentless motion of the ship gave Elizabeth a confused feeling. Sailing along the coast, she could see the smoke of native fires 20 kilometres away on shore.

Their provisions on the *Dromedary* were almost exhausted, and the last pig and sheep were killed for Christmas dinner, the fowls having all been eaten long before. When the Macquaries sat down with the officers, they were also able to share some 'salt beef and pork, and part of an old goat which was killed for the occasion'.[61] Macquarie brightened for the festive occasion, and Elizabeth noted that 'the kindest congratulation I ever received was this morning from my beloved husband who thank God feels himself better.'[62]

Pritchard gave the men an extra allowance of grog for Christmas, and while they were quiet and jovial for a while, three of the crew were soon in chains after a brawl.

Four days of 'very disagreeable baffling weather'[63] kept the two ships bobbing about off the mainland's coast and, on the evening of 27 December, the wind shifted to all points of the compass, blowing a hurricane with thunder, lightning and heavy rain.[64]

But then at 7 a.m. on 28 December 1809, the storm clouds blew away and those aboard the two ships could see the foaming blue ocean smashing against grand sandstone cliffs. Macquarie saw the flagstaff at the head of Port Jackson and the two ships sailed through Sydney Heads, with Pasco's *Hindostan* leading the way under full sail. Pasco fired a cannon to call for a pilot and announce their arrival.

The band again played 'God Save the King' but, as Macquarie looked out across the wide expanse of the harbour and the untamed bush all around him, he wanted to let everyone in Sydney know that there was a new king in town.

Chapter 18

DECEMBER 1809 TO MAY 1810, SYDNEY AND SURROUNDS

*I found the colony barely emerging from infantile imbecility ...
depressed by poverty ... the morals of the great mass of the
population in the lowest state of debasement ...*

MACQUARIE EXPLAINING WHAT NEW SOUTH WALES WAS LIKE WHEN
HE AND ELIZABETH ARRIVED[1]

SYDNEY DID NOT GREET Macquarie kindly. Just inside the Heads, an extraordinary wind powered straight towards the *Dromedary* and *Hindostan* from the west, and the two ships could not continue further. They anchored at 10 a.m., and half an hour later, former convict Isaac Nichols,[2] appointed by Sydney's military rulers to the post of Assistant to the Naval Office, came on board the *Dromedary* to welcome the colony's new master. Nichols had arrived in Sydney as a convicted thief, but since winning his freedom, had built a real-estate empire along what would become George Street, as well as establishing a shipyard and building his own trading vessel, the *Governor Hunter.* He also became the colony's first postmaster.

Nichols confirmed that Bligh 'had not been heard of for some time ... but was supposed to be on the Derwent River at Hobart on board the *Porpoise*'.[3] The orders of the Colonial Office to Bligh, which Macquarie had copied by hand, demanded that

Bligh receive Macquarie at Government House, hand over power and swear him into office.[4] Macquarie would have to change his arrival plans.

At noon, he was joined on board by ex lieutenant-governor Foveaux and John Mell, Paymaster of the 102nd Regiment. They were standing in for Lieutenant-Governor Paterson, who was ill. Ellis Bent described Foveaux, who ran Surry Hills Farm, just south of Sydney Cove, as *'pleasant looking and handsome, tho'* a *very corpulent* man'.[5] Foveaux had fresh meat, bread, vegetables and fruit sent out to the ships for dinner, which was more than welcome after so long at sea.

The new Australians remained anchored for two days, waiting for the wind to change as a variety of visitors came on board. Finally, at 5 p.m. on 30 December 1809, the *Dromedary* anchored in Sydney Cove, close to the Governor's Wharf.

The next morning, Macquarie commandeered the ship's barge, and at 10 a.m., he and his entourage were ferried to shore, as fifteen cannons on each of the two ships saluted the colony's new governor. The cannons' great roar echoed around the sparsely inhabited cliffs fringing the majestic harbour before the men on both ships gave Macquarie three cheers.[6] The battery at Dawes Point answered the salute with more cannon fire while the ground trembled like an earthquake had hit.

On shore, Paterson and Foveaux – along with most of the town's population, from its leading lights to its battlers – saluted as 'His excellency Lachlan McQuarrie Esquire, Captain General and Governor in Chief of this His Majesty's Territory of New South Wales and its dependencies, and his lady'[7] set foot on their new kingdom. The 102nd Regiment formed a red-coated line for 300 metres up the hill from the Government Landing Stairs to the freshly painted Government House,[8] and there was constant bowing from the onlookers as Macquarie passed.

Paterson's wife Elizabeth[9] welcomed the Macquaries to their new abode. It was a comfortable home, but no palace: an entrance hall led to a 30-square-metre reception room, an adjacent bedroom, dining room and two offices. There were two small bedrooms upstairs, and above them an attic with a floor so thin that servants could be heard walking around up there at night. The kitchen was detached to prevent the spread of fire.

Macquarie then joined Foveaux on a carriage ride through the sylvan setting of Sydney, a small and still rustic township circling a majestic waterway, a smattering of grand homes rising beside the dusty tracks but nature still dominating man, the wild of the New South Wales bush still breathing down the neck of this young European settlement.

THE NEXT DAY, the first of 1810, the soldiers of the 73rd disembarked from the two ships at 11 a.m. and marched to the Grand Parade Ground of the barracks. At noon they formed into a square with the 102nd, under a blazing summer sun.

New Year's Day had ushered in a new era for a new land, in the most remote corner of the British Empire.

Macquarie, resplendent in scarlet coat and gold braid, broke the wax seal upon the patent and opened the King's Commission, handing it to Judge-Advocate Ellis Bent, who unfolded it.[10] The Great Seal of the Territory was then displayed. The troops presented arms and the officers saluted as 'God Save the King' roared out once again from the small settlement and assaulted the bushland all around.[11] Ellis Bent, shaded by an umbrella, then read out Macquarie's commission, beginning with the words:

'George the Third … to our trusty and well-beloved Lachlan Macquarie, Esquire, greeting'.[12]

After Bent had finished, the soldiers fired three volleys. The summer sunlight glistened on the gold buttons of Macquarie's red coat and he puffed out his chest. Then, in his rich Scottish burr, he began his address by declaring: *'Fellow citizens, and fellow soldiers!'*

Macquarie had done a lot of soul-searching on the voyage from London about what it meant to take on full responsibility for a young, isolated colony, particularly following the upheaval of the Rum Rebellion. After a lifetime as a soldier, the moment had arrived for Macquarie to score his most important victory, to leave his mark on the world as a right-thinking leader who advanced the prospects and the people of a young land. He had put away his dodgy deals and was ready to present himself as a staunch moral guardian to the struggling settlers and the convicts of New South Wales. He planned to be fair but firm for rich and poor, man and woman, black and white.

He told his captive audience in a 'short, animated speech', delivered with 'peculiar energy', that he would exercise his 'authority from the king with strict justice and impartiality', and that he would not tolerate the misbehaviour that had toppled Governor Bligh.[13]

'I am sanguine in my hopes,' he said, hoping everyone would know what 'sanguine' meant, 'that all those dissentions and jealousies which have unfortunately existed in this colony, for some time past, will *now* terminate forever, and give way to a more becoming spirit of conciliation, harmony, and unanimity, among all classes and descriptions of the inhabitants of it.'

> I must strongly recommend to *all classes* of the community a strict observance of all religious duties, and a constant and regular attendance at divine worship on Sundays, and other holidays set apart for that purpose: and I trust, that the magistrates and all other persons of authority will exert themselves to the utmost in checking and preventing all species of vice and immorality.

He offered an olive branch to the first peoples of the land:

> I need not, I hope, express my wish that the natives of this country, when they come in the way in a peaceable manner, may not be molested in their persons or property by any one; but that, on the contrary, they may always be treated with kindness and attention, so as to conciliate them as much as possible to our government and manners.

From his troops, he demanded 'a most vigilant discharge of every part of *their duty*', hoping that their 'strict discipline' would be so exemplary as to 'preclude the painful necessity of resorting to punishment'.

He concluded by telling Sydney that it was 'the earnest wish of our most gracious king, and his ministers, to promote the welfare and prosperity of this rising colony in every way possible; and it will, therefore, be the fault of the inhabitants themselves if they are not as comfortable and happy as any other of His Majesty's subjects.'

It was not only Macquarie's 'duty', he said, but also his 'chief happiness' to see the colony prosper, and he assured his subjects that 'the honest, sober, and industrious inhabitant, whether free settler or convict, will ever find in *me* a friend and protector!'[14]

The troops gave Macquarie three more cheers, then there was a 'royal salute of 21 guns' from Dawes Point and from the two ships as the gunpowder stores in the colony took a savage hit.[15]

The 73rd Regiment then marched out to the area known as Grose Farm, which had been set aside for a military camp and which would later become the site of Sydney's first university. Macquarie returned to Government House, where Ellis Bent read out the oaths of allegiance, and where Macquarie issued his first proclamation, signed by his new private secretary John Thomas (J.T.) Campbell.[16]

It began by declaring that His Majesty felt the 'utmost regret and displeasure on account of the late TUMULTUOUS PROCEEDINGS in this his COLONY, and the MUTINOUS CONDUCT of certain PERSONS therein towards his late representative, WILLIAM BLIGH, Esquire'. Moreover, 'through his gracious anxiety for the welfare and happiness of his loyal subjects of New South Wales, for the complete restoration of quiet and harmony, and to remove every motive for future disturbance', the king was 'graciously pleased' to make Macquarie the new boss. Macquarie then signed the proclamation 'given under my hand, at Government House, Sydney, this First Day of January, 1810.

'LACHLAN MACQUARIE.

GOD SAVE THE KING!'[17]

After two years of turmoil in the colony, New Year's Day was one of rejoicing in Sydney. That night, celebratory blazes illuminated the settlement and sky rockets were let off on the transport ships.[18]

On 7 January, Macquarie's first Sabbath as governor, he and Elizabeth sat down under the 45-metre clock tower of St Philip's Anglican Church, on a high hill overlooking the rest of Sydney, as the heavens roared and flashed. The church had been named in honour of Governor Arthur Phillip,[19] and had replaced Sydney's first church, which convicts had burned down in 1798.[20] The Macquaries were joined by a large congregation, including Foveaux and other 'officers of rank, civil, military, and naval', as well as a large gathering of sailors and marines, paying 'the duties of respect and adoration to their beneficent Creator'.[21]

The slightly built thirty-one year old Lancashire clergyman, William Cowper,[22] delivered 'a most impressive sermon' based on 1 Samuel 16:12: 'Arise, anoint him: for this is he.' Macquarie could not have had a more impressive welcome.

On 16 January, the colonists sent him a collective address in which they could not but sincerely lament the unhappy differences and dissension under which this colony has unfortunately laboured', but cherished an anxious hope, that the union and harmony so forcibly recommended by Your Excellency will unanimously prevail; and that all party spirit may be buried in oblivion!'[23]

In response, Macquarie told the five men representing the colonists that, if 'the upper class of society ... set an example of subordination, morality, and decorum ... this country must inevitably increase in consequence, opulence, respectability, and importance'.[24]

That night, illuminated signs were displayed in the homes of Sydney's well-to-do. Merchant Garnham Blaxcell,[25] one of the plotters against Bligh, displayed a 'well executed portrait of His Majesty' at his front door.[26] Joseph Underwood,[27] whose business involved importing pork from Tahiti, whaling and hunting for sea-lion oil, had a huge bonfire in front of his house and a band in a corner of his veranda, playing 'God Save the King' and 'Rule, Britannia!' He threw open his home for the entertainment of spectators and 'tables everywhere were covered with refreshments'. A reporter watching the scene remarked that 'youth and beauty joined the lively throng and kept the merry dance alive'.[28]

MACQUARIE'S JURISDICTION was to cover the great land mass of New Holland – half the size of Europe – that Matthew Flinders had circumnavigated six and a half years earlier, as well as Van Diemen's Land, which Flinders had previously proved to be an island. It would also include the colony of Norfolk Island and unspecified 'adjacent islands', which Macquarie took to include New Zealand, Tahiti, the Solomon Islands and Fiji.

Save for interference from London, months away by sailing boat, Macquarie's power was absolute for thousands of kilometres in every direction, even if the population of his whole kingdom was less than that of a small English town.

Macquarie's first census, conducted in the early months of 1810, showed that Sydney had a European population of 6156, Parramatta 1807, the Hawkesbury 2389 and Newcastle just 100 'souls'. That made a total of 10,452: 5511 men, 2220 women and 2721 children. In total, there were 1437 prisoners being guarded by 1365 military personnel.[29] The free settlers and convicts of Van Diemen's Land totalled 1321 at the settlements of Port Dalrymple and Hobart Town. Only 177 people lived on Norfolk Island.[30]

They would all have to do as they were told. Macquarie did not support what he had once called 'the infernal and destructive principles of democracy' as wielded by the 'savages of France' during the revolution.[31] Here, Macquarie's word would be law.

He put a positive spin on the future whenever he spoke in public or delivered a proclamation, but privately he knew there was much work to be done. He was not at all pleased with what he had seen in Sydney so far.

He would later write that:

I found the colony barely emerging from infantile imbecility, and suffering from various privations and disabilities; the country impenetrable beyond forty miles from Sydney; agriculture in a yet languishing state; commerce in its early dawn; revenue unknown; threatened by famine; distracted by faction; the public buildings in a state of dilapidation and mouldering to decay; the few roads and bridges formerly constructed, rendered almost impassable; the population in general depressed by poverty; no public credit nor private confidence; the morals of the great mass of the population in the lowest state of debasement, and religious worship almost totally neglected.[32]

He set about fixing that immediately, rather than fixing old scores. The rebels who had overthrown Bligh would keep. Periodic flooding of the Hawkesbury River Valley, the fledgling colony's food bowl, meant the inhabitants of New South Wales were regularly at risk of starvation. Macquarie's first job was to make sure his subjects had enough food on the table, so his first orders were to have 3 or so hectares at Castle Hill, a fertile area away from the floodplain, prepared for planting potatoes and another 150 hectares prepared for sowing wheat.[33]

Soon, Macquarie could report that more than 8000 hectares of New South Wales were under cultivation and almost 30,000 hectares cleared for pasture, and that between them, the colony's farmers owned 33,818 sheep, 8992 hogs, 6351 cows, 4732 oxen, 1732 goats, 914 horses and 193 bulls.[34]

On 15 January, the almost providential arrival of the ship *Marian* from Bengal, carrying 3500 bags of wheat, 500 bags of rice and 100 bags of sugar,[35] brought what Macquarie called 'a most reasonable relief'[36] to a colony desperate for food. The fears of famine would soon be further allayed by a bumper crop of maize.[37]

But lack of food was not the colonists' only worry. Mr and Mrs Macquarie made a three-day visit to Parramatta, inspecting the almost uninhabitable government house there, with its rotting floorboards and staircase. Then they visited the sad institution that was Sydney Cove's Female Orphan School,[38] where 100 miserable young wretches tried to survive both poverty and sexual predators. Elizabeth eyed the children with pity. The orphanage was located next to a public works depot and she feared that the girls' close proximity to male workers and to the nearby slums and drinking houses of The Rocks put them at risk of moral corruption.[39] The orphanage would have to move because Sydney was full of sin.

But Macquarie could not put off the inevitable for long. Castlereagh's orders had made his first priority clear: to deal with the after-effects of the Rum Rebellion.

THUNDER AND LIGHTNING rocked Sydney a week after Macquarie's arrival, with a late-afternoon storm that threatened people's lives.

At the office of the colony's first newspaper, the *Sydney Gazette,* lightning repeatedly assailed a building full of metal type where six children cowered. One young man was knocked to the ground by the force of a lightning bolt, which sent a back door flying off its hinges and reduced the wood and brickwork around it 'to atoms'.[40]

George Howe,[41] who had escaped the noose as a convict to become the paper's publisher, was reading a page proof of his next edition when he was thrown backwards off his seat by an electric fireball that cannoned into the building, invading every opening with its flaming tongues. Howe rose from the floor to find himself looking like a ghost, enveloped in the dust of lime and mortar from the shattered brickwork.[42]

The storm was a portent for Macquarie's first conflict in his new post.

One of his first social visits as governor, on 4 January, was to John Macarthur's wife Elizabeth.[43] At least Macarthur was a problem he no longer needed to worry about – but William Bligh was another matter.

Early in the new year, he sent the *Estramina*, just down from Newcastle,[44] south to the Derwent to bring Bligh back to Sydney.

But the cranky old salt had already heard of Macquarie's arrival from the skipper of a whaling vessel. He and Mary, his hardiest supporter, sailed through the Heads aboard the old and battered *Porpoise* on 17 January 1810.[45]

Bligh was unimpressed by the formal thirteen-gun salute that greeted him, and declined a request to break bread with the new governor,[46] despite Macquarie's promise to bestow 'every respect and attention' on him while he remained in the colony.[47]

When Bligh did come ashore the next day, Macquarie ordered two companies of the 73rd to form a guard of honour at the wharf. Greeting his predecessor, Macquarie formally invited father and daughter to live with him at Government House for as long as they remained in Sydney.[48] Privately, Macquarie worried how he would cope with having Bligh and his daughter under their roof, and knew Elizabeth's brow would be furrowing over the potential for domestic disaster. Fortunately for their household, Bligh declined the invitation.

Macquarie handed back Bligh's sword and flintlock pistols, which the rebels had taken, as well as returning Bligh's papers, although Macarthur and Johnston had kept all the important ones for themselves.[49]

Bligh, however, continued to ceremonially thumb his nose at Macquarie, angry that his successor had taken command without waiting for his return from exile. He wanted command of the *Hindostan* and *Dromedary*. He demanded to be treated regally. He rented a cottage at £10 a month beside the Tank Stream near Government House and had Macquarie assign him a sergeant from the 73rd as his personal bodyguard. He would walk about Sydney with his guard close by, often to the hoots and jeers of the populace.

Above all, he wanted anyone who had supported his overthrow to be prosecuted. He demanded that sixteen witnesses to his demise return to England with him to ensure that Macarthur and Johnston were hanged.[50] Macquarie told Bligh that the expense of the travel and the inconvenience to families would be too great, and that Bligh should 'compress his evidence to a smaller number'.[51] Bligh eventually came up with six names.

Even though he regarded the ex-governor as a 'great plague',[52] Macquarie did his best to smooth over the troubles of the past. He removed the bureaucrats who had been appointed in Bligh's absence and restored the men who had held those roles during his reign. He also revoked the land grants, emancipations and pardons awarded by the rebel government.

The Rum Corps might have staged the mutiny, but Macquarie accommodated the soldiers who wanted to stay in New South Wales by merging some into the 73rd and forming a veterans' company for those who had performed long service. The 73rd was soon augmented by transfers from the departing 102nd, with more than half of them – 447 men – eventually choosing to remain in New South Wales.[53]

Like the men of the 102nd, Bligh seemed in no hurry to leave. He wrote to his wife that he wanted to be rid of 'this wicked place',[54] but it looked as if getting him to go home would be a tough task.

Already, Macquarie was heartily sick of him, telling his brother Charles that 'Govr. Bligh certainly is a most disagreeable person to have any dealings, or publick business to transact with; having no regard whatever to his promises or engagements, however sacred, and his natural temper is uncommonly harsh, and tyrannical in the extreme.' It was 'an undoubted fact' that Bligh was 'a very improper person to be employed in any situation of trust or command, and he is certainly very generally detested by high, low, rich and poor'.[55]

On St Patrick's Day, 17 March 1810, Bligh left Sydney to inspect his farms on the Hawkesbury at Green Hills (the original name of the town of Windsor). Since it was a glorious autumn day, he got out of his coach and planted his paunch on a poor pony for 'twenty miles'. A 'corpulent man and for some time unused to exercise', he became ill with fever and a swollen leg, which only made his temper and language more prickly than normal, so that he 'overpowered and affrighted every person that might have dealings with him'.[56]

At least he was faring better than David Collins, who died

suddenly of a stroke in Hobart a week later while talking to his doctor.[57] Macquarie had long wanted Foveaux to replace Collins, whose personal liaisons made him a figure of controversy. Macquarie told Castlereagh he had never met an officer more capable of 'conducting to maturity and perfection any infant colony committed to his charge'.[58] But Foveaux was out of favour in London for appearing to support the rebels. After the overthrow of Bligh, Foveaux had arrived back in Port Jackson from a visit to London as the senior British officer, faced with the dilemma of deciding whether to reinstate the despised Governor or take command himself pending orders from London. He had decided that restoring Bligh to power would only inflame a volatile situation. Macquarie was still talking up Foveaux's abilities to rule in Van Diemen's Land, even after his portly pal set sail for England on 18 March.[59]

A week after Foveaux's departure, the Macquaries joined Mary Putland on a two-day excursion in the governor's carriage to the Parramatta, Castle Hill and Baulkham Hills districts,[60] though Mary left them in Parramatta to meet her father on the Hawkesbury. Mary had been spending a lot of time at Government House, visiting her cousin Captain Antill and his commander, the debonair Lieutenant-Colonel O'Connell, Macquarie's second-in-command.

The Macquaries returned to Government House more in love with the countryside of New South Wales than ever, and Bligh returned to Sydney angrier than usual. He made the most of Macquarie's generous spirit, however, taking up his quarters on the *Hindostan* and enforcing strict discipline, with the crew obliged to present arms many times a day as he came and went. In one week, the guns of the ships in the harbour and at the battery saluted him in symphony six times.

Bligh had received instructions that the rebellion had been declared illegal, and that the British Foreign Office had declared it to be a mutiny. For the next few months, he set about collecting evidence for the coming court martial of Major Johnston in England. While it seemed that wild horses could not drag Bligh away until then, he was now eager to get going for the delicious prospect of seeing Johnston hang.

Bligh decided that when the *Hindostan* sailed in May alongside the *Dromedary* and *Porpoise*, he and Mary would sail with them.

Some disgruntled onlookers, such as naval surgeon Joseph Arnold,[61] who had come out on the *Hindostan* with the Macquaries to make sure the 73rd arrived shipshape on arrival, believed the new governor should be taking a much tougher line with the old curmudgeon. Arnold was dreading the voyage home to England with 'so boisterous and ostentatious a little old man as Commodore Bligh'.[62]

'Governor Macquarie,' Arnold wrote, 'is of too peacible a nature for his situation, he endeavours to conciliate all persons, and instead of showing a marked disapprobation of the principal men in the late revolt, he invited them to his table at Government House, put some of them in responsible situations and made others his confidants'.[63]

Arnold was a hard man to please, and so was Ellis Bent when it came to the Macquaries' hospitality. Elizabeth had brought a Broadwood three-pedal grand piano from England to entertain at her parties and dances but, at a Government House dinner only a few weeks after their arrival, Arnold noted that Mr and Mrs Macquarie were 'both Scotch & consequently close fisted' and that they 'kept a shabby table'.[64]

Ellis Bent described a farewell dinner for Colonel Paterson and his wife as 'stupid'. There was the obligatory curry as a nod to Macquarie's service in India and the presence in his family of George, but Bent was not impressed. He even described where everything was on the table and, though he felt the fare was meagre, it seemed there was plenty of variety:

Mrs Macquarie has not the art of making people feel happy and comfortable around her. There were in all Seventeen Persons present. Mrs M's dinners, are as much too small as the dinners usually given in the Colony are too profuse ... there was Soup removed by a very small Boiled Turkey at the Bottom (where Captain Cleaveland the Brigade Major sits). There was a piece of Roast Beef. The sides were fricassee, curried Duck, Kidneys & a Tongue, the Corners Vegetables. 2nd Course, at the Top, Stewed Oysters, bottom Wild Ducks, sides & corners tartlets, Jellies & vegetables, in the middle there was an Epergne. – The Table was very large, & one might have danced a Reel between the dishes.[65]

While ungrateful dinner guests were a mild annoyance to Macquarie, by now, Bligh was wearing out his welcome even with his most loyal supporter.

For two years, Mary had played the doting daughter, putting up with her father's foul temper and cruel tongue. But no more. While Bligh had been blustering around town, cursing everyone in sight, the fiery little twenty-seven year old, who in her own fashion statement modestly wore trousers under her delicate, almost translucent dresses, had been falling for the charms of forty-two year old Lieutenant-Governor O'Connell.

Bligh gave O'Connell's marriage proposal a 'flat denial', but Mary would not take no for an answer. Instead of returning to England with her on the *Hindostan*, Bligh gritted his teeth as he gave her away to the new regime. His last official act in New South Wales was to attend Mary and O'Connell's wedding at Government House on 8 May 1810 at 10 a.m.[66] Samuel Marsden performed the ceremony, and the Macquaries presided with an 'extraordinary degree of pleasure and even exultation'.[67] Convict poet Michael Robinson,[68] an Oxford lawyer turned blackmailer, composed some verses to serenade the happy couple:

In Australasia's genial clime proclaim,
That LOVE and VALOUR blend their spotless flame.[69]

Ellis Bent wasn't impressed with the situation, however, describing the lieutenant-governor's new wife as something of a hellcat: 'very small, nice little figure, rather pretty but conceited and extremely proud. God knows of what! Extremely violent and passionate, so much as now and then to fling a plate or candlestick at her father's head … I regret this marriage for I dislike her and in the next place it crushed any hopes I had formed of seeing comparative harmony restored to the colony.'[70]

Macquarie granted O'Connell 1012 hectares, which he called Riverston Farm, in what is now the suburb of Riverstone. Soon afterwards, Mary was granted 427 hectares in what is now the western Sydney suburb of Werrington, adjoining the property Frogmore, which Governor Philip Gidley King had given her. She was a wealthy young bride, with a personal fortune that included more than 1200 hectares and 7000 head of sheep and cattle.

Broken-hearted, Bligh prepared to leave Sydney without 'his inestimable treasure'. Three days after the wedding, he was ferried back out to the *Hindostan*, anchored beside the *Dromedary* and *Porpoise* at the Heads and ready to sail at a moment's notice.[71]

On 12 May 1810, Mr and Mrs Macquarie took their carriage out to the cliffs overlooking the Heads, along with a large gathering of colonists, to see the ships sail out into the open sea a little after noon.[72] On board along with Bligh were around half of the Rum Corps and his six witnesses[73] for the prosecution, as well as Colonel Paterson, who would die on the voyage, and Judge-Advocate Atkins, whom Macquarie wrongly thought unlikely to survive the long journey either, given his heavy drinking and feeble health.[74]

Macquarie stayed for three hours watching Bligh disappear over the horizon, just to make certain he was gone.

He turned to Elizabeth to say that the back of Bligh was 'a fine sight!'[75] and that he was 'heartily glad to get quit of him'.[76]

The last of the old order had disappeared. Macquarie was unopposed ruler of his new kingdom, a place with flora, fauna and potential like nowhere else in the world.

Now Governor Macquarie had a nation to build.

Chapter 19

*I have, nevertheless, taken upon myself to adopt a new line of
conduct, conceiving that emancipation, when united with rectitude
and long-tried good conduct, should lead a man back to
that rank in society, which he had forfeited.*

MACQUARIE DECLARING THAT HE IS ALL FOR GIVING CONVICTS
A SECOND CHANCE IN THEIR NEW HOME[1]

THE MOOD in New South Wales brightened as soon as
Bligh's dark shadow sank beneath the horizon, and Macquarie
set about cleaning up the mess his predecessor had left behind.

While that grizzled old salt was still fuming on the *Hindostan* as
it approached the Solent, between England and the Isle of Wight,
Sydney was celebrating like never before.

At a fair in May at Parramatta, cockfighting was one of the
entertainments, along with horse racing, trotting and a ladies'
sack race, as the population revelled in 'feats of humour and
fun'.[2] To celebrate the king's birthday on 4 June 1810, Macquarie
threw open the lawn in front of Government House and 'an
immense number of the inhabitants' gazed in astonishment at the
decorations on the veranda', while the band of the 73rd Regiment
provided entertainment.[3]

Then, on 6 October, Macquarie decreed that the unoccupied
area south of Sydney – variously called the Common, the Cricket

Ground and the Racecourse – would henceforth be known as Hyde Park, and would be devoted to the 'recreation and amusement' of the people and to the exercising of troops.[4]

Nine days later, during a glorious spring week, it appeared as though all of the colony's 11,000 inhabitants had turned out for Sydney's first spring racing carnival. There had been horse races in the colony before, but nothing like this event, in which the convict rubbed shoulders with the judge, and the thief cheered beside the land baron. The egalitarian arms of the track welcomed all.

While Macquarie had prohibited the sale of alcohol, as well as 'gaming, drunkenness, swearing, quarrelling, fighting or boxing taking place on or near the race-ground',[5] a good time was to be had by the masses. There were the obligatory entertainments between the gallops, with cockfights and several foot races, but none more entertaining than the sight of one Dicky Dowling carrying 90 kilograms on his back for 45 metres against an unfettered rival who had to run *two* lots of 45.[6]

Officers from the 73rd Regiment had put together a program that featured three race days over a five-day festival, held between Monday 15 and Friday 19 October.[7] Hyde Park's track was 1 mile and 40 yards in circumference and, appropriately, the finish line was close to the gallows. Some of the races covered two laps of the course and some three. Providing the pageantry, colour and thrills were horses owned by prominent citizens Ellis Bent, Maurice O'Connell, Simeon Lord, Captain John Piper[8] and Captain Thomas Cleaveland.[9] There were two celebration balls, setting racing on track to become a major social event of Australian life.

Captain John Ritchie's grey six-year-old gelding, Chase, won the 50-guinea Subscribers' Plate on the first day of racing and on the second day Elizabeth Macquarie, 'with her usual affability', presented him with the Ladies' Cup, after another win on the same horse. Elizabeth, with a smile almost as wide as the harbour, gave a short speech in which she said: 'In the name of the ladies of New South Wales, I have the pleasure to present you with this cup.

Give me leave to congratulate you on being the successful candidate for it; and to hope that it is a prelude to future success, and lasting prosperity.'[10]

On the final day, Gig, a horse ridden by D'Arcy Wentworth's son William,[11] crashed while avoiding a stray dog, badly injuring the jockey, but as Macquarie and Elizabeth graced that evening's celebration ball, the *Sydney Gazette* discerned 'a universal glow of satisfaction – the celebration of the first liberal amusement instituted in the colony and in the presence of its patron and founder. The ballroom was occupied till about two o'clock when part of the company retired'.[12] The rest partied on until dawn. Macquarie's racing carnival showed a spirit in Sydney that was missing in the old countries where the convicts had originated. In Sydney, Macquarie wanted the prisoners and the free settlers to know that there was a willingness to forget the wrongs of the past. That spirit of openness in society would characterise Macquarie's governorship.

MACQUARIE SET ABOUT building Sydney from the ground up, and hang the cost. He had never been too careful with the king's money, and there were projects and possibilities everywhere he looked. Sydney needed to be fed then housed and Macquarie realised he could make a statement about the potential of New South Wales in bricks and mortar.

Not long after his arrival in Sydney, Macquarie had written to Castlereagh, warning his superior that he was about to 'put the Crown to a very considerable expence in the erection of barracks and other essentially necessary public buildings'.[13] Word had not yet reached Macquarie that Castlereagh had resigned temporarily from his position as Secretary of War and the Colonies after blowing apart the thigh of Foreign Minister George Canning in a duel on Putney Heath on 21 September 1809.[14] Macquarie wrote to say the colony needed new roads and bridges, a new hospital, new granaries, accommodation for 1000 soldiers, and more barracks to deal with the arrival of more convicts. To get all this done, Sydney would also need a new government architect and surveyor-general.[15] Macquarie's constant tapping of the treasury would quickly wear thin and provide ammunition for his enemies, concerned by his rebellious Highland streak.

Further afield, Macquarie planned to construct a turnpike road to the Hawkesbury,[16] and then there were those impassable Blue Mountains, 70 kilometres west of Sydney, that needed to be overcome.

David Collins's grandiose funeral in Hobart, organised by his chief mourner Lieutenant Edward Lord,[17] had cost a staggering £507,[18] for such items of mourning as '107 yards of black cloth, 19 waistcoat fronts, 11 black gowns and five fine hats',[19] and had been a much 'greater expence' than Macquarie had deemed necessary.[20] He sent the bill to London.

When he first arrived in Sydney, he said, he had found the king's stores virtually empty of dry provisions and the convicts in rags. He had been forced to buy clothes at 'exorbitant' rates to cover the convicts' nakedness, and purchase canvas for hundreds of soldiers' hammocks. Then he had had to buy six months' provisions for the *Hindostan*, *Dromedary* and *Porpoise* for Bligh's return to England. He sent orders to England for wheat, rice, sugar and spirits.[21]

A new printing press was needed for the *Sydney Gazette*, the government's mouthpiece, and while he was at it, Macquarie asked for a copy of the 'Royal Arms of the United Kingdom in brass … about the size and form of the arms that head his Majesty's speeches to parliament' to use on proclamations. He also wanted 'a double complement' of capital letters in metal type because his fondness for them was wearing out the *Gazette's* supplies.[22]

The *Porpoise* was old and falling apart, and Macquarie needed two new vessels.[23] Even the flagstaff at Dawes Point was 'quite rotten and decayed'.[24] Because of the prevalence of handwritten promissory notes, which invited fraud, Macquarie also began thinking about a bank of New South Wales, much like the bank at the Cape of Good Hope.

Within the first three months of his rule, Macquarie was billing Castlereagh for £22,555, 12 shillings, fivepence and *a farthing*.[25]

But money was not the only thing he was angling for. He said his deputy, Maurice O'Connell, would need his annual salary doubled to £500.[26] He himself was not averse to a payrise when he could get one either, and given the way he himself had been passed over for promotion in years gone by, he thought it appropriate that the king make him a brigadier-general.[27]

He had served His Majesty for thirty-three years 'in the four different quarters of the globe' and had 'only attained the rank of lieut-colonel in the army, with the local rank of colonel in New South Wales'. Not only would promotion to brigadier make up for all Macquarie's previous disappointments, but it would be 'highly gratifying' to his feelings 'as an old officer' and 'it would give additional weight and consequence' to his position 'in this remote colony'.[28] Macquarie never stopped trying. He saw endless possibilities in Australia and he planned to keep attacking the British government with a fusillade of demands until they cracked.

ON 6 OCTOBER 1810, Macquarie sent out an order that, for the 'convenience, accommodation and safety' of the people of Sydney and for the town's 'ornament and regularity', he had divided it into five districts. There would be a watch-house in each one to preserve 'peace and tranquillity' and to guard against night-time robberies.[29]

It would be expedient, he declared, to name all of Sydney's streets, to order posts with the street names painted on them, and to have houses and buildings numbered at the cost of sixpence per property. The principal street in Sydney, leading from Dawes Point to the Brickfields (in what is now Surry Hills), would be called George Street 'in honour of our revered and gracious sovereign'. A prominent part of the town near the homes of wealthy former convicts Simeon Lord and Mary Reibey would be called Macquarie Place.

Streets were to be 50 feet wide, edged by paling fences 4 feet high. Buildings that encroached on the streets would have to be moved back at public expense. Pigs, dogs and goats would have to be fenced in. Stray pigs and goats would be sold to benefit the Orphan Fund, and dogs that chased horses would be killed. Men driving cattle through the streets would have to do so on foot, but avoid the footpaths under penalty of arrest. Shooting of guns in town, especially on Sundays, was prohibited, as was doing laundry in the Tank Stream, or polluting it in other ways.[30]

The home of the former convict Isaac Nichols – 'a most, zealous, active and useful man',[31] and the first to welcome Macquarie to New South Wales – became Sydney's first post office.[32] Soon Nichols created a postmark that read 'Sydney NSW', the precursor of the stamp in Australia.[33]

Ironically, though, Macquarie's greatest building project would be driven by what he believed was the colony's deadliest evil.

Macquarie had been given orders to stop the use of rum as an instrument of barter, but he knew mere prohibition would be useless. Rum was still vital to the colony as a means of payment and 'for the accommodation of the inhabitants'. He decided the best way to regulate the liquor trade was to allow unrestricted importation under a higher duty.

From 3 March 1810, Macquarie increased the tax on liquor imports from 1 shilling and sixpence to 3 shillings a gallon. He believed this would put an end to any monopoly, to the bartering of spirits for corn and to the 'very numerous' illegal stills in the colony.[34]

The old system of barter would continue for some time, though. Ellis Bent bought 57 gallons of brandy for £17 and sold them for £142 10s. When Macquarie contracted for a new bridge over the Tank Stream in September 1811, he would pay the builder with 660 gallons (2500 litres) of spirits.[35] Rum also lubricated Macquarie's deal to prevent New South Wales from starving. Because of fears that further flooding in the Hawkesbury would destroy crops, Macquarie formed a contract in April 1810 with Simeon Lord and his partner, Francis Williams,[36] to import 200 tons of Bengal wheat as a safeguard. They charged Macquarie a low price of £16 a ton in return for permission to import 20,000 gallons of Bengal rum.[37]

Soon afterwards, Macquarie would negotiate a much greater liquor deal that he saw as being vital to the colony's future.

Sydney's hospital was in worse condition than most of the eighty ailing patients it housed. Governor Phillip had overseen its building in 1790 from sections shipped from England, but twenty years later, it was in 'a most ruinous state'.

So it was that John Macarthur's business partner Garnham Blaxcell, the wealthy merchant Alexander Riley[38] and the rakish surgeon D'Arcy Wentworth, inexperienced in construction but full of the entrepreneurial spirit that Macquarie loved, proposed to build from stone and wood 'one of the finest public buildings in any of His Majesty's colonies'. It would be two storeys high, 87½ metres long, 8½ metres high and 11½ metres wide, with walls over half a metre thick and 'a viranda around each storey of the building 10 feet [3 metres] wide'. It would house two surgeons' quarters. There would be mahogany doors and 'every sort of judicious ornament', and it would be erected on 2.8 hectares of land high upon a hill, on a street Macquarie had just named after himself.[39]

In return, Blaxcell and Riley would receive twenty convict labourers, eighty oxen to feed them, twenty draught bullocks for the hard toil and – the sweetest part of the deal – permission to import 45,000 gallons (205,000 litres) of rum from India and sell it over the three years that it would take to build the new structure.[40]

The negotiations for the deal took several months. Mr and Mrs Macquarie wanted to give New South Wales the best medical help possible.

YET MACQUARIE KNEW that rum's most pernicious use was not as a tool for bartering. So he set about making Sydney a more sober and serious place and eliminating the evil influence of liquor on the morals of its people.

Macquarie quickly reduced the number of public houses from seventy-five to twenty, and cut the numbers by the same proportion in other settlements to 'arrest the progress of drunkenness'.[41] He banned 'the shameful and indecent custom' of working on the Sabbath and instructed all public houses to shut during divine service. He threatened to take away the liquor licence of any establishment ignoring that edict and to arrest anyone caught working on a Sunday.[42]

He promised to end, as far as possible, the 'scandalous and pernicious custom so generally and shamelessly adopted throughout the territory of persons of different sexes cohabiting and living together unsanctioned by the legal ties of matrimony'.[43] Macquarie knew the ways of the world; he was well acquainted with venereal diseases and mercury, and many of his high-powered associates had fathered children out of wedlock. Now, though, he saw himself as the colony's moral guardian. He described couples who merely lived together as a 'scandal to religion, to decency, and to all good government', and said the practice had to stop in Sydney because it was injurious to society and to the 'innocent offspring of misconduct'.[44]

He was fortunate to have had two loving marriages and marriage was the cornerstone for industry and decency, he said, adding that it was also a protection for women, especially when it came to inheriting property after these 'illicit connexions'[45] when a partner died intestate. Macquarie had more success with the marriage rate, though, when the licence fee was 3 guineas than he had when it was upped to 5.

The numbers of poor and neglected children in the streets of Sydney, which Macquarie attributed to 'illegal and criminal intercourse' rather than marriage, prompted him to immediately open charity schools under the control of the Reverend Cowper, so that the young, unlearned and unwashed could become 'honest, faithful and useful members of society'.[46]

Irishman Matthew Hughes[47] became the teacher at Macquarie's first charity school, a slab hut at Kissing Point on the Parramatta River, close to where St Anne's Church now stands at Ryde. He had arrived in the colony as a convict in 1796, sentenced to transportation for life while a militia corporal after a fight with civilians in which a man died.

With fifty students under his care, Hughes told Cowper the remuneration was so inadequate that he was compelled to leave his school at intervals to earn extra money 'to supply the necessary wants of me and my wife'.[48] Macquarie was always as keen to hand out payrises as he was to ask for them, and

Hughes, a strict Methodist who did not believe in sparing the rod, agreed to 'give six children education, free of all expense to their parents, and to continue to educate such other children as may come to my school at the rate of eight pence per week, for spelling and reading, and one shilling per week for writing and accounts'.[49] Macquarie soon appointed him to a new charity school at Windsor, where he was paid £60 a year and given a land grant of 25 hectares. He taught school for the next thirty-one years at Windsor and Richmond.

Next on Macquarie's list was the closing of Sydney's brothels – the 'most licentious and disorderly houses' – where abandoned members of both sexes were encouraged in 'dissolute and disorderly habits'.[50] The keepers of these 'houses of ill fame' were to be punished 'to the utmost extent allowed by the law'.[51] He also put a stop to the sex trafficking of female convicts, declaring that before he arrived, many unfortunate women had suffered from the 'depravity of manners and vicious habits' of their masters.[52]

Soon he would prohibit bathing near the government wharf and dockyard at any time of the day, because the sight of naked flesh close to the settlement was 'indecent and improper'.[53] Bathers were welcome to use beaches further up the harbour, but he warned Sydneysiders against swimming in the surf of the open ocean because of recent drownings.[54]

Macquarie appealed to his subjects to make the colony a more harmonious and godly place, hoping that:

> ... the higher classes will set an example of subordination, morality and decorum, and all those in an inferior station will endeavour to distinguish themselves only by their loyalty, their sobriety and industry: but which means alone the welfare and happiness of the community can be effectually promoted'.[55]

FROM THE SUNNY NORTH ROOM at Government House, where Macquarie could look out at the ships in the harbour, the new governor began to give instructions to his civil servants daily between 10 and 11 a.m., 'Sundays excepted'.[56] Between eleven and noon, he would devote himself to matters involving the 73rd. He would deal with written applications for land and stock grants every Monday at noon, and every Tuesday from noon until 2 p.m., he would be available for business meetings or visits of ceremony. He promised to be available 'at all hours and on all days' in case of emergency. Frivolous requests, though, would receive no notice 'whatever'.[57]

As he sought out officials with talent to help him rule his Antipodean kingdom, Macquarie began a concerted program of accepting emancipated convicts into the upper realms of New South Wales society.

With many of the colony's more capable men having sailed for England for the trial of Johnston, Macquarie would increasingly call on prosperous former convicts to perform important public roles. On Ulva and Mull, his noble yet impoverished kin had toiled alongside the poorest of the poor. He was conscious of his own misdemeanours, and of the 'second chances' that had seen him rise to become ruler of his own domain. After decades of playing by the British Army's class-conscious rules, now he could finally do things his way, and promote people on talent.

He wanted men of action and resilience to drive the colony's growth, and believed that, by promoting former prisoners, he was getting the best out of the best minds in the colony. He was determined to provide a pathway to redemption for ex-convicts who, by 'long habits of industry and total reformation of manners, had not only become respectable, but by many degrees the most useful members of the community'.[58] Each man should 'feel himself eligible for any situation which he has, by a long term of conduct, proved himself worthy of filling'.[59] As far as it was within Macquarie's power, New South Wales and its territories would be a meritocracy.

There was something almost messianic in his forgiveness of these 'evildoers', each man's former state 'no longer remembered or allowed to act against him'.[60] Macquarie would later explain his thinking as follows:

At my first entrance into this colony ... I certainly did not anticipate any intercourse but that of control with men who were or had been convicts; a short experience shewed me, however, that some of the most meritorious men of the few to be found, and who were most capable and most willing to exert themselves in the public service, were men who had been convicts! I saw the necessity and justice of adopting a plan on a general basis which had always been partially acted upon towards these people, namely, that of extending to them generally the same considerations and qualifications, which they would have enjoyed from their merits and situations in life had they never been under the sentence of the law ... I have never had cause to find I had mistaken the object I had in view, namely, holding out to the minds of men the greatest incentive to virtue which can be employed to promote that end.[61]

He announced that the Irishman D'Arcy Wentworth – tall, handsome, blue-eyed and charming – would be the colony's principal surgeon until Dr Jamison returned from giving evidence at George Johnston's trial in England. Wentworth had been acquitted of four armed robberies in England, despite having been caught carrying a pistol, black silk mask and wig near the scene of a hold-up in the wilds of London's Hounslow Heath.[62] But he could wield a scalpel well enough for Macquarie's purposes, regardless of his colourful private life, which included three sons he acknowledged and at least seven other children whom he supported.[63]

Later, he would also become Chief Police Magistrate, Superintendent of Police, Treasurer of the Police Fund and one of the contractors building Sydney Hospital.

Wentworth's assistant would be the long-faced William Redfern,[64] a kind but proud and impolite former convict who had been in New South Wales since 1801.[65] Redfern had been transported as a consequence of a mutiny at the Nore, an anchorage in the Thames Estuary, that had resulted in a death sentence,

William Redfern,
painted by George
Marshall Mather in
1832. State Library of NSW

commuted because of his youth. During his passage, he had assisted
the surgeon and kept the journal for the treatment of the sick.
Foveaux had recommended him to Macquarie 'in the strongest
terms, as to his conduct, character and professional abilities'.[66] It
was Foveaux who had appointed him the colony's assistant surgeon,
a position confirmed in 1811 by the Prince Regent, who had
taken over the duties of his father George III because of the king's
recurring mental illness.

Soon, Redfern was running the old and dilapidated hospital
at Dawes Point and building up a profitable private practice, as
well as conducting a daily outpatients' clinic for men from the
convict gangs.

Macquarie later pointed out that there were few families in
Sydney who had not availed themselves of Redfern's considerable
skills:

His duty in the general hospital has been laborious and most certainly fulfilled with a degree of promptitude and attention not to be exceeded. I have heard many poor persons, dismissed from the hospital, thank him for their recovery; but I have never known a patient complain of his neglect.[67]

Macquarie appointed free settler John Jamieson[68] as Principal Superintendent of Government Stock[69] and he gave the job of Chief Superintendent of Convicts to the ubiquitous former convict Isaac Nichols. Nichols's wife Rosanna was the daughter of former convict Esther Abrahams,[70] who, after long cohabitation, would marry George Johnston when he returned to the colony within a few years.

Soon the judicial benches were being filled by men who had once been in irons, more and more constables knew what it had been like on the other side of the bars. Sydney's road system was being put together by James Meehan,[71] a former Irish rebel, and colonists found themselves pleading with former prisoners for land grants.

Akin to Macquarie's compassion for the convict seeking to blot out the crimes of the past was his real empathy for the battling farmer working his few hectares, trying to grow a life from the soil. Macquarie had grown up on the land and later managed his uncle's estate. He had seen such hardships with his own eyes, and had already demonstrated his sympathy in his treatment of his tenants at Jarvisfield.

Pursuing this same policy of giving convicts a second chance, Macquarie began to commute death sentences for all crimes but murder.[72] He was appalled by the brutal floggings that laid bones bare.

After Ellis Bent sentenced convict James Hutchinson to hang for stealing from a shop, Hutchinson made a daring escape the night before his scheduled execution, getting away in what Macquarie called 'a most unaccountable manner, being in irons and lodged in one of the cells'.[73] Macquarie was so impressed with the convict's pluck that, when Hutchinson was captured, he amended his sentence to life with hard labour.

Hutchinson eventually reoffended and was strung up beside an accomplice.[74] There were limits even to Macquarie's generosity.

ON TUESDAY 7 AUGUST 1810, Macquarie made a note: '!!! — Mrs Macquarie had the misfortune of having a miscarriage this night after going to bed, which caused us both a great deal of uneasiness and mystification. She must have been gone with child between five and six weeks.'[75]

Soon, however, they stood as godparents at St Philip's for the son of the vicar, who named his boy William Macquarie Cowper: the first Australian child named in the governor's honour.[76] He became known as Macquarie Cowper and went on to become the Anglican Dean of Sydney.[77]

BY 27 OCTOBER 1810, Macquarie could report to Castlereagh's replacement, the Earl of Liverpool,[78] that there was a fair prospect of a good and plentiful grain harvest, that horned cattle and sheep were 'fast increasing', and that the general state of the colony was 'prosperous and improving'. Several new schools had been established, and there had been 'a very apparent change for the better in the religious tendencies and morals' of the population.[79] The turnpike road and bridges from Sydney to the Hawkesbury, 65 kilometres northwest, were well under way and the stone and gravel turnpike road to Parramatta, 28 kilometres west, was just about complete:[80] 10 metres wide, with a ditch on either side to keep it dry.

It was time to get travelling on it.

TWO WEEKS after writing to Liverpool, Macquarie climbed into his carriage behind Joseph Bigge and, with 'Mrs M', Captain Antill, Captain Cleaveland, Dr Redfern, his cousin Ensign John Maclaine and the Acting Surveyor, James Meehan, set off towards the setting sun for what he called 'Governor Macquarie's first Inspection of the Interior of the Colony Commencing on Tuesday the 6th. of Novr. 1810'.[81] Macquarie needed to know the land and its people, but he particularly enjoyed travelling about and naming things (usually after himself), and planning new towns and improvements along the way – an extension of the building work he'd already begun in Sydney. If he couldn't make tours of his beloved Jarvisfield for the time being, he might as well treat New South Wales as his own personal estate.

Trotting along through the bush and scrub on their new expressway, they were at Parramatta's Government House ninety minutes later. They were all up at daybreak the next morning, and at 6 a.m., Macquarie and Elizabeth climbed on horses and headed south, accompanied by Antill and Meehan. They crossed the Georges River by boat, and arrived for breakfast at Moorebank, the property of Thomas Moore[82] and his wife Rachel. A master boatbuilder and a devout Anglican, Moore had become one of the colony's biggest landowners.

After breakfast, the party rowed up river and landed near the house of Thomas Laycock,[83] a former officer of the Rum Corps. Macquarie surveyed the thick forest all around and later noted:

> I determined to erect a township on it and named it Liverpool in honour of the earl of that title – now the Secretary of State for the Colonies. – The Acting Surveyor Mr Meehan was at the same [time] directed to mark out the ground for the town, with a square in the centre thereof, for the purpose of having a church hereafter erected within it.[84]

For the next week, the party based themselves at Moore's house and, over the next week, inspected the farms and fields of wheat in the 'Minto District', down to the 'excellent' St Andrew's farm of Macquarie's friend, Magistrate Andrew Thompson, who had recently died at the Hawkesbury.[85]

They moved on through the wilds of the Banks Town district, 'wandering about in a boundless forest for upwards of three hours without knowing where we were',[86] and then on to Harris's Creek. On subsequent days, there were excursions to the different farms in the districts of the Ponds, Field of Mars, Dundas and Baulkham Hills. They rode to Gregory Blaxland's[87] Brush Farm, at what is now the Sydney suburb of Eastwood, and the nearby One-Tree-Hill property of Samuel Marsden, who gave a 'very good' sermon on the Macquaries' first Sunday away.[88] There was an inspection of the new roadworks to the Hawkesbury, and 'Mrs M' and Eliza Bent accompanied Macquarie in the carriage to Dr Wentworth's farm at Liberty Plains, then to Blaxland's salt pans,[89] at what is now the Silverwater Correctional Complex and which was soon providing Sydney with 8 tonnes of salt a week.

At daybreak on 16 November, Macquarie and Elizabeth headed southwest in Bigge's carriage towards the area known as the Cowpastures, near modern-day Camden. They would be camping under the stars on this leg of the journey, so a sergeant and three troopers joined them from Sydney as guards, along with servants in two carts carrying their Indian canvas tents, for which Macquarie had billed London £550.

They were accompanied by their original party from Government House, and by Blaxland, who was preparing to explore the Nepean River.[90] Governors King and Bligh had regarded the wealthy Blaxland and his brother John as pests who were always making demands, and Macquarie would increasingly agree. But Blaxland was an enterprising and determined man, and he wanted more land.

The countryside from Parramatta to the Nepean was mostly open forest. The governor's party met two or three small parties of the 'Cow Pastures natives – the chief of whom in this part is named Koggie; who with his wife Nantz, and his friends Bootbarrie, Young Bundle, Billy, and their respective wives, came to visit us immediately'.[91] Macquarie and his party camped on 'a beautiful eminence near a lagoon of fine fresh water' near the foot of Mount Taurus, and at dinner, 'Mrs M tho' so young a campaigner' had 'provided every requisite to make our tour easy, pleasant, and happy'.[92]

They placed a guard and fires around the camp as protection against wild cattle, which bellowed through the night.

Blaxland and ex-convict John Warby went out at dawn the next day and shot a wild bull for the servants to eat. Later in the day, the party caught five calves and sent three males home for veal, then watched wild bulls fighting.

They explored Stone Quarry Creek and were visited by Elizabeth Macarthur, who was in the area staying in 'a miserable hut', looking after her farms and 'fine numerous flocks of sheep'.[93] Her husband was still in London, fomenting future trouble for Macquarie in case he ever made it back home to New South Wales.

At Robert Campbell's sheep run at Menangle, the Macquaries were impressed by the friendly Indigenous men, women and children of the area and watched one climb 'a high tree to catch a guanna, which he did in a very dextrous manner'.[94]

On 21 November, they spent six hot hours on horseback before returning to their new headquarters at St Andrews, and Macquarie was afraid the long day in the saddle would 'knock up Mrs M as it is much too long a ride for her in such very hot sultry weather'.[95] The country was superb, however, 'the best and finest' Macquarie had yet seen in the colony. He named the area 'Airds' in honour of his 'dear good Elizabeth's family estate'.[96] Soon there would be a village there called Campbell-Town in honour of her family.

Joseph Bigge, although 'suffering great pain' after being kicked in the shin by a horse, drove them 'with his usual skill and dexterity' back to Parramatta, where they rested for five days, 'both a little indisposed after their late fatigues'.[97]

Soon they were heading to the Evan District, past Prospect Hill, and to South Creek, where Nicholas Bayly's farm impressed them with the neatness of its barn and stockyards. They stopped for breakfast at Blaxland's farm hut, then Macquarie and Blaxland rode on to see James Badgery's farms in the Bringelly district. Nearby was D'Arcy Wentworth's property, and another of Samuel Marsden's farms, Mary O'Connell's Frogmore, and a property belonging to Anna King,[98] the widow of former governor Philip Gidley King, who had died in London two years earlier while fighting the Colonial Office for a pension. Mrs King had 'fine numerous herds of horned cattle, of which she has upwards of 700 head of all descriptions'.[99]

With surveyor George Evans,[100] they moved on to Dr Jamison's farm on the Nepean and, at 5 p.m. on 28 November, launched John Maclaine's boat, which they called the *Discovery*, to explore a magnificent waterway a mile wide and very deep, with banks that were 'almost perpendicular, not being less than 400 feet in height and wooded to their very summits'.[101] The next day, they spent four hours rowing around the waterway and took a picnic breakfast to drink in the scenery.

One of the local natives told Macquarie the place was called Warragamba.[102]

Macquarie's group then moved north towards the Hawkesbury, passing a 'long extensive chain of farms along the Nepean belonging to Appledore, Westmore, Collett, Stanyard, Pickering, Field, Stephen Smith, Jones, Cheshire, Harris, Guy, Wm. Cheshire, Landrine, Stockfish, Oldwright, Ryan, Griffith, Kennedy etc, being the front line of farms on this river'.[103]

The governor's energy seemed boundless as the new sights and experiences of this new country stimulated him like nothing before. He sometimes rode 60 kilometres a day, making notes at night and imagining building towns where there was now virgin forest.

From the confluence of the Nepean and Grose Rivers, Macquarie and 'Mrs M' proceeded again in the carriage to the 'Yellow-Mundie-Lagoon, a noble lake of fine fresh water'. They mounted horses to explore the heights of Richmond Hill, the Kurrajong Brush and Richmond Terrace, but Macquarie had to send his horse Cato back after he hurt his leg crossing a river.

They visited the farm Belmont on the Hawkesbury, where Maria Bell was waiting for her husband Archibald,[104] a former Rum Corps lieutenant, to return from George Johnston's trial in London. They found plenty of wild raspberries on Kurrajong Hill, but they were without any flavour and not worth eating, and the descent was 'so very steep' that they 'had great difficulty' staying on their horses. Leeches attacked their mounts and made them fret, and 'Mrs M had two or three of them on her ankles at one time'.[105]

It was a relief to hit the area called Richmond Terrace, running parallel with the Hawkesbury for about 5 kilometres and 'commanding a very rich and beautiful prospect of the low grounds on each side' of the river, 'now looking very rich, being covered with luxuriant crops of wheat'. They crossed the river on the late Andrew Thompson's barge, while the horses swam across for 400 metres, and that night, the Macquaries slept in the government cottage on a 'sweet delightful spot'.[106]

On 6 December, Macquarie celebrated the end of the tour with a dinner for twenty-one guests, including Simeon Lord and Thomas Moore. All the time he had been travelling, he had been planning new settlements:

> After dinner I christened the new townships, drinking a bumper to the success of each. I gave the name of Windsor to the town intended to be erected in the District of the Green Hills, in continuation of the present village, from the similarity of this situation to that of the same name in England; the township in the Richmond District I have named Richmond ... the township for the Evan or Nepean District I have named Castlereagh in honour of Lord Viscount Castlereagh; the township of the Nelson District I have named Pitt-Town in honour of the immortal memory of the late great William Pitt, the minister who originally planned this colony; and the township for the Phillip District; on the north or left bank of the Hawkesbury, I have named *Wilberforce* – in honour of and out of respect to the good and virtuous Wm. Wilberforce Esqr. M.P. – a true patriot and the real friend of mankind.[107]

Soon, he was giving James Meehan detailed instructions for the laying out of the new towns, setting a regular width of 66 feet for the streets and telling him to find 'a square space of ground containing 396 feet on each side for the purpose of erecting a church, a school house, a gaol and guard house and ... 2 acres of ground on the rear of the central square for a burial ground'.[108]

MACQUARIE CELEBRATED HIS FIRST twelve months in Sydney by taking to the harbour on New Year's Day 1811 in a new barge named after Elizabeth, and reading a 'very handsome flattering address' presented to him by a committee of citizens.[109]

Soon, though, he was back visiting the sites for his new townships. Macquarie had planned Richmond 'on the most eligible and convenient spot of ground that could be found in the whole country', getting Nicholas Bayly to relinquish about 60 hectares in return for 120 hectares elsewhere.[110]

At Windsor, he gave former convict Richard Fitzgerald a large allotment in the square named after Andrew Thompson, 'on the express condition of his building immediately thereon a handsome commodious inn – of brick or stone – and to be at least two stories high'.[111] The inn is still known as the Macquarie Arms.

On 31 January 1811, back at Government House in Sydney, Macquarie hosted a public dinner for the officers of the 73rd and their ladies to celebrate his fiftieth birthday. That night, Elizabeth continued the celebrations by hosting a concert for him around her grand piano.[112]

After a year of triumph and tragedy in their new home, Mr and Mrs Macquarie made beautiful music together.

Chapter 20

NOVEMBER 1810 TO MAY 1812, NEW SOUTH WALES
AND VAN DIEMEN'S LAND

*My poor dear Elizabeth has suffered a great deal from sea sickness
during the storm and from the violent motion of the vessel – but she
makes a most excellent brave sailor, never expressing the
least fear or apprehension of danger.*

MACQUARIE ON HIS FIRST VOYAGE TO VAN DIEMEN'S LAND, AS ALWAYS,
IN AWE OF HIS WIFE'S COURAGE[1]

ALL ALONG THE FORESHORES of the pretty village
that was Hobart Town, the population of the remote outpost
cheered as the barge powered up the Derwent River under the
power of its well-muscled oarsmen. It was carrying Lachlan and
Elizabeth Macquarie, on their first visit to the governor's southern
territory of Van Diemen's Land.

The river looked to be at least 3 kilometres wide, the lofty hills
surrounding the glistening water were grand and picturesque,
and there was a magnificent mountain in the distance standing
sentinel. The colonial brig at anchor, the *Favorite*, unleased a salute
of cannon fire, and another echoed from the guns on parade near
Government House.

Twelve months after braving the wilds of Banks Town and
Baulkham Hills, Macquarie was investigating the potential of the

wild land separated from the rest of New South Wales by what he called 'Bass's Straits'.[2]

Macquarie's mother had died in November 1810, on the day the governor, 'Mrs M' and a party of attendants had been rowing around the Nepean at Warragamba, looking for the most 'beautiful romantic spot'[3] to have their breakfast. He did not hear of the 'most afflicting and distressing' news of Margaret Macquarie's passing, though, until the arrival of the September 1811 mail. Charles had gone to Mull for a short leave of absence from his 42nd Regiment just before their mother died, and he had conveyed the melancholy news to Macquarie in a heartfelt letter.

For most of his adult life, Macquarie had supported his mother financially, and though they were separated by great oceans and thousands of kilometres, she had always lived close by within his heart. He deeply lamented the loss of this 'most beloved and deservedly revered dear good and amiable' parent:

She breathed her last on the evening of the 29th. of Novr. last, at her own house at Oskamull at the advanced age of eighty-two, esteemed, beloved and respected by all who knew her. She was interred at Kilvickewen and buried in the same grave with her husband and three sons on the 5th. of December 1810, with every mark of honour and respect – her funeral being attended by all the gentlemen, & 125 of the commoners of Ulva & the neighbouring country, and her own dear good son Charles, and her nephew Lochbuy, presiding at and arranging everything relative to her funeral.[4]

Macquarie comforted himself that she was 'now in the blessed regions of the good & virtuous tho' we must ever deplore our loss of her!'[5]

The same mail ship brought better news, though, from the British parliamentarian and anti-slavery campaigner William Wilberforce, whom Macquarie had honoured with the naming of the town in the Hawkesbury region. Wilberforce assured

Macquarie that his campaign to promote marriage and 'the domestic virtues' would be an enormous benefit, and 'that attention to ye religious and moral state of ye colony would in a few years produce improvement which men could scarcely anticipate'.[6]

By 1811, Macquarie reported that New South Wales was in a state of 'the utmost peace and tranquillity'.[7]

Hobart Town, Port Dalrymple and Norfolk Island had never had it so good either, and the country at large was 'in a progressive state of improvement', the people 'becoming more temperate and more religious', and as a result, they were 'making considerable progress in the cultivation of their lands … taking much greater pleasure in honest industry' than before.[8]

Not that everyone saw it that way. There was trouble even in paradise.

The *Sydney Gazette* reported a crime at Windsor's Thompson Square 'which every sense of manhood should revolt from, with detestation':

A person (for a man I cannot call him) of the name of Ralph Malkins, led his lawful wife into our streets on the 28nd ultimo, with a rope round her neck, and publicly exposed her for sale; and, shameful to be told, another fellow, equally contemptible, called Thomas Quire, actually purchased and paid for her on the spot, sixteen pounds in money, and some yards of cloth. I am sorry to add, that the woman herself was so devoid of those feelings which are justly deemed the most valuable in her sex, [that she] agreed to the base traffic, and went off with the purchaser, significantly hinting, that she had no doubt her new possessor would make her a better husband than the wretch she then parted from.[9]

A bench of three magistrates 'sentenced this "no-man" to receive 50 lashes, and be put to hard labour in irons, in the gaol gang in Sydney for the space of three calendar months; and the woman to be transported to the Coal River for an indefinite time'.[10]

IN EARLY MAY 1811, Macquarie and 'Mrs M' were in Windsor naming streets, and watching boards with those names painted on them going up all over the village. They then moved on to Parramatta, where Macquarie named the main streets – George, Pitt, Phillip, Macquarie (of course) – as well as Church Street and Marsden Street, even though the Reverend Samuel Marsden was a continual headache to him, and there was every sign that the pain was only going to get worse.

On 29 May, Macquarie and Elizabeth made another three-day visit to Parramatta and, 'commiserating the unhappy condition of persons labouring under the affliction of mental derangement', Macquarie ordered that an asylum be built at the remote Castle Hill agricultural settlement, about 12 kilometres north of Parramatta, so that patients could be 'accordingly removed from their former place of confinement, which was in the town gaol at Parramatta'.[11]

He arranged for a two-storey sandstone granary, 30 metres by 8 metres, to be modified as the Castle Hill Lunatic Asylum, the first institution in Australia specifically designed to care for the mentally ill. As the *Sydney Gazette* reported, Macquarie instructed that 'every provision that humanity could suggest ... be made for their accommodation and comfort'.[12]

Macquarie wanted to be all things to all people. In February 1811, he directed that magistrate Alex Riley[13] take 'every possible pains ... to come at the facts, and strictly to redress the grievance' in the first documented case of an Indigenous man bringing a civil action to an Australian court. The case revolved around a dispute over a sea voyage to Van Diemen's Land. It was dismissed, but the *Gazette* noted: 'The care bestowed in the foregoing enquiry is satisfactory of the determination of government to afford every protection and support to the natives ... and particularly to encourage them to useful industry by requiring a scrupulous observance of every contract in which they may be interested'.[14]

Only a few weeks earlier, at the birthday celebrations for Queen Charlotte, the ballroom at Government House had featured as its centrepiece a painting of Indigenous men 'earnestly anticipating the blessing of civilization, while a striking full-sized figure, drawn

The abandoned village of Ormaig on the isle of Ulva, Macquarie's likely birthplace, with Mull in the background. *Sheila L Tough*

Moy House and Moy Castle, Lochbuie, Mull, seat of the ancient clan Maclaine. The patronage provided by Macquarie's uncle, the 18th chief, Murdoch Maclaine, offered an escape from a hard life of Hebridean poverty. *Alamy*

A kilted warrior from Clan MacQuarrie. Originally published in Robert Ronald McIan's *The Clans of The Scottish Highlands*, published in London by Ackermann and Co., 1845.

Fort Edward, Nova Scotia, circa 1900. Macquarie was posted here as a teenage soldier protecting Britain's maritime provinces from American rebels. From left to right: the blockhouse (fortification), officers' quarters, and soldiers' barracks. Only the blockhouse remains today. *Alamy*

Above: Tipu Sultan by an anonymous Indian
artist in Mysore, c 1790–1800.

Left: An Indian soldier of Tipu Sultan's army
using his rocket as a flagstaff. These were the
first iron-cased rockets successfully deployed
for military use. *Victoria and Albert Museum*

'The coming-on of the monsoons; – or – the retreat from Seringapatam'. Cartoon by James Gillray, published 6 December 1791. This retreat dashed the hopes of a young Macquarie for the 'laurels, fame, honour, riches and promotion' he expected to follow a successful attack on Tipu Sultan's great fortress.
National Portrait Gallery, London

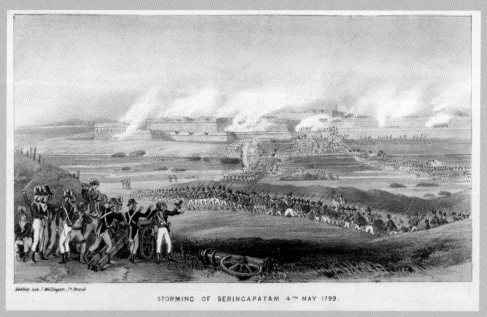

STORMING OF SERINGAPATAM 4TH MAY 1799.

More than seven years later, Macquarie had the satisfaction of witnessing the final defeat of Tipu Sultan. The storming of Seringapatam in May 1799 enabled Britain to take control of southern India with no serious opposition remaining. Hand-coloured lithograph, c 1800. *State Library of New South Wales*

Above: A British officer reading a book in an enclosed palanquin carried by Indian bearers – a preferred means of transport for Macquarie during his years in India. Unsigned watercolour c 1830. *Brown University Library*

Left: Jane Jarvis, date and artist unknown. *State Library of New South Wales*

Plate six from J M Gonsalves' 'Views at Bombay', 1833. The southern entrance of the Apollo Gate is close to St Andrew's Church, or the 'Scotch Church', shown on the left here. The yellow building at the centre is Admiralty House, where Macquarie lived for a time at the invitation of the Commander in Chief of the Indian Fleet. *British Library*

The arrest of Governor Bligh, Australia's famous first cartoon, or first example of political propaganda. *State Library of New South Wales*

Convict uprising at Castle Hill, 1804. Major Johnston with Quartermaster Laycock and twenty-five privates of the New South Wales Corps defeat two hundred and sixty-six armed rebels, 4 March 1804. Artist unknown. *National Library of Australia*

'View of the Town of Sydney in the Colony of New South Wales', c 1802 (after Thomas Watling, artist unknown). This was Sydney as Macquarie found it – a modest settlement wracked by corruption, coups and rebellion. *Art Gallery of South Australia*

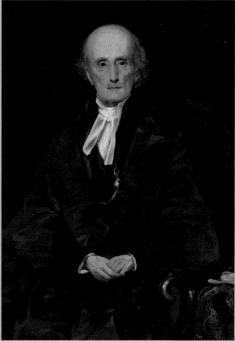

Brothers Ellis Bent (l) and Jeffery Hart Bent (r). Both clashed regularly with Macquarie over the application of the law in New South Wales. *National Library of Australia*

South-west view of Hobart Town, 1819, watercolour by George William Evans.
State Library of New South Wales

Hyde Park Barracks – one of Francis Greenway's finest designs. *Shutterstock*

The extravagant, castellated Fort Macquarie built where the Sydney Opera House now stands. A visitor in 1819 remarked, 'No one could tell us what the governor had in mind when he built it'. Drawn by Robert Russell, 1836. *State Library of New South Wales*

Elizabeth Macquarie, c 1819
State Library of New South Wales

Elizabeth and Lachlan's great joy, Lachlan
Macquarie Jr, c 1818.
State Library of New South Wales

First Government House, Sydney, c. 1807. Watercolour by John Eyre. *State Library of New South Wales*

A portrait of Governor Macquarie painted towards the end of his tenure by the colony's finest portrait painter, former convict, Richard Read Sr. *State Library of New South Wales*

The 'holey dollar' and 'dump' – Macquarie's ingenious solution to the colony's currency crisis. *State Library of New South Wales*

View of the government hut at Cowpastures (Camden area), 1804. At the time, this was at the hotly disputed frontier of white settlement. *State Library of New South Wales*

'The Plains', Bathurst by John Lewin, 1815, just two years after Blaxland, Lawson and Wentworth found a route across the Blue Mountains. *State Library of New South Wales*

Portrait of William Bligh, 1814.
National Library of Australia

Bligh's fiery daughter, Mary. For a time she was the first lady of the settlement, c 1805.
State Library of New South Wales

One of Macquarie's several nemeses, 'the flogging parson', Samuel Marsden, depicted in 1833.

Convict turned tycoon, Simeon Lord, c 1830.
State Library of New South Wales

Pugnacious British
lieutenant and wool
pioneer, John Macarthur,
artist and date unknown.
State Library of
New South Wales

A romanticised painting by Joseph Lycett of Macarthur's Elizabeth Farm viewed from the northern
riverbank of Parramatta River. *State Library of New South Wales*

'Fight between aborigines and mounted whites'. Samuel Calvert 1828–1913, date unknown.
State Library of New South Wales

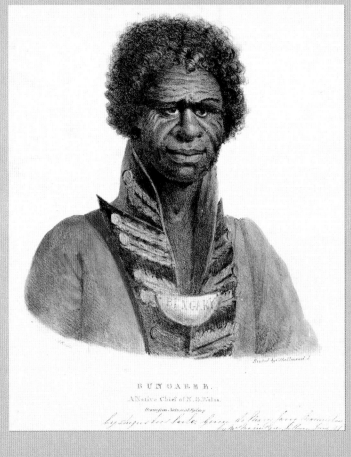

Bungaree was a Kuringgai man from the Broken Bay area north of Sydney. He circumnavigated Australia on the *Investigator* with Matthew Flinders. Later, going against the Aboriginal system of selecting elders, Macquarie appointed him as the 'Chief of the Broken Bay Tribe'. Portrait by Augustus Earle, c 1826.
State Library of New South Wales

Commissioner John Bigge, who arrived in Sydney in 1819 as Commissioner of Inquiry into the Colony of New South Wales. Macquarie's initial expectations that Bigge could not fail to see the merits of his administration were soon dashed. Portrait from 1819.
State Library of New South Wales

Macquarie Mausoleum on Mull, where he rests with his wife Elizabeth and his children Jane and Lachlan Jr. *CC BY-SA 4.0 / Gunther Tschuch*

in one of the most animated attitudes of the corrobori, pointed with his waddy at the Church of St. Philip … symbolical of the Christian religion inviting them to happiness'.[15]

THE FLOURISHING NEW settlements around Sydney Cove were a source for celebration, and the vice-regal couple continued to hold the best parties in the colony.

There were seventy-two guests at their dinner on 4 June to celebrate the king's seventy-third birthday at the 'new dining room or "great saloon"' in Government House.[16] Macquarie received letters from his old military commanders, Robert Abercromby and James Balfour, who told him that hopes were still entertained of 'His Majesty's recovery from the mental illness with which he had been for some time past afflicted'.[17]

Government House had the best view of the harbour in the settlement, and the waterway was teeming with life. One afternoon, the crew on the ship *Cato* harpooned a black whale upwards of 11 metres long near Pinchgut Island. They estimated that the great sea creature was only about two years old and 'would yield about 35 barrels of oil, valued at £45 per ton'.[18]

The following month came news that, although Macquarie had been pushing to become a brigadier, he had at least been promoted to colonel as of 25 July 1810. He also received word that Charles was now a lieutenant-colonel.

Macquarie visited Samuel Marsden's new Water Mill on the Toongabbie Creek[19] and went on an inspection tour of Parramatta's Female Factory, which had just received thirty-eight new prisoners fresh off the boat.[20]

The two-storey building, which housed male prisoners on the ground floor, had been commissioned by Governor King and the convict women began working there in 1804, producing cloth in linen and wool. Something would have to be done about the overcrowding, with as many as 200 women and children confined in a place that could house only sixty at night.

Elizabeth again presented the Ladies Cup to the winner of the 1811 Sydney racing carnival, this time held in August.

Maurice O'Connell's three-year-old Carlo romped home from Ellis Bent's chestnut gelding Match'em, but the disgruntled judge-advocate claimed the horse had suffered bloating from being given green feed in what was the first doping scandal of the Australian turf scene.

While the 1810 races had been a celebration of all that was good about the young town of Sydney and the enthusiasm of its new ruler, there was a darker air by 1811. In one trackside dispute, Macquarie's secretary J.T. Campbell shot and severely wounded Captain John Ritchie, the winner of the 1810 Ladies' Cup, in a duel.[21] It seemed Campbell's mood had not been improved by a recent grant of 800 hectares for a stud at Bringelly.

THERE WAS STILL an air of malevolence swirling around Sydney when, on 4 November 1811, Macquarie set sail for Van Diemen's Land with Elizabeth, Antill, John Maclaine and James Meehan on the brig *Lady Nelson,* commanded by Bryan Overhand. Macquarie thought Elizabeth deserved great praise for her 'taste and judgment' in making their quarters neat and comfortable, but a storm followed their little boat all the way south, and Macquarie was in for even rougher weather as governor.

The *Lady Nelson* pulled into Jervis Bay, 200 kilometres south of Sydney, but the passengers had to delay their breakfast because they were all seasick.

They walked on the dazzling white beach, picking up shells and pebbles. Three Aboriginal people, 'very stout well-made good-looking men' who 'seemed perfectly at their ease and void of fear', approached in canoes with fish, which they eagerly bartered for biscuits and tobacco. Overhand and his crew caught fish that looked like salmon, as well as many young sharks and, the next day, more Aboriginal men in canoes arrived, trying to communicate and understand the English words. One of the fishermen came on board and was intrigued to have his beard shaved off.

They continued on, but a week into the voyage, the *Lady Nelson* was battered by horrific storms that lasted three days. The travellers couldn't cook, and were forced to eat 'very common fare' while sitting on the floor like animals.[22]

Macquarie later recalled that their 'tight little bark … swam on the top of those terrific billows like a feather and surmounted all the dangers that threatened her',[23] but Elizabeth, despite her stoicism, became violently ill in weather 'which was enough to alarm most landsmen in so very small a vessel'. Overhand told Macquarie it was 'one of the worst and most violent gales he ever experienced'.[24]

The furious weather made repeated attacks throughout the voyage, but finally, after nineteen days of battling the wind and wild seas, the Macquaries were rowed up the Derwent to a grand reception in Hobart Town. Even if they had to stay in a pretty little cottage because Government House was 'much out of repair',[25] it was a relief to be on solid land at last, as the cannon salutes echoed across the Derwent and into the grand vistas behind the town. The troops prepared large celebratory bonfires, around which the colonists, soldiers and convicts sang and danced until dawn.[26]

Macquarie wanted to see as much of the island as he could. He went out to New Town and named the prettiest spot looking down the Derwent 'Macquarie Point'.[27] In the New Norfolk area, 35 kilometres northwest of Hobart, he named the site of a village Elizabethtown.[28] He rode and walked through 'beautiful picturesque company', inspected the farms of Sandy Bay then rode to the top of Mount Nelson,[29] where he ordered the immediate erection of a flagstaff and signal station.

He organised Hobart into a square, surrounded by seven main streets, chief among them being Macquarie Street (of course). Then there were Liverpool, Elizabeth, Argyle, Harrington, Collins and Murray Streets – the last named after Captain John Murray, the Commandant of Hobart Town. Later, there was Antill Street as well. He planned out new barracks, new hospitals and a new jail.

In a collective address at being allowed to draw rations from the king's stores, the 'inhabitants of New Norfolk' told Macquarie that their gratitude 'shall never be effaced from our memories and our children shall be instructed, as soon as their articulation commences, to lisp the name of Governor Macquarie'.[30]

That name was going to be remembered in other places, too, the way Macquarie was doling it out. In the first week of December, after a military parade down Hobart's Macquarie Street, he and his party set out on a 200-kilometre journey north. They were heading for the village of Launceston, about 40 kilometres southeast of Port Dalrymple, which was on the mouth of the Tamar River. Macquarie made notes of the places he named along the way.

There was a picturesque area over Constitution Hill, north of Hobart, that he called Glenforsa after Charles's Scottish estate, then they passed through Elizabeth Valley before stopping at what would thereafter be known as Governor Macquarie's Resting Place. There was Table Mountain, a name drawn from his time in Cape Town, Mount Dromedary, named after the ship that had brought him from England, Ben Lomond, which reminded him of the mountain in Scotland, and Jericho and the River Jordan, inspired by his time in the Middle East. Then they passed through Macquarie Springs, the Meehan Valley, York Plains and Antill Ponds.

Port Dalrymple (York Town), painted by J.W. Lewin in 1808. State Library of NSW

Mount Henrietta was a nod to Mrs M's middle name. Then there were the Argyle Plains that stretched to the banks of the Macquarie River, Mount Campbell, named after Mrs M's family, the Maclaine Plains, the Antill Plains, the Elizabeth River, which flowed through the Macquarie Plains, the Gordon Plains, the Henrietta Plains and the Corra-Linn Cascade, named after a cave in Lanarkshire that had once been a refuge for William Wallace, 'the patriot chief of Scotland', as Macquarie called him.[31]

Late on the afternoon of 8 December 1811, they took in a 'wild romantic view' before reaching Launceston, where the commandant, Major George Alexander Gordon, had the troops formed up, then a nineteen-gun salute echoed over the water as it cascaded through the area's river gorges:[32]

> The grand view, and noble picturesque landscape that presented themselves on our first coming in sight of Launceston and the three rivers, and fertile plains and lofty mountains by which they are bounded, were highly gratifying and truly sublime; and equal in point of beauty to anything I have ever seen in any country.[33]

Macquarie resolved to move the settlement of Port Dalrymple and make the village of George Town on the York Cove the principal town in northern Van Diemen's Land. On the night of 18 December 1811, he and Elizabeth slept in a tent on what he envisaged would be the 'future scite' of the town square.[34] The next day, he had two boards with 'GEORGE TOWN' painted on them and nailed to conspicuous trees, and marked out the places for a government house, government domain and government wharf, public stores and a granary.

That would be the last work done there for a while, because as Macquarie, Mrs M and their party boarded the *Lady Nelson*, which had sailed up from Hobart to join them, the wind was about to be knocked from his sails, as London baulked at his expenditure.

Still, Christmas was celebrated in Bass Strait with fine food and some grog for the sailors in honour of what Macquarie called 'this holy and sacred day!'[35]

Macquarie decided to extend his voyage of discovery and explore other areas of his command. So, on 30 December, they sailed past the Sydney Heads and headed for Port Stephens, 200 kilometres to the north, where four Aboriginal men, 'stout, tall, well-made people',[36] came on board from two canoes to sample Macquarie's biscuits. He named Elizabeth Island, called another Inchkenneth after an island near Mull, and called yet another Meredith after Mrs M's favourite friend, Henrietta Meredith.

The countryside around Port Stephens was not promising for a settlement, so Macquarie sailed back to Newcastle, 40 kilometres south, and journeyed 30 kilometres up 'Hunter's River'. With Newcastle's commandant, Lieutenant Thomas Skottowe, he inspected the troops, convicts, the hospital and barracks as well as the government flocks and herds, the coal mines and lime kilns. He marked the occasion with a holiday on Saturday, 4 January 1812, and ordered that the convicts be exempted from labour during the whole of the day, and that extra rations of beef be given to both the soldiers and convicts. He told the *Sydney Gazette* that he:

> ... was much gratified to find that this useful settlement, already furnishing the colony with cedar, coals and lime, also promises from the fertility of the soil higher up the river, to provide for the increasing population of the country, being fit for the purposes of agriculture and grazing.[37]

THE MACQUARIES ARRIVED back in Sydney on 6 January 1812 after a tour of just over two months, to find that Maurice O'Connell had assumed the caretaker role with 'zeal'.[38] Macquarie immediately sent surveyor George Evans off in the *Lady Nelson* to further explore the shores of Jervis Bay then take a small party on foot across rugged bushland to Appin, opening up the lush Illawarra district for farming. Evans would impress Macquarie with his 'tenacity' during an arduous journey, and he would be working overtime in the years ahead.

Less than two weeks after Macquarie's return from Newcastle, another 199 convicts arrived in Sydney Cove with a detachment of the 73rd,[39] and so did Maurice Charles O'Connell junior. Macquarie stood as the godfather when the baby was christened by the Reverend Marsden.[40] The son of the lieutenant-governor and grandson of Captain Bligh would later forge a great political career.[41]

THE JANUARY MAILS of 1812 brought the news that Macquarie's mentor Governor Jonathan Duncan had died the previous August, and that another old friend, Major-General Sir Samuel Auchmuty, had taken Java for the British after storming the Dutch garrison there.[42] But Macquarie and Elizabeth had their own battles at home.

On 22 April 1812, with his 'dearest Elizabeth' feeling poorly, Macquarie had a long conversation with Dr Redfern and was told that she was most likely pregnant. Macquarie noted 'the circumstance of her not having a return of her usual femenine complaint for six weeks past, it being this day six weeks she was last attacked with it – and being now five weeks and two days in perfect good health and free from a return of the complaint alluded to'. Redfern recommended that Elizabeth 'should take no exercise in the carriage or on horseback' and 'keep herself as quiet – and as free from any fear or alarm as possible'.[43]

Ten days later, she was still in pain, and a week later, experienced a 'considerable discharge' after getting out of bed at 7 a.m. She had abdominal pains and a 'good deal of fever'. Macquarie noted she 'continued extremely unwell' for three days, until finally 'she passed a small foetus with a large quantity of thick dark coagulated blood, and thus unhappily miscarried'.[44]

Her agony was not yet over. 'In the forenoon she passed what is called "the after Birth" – a large mass of coagulated blood, which gave her great pain and left her very weak ... this is no less than five miscarriages that poor Mrs M has had since the birth of our angelic dear baby Jane Jarvis whom we had the misfortune to lose at Perth.'[45]

But personal tragedy would soon be mingled with deep professional anxiety.

BRITAIN'S WAR WITH NAPOLEON was far more important to the London bureaucracy than Macquarie's grand vision for a penal colony at the other end of the world. The invoices Macquarie was sending home and his plans for infrastructure in his five new settlements raised serious alarm in Downing Street, where every farthing was being directed to stopping the French from crossing the English Channel.

In May 1812, Liverpool unloaded on the governor, demanding to know what game he was playing. Under Macquarie's watch, the burden of New South Wales upon the mother country had so dramatically increased that the Prince Regent wanted 'a more satisfactory explanation' of the 'unusual expenditure' he had sanctioned.[46]

Why had he racked up bills of £72,600 6s 10¼d in 1810, when under Governor King's watch, less than £14,000 had been spent in total? Even Bligh had billed the Crown for only £31,100 during his brief reign. If 1810 wasn't bad enough, from 1 January to 12 March 1811, Macquarie had asked his superiors to fork out £21,214 11s 8¾d. The spending had to stop, Liverpool ordered:

> I am to repeat to you the positive commands of his Royal Highness that while you remain in charge of the Colony of New South Wales you use the most unremitting exertions to reduce the expense at least within its former limits, that you undertake no public buildings or works of any description without having the previous sanction of His Majesty's Government for the construction …[47]

Macquarie's job, Liverpool said, was *relieving* the mother country of a substantial financial burden in running the colony, not adding to it! Macquarie was to provide much greater detail in his revenue statements every quarter. If free settlers – who were to receive the benefits of such things – were not able to finance quays, wharfs, roads and bridges, then they didn't deserve them.[48]

Liverpool had bought the two new brigs Macquarie wanted to replace the *Porpoise*, but he warned that Macquarie should not make him regret it. And what was that 'unauthorized charge of £551 10s 7d for camp equipage' and Indian tents for his expedition to the interior all about?[49]

But the biggest problem, Liverpool said, was this bizarre scheme to let contractors import 45,000 gallons of rum in exchange for building a hospital.

'I am surprised that you did not see the embarrassment which would inevitably be occasioned in the execution of this contract,' Liverpool thundered in ink, adding, 'It would have been advisable that engagement of this kind have not been entered into, until you had an opportunity of learning the sentiments of His Majesty's Government.'

Macquarie had proposed the free importation of rum under a high duty, but Britain's Privy Council for Trade had already issued licences to British traders to land large quantities of liquor in the colony under the same plan. There would be a lot of angry merchants when they found out what Macquarie had done, with the potential for outrageous oversupply and slashed prices. All that was now on the governor's head, too.[50]

Getting a regal kick up the backside had not been in Macquarie's job description when he became governor, and Liverpool's 'severe censure' caused him 'sincere sorrow and mortification'.[51] It had caught him totally off guard.

Rather than a rebuke, Macquarie told Liverpool he had been expecting 'nothing short of your Lordship's highest commendations', because the scheme was so 'advantageous to government'.[52]

He told Liverpool that, 'without the least apprehension or fear of contradiction', he could safely say that no governor 'here or in any other of His Majesty's colonies' had been 'more rigidly vigilant and watchful in the public expenditure'. He *was* a Scot, after all.

The 'apparent great increase of expense' had been unavoidable, he continued, because of 'imperious necessity'. There had been a revolution against Bligh and stores had been diminished by the rebel regime. The place had been in a state of decay when he arrived, with the convicts almost naked and more arriving all the time.[53]

Not only was New South Wales seen by London as a dumping ground for convicts, Macquarie complained, but it was also a refuge for 'a most troublesome and useless set of persons', namely, anyone looking to escape 'troublesome connections' at home by fleeing to Sydney to sponge off the colonial government. 'They imagine,' Macquarie told Liverpool, 'that they have done His Majesty's Government so very great a favour by coming to New South Wales, that no expense on behalf of the Crown can repay the obligation.'[54]

Macquarie complained that he had had to spend money to ward off famine while, at the same time, opening up the colony for pasture and cultivation.

'I believe I may also say without vanity and with great truth that I have already done more for the … improvement of the manners, morals, industry and religion of its inhabitants, than my three last predecessors, during the several years they governed it.'[55]

Macquarie sent off his reply, hopeful that his forceful arguments would win the day.

As it turned out, the war with Liverpool would soon end in quite an unexpected way. But other bitter battles would rise up to take its place.

Chapter 21

MAY TO DECEMBER 1812, NEW SOUTH WALES

What the governor's motive can be I cannot conceive. He issues public orders in favour of morality, while he appoints men magistrates whose general conduct and example militate as much as possible against it.

THE REV SAMUEL MARSDEN, AGHAST AT SEEING FORMER CONVICTS SIT IN JUDGMENT UNDER MACQUARIE'S RULE[1]

THE PRIME MINISTER of Great Britain, Spencer Perceval,[2] hurried towards the lobby of the House of Commons: small, slight, pale and with the bright, sharp, shining eyes of a bird. Powdered wigs and knee-breeches were going out of style, but Perceval, dressed entirely in black, hung on to the old ways as one of a dying breed.

His favourite moments were spent with his twelve children,[3] not under piles of correspondence and official orders, but in May 1812, the business of government took all his attention. The Luddites were busy destroying industrial machinery in their fight for better work conditions, and King George III was drowning in dementia. The French were causing mayhem in Spain and about to push towards Russia. Perceval was a man with too much work and too little time.

As the forty-nine year old statesman entered the House of Commons lobby, the morose John Bellingham, a merchant with a long-standing grudge against the government over a compensation claim, stepped forward, drew a short-barrelled .50 calibre pistol from inside his coat and shot Perceval in the chest.

'Oh my God, murder,' the Prime Minister exclaimed, a few minutes before he was pronounced dead.[4] Bellingham sat down on a bench and waited quietly to be arrested.

Perceval was buried at St Luke's Church in Charlton, London, on 16 May, and Bellingham, refusing to enter a plea of insanity, was publicly hanged in front of Newgate Prison two days later. His penis 'seemed to be in a state of semi erection',[5] and his skull was preserved in the Pathology Museum at London's St Bartholomew's Hospital for study by phrenologists, who believed that the shape of a skull could determine a person's character.

Perceval had not been an especially popular prime minister, and while the mandatory eulogies were delivered and a monument erected here and there, afterwards, it was business as usual in the halls of government.

At least the only assassination ever of a British prime minister got Lord Liverpool off Macquarie's back, however, because Liverpool became the new British leader and Earl Bathurst[6] replaced him as Secretary of State for War and the Colonies. Bathurst had a more relaxed manner than the ever-demanding Liverpool and Macquarie was able to breathe more easily over his accounts, even if the treasury still demanded that he watch their pennies.

THE NEWS of Perceval's assassination arrived in Macquarie's October 1812 mail delivery. With it came the distressing news that his sister's son, Hugh Maclaine, once part of Macquarie's bogus regimental commission scam, had finally made captain on his own merits, only to have his leg shot off in the Siege of Ciudad Rodrigo in Spain, when Arthur Wellesley's Anglo-Portuguese Army attacked the city's French garrison. Betty had already lost her son Hector to war, but Macquarie knew she would be comforted by the news that Hugh was 'likely to live and do well' despite his grave wounds.[7]

Macquarie opened a third envelope to find that his promotion to brigadier-general had come through. His joy was immense.

The poor boy from Mull was now a general in the British army and governor of a territory that seemed as big as Europe. But it would take more than a higher rank to help Macquarie fend off the attacks from the elite of New South Wales society, angered by his egalitarian ways.

MACQUARIE SURMISED that the most virtuous men and women of the colony would agree with his new 'meritocracy', and that the only objections would come from the 'malcontents' who, from Governor Phillip's time, had been nothing but 'burthen and turmoil'.[8]

Yet it was these 'malcontents' who often had the loudest voices. The appointment of former convicts to important colonial positions soon stirred up a bubbling stew of discontent.

Bathurst warned Macquarie that for the conservative elements of New South Wales society, the admission of convicts to the upper echelons would be the 'main point of resistance'. He highlighted 'the necessity of not compromising your authority by exerting it on the subject where resistance may be so well cloaked under a rigid sense of virtue or a refinement of moral feeling'. It would be useless, Bathurst counselled, trying to compel people to associate with those whom they disliked or despised. If Macquarie wanted to bring convicts into the upper ranks, he 'should trust to the gradual effect'.[9]

Macquarie's proposal to appoint former convicts as magistrates sparked particular fury among the establishment. Yet he assured Bathurst that 'to the high and important duties of the magistracy, I shall be particularly cautious not to advance any person, who shall not appear to me fully and respectably qualified'. He agreed that there were certainly 'some illiberal men' in 'this country, who would destine a fellow creature, who had once deflected from the path of virtue, to an eternal badge of infamy', regardless of the veil they had subsequently thrown over past errors. In the eyes of such persons, Macquarie said, 'no reform, no amendment however sincere, will be admitted as sufficient for this purpose. I am happy in feeling a spirit of charity in me, which shall ever make me despise such unjust and illiberal sentiments'. Macquarie despaired that most of the bigotry was to be 'found in the higher class, where more enlightened and liberal sentiment might have been reasonably expected to be cherished'.[10]

Joseph Arnold noted that much of Sydney was preoccupied with turning up its collective nose at these convicts-made-good, while being only too happy to do business with them. The rise of the late Andrew Thompson had been galling to the establishment:

> Some of the convicts, (their time having expired) are now very rich. Mr [Andrew] Thompson who was sent here for theft twenty years ago has elegant town and country houses, several thousand acres of cultivated land, and employs three hundred men year-round on his estates. Mr [Simeon] Lord (formerly a horse stealer) has built a house which he lives in that cost £20,000; but still these men are despised and any free settler would not deign to sit at their tables.[11]

Andrew Thompson,[12] a Scot from Kirk Yetholm in the Scottish border region, had been sent out to New South Wales for the theft of £10 worth of cloth, but had subsequently built a fortune from land acquisitions and from his five ships. For many years, he had also been the colony's chief constable.[13] Macquarie had considered him 'an excellent worthy man'[14] and had made him a magistrate.[15]

Yorkshireman Simeon Lord had also been transported for stealing cloth worth 10 pence[16] (not horses, as Arnold suggested), but as a merchant and trader, he had built a home in Sydney that made Macquarie's abode look like a cottage.[17] Macquarie made him and D'Arcy Wentworth magistrates, too, authorising them to sit in judgment on men who were once their jailers. Showing that he was very much a man of the people, Macquarie and 'Mrs M' were the honoured guests at the Bachelor's Ball, held at Lord's mansion. It marked the first time a governor had been entertained by a former convict.[18]

Lieutenant Archibald Bell, from the Hawkesbury, would later assert that the governor and his wife were kind to people whom others regarded as 'tainted, unfit for associating with', and that the Macquaries had the 'evident desire of introducing them with marked esteem to other visitors'.[19] Some would rise from the governor's dining table rather than break bread with ex-convicts.

Bell believed the Macquaries even showed favouritism to these 'undesirables', and complained that Elizabeth Macquarie once walked straight past him at Government House, though he was in the full uniform of his regiment, to shake the hand of a former prisoner. Macquarie countered this by declaring that Elizabeth showed 'as much kindness towards those persons as their good conduct can justify',[20] and that he had never forced any unconvicted person to associate with convicts or former convicts if they chose not to.

The Reverend Samuel Marsden, in particular, begged to differ.

Marsden was a dour Yorkshireman, the son of a blacksmith, with a fiery zeal for the gospel that matched his volatile temper, but often with a marked lack of charity. He had come to Australia in 1794 as assistant to the Reverend Richard Johnson under the blessing of William Wilberforce and came to see himself as the moral voice of the colony. By the time Macquarie had arrived in Sydney, Marsden had already been a resident for sixteen years and also possessed over 1000 hectares of land and more than 1000 sheep. Only John Macarthur had more stock.

In 1808, Marsden had his own wool made into a suit by the Thompsons of Horsforth in Yorkshire, and George III, during a moment of sanity, was so impressed that he gave him some merinos from his Windsor stud. Marsden would send more than 1800 kilograms of wool to England on the *Admiral Gambier* in 1812, and sell it all at a single trade.[21]

In February 1810, Marsden returned from London to discover that he had been appointed to Macquarie's board controlling the new Parramatta turnpike road, alongside Simeon Lord and Andrew Thompson. Marsden was furious. He saw wealthy emancipists such as Lord and Thompson only as rich riff-raff and accused Macquarie of trying to 'raise one class of the community and to lower the other, and to bring bond and free more upon one common level'.[22] He declared that the role was a 'degradation of his office as Senior Chaplain of the colony' and 'totally incompatible' with his sacred functions.[23]

Macquarie appointed D'Arcy Wentworth to the post instead, irrespective of the cloud hanging over those unsolved armed robberies. Marsden then claimed that Macquarie was 'possessed of sovereign power, and accustomed to being implicitly obeyed'. Macquarie told the chaplain that he would not forget this 'act of hostility to his government' and that, if he had been a soldier, rather than a civil servant, he would have had Marsden court-martialled.[24]

Marsden complained to the Archbishop of Canterbury and wrote to William Wilberforce to say that it was not consistent with 'morality, religion or sound policy' to have magistrates who had been convicts and who 'were still living in open profligacy'. He claimed that 'My refusal to act with persons whom the governor has appointed magistrate, gave great offence; my own conscience tells me I did right; and I have not repented, though perhaps I may feel the effects of my refusal in one way or other, while the governor remains in the colony.'[25]

Marsden was a hard marker. In 1806, he had started a New South Wales 'female muster' that only recognised women wed within the Church of England as legitimately married; most others were classed as concubines and their children as illegitimate.[26] He declared that Lord and Thompson were immoral men, both living with women though unwed. He pointed out that the circumstances of Lord's domestic life 'were very notorious in the colony',[27] and that the *Sydney Gazette* had investigated allegations that he had tried 'to seduce two of the girls of the orphan school at Sydney ... although these animadversions did not positively charge him with the crime'.[28]

None of the other magistrates in New South Wales objected to sitting beside Lord, though in later years, Judge Barron Field[29] would say that Lord appeared to be a man 'who would never pay anybody if he could help it and would take every advantage of a tradesman'.[30]

Macquarie argued that Lord's personality was so pleasing that, while aboard the convict transport vessel the *Atlantic* in 1791, 'he had received the most humane and indulgent treatment and almost paternal kindness'[31] from the skipper. After eighteen months' servitude, he had been employed as an assistant in the government stores, serving there for the rest of his sentence, 'in a manner highly satisfactory to his superiors'. By what Macquarie called 'his own exertions and economy', Lord had built two houses and cultivated about 4000 square metres of ground, raising pigs and poultry and engaging occasionally in trade. Even before the expiration of his sentence, he had 'property to the amount of several hundred pounds'.[32]

In time, Lord had bought 'a commodious house and warehouses', become an auctioneer and commission agent, and commenced business 'on a more extensive scale as a merchant and shipowner'. He was now a boon rather than burden to the colony. His ships were employed in procuring oil, sealskins, fish, sea cumber, pearl shells, sandalwood 'and other articles of export to the mother country and the East Indies, while the benefits derived by the settlers from his speculation, which opened a vent for their produce, for which there was otherwise no market, were by no means inconsiderable'.[33]

Thompson was also an exemplary member of society, Macquarie argued, if for no other reason than because he had risked life and limb 'over three successive days and nights', saving the lives and property of settlers inundated by the floodwaters of the Hawkesbury in 1806 and 1809.[34]

Macquarie told his critics that, since Thompson had been transported to the colony in 1792, every governor of New South Wales had put him in a position of trust and, when Macquarie arrived in Sydney, he had found 'Mr Thompson to be what he always has been, a man ever ready and willing to promote the public service'.[35]

Macquarie had made him a magistrate in recognition of both his merits and the fact that Macquarie could find no one else qualified, though he said that Thompson had already been doing the work of a magistrate for eight years.

He told Marsden and the other 'exclusives', who claimed Thompson made moonshine liquor on Scotland Island, north of Sydney,[36] that they had it all wrong. He had always found Thompson a 'sober, industrious and enterprising man', who had built several vessels for hunting seals and who over the last eight years of his life had employed from 80 to 120 men, and had up to 80 hectares under cultivation as well as hundreds of hectares for grazing.

When he had been convicted, Thompson's 'respectable' Scottish family had 'discarded' him, but Thompson 'felt so much gratitude for being restored to the society he had once forfeited,' Macquarie said, 'that in his will he bequeathed to me one fourth of his fortune'.[37]

Did he, now? This last detail would give Macquarie's enemies ammunition for years.

Thompson died suddenly on 22 October 1810 after catching a 'severe cold', and his friend Francis Williams arrived in Sydney soon afterwards to tell Macquarie that he had been left a quarter share of Thompson's estate, reckoned to be as much as £25,000. Macquarie regarded this gift as 'a most extraordinary instance of friendship & gratitude!'[38] He erected a tombstone over Thompson's Hawkesbury grave,[39] almost as wordy as that over Jane's in Bombay, extolling the 'generosity of his nature in assisting his fellow creatures'.[40]

When Thompson's creditors were paid, Macquarie's share of the estate only amounted to £500, still a princely sum for the time, and which caused Macquarie to remark: 'Poor man, he intended well'.

JOHN MACARTHUR had been Andrew Thompson's mortal enemy. Following the 1806 floods, Macarthur had demanded that Thompson pay him £341 for a supply of grain: ten times the normal price.[41] Bligh, who had employed Thompson to run his land on the Hawkesbury, had dismissed the writ.

While Macarthur's contacts in London were helping him avoid being brought to trial for his part in Bligh's downfall, he was spending much of his time gnashing his teeth over Macquarie's reign. The news that Macquarie had made Thompson a pillar of his administration sent Macarthur into a spin.

He wrote to his wife Elizabeth, lamenting that Macquarie was bringing men to the table 'who have been convicts, who have amassed fortunes by the most infamous frauds and have and continue to set the most shameful examples of dissoluteness and vice'.[42]

He did not mourn Thompson's passing, and certainly did not share the Macquaries' assessment of their 'good and most lamented departed friend'.[43] To him, Thompson's death was the 'interposition of Providence to save the colony from utter ruin'.[44]

> Never was there a more artful or a greater knave. How — how could Governor and Mrs Macquarie be imposed upon as they have been? I think the last stroke of leaving the governor part of his property is by far the deepest he ever attempted, whether I view it as an act done in contemplation of Death, or in expectation of raising himself to higher favour should he live.[45]

Macarthur thought about pulling his family out of New South Wales for a brief moment, telling Elizabeth: 'God alone knows how such a state of things as you describe may terminate, or how operate upon our affairs. Would to God I could withdraw you from the colony.'[46] Yet he knew that in England they would 'not find it very easy to realise an annual income of £1300 or 1400'.[47] In London, Macarthur fumed over the new governor's reign and thought about ways to bring him undone when he got the chance.

Macquarie's prospects were looking a lot better, though, on the other side of the world.

IN FEBRUARY 1812, a select committee of the House of Commons began sitting to discuss the viability of continuing to transport convicts, and to assess Macquarie's rule. Among those giving evidence and opinions about the penal colony were Matthew Flinders and former governors John Hunter and William Bligh.

Twenty-four years on from the First Fleet's landing, the prospects of 'New Holland' still seemed bleak, since the continent appeared largely uninhabitable beyond the narrow eastern coastal fringe. But at least Macquarie seemed to be doing a good job. His ideas on reformation and reward seemed noble, and he appeared to be a kind man with a firm grip on power. When his 'liberal views' had time to operate, the committee decided, 'the best effects are to be expected'.[48] His was already a significant improvement on previous regimes, with the committee finding:

> In the distribution of female convicts great abuses have formerly prevailed; they were indiscriminately given to such of the inhabitants as demanded them, and were in general received rather as prostitutes than as servants; and so far from being induced to reform themselves, the disgraceful manner in which they were disposed of, operated as an encouragement to general depravity of manners ... Governor Macquarie is directing his endeavours under orders from the government here, 'to keep the female convicts separate till they can properly be distributed among the inhabitants, in such manner as they may best derive the advantages of industry and good character'.[49]

Macquarie had advised London that 'as many male convicts as possible should be sent' to New South Wales, 'the prosperity of the country depending on the numbers; whilst, on the contrary, female convicts are as great a drawback as the others are beneficial'.[50]

The committee could not 'accede' to this. While, in many instances, the women were 'likely to whet and to encourage the vices of the men ... such women as these were the mothers of the great part of the inhabitants now existing in the colony, and from this stock only can a reasonable hope be held out of rapid increase to the population'.[51]

Macquarie was asked to take measures to ensure convict women could return to Britain after finishing their sentences if they so desired, without prostituting themselves on the ships to pay for their fare.[52] Writing to Bathurst in June 1813, Macquarie thought that, if the committee had known how rough some of the convict women were, they would have done everything they could to keep them away.[53]

Macquarie was much more agreeable to the idea of permitting a 'regular distillation of spirits to be established in this colony', and considered that it would improve the colony beyond any measure, though Bathurst demurred.[54] There was some to-and-fro over introducing a jury system to the courts, with Bathurst worried that there would not be enough free settlers for jury duty.

Macquarie told Bathurst that reformation of the convicts was his main priority, even if many settlers opposed the concept. It remained 'for His Majesty's Government' to consider whether they were more interested in pleasing 'free persons' coming to settle in New South Wales, or in constructing a system to 'hold out the greatest possible rewards to the convicts for reformation of manners', so that when redemption had been earned, they were 'entitled to the rights and privileges of a citizen, who has never come under the sentence of transportation'.[55]

Macquarie argued that no country in the world had been 'so advantageous to adventurers as New South Wales', and while many of the free settlers recoiled at the thought of welcoming convicts back into society, among them were a 'few liberal minded persons ... who did not wish to keep those unfortunate persons forever in a state of degradation'.[56]

Macquarie had managed to defend his program of emancipation. The minister and the Colonial Office were backing him and, as he and Elizabeth took their seats in church on Sundays and the convicts doffed their caps in respect to his authority and appreciation of a second chance, Macquarie could see the potential for greatness all around him.

A massive hailstorm hit Sydney on 7 November 1812, the stones more than 5 centimetres in diameter, but Macquarie could see sunny days ahead. On 18 December 1812, he made a special note that he and Elizabeth had slept the first night in their new bedroom, noting the occasion with an exclamation mark.

Like the prospects offered by the new bedroom, the colony's potential seemed limitless. And three intrepid explorers were about to find a priceless treasure that seemed to go on forever.[57]

Chapter 22

MAY TO NOVEMBER 1813, NEW SOUTH WALES

Mrs M felt the child, she is now pregnant of, quicken for the first time … and it has ever since continued very lively!!!

MACQUARIE'S UNBRIDLED JOY AT THE PROSPECT OF BECOMING A
FATHER AT THE AGE OF FIFTY-THREE[1]

THE BLUE MOUNTAINS LOOMED in the distance in all their colossal glory. In the morning sunlight, the miles upon miles of eucalypts, stretching outwards and upwards in a great wall, emitted a soft blue-grey haze over the rugged peaks.

On the morning of Tuesday, 11 May 1813, Gregory Blaxland, D'Arcy Wentworth's son William and Lieutenant William Lawson[2] of the 73rd Regiment set out from Blaxland's South Creek farm[3] on a journey of discovery and conquest. With them were five dogs, four packhorses 'laden with provisions, ammunition, and other necessaries'[4] and four servants, including a guide, James Burns,[5] who would have to wait six months for a £10 reward.[6] Ahead of them were huge sheer cliffs, deep gorges, thick scrub, fast-flowing rivers and high waterfalls that, as far as anyone could prove, had been more than a match for every European adventurer trying to reach the vast inland sea said to lie beyond.[7]

The convicts transported to Sydney were caught in a vast natural jail. There was the limitless Pacific Ocean to the east, the

Hawkesbury and Port Hacking Rivers, respectively, to the north and south, and the foreboding mountains to the west, rising up like a giant prison wall.

A First Fleet convict named John Wilson[8] had become a skilled bushman by living with Aboriginal people in the Hawkesbury district, and claimed to have travelled 100 miles (160 kilometres) from Sydney in every direction, including across the Blue Mountains.[9] He couldn't prove it, but judging by the descriptions he gave, he might have been telling the truth.

George Caley,[10] Joseph Banks's plant collector, made repeated trips into the mountains but never found what was on the other side, while Francis Barrallier,[11] aide-de-camp to Governor King, led two expeditions into the foothills of the mountains, but only that far, in 1802. He discovered Burragorang Valley, southwest of Sydney, but a large waterfall stopped him from travelling further.

Blaxland, Lawson and Wentworth resolved not to turn back until they had crossed the entire range.

Thirty-four year old Blaxland was a man of some wealth and social standing, who owned property in Kent. He was a family friend of Joseph Banks, and it was Banks who had persuaded Blaxland and his older brother John to emigrate, telling them of the prospect of great treasures in the vast south land.

Blaxland had arrived in Sydney on the *William Pitt* in 1806 with his wife, three children, two servants, an overseer, a few sheep, seed, bees, tools, groceries and clothing.[12] He had sold many of his goods at great profit, bought eighty head of cattle, put them on 1619 hectares of land at his South Creek farm and been given forty convict servants. Soon afterwards, he bought the 180-hectare Brush Farm from D'Arcy Wentworth for £1500. Blaxland had already made vain attempts to cross the mountains to find new pastureland for his sheep, only to be thwarted by the rugged landscape. This time, he was determined to find a way through.

Aged thirty-nine, William Lawson was a Londoner born of Scottish parents who had trained as a surveyor before he arrived in Sydney in 1800. He had spent six years on Norfolk Island and been the commandant at Newcastle. He now owned 150 hectares at Concord and another 200 at Prospect, and had just returned from giving evidence in England at Colonel Johnston's court-martial, where Johnston was lucky to escape the noose.[13]

Born on a convict ship, William Wentworth was the offspring of D'Arcy and a prisoner named Catherine Crowley, who had been convicted at the Staffordshire Assizes in July 1788 of feloniously stealing 'wearing apparel'. William's father had sent him to England for an education and he had returned to the colony in 1810. When young Wentworth was not riding winners at Hyde Park, he was a young man going places. Macquarie had made him Acting Provost-Marshal – the head of the military police – and presented him with 700 hectares at Camden between the Nepean River and Bringelly Creek.

Young Wentworth called his new estate Vermont.[14]

When Blaxland first approached Macquarie about their expedition in early 1813, the governor had been 'reserved'. Macquarie was more interested in helping small-scale farmers get a foothold on the aspirational ladder than in doling out more huge land grants from what might lie beyond that great blue-grey barrier.

Ever the diplomat, Macquarie had the tact to avoid unnecessary frictions. But men like Blaxland and his brother John – one of Macarthur's sidekicks in the overthrow of Bligh – were 'among the most discontented persons in the colony', who always had their hands out.[15] And at the start of 1813, Macquarie had a lot more on his mind than Blaxland's venture.

THE VIOLENT HAILSTORM that hit Sydney in November 1812 had heralded the arrival, later in the month, of the leaky and creaking[16] HMS *Samarang* from Madras. It brought with it 40,000 Spanish dollars in coins, worth £10,000, which Macquarie would use to create the colony's first currency of its own. But the *Samarang* also brought with it its own tempest.

Macquarie had a convicted forger named William Henshall cut the centres out of the coins and counter-stamp them, which made them worthless outside the colony. The central plug, known as a dump, was valued at 15 pence and was stamped with a crown on one side and the denomination on the other. The 'holey dollar' received an over-stamp around the hole that said 'New South Wales 1813' on one side and 'Five Shillings' on the reverse. The combined value in New South Wales of the holey dollar and the dump was 6 shillings and threepence, or 25 per cent more than the value of a Spanish dollar, making it unprofitable to export them from the colony.

Converting the 40,000 Spanish coins took more than a year. Of the 40,000 Spanish dollars imported, 39,910 holey dollars and 39,910 dumps were made. Ninety of the coins were ruined during the conversion process. On 1 July 1813, Governor Macquarie issued a proclamation 'that the said Silver Money shall be a legal Tender'. The coins went into circulation in 1814.

While the new currency was a godsend for the colony, Captain William Case of the *Samarang* and his crew were a constant headache, like boozy neighbours who had suddenly moved in next door, upsetting the ordered world Macquarie was creating with behaviour that was 'highly irregular and improper'.[17]

In terms of arrogance, Captain Case made Captain Bligh look wishy-washy. Over the Christmas period of 1812, when Sydney turned out its best festive decorations, Case allowed his men 'to ramble about the streets', bringing their grog with them in defiance of the law, 'thus greatly disturbing the peace and tranquillity of the town'.[18]

For the next few months, the sound of breaking glass and the whack of fence palings mingled with a cacophony that was already starting to plague Sydney. For some time, the dog population was exploding and the *Gazette* said that 'the evident increase of the canine race', made 'it now almost impossible for a stranger to enter within a gateway without undergoing the discipline of a mixed group of kangarooers [kangaroo dogs], curs, and terriers, to the great solacement of some, who can find amusement in the terrors which their four-footed favourites are capable of exciting'.[19]

IN THEIR NEW YEAR'S ADDRESS 'To His Excellency Brigadier General Macquarie', the citizens praised a morally upright leader who had 'braved all personal danger and dispensed with every comfort in visiting the most remote parts' of the colony.[20]

How could they not laud him 'when we behold the daily increasing beauty and improvement of our metropolis'?[21] He had brought about the 'improvement and construction of roads ... the great abundance of provisions, both animal and vegetable, an abundance rendering future supplies from the mother country unnecessary'.[22] There was wool on its way to England, as well as meats for the Royal Navy, shipped in casks made of local wood.

But the collective colonists also wondered how the holey dollars would impact on their trade, and what they could do with all the leftover produce. They wanted Macquarie to support an expansion of colonial trade, something at odds with Britain's exclusive support of its own merchants and the East India Company, a policy that had prompted Bathurst to threaten that it would be cheaper to import wheat and corn from Calcutta than support agriculture in New South Wales.[23]

The colonists wanted Macquarie to petition London for their own distillery, an idea he supported, but something London would definitely be against, given the money being made by British traders with a monopoly. And 'the daily increasing beauty and improvement' of the Sydney 'metropolis' wasn't something London was interested in either, with constant directions to rein in spending. If the colonists wanted grand buildings and bridges, Macquarie was still supposed to get them to pay for it.

Sitting at his portable writing desk, Macquarie wrote out an appeal to the 'liberal spirit'[24] of the colony's inhabitants to build a new combined town hall and courthouse, with a budget of £4000. He provided £500 in government funds and his own gift of £60 to kickstart the project. But despite their fawning new year's address, the colonists didn't seem interested in stumping up for the rest.

Macquarie told them that 'some of the various suggestions' were likely to be acted on without 'interfering with the interests' of England, but stressed there had to be 'an increased exertion ... by regularity of conduct and industry, to render the colony less burdensome to the mother country'.[25] A committee was formed to outline the colonists' requests to London, chaired by Simeon Lord and including John Blaxland, William Redfern, William Wentworth and the wealthy merchants Robert Jenkins[26] and Samuel Terry,[27] known as the 'Rothschild of Botany Bay'.[28]

Perhaps prompted by gratitude, Jenkins hosted a huge celebration for the third anniversary of the start of Macquarie's reign. He erected a large marquee in the front garden of his George Street home, with lavish displays of flowers and other decorations. Union Jacks flew proudly as the band of the 73rd let loose.

There were almost 150 revellers. A reporter covering the event said the 'company placed themselves promiscuously without respect to rank or difference of condition; and the challenge to "hob or nob" was proffered and accepted with a cordiality that was truly gratifying to the feelings of all present'.

After dinner at 6 p.m., they drank fifteen toasts. The toast to Macquarie was a bumper: 'Governor Macquarie! May the anniversary of his assuming the command of this territory be commemorated and reverenced by our latest posterity!'[29]

Despite the enthusiasm, the approach to London didn't materialise, and while there was a degree of cordiality at the anniversary celebrations, soon the 'exclusives' and the 'emancipists' were again at each other's throats.

SO TOO WERE MACQUARIE and the crusty Captain Case, whose ship was falling apart and whose men were falling over themselves to create mayhem on Sydney's streets. In February 1813, Macquarie spent his fifty-second birthday at Parramatta's repaired Government House[30] but, after the festivities he was soon complaining about Case to the Irish statesman John Wilson Croker, Secretary to the Admiralty. While he had greeted the old sea salt with 'every degree of respect and attention due to a commander of His Majesty's ships of war', he told Croker, the captain and his crew had replied with 'improper and disrespectful conduct' and Macquarie had been forced 'to forego all further intercourse with them'.[31]

Case was acting like a buccaneer. And he had form.

Eleven years earlier, as a lieutenant serving on the sloop *Beaver*, he had been charged with 'running the said vessel on shore through obstinacy, for tyranny and oppression and for having used language to his accuser, scandalous and unbecoming the character of an officer'. The first charge was declared to be frivolous and vexatious; the second was partly, and the third fully, proved.[32]

In Sydney, Case was immediately in a dispute with the harbourmaster Robert Watson[33] over the loading of 6 tons of coal onto his ship. Watson, who had arrived with the First Fleet on HMS *Sirius*, claimed that the crew of Case's *Samarang* were lying about the amount of coal being transferred from the collier *Estramina*, just arrived from Newcastle. Case had the harbourmaster put in irons.

Macquarie was ropeable at 'this disgraceful summary punishment', which was 'as illegal as it was unjust and arbitrary', and considered it 'highly disrespectful and insulting' to him as governor and His Majesty's representative.[34]

Case couldn't have cared less. He was a law unto himself. He sailed for India on 7 January 1813, but was forced to return soon afterwards when the *Samarang* sprung another leak.[35] Macquarie noted that a number of convicts had absconded at the same time, and suspected they had joined Case's crew. Case rebuffed Macquarie's demands to have someone search his boat to look for them,[36] but later coughed up five new sailors who turned out to be the escapees.[37]

One of the crew's servants knocked an ornament off the fence of publican Thomas Clarkson's property in Hunter Street, and was incarcerated in a watch-house for his pains.[38] On 16 March, three of Case's officers bowled up to the watch-house, waylaid the lone constable there 'with very threatening and abusive language'[39] and released the man, then went to Clarkson's house and tore out fence palings to send some more 'ornaments' rolling down the street.[40]

Case laughed it off as 'trifling damage unintentionally done to his fence in a frolic'.[41] Macquarie called the officers' explanations 'evasive and unsatisfactory'.[42] Case said 'see you in court'.[43]

In the end, one of the accused, Lieutenant Butcher, had a brother officer come forward and 'in a very handsome liberal manner'[44] say that it was he who had caused the trouble, introducing so much doubt that action against them all was forced to cease.

But Case wasn't finished yet, and his worst was still to come.

MEANWHILE, MACQUARIE had other worries. At Parramatta in March, he graced 'The first public fair ever held in this territory … with a great show of cattle',[45] but a crime wave had washed over the district, with a spate of livestock thefts from the government that highlighted poor record-keeping by Macquarie's officials. He was forced to dismiss John Jamieson from the post of Principal Superintendent of Government Stock, telling Bathurst that, while he was 'a very honest man', he was 'extremely ignorant and obstinate' and too conceited to take advice.[46] Kent-born George Thomas Palmer,[47] 'a young man of good education, high honour & integrity, active diligent & intelligent', took his place.[48]

The cattle thefts culminated when three members of the Kearns family organised a pair of hitmen to murder an informant in George Street, Parramatta.[49] All five men involved in the crime were hanged.[50]

Meanwhile, the bureaucracy of London was wearing Macquarie down, with the hospital contractors constantly badgering him for more concessions.

It was a sombre, reflective time for the governor on a personal level too. With a heavy heart and a wavering quill, he noted in his diary:

Saty. 1st. May!!!
    Mrs M was taken very ill this morning – and continued so till Wedy. 5th. May, when she had a miscarriage; being the sixth she has had at home & in this country since the birth of our darling little baby!!![51]

ON 11 MAY 1813, six days after Elizabeth miscarried, Blaxland, Lawson and Wentworth crossed the Nepean onto the fertile Emu Plains.[52] At 5 p.m., they set up camp in the shadow of the Blue Mountains to pass the first night of their expedition.

The following morning, the explorers began their climb, passing a large lagoon of good water full of very coarse rushes that now sits in the suburb of Glenbrook.

> The land was covered with scrubby brush-wood, very thick in places, with some trees of ordinary timber, which much incommoded the horses. The greater part of the way, they had deep rocky gullies on each side of their track, and the ridge they followed was very crooked and intricate. In the evening, they encamped at the head of a deep gully, which they had to descend for water; they found but just enough for the night, contained in a hole in the rock, near which they met with a kangaroo, who had just been killed by an eagle.[53]

The explorers had decided to adopt a systematic approach to the climb. They would wait until the morning sun had melted the dew. Then, leaving two servants in camp with the horses and supplies, they would hack or clamber their way through the thick scrub for 6 to 8 kilometres. They would mark the trees on either side of the trail, before turning back and cutting a path for the horses to follow the next day.

It was slow, gruelling work, and sometimes they had to go over the same foreboding scrub three times to make a path wide enough for the animals.

On the third day, 13 May 1813, they found a track marked by a European, with markings cut into tree bark. They spied 'several native huts' in the distance. Some of the horses fell several times under their loads on the rocky terrain, while a kangaroo suffered even more, dragged down and killed by the party's hunting dogs.

It was wet, cold and foggy, but the party kept moving onwards and upwards, cutting through the thick brushwood. They could find no food for the horses but, when they camped on the fifth night, they heard an emu calling continually from the other side of a gully.

The dogs were ruthless, killing two more small kangaroos and eliciting growls from dingoes in the distance as the explorers pressed on in their struggle, up and over the roughest country any of them had experienced. Water was so scarce that they had to fetch it in wooden pales that they hauled up a precipice almost 200 metres high, between modern-day Faulconbridge and Linden. The explorers could get scarcely enough for themselves and their servants, so that the animals had to go thirsty.

On Wednesday 19 May, they reached a high ridge with a clear view of the settlements below: Seven Hills, Windsor, Mount Banks near modern-day Mount Tomah, and Grose Head near modern-day Yellow Rock. They found a heap of stones shaped as a pyramid, which they believed another European had used as a marker. Blaxland thought that it might have been put there by George Bass,[54] though it was more likely John Wilson, or Henry Hacking,[55] the First Fleet quartermaster from HMS *Sirius*, who had also attempted a crossing. The cairn later became known as Caley's Repulse, even though George Caley had not been there.

On the 20th, they covered nearly 8 kilometres, and camped at the head of a swamp situated about midway between modern-day Hazelbrook and Lawson, and where the only fodder for the horses was swamp grass. Near a waterfall they named after Wentworth, they had a fright in the night, which they believed had been caused by marauding Indigenous people, chased away by the dogs.

Two days later, they reached an area of about 800 hectares on top of a ridge, clear of trees and covered with loose stones and short coarse grass, which reminded them of the commons in England. They camped beside a fine stream of water and had a wondrous view of all the settlements and country eastward.

At the Jamison Valley, between modern-day Leura and Katoomba, their progress was halted when they arrived at the edge of an impassable barrier of rock more than 150 metres high, 'which appeared to divide the interior from the coast as with a stone wall, rising perpendicularly out of the side of the mountain'.[56]

Lawson, putting his surveyor's training to use, remarked that the awe-inspiring landscape was 'no doubt ... the remnant of some dreadful earthquake'.[57] Wentworth agreed, stunned that the grand forces of nature had produced countryside both terrifying and sublime: 'A country of so singular a description could in my opinion only have been produced by some mighty convulsion in nature – those immense unconnected perpendicular masses of mountain'.[58]

They gradually worked their way around the great cliffs and passed through what is now Medlow Bath and Blackheath, spellbound by the mists rising from deep within the valleys. On the 26th, they saw fires warming a party of Aboriginal people below, which they counted to include thirty men, women and children.

On the 28th, they made it to the precipice of Mount York and saw a river below, delighted by the view of what looked like fertile country.

On the 29th, they began the dangerous descent through a pass in the rock, about 10 metres wide. The climb down was so steep that the horses stumbled under their loads and the men had to carry the equipment themselves. Blaxland thought that a 'cart road might, however, easily be made by cutting a slanting trench along the side of the mountain'.[59]

They scaled back to the top of Mount York to camp, and the next day, one of the party shot a kangaroo from 'a great distance across a wide valley'. The ground was covered with a thick frost, and 'a leg of the kangaroo was quite frozen'.[60]

They then proceeded down the mountain again, 'through forest land, remarkably well watered, and several open meadows, clear of trees, and covered with high good grass'. They found 'two fine streams of water', what would become known as the River Lett and Cox's River. There were the remains of Aboriginal cooking fires and stones used to sharpen spears.

They camped beside a fine stream of water, probably Lowther Creek, a tributary of Cox's River, at a short distance from a high hill in the shape of a sugarloaf, which would become known as Mount Blaxland.

In the afternoon, they climbed to its summit. Blaxland looked out at the surrounding countryside and thought it would 'support the stock of the colony for the next thirty years'.[61]

The men had not made it as far as the wide Bathurst Plains, but they had seen enough to create great excitement. They had covered 80 kilometres of rugged countryside more than twenty-one days and found undoubted treasure.

When they returned to Sydney the following week, sick and weak, their clothes and shoes tattered, the *Sydney Gazette* trumpeted their discovery of 'a prodigious extent of fine level country … which time may render of importance and utility'.[62] The news item appeared next to a paragraph about a cockfight.

But Macquarie was in no hurry to let prisoners or budding bushrangers know that there was a new avenue of escape to the west. As it was, three convicts soon 'formed the absurd idea of crossing the Blue Mountains, making for the western coast and there building a vessel to take them to the island of Timor'.[63] The escapees crawled through the rugged country for a week, ate their dogs out of desperation, and when recaptured, were sentenced to '300 lashes each, and to work for twelve months in the gaol gang, in irons'.[64]

TWO WEEKS AFTER the *Gazette* celebrated the feat of Blaxland, Lawson and Wentworth in finding a lifeline for the colony, two of Macquarie's lieutenants beat a man to death in Pitt Street.

Lieutenant Philip Connor and Lieutenant Archibald McNaughton, two of the men who had risen from the governor's table rather than eat with former convicts, were arraigned over the killing of William Holness,[65] who had gone to the aid of a damsel in distress.

According to witnesses, McNaughton had been dressed extravagantly in 'coloured clothing' for a night on the town when he came upon a seamstress he knew, named Elizabeth Winch, arm in arm with her beau John Brown, a humble house painter. The haughty McNaughton had pushed Brown aside and grabbed hold of the object of his 'affection'. She begged him not to take liberties with her.

Brown jumped in and told the two drunken officers: 'Gentleman, this young woman has no call to you.' McNaughton replied by hitting him in the neck. Miss Winch ran to the house of her employers, Mr and Mrs Holness, and let Brown in as the two officers hurled abuse and began smashing at the front door with fence palings.

It took every exertion of Brown, Elizabeth Winch and Mrs Ann Holness to keep the two officers from bursting in. Meanwhile, William Holness came home to find a riot on his doorstep. He asked the soldiers to go about their business, because nobody wished to offend them, but using the 'most indecent language', the lieutenants told him what they wanted to do to his wife and the young seamstress.

When Holness asked them not to use that kind of language, McNaughton broke a stick across Holness's back and Connor hit him across the back of the head with a fence paling. Then they both took turns in striking him.

Mrs Holness ran out into the street to help, but realising she could do nothing, screamed out: 'You've murdered my husband!'

As Connor hung his head in shame at what had just happened, McNaughton, replied: 'If he is dead let him die and be damned.'[66]

Macquarie had been pushing for a jury system in local courts but still without success. McNaughton and Connor appeared before the type of court that usually operated in the colony, before Judge-Advocate Ellis Bent and six of the accused's regimental colleagues, including Lieutenant William Lawson, whose feet were still sore.

The military and naval doctors told the court they could find no 'external marks of violence on the body sufficient to occasion death'.[67] Samuel Ross, surgeon of the ship *Fortune*, said Holness had probably died from 'some spasm or faction of the heart', and that the death was more likely 'occasioned by passion than by any blows inflicted on him by the prisoners'.

Ellis Bent pronounced the men not guilty of murder, but still guilty of the serious crime of 'Feloniously killing and slaying the said William Holness'. They were each fined the grand total of a shilling, payable to the king, and ordered to serve six months in Parramatta Gaol.[68]

Macquarie was outraged. He told Bathurst that the circumstances of the case were 'disgraceful'. The pair had 'murdered ... a very peaceable and unoffending man in the lower ranks of life'.[69] The evidence from the victim's widow was crystal-clear, and 'no doubt could have possibly existed of the conviction of the prisoners'. Strong suspicion 'arose against the credibility' of the defence witnesses. Popular sentiment, he regretted to say, was that 'little justice could be expected towards the poor whilst the court consists of brother offices to the prisoners at the bar'. Men who should have been 'prompt and steady of the laws of their country' had become 'the violators of them and the terror of that society'.[70]

> In fact, My Lord, the present construction of our criminal court is such as must necessarily induce a popular, if not a just, feeling against its decisions; especially when as in the present case, some of the members who constitute the court were the intimate friends of the prisoners. And I apprehend that this circumstance will tend to convince all unprejudiced persons that such a court is ill constructed ...[71]

Macquarie told Bathurst the behaviour of the 73rd Regiment over this 'deplorable event' had forced him to petition the Duke of York – back in the role of army commander-in-chief – to pull the 73rd out of New South Wales and to replace it 'with one from home'. He argued that none of the 73rd's officers should be allowed to swap regiments in order to stay either, because it would only 'prolong the evil, they have so much fostered'.[72]

He insisted that no regiment should spend more than three years in the colony, lest they lose sight of their duty and form connections with local women and 'the lowest class of the inhabitants'. Even

Murdoch Maclaine's son John, Macquarie's aide-de-camp, had fallen 11 metres from the masthead of the ship *Eugenia* 'in a state of extreme intoxication', and dislocated his left arm 'in a most shocking and dangerous manner'. It was, Macquarie said, 'the consequence of low drinking and intemperance', and 'this unfortunate young man deserves little pity!'[73]

The 73rd was also riven by internal enmities. Mary O'Connell, Macquarie said, 'had strong feelings of resentment and hatred against all those persons and their families, who were in the least inimical to her father's government', and while O'Connell was 'naturally a very well-disposed man, he allows himself to be a good deal influenced by his wife's strong-rooted prejudices against the old inhabitants of this country who took any active part against Governor Bligh'.[74]

Macquarie's chagrin over the 73rd couldn't stop a perpetual smile from cracking his stoic exterior, however, at some delighted and long-awaited personal news. When he took to his journal, he wrote with a flourish:

Sunday 25 July !!! —
    From present appearances, and from her being quite well and free from her usual monthly complaint since the 25th. of last month, now 30 days, there is some reason to hope that my dearest Elizabeth is pregnant, and that she has now been so for three weeks past! — She is at present in very good health – and may the Almighty Ruler of all events grant that our mutual fervent prayers and most earnest wishes to have offspring may at length be realized – and thereby complete our earthly happiness![75]

MARY O'CONNELL'S 'strong feelings of resentment and hatred' were about to be stirred up all over again by an unwelcome blast from the past.

George Johnston had escaped with his life at his court martial in London in June 1811. Macquarie's old friend David Baird, cranky at the best of times, had been one of the officers sitting in judgment. Johnston had tried to make a case out of the undeclared land grants Bligh had received from the outgoing Governor King, and of Bligh's use of government stock and provisions to improve his own farm. He had also tried to use the governor's bad temper and foul mouth as an excuse for the armed insurrection, and even claimed that Bligh had deserved it because of his cowardly display when he was arrested.

Nothing worked. Johnston was found guilty and was dismissed from the army with dishonour. The rebel leader was fortunate that illness from his war wound had forced Baird off the bench on the final day of the court martial, as the sentence would otherwise have been much more severe. Baird told Macquarie he could see no excuse for Johnston's behaviour.

Unlike David Baird, the Colonial Office had showed Johnston a degree of mercy. After repeated appeals, and with former governor John Hunter, now a vice-admiral, supporting him, the government had decided to reward his long and previously proud history in the force. They gave him a free passage back to New South Wales, ordering Macquarie to treat him as he would 'any other ordinary settler'.

Johnston arrived back in Sydney on 30 May 1813, bringing with him goods and stock for which he had borrowed heavily. Macquarie greeted him as an old comrade from the American War and gave him 600 hectares near Lake Illawarra. Only a little earlier, Macquarie had taken back the 800 hectares at Emu Island that Johnston had granted his son George junior following Bligh's overthrow.

In accordance with Macquarie's edicts on marriage, Johnston married[76] Esther, the former convict lass who had already borne him a large family. He retired to a quiet life away from the drama and turmoil amid which he once burned brightly.

Just two weeks beforehand, Simeon Lord too had married Mary Hyde, the mother of his eight children.

A MONTH after Johnston's return, while Macquarie was still dealing with the fallout from the 'intemperate and disgraceful'[77] conduct of McNaughton and Connor, Captain Case was gearing up for another attack on the besieged governor.

Despite the hostility between the pair, Case wrote a surprisingly pleasant letter to Macquarie on 11 June 1813, telling him that he needed to repair the *Samarang* before taking her back to India, and asking Macquarie to provide naval stores, timber and workmen to make the old ship seaworthy.[78]

Macquarie promised to provide everything that the colony could spare, but Case was soon complaining it wasn't enough. Macquarie replied that he feared Case would 'put the Crown to a very heavy expense in repairing this old decayed ship without ever being able to make her fit for His Majesty's service'.[79]

Macquarie began receiving complaints from 'respectable ship owners and merchants in Sydney that have sustained very severe loss and injury in their trading and shipping concerns from Captain Case's forcibly taking boats, seamen and carpenters from their ships, and private dockyards'.[80]

Macarthur's old partner Garnham Blaxcell, busy constructing the new hospital, was Case's chief target. Case was from the Samuel Marsden school, resentful of any jumped-up convict-made-good who didn't genuflect every time he came near. Case sent a party of armed marines to Blaxcell's shipyard to take by force two carpenters working there on whale boats. Then on 29 July, according to Blaxcell, Case sent an officer and crew alongside Blaxcell's sealing brig, the *Governor Macquarie*, to take the ship's launch by force.[81]

On 8 August, as Blaxcell's little ship, crewed by ten sailors, was leaving Sydney for Tahiti, Case ordered his men to fire a broadside at her for not dipping her colours in deference to his warship. Several musket balls were fired too, one missing a sailor's head by less than a metre. Then Case ordered his men to board the *Governor Macquarie*, brandishing cutlasses and forcing six of Blaxcell's men to join his crew.[82]

Case was furious at Blaxcell's lack of respect for his authority as 'the senior naval officer in New South Wales', angry at him for 'treating the flag with disrespect', and angry that Macquarie's artillerymen at Dawes Point hadn't fired on Blaxcell's ship as well.[83]

Macquarie breathed a heavy sigh of relief when, after another false start on 14 October, Case and his decrepit old tub finally disappeared over the horizon in November on their way back to Madras.

BLAXCELL WAS JUST AS UPSET that his deal to sell spirits had been diluted by the arrival into port of another 120,000 gallons under a licence from the Privy Council for Trade. Yet work on Sydney's 'rum hospital' continued unabated.

On 24 September, Macquarie laid the foundation stone of the Female Orphan School at Parramatta, then continued on another tour of New South Wales, climbing Grose's Head to take in the view, inspecting sites for new schools at Wilberforce and Richmond, and admiring the fertile ground of Emu Island.

On 9 October, the convict transport *Earl Spencer* arrived, bringing 196 male prisoners, but also news that Macquarie had become a major-general; that his brother Charles had married 'Miss Marianne Willison,[84] a highly accomplished young lady, wt. a fortune of £12000';[85] that young Murdoch Maclaine junior had married a daughter of Donald Maclean of Drimnin, and his sister Flora had married Dr Allan Maclaine; and that Elizabeth's beloved aunt, Mrs Campbell of Wigmore Street, London, had died.

But there was much happier news.

Twelve days later, Elizabeth felt the baby growing inside her jump, and it continued doing so 'very lively'.[86]

After half a dozen miscarriages, 'Mr and Mrs M' sat down to a dinner party at Government House on 3 November 1813 to celebrate their sixth wedding anniversary. Macquarie prayed to God that Elizabeth's pregnancy would 'come to maturity and prove fortunate'.[87]

Chapter 23

MARCH TO OCTOBER 1814, NEW SOUTH WALES

*A finer child could not be – being perfect in all his parts & limbs,
a good size, a sweet countenance, and surprizingly strong and
healthy. — Our mutual delight and reciprocal congratulations were
inexpressible, our happiness on Earth being now complete.*
MACQUARIE ON HIS NEW SON, LACHLAN JR[1]

'IT'S A BOY!'[2] exclaimed Dr William Redfern, his long equine face breaking into a rare smile as he held the crying mass of wet, wrinkled flesh aloft like a trophy.

For Macquarie, that pronouncement was the most joyful news he had ever heard. 'A finer child could not be,'[3] he gushed, as his heart soared and tears of pride welled in his fifty-three year old eyes at the cries of his firstborn son and heir.

Over the previous few months, the impending birth of a child to replace their darling infant Jane, dead now five years, had occupied all of Macquarie's waking thoughts and most of his dreams, pushing away all other concerns. In Van Diemen's Land, for one, Lieutenant-Governor Thomas Davey[4] was becoming more and more notorious for his hard drinking,[5] in part to deal with the stresses created by the Yorkshire-born bushranger Michael Howe.[6]

Macquarie wrote that Davey was 'so dissipated in his manners and morals, so expensive in his habits, so very thoughtless and volatile, and so very easily imposed upon by designing plausible characters, that I cannot but think him a very unfit man for so very important a situation as the one he now holds.'[7]

But Macquarie wasn't spending much time worrying about Davey or Howe.

Elizabeth's labour pains began at 3 p.m. on 28 March 1814, as she and Macquarie were taking soup together in the drawing room of Government House. She retired immediately to the Macquaries' grand bedroom, and with her midwife, Mrs Ann Reynolds, by her side, the labour pains continued at short intervals throughout the whole afternoon.

The pangs increased 'very much' six hours later, when they became 'stronger, quicker and more painful'. Redfern had arrived at 11 p.m., and Macquarie had become distressed as Elizabeth 'suffered very much' for the next hour.

But, to the couple's 'infinite joy and delight', Dr Redfern delivered their 'remarkable fine boy' two minutes before midnight.[8] Macquarie would recall that, as soon as Mrs Reynolds had washed and dressed the baby in an adjoining room, she brought him back and placed him in the arms of 'his doating mother and myself'.[9]

After all the years of wondering if syphilis had made him infertile, watching Jane dote on Dorothea's children because she remained childless, then finally becoming a father to Elizabeth only to see his firstborn die and witness another six miscarriages, Macquarie could not contain his pride and joy. His happiness on Earth was now complete, he wrote, and for he and Elizabeth, 'this joyful event was the only thing that was wanting.'[10]

The newest member of the Macquarie family could not have chosen a more inconvenient time to arrive. His parents had planned a large formal banquet to welcome Macquarie's new lieutenant-governor, George Molle,[11] whose commission had been read out that morning.

Molle, who came from an old Scottish landed family and would later have tropical islands named after him, was replacing Maurice O'Connell, now that the 46th Regiment was being shipped in to take the place of the troublesome 73rd. Macquarie had petitioned Bathurst to let his newly married brother Charles come to Sydney as his deputy,[12] but for now, he was happy enough with Molle, an old friend from his campaigns in India and Egypt, who had named his son, born on the voyage to Sydney, William Macquarie Molle.[13]

Thirty-eight people had sat down that night to eat Mrs Ovens's finest dinner, including Maurice and Mary O'Connell, who would soon be heading to Ceylon with the 73rd. The dinner had continued during Elizabeth's labour pains, with Macquarie forced to explain his distractedness and seeing off most of the guests half an hour before the birth.

The O'Connells stayed behind in the spare room to eagerly await the news, and Macquarie sent word to Molle and his wife Catherine of their joy. Macquarie sat up with 'Mrs M and the child' until half past two, when he stumbled blissfully into Elizabeth's dressing room and lay his head down on a pillow to sleep, the happiest man in the world.[14]

Macquarie had not made an entry in his memorandum book for the previous hundred days, but for the next thirty-five, he wrote of nothing else but the joy he and Elizabeth felt at the birth of this exquisite creature, 'being perfect in all his parts and limbs, a good size, a sweet countenance, and surprizingly strong and healthy'.[15]

Not even the news from David Baird that 'Bonaparte is going as fast to the D—l as his greatest enemy could wish'[16] could rouse much interest from this doting dad.

The next morning before breakfast, as Elizabeth showed off the golden child to Catherine Molle and Mary O'Connell,[17] Macquarie began writing notes to share his bliss with friends around the globe, letting them know his new son 'had a fine suck, milk having then flowed freely from his dear mother's breasts',[18] which were sadly becoming 'much swelled and inflamed'.[19]

Soon, however, tragedy loomed. The still-unnamed baby was two weeks old when gripe and phlegm in his throat led to 'frequent severe spasms and difficulty of breathing'. He was 'uneasy in his bowels' and one of his nurses, Mrs Frost, 'observed a visible falling off in his flesh and strength'.[20]

The Macquaries became 'dreadfully alarmed' at their 'beloved babe's appearance and general state of health'.[21] They had already buried one child, and were terrified at the prospect of burying another. With heavy hearts, they wondered whether every moment would be his last.[22]

MACQUARIE'S STRESS WAS OVERWHELMING and his own health was becoming precarious. His teeth were falling out, he had trouble with his bowels because of all the concoctions and potions he had taken for his illnesses since India, and his skin was yellowed by frequent fevers. His workload was heavy and the responsibilities enormous.

An abundance of produce was breeding complacency and waste. Macquarie had been able to drop the price of wheat at government stores from 10 to 8 shillings per bushel (25 kilograms), but with no other market for it and no distillery for the excess grain, many farmers were becoming 'indifferent' about their crops.[23] This in turn led to shameful, unnecessary shortages.

When the March rains did not arrive as expected, Macquarie feared that a famine would sweep the colony. He issued strict instructions to stop the colonists from spurning 'the blessings Providence had thrown in their way'.[24] The feeding of grain to dogs, pigs and cattle was prohibited; pigs should be killed quickly and cured to end the problem of feeding them; 'useless and unnecessary dogs' were to be destroyed; farmers should thatch their stacks of grain; and anyone with land was urged to promptly plant turnips, potatoes and French beans, and keep cabbage stalks in the ground, because the shoots would be valuable in times of need. Rations were to be given half in wheat and half in maize, and until the next harvest, there was to be a weekly allowance for each person of as much bread as could be made from a gallon of maize and a gallon of wheat.[25]

By August, New South Wales was in a state of severe drought. Ponds and rivers had dried up. Much of the grain crop had perished, and much of the other vegetation had withered.[26] Dead lambs dotted the paddocks and cattle perished in great numbers in the mud, on the 'exhausted borders of their usual watering places'.[27] Macquarie estimated that farmers could only glean 8 bushels of grain from an acre when they had once expected 24.

Macquarie lamented to Bathurst:

> Owing to the lazy negligence of the lower orders of the settlers, and their inexcusable and profuse waste of grain, in their feeding not only their horses and cows with it but also their pigs and dogs, there is now a great scarcity induced, and I am concerned that the quantity in the country will with great difficulty subsist the inhabitants until the next harvest.[28]

On 12 October, a desperate Macquarie wrote to the Governor of Bengal for an urgent shipment of 250 tons of wheat,[29] even though Bengal wheat was of an inferior quality and almost always full of weevils.

The situation worsened over the hot dry Christmas period as grain growers held out for better prices, even though the king's stores had become empty.

In one of his regular proclamations – this one to be read in all churches[30] to shame the tardy into action – Macquarie expressed his 'great regret' over 'the reluctance of the settlers in general throughout this colony in coming forward to supply His Majesty's stores with grain in the present alarming season of scarcity':

> ... instead of manifesting a due sense of gratitude for the repeated favours and indulgencies they have received from government, they seem determined to take every advantage of its necessities, by withholding their tenders to as late a period as possible, to give them an opportunity of exacting a most exorbitant price for their grain ... those who are in opulent circumstances, principally owing to the assistance they have derived from the bounty of government in originally granting them lands, stock, provisions, and government men to cultivate their grounds, ought to have

been the first to come forward at such a season to supply government with such grain as they could conveniently spare at a reasonable and moderate price.[31]

He offered 15 shillings per bushel of wheat and 9 shillings for maize.[32] Macquarie undergirded his offer with a threat: if the growers did not help the colony, he would buy all his wheat from overseas, where it sold for half the price of the going rate in New South Wales.

WHILE MACQUARIE had not previously been keen to publicise the successful crossing of the Blue Mountains, he now admitted to Bathurst that the drought had forced him to make an effort to find country 'where possibly nature might be more bountiful than in the present circumscribed limits of this colony'.[33]

On 19 November 1813, the colony's assistant-surveyor George Evans began a two-month tour to retrace the steps of Blaxland, Lawson and Wentworth, and prepare to build a road over the mountains. With him were convicts James Cooghan, John Grover and John Tygh, and free settlers Richard Lewis and James Burns, who had been part of the team for the first crossing six months earlier.[34]

Burns struggled to find the right track on the first day, and theirs was a wet journey through rain and fog, much of it over hard, slippery granite in which it was dangerous to travel at anything more than a walk.[35] Then they found open country, with 'the finest grass and intermixed with the white daisey as in England'.[36] They saw a fast-flowing stream teeming with food and called it Fish River, and they cut logs to form the first bridge west of the Blue Mountains to cross the raging Campbell. Evans gazed upon 'the handsomest country I ever saw … good and beautiful' and named one part Macquarie Plains and the other O'Connell Plains.[37] Then they followed the Campbell until it reached another river, and Evans called that the Macquarie. They camped beside it, on a site that would become the city of Bathurst.[38]

Macquarie sent Earl Bathurst samples of the pebbles and minerals Evans had collected on the tour, as well as pieces of timber. He reported that Evans had discovered 'a beautiful and champain country of very considerable extent and great fertility, thro' which a river of large size, abounding in large and very fine fish, takes a westward course'. He was confident that the region 'at no distant period' would 'prove a source of infinite benefit to this colony'.[39]

THE YEAR 1814 STARTED violently in Sydney. On 8 January, the *Sydney Gazette*, under a headline 'Pugilism', provided a report on the first known boxing contest in Australia, which had taken place the previous day 'in a field on the road to Botany, about half a mile from the Race Course'.

The two pugilists, convicts John Parton, aka John Berringer, and Charles Sefton, had both escaped the noose in England for minor thefts. The two of them had arrived in Sydney on 11 June 1813 with 198 other prisoners aboard the convict ship *Fortune* for the term of their natural lives. Berringer was 'about 20 and standing near 5 feet 9 [175 centimetres]' while Sefton 'was about 30, and about 5 feet 7 [170 centimetres]'.

The *Gazette* reported:

They set to with equal spirit and confidence (Sefton possessing greater skill but his adversary greater activity, and a longer reach), in a ring formed by a multitude of spectators, which was not less than 30 feet [9 metres] diameter. They fought two hours, and had upwards of 50 rounds, being timed to half minutes, so that out of two hours there was a full hour and a half of hard fighting ... Within the few last rounds Sefton's strength had observably declined much more than that of his adversary.[40]

Berringer won in the fifty-sixth round. Sefton lost several teeth and was unable to see out of his eyes, which were swollen from the blows of his younger rival.

TWO MONTHS LATER, a hailstorm assaulted Sydney with such force that almost every pane of glass in the town was smashed. To Macquarie, Sydney looked like it had been blown apart by an enormous explosion of gunpowder.[41] He warned London that he had 200 boxes of window glass on order, and that there would be other big, unavoidable expenses, too.

While the road to Windsor had now been completed, the Sydney–Liverpool turnpike was still not finished and Macquarie had grand plans for the road across the Blue Mountains to the land of milk and honey beyond. He estimated that it would take three months to build and need fifty convict labourers.[42] Toll roads would help defray some of the costs.

However, not all of Macquarie's improvements were costly. The convict transport *General Hewitt* had arrived in Sydney on 7 February, carrying seventy soldiers of the 46th Regiment and 266 male convicts, including the convicted forger Francis Greenway. Most of the prisoners were in 'a weak and sickly state', and another thirty-four had perished on the voyage,[43] mostly from contagious dysentery.

Horrified, Macquarie asked Dr Redfern to file a report on the sanitary problems of the convict ships. This report would eventually lead to a vast improvement in conditions, including the appointment of a medical officer for each voyage.

On 6 April, the same ship, exorcised of the stench of death, sailed for Ceylon bearing Maurice and Mary O'Connell and the 73rd. Even though he had always been cordial to him and his wife, Macquarie was glad to see O'Connell leave, considering him possessed of 'an irritable temper and overbearing disposition',[44] and there had not been much peace with Mary bearing a grudge against so many people in town.

MACQUARIE CERTAINLY WISHED that 'Mad Tom' Davey,[45] his alcoholic deputy in Van Diemen's Land, had left with the O'Connells.

A First Fleeter, Davey had returned to Britain late in 1792 and fought as an officer of the Royal Marines at the Battle of Trafalgar.[46]

Macquarie had been pushing for his brother Charles or Foveaux to replace David Collins after he died in March 1810, but Davey had received the position through the backing of his patron Lord Harrowby,[47] a prominent politician. Macquarie had used a series of commandants at Hobart until Davey arrived.

Henry Goulburn,[48] the Under-Secretary of State for War and the Colonies, wasn't a fan of the new man, however and wrote to Macquarie to warn him about Davey's character. Davey owed a considerable sum for debts contracted as a paymaster of the marines, and his salary as lieutenant-governor was being garnisheed until the money was paid back.[49]

Davey was three years older than Macquarie but hardly acted his age. He had arrived in Sydney in October 1812, but his baggage, in another ship, had been captured by an American privateer. He had shown the governor an 'extraordinary degree of frivolity and low buffoonery',[50] and Macquarie feared that, with 'no superior to control him', he would 'altogether lose sight of that manly and dignified deportment, which his rank in the service, his present high authority, and his advanced time of life should have all alike induced him to support'.[51]

Davey was granted 1200 hectares before he assumed government, but before he sailed for Hobart in early 1813, Macquarie warned him:

The Lt. Governor ought to be very much on his guard against some designing characters there, residents who will endeavour to impose upon him and mislead his judgment by artful insinuations and plausible but interested projects and speculations. Messrs. Knopwood, Fosbrook, Humphry, Loane, Bowden, and Kent, all come less or more under this description; and, having generally opposed the measures of the present commandant, the Lt. Govr. cannot be too much on his guard against their machinations. The chaplain is a man of very loose morals, by report, and ought to be severely admonished when guilty of any impropriety of conduct, and such reported to me. The [Deputy Commissary], is, I fear, a corrupt man, and must therefore be very narrowly watched as long as he remains in office.[52]

But Davey had not taken Macquarie's admonitions too seriously. According to tradition, on his arrival in Hobart, the new commander came ashore in his shirtsleeves with his coat over his arm, and interrupted the regal procession to stop for refreshment at the first pub he saw.[53] Macquarie later told Bathurst that he spent almost all his time 'drinking and every other species of low depravity with the basest and meanest of the people'.[54]

To make matters worse, Davey was surrounded by avarice and greed. According to Macquarie, Andrew Geils, the commandant at Hobart Town before Davey's arrival, had not only displayed 'a sordid, mean and covetous disposition', but had also shown himself to be 'venal and corrupt', stealing both spirits and building supplies from the government stores. Davey's deputy-commissary Leonard Fosbrook was court-martialled for fraud,[55] and so was Fosbrook's successor P.G. Hogan.[56]

In this atmosphere, crime flourished. Van Diemen's Land was being besieged by bushrangers, chief among them Michael Howe, who appeared to have a pathological hatred for authority.

In 1811, after robbing a miller, Howe was tried for a capital crime at the York Assizes, but received seven years' transportation instead. He was assigned as a servant to a Hobart merchant and grazier, but he ran away and joined twenty-eight other escapees on a crime spree, hiding in the forests and living off the land.

Macquarie had planned to crush the desperadoes but, realising the task was too great for his limited resources, in May he decided to offer pardons in the press to the twenty-nine offenders, so long as they had not committed murder and they surrendered by 1 December 1814.[57]

IN 1803, THE SECRETARY OF STATE, Lord Hobart, had called for the abandonment of the Norfolk Island settlement because it was too remote and expensive. Soldiers and convicts were to be moved to Van Diemen's Land.

In April 1814, Macquarie was able to report to Earl Bathurst that all the buildings on Norfolk Island had been destroyed, all the provisions and stores shipped out, and all the cattle, sheep and pigs slaughtered and salted, with the exception of a few pigs and goats that were wild and couldn't be caught.[58] The island would stay abandoned for another eleven years.

William Hutchinson,[59] a former Norfolk Island inmate, had become Macquarie's right-hand man on the demolition project. Now that the project was complete, he was promoted to Principal Superintendent of Convicts and Public Works in Sydney, replacing Isaac Nichols, who retired with Macquarie's esteem. Hutchinson became one of Macquarie's most trusted advisers.

ON 10 APRIL, the Macquaries' tiny son began to struggle for breath while lying beside Elizabeth late at night. Macquarie immediately sent a servant racing on horseback to bring Dr Redfern. The doctor stayed with the baby all night, but for three more days, the beloved child suffered badly while his parents bowed their heads and prayed. Gradually, though, his diarrhoea abated and he began to pick up.

When the baby was three weeks old, 'the dear little fellow' was baptised by the Reverend Cowper in the Macquaries' bedroom after dinner. Catherine Molle was the godmother and Captain Antill stood in for Macquarie's friend James Drummond, the M.P. for Perthshire, as the godfather. Drummond and Macquarie had formed a lifelong friendship in Macao, where Jane Macquarie had perished.

Cowper sprinkled the holy water on the baby's forehead, and as an enormous smile split Macquarie's ageing and weathered visage, Elizabeth named the adored child 'Lachlan Macquarie'.[60] He underwent a public christening together with four-month old William Macquarie Molle at St Philip's on 1 May. Macquarie gave £5 each to the two nurses, Mrs Reynolds and Mrs Frost.

On 24 May, Macquarie reported that he slept in the same bed as 'Mrs M' for the first time since she gave birth and that she was now 'thank God! perfectly recovered and quite well.

Our beloved Babe is also, thank God, in very good health, and thriving equal to our most sanguine expectations. He was last night eight weeks old!'

Despite his father's best wishes, young Lachlan would not have an easy life.

AS MACQUARIE'S PRIDE AND JOY continued to grow in strength, a newly launched convict transport, the *Three Bees,* sailed into Sydney Cove to cause terror, the likes of which the colony had never seen. It arrived on 6 May 1814 with 210 male convicts on board, guarded by forty-three officers and men of the 46th Regiment.

Nine of the convicts had died on the journey, and Macquarie was aghast when another fifty-five, most of them crippled by scurvy, had to be transported to the decaying hospital at Dawes Point. Others were lame and infirm from old age. Macquarie told Bathurst that 'the circumstance of several of those unfortunate men being embarked in a diseased or feeble state' showed that the examining surgeons had to lift their game 'as humanity demands'.[61]

But the state of the men was not the biggest shock the *Three Bees* provided.

Two weeks later, the total destruction of Sydney appeared nigh.

At 4.30 p.m. on 20 May, the *Three Bees,* carrying thirty casks of gunpowder, caught fire after a tailor extinguished a candle 'in a careless manner'. So 'rapid and violent' was the burst of flames that there was no hope of extinguishing them, and with the gunpowder stores ready to blow, the cry went up to abandon ship.[62]

Dozens of homes around the harbour were evacuated as men, women and children scurried for their lives, lest they be buried in the ruins.[63] As a nervous town watched, the blazing *Three Bees* drifted down the harbour like a mad assassin, swaying to and fro with the tide.

One by one, fourteen of the ship's loaded cannons fired their projectiles – some of them grapeshot and some cannon balls – in all directions as the terrified colonists ducked for cover behind trees. One ball went sailing through the front window of the resident naval officer, Captain Piper, on the point of land that now bears his name, and took the corner off his writing desk.[64]

With the sun going down and Sydney waiting for the biggest fireworks show of all time, the *Three Bees* drifted into the rocky outcrop called Bennelong's Point. The feared explosion occurred at 7.45 p.m., but much of the gunpowder was wet and the threat to Sydney had run out of puff.[65] The *Three Bees* burned to the waterline all night.

A few weeks after that scare,[66] another convict transport, the square-rigged fever-ravaged *Surry*, brought even more sick and infirm convicts to Macquarie's patch. One sergeant and three soldiers belonging to a detachment of the 46th Regiment had perished on the voyage, along with the ship's master, the first and second mates, the boatswain and ten sailors. Of the 200 male convicts who had left England, thirty-six had died. Macquarie was horrified and imposed a strict quarantine for three weeks as doctors Redfern and Wentworth went to work. 'With very few exceptions these unfortunate people recovered under the humane and skilful attention of those gentlemen,' Macquarie wrote, reporting to London of the carelessness of the *Surry*'s late commander James Paterson over the spreading of the disease on board.[67]

On the same day that the *Surry* arrived, the *Broxbornebury* also came through the Heads, along with 118 survivors from its original cargo of 120 female prisoners. The ship also brought a new judge to the colony – Jeffery Hart Bent,[68] the elder brother of Judge-Advocate Ellis Bent – as well as Sir John Jamison,[69] a doctor and the son of the old surgeon who had sailed away to his death after the overthrow of Bligh.

The brig *James Hay* was returning to Britain and Macquarie sent home, in the care of John Maclaine, a pair of black swans for his brother Charles, and a box of twenty-eight Norfolk pines to be planted on Jarvisfield and Glenforsa.[70] He had high hopes of seeing those lands again when his eight-year deal with the government came to an end, and expected to be drawing a pension of at least £500 a year.

MICHAEL HOWE, now starting to dress as a wild man in kangaroo furs like other bushrangers, was creating as much terror in Van Diemen's Land as the *Three Bees* had in Sydney. On 18 August 1814, he captured then released a posse of soldiers and sent them back to Hobart with a message for Mad Tom Davey, threatening to put some 'buckshot through his old paunch'.[71]

Howe was part of a gang of fourteen, all heavily armed, who robbed Ingle's farm, 20 kilometres from Hobart. They took £700 in loot and 'cruelly abused the person of a female'.[72]

The wild south had become a gangster's paradise, with even some of the government's most trusted employees downing tools and picking up guns in the hunt for spoils. At Port Dalrymple, Peter Mills, the Deputy Surveyor, and George Williams, deputy commissary in charge of stores, took off to form a bushranging gang.[73] Even Hobart's chaplain, Robert Knopwood,[74] was said to be consorting with bushrangers, while the soldiers who went hunting for them sometimes defected to the other side for a payrise. Even the senior Royal Navy officer in Hobart, Charles Jeffreys,[75] felt he was above the law, boarding a customs boat on the Derwent with a crew of armed sailors, then cutting the customs officer's head open with his cutlass, dragging him away and promising to have him flogged and put in irons.[76]

In October 1814, a brazen gang of bushrangers raided ex-convict Denis McCarty's New Norfolk home, where Macquarie and Elizabeth had stayed on their tour in 1811. McCarty had delivered the public address to welcome them. Now, however, McCarty, an emancipated convict, was back behind bars, serving twelve months in Sydney for smuggling.[77]

McCarty's wife, Mary Ann, was at home with some servants and friends – including Mrs Hibbins, who had a babe in arms – when a man walked into their kitchen with his face blackened with soot, pointing a musket at them. Three other bushrangers then followed.

Their leader spoke in a Yorkshire accent, and another one was dressed entirely in kangaroo furs with his cap pulled over his eyes. They said they didn't want to hurt anyone except 'that damned whore Mrs McCarty', whom they threatened to rape, before dragging her out from under a table where she was hiding.[78]

In the end, they let her alone after she told them where all her husband's valuables were. The gang made off with more than £600 worth of loot, including 25 kilograms of gunpowder, a double-barrelled pistol, three silk dresses, twelve muslin dresses (seven trimmed with lace), one chest of tea, 4½ kilograms of tobacco, two telescopes, three dozen buttons and all six pairs of McCarty's pantaloons.[79]

Before disappearing into the wilds, they told their captives that, while 'the old gentleman' Macquarie's terms of surrender were 'very favourable', they were damned if they were going to turn themselves in. They were planning on leaving the colony with £4000.[80]

Howe eventually availed himself of Macquarie's amnesty, however, along with John Whitehead, 'an equally desperate offender',[81] but it was only a temporary stay of proceedings, and Howe would soon cause the governor more grief than ever.

Crime was getting out of hand in Sydney too. With the 73rd Regiment having sailed for Ceylon, there were now just 372 soldiers in the colony, and only 167 in Sydney.

There were always dangerous criminals for the soldiers to chase and sometimes skirmishes with the 'natives', though Macquarie told Bathurst that, while some Aboriginal people manifested a spirit of hostility, 'it must be admitted that this rarely occurs, unless in retaliation for injuries done them wantonly by settlers or their servants'.[82]

For Macquarie, the most worrying aspect of the lack of military muscle was that Sydney was ripe for invasion by a foreign power, with rumours circulating that French ships might arrive at any time.[83] With news travelling slowly by ship, Macquarie had no knowledge that Napoleon had abdicated on 11 April, and asked for at least another 400 soldiers, as well as half a company of artillery, with some heavy cannons and another 1000 muskets and pistols.[84]

THE IMPACT OF THE DROUGHT was still being felt too. The shortage of wheat had pushed up the price to £2 a bushel, three times what it had been in the previous year of plenty, and the shipment of grain from Calcutta was not due to arrive until October 1814 on the ships *General Browne* and *Betsey*. The drought was part of what Macquarie called a 'total inversion of the natural order of the seasons',[85] and it called for urgent measures.

It seemed almost another lifetime ago that Macquarie had built roads over the ghauts in Mysore for Robert Abercromby's army, working at the rate of 8 kilometres a day. Now, he began to plan roads that would open up the 'champain' country across the mountains, and in the Cowpastures, where at the moment only Macarthur's sheep and wild herds of government cattle roamed.

The man tasked with building the Blue Mountains road was fifty-year-old William Cox, the former paymaster of the New South Wales Corps and more lately a magistrate on the Hawkesbury. Macquarie accepted his offer to build a carriage road from 'Emu Plains, on the left bank of the river Nepean, across the Blue Mountains, to that fine tract of open country to the westward of them', telling Cox on 14 July that he had 'full power and authority to carry this important design into complete effect'.[86] The Governor had toured the foothills of the mountains on 15 April 1814 and realised that Emu Island was not an 'island', but a plain that occasionally flooded.

Macquarie wanted a road 20 feet wide, in which two carriages could pass each other with ease, and on which a four-wheeled vehicle could safely negotiate any conditions. In the really rough patches, 12 feet wide would do. The road would stretch for 163 kilometres across rugged mountain country, rising almost 1200 metres and requiring a dozen bridges, hewn on the spot from nearby trees.

Cox was given a guard of eight soldiers, and thirty convict volunteers who looked capable of hard work for six to twelve months, with the promise of freedom when the road was built. Twenty of the convicts were labourers and the other ten included a doctor, blacksmith, constable, carpenter and two bullock drivers.[87]

The project was starting in the depths of winter, and the men would be perpetually wet, cold and sore. The weather was treacherous, and winds could rip trees apart in the highest areas. But Cox was the perfect manager, already known for his kindness and fairness in dealing with both convicts and Aboriginal people. He believed a pat on the back was more motivating than a kick up the bum, and his estates were a model of self-sufficiency.

Cox took as his assistant Lieutenant Thomas Hobby,[88] a veteran of the New South Wales Corps, and the local guide James Burns, who was now making his third crossing.

They set off on 18 July 1814 to begin one of the great engineering feats of early Australia.

The guards were more concerned about their own safety from 'the mountain natives'[89] than the threat of convicts absconding. One of Cox's properties near the start of the road had recently been attacked, with the *Sydney Gazette* reporting:

> Mr Cox's people at Mulgoa have been several times attacked within the last month, and compelled to defend themselves with their muskets, which the assailants seemed less in dread of than could possibly have been expected. On Sunday last Mr Campbell's servants at Shancomore were attacked by nearly 400; the overseer was speared through the shoulder.[90]

With Earl Bathurst's scales of economy weighing heavily upon him, Macquarie permitted Cox to take only the bare necessities from the government stores: one horse, six bullocks, two carts, ten axes, four sledgehammers, twelve knives and forks, twelve spoons, an anvil, a bellows and a set of scales to weigh the prisoners' rations. They had four muskets, forty rounds of ball cartridge, some buckshot and duck shot, as well as just 11 kilograms of blasting powder. It would be dirty work, so they also took with them 45 kilograms of Bengal soap, and Cox had a small caravan to sleep in. 'The expense of constructing this road,' Macquarie explained to Bathurst, 'would be trifling to government', because the cost of labour was only emancipation and rations.[91]

Cox marched his men up through the fog and rain, and the tangles of rock and forest, carving out their highway day after day. By the first week of October, they had covered 50 kilometres and built a second works depot.

They reported the good news to Macquarie. He had recently received a grey Arab pony from Charles Forbes in Bombay, seven years old and '14 hands 2 Inches high'. He had cost 700 rupees and arrived on the ship *Frederick* from Calcutta. Macquarie called him Abdulla,[92] and was eager to ride him along the new road, to see for himself this promised land.[93]

At the same time as Cox was cutting his way through the Blue Mountains scrub, seventeen-year-old Hamilton Hume[94] and his younger brother John were trekking south from their family's farm at Appin, along with a young Aboriginal friend named Doual. They reached the lush Wingecarribee River area that the Indigenous locals called Toom-Boong (Bong Bong), in what is

Part of Cox's Pass, sketched by E. Purcell, c.1819.
State Library of NSW

PART OF COX'S PASS, NEW SOUTH WALES

known today as the Southern Highlands. They saw great mobs of kangaroos grazing on pasture that was superior to anything nearer to Sydney.

DESPITE THE THREATS OF FAMINE and foreign invaders, and Elizabeth's new battle with the skin rash St Anthony's fire,[95] the months after the birth of young Lachlan were among Macquarie's happiest days. He journeyed to Liverpool and Parramatta in Molle's smart Landau carriage and had two Norfolk pines from D'Arcy Wentworth's farm at Homebush planted in the Government Domain.

But his joy over his son and heir, and the rich lands soon to be settled, came crashing to a halt at midday on 6 October 1814.

Elizabeth was seated behind her coachman Joseph Bigge in her light, open, two-wheeled curricle as it travelled at a mild trot along the gravel of George Street. Private William Thomas, a member of Macquarie's personal bodyguard, was on duty, riding alongside the carriage, which passed in front of his own home.

Bigge saw a group of children playing in the street and called out to them to get out of the way, drawing the vehicle to a halt. Private Thomas's three-year-old son Charlie rushed into the road to meet his father, and show him a set of whistling bells sent by Governor King's widow. Just as Charlie reached the street, Bigge started off again without seeing the little boy, and Charlie fell under a wheel.

Bigge jerked the reins back as Elizabeth screamed: 'Stop, there is a boy under the horse'.

She jumped from the carriage and carried Charlie, sporting a large bruise on his head, into his nearby home.

Mrs Thomas fainted. Dr Redfern was sent for. He tried to revive Charlie by bleeding him, but the boy died soon afterwards.

Elizabeth headed home in what Macquarie later called 'a state of anxiety and distraction of mind not to be described'.[96]

He told Henry Goulburn of the Colonial Office:

My coachman is a remarkable, good driver, and whatever could be done to avoid such an accident, I am confident he did do. He has now served me for ten years, and was coachman for several years in London to Mr Rolleston of the Foreign Office. I have never known him to shew any disposition to cruelty to his fellow creatures. On this unfortunate occasion, he said 'He would rather have broken his own neck than have been the cause of the death of the poor boy.'[97]

A coronial inquest cleared Bigge of any charges of negligence or reckless driving. But Elizabeth was still in a state of shock. As she cradled her eight-month-old son to her breast at Government House, it only exaggerated the grief she felt over a little boy lost. She suffered a nervous breakdown that confined her to bed for several weeks.[98]

Charlie's brother William Thomas alleged that Bigge had been driving drunk. Yet he would also recall:

A few days afterwards I remember going to the funeral and standing by the open grave holding my father's hand. Years afterwards, when we lived in Hobart Town, Lady Macquarrie often came to see my mother, and she always used to cry and blame herself for my brother's death. She was a very good woman, and most kind. Everybody liked her.[99]

Chapter 24

Those natives, who resort to the cultivated districts of this settlement … in general, are of free, open and favourable dispositions, honestly inclined, and perfectly devoid of that designing trick and treachery, which characterize the natives of New Zealand.

MACQUARIE COMMENTING ON WHAT HE SAW AS THE DIFFERENCES BETWEEN THE ABORIGINAL AND MAORI PEOPLE[1]

BLOOD STAINED THE CORNFIELDS to Sydney's southwest as the drought in New South Wales broke, only to signal a war between the white settlers and the colony's first people. The dry spell had cost the colony 1200 cattle, 12,350 sheep, 500 goats and 1000 hogs, and the colonists had become miserly in protecting what was theirs.

In his first proclamation upon arriving from England, Macquarie had expressed a wish that 'the natives of this country' would be treated with 'kindness and attention'.[2] He had developed a cordial relationship with Indigenous people, even if he considered their language 'gibberish',[3] and believed that their adopting European habits and Christian beliefs was the only future for them.

Like most others of his time, his attitude was paternalistic and patronising, and to him, the natives of New South Wales were 'prone like other savages to great indolence and indifference as to their future means of subsistence'.[4]

He wanted to change their attitude and make what he saw as improvements to their lot. But not all settlers had the welfare of the colony's first people at heart.

In Macquarie's first five years of government, there were killings on both sides, though the governor admitted 'that the *first* personal attacks were made on the part of the settlers, and of their servants',[5] and that the attacks by Aboriginal people were usually motivated by a desire for revenge. Dispossession of land and food sources, assaults, shootings, and the kidnapping of Aboriginal women and children were not infrequent.

Around the Nepean at Appin, settlers such as William Broughton,[6] his brother-in-law John Kennedy[7] and the family of Hamilton Hume had long experience of their Indigenous neighbours. Kennedy and Hume, especially, had close relationships with Aboriginal people, as did Dr Charles Throsby[8] at Glenfield (modern-day Casula) to the north.[9] Kennedy's 80-hectare Heston Farm and the rocky river gorges south of there were usually places of security for the Gandangara as well as other Aboriginal peoples.[10]

But in the winter of 1814, wandering Indigenous groups failed to comprehend why they were not welcome to partake of the fields of corn around Appin and nearby Airds; their concept of property was deeply at odds with European ways.[11] As they came down from the mountains to share in nature's bounty after the great drought, their hunger was met with gunfire.

On 7 May 1814, near Appin, three soldiers opened fire 'on a large body of the natives who were plundering the corn fields of a settler'.[12] A small Gandangara boy was killed. The startled warriors fired back with a volley of spears. Two of the soldiers escaped, but Private Isaac Eustace was too slow, and when his mangled body was found later, he had been stripped and one of his hands cut off.[13]

Atrocities followed. A party of settlers killed the wife of Bitugully, a Gandangara warrior,[14] and two children while they were sleeping.[15] The next day, in an attack by Indigenous warriors on a stock-keeper's hut at Bringelly, belonging to Elizabeth

Macarthur, her shepherd William Baker and a woman named Mary Sullivan were slaughtered.[16]

Fear gripped much of New South Wales, with the *Sydney Gazette* reporting on 4 June 1814 that many white women and children had been evacuated from the area around the Cowpastures. Aboriginal fighters from Jervis Bay had joined with the Cowpastures 'mountain tribes' and declared that, 'when the moon shall become as large as the sun [that is, a full moon], they will commence a work of desolation, and kill all the whites before them'.[17]

There were rumours that the people of the mountain tribes were cannibals, but Macquarie refuted that in a despatch to Earl Bathurst, saying that, in fact, the Indigenous peoples 'seem to have as great an abhorrence of practices of that kind as if they had been reared in a civilized state'.[18] Still, they were terrifying, killing the wife of James Daly and two of their children near Mulgoa in July, and tossing their baby onto the floor.[19] The men who had killed the Gandangara woman and children were speared on William Broughton's 400-hectare Lachlan Vale.[20]

In a proclamation in the *Gazette*, Macquarie pointed out that there had been cruel acts committed on both sides, but he warned the settlers against taking the law into their own hands, and counselled them to 'beware of wanton acts of oppression and cruelty against the natives, who are, in like manner with themselves, under, and entitled to the protection of the British laws'.[21] He urged 'patience and forbearance', because 'it must be evident that no deep rooted prejudice exists in their minds against British subjects or white men'.[22]

On 22 July 1814, Macquarie authorised the bushmen John Warby and John Jackson to lead an armed party of twelve Europeans and four Indigenous guides to track down and capture five Aboriginal men, who had been identified as responsible for attacks on white settlers. They were Goondel, chief of the Gandangara tribe, Murrah, Bitugully, Yelloming and Wallah.

The party found no one, but two months later, Warby and several Aboriginal trackers helped capture the bushranger Patrick

Collins. When Collins tried to escape, the trackers speared him in the leg and arm.[23] Three months later, he was hanged for murder.[24]

Macquarie told Earl Bathurst that the Aboriginal people had 'scarcely emerged from the remotest state of rude and uncivilized nature', but that they 'appear to possess some qualities, which, if properly cultivated and encouraged, might render them not only less wretched and destitute by reason of their wild wandering and unsettled habits, but progressively useful to the country according to their capabilities either as labourers in agricultural employ or among the lower class of mechanics'.[25]

The introduction of herds and flocks had not yet tempted them to alter their mode of living, and Macquarie lamented that 'the principal part of their lives is wasted in wandering thro' their native woods, in small tribes of between 20 and 50, in quest of the immediate means of subsistence, making opossums, kangaroos, grub worms, and such animals and fish, as the country and its coasts afford, the objects of their fare'.[26]

He was convinced that the Indigenous people near the principal settlements mostly lived in a state of 'perfect peace, friendliness, and sociality with the settlers', and even showed 'a willingness to assist them occasionally in their labours'. It needed only 'the fostering hand of time, gentle means, and conciliatory manners, to bring these poor unenlightened people into an important decree of civilization, and to instil into their minds, as they gradually open to reason and reflection, a sense of the duties they owe their fellow kindred and society'.[27]

He told Bathurst that, as 'a preliminary measure', he intended to establish a 'Native Institution at Parramatta',[28] with the aim of bringing up 'to habits of industry and decency, the youth of both sexes, commencing at the outset with six boys and six girls'.[29] They would be aged from four to seven.[30] Both sexes were to be instructed together in reading, writing and arithmetic; the boys would also be taught agriculture and mechanical arts, and the girls needlework.

No child, after having been admitted into the institution, was permitted to leave it, or be taken away by any person, even parents or other relatives, until the boys were sixteen and the girls fifteen.[31] Each child was to receive a weekly ration of 3½ pounds of meat, 2 pounds of rice, 2 pounds of wheat, 10 pounds of cornflower and half a pound of sugar, as well as pepper, salt and soap.[32]

The institution would be under the direction of Staffordshire-born William Shelley,[33] a 'moral, well-meaning man' and former missionary, who had just returned from Tahiti with a huge haul of pearls on his ship, the *Queen Charlotte*, after Raiatean pearl divers had temporarily seized her and murdered three of her crew.[34] Shelley's salary would be £100 per annum.

Macquarie also set aside a piece of harbour-front land on Sydney's north shore, which he divided into sixteen lots for 'a few of the adult natives, who have promised to settle there and cultivate the ground ... preferring the productive effects of their own labour and industry to the wild and precarious pursuits of the woods'.[35]

While writing to Bathurst about all this, Macquarie couldn't help taking a shot at the Reverend Marsden and his efforts to take Christianity to the Maori:

> Whilst it is well known that considerable sums of money are expended by the missionary societies of London and other parts of England in attempting to evangelize the natives of New Zealand and Otaheite [Tahiti], it may be allowed to be an object favourable to the interests of humanity to see an attempt of this kind made on a frugal and prudent scale in the territory of New South Wales, the natives of which appear to me to have peculiar and strong claims to the philanthropic protection of a British government.[36]

Macquarie claimed that 'in general', the Aboriginal people had 'free, open and favourable dispositions', which in an early strike for trans-Tasman hostility, he claimed was unlike 'that designing trick and treachery, which characterise the natives of New Zealand'.[37]

On 28 December, Macquarie and Elizabeth, now recovered from the effects the fatal road accident two months earlier, travelled to Parramatta for the first Aboriginal Feast Day, a public celebration between Europeans and the tribes of the Cumberland Plain. Sixty Aboriginal people gathered in a circle at the marketplace at 1 p.m. for a dinner of roast beef and a refreshing ale, before offering their children for the white man's education. Among the sixty was Yarramundi, 'Chief of the Richmond Tribes', one of the Dharug peoples, whose daughter Maria[38] was admitted to the school. Macquarie would come to regard Maria as one of its great success stories.

In next to no time, the positions for six boys and six girls were filled. William Shelley told Macquarie that many Aboriginal parents were keen to send their children to the school, wanting them to learn the ways of the Europeans.[39] Macquarie would soon tell Bathurst that 'in a short time these children appeared to be perfectly happy and reconciled to their new mode of life'.[40]

That would change.

A month later, as part of Macquarie's fifty-fourth birthday celebrations, he and 'Mrs M', accompanied by a large party, took a boat ride across the harbour to George's Head on the north shore, where the sixteen Indigenous families were assembled on their farm plots in the colony's first Aboriginal settlement.

Going against the Aboriginal system of selecting elders, Macquarie had appointed Bungaree[41] as the colony's leader and declared him 'Chief of the Broken Bay Tribe',[42] awarding him 6 hectares of harbour-front land. Bungaree had circumnavigated Australia on the *Investigator* with Matthew Flinders. To mark the occasion, Macquarie presented him with a 'breastplate', an honour the governor would bestow on at least thirty-eight 'chiefs' over the next few years.

Within three months, however, the natives were getting restless. Shelley told Macquarie that the parents of the students at his school had promised him they would never entice their children 'to run again into the bush'. Yet it's doubtful whether any of them had known their children would be taken from them for ten years. They soon began pining for their children, who seemed to be prisoners of the white men. Before long, Yarramundi, an elder of the Dharug people, spoke of the fear of 'men in black clothes' who came to take the children away to the Institution.[43] An open slat fence would be built early in 1815 to give parents the opportunity to look upon their children, but only from afar.

As Macquarie fielded reports from Shelley, he complained to Bathurst that:

> Some of their parents ... from an unaccountable caprice, have since decoyed away their children, and six only remain now at the institution instead of twelve ... The natives, naturally timid and suspicious, have not yet sufficient confidence in Europeans to believe that this institution is solely intended for their own advantage and improvement; but, by bearing with their caprices patiently and indulging them a little in their prejudices, I have no doubt but their repugnance to civilization will soon yield and be entirely overcome.[44]

Macquarie would soon make the Aboriginal people of New South Wales more timid and suspicious than ever. Because of his orders, they would, for many years, view European civilisation as even more barbarous and repugnant than before.

NOT LONG AFTER ARRIVING in Sydney, Ellis Bent had complained about the food on Mrs Macquarie's table[45] and that had just been the start of his grievances.

Lord Castlereagh had called him a 'barrister of eminence' when he sailed for Australia with Macquarie at the age of twenty-six. Yet that 'eminence' could not disguise his many personal flaws.

Ellis was the first lawyer to come to Australia of his own free will, but he did not enjoy the tyranny of distance. Overweight, delicate and prematurely balding, he suffered from pleurisy and rheumatic fever on the voyage, then took one look at Sydney and wanted to go home.

He regarded the Judge-Advocate's abode as a 'perfect pigstye', and his office, all 5 square metres of it, as totally unsuitable, with a lack of stationery and nowhere to lay his wig. He once remarked that, when he put on his black silk cap to pronounce the sentence of death on prisoners, 'they took it as coolly as I did', and while some judges might cry at authorising an execution, he said he would have felt much more tenderness if he had had a decent salary and a fine court to sit in.

'But good God,' Ellis wrote to his brother, 'if you could see, my dear fellow, the court I sit in and the crowd I am surrounded by you would split yourself with laughing'.[46]

He welcomed the Macquaries' friendship and their doting on his young son. Macquarie even named a prominent street after him. Yet he was earning much more than the governor. He gloated that, in addition to his salary of £800, he made £2300 a year[47] in a litigious society, for doing everything from hearing a case to copying a document.

Even though Ellis was an 'officer at the head of the Law Department' who should have known better, he soon made moves to cash in on Macquarie's generosity. Macquarie procured Andrew Thompson's Sydney mansion for Bent to live in while his own home and adjoining court office were being built. Bent procured rum and cash from Macquarie on the government tab to build this new base, billing the colony for £2950,[48] most of the money going on his personal quarters rather than the one room attached for court business. Macquarie told Bathurst it was a much finer home than his own.[49] Yet Ellis had hardly planted his wig in the vestibule of his new mansion when he wanted a bigger abode and a better courthouse.

Ellis demanded a grand palace of justice, complete with a Grecian Doric portico at the main entrance, copied from the Temple of Theseus at Athens. Soon Macquarie was doling out land to him too.

He later told Bathurst that he had given Ellis 500 hectares on the Nepean, as well as cattle and convict servants as a 'mark of my attention to his comfort and welfare', then given him another 300 hectares 'adjoining the former for the ultimate benefit of his two infant sons'.[50]

When Macquarie had petitioned Bathurst in 1813 over the issue of changing the court system in New South Wales to trial by jury, he had asked him not to 'overlook the great legal abilities and services of Mr Bent' when it came to appointing a chief justice, 'as I do not know any man more deserving of it, or fitter for that very high and important office'.[51] Ellis's brother, Jeffery Hart Bent, was also Macquarie's 'strong recommendation' as assistant judge, being 'a barrister-at-law' of seven years' standing, 'a man of considerable eminence as a lawyer, good sense and conciliatory manners, and as such would be a great acquisition for the colony, especially when united with the mild and conciliatory manners of his brother'.[52]

Macquarie soon changed his tune. After his attempts in early 1813 to raise £4000 for public works by subscription fell flat, Ellis grew angry at his refusal to withdraw his artisans and labourers from the many other buildings in progress to devote them to the ostentatious new courthouse.

According to Macquarie, Ellis ceased to make social visits to Government House, and when they met to discuss public business, the judge 'assumed a very marked degree of coolness of manner'.[53] Bent's usually mild demeanour turned to rage as he accused Macquarie of having 'a great want of feeling' when it came to the judge's 'personal comfort'.

Hoping he would 'become sensible of the impropriety of his conduct', Macquarie invited Bent to dine with him and Elizabeth, but Ellis told him what to do with the invitation 'in a pointedly rude manner'. Even in church, where it was the custom of the congregation to stand when the governor entered, Ellis stayed seated in his pew with a scowl on his face.[54]

In 'contempt' of Macquarie's authority, he declined to sit on the bench of magistrates any longer, saying that role had only been 'optional' and he now found it 'inconvenient'.[55] He refused to redraft new port regulations for Macquarie, claiming that they were unnecessary and arguing, incorrectly, that Macquarie had no authority over him, since he was no longer 'subject to military discipline'. He was.

Ellis's mood further darkened when the holey dollar came into circulation in 1814 and stopped his speculation on promissory notes. He began to believe Macquarie was trying to affect the independence of the judiciary. Meanwhile, Macquarie told Bathurst that Ellis was bitterly opposed to his liberal policies over emancipation, except 'in a few peculiar instances' when he found his own financial interests involved, 'and on such occasions, he is not at all scrupulous in associating with those, who had been convicts'.[56] Macquarie wanted to excise Ellis's insubordination before it became 'a dangerous contagion among all those persons, whose natural disposition leads them to be discontented or dissatisfied with the measures of government'.[57]

Ellis Bent allowed ex-convict lawyers to appear before his court, although they were prohibited from doing so in England, but he only allowed them as 'agents of the parties' rather than formal officers of the court. Most of the colonists saw this as a necessary measure given the scarcity of legal minds in the infant settlements. Ellis had sat on the magisterial bench beside Simeon Lord, and Bent's own clerk James Foster was a former convict. He had also employed an Irish lawyer transported for passing a forged note. Ellis, himself, had said that, if the selection of jurymen was only confined to those persons who had come to the colony free, 'many would be excluded who are now among the most useful and opulent members of the society here'.[58] But Bent was not prepared to give the emancipists all the concessions that Macquarie wanted.

The arrival of Jeffery Hart Bent only gave his older brother more ammunition for his battles with Macquarie. If Macquarie had thought Ellis was trouble, Jeffery took it to a new level. By the time he'd finished with the Ellis brothers, the colony wouldn't be big enough for the three of them.

The cadaverous Jeffery, his face gaunt and haunted, and his long, narrow nose always high in the air, had a lofty opinion of himself. He refused to get off the *Broxbornebury* until Macquarie had organised a formal salute of cannon fire,[59] and had complained bitterly to Bathurst for not procuring him a knighthood and audience with the Prince Regent before his departure.[60] In consequence, his nickname in the colony became 'Sir Jeffery'.

Under Macquarie's rule, New South Wales and Van Diemen's Land were changing rapidly from penal colonies to trading centres and the court system needed changing to accommodate that.

Jeffery Bent had been appointed judge of the new Supreme Court of Civil Judicature, on a salary of £800 a year. That court would deal with disputes of more than £50. Ellis, the new chief justice, had a payrise to £1200. His Governor's Court would have jurisdiction over civil matters. Before leaving England, Jeffery had nominated William Moore[61] and Frederick Garling[62] as two attorneys willing to migrate to New South Wales for a retainer of £300 each.

Jeffery brought with him a new charter of justice[63] and orders to economise. The rum hospital idea was troubling Bathurst, and he instructed Macquarie to fire all the officers' servants on the government payroll and to stop bureaucrats from using the government stores as a collective teat.[64]

Even if he had not requested it, the new charter of justice gave Macquarie the power to veto Supreme Court verdicts, should Jeffery disagree with both the magistrates sitting beside him and launch an appeal. Macquarie was also the absolute judge in civil appeal cases up to £3000, beyond which sum, appeal to the Privy Council was required. To the Bents' chagrin, Macquarie now decided court fees, too. In fact, as the military commander in chief, Macquarie had the authority to institute martial law if he decided it was appropriate.

To Ellis's further disdain, the new charter also meant that a large portion of the fees Ellis had been collecting for legal work would now go to his brother.

After demanding his grand reception, Jeffery did not open his court for months. He said there was no place for him to preside, or to reside, that befitted his dignity. Jeffery and his brother asked for the whole southern wing of the unfinished rum hospital as their courthouse, but Macquarie had already promised it to D'Arcy Wentworth.

Macquarie agreed to make two rooms in the wing available to Jeffery as his chambers, and half of the central wing as a courthouse for both the brothers until something better was available. The *Sydney Gazette* described the apartment set aside for the court as 'commodious': almost 50 metres long, 8 wide and 5 high, and positioned inside a 'stately' building with wide verandas and massive pillars.[65]

Bathurst supported Macquarie's plan, and as they licked their wounds, the Bents boiled with rage. Their thin lips were pursed as they surveyed the opulent quarters being occupied by Wentworth, a man they regarded as a 'notorious highwayman',[66] who had been named in the British Parliament for sticking a gun in the face of Sir Henry Russell, the late chief justice of Bengal, and taking his watch on Hounslow Heath.[67]

Writing to Henry Goulburn at the Colonial Office, Jeffery said Macquarie should not 'escape blame or punishment' for providing him with a room that 'was in a most disgraceful state from dirt and vermin', while busy 'expending the labour of the government servants and the public money upon buildings of luxury for himself and palaces for his favourites'.[68]

After Jeffery had been in the colony for five months without holding court, Macquarie felt obliged to ask the new judge if he had thought about giving the wig and gavel a run any time soon. Jeffery told him that William Moore was the only non-convict attorney in the colony and he would not be holding court before the arrival in August of the second solicitor from London, Frederick Garling. That would be thirteen months after Jeffery's arrival. Macquarie told Bathurst he found the delay 'frivolous and ridiculous', especially since there were rumours that Garling had been waylaid on his voyage by an American privateer.[69]

By April 1815, Jeffery had been in the colony for nine months and was still demurring about going to work. Macquarie told Jeffery that he had received petitions from three men who had acted as legal agents and wanted to practise law in New South Wales: George Crossley,[70] Edward Eagar[71] and George Chartres, a publican.

The sixty-six year old Crossley had been a solicitor in London for twenty-four years when he was charged in February 1796 with forging the will of Reverend Henry Lewin and defrauding the rightful heir on behalf of his client, Lady Briggs. According to one story, Crossley placed a live fly in the mouth of the deceased cleric before taking his cold dead hand and drawing the signature, so he could say there was still life in the body.[72] He was acquitted, but a few months later, transported for seven years for perjury in another case. In Ellis Bent's court, he had managed to plead a case for false imprisonment against the rebels who overthrew Bligh and win £500 in damages.

Eagar was a Dublin lawyer when he was convicted of forging a bill of exchange and sentenced to death. He was said to have undergone a remarkable conversion to Christianity while in a holding cell, saving him from the hangman and commuting his sentence to penal servitude in Sydney. George Chartres also practised law in Dublin before being convicted for fraud.

Macquarie told Jeffery that it was unfair to 'debar persons of a respectable profession' when it was their only means of earning a livelihood, and that the three men had paid their debt to society. Jeffery said he saw the issue 'in a very different light', and that he could not avoid expressing his 'poignant regret' at Macquarie's interference in his work.[73]

BLASTING THROUGH ROCKS with their limited supplies of gunpowder, and smashing the rest with sledgehammers, William Cox's workmen reached the Macquarie River on 14 January 1815 and raised the British flag. Writing to London, Macquarie said the feat of constructing 101½ miles of road from Emu Plains to what would become the site for the new town of Bathurst in six months did Cox and his party 'infinite credit, due consideration given to the extraordinary difficulties they had to surmount, and to the short period of time in which they completed it'.[74] Macquarie gave Cox £300 and a grant of land for his work, though Earl Bathurst, still watching every penny from London, ignored his request to authorise the money.[75]

Macquarie was eager to see the new sights for himself, and on 25 April 1815, he and Elizabeth left little Lachlan in the care of their Government House babysitters and headed off in their carriage to see the promised land. There were thirty-seven others with them, including Cox, Captain Antill, William Redfern, John Jamison, James Meehan and George Evans, as well as J.W. Lewin,[76] a painter and naturalist, who would capture in oils the grand vistas they all awaited with eager expectation. Also in the group was the surveyor-general John Oxley,[77] a Yorkshireman who had been aboard the *Porpoise* when Bligh sailed it to Van Diemen's Land. He had once been engaged to John Macarthur's daughter, until Macarthur broke it off when he realised the scale of Oxley's debts. Oxley was far more prosperous now, and land grants from Macquarie had seen him master of a 400-hectare estate near Camden that he called Kirkham after his home in England.

The party camped at South Creek for the night and, the next day, Macquarie and Elizabeth and their companions mounted their horses for the ride into the mountains, and stayed that night 'in a very pretty wooded plain near a spring of very good fresh water'. Macquarie called the place 'Spring-Wood'.[78] They breathed in the deep mountain air and gazed at the astonishing rock and cliff formations, the deep green valleys and the mystical blue haze above them. They named Mount York, Cox's River and Cox's Pass. Beside Cox's River, near its confluence with the River Lett, Macquarie had divine service performed on 30 April.

Four days later, the Macquaries arrived at the colonial depot on the Macquarie River, to be greeted by three cheers from the soldiers stationed there. To their 'great surprise, mixed with no small degree of fear', they also sighted three Aboriginal men and four young boys, all dressed in possum skins. The Indigenous onlookers were startled 'at seeing so many strangers, horses and carriages', but 'they soon appeared to be reconciled on being kindly spoken to'.[79]

On 7 May, with Oxley's help, Macquarie chose the site for the new town of Bathurst, the first town deep into the inland of the continent. Before an audience of seventy-five, Macquarie made a speech praising Evans and Cox for their extraordinary work; the Union Jack was raised on a new flagstaff, the military fired three volleys and everyone gave three cheers.[80] Before heading home, Macquarie spent three more days touring the fertile plains on horseback, assessing their grand potential. He met groups of Aboriginal people and gave them 'presents of black leather caps and tomahawks', and issued orders that they should have plenty to eat from the public stores.[81]

He sent George Evans 200 kilometres further west to see what other treasure he could find, and Evans came upon Mount Canobolas, almost 1400 metres high. The name 'Macquarie' was already on just about everything, so Evans called another great river the Lachlan, and named Cowra,[82] Mount Lachlan, Maclaine's Peak and the Oxley Plains.

Macquarie told Bathurst the glowing reports of the country had not been exaggerated. The rivers teemed with fish, some weighing more than 10 kilograms, and there was game everywhere. Kangaroos abounded, as did black swans, wild geese, ducks of various kinds, pigeons and a curious duck-billed creature that the people called a 'water mole or paradox' [the platypus].[83] Macquarie shot a black snake but missed a hawk.[84] Joseph Bigge killed an emu.

Macquarie ordered the new superintendent at Bathurst, Richard Lewis, to plant 3 hectares of wheat and a vegetable garden to test the soil quality. Soon, he happily reported abundant crops.[85]

On 21 July 1815, William Lawson crossed the Nepean and, shivering and covered in snow, drove 100 head of cattle and some weary horses that looked like they couldn't go much further up through the mountains and on to the fertile plains beyond. In October, 100 head of cattle, considerably fatter, came back across the mountains, the first from the west for the tables of Sydney.[86]

JEFFERY HART BENT finally went to work on 1 May 1815, while Macquarie was still in the mountains. Oaths were administered, and the first proceedings of the Supreme Court took place on 5 May.[87] Beside him on the bench were the magistrates Alex Riley and William Broughton (the highly respected First Fleeter). Jeffery did not rate either of them.

Eagar presented his petition to be admitted as a solicitor. Jeffery rebuffed it because Eagar had underlined parts of it for emphasis. When Magistrate Riley defended the practice as common in the colony, Jeffery told him to pipe down.[88] Later, in chambers, Jeffery told the magistrates that, according to an Act of Parliament from the reign of George I, a conviction for forgery or perjury prevented anyone from practising as a solicitor. With all due respect, the magistrates pointed out that, while they 'regretted they were compelled to differ from Mr Bent', that ruling only applied in England.[89] Bent bristled.

When the court met again, Crossley began by making his petition. Jeffery told him to sit down and shut up. When Crossley kept talking, Jeffery threatened to have him committed.[90] Magistrate Broughton interjected and said that he thought the petitioner should be heard.

Riley agreed, and though Bent was outvoted two-to-one, he told the magistrates they were 'destitute of common sense'.

Riley said he was sorry that Mr Bent had so little sense as to belittle him publicly.[91]

Jeffery asked Riley whether he had an opinion on admitting the petitioners, and as Riley began to answer, Bent cut him off, shouting: 'I want no Ifs, sir. It appears you cannot say yes or no.'

Riley replied: 'I can express those monosyllables with as much facility as you, Mr Bent.'[92]

The judge accused Riley and Broughton of being influenced by Macquarie, and insulting his feelings and the dignity of the court. He declared that his court would never be disgraced by such men as the petitioners. If they ever tried to practise law in New South Wales, he would severely punish them.

With no consultation, and with a series of insults to his fellow magistrates in front of an audience that included both convicts and colonists, Bent announced that he was adjourning the court, for another long spell, and he would report the two magistrates to London for not agreeing with him on the matter.[93]

The next day, Broughton and Riley wrote Jeffery a letter, complaining that he had 'publicly injured and insulted'[94] their feelings. Jeffery told them to suck it up, reminding them he 'was a barrister of nearly ten years standing',[95] a boast he made frequently.

Broughton outlined his opinions on the matter by writing to London, saying that Jeffery's unwavering opposition to emancipists was 'repugnant to the benevolent principles upon which His Majesty's Government found this colony, and in which I can see that they had a greater regard for the reformation of the people than the punishment of the criminal'.

He added:

These respective persons have received the royal pardon and the instrument, under which the same is manifested, expressly declares that they are restored to all the rights and privileges of free British subjects in this colony; to deprive them of the benefit of following their professions would destroy the effect of the pardon.[96]

ON MACQUARIE'S RETURN JOURNEY through the Blue Mountains to see his darling infant Lachlan, he named the Jamison Valley and an area of dark vegetation 'Black-Heath'. It had been an awe-inspiring trek, full of wonder and promise. But when he arrived back at Government House on 19 May 1815, wars raged on many fronts.

Napoleon was about to face his Waterloo but, in Van Diemen's Land, Michael Howe and his fellow desperadoes were causing their own mayhem.

Mad Tom Davey had declared martial law on 25 April 1815,[97] much to Macquarie's annoyance, because Macquarie was the only man authorised to do so, and he felt it was unwarranted. He told Davey to revoke the declaration at once,[98] and he would not let him forget his mistake.

Howe was now travelling with an Aboriginal woman known as Black Mary, and on the day martial law was announced, his gang, including John Whitehead and James Geary, a deserter from the 73rd Regiment, robbed another property at New Norfolk.

Denis McCarty, now out of prison, organised a posse. A shootout ensued in which five of the pursuers were wounded, two of them fatally. On 10 May, as Macquarie was preparing to leave Bathurst for home, the bushrangers attempted another raid on McCarty's property, only to find a party of the 46th Regiment waiting for them.

John Whitehead, mortally wounded, rushed to Howe and asked his comrade in arms to cut off his head so that the soldiers would be thwarted in taking it back to Lieutenant Governor Davey for a 50-guinea reward. Howe took out his sword and obliged. Whitehead's headless corpse was brought to Hobart Town and gibbeted on what is now Hunter Street.[99]

The bloodletting only emboldened Howe more, and the self-styled 'Lieutenant-Governor of the Woods' would continue his bloodshed for a long time to come.

JUSTICE JEFFERY BENT would not budge. Riley and Broughton, thoroughly sick of him, asked Macquarie to replace them on the bench, but Macquarie wanted them to stay, so on 25 May 1815, the three met in Jeffery's chambers to discuss the matter.

Broughton asked Jeffery what he would do if London sanctioned the admission of the emancipists to court. Jeffery said it would be a disgrace and he would not accept it.[100] Broughton and Riley said they would express their views in support of the idea in open court.

They entered the court and took their seats. Jeffery refused to come out of his room. He sent word that there would be no court without him.

Jeffery repeated his threat over the petitioners[101] the next day and shut down the Supreme Court. In support, Ellis Bent shut down the Governor's Court.

Macquarie asked Jeffery for a report on why the court had

been shut and Jeffery told the governor he wasn't entitled to a report because of the 'disrespect and indignity' shown to one of His Majesty's judges. Oh, and he didn't believe he was under Macquarie's command.[102]

Macquarie told Bent his felt his tone was 'highly disrespectful and offensive', and that he was ceasing all communication with the judge because 'a continuation of it would probably subject me to further insult'.[103]

Macquarie reported Jeffery's behaviour to London and asked the Colonial Office to give clear instructions on whether emancipists could practise as lawyers. But the Bent brothers had worn him down. He had spent a lifetime in the military and he was not about to be dominated by a pair of men he now saw as rat-faced hyenas. Sick of constant feuds with the Bents, he decided to hit London with an ultimatum.

He told Bathurst that it was now 'utterly impossible' for him to work with the 'Messieurs Bent', and that, for the good of the colony, 'they or I' should be removed from it.[104]

> I therefore most respectfully take the liberty to solicit, that, in the event of the conduct of the Messieurs Bent being approved of (which of course will be virtually disapproving of mine) by His Majesty's ministers, your Lordship will do me the favour to move His Royal Highness the Prince Regent to be graciously pleased to accept of my resignation as governor of the territory.[105]

It would take a voyage to London and back with official correspondence before Macquarie received an answer. Meanwhile, he prepared for war.

Chapter 25

OCTOBER 1815 TO MARCH 1816, NEW SOUTH WALES

There is no sin however serious which is not practised without remorse amongst us. Lying & perjury & theft, and whoredom, and blasphemy, and drunkenness, are daily committed amongst us.

THE REVEREND SAMUEL MARSDEN, OUTLINING WHAT HE SAW
AS THE EVILS OF NEW SOUTH WALES[1]

A S MACQUARIE WAITED for word from London over his threat to resign, he took a tour of the lush Cowpastures to assess 'how far it may be practicable to tame the wild cattle ranging there'. He set out in his carriage on 3 October 1815 for a nine-day journey, covering 277 miles (446 kilometres).

His team included William Cox, John Oxley, James Meehan and Major (formerly Captain) Antill. They travelled along the Georges River by boat from Thomas Moore's Moore Bank property to Liverpool and then through fine-looking open forest country all the way to the ford of the Nepean, where they camped close by a Government Hut that had recently been erected.

The area was home to three Indigenous tribes: the Gandangara mountain people, the Tharawal and the Dharug, who lived to the northeast of the Nepean River. A year earlier; there had been fatal skirmishes in the area as land grants saw fences built across the land, kangaroo feeding grounds given over to livestock and yam beds destroyed,[2] but Macquarie hoped that the current relative peace might remain.

He passed through John Macarthur's property at Camden. Macarthur was still in England, under orders not to return to Sydney, but Elizabeth Macarthur told Macquarie that 'by mistake' she had built a small cottage on a piece of ground adjoining their property, and would it be possible to have it added to their holdings? Macquarie gave her an extra 24 hectares.[3]

The governor inspected Walter Davidson's[4] farm Manangle,[5] the properties of James Harrex,[6] Reuben Uther[7] and Andrew Hume,[8] the Lachlan Vale estate of William Broughton, and the properties of Charles Throsby and David Allan.[9]

He shared bread and wine with John Kennedy[10] at Heston Farm and gave him 40 more hectares for working so hard.

Macquarie's horse Cato became lame, just as he had almost six years before when carrying the new governor over the hills of Kurrajong, and Macquarie was glad to rest him and explore the magnificent gorges and canyons around the Natai River on 5 October. The governor and his party were shown the way by local guides John Warby and young David Budbury, an Aboriginal teenager raised by a white family. Macquarie paid Warby 20 shillings a day for his work, including 10 shillings a day for the loan of a new horse. It took eighty minutes of a 'most tiresome scrambling walk' for them to descend the rocky cliffs and reach the right bank of the Natai, where Macquarie enjoyed a biscuit and a glass of cherry brandy, Antill having carried with him 'a pint bottle of this good stuff'.[11]

While he was busy rock-climbing, though, Macquarie's beloved greyhound Oscar had been badly hurt chasing a kangaroo, and Macquarie was ropeable at his servants for 'taking so daring a liberty' by letting the dog off his leash. Macquarie ordered the 'poor animal to be taken particular care of, and to be carried in one of the carts till he recovers.'[12] For three days, he doted on his four-legged friend, trying to nurse him back to health, but on 8 October he reported that 'between 9 and 10 o'clock this morning my poor favourite beautiful greyhound Oscar died in great agony, to my great concern and mortification, having had him now upwards of four years'.[13] Macquarie ordered him to be buried on Macquarie Grove,[14] the property of Rowland Hassall[15] that they were visiting, near modern-day Camden Airport.

Macquarie rode through the barren country south of Stone Quarry Creek called Great Bargo and inspected John Oxley's stockyard. He ordered the arrest of two men[16] who were each carrying a bag of fresh beef from a wild heifer, which Macquarie told them 'most scornfully' was the property of the Crown.[17] Macquarie was all for supporting a battler doing his best, but his laws must be obeyed.

On Ellis Bent's property, Moulsey, the party surveyed a 'large and beautiful' waterhole formed from the Nepean called Bent's Basin.[18] Then they rode through the nearby properties of Hannibal Macarthur, William Wentworth, D'Arcy Wentworth and Macquarie's secretary J.T. Campbell, who had 'one of the richest and best farms in the colony'. Macquarie and his entourage rode up the 'Kobbatty-Hills',[19] and inspected the land of Captain Daniel Woodriff,[20] Mary Birch,[21] George Palmer[22] and John Blaxland. At Mulgoa, they enjoyed some relaxation on the property of William Cox. They rode on to Castlereagh, then along the New Western Road near Eastern Creek and on to Rooty Hill, but not before Macquarie had organised a 'trusty party of men' to chase eight runaway convicts, heading west along the new road across the Blue Mountains.[23]

Soon, Macquarie would organise a party of men to chase troublesome Aboriginal men in the majestic gorges he had traversed around Appin.

Macquarie had found the cliffs and the deep water and the grand rivers and the thick forests sublime. The country was like a slice of heaven. Yet the terror his soldiers would soon cause to the local Indigenous population, and the legacy of brutality they would leave behind, would stain Macquarie's reputation forever.

JEFFERY HART BENT had continued to thumb his nose at the governor's authority. Despite pleasant diversions, such as tours of the countryside, Macquarie was constantly stressed by the Bent brothers as he waited on word from London over his threat to resign.

Macquarie and his staff were the only travellers exempt from paying the toll on the Sydney turnpike on George Street. One toll bar was at the George Street end in Haymarket and the other was at Boundary Road in Parramatta. Ellis Bent had framed the laws authorising the toll, and even refused Macquarie's offer of an exemption, saying he did not want to open the floodgates for every magistrate and officer of the Crown to follow.

Jeffery, though, felt he deserved a free pass. He told Macquarie the toll was illegal, and clip-clopped his way through the George Street toll gates, warning the coin collectors, Michael Wyer and Patrick Cullen, that he would jail them if they tried to slow his progress. It was alleged that at one point he used the line: 'You damned scoundrel, who are you? Do you know who I am?'[24]

In his role as police chief, D'Arcy Wentworth issued a summons against Jeffery.[25] But Jeffery replied that Wentworth had forgotten to mention in the writ that Jeffery was a Supreme Court

The George Street Toll Gate with the Benevolent Asylum in the background.
State Library of NSW

judge and that he was 'by no means amenable to any criminal jurisdiction in this territory', so he would not be paying any attention to the summons.[26] Wentworth fined him 40 shillings.[27] Jeffery refused to pay.

Instead, Macquarie tried to publicly shame this man with an elephant hide. Macquarie had a pretty thick skin himself, and had got away with outrageous behaviour in his earlier years. But he would be damned if Jeffery Bent got over him. On 9 September 1815, Macquarie had issued a government order and a couple of hard jabs into Jeffery's midsection:

> The governor has been officially informed, with much surprise and regret, that an officer of very high rank in the civil service of this colony has refused to pay the toll ordered in the proclamation under date the 30th of March 1811 ... Whilst the governor laments that any person should be found in the colony so wanting in public spirit as to wish to evade contributing his mite towards the support of so useful and beneficial an establishment for the country and the community at large, he cannot allow any person whatsoever, however high his rank may be, to break through or set at defiance the established regulations of the colony ...[28]

Macquarie stipulated that 'any person or persons attempting to use force or violence to evade paying such tolls or dues' was to be arrested. From 'motives of delicacy, and out of respect for the high office he holds', Macquarie said he wouldn't name the offender, but couldn't help expressing publicly 'his astonishment and regret, that he should be the first and only person in this colony' who had openly tried to flout the regulations the governor had deemed necessary for the improvement of the country.

From a person at the head of so high an office, 'the governor had just reason to hope and expect every degree of reasonable support, instead of opposition and violent resistance to his public measures'.[29]

Jeffery wrote letters of protest to Macquarie in response, but Macquarie said, since they were coated with disrespect, he would not even reply.[30]

AMID ALL THE TENSIONS with Macquarie, Ellis Bent's health had been failing for some time. In October 1814, suffering from what he called 'incipient dropsy of the chest', he had asked Bathurst to find him another position in the East Indies.[31] By July 1815, plagued by a severe decline in health, Ellis was complaining to Bathurst that, despite his legal standing, Macquarie treated him 'like a subaltern officer, a mere cypher, a person sent out simply for his convenience and merely to execute his commands as one of his staff'.[32] His health finally collapsed soon afterwards.

In October, as the governor returned from his tour of the Cowpastures, he gave Ellis leave to visit Europe in order to get well again. Ellis never made it but, as he was preparing to go, Jeffery immediately put his hand up, offering, with a payrise, to do Ellis's job as chief justice while Ellis was away. Macquarie told him that, after all the disrespect Jeffery had shown, he must be dreaming.[33] Instead, the role went to Frederick Garling, who had arrived in the colony on 5 August, safe from the privateer after all. Unsurprisingly, Jeffery responded that the new man was 'so inferior a person in the profession to me ... a barrister of ten years standing and to whom the high office of judge has been confided by the Crown'.[34]

Bathurst disagreed. When he sat down at his desk in Downing Street in January 1816, with Macquarie's letter of resignation in his hand, he decided to sack both the Bent brothers instead. They seemed, he said, 'too much disposed to resent the authority of the governor and to withhold from him that cordial co-operation without which the business of the colony could not be satisfactorily conducted'.[35]

Bathurst told Macquarie that, while the Bent brothers 'had clearly a right to protest against any act of yours which they conceived as illegal or improper, and to transmit that protest to His Majesty's Government ... they were not authorized on the ground of a difference of opinion, either to withhold from you the legal assistance which you required, or to interrupt the course of judicial proceedings'.[36]

His Royal Highness, the Prince Regent, had had no hesitation in removing the thorns from Macquarie's side and had been impressed by the way the governor had taken decisive action in suspending the officers under his command. Bathurst told him the whole incident had revealed that, 'even under circumstances of a most irritating nature', Macquarie prioritised working for the public good over his 'own private convenience'.[37]

Bathurst based his dismissal of Jeffery on his closing of his court, for though he approved of the judge's attitude to not allowing former convicts to practise as attorneys as a general principle, he thought that in the circumstances they might have been admitted temporarily as agents. In any event, 'the evil of the suspension of justice' was 'too serious'.[38]

Bathurst told Jeffery:

It is not necessary that I should enter into the question, on which your difference with Governor Macquarie appears to have originated; or whether convicts be or be not authorized to practice is a question of little importance, when compared with the consequences arising out of its agitation, the closing of the Supreme Court of the colony for at least twelve months. With every disposition to make allowance for your feelings in resisting the introduction of such persons into your court, I cannot find any apology for your refusal to accede to the qualified admission, recommended by Governor Macquarie. A gentleman having been appointed to succeed you as judge of the Supreme Court, you will be at liberty to leave the colony at any period best suited to your convenience.[39]

Bathurst sacked Ellis because he 'had no other alternative' given his 'refusal to draw the new port regulations'.[40]

By then, though, Ellis Bent was dead. He coughed his last on 10 November 1815, leaving a pregnant wife and four children under the age of eight. He had never uttered a word of regret to Macquarie, even though he'd known his time was short.[41]

Macquarie felt genuine sorrow. He told Bathurst that, while Ellis had become his 'bitterest enemy', he had always tried to treat him like a 'true friend'.[42] As a judge-advocate, 'he faithfully, indefatigably and ably administered justice, so long as his health enabled him to take the bench'. Macquarie said, despite the property Ellis had accumulated, his family would be left in dire circumstances without his income.[43]

THE PUGNACIOUS SAMUEL MARSDEN had supported the Bents' disdain for Macquarie. He had never forgotten Macquarie's request that he sit beside those 'immoral' ex-convicts, Simeon Lord and Andrew Thompson, on the turnpike board.

Marsden had been vigorously admonishing evildoers in the colony since arriving in 1794. Once, during divine service early in his tenure, he was furious to find several men digging up ground outside his church on the Sabbath. He gave them an impromptu sermon from the book of Revelation on the 'great wrath' to come.[44]

After Bent's death, he preached a fiery sermon[45] at his church, St John's at Parramatta, telling the sinners seated before him that 'God in his anger often removed from the Israelites an upright judge or king'.[46]

Marsden based his warnings to the flock on 2 Chronicles 29 verses 10 and 11, about making a covenant with the God of Israel so as to turn away his wrath.

Ellis Bent had been Marsden's friend, and Marsden had admired what he called his quiet manner and his strong Christian beliefs:

With respect to the doctrines of the Christian religion I had many conversations with him, both before and during his last sickness. He searched the scriptures daily like the Boreans[47], to see whether these things were so. He was very anxious to know the way to glory. The Psalms of David afforded him much consolation, and also the Esiples of St. Paul. We had much conversation on these doctrines … The word of God appeared to be very precious to him.[48]

The sermon itself, however, was not so much about Bent as about the calamities that had plagued New South Wales under Macquarie's rule. He called upon his congregation to turn away from sinfulness, so that the anger of the Lord would not 'wax hot' against them:

> We have reason to apprehend that God is angry with us for our sins, from the rains being withheld, the earth not bringing forth its increase, our cattle dying with famine, and ourselves threatened with the same calamity which is God's usual method of punishing nations for their iniquities and from God taking from us a just and upright judge.[49]

But if God was angry, then so was Macquarie. He gave Marsden a severe dressing-down in front of Major Antill and the Reverend Cowper.[50] While Marsden felt it was because he had heaped too much praise on Bent, one of Macquarie's enemies, an inquiry later found that:

> The governor reproached Mr Marsden [not] for eulogising the character of Mr Ellis Bent but for having declared in his sermon preached at Parramatta 'that no greater calamity could befall a country than the loss of an upright judge, and that no doubt the sins of this colony had been the cause of Mr Bent's death as a chastisement from the Almighty for the sins of the people'.[51]

JEFFERY BENT blamed Macquarie for his brother's death. Ellis had been 'compelled', he told Earl Bathurst, to sit in a confined courtroom – a courtroom whose construction Ellis himself had overseen – and the hellish Sydney heat had only added to the anxiety Macquarie gave him. Poor Ellis, his brother intoned, had little to show for a 'life of labour, anxiety and public duty'. He had been clearing a mere £720 a year since he arrived in Australia, and his life insurance would hardly cover his debts. His Majesty's Government owed him a debt of gratitude and some cold hard cash.[52]

Macquarie, on the other hand, considered Jeffery a waste of space, with his 'midnight cabals' and 'petty factions', and swore 'that no court of law, wherein Mr Bent shall preside, will ever render this colony a service'.[53]

He had told Bathurst there was 'only one part' of Jeffery's conduct that laid 'any claim to consistency', and that was 'the unqualified opposition, and the low mean resistance to all and every measure of my government'.[54]

Macquarie felt totally vindicated. John Wylde,[55] a lawyer of much greater standing than the Bent brothers, would become the new judge-advocate. Barron Field, a direct descendant of Oliver Cromwell, would take Jeffery's role in the Supreme Court.

MACQUARIE had bowled over two of his fiercest enemies. He was also beginning to succeed in his push to get rid of Mad Tom Davey in Van Diemen's Land. But there was a queue of others lined up behind the Bent brothers waiting to have a shot at Macquarie. And Samuel Marsden stood right at the front.

Despite Macquarie's elevation of convicts to positions of power, Marsden had a grudging respect for his morality. Marsden's daughter Ann[56] once called Macquarie 'a great friend to the gospel': 'Tho not pious, yet he is what the world calls a moral man, which is much more than any of his predecessors; he has also made great improvements in the colony particularly at Sydney.'[57]

However, Marsden and Macquarie clashed often. Although he was Marsden's mentor, William Wilberforce supported Macquarie against Marsden on the convict issue, telling the governor:

> I am sorry Mr Marsden differs from us on this subject. He is a very worthy man and has a sound understanding and in general good principles. Still like other men he is liable to

error and I have frankly told him, tho he had not mentioned the topic to me for a long time before, but I think his opinion erroneous in this instance, stating however that I thought some guard ought if practicable to be found against the abuse of the principle. I will take as early an opportunity as I can of pleading the cause of the colony with His Majesty's ministers they are always apt to be too pinching, especially in these days of great expenditure.[58]

A week later, Wilberforce wrote to Marsden to tell him that he should 'cultivate the governor's favour, so far as you can'. He explained that Macquarie had recently consulted him about the 'important and delicate topic' of admitting emancipists into society and 'even into office'. Wilberforce had talked the issue over with several friends whose 'understanding and principles' made them wise counsellors, and he told Marsden that, without a single exception, they were all of the opinion that 'persons who came out as convicts, should after giving sufficient proof of their having amended their ways, be admissible into office, but then we all agree in conceiving that in order to preserve the principal from abuse and to prevent the practice from becoming injurious instead of being beneficial, some previous recognition of their reformation should proceed their return into society'.[59]

Wilberforce agreed with the idea Macquarie had proposed to Bathurst, that there should be 'some public declaratory act' with which ex-convicts could demonstrate their reform. Macquarie felt it was a key issue for the future prosperity of the colony, because seven-eighths of the population of New South Wales, 'now upwards of fifteen thousand souls', depended on it.[60]

At the time of Wilberforce's conciliatory letters, Marsden was already knee-deep in another feud with Macquarie. In February 1814, Marsden had taken to the pulpit at St John's, defiantly refusing to read to the congregation Macquarie's government order castigating the farmers for not selling their wheat cheaply to the government stores in time of drought, and praising Thomas Gilberthorpe of Pitt Town for his example of generosity.[61] Marsden refused to read the order a second time, and Macquarie cautioned him to ignore the governor's commands at his peril. Marsden's defiance earned him a reprimand from the Colonial Office and, more painfully, from the Archbishop of Canterbury.

Then Marsden and Macquarie quarrelled over attacks on Marsden in the *Sydney Gazette*, of which Macquarie's secretary J.T. Campbell was the official censor.

While in London showing off his wool in 1808, Marsden had made a public appeal to support a lending library in New South Wales. The Bible Society had provided Bibles and New Testaments and, before long, there were 455 books from there and from Sydney benefactors, though the range of subjects was fairly narrow. There was an *Encyclopaedia Britannica* and a tome on Spanish rams, but after that, it was pretty much a hundred tracts each on subjects such as drunkards, swearers, Sabbath-breakers and unhappy women, as well as six sermons on original sin and twelve on the torments of hell.

Marsden kept his book collection at the back of his Parramatta house, a long way from the main population in Sydney, and some of the donors began complaining that their gifts were being hidden away. The *Gazette* began some gentle chiding that Marsden was keeping his public library a secret unto himself. Marsden, displaying the thin skin that seemed to be common to some of the hardiest colonists of the time, told Macquarie he was deeply offended, and that 'whosoever holds up the clergy and magistrates to public contempt stabs at the very vitals of that government which supports and protects him'.[62] Marsden accused Campbell of being the author of the 'libels'.

Macquarie told Marsden to get over it but that, if he was really so hurt, he should sue. Marsden would eventually bring the books out of the back room for the opening of a Sydney reading room in 1820.

Meanwhile, Macquarie and Marsden continued to spar.

Marsden bristled at Macquarie's government order of 10 September 1814, in which he scaled back the flogging of convicts and instead established jail gangs at Parramatta, Windsor and Liverpool, where the offenders would wear clothing that was 'a public mark of disgrace', a 'party' coloured uniform 'half black and half white' to 'distinguish them from the better behaved'.[63]

Magistrates were to inform Macquarie of all fines and punishments they meted out:

> The governor recommends in the strongest manner to the magistrates, to inflict corporal punishment as seldom as possible; but to substitute in its stead, confinement in the stocks for petty crimes, and either solitary confinement, or hard labour in the jail gangs, according to their judgement of the degrees of offence; still keeping in view the general conduct and character of the delinquents.[64]

He also banned magistrates sitting alone from inflicting more than fifty lashes, a figure that Marsden felt was far too low for some of the 'dangerous infamous characters' in the colony.[65] Marsden had once sentenced a man to 100 lashes for stealing a fowl, and he believed that, if the escapee Thomas Hill had been given hundreds of lashes at a time, he would have turned from his wicked ways and not been hanged for stabbing Constable Thomas Smith near Parramatta.[66]

In September 1800, Marsden and his fellow magistrate, the often-sloshed Richard Atkins, had sentenced 20-year-old Irishman Paddy Galvin to 300 lashes a day until he gave up information on home-made weapons believed to have been hidden by convicts planning a rebellion. It was a windy day, and pieces of skin and splashes of blood hit onlookers more than 10 metres away. After Galvin's body was reduced to a quivering bloody mess on the first day, the young Irishman told the flogger: 'You may as well hang me now, for you never will get any music from me.' He was carted away to the hospital.[67]

Macquarie was ready to give Marsden a public flogging, at least verbally, and was just waiting for the chance. The English evangelist William Goode the elder[68] provided the ammunition when he published *An Entire New Version of the Book of Psalms* in two volumes.[69] Macquarie couldn't wait to tell Bathurst that Marsden was trying out this controversial 'innovation' on his flock:

> A few months ago, Mr Marsden either imported or received from a missionary society, a number of copies of Dr Goode's version of the Psalms, and without any previous communication or reference to me on the subject, he caused them to be sung for some Sundays in our churches to the exclusion of those attached by authority to the Bible and Book of Common Prayer. It appearing to me that this was a very unwarranted violation of the service of the established church, and one which would probably lead to still further and greater innovations on its sacred ceremonies, I have deemed it my duty to prohibit this version, or any other than that attached to the Bible and Prayer Book of the Church of England, from being any longer used until such time as reference could be made to the supreme authority of our church, and the commands of His Royal Highness the Prince Regent should be communicated to me.[70]

Macquarie told Bathurst that Marsden and 'some of assistant chaplains are originally of low rank', and 'not qualified in the usual way for the sacred functions entrusted to them, and are also much tinctured by Methodistical and other sectarian principles, which dispose them to a hasty adoption of new systems or at least of new forms to the exclusion of the old establishment of the Church of England'.[71] Tolerating these new ways would 'give latitude to dissent' in this 'young and unschooled colony'.[72]

Bathurst gave Macquarie his blessing to tell Marsden to stick, with 'strict adherence',[73] to the Bible that everyone else was reading. Marsden still tried to sneak a few new hymns into his Sunday service and Macquarie took special delight in admonishing him.[74]

Still, superficially he treated the chaplain with respect, and in July 1815, gave him 400 more hectares as a reward for his work as a magistrate, planned churches in all his new townships and made expensive repairs to St John's. He also cooperated with Marsden in planning a new St Andrew's Cathedral for Sydney, and gave official recognition to his missionary work with the Maori as Marsden set out for New Zealand in November 1814 on the brig *Active*.

THE RELATIVE PEACE that had prevailed around the Cowpastures was soon being shattered. On 2 March 1816, a group of about thirty Aboriginal men attacked the servants' quarters on George Palmer's property on the Nepean, and the following day, four of Palmer's men crossed the river with three other locals to take back what had been stolen.

When their progress was slowed in a marshy flat near Captain Fowler's farm, a large group of Indigenous men circled them and hailed down 'a shower of spears'.[75] Some of the men picked up guns that had fallen and used the white man's weapons back on them.

In a 'terrible attack', Patrick McHugh, Dennis Hagan, John Lewis and John Murray 'fell in an instant, either from shot, or by the spear', and a teenager named William Brazil received a spear in the back. The Aboriginal men chased the survivors as they took refuge in the farmhouse of Edmund Wright, but again the next day, another sixty of them attacked, destroying the farm buildings. The Wrights' house was ransacked, and as Mrs Wright hid in the loft with William Bagnell, one of the farm labourers, 'every possible endeavour [was] made to murder them'.[76] The attackers darted spears through the roof and through a temporary bark ceiling, missing the pair of terrified locals by 'a hair's breadth'.

Bagnell, fearing that they would be killed at any moment, threw open a window and begged for their lives. One of the young Indigenous warriors, mistakenly identified in initial accounts as the guide David Budbury, managed to convince the raiders that the white people 'should not be killed this time'.[77]

Reluctantly, after destroying everything in the house, and taking all the food and much of the corn in the fields, the attackers recrossed the river, 'very dispassionately bidding Mrs Wright and Bagnell a good bye!'[78]

Soon, a great arc around the Cumberland Plain, from Lane Cove on Sydney's north shore to Bringelly in the west and Camden in the south, became a battleground in what the *Gazette* called a co-ordinated plan of the 'mountain natives' and the 'nearer hordes' to plunder the settlers' maize fields. Even on the Bathurst Plains, a group of Aboriginal men had stopped and robbed a government cart taking provisions to the new settlement, and the *Gazette* warned that they demonstrated 'considerably less apprehension than formerly from the effect of firearms'.[79]

Then, at about 5 p.m. on 10 March 1816, a startling report reached the Hassall family's Macquarie Grove property, where the Governor had buried his beloved greyhound some months earlier. Nineteen-year-old Samuel Hassall was in his 'little room composing and committing to paper a morning prayer' when a messenger arrived with the terrifying news that 'the whole body of Gundenoran [Gandangara] natives' intended to attack the Macarthurs' nearby farm to 'plunder and murder all before them'.[80] They then planned to 'proceed down to Mr Oxley's to act with them in the same manner', before attacking the Hassall property. Hassall sent his young sisters away to safety.

A small detachment of soldiers arrived at magistrate Robert Lowe's farm, Birling, where 'all the arms and ammunition in his district' were being gathered. News spread that three of the Macarthurs' servants at Upper Camden had 'fallen victim to the dreadful atrocities of the savage natives'. The armed party immediately distributed their ammunition, though each man only received a small portion.

Hassall would recall that the soldiers 'mustered about forty armed men, some with muskets some with pistols some with pitch forks some with pikes and others with nothing', and they marched to Lower then Upper Camden, where a 'small company of the more friendly natives' said they could guide them to the warriors who had committed the 'dreadful atrocities'. They also warned the militia that these warriors 'would show fight whenever attacked'.

On the nearby Razorback Range, they came face to face with their enemy, who had apparently stockpiled spears and lured the white men into a trap.

Hassall would remember that the Aboriginal warriors were 'posted on a high perpendicular rock' and 'began to dance in a manner daring our approach'. Lowe's men fired their muskets, but the natives, knowing that the guns were good for just one shot, fell down as soon as the men aimed at them, only to 'get up and dance' after the explosion.

Spears and stones then rained down on the colonists 'in great abundance'.

Realising they had no chance, the colonists ran away as fast as they could. Hassall, on horseback, 'could scarce keep up with some of them', who 'even threw off their shoes to enable them to run fast'.[81]

Refugees from the various scattered farms huddled together at Narellan and were told to flee, as 'the natives had obliged us to retreat', but one woman said 'she would not go till her husband went with her, or she would die with him'.

Reinforcements arrived with ammunition but Hassall remained 'in daily expectation' of the warriors 'paying another visit'.[82]

Three weeks later, the *Gazette* reported:

At the beginning of the week an attack was made by a body of natives upon the farm of Lewis, at the Nepean, whose wife and man servant they cruelly murdered. The head of the unfortunate woman was sever'd from the body, and the man was dreadfully mangled with a tomahawk. The furious wretches afterwards plundered the house, and wantonly speared a number of pigs ... A number of the natives, supposed 80 or 90 at the least, a few days since made their appearance at Lane Cove, and committed depredations on several farms.[83]

The attacks were becoming more and more frequent and widespread. Colonists were advised only to travel in numbers.

Even Macquarie's vision splendid of opening up the country west of the Blue Mountains was being threatened. He had long conceded that most of the attacks by the Indigenous peoples had started when cruelties were heaped upon them by the settlers, but now he would tolerate no excuses for their barbarity. Many settlers had already abandoned their farms.[84]

He wrote to Bathurst to say that he had consistently shown 'much kindness' to the Aboriginal people.[85] He had given them some of their own land back, set up his Native Institution at Parramatta and always tried to remain on 'friendly terms', overlooking 'many of their occasional acts of violence and atrocity'. Though it was clearly going to be a 'more arduous task' than he had first imagined, he told Bathurst he was still determined 'to domesticate and civilize these wild, rude people'.[86]

While he had wanted New South Wales to be a colony run on civil, rather than military lines, Macquarie was still a major-general in the British Army. He had been a soldier all his life, and this was a war he was determined to win.

He began to mobilise the biggest military expedition in the history of the colony.

His plan was to strike the Aboriginal people 'with terror against committing similar acts of violence in future'.[87]

His orders are still chilling more than two centuries later.

Chapter 26

APRIL TO JULY 1816, NEW SOUTH WALES

*In the event of the natives making the smallest show of resistance –
or refusing to surrender when called upon so to do – the officers
commanding the military parties have been authorized to fire on them
to compel them to surrender; hanging up on trees the bodies of such
natives as may be killed on such occasions, in order to strike
the greater terror into the survivors.*

MACQUARIE INSTRUCTING HIS TROOPS ON HOW TO DEAL
WITH ABORIGINAL FIGHTERS[1]

IT WAS A COLD, moonlit morning. The Cataract River
flowed rapidly northwards from its source near Mount Pleasant
in the Illawarra. The deep water cascading over the boulders was
caught in the stream, before rushing through the deep canyons.
The mossy crags and thick forest carpeted the whole area in a sea
of dense, dark foliage, ending in sheer cliffs 60 metres high.

The air was heavy with menace. There was no sound of an owl,
no rustle of a kangaroo, no lowing of cattle in the distance – just
the burbles of the fast-flowing water, punctuated by the thump of
boots striking the rocky ground as the red-coated soldiers of the
46th prepared to administer frontier justice.

The pocket-watch of Captain James Wallis[2] had told him it
was just after 1 a.m. when he ordered the shadowy march from
the camp at the Cowpastures to this spot. It was 17 April 1816,

and Wallis had been hunting Aboriginal people in vain for a frustrating week. Now, his native guides had led him to this majestic campsite, shrouded in the soft moonglow.

The camps were deserted but their fires were still burning. Wallis, a talented artist and ambitious young officer from Gloucestershire, crept forward to where he hoped the locals were hiding. He feared that, knowing this country better than he did, his quarry had escaped once again to make his pursuit look like a folly.

Then he heard a child cry.

APRIL 1816 WAS SUPPOSED to be a joyful time in New South Wales. Macquarie had now been governor for longer than any of his predecessors, and was proud of how he had shaped the colony in accordance with his vision for an enlightened, liberal outpost of empire, a place where anyone could get a fair go.

Patients from the decrepit Dawes Point infirmary were about to be transferred to his rum hospital, the grandest building in Sydney. The year 1816 had started in jubilation, with a victory dinner for 120 elegantly attired ladies and gentlemen in one of the hospital halls, which was festooned with native flora and exquisitely crafted decorations that spelled out 'WATERLOO, WELLINGTON, and VICTORY'[3] as Sydney celebrated the final defeat of Napoleon.

But Macquarie was overloaded with stress. In a private letter, he complained to Earl Bathurst about Lieutenant-Governor Davey's behaviour in Hobart, with fresh reports of Davey's 'dissipation and profligacy' in almost every despatch from Van Diemen's Land: 'He spends almost his entire time in drinking, and every other species of low depravity, in company with the basest and meanest of the people ... what renders this debasement the more gross and offensive is that he is a married man, and his wife and daughter, who live with him, are both very amiable and highly respectable.'[4]

Macquarie claimed that Davey was idle, indolent, always inebriated and 'incapable of executing the public duties of his station'. There were reports that he was not only 'profligate in his private life ... but also that he is extremely venal and corrupt in his public capacity. Among other abuses of power with which he is taxed, he is charged with having been privy to and sanctioning a great deal of clandestine trade and smuggling of spirits at the Derwent'.[5]

The Reverend Samuel Marsden was always on Macquarie's mind as well. They had recently clashed yet again, this time over accommodation for convicts.

Marsden complained to Macquarie about the wicked mood in the colony. Macquarie pointed out that crime was worst at Parramatta, where Marsden was both chaplain and magistrate, and that he should do more to stop it.

Marsden wrote a public letter to Macquarie, as Principal Chaplain of New South Wales, and sent a copy of it to be published in London, knowing it would embarrass the governor. It said: 'During more than 20 years' residence in this town, I do not remember any former given period, when so many offences were committed against the peace, as there have been for some time past. House-breaking, highway-robberies, and other daring crimes have increased to a very alarming degree.'[6]

Marsden went on to highlight the urgent need for a convict barracks at Parramatta, instead of the current system in which many male convicts were scattered all over town in different lodgings, procuring beds 'amongst the lower order of people who live upon their vices'.

He told Macquarie, and the world at large, that female convicts in particular were in 'a miserable situation' without proper accommodation; they were the most 'infamous and abandoned characters composed of the very dregs' of the colony, glad to cohabit with any 'poor wretched man' who would give them shelter for a night, often relying on prostitution to survive.[7]

Macquarie had put a stop to sex trafficking as soon as he arrived in Sydney, and convict women were now housed at the Female Factory in Parramatta before being assigned work with approved families. While the prisoners waited, they toiled in the tattered overcrowded woollen factory run by Marsden and Hannibal Macarthur,[8] John's nephew. It consisted of one long room, 25 metres by 6 metres, where the women slept on the boards atop fleeces dragged from the storeroom, surrounded by looms and spinning wheels.[9]

The factory was directly above the men's jail, so the women were forced to endure the constant lewd jests of the male prisoners below them, the smutty lines wafting up like poisonous fumes through the many cracks in the decade-old wooden floor. They did their best to avoid Marsden's wrath, lest he have their heads shaved or chain two prisoners together for a month, as he sometimes did.

Macquarie had actually been petitioning Bathurst to build better female barracks for three years, but Marsden made no mention of this in his letter.[10] Macquarie could only lament that Marsden was apparently trying to make a name for himself at his own expense.

Their war would continue.

IN APRIL 1816, as his soldiers chased Indigenous people across the colony, Macquarie was still awaiting word from London on the future of Jeffery Hart Bent, who sulked at his home and fomented trouble, and encouraged his friends to do the same.

One of those friends, the Reverend Benjamin Vale,[11] Chaplain of the 46th Regiment, had been a constant pain for Macquarie since setting foot on Sydney Cove a year earlier. Like Jeffery Bent, he found fault everywhere. He had repeatedly expressed 'much feeling of disappointment and discontent at the situation' in Sydney, where the pay and conditions were 'much inferior' to what he had been led to expect when he received his appointment. He wanted a separate parish, his own church, and 'a well-furnished parsonage house, with an allowance of government servants, rations, fuel, etc.' He didn't get them, and became 'discontented and miserable'.[12]

Macquarie had tried hard to help out Vale. He made him assistant to the Reverend Cowper, put him and his family on the government stores tab, assigned him a government servant and gave him the same rent allowance as an army captain:

> I have even gone so far as to say that I would give him a grant of land with the indulgences, usually extended to free settlers, whenever he would chuse to select a situation for that purpose. All this I have done in order to reconcile this poor man to his situation, but all has been in vain, for he still continues to be discontented ... Everything further in my power shall, however, be done to render him as comfortable as his own temper and my ability will admit.[13]

Yet in April 1816, Vale and his friend, the lawyer William Moore, committed a rash act that looked like it had been expressly designed to embarrass Macquarie internationally. As soon as the governor left Sydney on an inspection tour, Vale and Moore rushed down to the dock with legal papers to arrest the visiting American ship, the *Traveller,* which was bringing tea, sugar and other goods that were in short supply in Sydney.

Vale and Moore cited the *Navigation Act*, which was designed to protect East India Company trade. Even though the American war with Britain was long over and both Macquarie and the East India Company had approved the visit, they declared the *Traveller* an enemy vessel.

When Macquarie returned from his tour a week later and heard what had happened to the American ship, he was furious. He immediately 'removed the arrest', sent for Vale and harshly rebuked him. Instead of apologising, though, the chaplain 'attempted by argument to vindicate the measure',[14] so Macquarie ordered his arrest and trial by court martial.

The result would prove a great embarrassment to Macquarie.

ALL THIS TURMOIL was swirling through Macquarie's head on the morning of 17 April, as he slept at Government House beside Elizabeth and with little Lachlan peacefully nearby, his long blond hair and rosy cheek resting lightly on the pillow.

At that same hour, the Dharug people were much less comfortable as they tried to shelter amid the rugged rocks and cliffs near Appin, knowing that their lives were in danger.

Macquarie's foot soldiers were about to perpetually stain the governor's record with the blood of innocent men, women and children.

MACQUARIE HAD written a précis in his memo book on 10 April of the orders that he had given to three officers. Their mission was to take place the next day.

He had resolved to send a grim warning to the native population of the colony. His reputation for mercy was set aside. He wrote that he felt 'compelled, from a paramount sense of public duty', to 'chastise these hostile tribes' by inflicting 'terrible and exemplary punishments'.[15]

Macquarie might have been psychologically unhinged. Certainly, his health was in decline. The years of heavy drinking, the medications he had taken and the enormous stress of his battles with the Bents, Vale and Marsden might all have contributed to his 180-degree turn in relation to a people he had always viewed with benign paternalism. His authority was being threatened by the Aboriginal raids and, as the leader of an army, he was not going to let enemy forces gain the upper hand even for a moment.

Once, he had apologised for the Aboriginal attacks on settlers. Now, he would not be swayed by moderate voices.

Dr Charles Throsby, who had hosted Macquarie at his property Glenfield, counselled the governor against reprisals.

On 5 April 1816, Throsby had written to Acting Provost-Marshall William Wentworth, expressing his concerns for the safety of the Aboriginal men Yelloming and Bitugully and the young Doual, who two years earlier had explored the Bong Bong area with his friend Hamilton Hume. Throsby outlined the horrific treatment of Yelloming's wife and children that had occurred during earlier battles with settlers:

The people not content at shooting at them in the most treacherous manner in the dark, actually cut the woman's arm off and stripped the scalp of her head over her eyes, and on going up to them and finding one of the children only wounded one of the fellows deliberately beat the infant's brains out with the butt of his musket, the whole of the bodies then left in that state by the (brave) party unburied![16]

Was it any wonder, Throsby asked, that the natives went looking for revenge?[17]

Yet Macquarie would tolerate no excuses:

The Aborigines, or native blacks of this country, having for the last three years manifested a strong and sanguinary hostile spirit, in repeated instances of murders, outrages, and depredations of all descriptions against the settlers and other white inhabitants residing in the interior and more remote parts of the colony, notwithstanding their having been frequently called upon and admonished to discontinue their hostile incursions and treated on all these occasions with the greatest kindness and forbearance by government; — and having nevertheless recently committed several cruel and most barbarous murders on the settlers and their families and servants, killed their cattle, and robbed them of their grain and other property to a considerable amount, it becomes absolutely necessary to put a stop to these outrages and disturbances, and to adopt the strongest and most coercive measures to prevent a recurrence of them, so as to protect the European inhabitants in their persons & properties.[18]

Macquarie ordered three separate military detachments to march into the 'interior and remote parts of the colony' to punish 'the hostile natives, by clearing the country of them entirely, and driving them across the mountains; as well as if possible to apprehend the natives who have committed the late murders and outrages, with the view of their being made dreadful and severe examples of, if taken alive'.[19]

> I have directed as many natives as possible to be made prisoners, with the view of keeping them as hostages until the real guilty ones have surrendered themselves, or have been given up by their tribes to summary justice. In the event of the natives making the smallest show of resistance − or refusing to surrender when called upon so to do − the officers commanding the military parties have been authorized to fire on them to compel them to surrender; hanging up on trees the bodies of such natives as may be killed on such occasions, in order to strike the greater terror into the survivors.[20]

Hanging the bodies of those deemed to be criminals was not an uncommon thing in Macquarie's lifetime. It had occurred in Scotland during his formative years and still took place in Van Diemen's Land. Even in Sydney, the body of convict Francis Morgan had been left dancing in the wind for four years on a gibbet at Fort Denison as a perpetual warning after his execution in 1796.[21]

Macquarie's plan called for men of his 46th Regiment to scour the country from Kurrajong on the north side of the Hawkesbury, to the 'Five Islands, alias Illawarra, on the south' and 'eastward of the Cowpastures and River Nepean'. Each of the detachments would have local guides, including some Aboriginal men friendly to the colonists.

Macquarie ordered Captain W.G.B. Schaw to hit the 'hostile natives' hard around the Nepean, Grose and Hawkesbury Rivers. Schaw was to treat the first peoples like enemies in war:

> On any occasion of seeing or falling in with the natives, either in bodies or singly, they are to be called on, by your friendly native guides, to surrender themselves to you as prisoners of war. If they refuse to do so, make the least

show of resistance, or attempt to run away from you, you will fire upon and compel them to surrender, breaking and destroying the spears, clubs, and waddies of all those you take prisoners. Such natives as happen to be killed on such occasions, if grown up men, are to be hanged up on trees in conspicuous situations, to strike the survivors with the greater terror. On all occasions of your being obliged to have recourse to offensive and coercive measures, you will use every possible precaution to save the lives of the native women and children, but taking as many of them as you can prisoners.[22]

If women and children were killed, they were to be buried 'where they fell'.

Lieutenant Charles Dawe was ordered to do the same in reprisals around the Cowpastures, while Captain Wallis took his men towards Liverpool, before heading further south to Appin and Airds. All of the officers carried the names of known offenders.

Schaw's troops came up empty-handed, the Aboriginal people one step ahead of them the whole time. The soldiers didn't even see any Indigenous men, let alone get the chance to kill some. They marched south, but realised their pursuit of the warriors on the Wingecarribee River was in vain after the Indigenous guide Colebee, who had helped William Cox cross the Blue Mountains, told him that the tracks they spotted were two days old.

Maybe they were, maybe they weren't. Colebee might have been helping his own kin. He was the son of Yarramundi and the brother of Maria, one of the students at Macquarie's Native Institution.

At the Cowpastures, the Aboriginal guide Tindale, from the Muringong people, seemed happy to point Dawe's men in the wrong direction, too, though a local stock-keeper said there were some Aboriginal people staying on the Macarthur estate. Two warriors were subsequently killed and a boy was taken prisoner.[23]

Wallis was accompanied by the bushman John Warby, and two Dharawal men – young David Budbury, who had helped

Warby show Macquarie the gorges south of Appin, and Bundle, who had been orphaned as a child soon after the colony was established, and who had worked variously as an interpreter, tracker and constable.[24]

When Budbury and Bundle realised what the mission was all about, they went AWOL after the first day, most likely to warn the Aboriginal tribes. Warby winked at their escape and did his best to muddy the tracks as well, which made Wallis 'exceedingly annoyed'.[25] Soon Warby went missing for a day. When he returned, he was less than helpful.

On the second day of the mission, 12 April, Wallis arrived at Appin, where he found Aboriginal men on John Kennedy's Heston farm. Among the group were Yelloming and Bitugully, who were both among Macquarie's 'most wanted'.

Kennedy pleaded their case. He told Wallis – wrongly – that the two had actually been removed from Macquarie's list, and that the men were actually helping him protect the local farms from attack. Wallis let the men be, and sent word to Sydney for instructions.[26]

An overseer on Dr Redfern's farm by the name of McAllister told Wallis that there was a group of Aboriginal people camped there, so the soldiers marched along the Georges River to the property, only to find nothing but water, trees and rocks. Wallis 'reprobated McAllister's conduct most highly'.[27]

Wallis then marched the soldiers to various neighbouring farms, then back to Charles Throsby's Glenfield. The Indigenous people were always ahead of the game, however, as hard to catch as smoke.

Finally, a message arrived from the local pound-keeper William Tyson on the night of 16 April that there were Aboriginal people camped near Appin at William Broughton's Lachlan Vale farm, beside some ravines.

At a little after one o'clock on the morning of 17 April, Wallis's troops headed to the spot. Ex-convict guide Thomas Noble joined them, and led them to where he had seen the Aboriginal people encamped.

The deserted fires suggested that they had fled. But then the soldiers heard the cries of a cold child stab the morning air.

Their ears pricked up and their fingers reached for the triggers on their muskets.

Wallis ordered them to form a line, and they pushed on as quietly as they could through thick bush towards the 'precipitous banks of a deep rocky creek'.

Then the Aboriginal people's dogs began to bark, and the horror unfolded.

Trapped against the backdrop of the steep cliffs, the terrified Dharawal people could do nothing as Macquarie's soldiers opened fire. They ran for cover in desperation as the grey dawn of morning began to shine light on them.

The soldiers cut down some of them with rifle fire but, in the half-light, Wallis could only make out thin, dark shapes bounding from rock to rock, some shot, some falling inadvertently to their deaths with ear-splitting screams that echoed down the canyons. Others were seen 'rushing in despair over the precipice'[28] rather than surrender.

Wallis later said that he ordered his men to take as many prisoners as possible, and to be careful in sparing the women and children, but he 'regretted' to say some had been shot, and others met their fate by leaping to their deaths.

> I was however partly successful, I led up two women and three children. They were all that remained to whom death would not be a blessing. It was a melancholy but necessary duty I was employed upon. I regretted the death of an old native [Balgin] and the unfortunate women and children from the rocky place they fell in, I found it would be almost impossible to bury them.[29]

Wallis counted fourteen dead bodies strewn about in every direction, but no one could be sure how many men, women and children had been lost in the craggy rocks among the steep cliffs. The soldiers found a large quantity of potatoes and corn, and many spears and clubs left behind.

John Kennedy, who had promoted peaceful relations with the

Aboriginal people, supplied ropes and carts for the soldiers to cart away the prisoners. With great difficulty, Wallis had the mangled bodies of Durelle and Cannabayagal hauled up the precipice. Durelle was said to have been a Dharawal speaker, probably of the Muringong people, and Cannabayagal[30] was a well-known Gandangara warrior and leader from the Burragorang Valley.[31]

Wallis said he sent Lieutenant Adamson George Parker[32] with the bodies of Durelle and Cannabayagal to a prominent hill on Broughton's farm. There, Parker had the two warriors hauled up by their necks to hang from tree branches for days, as a warning to any of the other Indigenous people who thought about disobeying Macquarie again.

William Byrne, who was a local boy of eight at the time, remembered the massacre and its aftermath differently from Wallis. In his old age, Byrne recalled the slaughter, saying that 'The government ... sent up a detachment of soldiers who ran a portion of them into a drive, shot sixteen of them, and hanged three on McGee's Hill.' Byrne said *three* bodies were strung up, and that the soldiers 'cut off the heads and brought them to Sydney, where the government paid 30 shillings and a gallon of rum each for them'.[33]

Though Macquarie did not authorise it, there is compelling evidence that three of the dead *were* decapitated. One scholarly report claims that Cannabayagal's severed head left New South Wales in the luggage of naval surgeon Patrick Hill, and that Hill himself claimed that Adamson George Parker had supplied him with the skull.[34] Some time shortly after his return to Britain, Hill is said to have given Cannabayagal's skull to Sir George Mackenzie, a mineralogist who had developed a strong interest in the emerging field of phrenology.[35]

Adding to the weight of evidence, in 1991, the National Museum of Australia in Canberra received three skulls that had been held in the Anatomy Department of the University of Edinburgh for the previous 175 years. One was said to be Cannabayagal's, still bearing the cut marks where the head was severed from the body. The other two were thought to be those of Durelle and an unnamed woman.[36]

SOME OF THE SOLDIERS were certain that one of the Aboriginal men who ran through the bush to escape the massacre was David Budbury, the guide who had absconded, and Adamson was sent to wait in ambush for him and other warriors at a river crossing called Broughton's Pass just to the south. Adamson returned, saying he hadn't seen a thing.

Wallis sent Warby with the two women and three child prisoners to the property of former convict Henry McCudden at Airds, then McCudden took them to Liverpool. Meanwhile, Macquarie ordered the arrest of Bitugully and Yelloming, who were still at Kennedy's farm. They were tied up and taken in a cart to Sydney, along with the women and children who survived the massacre. Wallis left a corporal and three privates to protect Kennedy from 'the revengeful fury of the natives'.[37]

Five days later, in response to a report of Aboriginal sightings, Adamson headed a search around the farm of George Woodhouse,[38] who had been Ellis Bent's chief clerk. The same night at John Kennedy's farm, Parker took into custody Hamilton Hume's friend Doual and another 'hostile native', ironically known as Quiet.[39] Some of the Aboriginal men gave themselves up rather than face another massacre.

Macquarie noted in his journal on 4 May that:

The three separate military detachments ... sent out on the 10th. of last month to scour the interior of the country and drive the natives from the settlements of the white inhabitants, returned this day to headquarters, after having executed the several parts of their instructions entirely to my satisfaction; having inflicted exemplary punishments on the hostile natives, and brought in a few of them as prisoners to Sydney.[40]

Macquarie, looking to expand his re-education of Aboriginal children to become peaceable members of society, told Captain Schaw: 'Select and secure [twelve] fine healthy good-looking children from the whole of the native prisoners of war taken in the course of your operations and direct them to be delivered to ... the Native Institution at Parramatta.[41]

He issued a proclamation, telling the colony that while 'a few innocent men, women, and children may have fallen in these conflicts', it was hoped that 'this unavoidable result, and the severity which has attended it, will eventually strike terror amongst the surviving tribes, and deter them from ... further outrages and barbarities'.[42]

He then issued new rules for the native population, even if the vast majority did not speak or read English:

No native shall ever appear at or within one mile of any town, village, or farm, occupied by, or belonging to any British subject ... armed of any description, such as spears, clubs, or waddies, on pain of being deemed and considered in a state of aggression and hostility, *and treated accordingly.*

No group of more than six natives, being entirely unarmed, shall ever come to *lurk or loiter* about any farm in the interior, on pain of being considered enemies, *and treated accordingly.*

That the practice among the native tribes, of assembling in large bodies or parties armed, and of fighting and attacking each other on the plea of inflicting punishments on transgressors of their own customs and manners, at or near Sydney, and other principal towns and settlements is abolished, as a barbarous custom, repugnant to the British laws.

Natives who wish to be considered under the protection of the British Government, and disposed to conduct themselves in a peaceable, inoffensive, and honest manner, shall be furnished with passports or certificates to that effect, signed by the governor ... which they will find will protect them from being injured or molested by any person, so long as they conduct themselves peaceably, inoffensively, and honestly.

Settlers have the right to drive away groups of Aborigines by 'force of arms' and there are always troops at Sydney, Parramatta and Windsor to help.[43]

Macquarie said he wanted the native population to 'obtain an honest and comfortable subsistence by their own labour and industry'. He was always willing to help, he said, and ready to grant 'small portions of land' to 'friendly natives' who wanted to cultivate their own farms. They would be supplied by the king's stores for six months, and furnished with 'the necessary agricultural tools; and also, with wheat, maize, and potatoes for seed; work clothes and one colonial blanket for each family member'.

He urged all native parents to send their children to his Native Institution, a 'desirable and good opportunity of providing for their helpless offspring, and of having them brought up, clothed, fed, and educated in a seminary established for such humane and desirable purposes'.[44]

As a self-styled benevolent dictator, he saw the future of Indigenous Australia as a life of working small farms or becoming labourers or servants of the white man. He urged them to 'relinquish their wandering, idle, and predatory habits of life, and to become industrious and useful members of a community where they will find protection and encouragement'.[45] Macquarie had done little of late to encourage the Aboriginal people to trust in these promises, though.

He reported to Earl Bathurst that 'in consequence of the hostile and sanguinary dispositions of the natives', he had 'determined to send out some military detachments into the interior, either to apprehend or destroy them ... giving them instructions to make as many prisoners as possible; this service occupied a period of 23 days'. Macquarie told Bathurst that Wallis and his men had met some 'resistance', and that fourteen natives had been killed. 'This necessary but painful duty,' he wrote, 'was conducted by the officers in command of the detachments, perfectly in conformity to the instructions I had furnished them.' Two of the most 'ferocious and sanguinary of the natives', he said, were among the dead.[46]

Macquarie handed out £80 5s in cash rewards to some of the white trackers who had led the troops. John Warby and

John Jackson each received £12, Thomas Noble £3. Henry McCudden received £9 5s for cart hire to carry the prisoners.[47] The Aboriginal guides Bidgee-Bidgee, Harry, Bundle, Tindale, Colebee and Nurragingy (Creek Jemmy) each received shoes and blankets, four days of provisions, half a pint of spirits and half a pound of tobacco. Colebee and Nurragingy were each later given 12 hectares of land to farm at what is now Blacktown,[48] and Macquarie presented Nurragingy with his 'Order of Merit', handing him 'a handsome brass breastplate, having his name inscribed thereon in full as Chief of the South-Creek-Tribe'.[49] Macquarie appointed Bidgee-Bidgee 'Chief of the Kissing Point Tribe', complete with another engraved breastplate, as a reward for encouraging 'Coggie, the late Chief of the Cowpasture Tribe' to 'deliver up his arms', and had him promise 'to be friendly in future to all White People'.

Captains Wallis and Schaw each received 15 gallons of rum as a prize and Wallis was given the command of the Newcastle base for his 'zealous exertions and strict attention to fulfilling of the instructions' at Appin.[50]

THE HAWKESBURY AND NEPEAN experienced great flooding at the end of May 1816, wiping out the wheat crops and threatening food shortages, but Macquarie was satisfied that the immediate threat of mass Aboriginal attacks was over.

To celebrate the king's birthday on 4 June, Elizabeth hosted a dinner party for seventy-eight followed by coffee and a dance, while Macquarie ordered the release of fifteen men, women and children, the last of the 'black native prisoners' who had been in jail on suspicion of being concerned in the 'recent hostilities'.[51]

Two Aboriginal boys named Nalour and Dooro, and two girls named Mybah and Betty, all about eight years of age, had been among the prisoners, and Macquarie had them packed off to the Native Institution. They seemed happy to go, travelling up the Parramatta River by boat under the supervision of a constable.[52]

The only Aboriginal person who remained a prisoner after Macquarie's war was Hamilton Hume's friend, the young

Aboriginal guide Doual.[53] Macquarie told him he was lucky not to hang, and banished him to Port Dalrymple in Van Diemen's Land for seven years, 'in remittance of the death sentence imposed upon him'. He was willing to show compassion to the young man 'in consideration of his ignorance of the laws and duties of civilized nations', but if he somehow made it back to New South Wales within seven years, he would suffer the penalty of death.[54]

Macquarie's military offensive had killed a lot of people, but most of the Aboriginal leaders remained free. Settlers at the Kurrajong Brush, in the foothills of the Blue Mountains, were attacked with such ferocity and frequency that, by the end of the month, Joseph Hobson was the only one still farming there. On 7 July, he was killed with a spear through the heart.[55]

Attacks on William Cox's Mulgoa farm resulted in the murder and mutilation of a shepherd. Two hundred 'very fine sheep' were hurled down an 'immense precipice'.[56] At Glenroy on the Cox's River, on the western side of the Blue Mountains, Sergeant Jeremiah Murphy was ordered not to allow Aboriginal people nearer to the settlement than 60 yards, and to send any whom he captured, either handcuffed or with their hands tied with rope, to the depot at Springwood and then on to Parramatta.

The governor issued another proclamation on 20 July 1816, declaring ten Aboriginal warriors[57] as outlaws and giving anyone – 'whether free men, prisoners of the Crown, or friendly natives' – 'the power to kill and utterly destroy them'.[58]

Some individual Aboriginal men, he wrote, were 'far more determinedly hostile and mischievous than the rest', and had 'lately instigated their deluded followers to commit several further atrocious acts of barbarity'. As a consequence, Macquarie had now declared the ten outlaws 'avowed enemies to the peace and good order of society'.

He offered 'a reward of ten pounds sterling' for each of them, dead or alive.[59]

The bounties went unpaid, but Macquarie announced that several rebel leaders had 'been either killed or taken prisoners', and he called a truce. The ten outlaws would be forgiven if they surrendered, and 'from and after the 8 November 1816, all hostile operations, military or other, against the said native tribes will cease'.

Everyone was invited to the annual post-Christmas feast day at the Parramatta marketplace, where Macquarie assured the Aboriginal people that the meat and drink would be 'plentiful'. He would personally advise them on the 'plan of life' they might 'be inclined to adopt for their own comfort and happiness'.[60]

On 28 December 1816, he was pleased to write:

Pursuant to Public Notice and Invitation, a number of friendly Natives or Aborigines of the Colony, amounting in all to 179 Men, Women, and Children, assembled at Parramatta in the forenoon of this day – and were most hospitably and plentifully regaled and entertained with dinner and punch at the expence of government – in presence of myself and the gentlemen of the Committee for the Civilization of the Natives; the Children (15 Boys & Girls) at the School or Institution, having been presented and shewn to their friends and relatives now assembled – who were much pleased with their clean healthy appearance – and progress in education.[61]

Macquarie told Bathurst that the Indigenous population of New South Wales was now 'living peaceably and quietly in every part of the colony'.[62]

He declared that he had won the war on terror.

The wounds, however, would never really heal. They still fester today.

Chapter 27

NOVEMBER 1816 TO SEPTEMBER 1817,
NEW SOUTH WALES

*Australia which I hope will be the name given to this country
in future, instead of the very erroneous and misapplied name,
hitherto given it, of 'New Holland'.*

MACQUARIE MAKING THE FIRST OFFICIAL USE OF THE NAME 'AUSTRALIA'
FOR WHAT HE ENVISAGED WOULD BECOME A MAGNIFICENT NATION[1]

O N 5 APRIL 1817, Sergeant Jeremiah Murphy of the 46th
Regiment, back from patrol on the other side of the Blue
Mountains, had £50 in his hand as he walked into Entally
House, a dark candlelit building on Macquarie Place owned by
the convict success story Mary Reibey. Mary had been sent to
Australia at thirteen, for pinching a neighbour's horse as a lark, but
now the forty-year-old widow was a dynamic businesswoman: a
merchant trader, and one of the wealthiest people in the colony.

Sergeant Murphy handed over his money in exchange for a
receipt and watched his name entered into a thick ledger bound
with kangaroo hide, as the first customer of Macquarie's new
Bank of New South Wales.

The bank was Macquarie's baby. From almost the moment he
had set foot on Sydney, Macquarie had feared that the prevalence
of promissory notes would plunge the colony into bankruptcy
'unless some remedy [were] speedily applied to this growing evil'.[2]

The promissory notes had begun to come back into circulation under the jurisdiction of Ellis Bent, and Macquarie suspected that Jeffery's bizarre conduct in closing the Supreme Court had been a way of protecting Ellis and his friends from litigation.

On 22 November 1816, Macquarie had held talks about the new bank with prominent business and government figures. J.T. Campbell, who had previously helped found the Cape of Good Hope Bank, offered his advice, and Lieutenant-Governor Molle presided.

Macquarie had grown in confidence in dealing with London. In 1810, he had vainly sought the permission of the English Government to establish a bank; in 1817, he formed one and sought approval for it afterwards.

He told Earl Bathurst that his plan was for a 'subscription bank with a capital of £20,000, divided into £100 shares', and that 'the bank will be opened for the usual purposes of loan, discount, and deposit' under the management of seven directors.[3] On 29 November, it was agreed to fix an exchange rate for the local currency of 13 shillings and fourpence to the pound sterling, and Macquarie issued an order that all wages must now be paid in that currency. Major investors included Edward Eagar, Dr William Redfern, *Gazette* publisher George Howe, poet laureate Michael Robinson and later, Elizabeth Macquarie, who had five £100 shares by 1820.

An iron chest was purchased and banknotes were printed – there were 639 £5 notes, 1794 at £1, 440 at 10s, 1192 at 5s and 809 at 2s 6d. It was decided that the bank would be housed in one of the many buildings owned by Mary Reibey. The fact that she was a former prisoner made it doubly satisfying to the 'friend and protector'[4] of the colony's emancipists.

When Sergeant Murphy deposited his money on 5 April, the Bank of New South Wales was still three days away from its official opening, but all of the colony already seemed in a hurry to get things done.[5]

New South Wales was booming, with new, ornate and elegant buildings springing up everywhere, and a wave of trade and prosperity that Macquarie was driving. The self-appointed minister for infrastructure had enemies snapping at his heels, but he had his feet firmly planted and was making the colony grow.

Throughout the winter of 1816, following the massacre at Appin, Macquarie had been plagued with months of stress-related illness. An inflammation of the bowels gave him agony, and Doctors Wentworth, Redfern and Thomas Forster all attended to him day and night during the first week of September.[6]

The colony's prosperity proved to be his tonic.

Macquarie named the new 150-ton government brig, the *Elizabeth Henrietta,* in honour of Mrs M and donated 8 gallons of spirits to the builders from the king's store. On that same day, he gave 5 gallons to Nicholas Delaney and his ten-man working gang to share after they had completed the '3 miles and 377 yards' of Mrs Macquarie's Road, to transport the vice-regal carriage from Macquarie Place to a seat that convicts had carved into rock, from which the eponymous lady could gaze across the most magnificent harbour in the world.[7] Mrs M's road ran through the Government Domain, where Macquarie envisioned a magnificent garden under the care of his fellow Scot, Charles Frazer[8] of the 46th Regiment, who would soon be known as the Colonial Botanist.

Just up Bent Street from Macquarie Place was Macquarie's new General Hospital, the most spectacular building in the colony which, overlooking the ships on the grand harbour, he regarded as the sale of the century. Macquarie had charged the contractors £9000 in duties on their imported spirits, which eventually amounted to 65,000 gallons, and provided them with £4200 in convict labour and bullocks. In this way, he had poured nearly £4800 profit back into the government coffers, and into the bargain, he received for free a series of buildings with an estimated worth of £40,000 that would house not only a hospital but later, the colonial mint and the New South Wales Parliament.[9]

All three contractors complained that Macquarie's masterstroke had sent them to the wall. Alex Riley became a bitter rival of the governor and an ally of Marsden, D'Arcy Wentworth was flat out

The Rum Hospital. Sydney Living Museums

paying his son's allowance,[10] and Garnham Blaxcell was only saved from court action because Jeffery Bent had shut down the court.

Blaxcell was broke, with liabilities of £6373 against assets of £5255. He was unable to pay the government £2385 in import duties. Realising that the courts would soon be back in business, Blaxcell fled for England, promising to recover money owed to him when he arrived in London. He never made it. The man who was once one of Sydney's richest merchants, with a 'fine house' in Sydney, a warehouse in George Street, a windmill at Pyrmont, a farm at Petersham and at different times seven trading vessels, drank himself to death in Batavia.[11]

The hospital builders were not the only ones in a state of near-collapse. While the hospital looked magnificent from the *outside*, with its wide verandas a nod to Macquarie's time in India, there were concerns about shoddy building work caused by the contractors' cutting corners. The central block was 60 centimetres lower than planned, while the front verandas did not extend to a large flight of steps in the middle of the building, as had been intended.

The governor called in Samuel Bradley, the Superintendent of Government Carpenters, and Ambrose Bryan, Foreman of Government Stonemasons, to shore up its structure, along with the brilliant young convict architect Francis Greenway.[12]

Greenway came from a long line of stonemasons and builders around Bristol, and had been working as an architect in 1812 when he was sentenced to death for forging a document. The sentence was commuted to transportation for fourteen years. He had hardly arrived in the colony when Macquarie gave him a ticket of leave, and he opened an office at 84 George Street. His first colonial commission was overseeing extensions to Ultimo House for Dr John Harris, whom the Macquaries had met in Rio and who had returned to Port Jackson in February 1814.

When Macquarie first met Greenway, the governor had asked him to copy a design for a new courthouse from an architectural pattern book. Greenway told Macquarie the design was in poor taste, and suggested that he himself should be employed as the governor's public works architect. Although Greenway was eventually compelled to copy the design as originally requested, he was soon the colony's civil architect.[13]

Greenway and his team examined the structure of the two-storey rum hospital and announced that it required 'early attention'.[14] The stone flagging under the colonnade was laid upon wooden battens that were likely to rot; the tie beams across the roof were made in three pieces, instead of one as specified; no space had been allowed for air flow under the floor joists to prevent dry rot; and the roof gutters were too thin and poorly installed.[15] The columns of the three buildings, on the lower level cut from stone, and on the upper level carved timber, were particularly criticised.[16]

Stonemason John O'Hearne, a former convict, and the other builders defended their work against some of the committee's criticisms, and claimed that it was not possible to procure straight timber in the colony in the 46-foot lengths required for single-length tie beams.[17] Greenway said you could actually get colonial timber in even longer lengths than that, and he was about to use some in the adjoining Hyde Park Barracks.

Greenway and the committee recommended extensive repair works, which would be financed by the contractors, but the repairs were not carried out until more prompting from Greenway[18] some years later.[19]

D'Arcy Wentworth was both one of the contractors and the colony's principal surgeon, with the north wing set aside for his use, but he spent most of his time living at his home in the bush, in an area now called Homebush. It was left to William Redfern, the assistant surgeon, who had the most extensive private practice in the colony, to run the hospital. He would make daily rounds from 8 a.m. to noon, before working at his daily outpatients' clinic for men from the convict gangs. He toured the wards with a convict clerk, who would write down prescriptions. Female nurses often came on duty intoxicated, despite frequent punishments, while it was necessary to have convict constables patrolling the grounds to stop patients escaping over the 2-metre hospital wall.[20]

Medical treatments were still primitive.

Redfern's notebook included a 'cure for the evil' — scrofula, or tuberculosis of the neck — that involved rubbing the sores with a leg cut from a live toad, which he noted would 'cause the parts to swell very much for about 12 hours, and give violent pain'.[21] There were instructions on making tincture of opium, a poultice for cancer made from Turkish figs boiled in milk, instructions for making a wash for sore eyes from lead, opium and white vitriol, and a recipe for peppermint oil used to treat toothache. Onion juice was prescribed as a remedy for baldness. There was also a recipe for making gold.[22]

Sanitation was not a high priority. Pedestrians knew to stay clear of open windows because of what might be tossed out. An oversight in providing a mortuary meant one kitchen was converted to a 'deadhouse'. The other kitchen housed the overseer and attendant, leaving patients to cook for themselves in the wards. Medications were often given to the wrong patients and bloodletting was standard practice. An early history of the hospital related:

Cupping was a prevalent remedy, and it is recorded that one patient suffering from brain fever had 2 lb. of blood removed in the morning and 3 lb. in the evening– ; he was then allowed to get up, and died. Dysentery was also treated by bleeding and small doses of calomel [mercury chloride]. There was no dietary scale, and all patients, no matter what disease they suffered from, received rations at the rate of 1 lb. of meat and 1 lb. of flour per diem. The rations were issued to the patients individually three times a week, and many, not desiring their full meat supply, sold it to the townspeople, who came to the Hospital verandahs for that purpose.[23]

Convicts dreaded having to go there. Redfern's apprentice, sixteen-year-old Yorkshire lad Henry Cowper,[24] reported that they 'did not like the mode of treatment by such copious bleedings as were in practice ... They used to call the hospital the Sidney Slaughter House'.[25] Redfern conducted three amputations in the hospital's early years, in an era when grog was about the only available anaesthetic.[26]

Despite the rudimentary medicine, Macquarie considered his hospital a great achievement, and he and Greenway set about building other lavish structures that, with convict backbone and an eye to posterity, would change the face of the colony.

Macquarie had told Bathurst that he had no doubt Sydney would one day 'be as fine and opulent a town' as any in His Majesty's empire,[27] and he set about making this vision a reality. Macquarie was so enthusiastic about the potential for the colony, he discussed with secretary J.T. Campbell the possibility of writing the history of the place the governor was now calling 'Australia',[28] the name first used by Matthew Flinders that Macquarie encouraged Britain to adopt.[29]

Before long, Greenway had started work on Fort Macquarie — not to be confused with Port Macquarie, a village that surveyor John Oxley would soon name in honour of his boss. The fort was built on the end of Bennelong Point, where an even more lavish building, the Sydney Opera House, now stands. It used stone quarried from the Domain, and had fifteen large cannons and a small garrison. The powder magazine beneath the tower could store 350 barrels of gunpowder.[30]

The castellated fort was built along the lines of a medieval

Scottish castle, and the whole time convicts were piecing it together, Greenway was harking back to his childhood, playing soldiers in an English country garden.[31] 'Mrs M' was a keen participant in the design, too. Its impressive towers echoed Inveraray Castle,[32] the property of her relatives, the Campbells.

Elizabeth also had a copy of Edward Gyfford's 1806 book, *Designs for Elegant Cottages and Small Villas*, complete with its twenty-six sepia plates displaying the latest in stylish living.[33] Not only did she take a keen interest in the gardens of the Domain, which would become a jewel beside the harbour for more than two centuries, but she also had a key role in planning the park surrounding Government House at Parramatta, where the Macquaries began to spend more and more time after extensive repairs were completed in October 1816.[34]

Elizabeth turned the Parramatta property into a grand country estate, with a corridor of lemon trees, a hedge with masses of downy yellow mimosa flowers and 'Mrs Macquarie['s] beautifully contrived Bark Hut'.[35] She erected a dove house, a hen house, an enclosure for their emu, rabbit hutches and a deer house. Elizabeth once walked the garden with Rose de Freycinet, a French explorer's wife, who was impressed by the simple elegance of the design, and by the smiles on the faces of the thirty native children, many from Macquarie's school, playing in the grounds.[36]

Much of the restoration work at Parramatta was overseen by John Watts,[37] who had replaced Macquarie's relative John Maclaine as aide-de-camp. He built a new hospital and military barracks there; the latter is still in operation as the Lancer Barracks on Smith Street. Watts also designed a new military hospital to be erected on Sydney's Observatory Hill,[38] a building that is now the headquarters for the National Trust of Australia.

Again, Elizabeth took a keen interest in the work: according to Watts's daughter, he added two steeples to St John's Church after Elizabeth showed him a watercolour sketch of St Mary's, a ruined church at Reculver in Kent.[39] The female orphanage that opened at Parramatta in 1818 was based on the design of Elizabeth's family home in Airds, Scotland.

Greenway took over from Watts on the biggest projects in Sydney, and Bathurst allowed Macquarie to pay him three shillings a day – 'but I cannot consent to his being considered as holding a permanent office'.[40] He'd come to the colony as a convict, after all.

Soon, there was a Greenway-designed obelisk at Macquarie Place,[41] explaining the distances from there to principal parts of the colony, and later a sandstone Doric fountain[42] was built nearby. Greenway designed a new courthouse and a new St Matthew's Anglican Church at Windsor, and the magnificent Macquarie Lighthouse[43] near the entrance to Sydney Harbour, the first in Australia, named by Macquarie after Macquarie.[44]

The stonework was finished in December 1817,[45] and Macquarie was so pleased with the result that he presented Greenway with conditional emancipation, and they both drank a toast of cherry brandy to its success.[46]

The cost of the lighthouse and its revolving lantern was to be paid by a tax on ships entering the harbour, however, as a gift to Sydney, Macquarie declared that local vessels would be exempt.[47] The governor told Bathurst that it was a 'very elegant and strong stone tower' and it was 'greatly wanted for the use, safety and direction of shipping, trading to and from this port'.[48] Bathurst replied that that was all well and good, but Macquarie had been warned about wasting money on a place that was supposed to be a prison, after all.[49]

However, Macquarie and Greenway were on a roll. Macquarie asked his colonial architect to expand the fortifications at Dawes Point with a semicircular battery and a decorative guardhouse that resembled the one on Fort Macquarie.

Greenway designed the Hyde Park Barracks on Macquarie Street to house 600 convict men in hammocks, and Macquarie laid the foundation stone on 6 April 1817. There was going to be a great influx of convicts to New South Wales with the end of the Napoleonic Wars creating mass unemployment, and Macquarie wanted to be ready to accommodate them.

Macquarie would grant Greenway a full pardon on the day the barracks were opened, 20 May 1819.

Although stealing was rife within the compound, Macquarie would boast to Bathurst that, since the prisoners were no longer housed in lodgings around Sydney, 'not a tenth of the former night robberies and burglaries' were being committed.[50]

Across Macquarie Street, Greenway designed the grand St James' Church, which, when finally constructed, would be the tallest building in Sydney for almost half a century, its copper steeple rising to 52 metres.[51]

Greenway also designed the Georgian-style courthouse next door, originally intended as Macquarie's Georgian Public School, an institution to care for neglected children. It was modified during construction to accommodate the Supreme Court instead.

Greenway's greatest decorative masterpiece, however, was the Government Stables, a huge project that Macquarie tried to slip in under the nose of the London bean-counters.

He had been so keen to get his many building projects under way that, for a long time, he had been willing to put up with less-than-salubrious accommodation himself. All that was about to change. In March 1816, he wrote to Bathurst:

> The old government house and offices, originally built by Governor Phillip twenty-eight years ago, remain exactly as I found them ... much decayed and rotten as to render them extremely unsafe any longer to live in ... All the offices ... exhibit a most ruinous mean shabby appearance ... the stables, if possible, are still worse than the other offices, it having been of late frequently necessary to prop them up with timber posts to prevent their falling, or being blown down by the winds.[52]

But Bathurst told Macquarie to hold his horses when it came to a new home and stables – and rein in the other public buildings works, too.

Regardless of Bathurst's directions, Macquarie had a bakehouse and mill erected on his proposed site for the new government house, and on 4 July 1817, he told Greenway to prepare plans for offices and stables. Mrs Macquarie gave him details of the number of rooms needed.

Work commenced on the stables on 9 August 1817, though four months later, Macquarie told Bathurst that no construction had commenced due to heavy rains. He said Government House was infested with white ants and would 'inevitably tumble down of itself in a very few years', but he would honour Bathurst's wishes and leave it to his successors to repair the 'inadequate accommodation I now occupy'.[53]

No sooner had he sealed the letter than he told Greenway to get out his pencil and slide-rule, because they had a lot of work to do before Bathurst found out what was going on.

They discussed the design for the new government house and Greenway, 'allowed to design it in the castellated style', based his sketch on Thornbury Castle, which he knew from growing up in Bristol. Except that Greenway, now enjoying more free rein than he could ever have imagined when he was on the convict ship *General Hewitt*, decided to make the design much bolder when he started on the stables.

Macquarie didn't confess to Bathurst that he had commenced building the stables until two years after work had started, by which time they were nearly finished. He explained: 'I had so long suffered such very great inconvenience from the want of a secure stables for my horses and decent sleeping places for my servants.'[54]

He might not have been sold on the stables' ornate towers,[55] but the building – now The Sydney Conservatorium of Music – showed that he wanted Sydney to be the jewel in the crown of his kingdom.

Greenway worked quickly and had the ability to make snap decisions. That was never more evident when Captain John Piper, a brother freemason of Macquarie's, started building his mansion in November 1816.[56] The foundation stone was laid in a masonic ceremony, to the accompaniment of a seven-gun salute.

Greenway sparked the wrath of 'the powerful and athletic' Captain Edward Sanderson of the 46th, who shook with rage at the convict's impudence when tasked with designing the Masonic aprons for the ceremony. Later, in the presence of witnesses, Sanderson took to Greenway with a riding whip and his fists.[57]

'Mr Sanderson, sir, recollect,' cried Greenway, 'Consider my situation, sir. I dare not run the risk of resisting, were I able.'

As Sanderson lashed at his helpless victim, Greenway could then only blurt out: 'You know how I am circumstanced.'[58] Greenway – still a convict at that point – knew that if a prisoner retaliated against a soldier, he could have his back torn to pieces with the lash.

Instead, he managed to have Sanderson fined £5 in court and won £20 in damages. Macquarie reprimanded Sanderson in private for using 'the most unbecoming and disrespectful language' to the chief magistrate.[59]

THERE HAD BEEN no talk for a long while of the massacre near Appin, but Macquarie was delighted that peaceful relations with the Aboriginal population seemed to have been restored at the 1816 post–Christmas feast day.[60] Two weeks later, Macquarie noted:

> Nurragingy (als. Creek Jemmy) the Chief of the South Creek, and Mary-Mary the Chief of the Mulgowy natives with their respective tribes amounting to 51 (men, women & children) persons, paid me a visit at Parramatta and were entertained in the Govt. Domain there by direction of Mrs Macquarie with breakfast and dinner this day; the 17 native children at the institution having also been entertained with fruit and presented to their parents & relatives belonging to those two tribes. Narrang Jack, one of the hostile natives some time outlawed, came in on this occasion and gave himself up …[61]

Later that day, Macquarie and Mrs M took the government barge to the 'native farm at George's Head', with Elizabeth presenting Chief Bungaree with a breeding sow, seven pigs and a pair of Muscovy ducks.

Not that everything was going swimmingly for the first Australians. Daniel Moowattin,[62] who had been raised by the colonial hangman and visited Norfolk Island, Van Diemen's Land and England with the botanist George Caley, became the first Indigenous man to be legally executed in New South Wales, when he was hanged – not by his adoptive father – for the rape and robbery of fifteen-year-old Hannah Russell.[63]

MEANWHILE, Macquarie's lieutenant-governors were almost as troublesome to him as Tipu Sultan had been a quarter of a century before. He was sick of having to censure Thomas Davey's conduct in every dispatch, and in July 1816, wrote to him in Hobart to tell him so.[64] Four months later, he let Mad Tom have it with both barrels, telling him that Bathurst was about to sack him.

Macquarie had never forgiven Davey for having declared martial law in Van Diemen's Land 'contrary to my orders and in contempt of my authority as Governor in Chief'. He also condemned Davey's 'almost total disregard to the instructions I had furnished you with on your proceeding from hence to Van Diemen's Land … your lavish expenditure of the public money and your injudicious and extravagant purchases and contracts made and entered into on the behalf of government'.[65]

To cushion the blow, and because he felt sorry for Davey's wife and daughter, Macquarie offered the miscreant 800 hectares in addition to the 1200 he had already granted him. It wasn't enough to suit Davey, though, and he ended up securing another 2400 hectares after he left his post on 9 April 1817, including 800 in the lush Illawarra.

The new Lieutenant-Governor of Van Diemen's Land would be William Sorell, whom the Macquaries had met at the Cape of Good Hope on their way to New South Wales. He had left his wife and seven children in England when he arrived at the cape and begun an affair with Louisa, the wife of his friend Lieutenant William Kent – not to be confused with the Lieutenant William Kent who had shipped the first merinos from the Cape of Good

Hope in 1797. Sorell and Louisa had openly lived together since Sorell left the cape in 1811, and now had two sons.

It had proved a costly affair, with Kent commencing proceedings against Sorell for criminal conversation in 1812. Within months of his arrival in Van Diemen's Land, the white-haired autocrat, known as 'the old man', would be forced to pay Kent £3000 in damages.

Kent wasn't the only one who had it in for the new lieutenant-governor, with Michael Howe now threatening to burn Van Diemen's Land from end to end.

A CAVERNOUS DIVIDE had also formed between Macquarie and the fiery redhead Lieutenant-Governor Molle, once Macquarie's comrade in India and Egypt.

Even before arriving in the colony, Molle and the men of his 46th Regiment, perhaps influenced by their association with the exiled John Macarthur in London, had refused to allow emancipists into their regimental mess.[66] They scoffed at Macquarie's idealism: his instructions to manage the convicts, 'these children of misfortune ... so as at once to make them feel sensibly the weight of their crimes ... and to hold out to them the distant prospect of relaxation from their chains, and even of eventual restoration to their original rank in society'.[67]

More recently, the soldiers had begun to openly mock Macquarie, with one young officer drawing 'a full length caricature' of Macquarie on the guard room wall in July 1816, 'in a position of ignominy, with indecent scurrilous labels underneath it'. The cartoon stayed there for days and was an endless source of amusement for officers and soldiers going by. While Macquarie forgave the young officer, Ensign Bullivant, because of his youth and immaturity, and decided not to order a court martial, he took a much harder line with all those senior officers who had tolerated it.[68]

The situation worsened when 'a scurrilous lampoon in manuscript' attacking Molle – or a 'pipe', as written barbs were known at the time due to the fact they were rolled up – was tossed into the yard of the military barracks. Rather than suffering the mocking verses 'by silent contempt', Molle began such a frenzied investigation that there were soon copies of the verses everywhere, and they were the topic of daily conversation.[69]

Suspicion first fell on the army-officer-turned-convict-bigamist Captain Robert Lathrop Murray,[70] and then Molle turned his ire on D'Arcy Wentworth, not realising that the real culprit was D'Arcy's son, William.

Molle demanded that D'Arcy, still a commissioned officer, be court-martialled. Macquarie instead appealed to the Duke of York to give him a new lieutenant-governor. His experiences with Molle and Maurice O'Connell before him – to say nothing of the incompetent Davey – had convinced him the role was 'inefficient and altogether useless'. Rather than aid to the governor, Molle and O'Connell had provided 'jealousy of the power of a superior'.[71]

The 46th, of course, backed Molle to the hilt, and made a written declaration to him that said:

'And here, sir, allow us still more to approve and applaud that system of exclusion [of former convicts] … which, altho' it may have prompted the malignity of those whom we have kept aloof, has established the name of the 46th Regiment on a most respectable basis.'[72]

The court ruled that Wentworth, as Principal Surgeon, was not eligible for court martial, so Macquarie cancelled it.[73] Under Macquarie's rotation system for troops, the 48th Regiment arrived in August 1817 to replace Molle's 46th, and the following month, Macquarie ordered his former friend onto the *Matilda*, bound for Madras. Molle died in India six years later.

MACQUARIE might have farewelled a couple of insubordinate lieutenant-governors, but he still had a list of enemies a mile long. The mood against him had been souring ever since the court martial of the Reverend Benjamin Vale back in March 1816, over the aborted seizure of the American ship, the *Traveller*. Macquarie had long suspected the involvement of his old sparring partner, Jeffery Hart Bent.

Macquarie had told Bathurst that Vale's conduct and that of his co-conspirator, lawyer William Moore, '(both officers receiving the pay under this government)', was 'highly disrespectful, insolent and insubordinate, in making seizure of a vessel during my absence, which they were fully aware had received my sanction for entry and discharge'.[74]

The court ruled that Vale should be 'publickly and severely reprimanded and admonished'. Macquarie, 'in consideration of his sacred character as a clergyman', softened the blow by telling Vale off in private.[75]

The perpetually perturbed Vale had left New South Wales and all its miseries on the *Alexander* on 16 June 1816, but he carried with him an explosive device primed by Macquarie's many enemies.

Macquarie had sacked Moore from his £300-a-year role, and Moore had responded by gathering signatures for a petition against the governor. Bent had been shown the original petition and, calling it 'niminy-piminy', beefed up the accusations.[76]

Bent himself did not go quietly either. The new judge-advocate, John Wylde, had arrived in Sydney on 5 October 1816 with his wife and six children. Also with him were his father Thomas, who would be his clerk of the peace, and his brother-in-law Joshua John Moore,[77] who would be the sessional clerk, and who would build the first house in Canberra, known as Acton House.

Bent hardly handed over the judicial baton with enthusiasm. One of his last acts in office was to jail magistrate William Broughton without bail for contempt of his authority, before Macquarie ordered Broughton's immediate release.[78] Bent would also not give up the house he now shared with his brother Ellis's widow, Eliza, so that Wylde could move in.

In December, Bent called on Alex Riley, one of the other magistrates with whom he had quarrelled, to constitute the Supreme Court once more as he was determined to retain power and status for as long as he could, but Riley told him where to get off. So Bent ordered Riley's arrest and the arrest of Provost-Marshal William Gore – head of the military police – for not recognising his judicial authority (even though he'd been sacked).[79] Macquarie finally had Bent ejected from the chambers and published a government order in the *Gazette* to say that His Royal Highness the Prince Regent had recalled Jeffery to England, and that the former judge 'has no authority or jurisdiction whatever in this territory'. Bent would try to assume or exercise 'any authority or jurisdiction whatever as the judge of the Supreme Court, or as a magistrate of this territory' *at his peril!*[80]

The besieged governor finally saw the back of Jeffery and Eliza Bent when they sailed away on 18 May 1817 on the *Sir William Bensley*, but not before Macquarie had bought Eliza's fire irons (£47 5s), external Venetian blinds (£60) and green doors (£28).

Jeffery spent most of the voyage home arguing with the skipper and nearly drowned in the Bay of Biscay. Yet he was nothing if not resilient. He lodged an unsuccessful request to replace Macquarie as governor and to secure a high position in India before being shipped off in April 1819 to become Chief Justice of Grenada, one of several posts in the West Indies, where trouble followed close behind him.[81]

He could not comprehend the stupidity of the government's decision to withdraw him from Sydney. He complained to Henry Goulburn that 'I was most clearly right in point of law; and yet my perseverance, in not abandoning what was right in principle and right in law, has been exclusively punished, while the obstinacy of Governor Macquarie and his creatures who were confessedly in the wrong, and to whom alone ought to be imputed the consequence of the dispute, has been scarcely, if at all, reprimanded'.[82]

CONVINCED that the Colonial Secretary's confidence in him had been eroded by the slanders of 'evil minded persons',[83] Macquarie submitted a table to Bathurst of the 'dirty dozen' at the top of his long list of enemies.

The Reverend Samuel Marsden sat on the top spot, with a note next to his name that said he was discontent, intriguing and vindictive.

Next on Macquarie's hit list, under the heading 'Discontented' were Dr Robert Townson,[84] Nicholas Bayly, John and Gregory Blaxland, Dr Charles Throsby and John Horsley.[85] Sir John Jamison, David Allan and John Oxley were 'intriguing and discontented', while Macquarie marked William and Thomas Moore as 'seditious, intriguing and discontented'.[86] Macquarie believed that they all resented the rise of convicts in the colony, and stirred up trouble by whispering slanders against him.

Macquarie had long had his suspicions about Oxley, but had appointed him to lead an expedition that included botanists Allan Cunningham[87] and Charles Frazer to explore the area west of the Blue Mountains. One of their chief assignments was to ascertain the real course of the Lachlan, if possible, and confirm whether it fell into the sea, or into some inland lake.

Leaving Bathurst on 28 April 1817, the explorers followed the Lachlan for more than two months, then in July, impassable marshes prevented further progress. Oxley theorised that much of the interior was marshland and unsuitable for settlement, not realising he was only a few days away from the fertile lands around the Murrumbidgee. He arrived back in Bathurst on 29 August 1817. Macquarie praised Oxley's 'zealous, indefatigable and intelligent exertions' and suggested he be awarded £200 for his 'meritorious services'.[88]

Oxley might have earned himself a spot lower down Macquarie's list, but Samuel Marsden was still Enemy Number One. A confrontation with Marsden had been brewing ever since the chaplain had refused to sit on the turnpike board with former convicts, and the relationship had been in freefall throughout 1817.

Macquarie had long been a supporter of charitable works in the colony. He played an active role in supporting the New South Wales Society for Promoting Christian Knowledge and Benevolence,[89] founded in 1813 by philanthropist Edward Smith Hall[90] and the forerunner of today's Benevolent Society. Macquarie would later help Hall build an asylum in 1821 for the blind, homeless, infirm and mentally ill at the entrance to Sydney, on the corner of Pitt and Devonshire Streets.[91]

But in Marsden, he saw a religious hypocrite. And a hostile one.

On 4 January 1817, a letter had appeared in the *Sydney Gazette and New South Wales Advertiser*, signed by 'Philo Free, a settler at Bradley's Head'. It was 1285 words of sarcasm directed at Marsden, highlighting the fact that, four years earlier, he had formed the New South Wales Philanthropic Society and called for donations to help with the 'laudable purpose of extending protection and civilization' to Polynesians.[92] Macquarie's secretary J.T. Campbell had been on the committee and Robert Jenkins,[93] a director of the Bank of New South Wales, had been the collector of funds. But the letter – which contained a surprising amount of insider knowledge – claimed donors had 'never been favoured even with a single report of the application of the funds'.

It insinuated that Marsden had been making money for himself as an evangelical gun-runner, selling 'muskets and cutlasses' to the 'natives' for their battles with settlers in New Zealand and Tahiti. It was also alleged that Marsden was expanding efforts to evangelise the peoples of the South Pacific, while ignoring the spiritual needs of the local Indigenous inhabitants.

Philo Free claimed that: 'The active exertions of him who is the worthy head of these sectarian visionaries or missionaries (whichever you please, Mr Editor), in propagating the gospel by such means, and the transmission from time to time of muskets and cutlasses, will, no doubt, redound much and highly to the honour of the Christian Mahomet'.

There was a general wish, he wrote, that the donations be returned 'and appropriated to the establishment of schools and the children of the poor within the colony, and the diffusion of Christian knowledge among the heathen natives'.[94]

In a letter to the *Gazette* a week later, agreeing with Philo and displaying a remarkable knowledge of Marsden's finances, 'A Spectator' asked what had happened to the £238 7s that had been donated to Marsden's fund, including his own 10-guinea contribution. 'As a single shilling has never been applied that I can learn of,' he wrote, 'I can perceive no pressing reason why it should have been collected.'[95]

Marsden demanded that George Howe, the editor of the *Gazette*, be prosecuted for criminal libel. It soon emerged that J.T. Campbell, who had final say over a newspaper that was the Government's official voice, had approved the letter's publication, but he claimed that he had been so busy, he had only looked at the beginning and end of it before passing it on to the paper. There were suspicions that Campbell was reprising the attacks he had launched against Marsden over the missing lending library, three years earlier.[96]

Macquarie was quick to distance himself from the affair and assure the colony that he did not sanction the letters' sentiments. He offered his support to the 'highly respectable and benevolent persons and societies engaged in missionary labours and purposes', and expressed his regret that the letter 'should inadvertently, from the great pressure of government business in the secretary's office, have got admission into the *Gazette*'.[97]

Marsden now demanded that Judge-Advocate Wylde prosecute Campbell, and the case came to trial in October 1817, before a bench consisting of Wylde and six military officers. Among Marsden's many grievances, Campbell was charged with:

> ... designing and intending ... to defame and vilify the good character and reputation of the said Samuel Marsden and to insinuate and cause it to be believed that the said Samuel Marsden was of a sordid and avaricious disposition ... [and] was a religious impostor and not a preacher and believer of the Christian religion, according to the usages and ceremonies of the Church of England ...[98]

Gazette compositor George Williams swore that Campbell had come to the newspaper's office with the letter in his hand, ordering that no one see it and that it be returned to him after it was set in type.[99] Williams had suspected it was in the secretary's own handwriting.

Not long after the letter's publication, and well before the trial, Williams had shown his support for Jeffery Bent and William

Moore's efforts to discredit Macquarie with their petition. Williams had turned back an advertisement from Samuel Terry, the Rothschild of Botany Bay, offering a reward for any man who came forward and admitted to forging his signature on the Vale–Moore petition. Macquarie ordered that Williams be sacked, and suggested that the ex-compositor might have had an axe to grind against Campbell.

Robert Jenkins did not appear during the case to shed light on the whereabouts of the subscribers' money, and Judge-Advocate Wylde decided there was no proof that Campbell had written the letter. Instead, the court found him guilty of the lesser sin 'of having permitted a public letter to be printed in the *Sydney Gazette*, which tends to vilify the public conduct of Mr Marsden ... and which it was in the power of the defendant in his official capacity, as secretary to His Excellency the Governor of this Territory, to have prevented the publication of'.[100]

With a red flush all over his almost bare pate, the angry Marsden then instigated a civil action, applying for damages of £3000. The case was heard before Jeffery Bent's successor, Mr Justice Barron Field, a former drama critic on *The Times* of London, who counted among his associates there the literary lions William Wordsworth and Charles Lamb.

Into his world came Macquarie's poet laureate, Michael Robinson, who was Campbell's clerk. Robinson showed no fear of what the governor or his immediate boss might say or do, and told the youthful Mr Justice Field that he had seen the letter and that it had undoubtedly been in Campbell's handwriting. He said Campbell had told him that he had copied it from an almost illegible document.

Field awarded Marsden a modest £200 in damages and the whole saga, including legal fees, set Campbell back £476.[101] Campbell apologised profusely to Macquarie 'for the hasty and inconsiderate letter',[102] which had embarrassed the governor. He said it had been written because of his 'indignation at the marked disrespect shown by Mr Marsden' to Macquarie's 'orders and establishments'. He also resented the chaplain's 'marked disinclination' to be involved in 'the civilization of the natives of this country', and his snubbing of Macquarie's annual Aboriginal feast day. Campbell admitted he had further damaged Macquarie's standing in the eyes of London.[103]

AS 1817 WORE ON, Macquarie geared up to wage war on an increasing number of fronts. He had recently paid £22,000 – all his liquid assets – for a piece of the Duke of Argyll's diminishing Scottish estate on the shores of Loch na Keal, near the Mull village of Laggan Ulva. He wanted to call it Jarvisfield Castle and take his wife and son there, far away from the accusations of the Marsdens, Bents, Moores and Vales.

Then, in September 1817, after almost a decade in exile for toppling a governor, and ignoring all warnings not to interfere in the politics of New South Wales again, John Macarthur breezed back into town aboard the *Lord Eldon*. While Macquarie was wary of him because of his role in toppling Bligh, the Governor had many more immediate threats to worry about.

Soon afterwards, Lachlan Junior was violently ill with heat stress and spasms. Wentworth and Redfern recommended the skin on his neck be blistered and bled.[104]

The little boy cried his eyes out, but Macquarie's enemies would give him far more pain.

Chapter 28

DECEMBER 1817 TO OCTOBER 1818, NEW SOUTH WALES

*If my Lord Bathurst encourages every disaffected unprincipled man
in this colony to set themselves up in open opposition to the legal
authorities of this place, he will soon have a fine commotion among
the set of villains with which the governors of this
colony ever have been surrounded.*

ELIZABETH MACQUARIE ON THE KNIVES BEING
THRUST INTO HER HUSBAND'S BACK[1]

MACQUARIE KNEW he was out of favour with Bathurst
from the harsh tone of the letters coming his way.

Bathurst had been in no good humour when he wrote to
Macquarie in early 1817 to say that court-martialling Vale, a
military chaplain, over the *Traveller* incident had been illegal:

> ... although I feel that Mr Vale's conduct was in many
> points of view extremely reprehensible ... yet I have now
> only to lament that you should, in a moment of irritation,
> have been betrayed into an act which, at the same time that
> it exposes you personally to considerable risk, cannot fail to
> diminish your influence among the more respectable part of
> the community, who justly look upon the law as the only
> true foundation of authority.[2]

Macquarie flatly refused Bathurst's direction to reinstate Moore, telling his boss with an air of defiance that 'this man has acted in a most daring and insulting manner in direct opposition and open violence to my authority'.[3]

Nor was he going to give ground over the 'depraved, hypocritical, unprincipled'[4] Vale.

Responding to Bathurst in November, he told him that 'It grieves me to find that the line of conduct I had deemed to pursue in regard to Vale … should be considered by Your Lordship as illegal, and consequently meriting your Lordship's displeasure and censure, conveyed to me in terms truly mortifying to my feelings.'

There was a hint of sarcasm as the liberal-minded major-general, who so often flouted authority, told the conservative Tory politician:

> However much I esteem and respect your Lordship's superior judgment, good feelings, and high station, and however much I may consider myself bound to submit to your Lordship's authority and opinions, I trust that on a further review and consideration of my conduct in this instance, it will not be deemed presumption, in a case where my public authority and character and feelings as a man are so deeply involved, if I take the liberty to dissent from the conclusions your Lordship has been pleased to draw … on the contrary I feel the consciousness of having treated him with much more lenity than his mutinous, seditious conduct deserved … for I believe there is not one respectable person now in this country who did not highly disapprove and execrate the mutinous, seditious and insolent conduct, pursued towards me …[5]

Macquarie said he had been 'bred in the School of Subordination too long, not to respect it; and Your Lordship must be fully aware, how necessary it is to support it in a distant colony like this'.[6]

But there was a lot more at stake than the future of an insubordinate former chaplain and Crown solicitor. The mood in Britain towards the transportation of convicts was changing dramatically. Napoleon had met his Waterloo but, faced with masses of returning troops, Britain was now experiencing a sharp downturn in its economy, bringing mass unemployment and distress. The Spa Fields Riots in London at the end of 1816 had given the aristocracy a fearful warning about the spreading mood of democracy that had already seen heads roll in France.

The petition William Moore had started, and Jeffery Hart Bent had redrafted, was just what Britain's progressive Whig opposition needed to attack the government over the exorbitant cost of housing convicts. Bent had made sure Macquarie would suffer after he was gone.

Henry Grey Bennet, an old friend of Marsden's, argued that New South Wales was becoming too costly an exercise, and that the man in charge of the venture was all at sea. On 10 March 1817, Bennet tabled the Vale–Moore petition in the House of Commons, opening up the floodgates of criticism against Macquarie and fuelling controversy among enemies of the British Government.

Meanwhile, Macquarie had got hold of a copy of the petition that had been floating around the colony, and argued to Bathurst in April that the charges against him were 'of the most false and malicious nature'.[7] He called Moore 'a worthless and unprincipled reptile' and said he was treading in 'the steps of his preceptor and patron, Mr J.H. Bent, in rendering indiscriminate opposition to all the measures of my government, as far as a weak head and a bad heart could impel him'.[8]

He told Under-Secretary Goulburn a month later that, though there was no proof, there was good reason to believe that:

[Moore] was only employed as a tool by Mr Justice Bent, who was the grand mover of this vile libel but who cautiously kept in the background. The means, now well known to have been used by Mr Solicitor Moore and two or three other unprincipled disaffected persons here, to obtain the signatures of 30 or 40 common low drunken fellows to this seditious address, were most disgraceful, many of the persons who signed it having since acknowledged that they were quite drunk, when taken to Mr Moore's house for that purpose.[9]

Macquarie had already cancelled the land grants of all those whose signatures appeared on the petition,[10] and Wentworth refused to sign the renewal of a liquor licence for one of them. When Moore's brother and clerk, Thomas Moore (not to be confused with the Liverpool landowner), was refused a land grant, Moore came forward and said he had forged his brother's signature on the petition: odd behaviour for a former Crown solicitor.

He begged Goulburn to send him an official copy of this 'wicked, libellous, and seditious' petition, compiled by a 'few discontented wretches here, of the lowest and most infamous description'.[11]

Meanwhile, he felt compelled to clear his name, and in the same letter, began answering the accusations against him.

Bent's charges against Macquarie went way beyond the costs of accommodating criminals. Many of them related to diverse incidents that had occurred during Bent's three disastrous years in the colony.

A day after the Appin massacre, three men, William Henshall, Daniel Read and William Blake, were each arrested for trespassing in the garden of the Domain. They were eventually given twenty-five lashes by the official hangman on the bare back, 'with the view of deterring others from similar practices'.[12] There had been no trial.

All three had protested loudly before and after the flogging, though Macquarie defended his actions by calling them 'depraved low vicious characters, and consequently proper objects to be made examples of'.[13]

Henshall was actually the man who had spent seven months punching out almost 40,000 holes for almost 40,000 holey dollars.[14] He said he had only been in the Domain to find white sand for his work as a silversmith. Blake, a blacksmith, was probably there to receive stolen goods, but Read, a stonemason, said he was just looking for a stone to use for the *Sydney Gazette*'s press and had no idea why he was being flogged, except that it was on the governor's orders.[15]

While Britain was unconcerned about the deaths of 'hostile natives' the day before, the petitions of the three victims caused a stir in the House of Commons.

Macquarie told Under-Secretary Goulburn that while, technically speaking, he might have acted illegally, there had been a long history of similar incidents in the Domain. Part of the garden had been enclosed with an expensive stone fence to improve the area with plantings. Despite warning signs about keeping out, trespassers scaled the fence to hide stolen goods. 'Lewd, disorderly men and women' also made their way into the thick bush 'for most indecent improper purposes'.[16] Only after the wall had been repeatedly broken down and 'much injury done to the shrubbery and young planting' did Macquarie resolve to make an example with a 'slight summary punishment' for the three trespassers.

The three men had sought help from Jeffery Bent, who made their complaints part of his petition. Bent also acted for Lieutenant Philip Connor, who accused Macquarie of 'prohibiting banns of marriage'.

Macquarie had been furious at the lenient six-month sentence imposed when Connor and fellow lieutenant, Archibald McNaughton, were convicted of the manslaughter of William Holness in 1813. Connor had left with the rest of the 73rd Regiment the following year, but had returned to the colony to marry in 1816. Considering Connor an undesirable immigrant, Macquarie ordered him out of the country before Connor could fulfil his marriage contract.

Bent's petition also accused Macquarie of interfering in the proceedings of the courts over the fatal road accident involving Elizabeth's carriage and his support for the convict lawyer George Crossley to practise in Sydney; and of pulling down houses. Macquarie said all the accusations against him were baseless.

He had not interfered in any cases, and the only houses he had ordered to be torn down were those that had been erected illegally.

THEN, ON 31 AUGUST, the ship *Almorah* arrived in Port Jackson with a series of explosive pages from Bathurst, written back on 24 January. The handicaps of sea transport meant they had taken eight months to reach him. But it was an even older document enclosed with Bathurst's letter that most upset Macquarie.

The Colonial Secretary had included extracts from a letter written on 13 March 1816, containing damning claims of Macquarie's mismanagement. Bathurst didn't reveal the author, just a list of deep grievances and wild exaggerations that suggested Macquarie had worn out his welcome in both New South Wales and Britain.

The letter had been forwarded to Bathurst by Sir Henry Bunbury, who ran the transport department of the British Government responsible for the shipment of all convicts. But Bathurst would not divulge anything about the original author, except that he was a 'most intimate friend' of the late Ellis Bent. Macquarie thought the author was Samuel Marsden,[17] but it was actually Nicholas Bayly, Number Three on Macquarie's list of enemies.

Bathurst demanded answers to the letter's accusations, 'affecting as they do to a great degree your character and conduct in the administration of the colony'.[18]

The letter charged that D'Arcy Wentworth, head of the police force and Principal Surgeon, was the 'greatest dealer of spirits in the colony'.[19] It further declared that the women at the Parramatta Female Factory, 'bad as they are', were to be pitied because, in the fight for lodgings, they would 'pick up' men for a bed; 'robberies are the result, the inhabitants are continually upon the alarm, and every vicious propensity is gratified by these disgraceful means'.[20]

Bathurst also demanded an answer to the letter's allegations of convict prostitution, 'in which it is stated that the female convicts during their voyage to the colony are permitted to live with the officers and seamen of the ships, in which they are embarked'.[21]

Henry Bathurst, 3rd Earl Bathurst by William Salter, date unknown. National Portrait Gallery, London

The letter writer said he had visited Parramatta Gaol with Marsden and the experience was almost 'too horrid to relate': a prisoner 'who had nearly lost the use of his limbs and faculties by confinement on bread and water', a prisoner perfectly mad, chained to a wall, and four other men facing twelve months in solitary confinement on bread and water, two years' imprisonment in the jail should they survive, 'and after that transportation to New Castle for life'.[22]

The accusations cut Macquarie to the core. He believed he had built a sterling reputation for the humane treatment of prisoners, and for encouraging them to improve their lot after being granted a ticket of leave.

Only a month before Bathurst's fusillade, Macquarie had been appalled by the treatment of the Irish convicts aboard the transport *Chapman* by guards from the 46th Regiment. On the night of 17 April 1817, and again on the 28th, guards had fired on the prisoners, fearing mutiny. Seven convicts later died of their wounds. Survivors claimed they were stabbed, starved, kicked, robbed, shot while lying in bed, chained naked, threatened with smothering by brimstone and charcoal, flogged for speaking Irish and beaten with bayonets and cutlasses, and that lemons had been squeezed into their eyes.[23]

Macquarie had wanted all those responsible to hang, but an investigation by Wylde, D'Arcy Wentworth and J.T. Campbell found the ship's officers, crew and guards only guilty of a misdemeanour, with Campbell dissenting. Campbell had prevailed on Macquarie to order a retrial in England, but the men were acquitted, the court finding that the defendants' fears *excused* the acts of homicide, even if they did not *justify* them.

On top of all the other accusations that had been levelled against Macquarie, Bathurst's insult in taking these outrageous charges seriously was too much. On 1 December 1817, Macquarie wrote to him to tender his resignation for the second time. As the pressure increased on Macquarie and his health worsened, he wore his heart on his sleeve more and more, even in official correspondence. Bathurst was clearly prepared to overlook Macquarie's outbursts because of his other stirling qualities. But his patience was wearing thin.

Macquarie told Bathurst that he had originally hoped to stay another two or three years to see 'the matured effects of that system of government I had unceasingly and laboriously endeavoured to establish for the reformation of the inhabitants, and improvement and prosperity of this young colony'. But with the sudden change in Bathurst's sentiments towards him, he felt the slings and arrows more poignantly.

He was sick of the servants of government 'who generally speaking are men who have at all times attempted a most indecent and insubordinate interference with the governors of this colony by opposing their measures here, and writing home false and malignant representations, with the sole view of creating mischief and dissatisfaction in the minds of His Majesty's ministers.'[24]

In a longer letter three days later, with more than a dash of mockery, Macquarie thanked 'Your Lordship for sending me the anonymous extract … in order to give me an opportunity of refuting the false and malicious accusations'.[25]

On the question of prostitution aboard convict transports, Macquarie asked how he could be expected to do anything about incidents occurring on the high seas while he was dwelling in New South Wales. And how could he be expected to control the sentences that courts imposed?[26]

> I have never for an instant, directly or by connivance, sanctioned or allowed any prostitution of female convicts after their arrival in this colony. Nor have I on any occasion sanctioned or allowed sanguinary or cruel punishments to be inflicted on any criminals. Altho' I have frequently interposed my authority, either in mitigation or total suspension of sentences, when … the circumstances of the case merited humane consideration and the mingling of mercy with justice.[27]

Prisoner Michael Hoare, who was said in Bathurst's letter to have been on bread and water for twelve months, had only been confined in a cell for thirteen days, and 'no cruelty or severity whatever was exercised towards him'. Hoare had actually acknowledged that he deceived Magistrate Samuel Marsden by pretending to be insane.[28]

Macquarie blamed the undermining of his rule on the sort of characters who had plagued every governor since Phillip:

> Men … totally unworthy to be employed in the several situations to which their interest, unhappily not their merits, had promoted them. These men soon coalesce with the old and experienced evil minded persons: for nowhere is the justice of the old saying, that birds of a feather flock together, more certainly proved than in this place …
>
> It cannot be a matter of surprize to any reasonable person that they have by dint of perseverance lessened, if not entirely destroyed that degree of confidence in me which I felt you possessed and which I have ever felt to deserve.[29]

Marsden was the worst of them, Macquarie wrote, a man who 'set out systematically, from the commencement of my government of the colony, to oppose, both publickly and privately, every measure and regulation of mine however beneficial they may have been for the best interests of the colony'.

> I am grieved to be compelled to say so of any man of his sacred profession, but I do firmly believe that there is not a more malicious or a more vindictive unfeeling character in existence than the Revd. Mr Marsden.
>
> With this impression on my mind, your Lordship cannot wonder at my deprecating your giving too easy credit to the artful and insidious representations, clothed in the garb of humanity and hypocritical religious cant of this malevolent man … had your Lordship reposed the same degree of confidence in my administration and integrity, that you appear to have done in his representations respecting the affairs of this colony, I should not now have to lament the sudden change in your Lordship's sentiments towards me; and the consequent necessity I feel of tendering my resignation as governor of this country, which I could not, on any principle of honour and justice, reconcile to myself to hold any longer.[30]

Macquarie thought it was extraordinary that men such as Marsden, who had ordered convicts to be flogged almost to death before Macquarie's arrival in the colony, would be complaining about the governor's harsh treatment of them.

He told Bathurst that 'instead of censure' he had looked forward with a 'confident hope for praise and approbation on the termination of my government of this country; for, I can safely venture to affirm that no governor of any of His Majesty's colonies has ever laboured harder in the discharge of his various, arduous, public duties'.[31]

At the same time, Macquarie confided to Bathurst on 13 December that he was leaving office just about broke. His

£2200 a year as Governor and his £1400 a year as a major-general were eaten up by all the government dinners and functions he had to pay for out of his own pocket. And all his savings had gone on buying the so-far unproductive land from the Duke of Argyll.

He admitted it grieved him to see Marsden not only earning a salary as Principal Chaplain, but having huge landholdings and valuable flocks, when the Governor saw himself as the worker doing all the heavy lifting to improve the colony.

Castlereagh had told Macquarie before he left London that he would be given a pension if he stayed eight years as governor, and on 1 December 1817, within a month of that period, Macquarie tendered his resignation. Macquarie was a proud man, but not too proud to ask Bathurst to give him that pension and a 6000-hectare land grant, including the disused 'Government Farm of Toongabbee'.[32] The Governor had a grand vision of retiring to become a laird on his great Highland estate but that vision was looking increasingly blurry round the edges.

BUSHRANGER MICHAEL HOWE had all of Van Diemen's Land afraid, but he was sick of living in the bush like an animal. Although his crimes carried the death penalty many times over, he wrote to Lieutenant-Governor Sorell, offering 'to give himself up to an officer, as well as to furnish important information of the friends and supporters of the old gang', chiefly the Reverend Robert Knopwood.[33] In return, he asked for a pardon. Captain William Nairn[34] of the 46th Regiment was dispatched to a rendezvous point on 29 April 1817 to convey Howe to Hobart Town's jail.

Sorell wrote to Macquarie with the good news that the island's arch villain was under lock and key with a 'conditional pardon'. Macquarie replied:

I approve of all the measures you have thought fit to adopt in respect to the banditti of bush rangers. I rejoice to find you have got hold of their chief and principal leader Michael Howe, as I hope it will be the means of all the rest of the banditti being either taken or destroyed ... Now that he is come in, he may be made most useful; and I shall not fail to employ my best endeavours to obtain the king's pardon for him for his past crimes and misdemeanours.[35]

Howe waited on word of Macquarie's pardon for five months, but hearing misinformation that it had been refused, he escaped from prison in September 1817. Knopwood was pronounced innocent of Howe's claims for lack of evidence.[36]

On 10 October, Howe was betrayed for the £110 reward on his head and captured by a shepherd and a shopkeeper near New Norfolk.

With his hands tied, and one of the two men following behind him with a loaded gun, Howe managed to free his hands, draw a knife that had been secreted in his trousers, stab the man carrying the gun and use that weapon to shoot his other captor.

He then hid at a remote stock hut on the Shannon River, wearing kangaroo skins like a wild man, committing his thoughts in blood to a kangaroo-skin diary, and making a list of the flowers he had known in Yorkshire and which he hoped to grow in his hiding place.

AS 1817 DREW TO A CLOSE, Elizabeth Macquarie found herself deeply affected by the issues her family was facing. Lachlan junior had suffered more than his fair share of sickness, and the summer heat of New South Wales was continually painful for him.

The political heat on his father, though, was even more intense.

In December 1817, Elizabeth wrote to Lachlan junior's godfather, James Drummond, the M.P. for Perthshire and one of Macquarie's most trusted friends since the days he was married to Jane, telling him that 'it has ever since the commencement of this colony been the custom of some designing and truly wicked men here to carry on underhand correspondence with the clerks at the Colonial Office; and everywhere they can think of, to propagate falsehoods, and represent the conduct of the different governors in as unfavourable a light as they can'.[37]

All the previous governors, she wrote, had 'been compell'd or induced to relinquish the command at the instigation of these false spies — we have long known the exertions they were making to poison the minds of H.M. ministers, but the governor consider'd them too contemptible to take any notice of their cabals, nor did Lord Bathurst until now'. She continued:

> It was Macquarie's intention to have remain'd here two or three years longer till lately, when he received some letters from Lord Bathurst disapproving of his conduct and written in such a strain, as he considers very insulting; this is quite new from his Lordship, who till now, has express'd himself in the most agreeable manner on all subjects ...
>
> Lord Bathurst is so far from approving of the governor's conduct that he has written in a very (as we think) extraordinary manner on the subject, disapproving of Mr Vale's being tried by a court martial, and has desired the governor to restore Mr Moore's salary. — This the governor never will do — as he considers it inconsistent with the due support of the executive authority intrusted to him in this country.[38]

(In fact, Macquarie *would* later relent and reinstate Moore, but it would take until 1819, and it would only happen after Moore apologised.)

Elizabeth told Drummond that, if he 'knew what the governor has done for these persons', he would be 'astonish'd at their conduct':

> The two most artful and indefatigable among them is the Revd. Mr Marsden principal chaplain; and Mr Oxley the Surveyor General, this latter gentleman was one of the most active underhand agents in the arrest of Governor Bligh, and who I have reason to believe was the person who influenced Mr Bent's mind to the destruction of his own happiness, and the disgrace of his heart and understanding, in being blinded by a villain to become

jealous of the governor in regard to the attentions he shew'd him, and forgetful of the numberless kindnesses which had been conferr'd on him and his family, from our first acquaintance.

Elizabeth thought the Macquaries would be back in Britain within twelve months, upon the arrival of her husband's successor as governor. There were 'many persons' in New South Wales, she said, who were sensible of Macquarie's merits, 'and I cannot but think that when he is gone his absence will be felt; many as honest and as clever men may be found to succeed him, but I could venture to forfeit my head, that no one will take the extraordinary pains, and never ceasing fatigues which he has done, to promote the public service'.

However, she lamented that he would return to Britain poorer than he had been in India: 'The income of the governor is not adequate to the necessary expences attending the situation, according to the present extended society; I am afraid that we have not lived on it'. As well as that, Macquarie's property purchase in Mull had proved 'ruinous and expensive', with the land not returning much in rent.[39] Macquarie still cherished the prospect of his Highland kingdom, but he feared he would be going home to Scotland a pauper rather than a prince.

MACQUARIE WOULD SPEND months waiting for word from Bathurst over his resignation. In the meantime, he still had a colony to grow. He ushered in the new year of 1818 at the Aboriginal Feast Day at Parramatta, and two days later, his 'dear boy Lachlan was inoculated with the cow-pock by Dr Redfern from a very healthy child in the Female Orphan School'.[40]

On 8 January, however, Macquarie was back at war. The pressure was mutating into paranoia as Macquarie felt surrounded by malice everywhere he turned. It was not just affecting his physical health, but he now had trouble controlling his own rage. He was now ready for a showdown with his bitterest enemy.

As Samuel Marsden hauled his squat, balding form into a seat in Macquarie's office, he had defiance carved into his round, rock-hard face.

There were four chairs behind the governor's desk. Macquarie sat imperiously in one, and beside him were the Reverend Cowper, J.T. Campbell and John Watts, whom he had brought in as witnesses to what was about to occur. Macquarie also had his portable mahogany writing desk open with a prepared speech on top of it. He was so angry that he had already prepared a statement to read to the flogging parson, because every nerve in his body was at breaking point, and he was not confident he could choose his words correctly. Marsden's act of taking statements for Bent's case involving the three trespassers was so galling: it played into all Macquarie's fears over his reputation in England, and showed just what he was up against.

The chaplain could see that Macquarie was 'much agitated'. He tried to stare the governor down and Macquarie's breathing became shallow as he tried to contain the anger inside him. For 'the sake of brevity and perspicuity', Macquarie started reading from his script. It was high noon.

> I have long known, Mr Marsden, that you are a secret enemy of mine … I despised too much your malicious attempts to injure my character to take any notice of your treacherous conduct; but now that you have thrown off the mask, and have openly and publickly manifested your hostile and factious disposition towards me, I can no longer consistently with what I owe to my own high station, and the tranquillity of the country I have the honour to govern, pass over unnoticed, a recent most daring act of insolence and insubordination, of which you have been guilty.[41]

As the governor kept reading, Marsden tried to cut him off. He protested, demanding to have a friend brought in as his own witness.

Macquarie's accusation was that Marsden had gone behind his back to interview the colony's executioner, Thomas Hughes, and then to take depositions over the flogging of the three Domain trespassers.

Marsden received his reprimand 'very callously'. He stared back at Macquarie and said he did not consider that he had done anything wrong.

Macquarie became 'extremely violent'. Marsden stood up to make his escape but Macquarie roared: 'I command you as governor of this colony to sit down.'[42]

Then Macquarie fired his broadside, reading loudly and quickly as every nerve and fibre in his aging frame shuddered with fury.

> I consider, Sir, that act of yours, not only as most insolent and impertinent as it respects myself personally; but also, as highly insubordinate and seditious; in as much as such conduct, on your part, tends to inflame the mind of the inhabitants, excite a clamour against my government, bring my administration into disrepute, and disturb the general tranquillity of the colony. Such conduct, sir, would be highly criminal in any man; but still much more so in you as being both a magistrate and a clergyman who ought to be the first to set an example of loyalty, obedience, and proper subordination![43]

Now that Marsden had 'transmitted home' his attack on Macquarie by sending off his missive to London, the governor wanted rid of the chaplain's big round head.

> Viewing you now, sir, as the head of a seditious low cabal − and consequently unworthy of mixing in private society or intercourse with me, I beg to inform you that I never wish to see you excepting on public duty; — and I cannot help deeply lamenting, that, any man of your sacred profession should be so much lost to every good feeling of justice, generosity and gratitude, as to manifest such deep rooted malice, rancour, hostility and vindictive

opposition towards one who has never injured you – but has, on the contrary, conferred several acts of kindness on both yourself and family!⁴⁴

Marsden said he would resign as magistrate. Macquarie wouldn't let him. He wanted his enemy to stay in office where he would remain under the Governor's control. Then he told Marsden to get out.

As Marsden got up to go, Macquarie snarled: 'I command you, sir, that you never again set foot in Government House, except upon public duty.'

But Marsden got the last word. He told Macquarie he would gladly comply. Then he went home and wrote to Wilberforce that there was no more 'infamous brothel in the whole universe'⁴⁵ than Parramatta Hospital, with its 'debaucheries committed by the dying bed ... drunkenness, whoredom, sickness and death', the living forced to lie in rooms next to the dead.⁴⁶ He said Macquarie rarely visited there, even though Marsden had not been at the hospital for six years himself. Wilberforce saw the accusations as the anger of a bitter man.

MARSDEN WAS a notable absentee when 158 people sat down to dinner at Government House on 19 January 1818 to celebrate Queen Charlotte's birthday with a feast and dancing until 4 a.m. He was missing again seven days later, when Macquarie organised Foundation Day, the first major Australia Day celebrations: a dinner, ball and supper to the tune of thirty cannon blasts from Dawes Point, to commemorate the thirtieth anniversary of Arthur Phillip's establishment of the Colony of New South Wales.⁴⁷

Even though he had tendered his resignation, Macquarie was determined to maintain his regal presence in New South Wales. So he kept up the visits to such places as the new Female Orphan School,⁴⁸ though on his return from there on one occasion, he was met with the 'afflicting and melancholy intelligence' that his former aide John Maclaine, his cousin and Elizabeth's nephew, had been killed fighting insurgents in Ceylon.⁴⁹

That colony was opening up more and more. On 28 May, John Oxley set out from Bathurst to explore the Macquarie River, departing from Bathurst with George Evans, Dr John Harris, Charles Frazer and twelve convicts.[50] They marched through areas that would become the cities of Wellington and Dubbo, named the Castlereagh River, crossed the Warrumbungle Mountains and came upon the rich soil of the Liverpool Plains. They reported on the fertile land around what is now Tamworth before reaching the Hastings River and naming Port Macquarie.

Hearing that there was another magnificent part of New South Wales bearing his name was music to Macquarie's ears, though perhaps not as gratifying to the senses as the words he had read in the *Sydney Gazette* on 28 March.

Judge-Advocate Wylde had begun an investigation into the harshness of the sentences Marsden was handing out. Marsden became enraged and offered his resignation. This time Macquarie accepted it, and made sure the whole colony knew, with a short, succinct paragraph in Sydney's newspaper:

HIS EXCELLENCY the GOVERNOR is pleased to dispense with the services of the Rev. SAMUEL MARSDEN, as Justice of the Peace and Magistrate at Parramatta, and its adjoining districts.
By His Excellency's Command.[51]

BY THE END OF 1818, Macquarie could report that 'the whole population of the territory (including Van Diemen's Land) amounts to 25,054 souls !!!'[52] He had constantly tried to bring a spirit of civilisation and progress to his domain.

That included its native inhabitants. Macquarie wrote to Bathurst in early 1819 to say that some Aboriginal people had travelled more than 100 miles (160 kilometres) to attend the annual feast day, 'manifesting thereby their pacific disposition and confidence in the protection of this government'. They had danced with feathers in their hair and with the teeth of wild animals strung around their necks, their bodies painted with red and white ochre, their bellies full with the white man's roast beef and plum pudding.

'In short these people are now perfectly peaceable and inoffensive, and some few men amongst them have become settlers and cultivate land on their own account, which I do everything in my power to encourage.'[53]

He asked Bathurst to send him 350 suits of clothes each year for the Indigenous tribes, because New South Wales was cold in winter.[54]

IN MANY PLACES, though, the colony remained a wild frontier. But one of its wilder habitants was about to meet his match.

On 21 October 1818, Michael Howe was tricked into visiting a hut on the Shannon River where a stock-keeper, Thomas Worrall, and William Pugh of the 48th Regiment were hidden. Howe was wearing kangaroo skins, and had long hair and a long black beard. He had a haversack and powder horn slung across his shoulders.[55]

As he entered the hut, Pugh fired his musket at him and missed.

Howe screamed: 'Is that your game?' and fired back.

His shot went awry and he took off on foot. But Worrall and Pugh chased after him.

Pugh knocked him down with the butt end of his musket and then literally bashed Howe's brains out as the desperado tried to open a clasp knife.[56]

The two bounty hunters cut Howe's head off and took it back to Hobart for the reward.

Chapter 29

*Doctors Wentworth and Redfern both attended me during my severe
and dangerous illness … But had it not been for the extraordinary
exertions, unwearied solicitude, and most affectionate attentions …
of my good and beloved Mrs M I think I should have
fallen a sacrifice to my disease.*

MACQUARIE ON HIS WIFE'S DEVOTIONS IN THE TWILIGHT OF HIS REIGN[1]

THE STRESS WAS KILLING MACQUARIE. With his
fifty-ninth birthday fast approaching, he was bedridden with
dysentery, and for almost all of December 1819 he was confined
to Government House. His weight fell away and his strength left
him. He feared he would die. He felt it was only through the
grace of God and Mrs M's loving care that he eventually regained
the appetite to fight on.

EVER SINCE he had sent Bathurst his resignation in December
1817, Macquarie had fielded criticism from all directions. New
South Wales, for so long a forgotten outpost on the other side of
the globe, had become a British political pawn.

On 18 February 1819, Henry Grey Bennet had risen in the
House of Commons and called for a parliamentary inquiry into
the management of the prison hulks in England, the convict

439

transport system, and the government of New South Wales,[2] which had already attracted so much criticism as a result of the Vale–Moore petition.

Bennet had previously declared that 'a better natured man than Macquarie did not exist', praising his humanity and his treatment of women in particular,[3] but he also considered that the governor's role was merely to be 'a keeper of a large gaol occupied by criminals'.[4]

On 1 March, it was moved that the parliament should establish a Select Committee on the State of Gaols and Other Prisons. Lord Castlereagh, now the Secretary for Foreign Affairs, said the committee should inquire into whether Botany Bay 'had not outgrown the object for which it was originally intended', and that some place nearer to Britain might allow for the transportation of convicts 'at a more moderate expense than at present'.[5]

Former prime minister Viscount Sidmouth, now the Home Secretary, led the debate in the House of Lords. Faced with a populace protesting over Britain's grim living conditions, Sidmouth had suspended the right of *habeas corpus*, which meant prisoners could now be detained without charge. He would soon usher in repressive laws banning protesters from assembling in large numbers after Manchester's Peterloo Massacre,[6] in which cavalry charged into a wave of demonstrators, killing eighteen people and injuring as many as 700. In such a climate, it was inevitable that the penal system would bear increased scrutiny.

In the House of Commons, Bennet repeated all manner of wild stories that he had heard from Macquarie's enemies: how Macquarie had imported wheat in 1813 to ruin the colonists – there was no shipment of wheat that year – and how one of Macquarie's magistrates named 'Laud' – Simeon Lord – would come down from the seat of justice, get into a cart and sell blankets as an auctioneer. Bennet called this 'one of the most indecent acts that could possibly be exhibited'.[7]

On 20 May 1818, Macquarie expelled 'the Popish Priest',[8] Jeremiah O'Flynn,[9] a Roman Catholic cleric who had a history of run-ins with authority. He had arrived in Sydney six months earlier, even though Bathurst had denied him permission to visit. Macquarie feared that, with a reputation as a troublemaker, he could spark the kind of dissent among Irish convicts that had led to the Castle Hill uprising of 1804.

Even though the Prince Regent had supported Macquarie's decision to expel O'Flynn, Bennet told Parliament that 'the poor Irish lamented exceedingly the departure of their clergyman. They shed tears as he left them, and appeared rather to be following some beloved friend to his grave.'[10]

Opinion in Britain was divided: many thought Macquarie had been too harsh on convicts – Bennet asserted that Macquarie believed he had the right to order 500 lashes for prisoners[11] – and many others thought he was far too lenient, allowing convicted criminals such as Mr 'Laud' to gain important positions.

Macquarie himself preferred the latter description.

On 4 June 1819, he was deeply gratified to attend the first dinner at Greenway's new Hyde Park Barracks, where 589 convicts sat down 'to a most excellent dinner; plum pudding and an allowance of punch being allowed to them, in addition to their regular meal on this auspicious day.'

Macquarie addressed them in 'a short, plain speech' and he and Mrs M 'drank to their health & prosperity'. There wasn't a whip in sight.

'They all appeared very happy and contented,' Macquarie noted, 'and gave [us] three cheers'.[12]

Sydney now had a population of 11,209, and despite the political machinations in London over his tenure, Macquarie felt a glowing sense of self-satisfaction over his ten years of hard work. He and Greenway were now planning a grand Gothic cathedral in George Street, because Sydney would soon be a city big enough to need one.[13]

Unlike the poorer classes in Britain, who were battling unemployment, food shortages and a government that was prepared to massacre its own, Macquarie's convicts were always well fed, worked a regular nine-hour day and were clothed at public expense.

Macquarie had done his best to make sure the deplorable working conditions in English mills and factories, where small children laboured until they dropped, did not exist in his new world. The health of both prisoners and free settlers in the Australian sunshine left standards among the smoggy mills of home for dead.

Indeed, many of Britain's poor would have been better off coming to New South Wales in chains than staying home to die. Sidmouth argued in the House of Lords that the crime rate in Britain would never drop when there was a working holiday in the sunshine awaiting all evildoers.

Macquarie's kindness came at a cost, too.

Though Bathurst was constantly telling Macquarie to be frugal, Britain spent £717,000 on New South Wales and Van Diemen's Land between 1816 and 1818 [about $A130 million in 2019 values], including £335,801 on provisions and stores.[14]

But the numbers didn't tell the whole story. Expenditure was only rising so dramatically because so many convicts kept arriving. In just five months from August to December 1819, 2559 prisoners were landed in Sydney on fifteen transports.[15] Macquarie had actually managed to reduce the cost of each convict to the government from £30 per annum in 1816 to £25 in 1819.[16]

The powers-that-be in Britain were not interested in the fine details, though. On 18 February, Castlereagh told Parliament that Earl Bathurst had 'instituted a commission, and had obtained the consent of an individual … to go out to the colony and make a detailed inquiry on the spot, for the purpose of ascertaining whether the colony could be made more auxiliary to the administration of justice in this country; and how far its religious and moral improvement might be promoted'.[17]

MACQUARIE WAS at Windsor for the General Muster – census – when John Thomas Bigge,[18] a former chief justice of Trinidad, now Commissioner of Inquiry into the Colony of New South Wales, sailed into Sydney on 26 September 1819.

Accompanying Bigge on the ship *John Barry* was his secretary, Thomas Hobbes Scott,[19] a bankrupt wine merchant whose sister had married Bigge's brother. Also on board were 142 male convicts, and James Bowman,[20] the new principal surgeon, replacing the retiring D'Arcy Wentworth.

Bowman would begin an immediate investigation into the rum hospital, reorganising the wards, nursing staff and patients' diets. He would add a separate mortuary and dissecting room, and order new supplies of instruments.

And Bigge would begin investigating Macquarie.

Before leaving for Windsor, the governor had left behind a welcoming letter and instructions for a thirteen-gun salute from Dawes Point. But in truth, Macquarie was dumbfounded by Bigge's presence. He had not yet received a reply to his resignation letter sent twenty-one months earlier, unaware that a letter Bathurst wrote in October 1818, telling Macquarie that he was doing a good job and asking him to reconsider his decision to quit,[21] had been lost somewhere on its final leg between Hobart and Sydney. He *had* received another letter from Bathurst, informing him of Bigge's arrival – but it had reached him just five days previously.

Bigge arrived in Windsor a day after reaching Sydney and gave Macquarie his instructions from Bathurst: explicit orders that Macquarie was to comply with Bigge's every direction and give him the same standing as himself as governor. He was also ordered to appoint Bigge a justice of the peace and magistrate, and to give him full access to official documents.[22] Even though the orders were a humiliation to Macquarie, a slap in the face after all he had done in developing the colony, he was impressed by the 'manners and polite address of Mr Bigge' and much pleased with 'Mr Scott's manners and mild address'. After introducing them to Mrs M, he showed Bigge and Scott to their temporary lodgings at the Macquarie Arms.[23]

Macquarie spent the next few days showing Bigge and Scott around the Hawkesbury. Macquarie's nephew Hector, the illegitimate son of Charles Macquarie, had replaced John Watts as Macquarie's aide-de-camp[24] and he escorted the visitors back to Sydney in a four-horse carriage.[25] Macquarie didn't let Bigge know, but Hector had just completed a month's confinement in the military barracks after being accused of raping a servant girl at Parramatta.[26]

Despite being taken off guard by his arrival, Macquarie was convinced that Bigge could not fail to see the merits of the colony and of the work that was being done by both the free settlers and the emancipists. He told his brother Charles:

> Commissioner Bigge arrived here ... with full powers to investigate and inquire into everything connected with the government of this colony, which is a most fortunate thing for me, as it will place my conduct at home on an eminence beyond the reach of faction malevolence and gross envious misrepresentations ... I certainly feel much obliged to H.M.'s ministers for sending out a commissioner as his reports *must* be favourable to my administration of the colony and highly honourable to my character.[27]

At Government House on 7 October, Judge-Advocate Wylde administered the oaths of office to appoint Bigge as a magistrate. A royal salute was fired at the end of the ceremony. Bigge addressed the gathering, delivering what Macquarie thought was a 'very beautiful appropriate speech, pointing out the principal objects of his mission to this colony'.[28] Then the governor introduced him to some of the civil and military bigwigs as wine and cake were passed around.

Macquarie was proud as punch as he showed Bigge the splendour of the colony he was building. He escorted the commissioner to the site of the new courthouse adjacent to Hyde Park for the laying of the foundation stone, and then on to the Hyde Park Barracks. Bigge couldn't help but be impressed. Or so Macquarie thought.

While Macquarie was initially impressed by Bigge's manners and quiet disposition, the admiration would wane after only a few weeks, once Macquarie discovered the true nature of the man and his mission.

Bigge's royal commission, issued on 5 January 1819, authorised an investigation of 'all the laws, regulations and usages of the settlements', notably those affecting civil administration, management of convicts, development of the courts, the Church, trade, revenue and natural resources.[29] Bathurst told Bigge that transportation needed to become 'an object of real terror', and that any weakening of this by 'ill-considered compassion for convicts'[30] in Macquarie's humanitarian policies should be reported. He was also to disclose confidences of the private or public lives of servants of the Crown and leading citizens, 'however exalted in rank or sacred in character'.[31] He was to be both public commissioner and private investigator.

Then there was the constantly vexing question of admitting into society 'persons, who originally came to the settlement as convicts'. The Prince Regent supported Macquarie's principles, but Bathurst noted that 'I am aware that the conduct of the governor in this respect, however approved by the government at home, has drawn down upon him the hostility of many persons, who hold association with convicts under any circumstances to be a degradation. Feelings of this kind are not easily overcome'.[32]

To Bigge, Macquarie's emancipist leanings were incompatible with the Tories' support for tough action against criminals. Bigge had just come from administering rough justice in a slave colony.

He was still administering rough justice when he got to work in New South Wales. His methods of inquiry were hardly in keeping with a royal commission. Evidence was taken informally, often in private, with no distinction made between sworn and unsworn testimony. Often the main line of questioning was: 'Have you any complaint to make against Governor Macquarie?'

The Governor had installed the colony's first flush toilet for Elizabeth at Parramatta, but Bigge was more critical of his expenditure on grand buildings such as the Government Stables. He saw them as a waste of money and resources. Architect Henry Kitchen, Francis Greenway's rival, concurred.

Bigge supported the views of the colony's landowners that convict labour would be better employed on farms than in the erection of colossal city structures. He cancelled many of Greenway's projects as being too extravagant, and interfered with others.

Later, he began to issue orders to Greenway as though Macquarie did not exist, creating a wedge between the governor and his colonial architect. In his report, Bigge would comment favourably on Greenway's abilities, if not his arrogance, and would blame the expensive buildings on the governor.

BIGGE AND MACQUARIE were also very different men. Macquarie was a professional soldier born in a dirt-floor hut. He was practical, far-sighted and humane, and no one knew more about the unique difficulties of governing in New South Wales. Bigge was an aristocratic lawyer, very much a man of the English establishment, with no experience of the problems of New South Wales. He was twenty years younger than Macquarie, and socially the academic and the soldier were incompatible. Bigge preferred the company of the Marsdens and Macarthurs.

He also found Macquarie stubborn, and soon he had 'nearly abandoned the hope of being able to influence him in any changes'. Private differences of opinion between Macquarie and Bigge became embarrassingly public.

One such dispute occurred over Macquarie's beloved physician William Redfern. Macquarie had wanted to appoint him to the post of magistrate at Airds in the Cowpastures district, where the doctor owned land. Redfern had also been hoping to succeed D'Arcy Wentworth as Principal Surgeon, but London had said no, because Redfern had been transported for his minor role in the Nore naval mutiny twenty-three years earlier. Redfern missed out on the magistracy, too, because Bigge wouldn't allow an ex-convict a place on the bench.

Redfern had brought Macquarie's son into the world and saved the life of John Macarthur's daughter Elizabeth.[33] Macquarie decided to write Bigge an impassioned letter on

Redfern's behalf, summing up the feelings he had towards convicts who had found redemption through honest work. What danger could arise, he asked, 'from availing myself of the services of a man of the first talents in this country, whose conduct, as a public servant of the Crown, since his arrival in it had been irreproachable'?[34]

> I have availed myself of the services of persons in a similar predicament for nine years past, without any evil having resulted from that measure, but on the contrary much good, I am at a loss to discover the grounds on which you have formed so decided an opinion. With all due deference to your acquirements and the superior faculties of your mind, I consider myself at least your equal in the consideration of a subject new to you, but familiar to me in my daily and hourly duties for now nearly ten years; and I cannot let this opportunity pass without dwelling a little longer on the subject which has given rise to this communication. At my first entrance into this colony, I felt as you do, and I believe I may add, everyone does; at that moment I certainly did not anticipate any intercourse but that of control with men who were, or had been convicts; a short experience showed me, however, that some of the most meritorious men of the few to be found, and who were most capable and most willing to exert themselves in the public service, were men who had been convicts![35]

He advised to beware of the 'exclusives' who had 'free access' to him. They had 'raised themselves by the labour' of convicts but wanted to keep this free workforce 'in a state of depression'.[36]

But Bigge still wouldn't have a bar of Redfern as a magistrate. He was angry at Macquarie for questioning his judgment, and told the governor that Redfern's crime of mutiny was 'the most foul and unnatural conspiracy that ever disgraced the page of English history'. While it might 'be forgiven by Englishmen, it never can be forgotten'.[37]

He asked Macquarie to forget about friendships, remember whom he served, and to make 'a magnanimous sacrifice of your personal feelings to your public duty'.[38]

Macquarie made Redfern a justice of the peace instead.

Bigge already knew the names of the 'exclusives' on Macquarie's list, but the governor furnished him with another list as a reminder. To Macquarie's chagrin, these same men clearly had Bigge's ear from the start, and formed a queue to slander the governor.

Samuel Marsden couldn't wait to tell Bigge that his reputation was being 'torn to pieces by the hand of power and scattered in blotted scraps by an official engine over the face of the whole earth'.[39]

John Macarthur gave Bigge and his secretary Scott 'two beautiful valuable horses' on loan, 'two such as could not be equalled in the colony', and remarked that the commissioner was an accomplished horseman who rode 'his prancing Arab with no little satisfaction'.[40]

He told Bigge that he was worried about the spirit of democracy that Macquarie was promoting among the convict class. Macarthur told Bigge that the future of New South Wales was as an extensive exporter of wool. Rather than a colony full of emancipists in important positions, Macarthur argued that it was big landowners like him and men of capital, using convicts as cheap labour, that would drive the future of His Majesty's possession. Macquarie's fanciful idea of trial by jury, Macarthur said, would never work in the colony because the convict class could only be relied upon for dishonesty.

BY DECEMBER 1819, the stress was overwhelming Macquarie. He was violently ill with dysentery and afraid he would die if not for the medical treatment from Redfern and Wentworth, and from Elizabeth's loving care.

The day after he rose from what he had feared would be his deathbed, Macquarie hosted Bigge and Scott at the 1819 Aboriginal Feast Day at Parramatta. Macquarie was proud to note that there were 231 Aboriginal men, women and children assembled in the marketplace, and that there were now twenty children attending his Aboriginal school.[41]

IN LONDON, a letter written by Henry Grey Bennet to Viscount Sidmouth was published as a pamphlet in 1819. Much of the information within it, claiming that New South Wales was a godless, corrupt colony in chaos, had been provided by the man Bennet called a 'respectable minister of the gospel … one of those distinguished persons, who, praise be to God, are daily raised up among us'.[42]

Unsurprisingly, the 'respectable minister of the gospel' who had written of the debauchery of the female convicts, the riff-raff who held government positions and the stench of the governor's democratic thinking was one Reverend Samuel Marsden. Bennet had claimed in parliament that a 'letter from Mr Marsden, the chaplain-general of the colony, set at rest all loose assertions with respect to the moral state of the colony, and what was to be expected from exporting annually such a quantity of vicious matter to the New South Wales'.

By February 1820, the pamphlet had found its way to New South Wales. Macquarie wrote to Bathurst to tell him the attacks on him came 'from the most polluted sources and the false communications of unprincipled individuals … A man must therefore be devoid of all feeling, who could tamely submit to have his character thus cruelly slandered … without making some attempt to repel and refute such false accusations, when perfectly conscious of his own innocence'.[43]

Macquarie told Bathurst he had tried to canvass the support of magistrates friendly to him, but Bigge had taken 'violent umbrage' at the move, accusing Macquarie of 'very improper interference with the objects of his commission' and telling him that he would not speak to him again.[44]

Macquarie had a generous nature, though. As he had shown with Ellis Bent, he had the grace to praise even his enemies. In the case of Bigge, he had the facility not only to forgive his most strident critic but also to praise him, telling Bathurst that he had received:

> a very angry letter from Commissioner Bigge, written in a very offensive style ... I can with truth assure your Lordship that it has occasioned me a very sincere distress of mind to be compelled in my own vindication to carry on so unpleasant a correspondence with Commissioner Bigge, and to be at variance with that gentleman; for I have rarely met in public life any gentleman, of whom I thought more highly, nor one whose friendship and good opinion I was more solicitous to cultivate and possess.[45]

Macquarie patched things up, but he knew he had made a powerful enemy.

That same month, Bigge sailed for Hobart. He spent three months there, and gained a favourable impression of Sorell's work in Van Diemen's Land. After the madness of Tom Davey, Sorell had done a stirling job of cleaning up the colony, ridding it of its most dangerous bushrangers and founding the Macquarie Harbour Penal Settlement to house the worst offenders in the colony.

Despite his regard for Sorell's administration, Bigge refused to enter Hobart's Government House because Sorell was living there with another man's wife.

By May, Bigge was back in Sydney. But by then, Macquarie had seen and heard enough. Since arriving in Sydney, he had cleaned up Bligh's chaotic mess and finally sent him packing, only to be met with constant criticism and backstabbing over the improvements he began to make to a wild frontier. Ten years of stress had eroded his health and the job was costing him money in entertainment expenses. Now his bosses in Britain had started believing the scuttlebutt about him and had stuck an officious lawyer on his back to investigate and insult him! Macquarie had become thin-skinned and the job was bleeding him dry.

On 29 February 1820, he had written to Bathurst:

After the arduous and harassing duties I have had to perform in the administration of this colony for now upwards of ten years, the constant counteraction I have experienced here to my best measures, and the cruel and base calumnies circulated to the prejudice of my character at home, I must confess, my Lord, I am now heartily tired of my situation here, and anxiously wish to retire from public life as soon as possible. I therefore most earnestly entreat your Lordship will be so good as to move His Royal Highness, the Prince Regent, to accept this second tender[46] of my resignation, and to be graciously pleased to appoint another governor to relieve me here as soon as a competent person can be selected for that purpose.[47]

For Macquarie, the arrival of a new Governor could now not come soon enough.

AT LEAST there were still some events in the colony that brought him joy. On 22 March 1820, at St Philip's Church, George Jarvis, the Indian slave Macquarie had purchased at Cochin and whom he now treated like a son, married Mary Jelly, a convict chambermaid, at Government House. The Reverend Cowper performed the ceremony. George was now 30 years old and it had been a quarter of a century since he had become part of Macquarie's household, a twist of fate that took him around the world and provided him with opportunities he would never have experienced in poverty on the subcontinent.

George accompanied Macquarie on his next travels in October 1820, this time exploring the lush land south of the Cowpastures, and bringing with him wine, biscuits and oranges for their fellow travellers.[48]

Macquarie wanted to see the great lake that had been reported on by Joseph Wild,[49] a former convict burglar employed by Charles Throsby. On 27 October, the party reached the north shore of the lake, 'most highly gratified and delighted with this noble expanse of water, and the surrounding scenery',[50] though

Macquarie was surprised to learn from Throsby's Aboriginal guide, Taree, that it was not the source of the 'new river' Murrumbidgee. Joseph Wild sold Macquarie 'four very pretty young emus and a very little rock kangaroo' as well as a young swan 'as presents for my beloved Lachlan'.

On 28 October 1820, Macquarie sat down to dinner at their bush camp, and he and his party drank a bumper toast to the success of the future settlers of the magnificent sheet of water that he now named 'Lake George', in honour of the king – and perhaps of his humble servant–cum–son as well.

George and Mary's first child was born on 19 December but died on Christmas Day.

ON THE LAST DAY of 1820, Major Frederick Goulburn,[51] a younger brother of the Under-Secretary of State for War and the Colonies, arrived in Sydney as the new Colonial Secretary. Goulburn was a veteran of Waterloo. He was replacing J.T. Campbell, who had become the new provost-marshal after William Gore was declared bankrupt and thus ineligible for the position.

Goulburn brought with him news that Macquarie's resignation had been accepted. The day after his arrival – 1 January 1821 – Goulburn was one of twenty-six revellers at a Government House dinner celebrating Macquarie's eleven years in the colony. Macquarie had made enemies in New South Wales but he had also made many friends.

Later that month, he lent his support to the campaign organised by Edward Eagar to ensure that Macquarie's pardons legally restored the rights of former convicts. Justice Barron Field had argued, that under English law, only a royal pardon restored a convict's civil rights, and that Macquarie's pardons were therefore invalid, which threw the outcomes of legal disputes and property claims into chaos. Eagar organised the signatures of 7556 emancipists from New South Wales on a petition that he and Dr Redfern would take to England[52] in their fight to have the New South Wales emancipists protected by English law.[53]

ON 1 FEBRUARY 1821, Bigge was on hand to see 109 female convicts and seventy-one children moved to the New Factory at Parramatta, which had much more commodious accommodation for the prisoners. Six days later, at Government House, Bigge gave a farewell speech before making a move himself. His investigation was now complete.

Despite their differences, and the big knife that Macquarie suspected was coming for his back, the governor magnanimously described Bigge's words as 'very handsome, complementary and gratifying'.[54] On 8 February, Macquarie organised two companies of the 48th and the boys from the male orphanage into a guard of honour for Bigge to walk through on his way to board the *Dromedary*. Bigge left for England to the sounds of another thirteen-gun salute.[55]

Recent dispatches from Bathurst had warned Macquarie against making Redfern a magistrate. They also banned him from allowing another former convict, Laurence Halloran,[56] back into the teaching profession, because he had once forged a frank in return for tenpence.

But Macquarie wasn't going to be told what to do any more. He saw Halloran as 'a very unfortunate old man, deserving of sympathy'.[57] With help from Simeon Lord and John Macarthur, who saw potential in Halloran as an educator despite his background, he opened a private school, 'Dr Halloran's establishment for liberal education, now better known as Sydney Grammar School.[58]

MACQUARIE, NOW SIXTY, started a farewell tour of Australia on 4 April 1821 with Mrs M, Lachlan and a large entourage, including George Jarvis, Lachlan's teenage tutor Theodore Bartley[59] and a complement of servants aboard the private merchant vessel *Midas*. Macquarie loved Australia and its unique landscapes, and went bush every chance he got. Their first few days travelling towards Van Diemen's Land 'nearly proved fatal' in heavy winds, and Greenway's lighthouse near South Head was a welcome sight for the skipper, Captain Beveridge.

It took them twenty days to finally reach Hobart, where they were greeted by the glory of Mount Wellington covered in snow. Less edifying was the sight of ten men being hanged on a public scaffold at the top of Macquarie Street on 28 April, and the plight of Macquarie's faithful old carriage horse, Ajax, who impaled himself on the end of a plough after breaking loose from his stable.

They continued on to Port Dalrymple, Launceston and George Town, retracing much of the journey from a decade before. In Launceston, Macquarie signed nine death warrants,[60] but had much more pleasant papers put before him when he opened his official mail in Hobart on 11 June.

A letter from Henry Goulburn informed him that a fellow Scot, Major-General Thomas Brisbane, graduate of Edinburgh University and almost as well travelled in the military as Macquarie, was on his way to become the new governor.

Brisbane was a keen astronomer, and had first expressed an interest in Macquarie's job in 1815, keen to chart the stars from the Southern Hemisphere. He had even built an observatory at his home, Brisbane House at Largs in Ayrshire. Brisbane was close friends with the Duke of Wellington from their days as young subalterns in Ireland. He had served in Flanders, France, the West Indies and America, and had most recently had command of the military in Munster Province in Ireland.

The Macquaries returned to Sydney on 12 July 1821, to a welcome of fireworks, bonfires and balls. Later that month, Macquarie attended the funeral of his old magistrate, the First Fleeter William Broughton, at Liverpool.[61] Though it would be months before Thomas Brisbane arrived to relieve him, Macquarie began packing off gifts bound for England: a pair of emus for Lord Bathurst, another pair for Lord Castlereagh, a pair of black swans to General Sir George Nugent, who had been commander-in-chief in India, and a box of stuffed birds for Kitty, the daughter of Charles Forbes, now a member of the British Parliament.

Lachlan junior, now seven, was enrolled in the Reverend Thomas Redall's[62] new school at Macquarie Fields, near Campbelltown.

Elizabeth went with the little boy as he prepared to begin his schooling there, with a class that included Edmund Sorell, son of the lieutenant-governor. Mrs Macquarie had strawberries sent to the school twice a week, while Macquarie donated a cricket set and gardening tools.

On 1 September 1821, Macquarie granted George Jarvis's wife Mary an absolute pardon so that she could travel to Britain with him when the Macquaries sailed.

Macquarie wanted to see the new site for the town and penal settlement of Port Macquarie, 400 kilometres to the north, before he was finished in New South Wales. He embarked on 1 November aboard the *Elizabeth Henrietta*, while Elizabeth and Lachlan stayed behind. He drank a toast to their fourteenth wedding anniversary en route.

On 6 November, Macquarie found a 'most convenient site for the future town, it being so very close to the harbour, and very well supplied with fresh water ... There is also [an] abundance of most excellent timber for building growing close in the vicinity of the town.'[63]

After another rough voyage, in which the boat dragged her anchor and lost her rudder, Macquarie made it to Newcastle, where a great pier – Macquarie Pier, of course – impressed him as a 'Herculean undertaking'.

Elizabeth welcomed Macquarie back to Sydney on 21 November with the news that Thomas Brisbane had been in the colony for two weeks. He had been staying at Parramatta, but had come down to Sydney that morning, and he and Macquarie met while walking in the Domain. On 30 November, Macquarie officially handed over Government House at Parramatta to serve as Brisbane's home until Macquarie left Government House in Sydney.

THE NEXT MORNING, 1 December 1821, Macquarie prepared his farewell speech as all of Sydney prepared to say goodbye to a governor who had dramatically changed the colony – its outlook, its surrounds and its prospects. The drums were beating outside Government House, and at Dawes Point, the artillerymen were loading black powder and wadding into nineteen cannons for Macquarie's farewell salute. On this first day of summer in 1821, Macquarie congratulated himself on his work in transforming this thriving settlement from a prison camp into a budding nation.

When Macquarie had taken control of New South Wales in 1810, the total population of the colony, including soldiers, had been 11,590. Now it was 38,778. The number of cattle had increased nine-fold to more than 100,000. Sheep numbers had grown from 25,000 to 290,000, with similar dramatic rises in the numbers of pigs and horses. Back then, there had been 3000 hectares of land under cultivation; now there were more than 12,000.[64] The 'awkward, rusticated, Jungle-Wallah'[65] believed that he had put this burgeoning colony on the pathway to a grand future.

Macquarie was running out of steam fast, but he still wanted a big finish after more than a decade of hard work. The short carriage ride from Government House to Hyde Park gave him the chance to admire the way Sydney had changed, growing up as he had grown old. While many in Britain still wanted this town to resemble a place of terror and punishment, Macquarie saw a world of possibilities on the shining, shimmering harbour, and among the hardy, enterprising people who were making it home.

As the carriage arrived at Hyde Park and a large gathering stood to attention to hear the governor's final public address, Major-General and Mrs Macquarie looked around at the new world they had created over the last eleven years. The convict stood next to the captain of industry, the banker next to the baker, in this egalitarian home of the fair go.

Macquarie stepped forward, and cleared his throat. In his booming Scottish burr, he used the name he was determined to see as the official title for this land.

'Fellow citizens of Australia!' he began:[66]

On the occasion of my own commission, as governor in chief of this territory, being read, now nearly twelve years ago, I pledged myself to administer the affairs of this government with strict justice and impartiality; and I trust, that every liberal and unprejudiced person will admit that I have redeemed that pledge: my constant maxim and principle being, to reward merit and punish vice, wherever I found them, without regard to rank, class or description of persons. When I took charge of this government, on the 1st. of January 1810, I found the colony in a state of rapid deterioration; threatened with a famine; discord and party spirit prevailing to a great degree; all the public buildings in a state of dilapidation and decay; very few roads and bridges, and those few very bad; the inhabitants, generally very poor; and commerce and public credit at the lowest ebb. I now have the happiness to reflect, that I leave it in a very different condition: to have been instrumental in bringing about so favourable a change, will ever be to me, a source of sincere delight.[67]

He told the crowd that his health had been 'greatly impaired' by the pressures of the job, and that he had made enemies as every man in public life must do. But he was proud of forty years' service spent 'in honourable pursuits, and stained with no action which can give me remorse'.

His attachment to Australia was all that much stronger on account of the fact that it was the birthplace of his only surviving child. Although still only young, Lachlan already expressed 'the strongest affection for his native Australian land'.

Concluding his address, he declared that the colony had found a good man in Brisbane, and Macquarie hoped he would use all his abilities and talents to promote the prosperity and improvement of the colony, and the happiness and unanimity of its inhabitants.

'In these sentiments and wishes, deeply engraved on my heart, I now bid you all – farewell!'[68]

Chapter 30

FEBRUARY 1822 TO JUNE 1824, NEW SOUTH WALES,
SCOTLAND AND ENGLAND

*Finally, when he took leave of me, he burst into tears, which he never
did before. The recollection of this, is one of the most agreeable
I have to reflect on, being to me, a convincing proof
(had such been required), of his affection.*

ELIZABETH MACQUARIE SAYING HER LAST GOODBYE TO HER HUSBAND[1]

SYDNEY HARBOUR was such a wondrous sight that
Macquarie found it hard to leave. All over its waters and
around its banks on 12 February 1822 – on Greenway's new Fort
Macquarie, the Dawes Point Battery and the rocks on the western
side of Sydney Harbour – men, women and children, ex-convict
and free, turned out to farewell the governor. Wooden boats,
under sail and oar, crowded the vast waterway. Macquarie and
Mrs M had tears in their eyes aboard the convict transport *Surry*;[2]
they felt touched by the deepest emotions at saying goodbye to
their people.

Following his farewell speech to Australia on 1 December
1821, Macquarie had spent ten weeks savouring every bit of the
countryside that he could. He knew that, with his health having
faltered so much of late, he was unlikely ever to see it again.[3]

He had ridden over the majestic Blue Mountains one last time
and crossed the Macquarie River to Bathurst, where a group of

fifteen Aboriginal people had entertained him with what he called 'a very good karauberie' (corrobboree).[4] But there were perils in the Australian bush, too, and on the return journey towards Mount York, one of the cart horses had become ill. He was immediately bled and a draught of hot port wine poured down his throat. He had died in great agony, despite (or perhaps because of) the treatment.[5] Macquarie felt pity for animals just as he always did for the convicts who were often regarded as beasts by the establishment.

Macquarie had attended his last Native Feast Day on 28 December 1821, and though future generations would condemn him for his role in the Appin massacre, he took pleasure in taking Mrs M, Lachlan and Brisbane along to meet 'these poor inoffensive people'. There were 340 Aboriginal men, women and children: over five times as many as had attended the first feast. Macquarie introduced several chiefs to the new governor and showed off the progress of the twenty children at the Native Institution. In his luggage for the return to Britain was a portrait of a proud young Aboriginal warrior.[6]

He had taken Elizabeth and Lachlan on one last tour of the south and southwest: Liverpool, Campbelltown, Cawdor, Camden, Appin and the area named Minto after his friend the Earl of Minto, the former governor-general of India.[7]

On 15 January, they had crossed the Cataract River near its source, and 'arrived at the summit of the great mountain' that overlooks the ocean and 'the pass to the low country of Illawarra', now the city of Wollongong. The whole face of the mountain was clothed with the largest and finest forest trees Macquarie had seen in the colony. He named it Regent Mountain. The descent of just a mile took an hour over rocky, slippery terrain that made the packhorses stumble again and again.[8]

THE MACQUARIES had to hire a second ship to carry all their luggage and possessions back to Britain, but they gave some things away, including Elizabeth's violoncello to Captain Piper's wife Eliza. They offloaded a lot of others in a vice-regal sale, with ads appearing in the *Sydney Gazette*:

AUCTION

THE SALE of the HOUSEHOLD FURNITURE, BOOKS, PLATE, TABLE LINEN, CHINA WARE, CARRIAGES, &c. &c. &c. belonging to Major General MACQUARIE, will commence at Government House, in Sydney, on Tuesday, the 15th inst. and be thence continued, daily, until the whole will be disposed of.

Sale will commence each day at ten in the forenoon; and printed catalogues of the articles to be sold, will be distributed previous to the auction.

The terms of sale will be announced each day, by S. Lord, auctioneer.[9]

At 11 a.m. on the bright summer's day of 12 February 1822, the 48th Regiment paraded under arms in the Government Domain, forming a lane from Government House to the private landing place below Lachlan's Garden on Bennelong Point. All of Sydney's dignitaries were there, and 'an immense concourse of the other inhabitants of Sydney', who followed the Macquaries to the waterside with melancholy looks at having to say goodbye.[10]

The Macquaries, George Jarvis, the heavily pregnant Mary, and outgoing aide-de-camp Hector Macquarie, perpetually on the run from creditors, climbed into the government barge and were slowly rowed through the throng of ships as the Dawes Point Battery cut loose with nineteen guns and other ships saluted in response. The military band played 'God Save the King' and, as the ship headed for the open sea, Macquarie stood on the opening deck 'bowing adieu' as he passed by the cheering crowds.[11]

The winds were so vicious, however, though, that they had to remain anchored off Watson's Bay, and Judge-Advocate Wylde, who had come on board to say a private goodbye, was forced to spend the night. Little Lachlan was reduced to tears at saying goodbye to Macquarie's chief bodyguard, Sergeant Charles Whalan, and his two young sons, Charley and James, before the ship finally cleared the heads on 15 February.

There would be plenty of pets for Lachlan to play with, though. Macquarie methodically listed them (as well as every passenger, crew member and plant on board):

1 horse Sultan [Macquarie's dun-coloured horse, 15½ hands high]
1 cow – Fortune
3 goats
42 sheep
9 pigs
21 turkeys
47 geese
60 ducks
106 fowls …
7 kangaroos
6 emus
7 black swans
4 Cape Barren geese
2 native companions [an early name for the long-necked bird, the brolga]
1 Narang emu
2 white cockatoos
2 bronze-wing pigeons
4 wanga-wanga pigeons
and also several parrots and lowries belonging to Lachlan.[12]

By the time they left Australia, there were only six kangaroos, though, Macquarie explaining that the others had beaten one of their own to death. Even though Macquarie had ensured the *Surry* was equipped with cedar cages and roomy pens, many of the animals died on the voyage.

As they neared Cape Horn, the Macquaries celebrated Lachlan's eighth birthday with a lavish dinner and fireworks. On 5 May, they reached the port of San Salvadore, Brazil, where Macquarie was delighted to report that, at midnight, George and Mary Jarvis had become the proud parents of a daughter, Elizabeth.

The Macquaries went shopping and visited a sugar plantation, but came away disappointed after Lachlan's fine straw hat was stolen.

Macquarie's cook James Wait,[13] a former convict, went on the mother of all benders while in port and never recovered. As the ship breezed on, he became weaker and weaker, and he died on 20 May, deeply lamented by Macquarie who wrote that, while the man had become 'violently intoxicated with the ardent poisonous spirits' of Brazil, he was 'in all other respects, a very well behaved man'.

Wait's remains were committed to the deep, which on 13 June turned on all sorts of entertainments for Mrs M's forty-fourth birthday. A great pod of sperm whales, frolicking and leaping from the water, kept everyone on deck astonished, while a large shark circling ominously provided more sinister thrills. A 20-kilogram turtle that was chased down by boat provided a delicious soup.

Macquarie caught sight of Britain for the first time in thirteen years when he saw the Isle of Wight on 1 July, and three days later, after spying the glorious sight of St Paul's Cathedral and the spires of other churches in London, they were disembarking at Deptford on the Thames.

MACQUARIE WITHDREW £50 from Messrs Coutts & Company's Banking House and arranged lodgings for the family in Fludyer Street, Westminster.[14] He had been back in London for just a day when he called on Bathurst, who gave him a measly half-hour to discuss twelve years of work for the Crown on the other side of the world. However, Macquarie was pleased enough that the minister 'received me immediately on my name being announced to him, and gave a very kind and gracious reception'.[15]

Three weeks later, Macquarie submitted his formal report of the work he had done on behalf of His Majesty, and how the colony was now 'reaping incalculable advantages from my extensive and important discoveries in all directions, including the supposed insurmountable barrier called the Blue Mountains, to the westward of which are situated the fertile plains of Bathurst, and, in all respects, enjoying a state of private comfort and public prosperity, which I trust will at least equal the expectation of His Majesty's Government'.[16]

He had saved the population from famine after great floods by importing grain from Bengal; he had ordered the planting of great fields of wheat and maize on high ground; flocks and herds had multiplied many times over, and duties on trade had increased from £8000 to £30,000 per annum. There was now a Bank of New South Wales with its own currency.

He had numbered buildings, turned the Sydney roads from dirt to gravel and raised them in the centre to carry off water to the sewers. He had established the rule of keeping traffic to the left, according to the English custom. He had built additional schools, major roads, bridges, hospitals, churches, forts and a lighthouse. He had established Windsor, Richmond, Wilberforce, Pitt Town, Castlereagh, Penrith, Appin, Airds, Campbelltown, Liverpool, Rooty Hill, Bathurst, Blackheath and Springwood. He had remodelled Hobart. He listed sixty-seven buildings whose erection he had presided over.

He had tried to make peace with the Aboriginal people through the annual feast day, because of the pity he felt for them in being driven from the coast, then having their hunting grounds occupied by farmers in the interior. Macquarie felt that attempting to educate Aboriginal children in the ways of the white world was the right thing to do, because it proved that 'the children of the natives have as good and ready an aptitude for learning as those of Europeans'.[17]

He had promoted marriage over cohabitation and encouraged religious feeling among all classes. But he said his 'policy in endeavouring to restore emancipated and reformed convicts to a level with their fellow subjects' was the work he would always 'value as the most meritorious part of my administration'. He had done his best to eliminate free settlers' discrimination against former convicts, whether the government had wanted that or not.

He had made mistakes, he said, but his great legacy to Australia was humanity. The worst thing anyone could say about his administration was that he was too kind.[18]

In response, Bathurst passed on the king's praise and gave Macquarie credit for the great increase of population, and the advances New South Wales had made in 'agriculture, trade and wealth of every kind'. 'If, as a place of punishment, it has not answered all the purposes for which it was intended,' Bathurst wrote, 'this is certainly not owing to any deficiency of zeal or solicitude on your part.'[19]

Macquarie saw the colony, however, not as a place of punishment but a place of promise. That had always put him at odds with those of a different view – from Bigge and Marsden down. Macquarie was ahead of his time when it came to social justice, fathering an experiment in a new land to reform criminals and make a successful, productive society. He was an Indian army veteran, a pillar of the established Church and an orthodox Tory in politics, but he became the great evangelist, preaching a second chance for those with drive and ambition. His years of struggle had given him a clear vision for the potential in all humanity.

He would be penalised for this until the last. He sought the pension Castlereagh had promised him but was, instead, given £1000 passage money. Macquarie would have to keep fighting for a fair reward.

ON 5 AUGUST 1822, thirteen years after he had offered Macquarie the governor's job, Lord Castlereagh, now the Marquess of Londonderry, presented him at Carlton House, the London residence of the Prince Regent, who had finally become King George IV in January.

But it was not an altogether pleasant meeting.

Castlereagh was highly agitated. He had been complaining of overwork for a long time and had become increasingly paranoid, regularly succumbing to fits of rage.

Four days later, at another meeting with the king, Castlereagh kept looking over his shoulder and saying that he was being watched. He told the king he had been accused of being homosexual. Friends and family were alarmed and hid his razor, but on 12 August, as Macquarie was doing the rounds looking up old friends, such as Charles Forbes, James Drummond and Archibald Campbell, Castlereagh found a small penknife and cut his own throat.[20]

FINALLY, MACQUARIE took the family north to Scotland. He introduced Lachlan to his sister Betty at Oskamull, who, having suffered agonies as the mother of soldiers, had just lost her husband, Farquhar, whom Macquarie called 'as good and honest a man as ever spelt the name of Maclaine'.

But Macquarie's return home was not what he expected. His long-held dream of building a castle on Jarvisfield, or even a new cottage by the stream at Gruline would have to wait. There had been bad harvests and a collapsed local economy. His tenants could pay no rents and Jarvisfield was in ruins.

Macquarie asked his brother Charles just to glaze the windows of the existing house and ensure it was watertight, but not to paint it because 'poor Elizabeth cannot stand painted houses'. He wanted to make sure Fortune, 'our poor old useful cow' from Sydney, was being treated royally and kept under cover at night.

Elizabeth's health had been in decline since embarking on the great voyage home, and Macquarie's own health was as bad as ever. They decided warmer climes and a change of scenery was the remedy, especially given they had become accustomed to the Australian sun.

With the threat of a severe winter coming to Scotland and Macquarie's own strong desire to travel through Europe, the family, along with George Jarvis, Elizabeth's maid Fanny and Lachlan's new tutor, Robert Meiklejohn, began preparations to set off for the continent. George's wife Mary would stay in London with their six-month-old daughter.

Before they left, however, Macquarie caught up with George Jarvis Mark One, the brother of Macquarie's beloved first wife Jane. Now Colonel George R.P. Jarvis, he was settled at Dover as a partner in a bank. The pair had 'a most affectionate happy meeting after a separation of fifteen years'.[21]

IN BOISTEROUS WEATHER on 4 December 1822, Macquarie's party boarded the *Dasher* steamboat for a perilous ride from Dover to Calais.

Unable to remain in the cabin below because so many ladies around her were violently seasick, Mrs M felt compelled to remain on deck with Lachlan, exposed to heavy rain, which wet them to the skin.[22]

Feeling the solid ground of Calais was a relief, but then they had to walk through dark, dirty streets in heavy rain towards a warm fire and good fare at Hôtel Dessin in the Rue Royale.

Macquarie hired a carriage and horses for 300 francs to convey them and their baggage to Paris, 300 kilometres to the south. They took in the sights along the way for a week, before arriving at the Prince Regent Hotel in Rue Hyacinthe, where to Macquarie's Scottish sensibilities, the prices were 'high and even extravagant'.[23]

They admired the opulence of the Palace of Versailles, and at the Sèvres porcelain factory, Macquarie allowed Lachlan to buy an exquisite bust of the Duchess of Angoulême, the daughter of Marie Antoinette.

Macquarie hired a coach with three horses so they could take in the warmer weather in the south of France. The roads were rough and snow falls made them worse, but along the way, they received a warm welcome when they called in on the Drummonds at their château near Montereau.

They approached Lyon on New Year's Day to behold a view that was 'beautifully romantic and picturesque',[24] but the roads around Avignon and Vaucluse were almost impassable because of heavy rains. At Aix-en-Provence, they put up at the Hôtel du Prince, 'a very large fine inn – but a very dear one in their charges',[25] and at Marseilles, the Hôtel de Beauvau was 'most extravagant' with its bill.[26]

On 15 January 1823, they arrived at the small Mediterranean town of Hyères, near Toulon, and here, on the southernmost point of Provence, surrounded by vineyards, olive groves and orchards, they decided to spend the rest of the winter at the Hôtel des Ambassadeurs.

Macquarie thought 40 francs a day for board and lodging for his group, including two bottles of good wine, was a fair price, and he agreed to pay an additional 18 francs a day to keep the driver, carriage and horses that had brought them there. But sadly, he was laid low in bed again for two weeks with a severe cold and fever, and an ulcerated throat.[27]

In the middle of March, with the spring sunshine thawing out his illness and with Mrs M's health 'being considerably improved', they headed to Italy. At the border on the River Var, though, they were detained for nearly an hour as their passports were examined, their names and ages recorded, and a note made of the description, size and age of their horses.[28]

MEANWHILE THOMAS BRISBANE had begun putting his own stamp on Australia.

Macquarie had hardly left Sydney Heads when the amateur astronomer unveiled his Parramatta Observatory near Government House.[29]

Believing that Macquarie had been too lenient and too extravagant, he stopped the premature granting of tickets of leave, reduced the number of road gangs and, instead, made the convicts clear land for farmers, who paid a fee to the government for their services. He established a harsh prison at Moreton Bay and reopened the one on Norfolk Island. Acting on Bigge's recommendation, he cancelled all ornamental work on buildings in New South Wales.

The old republican John Dunmore Lang,[30] first Presbyterian minister in Sydney, noted that, while Macquarie had suffered from vanity, and took a 'singular delight in having his name affixed to everything that required a name in the colony', he was immensely popular. Emancipists lamenting the changing scene in their town began singing a tribute to their hero, 'The Old Viceroy', on Foundation Day, 26 January 1824:

Macquarie was the prince of men!
Australia's pride and joy!
We ne'er shall see his like again;
Here's to the old Viceroy![31]

THE MACQUARIES journeyed through Nice, which was then an Italian city, then Genoa, Spezia and Lucca, before celebrating Lachlan's ninth birthday in Leghorn (Livorno), where they were joined by Macquarie's old friend and distant relative Lieutenant-General Lachlan Maclean, who would become the Lieutenant-Governor of Quebec. It being young Lachlan's birthday, the 'dear boy' was 'allowed to order the dinner he liked best'.[32]

Pisa was fascinating, but not so the village of 'Lascalles', where they stayed a regrettable night at 'a very poor miserable dirty little inn'.[33] They strolled through Florence, captivated by the history and the art treasures, and by 12 April, were fighting all the other English tourists to get a room in Rome during the holiday season. Turned away from three establishments with no vacancies, they settled into the Hotel du Grand Vaisseau on the Via Condotti, where Macquarie read his latest correspondence, saddened by the news that his nephew Major Murdoch Maclaine, his sister Betty's son, and his friend General James Balfour had both recently died.

Macquarie hired two Neapolitan dragoons at Mola to protect his family from the threat of *banditti* on the way to Mount Vesuvius and the ruins of Pompeii. Back in Rome, after finding reasonably priced lodgings at 79 Via di Capo le Case, he and his family began sightseeing in earnest at the Forum, Colosseum, Capitol and Palatine Hill. Lachlan began studying Latin and they heard mass at St Peter's.[34] Accompanied by Meiklejohn and Lachlan, Macquarie descended into the subterranean part of the church to view the Shrine of St Peter, the numerous tombs of the popes and the burial places of the three last royal Stuarts.

By special appointment, on 8 May, the Macquaries and Meiklejohn were presented to Pope Pius the 7th at Quirinal Palace. They walked in the Pope's gardens and were present at the cardinals' celebration of high mass.

Their carriage carried them back through Florence, then to Bologna, Padua, Venice and Milan, and by 11 June, they were surrounded by immense snow-covered mountains, torrents, cataracts and waterfalls as they journeyed on Napoleon's road to cross the Simplon Pass into Switzerland. They toasted Elizabeth's forty-fifth birthday with champagne in Sion.

Back in the French town of Fontainebleau on 2 July, Macquarie settled his accounts with their coach driver, who had now been with them fifty days, pressing a handy tip into the man's hand 'for his good conduct and attention'.[35]

The Macquaries spent twelve days there, while Macquarie wrote his answer to what he called 'Bigge's false, vindictive, & malicious report on N. S. Wales',[36] which had just been tabled in parliament.

BIGGE HAD COMPILED 300 pages in three parts, together with twenty-eight big boxes of statements. Most of these had been taken from Macquarie's foes, who bore grudges, mainly over petty incidents. There were many errors in the report, including wrong names and wrong crimes.

William Charles Wentworth later wrote that every page dripped with 'private scandal and vituperation', that Bigge had made up his mind about Macquarie even before he left England and that his motives were purely political.[37]

Bigge reported that one of Macquarie's favourites, Simeon Lord, had been accused of trying to seduce female orphans, and that Dr Redfern was hot-tempered and forward. Appointing criminals such as these men to important positions, Bigge said, exposed the colony to contempt. He recommended a much tougher line on convicts, and the end of land grants to men or women who had been prisoners. The idea of having trial by jury in a land where so many inhabitants had been criminals was absurd. In Bigge's view, punishment was supposed to be harsh.

Some of Bigge's criticisms, however, displayed insights that Macquarie was in no position to grasp. Bigge could see how the mutual animosity between Macquarie and Marsden had clouded both their judgments. He could also see that Macquarie took criticism far too personally, making it difficult for him to accept advice that was in opposition to his own opinions.

Bigge revealed another side, however, in his orders to change Macquarie's courthouse at Hyde Park into St James' Church. On 2 October 1824, Thomas Hobbes Scott, the bankrupt wine merchant who was Bigge's relative by marriage, was appointed Archdeacon of St James' on £2000 a year, the same salary Macquarie had started on.

After his European vacation, Macquarie returned to London on 31 July, ready for a fight.

He protested to Bathurst about Bigge's report. He denounced Bigge's statement that his three principal advisers were ex-cons as a lie. He threatened to sue the *Edinburgh Review* newspaper for libel.

All to no avail. He could not make his protests heard, and the frustration ate away at him.

MACQUARIE NOW HAD a massive land holding on Mull, more than 8000 hectares, but it was producing little income. After blowing what cash he had on his family holiday, he was not only broke, but in fact owed £500 to Coutt's.

With heavy hearts and empty purses, he and Elizabeth returned to Mull with Lachlan, George and Mary Jarvis, and their daughter Elizabeth.

They couldn't even afford a carriage, so they went by sea to Leith.

The Scottish Highlands was a grim place for an ageing man in poor health, who felt that he had been used, abused and thrown away by a government that had never appreciated him and no longer needed him. The weather was so stormy that the ship bringing the Macquaries' belongings to Mull couldn't land for two months and they had to lodge with one of Elizabeth's relatives.

When they finally moved into the tumbledown home at Gruline, it was a 'truly uncomfortable house'.[38] The walls were constantly as damp as a wet sponge, and the wind continually howled through the doorways and extinguished the fires. Macquarie, with no privacy even to write a letter, had to spend most of the time in the dining room, where the drafts were not so bad.[39]

Elizabeth never heard him utter a complaint. Each day, just as he had done in Australia, he would ride around his land, planning where his mansion would sit and where his crops would be planted. Her own spirits were low, but Macquarie would try to cheer her up. He would ride three miles into Salen every day, regardless of the weather, to sit as one of the local justices, devoting himself to the community just as he had done on a much wider scale in Australia.

Even in a raging storm, he felt a duty to others. Though Elizabeth was too ill to accompany him, Macquarie went to visit her sister Jane, Murdoch Maclaine's widow, who was in as bad a state of health and as poor as the Macquaries. He spent four days in the saddle, soaked through with rain. Soon, he had developed a dreadful cold and was shaking with fever.

On 28 March 1824, Lachlan's tenth birthday, Macquarie ignored the fact that it was wet and stormy, and rowed his family out onto a nearby lake in a boat that he had given Lachlan.

He reached a distant part of the lake and, looking about at the land surrounding it, said: 'My reason for bringing you thus far is to show you the extent of your estate.' It surprised Elizabeth that he said '*your* estate' instead of '*our* estate'.[40]

Around that time he began receiving letters from friends in London, urging him to come down and deal with an application he was pursuing to open a new church at Salen,[41] as well as making another attempt to secure his pension from Bathurst.

He did not want to leave Elizabeth, but she had a bad cold, and Lachlan, still being tutored by Robert Meiklejohn, was busy with his studies. So Macquarie decided to go to London with only George as his companion.

He cleaned out his writing desk and, to Elizabeth, he seemed to be acting like a man who didn't plan to come home. Before leaving, he put into Elizabeth's hand a little box she had never seen before.

It contained trinkets, pocket books, and different little things of that sort, which. had belonged to Mrs Mc.Quarrie, his former wife. He always had this box in the trunk with his most particular and private papers. He said 'I give you this; there are things in it, wch. may be useful, to you, and Lachlan'. I was so astonished and alarmed, that I exclaimed 'My God! You terrify me out of my senses, by the way you are going on –'.[42]

Macquarie left home on 15 April 1824, promising Elizabeth he would only be away a short time. He burst into tears saying goodbye. Lachlan followed his father to the top of a hill, from which there was a view of Mull and Loch na Keal and, with tears in his eyes, the little boy watched his father ride away.

The days of the private cabin were over for Macquarie, and now, on the most violent ocean journey he had experienced, he travelled cattle class, sharing a four-man berth with at least one passenger who kept 'caskading' his dinner through violent sea sickness. The sixty-two year old Macquarie vowed never to get on a steamboat again as long as he lived.[43]

Finally, sick with fatigue, he checked into Hatchett's Hotel in Piccadilly on 24 April. Later, he found more permanent lodgings at 49 Duke Street, St James's, noting that it would cost 34 shillings per week, including a bedroom for George, with extra for meals.[44] He wrote to Elizabeth to say he hoped to conclude his business in three weeks, and to 'kiss our darling Lachlan for me, and accept the same yourself'.[45]

He spent his first day in Duke Street in bed, still sick from the voyage and, over the next few days, he visited old friends, some from decades before, as though wanting to say goodbye.

After dinner with his old boss, the Earl of Harrington, on 29 April, Macquarie came back to Duke Street to find a letter from Bathurst, confirming a pension of £1000 per annum for life. He would have jumped for joy if he wasn't feeling so low.

He wrote to Elizabeth to say that, while the news was gratifying, he did not have the means of publishing it widely, so that the only information circulating about him was in the 'vile insidious Bigge Report', which was 'everywhere in the hands of everyone and has gone all over the world'.

Still, at least his friends believed in him. He dined with General Dunlop, with whom he had served in the American War forty-five years before, then with Henry Oakes, his friend from Bombay. They drank a bumper to the storming of Seringapatam.

He had a late dinner with Charles Forbes, now a baronet, and met up with Miles Nightingall, Elizabeth's friend Miss Meredith and David Baird. He called in to give his condolences to Castlereagh's widow but, to his surprise, she did not seem to be suffering from his suicide but, instead, had 'grown amazingly fat and appears very gay'.[46]

He visited silversmiths in Ludgate Hill, and ordered plates for Mrs M and bought two second-hand silver dishes. He also bought a huge vase with £500 that the colonists of Sydney had donated to him by subscription as their thank you for his work in New South Wales. After having had to watch his pennies since returning from his European vacation, he was able to spend big again.

Macquarie hoped that the king might bestow a title on him as a rebuff to the Bigge report but, within a week of applying, Bathurst told him no.[47] The Bigge report was an albatross around his neck and Marsden had done much to sully Macquarie's reputation. Macquarie then had a long interview with the Home Secretary and future prime minister Robert Peel. They spoke about the new bill for the future transportation of convicts, and Macquarie's support for the emancipists of New South Wales.

'I took this opportunity of explaining to Mr Peel his error in supposing that I had been too lavish in granting pardons in N. S. Wales,' Macquarie wrote. 'He was very civil, and appeared to be satisfied with my explanations.'[48]

Meanwhile, the weather blossomed in Mull. The birch trees began to show their leaves, and the ground was enamelled with primroses. Elizabeth's health had improved and she started renovating the old house, having some new rooms built and adding new wallpaper for her husband's return. She was finally well enough to visit her sister Jane, now dying, on two separate occasions.

Jane was being comforted by her son, Hugh Maclaine, who had started his military career as an infant under Macquarie's bogus-commission rort. Hugh was now a lieutenant-colonel commanding the 77th, one of Macquarie's old regiments. But Elizabeth was so spooked by the premonitions she was having about Macquarie in London that she was not with Jane when she died, having instead rushed back to Jarvisfield in the vain hope that her husband might have returned.

He had written to say he was on his way.

On 1 June 1824, he said goodbye to Bathurst and the Duke of York, telling His Highness about Mull and his plans for the island. Eight days later, he was at Carlton House, where the king 'received me most graciously, and spoke to me in a very kind manner'.[49]

Then two days later, as he prepared to return to his family, he picked up his journal and in a shaky hand wrote: 'Between 2 and 3, OClock this morning I awoke very ill, with a severe headache, pains in my bowels, and a difficulty of making urine. I sent immediately for Dr Andrews.'[50]

He spent the day in bed but, thanks to some diuretics, he recovered enough to take a ride in a glass coach, even though Elizabeth might think he had 'become so extravagant'. He stayed in contact with Elizabeth constantly, telling her not to worry.

On 12 June, he sent her a long letter, the first two pages devoted to her sister, his Aunt Jane.

Finally, later in the letter, he admitted to her that the previous morning he had become violently ill, and George had summoned a doctor at 4 a.m.:

The surgeon instantly ordered hot water, and flannel, and the parts to be fomented to remove the pain, giving me some diuretic draughts, at the same time … It was really a very smart and painful attack, whilst it lasted. The doctor called it spasms in the bowels, with something bordering on a strangury … Poor George was greatly alarmed, but still remained cool and collected … His kindness assiduity and attention could not possibly be exceeded, except by yourself.

Indeed more than ever I prayed inwardly, that you had been by me, to soften those painful sensations.[51]

Two days later, Elizabeth received:

49 Duke St. St. James' London
14th. June 1824
I kept my bed all yesterday, and also all this day, having merely got up to write this hurried scrawl, to you, to keep my promise; I have the happiness of assuring you, however, that the two main points in this attack have been overcome, namely the attack on my bowels, and strangury ... I certainly suffered much pain, and now feel extremely weak in consequence, but you may assure yourself, I am not in the smallest danger. I shall write to you again, tomorrow ... With my love to yourself, and Lachlan, and kind regards to Mr Meiklejohn, I remain my dear Love, your affectionate husband. L.M.[52]

Elizabeth could wait no more. She grabbed Lachlan and Meiklejohn and, money or no money, they raced to London as quickly as they could, arriving on 25 June.

They found Macquarie thin and pale, and not happy with them for having gone to so much trouble on his behalf. His doctor said it would be a month before he would be well enough to go home. The next morning, he rose early to write letters of introduction for a young man going to India, and he was quickly fatigued and shivering.

Lachlan was staying with Charles Forbes, and on the morning of 1 July, Elizabeth sent word for them to rush to Duke Street. Lachlan came first, roaring through the streets in a hired coach and crying all the way into the lodging house.

Elizabeth whispered to her husband, 'my love here is Lachlan come to see you', and father and son kissed each other. Charles Forbes arrived soon afterwards. Macquarie fixed his eyes upon his old friend with what Elizabeth called: 'an expression as extremely tender, benevolent, and kind, that I never saw anything so benign and beautiful in my life; but once, and that was, when our little darling daughter, regarded me with intelligence – her eyes were exactly like him.'

When Charles Forbes left the room, Elizabeth 'saw my husband, looking for him. I called him back. The same extraordinary expression was renewed, and I observed him, to say, "fine fellow, fine fellow"'.[53]

Elizabeth knelt beside Macquarie's bed and placed her hand upon his shoulder:

At that moment his eyes, were turned up to heaven. He continued to breathe gently, for some time, and at length, it ceased, without a groan, or struggle of any kind … The moment of his departure was to me the most sublime of my life. I felt as though my soul was ascending with his to heaven. His countenance remained the same as usual, but strongly expressive of exhaustion, and resignation.[54]

THE SURGEONS wanted to open up Macquarie's body to study the cause of his death, but Elizabeth said no. She believed that had Wentworth and Redfern been treating him, he might have survived.[55] Charles Forbes had a plaster death mask made, and though she was reluctant to take it at first, it later became her most treasured possession.

Ten days after Macquarie died, Elizabeth and Lachlan followed the hearse to the Hermitage Wharf. Bathurst and the Duke of Wellington provided empty carriages as a mark of respect but did not come, though there was a good crowd of friends, many from his days in India.

Charles Macquarie, George Jarvis and Robert Meiklejohn accompanied the coffin home through wild seas. Elizabeth then took Lachlan by coach. At Perth, she had the coffin containing their daughter Jane exhumed so that she could be reburied with her father.

Macquarie was laid out at Gruline in one of the new rooms Elizabeth was preparing for him, with the coffin of the infant Jane on his breast. The great vase bought with the subscriptions from Australia was placed at his head. His tenants on Mull and a few family and friends followed him and baby Jane to their shared grave on the Jarvisfield estate.

When the news reached the colony that the Old Viceroy was gone, the *Sydney Gazette* said Australia would forever hold the name of Governor Macquarie sacred, and appreciate his value; it would always proclaim 'the excellencies of an eminently good man'.[56] It reported that on Sunday, 14 November, the streets of Sydney were lined with thousands of grateful people watching a procession from Castlereagh Street that paid its respects to the memory of their dear departed governor.

The Reverend Cowper, who had welcomed Macquarie with a sermon fourteen years earlier that declared 'Arise, anoint him; for this is he' now used one of the Proverbs as his text at Macquarie's memorial service: 'Seest thou a man diligent in his business? he shall stand before kings; he shall not stand before mean men.'[57]

Cowper led the procession, with Macquarie's old staff, Antill, John Thomas Campbell and William Redfern, as the chief mourners. Governor Macquarie, Cowper observed, 'was subject to the fallibilities of man; but his principles and character demanded our esteem, and called upon us to revere his memory'.[58]

In the mail that brought the news of Macquarie's death came a private letter for William Wentworth, marked with the Macquarie signature of three exclamation marks. He had been writing letters in his final days, even though it had greatly fatigued him.

I have had two interviews with Mr Peel. I found him most polite and a man of business. He has acceded to all my wishes; and the [Transportation Continuance] Act, in which there is a clause restoring the emancipists to all substantial rights and privileges, not only in New South Wales, but in all His Majesty's dominions, has passed both houses of parliament and will receive the Royal Assent this week!!![59]

THE WINDS continued to howl on Mull. Elizabeth remained devoted to her husband even after he was gone, and fought Bathurst over publishing Macquarie's reply to the Bigge Report.

Most of Jarvisfield was held in trust for ten-year-old Lachlan junior, and his godfather James Drummond, now Viscount Strathallan, was appointed his guardian and the principal executor of the estate. Macquarie's will provided an annuity of £300 per annum for Elizabeth for life, along with £700 bequeathed to her by her father, the dilapidated home at Gruline and 40 hectares around it. But Elizabeth and Drummond soon clashed over the management of the estate and Lachlan junior's education.

Macquarie had died before he could draw any of his £1000 pension, and Charles Forbes began a campaign to secure Elizabeth her own money from the government. When Bathurst offered her £400 a year from September 1825, she proudly said that 'no necessity whatever exists on my part' for financial help. Forbes hastily explained to Bathurst's office that her response was due merely to 'the independence of the Highland character', but Elizabeth refused to accept any money until Macquarie's response to Bigge's attacks was published.

Elizabeth sold Macquarie's military commission to a son of the Duke of Sussex for £4500, and from 1825, she lived in modest circumstances at Barnes in London, while Lachlan junior attended school at Woodford, 16½ miles away. Each summer, she would bring this Australian-born son back to Scotland to stay at Jarvisfield.

Finally on 25 June 1828, the Colonial Office agreed to have Macquarie's reply to Bigge printed as a parliamentary paper, and the former first lady of Australia accepted a £400-a-year pension.

Her financial situation improved dramatically.

Her best friend, Henrietta Meredith, had died in 1825 and left her £2000, as well as a small house at 58 Upper Charlotte Street in London. Elizabeth lived there throughout 1828 and 1829, while Lachlan junior attended school in Finchley, to the north of the city.

Elizabeth gave Richard Fitzgerald, the former convict who had built the Macquarie Arms at Windsor, power of attorney over the

Macquaries' shares in the Bank of New South Wales and livestock they had left on Henry Antill's property at Picton. She had £500 in the bank and 950 head of cattle, and between 1829 and 1835 Fitzgerald sent her a total of £869, as interest on her account and profits from the livestock.

Elizabeth also wanted to do something for George Jarvis, who had been Macquarie's constant companion from the time he had been sold as a small child at a slave market in Cochin. George had been with Macquarie through heartbreaks and triumphs, through two marriages, and on all his journeys from the Garden of Eden to Government House, from Baghdad to Bathurst. He had summoned the doctor on Macquarie's last day, had been with him when he died and was beside his coffin on his journey home.

In his will, Macquarie left George a £25 annuity 'during his natural life', and declared that should he 'prefer living on my estate in Mull after my decease … he may be allowed to do so on my farm of Gruline and that he shall be comfortably fed, clothed and lodged there at the expence of my heirs and successors during his natural life independent of the annuity herein already allowed him'.

Elizabeth set up a trust fund for George and his descendants, but sadly Macquarie's faithful servant died in 1825 only a few months after his mentor, aged in his early-thirties, and was buried near Macquarie at Jarvisfield.[60] In 1830, Elizabeth moved north to Aberdeen, where she rented a house for six months at Sunny Bank at 7 guineas a month.

The following year, Lachlan junior, now sixteen, insisted on joining the army like his father, and Elizabeth purchased an ensigncy for him in the 42nd Regiment of Foot. He joined his regiment at Birmingham and Elizabeth returned to live at Jarvisfield. She commissioned a granite headstone to sit over Macquarie's lonely grave.

Life for her there was grim. Although she had the use of the house at Gruline for life, she clashed with James Drummond, who insisted that, if she wanted to buy cattle, she had to purchase them from the Macquarie estate, which he oversaw.

Her health declined in the cold and damp. Her dear brother John Campbell died on 7 November 1834, and she herself died peacefully at Gruline House at 2 p.m. on 11 March 1835, aged fifty-six, with George's widow Mary Jarvis and the family solicitor Donald McLean beside her.[61]

She was fortunately spared the worst excesses of Lachlan junior, who would prove a grave disappointment to his father's memory. Elizabeth and Macquarie had had high hopes for their 'dear boy', but before long, Lachlan was 'addicted to drink, and had many eccentricities' with 'an insane propensity to indulge in intoxicating liquors'.[62] He married Isabella Campbell, a distant relative of his mother's in 1836, and she stayed with him even though her brother Archibald suggested Lachlan should be certified and that she should run away.

His drinking commenced after breakfast, when he sculled wine and ale from a tumbler. His bizarre behaviour included ordering everyone at Jarvisfield to grow moustaches or be sacked, and herding his wife's ducks together and decapitating as many as he could with his sword.[63]

On 7 May 1845, thirty-one years after he was born overlooking Sydney harbour,[64] and most likely rolling drunk, Lachlan fell down stairs at Craignish Castle, the home of his wife's family, and died childless. The Macquarie lineage thus ended in a crumpled heap.

Lachlan's cousins from the Macquarie side were startled to find that, in order to cover his gambling debts to James Drummond's son William, Lachlan had bequeathed him Jarvisfield. In 1851 a court ruled that, even though Lachlan had been 'morally insane', his will was valid.

On what was now their land, the Drummonds soon erected a handsome mausoleum over the Gruline burial plot, which now contained Macquarie, Elizabeth, Lachlan junior and baby Jane.

Almost two centuries after his death, though, Macquarie's name lives on in the titles of towns, harbours, lakes and rivers throughout Australia – the island continent he loved that is now known by the name he promoted. 'Macquarie' is also perpetuated through the names of a major bank that uses the holey dollar as its symbol, a university, a dictionary, a vast radio network and countless other institutions.

In October 1948, the Macquarie mausoleum site was gifted by Lady Yarborough, the new owner of Jarvisfield, to the people of New South Wales, and it is now jointly administered by the national trusts of Scotland and Australia.

One side of the mausoleum bears the headstone that Elizabeth Macquarie commissioned in 1832, when she finally had the money to erect a memorial to her husband.

It described the man she loved as a 'most beloved husband, father and master, and a most endearing friend'.

But to Elizabeth, the final words summed up the life's work of Lachlan Macquarie.

'THE FATHER OF AUSTRALIA.'

Author's Note

More than two centuries after he arrived as ruler over the land he would call 'Australia', Lachlan Macquarie's influence remains huge.

Macquarie lived an enormous life and, in a biography of this size and scope, many people contributed invaluable assistance.

Thank you firstly to Macquarie University and its Lachlan & Elizabeth Macquarie Archive (LEMA) Project which provides such a wealth of material about Macquarie's life, loves and times.

Thank you also to the staff at the State Library of New South Wales and the National Library of Australia where so much of Macquarie's correspondence is stored.

I am indebted to previous Macquarie biographers Malcolm Ellis and John Ritchie for shining a light for my path, to the writings of Robin Walsh and Grace Karskens, and to those wonderful historians Fred Watson and Frank Bladen for their historical records of Australia and New South Wales.

Thanks to my friend and editor Kevin McDonald for his patience.

I will always be grateful to the team at HarperCollins/ABC Books who made this biography come to life – Brigitta Doyle, Jude McGee and Matt Howard – and to Emma Dowden and Lachlan McLaine who did so much to shape my words.

Bibliography

Roy Adkins, *Trafalgar: The Biography of a Battle*, Hachette UK, 2011.

Anna Agnarsdóttir (ed.), *Joseph Banks, Iceland and the North Atlantic 1772–1820: Journals, Letters and Documents*, Taylor & Francis, 2017.

Henry Colden Antill, *Early History of New South Wales*, W.A. Gullick, Government Printer, 1914.

Val Attenbrow, *Sydney's Aboriginal Past: Investigating the Archaeological and Historical Records*, University of New South Wales Press, 2010.

Alexander Beatson, *A View of the Origin and Conduct of the War with Tippoo Sultaun*, G. & W. Nichol, 1800.

Henry Grey Bennet, *A Letter to Earl Bathurst, Secretary of State for the Colonial Department*, J Ridgway, 1820.

George Birkbeck and Norman Hill (eds), *Boswell's Life of Johnson, Volume 3: The Life, 1776-1780*, Pembroke College, Oxford, 1887.

Gregory Blaxland, *A Journal of a Tour of Discovery Across the Blue Mountains, New South Wales, in the Year 1813*, B.J. Holdsworth, 1823.

James Boswell, *The Journal of a Tour to the Hebrides: With Samuel Johnson, Ll.D.*, Henry Baldwin, 1785.

Lewin B. Bowring, *Haider Ali and Tipu Sultan*, Clarendon Press, 1893.

J. Brook and J.L. Kohen, *The Parramatta Native Institution and the Black Town: A History*, University of New South Wales Press, 1991.

Richard Broome, *Aboriginal Australians: A history since 1788*, Allen & Unwin, 2010.

Nancy Gardner Cassels, *Social Legislation of the East India Company*, SAGE Publications India, 2010.

Ernest Clarke, *Siege of Fort Cumberland, 1776: An Episode in the American Revolution*, McGill–Queen's Press, 1995.

John William Cole, *Memoirs of British Generals Distinguished During the Peninsular War*, R. Bentley, 1856.

David Collins, *An Account of the English Colony in New South Wales from Its First Settlement, in January 1788, to August 1801*, T. Cadell jun. and W Davies, 1802.

John Connor, *The Australian Frontier Wars, 1788–1838*, UNSW Press, 2002.

Calvin Lee Craig, *The Young Emigrants and the Craigs of Magaguadavic*, C.L. Craig, 2005.

T. Crofton Croker, *Memoirs of Joseph Holt: General of the Irish rebels, in 1798*, Vol. 2, Henry Coulburn, 1838.

Jo Currie, *Mull: The Island and Its People,* John Donald, 2010.

Robert J.L. Darby, *A Surgical Temptation: The Demonization of the Foreskin and the Rise of Circumcision in Britain*, University of Chicago Press, 2005.

Aditi De, *Multiple City: Writings on Bangalore,* Penguin, 2008.

Joshua Dickson (ed.), *The Highland Bagpipe: Music, History, Tradition*, Ashgate Publishing, 2013.

James Douglas, *Bombay and Western India*, Sampson Low, Marston & Co, 1893.

Tom Dunne, *Rebellions: Memoir, Memory and 1798*, Lilliput Press, 2004.

Stephen Meredyth Edwardes, *The Rise of Bombay: A Retrospect*, Cambridge University Press, 2011.

Thibault Ehrengardt, *The History of Jamaica from 1494 to 1838*, Lulu, 2015.

M.H. Ellis, *Lachlan Macquarie; his life, adventures, and times*, Angus & Robertson, 1952.

Herbert Vere Evatt, *Rum Rebellion: A Study of the Overthrow of Governor Bligh by John Macarthur and the New South Wales Corps*, Angus & Robertson, 1965.

Elizabeth L. Ewan, Sue Innes, Sian Reynolds and Rose Pipes (eds), 'Janet Horne', *The Biographical Dictionary of Scottish Women*, Edinburgh University Press, 2006.

Edna Fernandes, *The Last Jews Of Kerala*, Granta Books, 2011.

Harald Fischer-Tiné and Michael Mann, *Colonialism as Civilizing Mission: Cultural Ideology in British India*, Anthem Press, 2004.

Phineas Fletcher, *The Purple Island, Or, The Isle of Man: An Allegorical Poem*, Frys & Couchman, 1783.

Antonia Fraser, *Mary, Queen of Scots*, Weidenfeld & Nicolson, 1969.

Sylvia R. Frey, *The British Soldier in America: A Social History of Military Life in the Revolutionary Period*, University of Texas Press, 2012.

James L. Garlow and David Barton, *This Precarious Moment,* Simon & Schuster, 2018.

Thomas Garnett, *Observations on a Tour Through the Highlands and Part of the Western Isles*, J. Stockdale, 1811.

Walter Gilbey, *Horses Past and Present*, Library of Alexandria, 1910

Henry Grey Graham, *The Social Life of Scotland in the Eighteenth Century*, A & C Black, 1899.

David Horspool, *The English Rebel*, Penguin, 2009.

Richard Hough, *Captain Bligh and Mr Christian: The Men and the Mutiny*, Hutchinson, 1972.

William James, *The Naval History of Great Britain, Volume 1, 1793–1796* (originally published 1827), Conway Maritime Press, 2002.

James M. Johnson, Christopher Pryslopski and Andrew Villani (eds), *Key to the Northern Country: The Hudson River Valley in the American Revolution*, SUNY Press, 2013.

Samuel Johnson, *A Journey to the Western Islands of Scotland: A New Edition*, A Strahan & T Cadell, 1791.

Thomas Brumby Johnston, James Alexander Robertson and William Kirk Dickson, *Historical Geography of the Clans of Scotland,* W. & A.K. Johnston, 1899.

David J. Cathcart King, *Catellarium Anglicanum: An Index and Bibliography of the Castles in England, Wales and the Islands, Volume I: Anglesey–Montgomery,* Kraus International Publications, 1983.

Hubert H. Lamb, *Climate, History and the Modern World,* Routledge, 2002.

Carol Liston, *Campbelltown: The Bicentennial History,* Allen & Unwin, 1988.

Michael O. Logusz, *With Musket and Tomahawk: The Saratoga Campaign and the Wilderness War of 1777,* Casemate, 2010.

Edward Long, *The History of Jamaica, Volume 2,* T. Lowndes, 1774.

Sibella Macarthur Onslow (ed.), *Some Early Records of the Macarthurs of Camden,* Angus & Robertson, 1914.

R.C. MacDonald, *Sketches of Highlanders,* Nenry Chubb & Co., 1843.

Anne MacKenzie (ed.), *Island Voices: Traditions of North Mull,* Birlinn, 2017.

Donald MacKenzie, *As It Was: Sin Mar a Bha – An Ulva Boyhood,* Birlinn, 2000.

Thomas Maclauchlan and Sir John Scott Keltie, *A History of the Scottish Highlands, Highland Clans and Highland Regiments, Volume 2,* A. Fullarton & Co., 1875.

David McCullough, *John Adams,* Simon & Schuster, 2008.

James McGrigor, *Medical Sketches of the Expedition to Egypt from India,* J. Murray, 1804.

J. P. MacLean, *A History of the Clan MacLean,* Heritage Books, 2009.

Rob Mundle, *Bligh: Master Mariner,* Hachette Australia, 2010.

M.S. Naravane, *Battles of the Honourable East India Company: Making of the Raj,* A.P.H. Publishing Corporation, 2006.

Stephen Neill, *A History of Christianity in India: 1707–1858,* Cambridge University Press, 2002.

Charles Boswell Norman, *Battle Honours of the British Army,* John Murray, 1971.

Herbert James Paton, *The Claim of Scotland,* Allen & Unwin, 1968.

Orlando Patterson, *The Sociology of Slavery,* MacGibbon & Kee, 1967.

Clive Ponting, *World History: A New Perspective,* Chatto & Windus, 2000.

Bruce Redford (ed.), Samuel Johnson, *The Letters of Samuel Johnson, Volume II: 1773–1776,* Princeton University Press, 2014.

John Ritchie, *Lachlan Macquarie,* Melbourne University Press, 1986.

John Ritchie, *The Evidence to the Bigge Reports, Volume 1, The Oral Evidence,* Heinemann, 1971

A. Maclean Sinclair, *The Clan Gillean,* Haszard & Moore, 1899.

William Forbes Skene, *The Highlanders of Scotland, Their Origin, History, and Antiquities: Volume 2,* Murray, 1837.

Thomas Smibert, *The Clans of the Highlands of Scotland,* James Hogg, 1850.

John Sugden, *Nelson: A Dream of Glory,* Jonathan Cape, 2004.

Tom Taylor, *Leicester Square: Its Associations and Its Worthies,* Bickers and Son, 1874.

Watkin Tench, *A Complete Account of the Settlement at Port Jackson: In New South Wales,* G Nicol & J. Sewel, 1793

Watkin Tench, *A Narrative of the Expedition to Botany Bay*, published as *Sydney's First Four Years*, edited by L. F. Fitzhardinge, Library of Australian History, 1979 (f.p. 1789).

Horace Kent Tenney, 'The Trial Of Mary Queen Of Scots', *American Bar Association Journal*, Vol. 17, No. 5 (May 1931).

Evan Thomas, *John Paul Jones: Sailor, Hero, Father of the American Navy*, Simon & Schuster, 2010.

Uno von Troil, *Letters on Iceland, Containing Observations Made in 1772 by Joseph Banks, Assisted by Dr Solander,* W. Richardson, 1780.

Peter Turbet, *The First Frontier*, Rosenberg Publishing, 2011.

Tim Voelcker, *Admiral Saumarez Versus Napoleon: The Baltic, 1807–12*, Boydell & Brewer, 2008.

Robin Walsh, *In Her Own Words: The Writings of Elizabeth Macquarie*, Exisle, 2011.

Thomas E. Wells, *Michael Howe, The Last and Worst of the Bush-Rangers of Van Diemen's Land*, Andrew Bent, 1818.

Estefania Wenger, *Tipu Sultan: A Biography,* Vij Publishing, 2017.

John White, *Journal of a Voyage to New South Wales,* J. Debrett, 1790.

Franklin B. Wickwire and Mary B. Wickwire, *Cornwallis: The Imperial Years*, University of North Carolina Press, 2017

Arthur Wilberforce Jose, Herbert James Carter, *Australian Encyclopedia*, Angus & Robertson, 1926.

INTERNET RESOURCES

AmericanRevolution.org

api.parliament.uk

arc.parracity.nsw.gov.au, (City of Parramatta Council Research & Collection Services)

arrow.latrobe.edu.au, (La Trobe University Research Online)

atlasobscura.com, 'Fingal's Cave'

australianmerino.net.au

boundforsouthaustralia.com.au

britainforaussies.weebly.com, 'Where was he born?'

cambridge.org

cityartsydney.com.au

cityofsydney.nsw.gov.au

clanmacfarlanegenealogy.info

collection.maas.museum, (Museum of Applied Arts & Science. Sydney)

dictionaryofsydney.org

digital.nls.uk/histories-of-scottish-families

domain.com.au, Sue Williams, 'Scottish island where Lachlan Macquarie was born may be bought by locals for $8m'

environment.gov.au/heritage/places/national/first-government-house eyewitnesstohistory.com, 'The Execution of Mary, Queen of Scots, 1587'

experiencesydneyaustralia.com

gutenberg.org

historyofparliamentonline.org

jamaicans.com.

jstor.org

lmacivilwar.weebly.com/typhoid-fever.html, 'Going to War: Louisa May Alcott's Experience as a Civil War Nurse'

merriam-webster.com.

michellescotttucker.com/2016/08/20/mrs-macquarie-and-the-tragic-accident

mq.edu.au

mull-historical-society.co.uk. 'Dr Samuel Johnson and Mr Boswell'

mullgenealogy.co.uk

newspapers.com

ngv.vic.gov.au, Elizabeth Cross, 'Early French explorers and Australia'

nla.gov.au, (Natuional Library of Australia)

outlookindia.com

paulineconolly.com/2015/bitter-legacy-the-dispute-over-the-macquarie-estate

rajbhavan-maharashtra.gov.in/rajbhavan.

records.nsw.gov.au

researchlibrary.agric.wa.gov.au

robertjacobgordon.nl

sath.org.uk, (Scottish Association of the Teachers of History), 'Execution at Fotheringay'

scholar.library.miami.edu

scotsman.com, 29 October 2015, Alison Campsie, 'How Aberdeen children were sold into slavery'

smithsonian.com, 8 March 2017, Erick Trickey, 'The Polish Patriot Who Helped Americans Beat the British'

stirlingcentrescottishstudies.wordpress.com, Nicola Martin, 'After Culloden'

sydneylivingmuseums.com.au

telegraph.co.uk

trove.nla.gov.au

umac.icom.museum, (International Committee for University Museums and Collections)

www.uelac.org, (United Empire Loyalists Association of Canada)

library.ydney.edu.au, (University of Sydney Library)

visitsydneyaustralia.com.au

warfarehistorynetwork.com

westernsydney.edu.au/femaleorphanschool

Endnotes

Prologue

1 'His Excellency's Address', *Sydney Gazette and New South Wales Advertiser*, 1 December 1821, p. 2.

2 'Sales by Auction', *Sydney Gazette and New South Wales Advertiser*, 1 December 1821, p. 3.

3 Lachlan Macquarie, born 31 January 1761, Ulva, Scotland; died 1 July 1824, St James's, London, England.

4 'Sydney History Overview', experiencesydneyaustralia.com.

5 Elizabeth Macquarie, born Elizabeth Henrietta Campbell, 13 June 1778, Kilcalmonell, Scotland; died 1 March 1835, Mull, Scotland.

6 Lachlan Macquarie to Dorothea Morley, 'Letterbook 22 November 1802 to 14 February 1804', 5 May 1803, Vol. Z A792, Lachlan Macquarie and Macquarie Family Papers, State Library of New South Wales, pp. 31–33.

7 'The Good Old Days: Recollections of Macquarie', *Windsor Richmond Gazette*, 29 July 1893, p. 6, quoting Dougall McKellar (1812–1901), whose father served with Macquarie in India and Australia, and whose mother was a servant to Elizabeth Macquarie at Government House.

8 *Ibid.*

9 William Temple (1779–1839) and John Webster (1798–1842). From 'Armchair owned by Governor Lachlan Macquarie', Museum of Applied Arts & Sciences, Sydney, collection. maas.museum.

10 Lachlan Macquarie, 'The Governor's Diary & Memorandum Book Commencing on and from Wednesday the 10th. Day of April 1816. — At Sydney, in N. S. Wales', 10 April 1816, Vol. Z A773, Lachlan Macquarie and Macquarie Family Papers, State Library of New South Wales, pp. 1–8.

11 Major-General Sir Thomas Makdougall Brisbane, born 23 July 1773, Largs, Ayrshire, Scotland; died 27 January 1860, Largs.

12 Lachlan Macquarie junior, born 28 March 1814, Sydney; died May 1845, Craignish Castle, Argyll, Scotland.

13 'His Excellency's Address', *Sydney Gazette and New South Wales Advertiser*.

14 Lachlan Macquarie to Mr Hobby, boot and shoemaker, St James's Street, London, 'Colonial Secretary: Main Series of Letters Received, 1788–1826', NRS 897, 4/1742, New South Wales State Archives, p. 359.

15 'His Excellency's Address', *Sydney Gazette and New South Wales Advertiser*.

16 *Ibid.*

17 Francis Greenway, born 20 November 1777, Mangotsfield, near Bristol, England; died September 1837 near Newcastle, New South Wales.

18   Simeon Lord, born about 29 January 1771, Dobroyd, Yorkshire, England; died 29 January 1840, Banks House, Botany, Sydney.
19   Mary Reibey, born 12 May 1777, Bury, Lancashire; died 30 May 1855, Newtown, Sydney.
20   D'Arcy Wentworth, born 1762, Portadown, Armagh, Ireland; died 7 July 1827, Homebush, Sydney.
21   Report by hospital assistant Henry Cowper, in John Ritchie, *The Evidence to the Bigge Reports, Volume 1: The Oral Evidence,* Heinemann, 1971, p. 142.
22   Henry Kitchen to John Thomas Bigge, 29 January 1821, BT, Box 26, Bonwick Transcripts 1641–1892, State Library of New South Wales, pp. 5947–5960.
23   'His Excellency's Address', *Sydney Gazette and New South Wales Advertiser.*

Chapter 1
1   Lachlan Macquarie to Murdoch Maclaine, 4 April 1788, MS 772, Item 4, National Library of Australia.
2   *Beinn Mhòr* in Scottish Gaelic, meaning 'Great Mountain'.
3   *Ullfur* in Norse.
4   William Shakespeare, *Macbeth,* Act IV, Scene 1, from Howard Staunton (ed.), *The Globe Illustrated Shakespeare: The Complete Works Annotated*, Gramercy Books, 1993.
5   'Ulva', undiscoveredscotland.co.uk.
6   Isabelle Fraser, 'Get Away from It All: The Scottish Island Up for Sale for £4.25m', telegraph.co.uk, 14 July 2017.
7   Some historians claim Macquarie was born in 1762, but his diary entry for 31 January 1794 marks this date as his thirty-third birthday.
8   Margaret Macquarie (1728–1810), the daughter of Lachlan Maclaine and Flora MacQuarrie.
9   J.C. Bonsall, 'Pleistocene Funeral Remains and Possible Food Processing Area', Canmore National Record of the Historic Environment, canmore.org.uk.
10   'Ulva', undiscoveredscotland.co.uk.
11   'Vikings were Warned to Avoid Scotland', telegraph.co.uk, 20 September 2009.
12   *Ibid.*
13   Ketill Björnsson, nicknamed Flatnose, Norse King of the Isles in the ninth century.
14   Magnus Olafsson, born 1073; died 24 August 1103. Better known as Magnus Barefoot or Magnus Barelegs, King of Norway (as Magnus III) from 1093 until his death in 1103.
15   'MacQuarrie' means 'Son of Guaire', while 'Macquarie' means 'Descendant'.
16   William Forbes Skene, *The Highlanders of Scotland, Their Origin, History, and Antiquities: Volume 2,* Murray, 1837, pp. 263–264.
17   Thomas Smibert, *The Clans of the Highlands of Scotland,* James Hogg, 1850, pp 113–117.
18   Thomas Brumby Johnston, James Alexander Robertson and William Kirk Dickson, *Historical Geography of the Clans of Scotland,* W. & A.K. Johnston, 1899, p. 14.
19   Antonia Fraser, *Mary, Queen of Scots,* Weidenfeld & Nicolson, 1969, p. 540, reproducing an account by Pierre de Bourdeille published in 1665.
20   'The Execution & Death of Mary, Queen of Scots, 1587', contemporary account by Robert Wynkfielde, englishhistory.net.
21   The nephew of William Cecil, Queen Elizabeth's principal advisor, from Antonia Fraser, *Mary Queen of Scots,* Weidenfeld and Nicolson, 1994, p. 540.
22   Phineas Fletcher, *The Purple Island, Or, The Isle of Man: An Allegorical Poem,* Frys & Couchman, 1783, p. 113.
23   Thomas Maclauchlan and Sir John Scott Keltie, *A History of the Scottish Highlands, Highland Clans and Highland Regiments, Volume 2,* A. Fullarton & Co., 1875, pp. 263–264.
24   Donald MacKenzie, *As It Was: Sin Mar a Bha – An Ulva Boyhood,* Birlinn, 2000.
25   Anne MacKenzie (ed.), *Island Voices: Traditions of North Mull,* Birlinn, 2017.

26 *Ibid.*

27 Alison Campsie, 'How Aberdeen Children Were Sold into Slavery', scotsman.com, 29 October 2015.

28 Henry Grey Graham, *The Social Life of Scotland in the Eighteenth Century*, A & C Black, 1899, p. 229.

29 Elizabeth L. Ewan, Sue Innes, Sian Reynolds and Rose Pipes (eds), 'Janet Horne', *The Biographical Dictionary of Scottish Women*, Edinburgh University Press, 2006, p. 170.

30 David Horspool, *The English Rebel*, Penguin, 2009.

31 Under the *Act of Proscription* 1746.

32 Herbert James Paton, *The Claim of Scotland*, Allen & Unwin, 1968, p. 161.

33 Thoracic aortic dissection.

34 On 11 August 1761.

35 On 30 October 1761.

36 'Where Was He Born?', britainforaussies.weebly.com.

37 Thomas Garnett, *Observations on a Tour Through the Highlands and Part of the Western Isles*, J. Stockdale, 1811, pp. 159–160.

38 *Ibid.*

39 Lauchlan Macquarrie (1715–1818), clanmacfarlanegenealogy.info.

40 Murdoch Maclaine (1730–1804).

41 Keith Sanger, 'One Piper or Two: Neil MacLean of the 84th Highlanders', Joshua Dickson (ed.), *The Highland Bagpipe: Music, History, Tradition*, Ashgate Publishing, 2013, p. 131.

42 MacLaine of Lochbuie Papers 1630–1904, GD 174/2405/2, National Records of Scotland.

43 Keith Sanger, 'One Piper or Two: Neil MacLean of the 84th Highlanders', p. 131.

44 John Ritchie, *Lachlan Macquarie*, Melbourne University Press, 1986, p. 16.

45 Lachlan Macquarie to Charles Macquarie, 'Letterbook 3 August 1797 to 22 November 1802', 24 August 1797, Vol. Z A790, Lachlan Macquarie and Macquarie Family Papers, State Library of New South Wales, p. 44.

46 Then called Drumnen House.

47 Uno von Troil, *Letters on Iceland, Containing Observations Made in 1772 by Joseph Banks, Assisted by Dr Solander*, W. Richardson, 1780, p. 288.

48 Anna Agnarsdóttir (ed.), *Joseph Banks, Iceland and the North Atlantic 1772–1820: Journals, Letters and Documents*, Taylor & Francis, 2017.

49 First published 1703.

50 'Dr Samuel Johnson and Mr Boswell', mull-historical-society.co.uk.

51 First published on 4 April 1755, Johnson's *A Dictionary of the English Language* was viewed as the leading dictionary of English until the completion of the *Oxford English Dictionary* in 1928.

52 Samuel Johnson, *A Journey to the Western Islands of Scotland: A New Edition*, A Strahan & T Cadell, 1791, p. 323.

53 James Boswell, *The Journal of a Tour to the Hebrides: With Samuel Johnson, Ll.D.*, Henry Baldwin, 1785, p. 400.

54 Bruce Redford (ed.), Samuel Johnson, *The Letters of Samuel Johnson, Volume II: 1773–1776*, Princeton University Press, 2014, p. 103.

55 Boswell, *The Journal of a Tour to the Hebrides*, p. 400.

56 Redford (ed.), *The Letters of Samuel Johnson, Volume II*, p. 104.

57 Johnson, *A Journey to the Western Islands of Scotland*, p. 232.

58 *Ibid*, p. 233.

59 Near the Ulva ferry crossing.

60 John Campbell, born June 1723; died 24 May 1806.

61 On 30 July 1796.

62 Hector Macquarie, died January 1778.

63   Donald Macquarie (1750–1801).

64   Charles Macquarie (1771–1835).

65   mullgenealogy.co.uk; Macquarie Memoranda A772, 29 September 1811.

66   N.D. McLachlan, 'Macquarie, Lachlan (1762–1824)', *Australian Dictionary of Biography*, National Centre of Biography, Australian National University, adb.anu.edu.au, published first in hard copy 1967.

67   Lachlan Macquarie to Murdoch Maclaine, 'Letter Book of Private and Familiar Correspondence Commencing at Bombay on the 31st Day of August 1793', 1 January 1794, Vol. Z A787, Lachlan Macquarie and Macquarie Family Papers, State Library of New South Wales, p. 47.

68   *Ibid.*

69   Lachlan Macquarie, 'Memoranda and Letters', 29 September 1811, Vol. Z A772, Lachlan Macquarie and Macquarie Family Papers, State Library of New South Wales.

70   Alexander Adam, born 24 June 1741; died 18 December 1809.

71   Ritchie, *Lachlan Macquarie*, p. 18.

72   Lachlan Macquarie, 'Journal – No. 1, Kept by L. Macquarie, Commencing 15th Decr. 1787', 24 August 1788, Vol. Z A768-2, Item 1, Lachlan Macquarie and Macquarie Family Papers, State Library of New South Wales.

73   Macquarie to Murdoch Maclaine, Letterbooks, 1 January 1794, Vol. Z A787, State Library of New South Wales, p. 33.

74   Macquarie to Murdoch Maclaine, Memoranda, 2 August 1783, Vol. Z A772, State Library of New South Wales.

75   Sanger, 'One Piper or Two: Neil MacLean of the 84th Highlanders', p. 131.

76   Later Major-General John Small, Lieutenant-Governor of Guernsey, born 13 March 1726, Strathardle, Athole, Scotland; died 17 March 1796, Saint Peter Port, Guernsey.

77   Later General Allan Maclean of Torloisk (1725–1798).

78   The Battle of Bunker Hill was fought on 17 June 1775 during the Siege of Boston, in the early stages of the American Revolutionary War.

79   John Trumbull (1756–1843), *The Death of General Warren at the Battle of Bunker's Hill, June 17, 1775*, Wadsworth Atheneum, Hartford, Connecticut, United States.

80   Muster Books and Pay Lists (WO 12/8741 & 8806): 84th (Royal Highland Emigrants) Regiment of Foot: 1778–1798, loyalist.lib.unb.ca.

81   Alexander McDonald to Colonel McLean, July 1776, 'Letter-book of Captain Alexander McDonald, of the Royal Highland Emigrants, 1775–1779', *Collections of the New York Historical Society for the Year 1882*, New York Historical Society, 1882.

82   Alexander McDonald to John Small, 9 January 1776, *ibid.*

Chapter 2

1   Macquarie to Charles Macquarie, Letterbooks, 26 January 1800, Vol. Z A787, State Library of New South Wales.

2   Evan Thomas, *John Paul Jones: Sailor, Hero, Father of the American Navy*, Simon & Schuster, 2010, p. 67.

3   Barry L. Hatt, 'A Look at Our Seafaring Past', new-brunswick.net/writer's%20corner.

4   John Paul Jones, born 6 July 1747, Arbigland, Scotland; died 18 July 1792, Paris, France.

5   R.C. MacDonald, "Sketches of Highlanders, Nenry Chubb & Co., 1843, pp. 44-45.

6   John MacDonald (1742-1810).

7   Brian McConnell, 'Captain John MacDonald of the Royal Highland Emigrants', Loyalist Trails, UELAC Newsletter, December 13, 2015, academia.edu.

8   Calvin Lee Craig, *The Young Emigrants and the Craigs of Magaguadavic*, C.L. Craig, 2005, p. 53.

9   Extract from letter from Captain Murdoch Maclaine to a gentleman in Edinburgh, 15 November 1776, reprinted in *Public Advertiser* (London), 8 January 1777, p. 2.

10 *Ibid.*

11 Kim R. Stacy, 'Royal Highland Emigrants', *Journal of the Society for Army Historical Research*, Vol. 77, No. 310 (Summer 1999), pp. 129–131.

12 Ernest Clarke, *Siege of Fort Cumberland, 1776: An Episode in the American Revolution*, McGill–Queen's Press, 1995, pp. 265–266.

13 Stacy, 'Royal Highland Emigrants', pp. 129–131.

14 Kim R. Stacy, 'Enlisted Uniforms of the 84th Regiment of Foot (Royal Highland Emigrants), 1775–1784', *Journal of the Society for Army Historical Research*, Vol. 73, No. 295 (Autumn 1995), pp. 181–183.

15 Hatt, 'A Look at Our Seafaring Past'.

16 Extract from letter from Captain Murdoch Maclaine to a gentleman in Edinburgh, 15 November 1776, reprinted in *Public Advertiser* (London), 8 January 1777, p. 2.

17 *Ibid.*

18 *Ibid.*

19 *Ibid.* Murdoch estimated it was about 40 leagues.

20 *Ibid.*

21 Hatt, 'A Look at Our Seafaring Past'.

22 Extract from letter from Captain Murdoch Maclaine to a gentleman in Edinburgh, 15 November 1776.

23 Extract from letter from Major-General Eyre Massey to Alderman Baker of Corke, published in *London Chronicle*, 14 to 16 January 1777, from Peter Force and Matthew St Clair Clarke, *American Archives: Consisting of a Collection of Authentick Records, State Papers, Debates, etc*, American Congress, 1843, p. 537.

24 Extract from letter from Captain Murdoch Maclaine to a gentleman in Edinburgh, 15 November 1776.

25 Hatt, 'A Look at Our Seafaring Past'.

26 Extract from letter from Major-General Eyre Massey to Alderman Baker of Corke, published in *London Chronicle*, 14 to 16 January 1777.

27 Ritchie, *Lachlan Macquarie*, p. 19.

28 Extract from letter from Captain Murdoch Maclaine to a gentleman in Edinburgh, 15 November 1776.

29 *Ibid.*

30 *Ibid.*

31 Jo Currie, *Mull: The Island and Its People,* John Donald, 2010.

32 Ritchie, *Lachlan Macquarie*, p. 19.

33 Eyre Massey, 1st Baron Clarina, born 24 May 1719; died 17 May 1804.

34 Extract from letter from Major-General Eyre Massey to Alderman Baker of Corke, published in *London Chronicle*, 14 to 16 January 1777.

35 Captain Alexander McDonald to Major Small, from Halifax, 6 January 1776, from *Letterbook of Captain Alexander McDonald of the Royal Highland Emigrants 1775–9,* from New York Historical Society. From americanrevolution.org.

36 Born in County Limerick, Ireland.

37 Captain Alexander McDonald to Major Small, from Halifax, 9 January 1776.

38 John Small to Murdoch Maclaine, 28 May 1789, MacLaine of Lochbuie Papers 1630–1904, GD174, National Records of Scotland.

39 Lachlan Macquarie to Cox, Mair & Cox, 12 March 1782, Australian Joint Copying Project miscellaneous series M460, National Library of Australia.

40 *Ibid.*

41 George Birkbeck and Norman Hill (eds), *Boswell's Life of Johnson, Volume 3: The Life, 1776–1780*, Pembroke College, Oxford, 1887, pp. 126–127.

42 He died on 14 January 1818.

43 Transcript of the Muster Roll of the 1st (or Major Commandant John Small's) Company of the Young Royal Highland Regiment of Foot: 21 January 1778 [Library and Archives Canada: Ward Chipman Fonds MG23-D1, Microfilm C9818, vol. 27, pages 312-313].

44 Hatt, 'A Look at Our Seafaring Past'.

45 Lachlan Macquarie to Murdoch Maclaine, 24 August 1783, MS 771, National Library of Australia.

46 Major Small later built a manor house in Nova Scotia called Selmah Hall, commemorated in the name of the local community of Selma.

47 Macquarie to Murdoch Maclaine, 24 August 1783, MS 771, National Library of Australia.

48 *Ibid.*

49 Kim R Stacy, 'Crime And Punishment in the 84th Regiment Of Foot, 1775-84', *Journal of the Society for Army Historical Research*, Vol. 79, No. 318 (Summer 2001), p. 116.

50 *Ibid.*

51 *Ibid.*

52 Also known as Samuel Graham.

53 Bible originally belonging to Hector Macquarie, B1685 vols 1–2, Macquarie Family Bibles 1762–1824, State Library of New South Wales.

54 McLachlan, 'Macquarie, Lachlan (1762–1824)'.

55 Walter Gilbey, *Horses Past and Present*, Library of Alexandria, 1910, p. 54.

56 Joseph Banks's evidence to the Bunbury Committee, 10 April 1779, *Journal of the House of Commons*, Vol. 37, p. 311.

57 *Ibid.*

58 *Ibid.*

59 *Ibid.*

60 Sylvia R. Frey, *The British Soldier in America: A Social History of Military Life in the Revolutionary Period*, University of Texas Press, 2012, p. 147.

61 Tadeusz Kościuszko, born 4 February 1746 in Mieračoŭščyna, Polish–Lithuanian Commonwealth (now in Belarus); died 15 October 1817 in Solothurn, Switzerland.

62 Charles Cornwallis, 1st Marquess Cornwallis, born 31 December 1738; died 5 October 1805.

63 David McCullough, *John Adams,* Simon & Schuster, 2008, p. 267.

64 Joseph W. Barnwell, 'The Evacuation of Charleston by the British in 1782', *South Carolina Historical and Genealogical Magazine*, Vol. 11, No. 1 (January 1910), p. 4.

65 List of Transports for the Evacuation of Charleston, 19 November 1782, Colonial Office, CO 5/108, National Archives, United Kingdom, folios 37–42.

66 Barnwell, 'The Evacuation of Charleston by the British in 1782', p. 4.

Chapter 3

1 Macquarie to Murdoch Maclaine, 24 August 1783, MS 771, National Library of Australia.

2 Clive Ponting, *World History: A New Perspective*, Chatto & Windus, 2000, p. 510.

3 Spelled Takyi in his native language, Akan.

4 Bill Evans, 'Tacky's Rebellion', jamaicans.com.

5 Richard B. Sheridan, 'The Jamaican Slave Insurrection Scare of 1776 and the American Revolution', *Journal of Negro History*, Vol. 61, No. 3 (July 1976), p. 292.

6 Orlando Patterson, *The Sociology of Slavery*, MacGibbon & Kee, 1967, p. 271.

7 Thibault Ehrengardt, *The History of Jamaica from 1494 to 1838*, Lulu, 2015, p. 181.

8 Edward Long, *The History of Jamaica, Volume 2*, T. Lowndes, 1774, pp. 465–469.

9 *Ibid*, p. 291.

10 *Ibid.*

11 Suzette Benitez, 'Maroons in Jamaica; Their Origins and Development', scholar.library. miami.edu/slaves.

12 Patterson, *The Sociology of Slavery*, pp. 273–274.

13 James L. Garlow and David Barton, *This Precarious Moment,* Simon & Schuster, 2018.
14 Sir Basil Keith to Lord George Germaine, 6 August 1776, Colonial Office, CO 137/71, National Archives, United Kingdom, folios 230–231.
15 Sheridan, 'The Jamaican Slave Insurrection Scare of 1776 and the American Revolution', p. 298.
16 As reported by the French governor in the West Indies, François Claude Amour, Marquis de Bouillé. Some British reports claimed there were 4500 French troops. From Joseph Boromé, 'Dominica During French Occupation, 1778–1784', *English Historical Review*, Vol. LXXXIV, Issue CCCXXX (1 January 1969), p. 38.
17 John Sugden, *Nelson: A Dream of Glory,* Jonathan Cape, 2004, p. 131.
18 *Ibid*, p. 168.
19 Macquarie, Journals, 5 November 1788, Vol. Z A768-2, Item 1, State Library of New South Wales, pp. 1–10.
20 Anne Learmonth (1743–1780).
21 Macquarie to Murdoch Maclaine, 24 August 1783, MS 771, National Library of Australia.
22 *Ibid.*
23 Hubert H. Lamb, *Climate, History and the Modern World*, Routledge, 2002, p. 246.
24 Macquarie to Murdoch Maclaine, 17 May 1784, MS 771, National Library of Australia.
25 Lachlan Macquarie to Earl Bathurst, 30 April 1824, Colonial Office, CO 201/156, National Archives, United Kingdom, folios 343–344.
26 McLachlan, 'Macquarie, Lachlan (1762–1824)'.
27 Also known as Lochbuy.
28 Archibald Maclaine (1749–1784).
29 A. Maclean Sinclair, *The Clan Gillean*, Haszard & Moore, 1899, pp. 267–268.
30 Stacy, 'Crime and Punishment in the 84th Regiment of Foot, 1775–84', p. 117.
31 *Ibid.*
32 Sometimes called Daniel Monroe, *The Political Magazine and Parliamentary, Naval, Military, and Literary Journal,* Volume 8, 1784, p. 385.
33 Sinclair, *The Clan Gillean*, p. 268.
34 Archie Maclaine had been due to become 18th Laird of Lochbuie, but his father John, who died a few months after him, had remained the clan chieftain.
35 Macquarie to John Abercromby, Letterbooks, 12 January 1794, Vol. Z A787, State Library of New South Wales, p. 85.
36 Sinclair, *The Clan Gillean*, p. 270.
37 On 28 January 1787.
38 Macquarie to Murdoch Maclaine, 25 July 1786, MS 772, National Library of Australia.
39 Macquarie to Murdoch Maclaine, 2 August 1783, *ibid.*
40 Macquarie to Murdoch Maclaine, 8 August 1786, *ibid.*
41 Charles Macquarie to Murdoch Maclaine, 1793, Australian Joint Copying Project miscellaneous series M460, National Library of Australia.
42 Later Admiral Arthur Phillip, born 11 October 1738; died 31 August 1814.
43 Macquarie, Journals, 15 December 1787, Vol. Z A768-2, Item 1, State Library of New South Wales.
44 J.L. Pimlott, 'The Raising of Four Regiments for India, 1787–8', *Journal of the Society for Army Historical Research,* Vol. 52, No. 210 (Summer 1974), p. 68.
45 William Pitt the Younger, born 28 May 1759; died 23 January 1806.
46 The Vereenigde Oostindische Compagnie (VOC).
47 Major-General Robert Clive, 1st Baron Clive (29 September 1725 – 22 November 1774).
48 Sepoy, from the Persian word 'Sipahi' means 'army man'.
49 By 1803.
50 *Journal of the Royal United Service Institution, Vol 2,* W. Mitchell & Son, 1859, p. 181.

51 Later General James Marsh, died 12 June 1804.

52 Macquarie, Journals, 15 December 1787, Vol. Z A768-2, Item 1, State Library of New South Wales.

53 Lachlan Maclean (1720-1799).

54 Macquarie, Journals, 15 December 1787, Vol. Z A768-2, Item 1, State Library of New South Wales.

55 Macquarie, Journals, 15 January 1788, Vol. Z A768-2, Item 1, State Library of New South Wales.

56 Macquarie, Journals, 7 February, *ibid.*

57 Macquarie, Journals, 29 January 1787, *ibid.*

58 Arthur Phillip to Lord Sydney, 15 May 1788, Frederick Watson (ed.), *Historical Records of Australia, Series I: Governors' Despatches to and from England, Volume I: 1788–1796*, Library Committee of the Commonwealth Parliament, 1914, p. 18.

59 Governor Phillip's Instructions, 17 April 1787, *Historical Records of Australia,* series 1, vol. I, pp. 13-14.

60 Arthur Phillip, Memorandum, October 1786, *Historical Records of New South Wales*, vol. 1, p. 52.

61 Grace Karskens, 'Governor Phillip and the Eora', dictionaryofsydney.org.

62 Richard Broome, *Aboriginal Australians: A history since 1788*, Allen & Unwin, 2010, p. 16.

63 Later Lieutenant General Watkin Tench (6 October 1758 – 7 May 1833).

64 Watkin Tench, *A Narrative of the Expedition to Botany Bay*, published as Sydney's First Four Years, edited by L. F. Fitzhardinge, Library of Australian History, 1979 (f.p. 1789), p. 37.

65 *Ibid.*

Chapter 4

1 Macquarie, Journals, 17 February 1788, Vol. Z A768-2, Item 1, State Library of New South Wales.

2 Macquarie, Journals, 31 January 1787, *ibid.*

3 Troil, *Letters on Iceland*, p. 288.

4 Macquarie, Journals, 7 February 1788, Vol. Z A768-2, Item 1, State Library of New South Wales.

5 *Ibid.*

6 Macquarie, Journals, 5 March 1788, Vol. Z A768-2, Item 1, State Library of New South Wales.

7 Macquarie, Journals, 2 March 1788, Vol. Z A768-2, Item 1, State Library of New South Wales.

8 David J. Cathcart King, *Catellarium Anglicanum: An Index and Bibliography of the Castles in England, Wales and the Islands, Volume I: Anglesey–Montgomery*, Kraus International Publications, 1983, p. 230.

9 Macquarie, Journals, 5 March 1788, Vol. Z A768-2, Item 1, State Library of New South Wales.

10 Later Lieutenant-General James Wallace Dunlop (1759-1832).

11 Later General James Balfour, born 3 November 1743; died 18 March 1823. On 25 October 1809 received the rank of general.

12 Macquarie, Journals, 12 March 1788, Vol. Z A768-2, Item 1, State Library of New South Wales.

13 *Ibid.*

14 Macquarie, Journals, 15 March 1788, Vol. Z A768-2, Item 1, State Library of New South Wales.

15 *Ibid.*

16 Macquarie, Journals, 18 March 1788, *ibid.*

17 Macquarie, Journals, 24 March 1788, *ibid.*

18 Macquarie, Journals, 25 March 1788, *ibid.*

19 *Harris's List of Covent Garden Ladies*, published annually from 1757 to 1795.

20   Macquarie, Journals, 26 March 1788, Vol. Z A768-2, Item 1, State Library of New South Wales.

21   *Dublin, Northumberland, Prince William Henry* and *Winterton.*

22   *Ibid.*

23   Colin Anderson, Commissioned Surgeon (15th Regiment of Foot) 8 April 1782; died 28 July 1804, drowned in the sinking of the *Candidate* in the Bay of Bengal.

24   Macquarie, Journals, 30 March 1788, Vol. Z A768-2, Item 1, State Library of New South Wales.

25   Macquarie, Journals, 24 July 1788, *ibid.*

26   Macquarie, Journals, 4 April 1788, *ibid.*

27   General Sir William Medows, born 31 December 1738; died 14 November 1813.

28   Macquarie to Murdoch Maclaine, 4 April 1788, MS 772, National Library of Australia.

29   Named after his convict ship, *Charlotte.*

30   Philip McCouat, 'Colonial Artist, Thief, Forger and Mutineer: Thomas Barrett's Amazing Career', *Journal of Art in Society* (2015), artinsociety.com.

31   The area became known as Hangman's Hill, part of The Rocks. A plaque on the corner of Essex and Harrington Streets marks the location.

32   They were not recaptured until November 1795.

33   Their bodies were discovered on 30 May 1788.

34   John White, *Journal of a Voyage to New South Wales,* J. Debrett, 1790, p. 160.

35   Henry Hacking (c.1750-1831). He gave his name to Port Hacking, south of Sydney, and died in Hobart.

36   John Connor, *The Australian Frontier Wars*, 1788-1838, UNSW Press, 2002, p. 26.

37   Val Attenbrow, Sydney's Aboriginal Past: Investigating the Archaeological and Historical Records, University of New South Wales Press, 2010, p. 21.

38   Louis XVI of France (1754–1793).

39   Jean-François de Galaup, Comte de La Pérouse (1741–1788).

40   Two 500-ton store ships were reclassified as the frigates *La Boussole* (under La Pérouse) and *L'Astrolabe* (under skipper Fleuriot de Langle).

41   Napoleon Bonaparte, born 15 August 1769; died 5 May 1821.

42   Both ships were wrecked on the reefs of Vanikoro in the Solomon Islands. Some of the survivors were massacred by the local inhabitants, while others survived in their island home for nine months before building a two-masted craft from the wreckage of *L'Astrolabe.* They disappeared without trace.

43   Macquarie, Journals, 29 March 1788, Vol. Z A768-2, Item 1, State Library of New South Wales.

44   Macquarie, Journals, 10 April 1788, *ibid.*

45   Macquarie, Journals, 30 March 1788, *ibid.*

46   *Ibid.*

47   Macquarie, Journals, 6 April 1788, Vol. Z A768-2, Item 1, State Library of New South Wales.

48   Macquarie, Journals, 20 April 1788, *ibid.*

49   *Ibid.*

50   *Ibid.*

51   Macquarie, Journals, 6 May 1788, Vol. Z A768-2, Item 1, State Library of New South Wales.

52   Macquarie, Journals, 10 June 1788, Vol. Z A768-2, Item 1, State Library of New South Wales.

53   *Ibid.*

54   Koeëlberg (Bullet Mountain) stands at 1289 metres high.

55   Macquarie, Journals, 12 June 1788, Vol. Z A768-2, Item 1, State Library of New South Wales.

56   Later Vice-Admiral William Bligh, born 9 September 1754; died 7 December 1817.

57   Macquarie to Charles Macquarie, 10 March 1810, *Royal Australian Historical Society Journal*, XVI, I, p. 27.
58   Macquarie, Journals, 13 June 1788, Vol. Z A768-2, Item 1, State Library of New South Wales.
59   Macquarie, Journals, 14 June 1788, *ibid*.
60   Cornelis Jacob van de Graaff, born 14 February 1785; died 24 June 1791.
61   Macquarie, Journals, 15 June 1788, Vol. Z A768-2, Item 1, State Library of New South Wales.
62   *Ibid*.
63   Macquarie, Journals, 14 June 1788, Vol. Z A768-2, Item 1, State Library of New South Wales.
64   Macquarie, Journals, 15 June 1788, *ibid*.
65   Robert Jacob Gordon, born 29 September 1743, Doesburg, Gelderland, the Netherlands; died 25 October 1795, Cape Town, Cape Colony.
66   Francis Masson, born August 1741; died 23 December 1805.
67   Macquarie, Journals, 18 June 1788, Vol. Z A768-2, Item 1, State Library of New South Wales.
68   *Ibid*.
69   *Ibid*.
70   'Merino Sheep Introduced', Defining Moments in Australian History, National Museum of Australia, nma.gov.au/defining-moments.
71   Macquarie, Journals, 18 June 1788, Vol. Z A768-2, Item 1, State Library of New South Wales.
72   Macquarie, Journals, 24 July 1788, *ibid*.
73   Macquarie, Journals, 2 August 1788, *ibid*.
74   Macquarie, Journals, 4 August 1788, Vol. Z A768-2, Item 1, State Library of New South Wales.
75   Macquarie, Journals, 3 August 1788, *ibid*.

Chapter 5
1   Macquarie, Journals, 5 August 1788, Vol. Z A768-2, Item 1, State Library of New South Wales.
2   By his reckoning, 9 miles long and 24 miles in circumference.
3   Charles II of England married Catherine of Braganza, daughter of King John IV of Portugal, on 11 May 1661.
4   Macquarie, Journals, 7 August 1788, Vol. Z A768-2, Item 1, State Library of New South Wales.
5   *Ibid*.
6   James Douglas, *Bombay and Western India*, Sampson Low, Marston & Co, 1893, p. 13.
7   Macquarie, Journals, 5 August 1788, Vol. Z A768-2, Item 1, State Library of New South Wales.
8   Macquarie, Journals, 24 August 1788, *ibid*.
9   'Raj Bhavan, History of Mumbai', Raj Bhavan Maharashtra, rajbhavan-maharashtra.gov.in/rajbhavan.
10   Macquarie, Journals, 5 October 1789, Vol. Z A768-2, Item 1, State Library of New South Wales.
11   Macquarie, Journals, 14 September 1788, *ibid*.
12   Also called Jawahar Dweep.
13   Also called Uran Island.
14   Also called Gharapuri Island.
15   Macquarie, Journals, 13 December 1788, Vol. Z A768-2, Item 1, State Library of New South Wales.
16   The sculpture is now displayed at Mumbai's Dr Bhau Daji Lad Museum. In 1864, the British attempted to carry it back to England, but their crane broke and the elephant shattered into several pieces. The fragments were eventually pieced back together.
17   Macquarie, Journals, 14 October 1789, Vol. Z A768-2, Item 1, State Library of New South Wales.
18   Macquarie, Journals, 5 November 1788, *ibid*.
19   Macquarie, Journals, 6 August 1788, *ibid*.

20 Walter Ewer to Henry Dundas, 30 November 1796 and 16 April 1797, Papers of Walter Ewer, Home Miscellaneous Series 438, India Office Records, British Library: Asian and African Studies, folios 19–20 and 72–73, as quoted in Ritchie, *Lachlan Macquarie*, p. 28.

21 Douglas M. Peers, 'Soldiers, Surgeons and the Campaigns to Combat Sexually Transmitted Diseases in Colonial India, 1805–1860', *Medical History*, Vol. 42, Issue 2 (April 1998), p. 144.

22 'Going to War: Louisa May Alcott's Experience as a Civil War Nurse', lmacivilwar.weebly.com/typhoid-fever.html.

23 Macquarie, Journals, 13 December 1788, Vol. Z A768-2, Item 1, State Library of New South Wales.

24 Macquarie, Journals, 20 August 1788, *ibid.*

25 Macquarie, Journals, 30 November 1788, *ibid.*

26 Macquarie, Journals, 9 August 1788, *ibid.*

27 Macquarie, Journals, 5 August 1788, *ibid.*

28 Macquarie, Journals, 14 August 1788, *ibid.*

29 *Ibid.*

30 Macquarie, Journals, 1 October 1788, *ibid.*

31 *Ibid.*

32 Macquarie, Journals, 13 October 1788, Vol. Z A768-2, Item 1, State Library of New South Wales.

33 Macquarie, Journals, 5 November 1788, *ibid.*

34 Macquarie, Journals, 14 January 1789, *ibid.*

35 Macquarie, Journals, February 1789, *ibid.*

36 The senior subaltern rank, above lieutenant and below captain.

37 Macquarie, Journals, 30 March 1789, Vol. Z A768-2, Item 1, State Library of New South Wales.

38 Macquarie, Journals, 30 March 1789, *ibid.*

39 Macquarie, Journals, 14 April 1789, *ibid.*

40 Richard Hough, *Captain Bligh and Mr Christian: The Men and the Mutiny*, Hutchinson, 1972, p. 189.

41 Macquarie, Journals, 16 May 1789, Vol. Z A768-2, Item 1, State Library of New South Wales.

42 Macquarie, Journals, 31 August 1789, *ibid.*

43 Macquarie, Journals, 13 January 1790, *ibid.*

44 Maximilien François Marie Isidore de Robespierre (6 May 1758 – 28 July 1794).

45 'Liberty, Equality, Fraternity', diplomatie.gouv.fr.

46 The British referred to the town as Anjengo. The East India Company had built a fort near the town in 1696.

47 Tipu Sultan, born Sultan Fateh Ali Sahab Tipu, 20 November 1750; died 4 May 1799; also known as Tippoo Sultan and the Tipu Sahib.

48 Macquarie, Journals, 13 January 1790, Vol. Z A768-2, Item 1, State Library of New South Wales.

49 Hyder Ali (also spelled Haider Ali), born *c.* 1720; died 7 December 1782.

50 Lewin B. Bowring, *Haider Ali and Tipu Sultan*, Clarendon Press, 1893, pp. 33–34.

51 *Ibid*, pp. 221–222.

52 *Ibid.*

53 Francois Gautier, 'The Tyrant Diaries, From the memoirs of a French adventurer who served at Tipu's court', outlookindia.com, 15 April 2013.

54 On 27 August 1781.

55 Robert J.L. Darby, *A Surgical Temptation: The Demonization of the Foreskin and the Rise of Circumcision in Britain*, University of Chicago Press, 2005, pp. 32–33.

56 M.S. Naravane, *Battles of the Honourable East India Company: Making of the Raj*, A.P.H. Publishing Corporation, 2006, p. 175.

57   Estefania Wenger, *Tipu Sultan: A Biography,* Vij Publishing, 2017.
58   The *East India Company Act* 1784, also known as Pitt's India Act.
59   Macquarie, Journals, 14 April 1790, Vol. Z A768-2, Item 1, State Library of New South Wales.
60   Macquarie, Journals, 10 November 1790, *ibid.*
61   Macquarie, Journals, 20 September 1790, *ibid.*
62   Macquarie, Journals, 20 to 22 November 1790, *ibid.*
63   Macquarie, Journals, 8 November 1790, *ibid.*
64   Later General Sir John William Floyd, 1st Baronet, born 22 February 1748; died 10 January 1818.
65   Macquarie, Journals, 10 November 1790, Vol. Z A768-2, Item 1, State Library of New South Wales.

Chapter 6
1   Macquarie, Journals, 27 March 1791, Vol. Z A768-2, Item 1, State Library of New South Wales.
2   Macquarie, Journals, 24 November 1790, *ibid.*
3   *Ibid.*
4   Macquarie, Journals, 6 December 1790, *ibid.*
5   Macquarie, Journals, 10 December 1790, *ibid.*
6   Macquarie, Journals, 11 December 1790, *ibid.*
7   General Sir Robert Abercromby, born 21 October 1740; died 3 November 1827.
8   Macquarie, Journals, 17 December 1790, Vol. Z A768-2, Item 1, State Library of New South Wales.
9   Macquarie, Journals, 14 December 1790, *ibid.*
10   *Ibid.*
11   *Ibid.*
12   *Ibid.*
13   *Ibid.*
14   Macquarie, Journals, 15 December 1790, Vol. Z A768-2, Item 1, State Library of New South Wales.
15   Macquarie, Journals, 17 December 1790, *ibid.*
16   *Ibid.*
17   *Ibid.*
18   *Ibid.*
19   *Ibid.*
20   *Ibid.*
21   Macquarie, Journals, 20 December 1790, Vol. Z A768-2, Item 1, State Library of New South Wales.
22   *Ibid.*
23   Aditi De, *Multiple City: Writings on Bangalore,* Penguin, 2008.
24   Now known as Srirangapatna.
25   Now known as the Kaveri River.
26   The cities are now respectively called Mysuru and Bangaluru.
27   Macquarie referred to it as the Billiapatam; now called Valapattanam; Macquarie, Journals, 28 January 1791, Vol. Z A768-2, Item 1, State Library of New South Wales.
28   Macquarie, Journals, 23 February 1791, Vol. Z A768-2, Item 1, State Library of New South Wales.
29   *Ibid.*
30   Macquarie, Journals, 31 March 1791, Vol. Z A768-2, Item 1, State Library of New South Wales.

31   Macquarie, Journals, 25 February 1791, Vol. Z A768-2, Item 1, State Library of New South Wales.

32   Macquarie, Journals, 27 March 1791, *ibid.*

33   Known originally by the British as Rose Hill; renamed Parramatta on 4 June 1791.

34   John Macarthur, born 1767; died 10 April 1834. He spelled his surname 'M'Arthur' for most of his life and sometimes 'MacArthur'. He only began using the now-standard 'Macarthur' late in life.

35   Woollarawarre Bennelong (c. 1764 – 3 January 1813).

36   Pemulway (c.1750 – 2 June 1802).

37   Watkin Tench, *A Complete Account of the Settlement at Port Jackson: In New South Wales*, G Nicol & J. Sewel, 1793, p. 90.

38   In 1803, the year after Pemulwuy's death, Hacking was sentenced to death for shooting and wounding his mistress Ann Holmes. He faced the death sentence again in 1804 for stealing naval stores from the HMS *Investigator*. He was pardoned in both cases by his old shipmate, the Governor, Philip Gidley King.

39   *The Journal and Letters of Lt. Ralph Clark 1787–1792*, 3 May 1791, University of Sydney Library, 2003, setis.library.usyd.edu.au/ozlit/pdf/clajour.pdf.

40   *Ibid*, 5 July 1787.

41   Macquarie, Journals, 4 April 1791, *ibid.*

42   Macquarie, Journals, 20 April 1791, *ibid.* Now called Dharwad.

43   Macquarie, Journals, 16 May 1791, *ibid.*

44   Macquarie, Journals, 16 May 1791, *ibid.*

45   Franklin B. Wickwire and Mary B. Wickwire, *Cornwallis: The Imperial Years*, University of North Carolina Press, 2017.

46   Macquarie, Journals, 23 May 1791, Vol. Z A768-2, Item 1, State Library of New South Wales.

47   *Ibid.*

48   Macquarie, Journals, 24 May 1791, Vol. Z A768-2, Item 1, State Library of New South Wales.

49   *Ibid.*

50   *Ibid.*

51   Macquarie, Journals, 26 May 1791, Vol. Z A768-2, Item 1, State Library of New South Wales.

52   Macquarie, Journals, 29 May 1791, *ibid.*

53   *Ibid.*

54   Macquarie, Journals, 30 May 1791, Vol. Z A768-2, Item 1, State Library of New South Wales.

55   Macquarie, Journals, 3 June 1791, *ibid.*

56   Macquarie, Journals, 4 June 1791, *ibid.*

57   *Ibid.*

58   Macquarie, Journals, 7 June 1791, Vol. Z A768-2, Item 1, State Library of New South Wales.

Chapter 7

1   Macquarie to Murdoch Maclaine, 20 September 1792, MS 772, Item 15, National Library of Australia.

2   Macquarie, Journals, 6 October 1791, *ibid.*

3   Macquarie, Journals, 8 June 1791, *ibid.*

4   *Ibid.*

5   Macquarie, Journals, 6 July 1791, Vol. Z A768-2, Item 1, State Library of New South Wales.

6   Macquarie, Journals, 6 September 1791, *ibid.*

7   Macquarie, Journals, 9 January 1792, *ibid.*

8   Macquarie, Journals, 3 to 4 February 1792, *ibid.*

9   Macquarie, Journals, 6 September 1791, *ibid.*

10   *Ibid.*

11   Macquarie, Journals, 12 August 1791, Vol. Z A768-2, Item 1, State Library of New South Wales.

12   Later known as the Bombay Marine Corps, then as the Indian Navy.

13   Macquarie, Journals, 12 August 1791, Vol. Z A768-2, Item 1, State Library of New South Wales.

14   Macquarie, Journals, 13 August 1791, *ibid*.

15   Macquarie, Journals, 5 October 1791, *ibid*.

16   Macquarie, Journals, 5 December 1791, *ibid*.

17   *Ibid*.

18   Macquarie, Journals, 7 December 1791, Vol. Z A768-2, Item 1, State Library of New South Wales.

19   *Ibid*.

20   Macquarie, Journals, 16 December 1791, Vol. Z A768-2, Item 1, State Library of New South Wales.

21   Macquarie, Journals, 13 February 1792, *ibid*.

22   Macquarie, Journals, 14 February 1792, *ibid*.

23   On 6 February 1792.

24   Macquarie to Murdoch Maclaine, 4 March 1792, MS 772, Item 14, National Library of Australia.

25   Wickwire and Wickwire, *Cornwallis: The Imperial Years*, p. 167.

26   Macquarie, Journals, 16 February 1792, Vol. Z A768-2, Item 1, State Library of New South Wales.

27   Macquarie, Journals, 20 February 1792, *ibid*.

28   Macquarie, Journals, 23 February 1792, *ibid*.

29   Macquarie to Murdoch Maclaine, 4 March 1792, MS 771, National Library of Australia.

30   *Ibid*.

31   *Ibid*.

32   Macquarie, Journals, 24 February 1792, Vol. Z A768-2, Item 1, State Library of New South Wales.

33   *Ibid*.

34   Macquarie, Journals, 26 February 1792, Vol. Z A768-2, Item 1, State Library of New South Wales.

35   Robert Home (1752–1834), *The Reception of the Mysorean Hostage Princes by Marquis Cornwallis*, National Army Museum, London.

36   Macquarie, Journals, 26 February 1792, Vol. Z A768-2, Item 1, State Library of New South Wales.

37   Wickwire and Wickwire, *Cornwallis: The Imperial Years*, p. 173. Some reports say that Medows's aid, Colonel George Harris, had actually removed the balls from the pistols.

38   Macquarie, Journals, 26 February 1792, Vol. Z A768-2, Item 1, State Library of New South Wales.

39   He was made a knight of the Bath on 14 December 1792.

40   Medows was promoted on 12 October 1793. In 1798, he was made a full general and in 1801, succeeded Cornwallis for a short space as Commander-in-Chief of Ireland.

41   Macquarie to Murdoch Maclaine, 20 September 1792, MS 772, Item 15, National Library of Australia.

42   Lachlan Macquarie, 'Journal No. 2 Kept by L. Macquarie Commencing 26th March 1792', 10 April 1792, Vol. Z A768-2, Item 2, Lachlan Macquarie and Macquarie Family Papers, State Library of New South Wales, pp. 66–115.

43   Macquarie to Murdoch Maclaine, 20 September 1792, MS 772, Item 15, National Library of Australia.

44 Macquarie, Journals, 16 February 1792, Vol. Z A768-2, Item 1, State Library of New South Wales.

45 Macquarie to Murdoch Maclaine, 20 September 1792, MS 772, Item 15, National Library of Australia.

46 Macquarie, Journals, 2 April 1792, Vol. Z A768-2, Item 2, State Library of New South Wales.

47 *Ibid.*

48 Macquarie, Journals, 10 April 1792, *ibid.*

49 Macquarie, Journals, 13 April 1792, *ibid.*

50 Macquarie, Journals, 21 April 1792, *ibid.*

51 Macquarie, Journals, 1 May 1792, *ibid.*

52 Macquarie, Journals, 15 May 1792, *ibid.*

53 Macquarie to Murdoch Maclaine, 20 September 1792, MS 772, Item 15, National Library of Australia.

54 *Ibid.*

55 Macquarie, Journals, 23 May 1792, Vol. Z A768-2, Item 2, State Library of New South Wales.

56 Macquarie, Journals, 22 October 1792, *ibid.*

57 Macquarie to Murdoch Maclaine, 20 September 1792, MS 772, Item 15, National Library of Australia; Macquarie, Journals, 6 July 1792, Vol. Z A768-2, Item 2, State Library of New South Wales.

Chapter 8

1 Macquarie, Journals, 7 August 1793, Vol. Z A768-2, Item 2, State Library of New South Wales.

2 James Morley, born September 1742, Bombay, India; died 22 February 1798, Bath, England.

3 Macquarie, Journals, 4 August 1793, Vol. Z A768-2, Item 2, State Library of New South Wales.

4 Dorothea Morley, née Jarvis, born 1768, Antigua; died 1 November 1850, Winchester, England. Married James Morley 11 March 1789, Parish of Westminster, Middlesex, London.

5 Jane Macquarie, née Jarvis, born 16 October 1772, Antigua; died 15 July 1796, Macao, China.

6 Macquarie, Journals, 2 September 1793, Vol. Z A768-2, Item 2, State Library of New South Wales.

7 Thomas Jarvis (1722–1785).

8 Jarvis Family Papers, William L. Clements Library, University of Michigan.

9 Rachel Jarvis, née Thibou, born Antigua 1728; died London 1794.

10 Macquarie to Murdoch Maclaine, Letterbooks, 1 January 1794, Vol. Z A787, State Library of New South Wales, p. 33.

11 Macquarie, Journals, 7 November 1792, Vol. Z A768-2, Item 2, State Library of New South Wales.

12 Macquarie, Journals, 20 November 1792, *ibid.*

13 Macquarie, Journals, 24 November 1792, *ibid.*

14 Macquarie to Murdoch Maclaine, Letterbooks, 1 January 1794, Vol. Z A787, State Library of New South Wales, p. 33.

15 *Ibid.*, p. 36.

16 Macquarie, Journals, 25 December 1792, Vol. Z A768-2, Item 2, State Library of New South Wales.

17 Macquarie, Journals, 4 June 1793, *ibid.*

18 Macquarie, Journals, 14 May 1793, *ibid.*

19 *Ibid.*

20 Macquarie, Journals, 29 June 1793, Vol. Z A768-2, Item 2, State Library of New South Wales.

21 On 22 September 1792.

22 Macquarie, Journals, 15 July 1793, *ibid.*

23 Macquarie to John Abercromby, Letterbooks, 12 January 1794, Vol. Z A787, State Library of New South Wales, pp. 82–83.

24 *Ibid*, the object of the fictional Don Quixote's hopeless devotion and love. Miguel de Cervantes, *Don Quixote de La Mancha*, Francisco de Robles, 1605.

25 Macquarie, Journals, 16 July 1793, Vol. Z A768-2, Item 2, State Library of New South Wales.

26 *Ibid.*

27 *Ibid.*

28 *Ibid.*

29 *Ibid.*

30 Macquarie, Journals, 2 August 1793, Vol. Z A768-2, Item 2, State Library of New South Wales.

31 *Ibid.*

32 Macquarie, Journals, 3 August 1793, Vol. Z A768-2, Item 2, State Library of New South Wales.

33 *Ibid.*

34 *Ibid.*

35 Macquarie, Journals, 4 August 1793, Vol. Z A768-2, Item 2, State Library of New South Wales.

36 *Ibid.*

37 *Ibid.*

38 *Ibid.*

39 *Ibid.*

40 *Ibid.*

41 *Ibid.*

42 Macquarie, Journals, 5 August 1793, Vol. Z A768-2, Item 2, State Library of New South Wales.

43 *Ibid.*

44 Macquarie, Journals, 6 August 1793, Vol. Z A768-2, Item 2, State Library of New South Wales.

45 Macquarie, Journals, 7 August 1793, *ibid.*

46 Charles Morley, born 3 October 1791, Bombay, India; date and place of death unknown.

47 Macquarie, Journals, 7 August 1793, Vol. Z A768-2, Item 2, State Library of New South Wales.

48 *Ibid.*

49 Macquarie, Journals, 12 August 1793, Vol. Z A768-2, Item 2, State Library of New South Wales.

50 *Ibid.*

51 Macquarie, Journals, 13 August 1793, Vol. Z A768-2, Item 2, State Library of New South Wales.

52 Later Colonel George Ralph Payne Jarvis, born 13 May 1774; died 14 June 1851.

53 Macquarie, Journals, 14 August 1793, Vol. Z A768-2, Item 2, State Library of New South Wales.

54 Macquarie, Journals, 31 August 1793, *ibid.*

55 *Ibid.*

56 Stephen Neill, *A History of Christianity in India: 1707–1858,* Cambridge University Press, 2002, p. 114.

57 Macquarie, Journals, 8 September 1793, Vol. Z A768-2, Item 2, State Library of New South Wales.

58 *Ibid.*

59 *Ibid.* 'Benedict': a newly married man who has long been a bachelor, based on Benedick, a character in William Shakespeare's *Much Ado About Nothing* (1600).

60 *Ibid.*

61 *Ibid.*

Chapter 9

1 Lachlan Macquarie, 'Journal – No. 3 Kept by L. Macquarie Commencing at Calicut in the Province of Malabar, 29th December 1794', 14 January 1795, Vol. Z A769-1, Item 1, Lachlan Macquarie and Macquarie Family Papers, State Library of New South Wales, pp. 7–15.

2 Macquarie, Journals, 9 September 1793, Vol. Z A768-2, Item 2, State Library of New South Wales.

3 *Ibid.*

4 John Tasker (*c.* 1742–1800).

5 Macquarie, Journals, 17 September 1793, Vol. Z A768-2, Item 2, State Library of New South Wales.

6 *Ibid.*

7 *Ibid.*

8 Macquarie to Murdoch Maclaine, 'Letterbook 1 November 1794 to 16 May 1796', 20 March 1795, Vol. Z A788, Lachlan Macquarie and Macquarie Family Papers, State Library of New South Wales.

9 Macquarie to Rachel Jarvis, Letterbooks, 28 September 1793, Vol. Z A787, State Library of New South Wales.

10 *Ibid.*

11 *Ibid.*

12 Macquarie to Zachariah Hall, Letterbooks, 4 December 1793, Vol. Z A787, State Library of New South Wales.

13 Macquarie, Journals, 7 to 30 October 1793, Vol. Z A768-2, Item 2, State Library of New South Wales.

14 Macquarie, Journals, 1 November 1793, *ibid.*

15 Macquarie, Journals, 20 December 1793, *ibid.*

16 Macquarie, Journals, 24 October 1793, *ibid.*

17 Macquarie to Murdoch Maclaine, Letterbooks, 20 March 1795, Vol. Z A788, State Library of New South Wales.

18 *Ibid.*

19 Macquarie, Journals, 6 November 1793, Vol. Z A768-2, Item 2, State Library of New South Wales.

20 Macquarie, Journals, 4 September 1794, *ibid.*

21 Macquarie to Murdoch Maclaine, Letterbooks, 1 January 1794, Vol. Z A787, State Library of New South Wales, pp. 44–45.

22 Macquarie, Journals, 4 September 1794, Vol. Z A768-2, Item 2, State Library of New South Wales.

23 Macquarie, Journals, 21 December 1793, *ibid.*

24 Macquarie, Journals, 29 December 1793, *ibid.*

25 *Ibid.*

26 *Ibid.*

27 Macquarie, Journals, 15 January 1794, Vol. Z A768-2, Item 2, State Library of New South Wales.

28 Macquarie, Journals, 16 January 1794, *ibid.*

29 Macquarie, Journals, 30 June 1794, *ibid.*

30 Yemmerrawanne (c.1775-18 May 1794). He and Bennelong were provided with fashionable clothes to wear in London and they stayed at a fine home in Mayfair. Tutors were hired to educate them in reading and writing in English, and they visited the theatre as well as St Paul's Cathedral and the Tower of London. In September 1793, Yemmerrawanne fell ill and, despite the ministrations of noted doctor Gilbert Blane, he died on 18 May 1794, aged about 19, from a lung infection. The ailing Bennelong returned to Sydney in 1795 on the HMS *Reliance* under the care of surgeon, sailor and explorer George Bass.

31 Elizabeth Macarthur to Relatives and Friends in England, 21 December 1793, in F.M. Bladen (ed.), *Historical Records of New South Wales, Vol. II: Grose and Paterson, 1793–1795*, Charles Potter, Government Printer, 1893, p. 508.

32 Macquarie, Journals, 16 January 1794, Vol. Z A768-2, Item 2, State Library of New South Wales.

33 Macquarie, Journals, 31 January 1794, *ibid*.

34 Macquarie, Journals, 16 March 1794, *ibid*.

35 Macquarie, Journals, 22 February 1794, *ibid*.

36 Later Lieutenant-General Sir Henry Oakes, 2nd Baronet (1756–1827).

37 Macquarie, Journals, 19 to 25 March 1794, Vol. Z A768-2, Item 2, State Library of New South Wales.

38 Macquarie described the vessel as a 'snow'.

39 Macquarie, Journals, 29 March 1794, Vol. Z A768-2, Item 2, State Library of New South Wales.

40 The guns were known as 'musquetoons'.

41 Macquarie, Journals, 29 March 1794, Vol. Z A768-2, Item 2, State Library of New South Wales.

42 Macquarie, Journals, 31 March 1794, *ibid*.

43 Francisco da Cunha e Meneses, born 10 April 1747; died 12 June 1812.

44 Macquarie, Journals, 1 April 1794, Vol. Z A768-2, Item 2, State Library of New South Wales.

45 Macquarie, Journals, 31 March 1794, *ibid*.

46 Macquarie, Journals, 8 April 1794, Vol. Z A768-2, Item 2, State Library of New South Wales.

47 Macquarie, Journals, 14 June 1794, *ibid*.

48 *Ibid*.

49 *Ibid*.

50 *Ibid*.

51 Oliver Goldsmith, *She Stoops to Conquer*, first performed in London in 1773.

52 Macquarie, Journals, 8 August 1794, Vol. Z A768-2, Item 2, State Library of New South Wales.

53 Dated 12 February 1794.

54 'Legacies of British Slave Ownership', PROB 11/12141/157, University College London, ucl.ac.uk/lbs.

55 Macquarie to John Tasker, Letterbooks, 6 May 1795, Vol. Z A788, State Library of New South Wales.

56 Macquarie, Journals, 3 August 1794, Vol. Z A768-2, Item 2, State Library of New South Wales.

57 *Ibid*.

58 Later Lieutenant-General James Wallace Dunlop, born 19 June 1759; died 30 March 1832.

59 Macquarie to Allan Maclean, Letterbooks, 4 January 1794, Vol. Z A787, State Library of New South Wales, p. 60.

60 Macquarie to John Abercromby, Letterbooks, 12 January 1794, *ibid*, p. 84.

61 Macquarie to Dorothea Morley, Letterbooks, 12 August 1794, *ibid*, pp. 161–162.

62 *Ibid*, pp. 162–163.

63 *Ibid*.

64 Macquarie, Journals, 16 July 1794, Vol. Z A768-2, Item 2, State Library of New South Wales.

65 Macquarie, Journals, 15 July 1794, *ibid*.

66 Macquarie, Journals, 4 September 1794, *ibid*.

67 *Ibid*.

68 Macquarie to Charles Macquarie, Letterbooks, 6 September 1794, Vol. Z A787, State Library of New South Wales, pp. 183–184.

69 Macquarie, Journals, 24 September 1794, Vol. Z A768-2, Item 2, State Library of New South Wales.

70 Macquarie, Journals, 10 October 1794, *ibid.*

71 Macquarie, Journals, 25 October 1794, *ibid.*

72 *Ibid.*

73 Macquarie, Journals, 26 November 1794, Vol. Z A768-2, Item 2, State Library of New South Wales.

74 A ship of 280 tonnes of unknown provenance, *not* the *Endeavour* of Captain Cook fame. That *Endeavour* was sold in 1775 and renamed *Lord Sandwich*. She was hired as a British troop transport during the American War of Independence and was scuttled in a blockade off Narragansett Bay, Rhode Island, in 1778.

75 Macquarie, Journals, 20 December 1794, Vol. Z A768-2, Item 2, State Library of New South Wales.

76 Macquarie to James Dunlop, Letterbooks, 1 January 1795, Vol. Z A788, State Library of New South Wales.

77 Macquarie, Journals, 25 December 1794, Vol. Z A768-2, Item 2, State Library of New South Wales.

78 Macquarie, Journals, 30 December 1794, Vol. Z A769-1, Item 1, State Library of New South Wales.

79 *Ibid.*

80 Macquarie, Journals, 24 May 1795, *ibid.*

81 Macquarie to Murdoch Maclaine, Letterbooks, 20 March 1795, Vol. Z A788, State Library of New South Wales.

82 Macquarie, Journals, 24 May 1795, Vol. Z A769-1, Item 1, State Library of New South Wales.

83 Macquarie, Journals, 4 June 1795, *ibid.*

84 Macquarie to Zachariah Hall, Letterbooks, 24 February 1795, Vol. Z A788, State Library of New South Wales.

85 Now known as Kochi.

86 Macquarie, Journals, 14 January 1795, Vol. Z A769-1, Item 1, State Library of New South Wales.

87 Macquarie, Journals, 24 January 1795, *ibid.*

88 Macquarie to Nash, Grantham & Co., Letterbooks, 18 May 1795, Vol. Z A788, State Library of New South Wales.

89 Macquarie to Murdoch Maclaine, Letterbooks, 20 March 1795, *ibid.*

90 Macquarie, Journals, 6 July 1795, Vol. Z A769-1, Item 1, State Library of New South Wales.

91 Macquarie to John Murray, Letterbooks, 17 March 1795, Vol. Z A788, State Library of New South Wales.

92 Macquarie to Hadjee Eesooff, Letterbooks, 23 July 1795, *ibid.*

93 Macquarie to James Dunlop, Letterbooks, 19 January 1795, *ibid.*

94 Macquarie to John Forbes, Letterbooks, 24 July 1795, *ibid.*

95 Macquarie to James Dunlop, Letterbooks, 19 January 1795, *ibid.*

96 Macquarie to James Dunlop, Letterbooks, 24 July 1795, *ibid.*

97 Macquarie to John Forbes, Letterbooks, 24 July 1795, *ibid.*

98 Later Colonel Bulstrode Whitelocke (1760–1826). His grandfather was Sir Bulstrode Whitelocke (1605–1675), an English lawyer, writer and parliamentarian, Lord Keeper of the Great Seal of England and an important figure in the English Civil War.

99 Macquarie to John Halkett, Letterbooks, 25 January 1795, Vol. Z A788, State Library of New South Wales.

100 Macquarie to Marlborough Parsons Stirling, Letterbooks, 31 January 1795, *ibid.*

Chapter 10

1   Macquarie to Marlborough Parsons Stirling, Letterbooks, 9 March 1795, Vol. Z A788, State Library of New South Wales.

2   Macquarie to Christopher Lundin, Letterbooks, 20 March 1795, *ibid.*

3   William V of Orange, born Willem Batavus, 8 March 1748; died 9 April 1806.

4   Macquarie, Journals, 21 July 1795, Vol. Z A769-1, Item 1, State Library of New South Wales.

5   War Office, *Rules and Regulations for the Formations, Field-Exercise, and Movements, of His Majesty's Forces*, J. Walter, 1792.

6   General Sir David Dundas, born 1735; died 18 February 1820.

7   Macquarie to Marlborough Parsons Stirling, Letterbooks, 31 January 1795, Vol. Z A788, State Library of New South Wales.

8   *Ibid.*

9   *Ibid.*

10 Macquarie to Marlborough Parsons Stirling, Letterbooks, 31 January 1795, *ibid.*

11 Macquarie to James Dunlop, Letterbooks, 24 July 1795, Vol. Z A788, State Library of New South Wales.

12 Macquarie to George Mackenzie, Letterbooks, 29 July 1795, *ibid.*

13 *Ibid.*

14 Macquarie, Journals, 23 July 1795, Vol. Z A769-1, Item 1, State Library of New South Wales.

15 Macquarie, Journals, 19 August 1795, *ibid.*

16 *Ibid.*

17 Now known as the Chaliyar River.

18 Macquarie, Journals, 18 September 1795, Vol. Z A769-1, Item 1, State Library of New South Wales.

19 Macquarie, Journals, 8 September 1795, *ibid.*

20 Macquarie, Journals, 9 September 1795, *ibid.*

21 Known today as Mattancherry.

22 Macquarie, Journals, 16 October 1795, Vol. Z A769-1, Item 1, State Library of New South Wales.

23 Macquarie, Journals, 18 October 1795, *ibid.*

24 *Ibid.*

25 Macquarie, Journals, 19 October 1795, Vol. Z A769-1, Item 1, State Library of New South Wales.

26 *Ibid.*

27 *Ibid.*

28 Macquarie, Journals, 20 October 1795, Vol. Z A769-1, Item 1, State Library of New South Wales.

29 *Ibid.*

30 Macquarie, Journals, 30 October 1795, Vol. Z A769-1, Item 1, State Library of New South Wales.

31 *Ibid.*

32 Macquarie, Journals, 31 October 1795, Vol. Z A769-1, Item 1, State Library of New South Wales.

33 Macquarie, Journals, 13 September 1795, *ibid.*

34 Macquarie, Journals, 14 November 1795, *ibid.*

35 Now called Sri Lanka.

36 Macquarie, Journals, 23 December 1795, Vol. Z A769-1, Item 1, State Library of New South Wales.

37 *Ibid.*

38 Macquarie, Journals, 1 January 1796, Vol. Z A769-1, Item 1, State Library of New South Wales.

39 Macquarie, Journals, 23 December 1795, *ibid.*

40 Macquarie, Journals, 31 December 1795, *ibid.*

Chapter 11

1 Macquarie, Journals, 3 January 1796, Vol. Z A769-1, Item 1, State Library of New South Wales.

2 *Ibid.*

3 Later General James Stuart, born 2 March 1741, Perthshire, Scotland; died 29 April 1815, London, England.

4 Macquarie, Journals, 12 February 1796, Vol. Z A769-1, Item 1, State Library of New South Wales.

5 *Ibid.* Macquarie called them 'creesses'.

6 *Ibid.*

7 Johan van Angelbeek, born 1727, Wittmund, Germany; died 2 September 1799, Columbo, Ceylon.

8 Patrick Alexander Agnew (1765-1813).

9 Macquarie, Journals, 14 February 1796, Vol. Z A769-1, Item 1, State Library of New South Wales.

10 The British took the Ceylonese kingdom of Kandy in 1815 and held Ceylon until independence in 1948.

11 Macquarie, Journals, 16 February 1796, Vol. Z A769-1, Item 1, State Library of New South Wales.

12 Now known as Jakarta, the capital and largest city of Indonesia.

13 Macquarie, Journals, 16 February 1796, Vol. Z A769-1, Item 1, State Library of New South Wales.

14 Macquarie, Journals, 19 February 1796, *ibid.*

15 Dietrich Thomas Fretz (1743–1815).

16 Macquarie, Journals, 22 February 1796, Vol. Z A769-1, Item 1, State Library of New South Wales.

17 *Ibid.*

18 Macquarie, Journals, 23 February 1796, Vol. Z A769-1, Item 1, State Library of New South Wales.

19 *Ibid.*

20 *Ibid.*

21 Macquarie to James Stuart, Letterbooks, 23 February 1796, Vol. Z A788, State Library of New South Wales.

22 Macquarie, Journals, 23 February 1796, Vol. Z A769-1, Item 1, State Library of New South Wales.

23 *Ibid.*

24 *Ibid.*

25 Macquarie, Journals, 17 March 1796, Vol. Z A769-1, Item 1, State Library of New South Wales.

26 Macquarie to Dietrich Thomas Fretz, Letterbooks, 29 March 1796, Vol. Z A788, State Library of New South Wales.

27 *Ibid.*

28 Anna Diederica Fretz, born 1772.

29 Pieter van Spall (1772–1804).

30 Macquarie to Dietrich Thomas Fretz, Letterbooks, 29 March 1796, Vol. Z A788, State Library of New South Wales.

31 Macquarie, Journals, 24 February 1796, Vol. Z A769-1, Item 1, State Library of New South Wales.

32 *Lists of the Officers of His Majesty's, and the Hon. Company's Troops, Serving Under the Presidency of Bombay*, Adjutant General's Office, 1798.

33 Macquarie, Journals, 15 March 1796, Vol. Z A769-1, Item 1, State Library of New South Wales.

34 *Ibid.*

35 Macquarie, Journals, 18 March 1796, Vol. Z A769-1, Item 1, State Library of New South Wales.

36 Macquarie, Journals, 19 March 1796, *ibid.*

37 Macquarie, Journals, 21 March 1796, *ibid.*

38 Macquarie, Journals, 15 April 1796, *ibid.*

39 *Ibid.*

40 *Ibid.*

41 *Ibid.*

42 Macquarie to Colin Anderson, Letterbooks, 7 to 8 May 1796, Vol. Z A788, State Library of New South Wales.

43 *Ibid.*

44 *Ibid.*

45 Lachlan Macquarie to Samuel Auchmuty, 'Letter Book Commencing 16th June 1796 and Ending 28th July 1797', 16 June 1796, Vol. Z A789, Lachlan Macquarie and Macquarie Family Papers, State Library of New South Wales.

46 Lestock Wilson (1749-1821); Macquarie to Lestock Wilson, Letterbooks, 10 July 1796, *ibid.*

47 *Ibid.*

48 From Jane Macquarie's tombstone, Macquarie, Memoranda, Vol. Z A772, State Library of New South Wales, p. 220.

49 Macquarie to Dorothea Morley, Letterbooks, 24 October 1796, Vol. Z A789, State Library of New South Wales.

50 Then known as the Canton River and also by its Chinese name, Zhujiang.

51 James Drummond, later Lord Strathallan (1767–1851).

52 Macquarie to Dorothea Morley, Letterbooks, 24 October 1796, Vol. Z A789, State Library of New South Wales.

53 *Ibid.*

54 *Ibid.*

Chapter 12

1 Macquarie to George Jarvis, Letterbooks, 24 August 1796, Vol. Z A789, State Library of New South Wales.

2 Macquarie to Dorothea Morley, Letterbooks, 24 October 1796, Vol. Z A789, State Library of New South Wales.

3 *Ibid.*

4 Macquarie to George Jarvis, Letterbooks, 24 August 1796, Vol. Z A789, State Library of New South Wales.

5 Sarah Morley, born 15 April 1776, Bombay, India; died 26 May 1854, Inverquharity, Scotland.

6 *Parliamentary Papers: 1780–1849, Volume 8*, House of Commons, Great Britain, H.M. Stationery Office, 1840, p. 609.

7 Macquarie to Dorothea Morley, Letterbooks, 24 October 1796, Vol. Z A789, State Library of New South Wales.

8 Sailing from Columbo to China under full sail with a cargo of cotton and sandalwood on 1 July 1805, McIntosh encountered a French attack and, to save his crew, was forced to run the *Sarah* into the breakers north of Point de Galle, where she was wrecked.

9   Macquarie to Dorothea Morley, Letterbooks, 24 October 1796, Vol. Z A789, State Library of New South Wales.

10   Stephen Meredyth Edwardes, *The Rise of Bombay: A Retrospect*, Cambridge University Press, 2011, p. 190.

11   The cemetery was closed in 1866 for new burials and, in 1961, was transformed into a children's park for the well-to-do.

12   *Bombay Courier*, 21 January 1797, republished in *Morning Chronicle* (London), Issue 8631, 13 September 1797, and *Gentleman's Magazine* (London), Vol. 67, Pt 2 (September 1797), p. 800.

13   Macquarie to John Forbes, Letterbooks, 22 January 1797, Vol. Z A789, State Library of New South Wales.

14   Macquarie to Cox and Greenwood, Letterbooks, 31 January 1797, *ibid.*

15   Macquarie to George Jarvis, Letterbooks, 10 December 1797, Vol. Z A790, State Library of New South Wales.

16   From Jane Macquarie's tombstone, Macquarie, Memoranda, Vol. Z A772, State Library of New South Wales. The last description of the tomb was recorded in about 1944 by the Scottish author R. W. Munro, before the tomb was demolished.

17   Macquarie to John Forbes, Letterbooks, 25 April 1797 Vol. Z A789, State Library of New South Wales.

18   From Jane Macquarie's tombstone, Macquarie, Memoranda, Vol. Z A772, State Library of New South Wales.

19   Drawn up by Mr Phineas Hall and signed at Calicut on 5 May 1795, *ibid.*

20   Macquarie to George Jarvis, Letterbooks, 12 February 1798, Vol. Z A790, State Library of New South Wales.

21   Macquarie to Dorothea Morley, Letterbooks, 18 August 1797, *ibid.*

22   Macquarie to Charles Macquarie, Letterbooks, 31 January 1797, *ibid.*

23   Macquarie to Dorothea Morley, Letterbooks, 13 February 1798, *ibid.*

24   Macquarie to Murdoch Maclaine, Letterbooks, 15 December 1798, *ibid.*

25   *Ibid.*

26   Macquarie to John Forbes, Letterbooks, 25 April 1797, Vol. Z A789, State Library of New South Wales.

27   Macquarie to Dorothea Morley, Letterbooks, 13 February 1798, Vol. Z A790, State Library of New South Wales.

28   Jonathan Duncan, born 15 May 1756; died 11 August 1811; Governor of Bombay from 27 December 1795 until his death.

29   Pazhassi Raja, also known as Cotiote Rajah and Pychy Rajah, born 3 January 1753 (as Kerala Varma); died 30 November 1805.

30   Harald Fischer-Tiné and Michael Mann, *Colonialism as Civilizing Mission: Cultural Ideology in British India*, Anthem Press, 2004, p. 60.

31   Major Donald Cameron, born 1754, Salachry, Argyll, Scotland; died 20 March 1797, Periya Pass, India.

32   Macquarie, Journals, 5 May 1797, Vol. Z A769-1, Item 1, State Library of New South Wales.

33   Henry Waterhouse (1770–1812).

34   William Kent (1760–1812).

35   Macquarie, Journals, 18 June 1788, Vol. Z A768-2, Item 1, State Library of New South Wales.

36   On 25 October 1795, at his house Schoonder Sight.

37   J.A. Mallett, 'Famous Sheep Breeds: The Merino', *Journal of the Department of Agriculture, Western Australia*, Series 4, Vol. 1, No. 1 (January 1960), Article 6, researchlibrary.agric. wa.gov.au/journal_agriculture4/vol1/iss1/6, p. 35.

38   Kent's *Supply* arrived back in Port Jackson on 16 May 1797; *Reliance*, commanded by Waterhouse, arrived on 26 June 1797.

39 Macquarie to George Jarvis, Letterbooks, 7 May 1797, Vol. Z A789, State Library of New South Wales.

40 *Ibid.*

41 *Ibid.*

42 Macquarie, Journals, 3 May 1797, Vol. Z A769-1, Item 1, State Library of New South Wales.

43 Macquarie, Journals, 12 May 1797, *ibid.*

44 Macquarie, Journals, 9 May 1797, *ibid.*

45 *Ibid.*

46 *Ibid.*

47 Macquarie, Journals, 10 May 1797, Vol. Z A769-1, Item 1, State Library of New South Wales.

48 *Ibid.*

49 Macquarie, Journals, 12 May 1797, Vol. Z A769-1, Item 1, State Library of New South Wales.

50 Macquarie, Journals, 14 May 1797, *ibid.*

51 *Ibid.*

52 *Ibid.*

53 Field Marshal Arthur Wellesley, 1st Duke of Wellington from 1814, Prime Minister of the United Kingdom 1828–1830 and 1834, born 1 May 1769; died 14 September 1852.

54 Macquarie, Journals, 22 May 1797, Vol. Z A769-1, Item 1, State Library of New South Wales.

55 Macquarie to George Jarvis, Letterbooks, 1 June 1797, Vol. Z A789, State Library of New South Wales.

56 Macquarie to Dorothea Morley, Letterbooks, 18 August 1797, Vol. Z A790, State Library of New South Wales.

57 Macquarie to Charles Macquarie, Letterbooks, 24 August 1797, *ibid.*

58 *Ibid.*

59 *Ibid.*

60 Lieutenant-General Sir John Abercromby (2 April 1772 – 14 February 1817).

61 Macquarie to Jane Maclaine, Letterbooks, 15 December 1798, Vol. Z A790, State Library of New South Wales.

62 Macquarie, Journals, 9 January 1798, Vol. Z A769-1, Item 1, State Library of New South Wales.

63 Macquarie to Colin Anderson, Letterbooks, 25 April 1797, Vol. Z A789, State Library of New South Wales.

64 Macquarie to Jane Maclaine, Letterbooks, 15 December 1798, Vol. Z A790, State Library of New South Wales.

65 *Ibid.*

66 *Ibid.*

67 Macquarie to Alexander Duncan, Letterbooks, 13 December 1798, Vol. Z A790, State Library of New South Wales.

68 Macquarie to Jane Maclaine, Letterbooks, 27 January 1799, *ibid.*

69 Richard Colley Wellesley, 1st Marquess Wellesley, born 20 June 1760; died 26 September 1842. Brother of the Duke of Wellington.

70 Lachlan Macquarie, 'Major Macquarie's Journal of the Campaign & Capture of Seringapatam', Notes for Journal, 19 February 1799, Vol. Z A769-2, Lachlan Macquarie and Macquarie Family Papers, State Library of New South Wales, pp. 5–27.

71 Macquarie to Charles Macquarie, Letterbooks, 9 February 1799, Vol. Z A790, State Library of New South Wales.

72 George Harris, 1st Baron Harris, born 18 March 1746; died 19 May 1829.

73 Charles Hilbert, 'The Fall of Seringapatam', 16 January 2019, warfarehistorynetwork.com/daily.

74 Macquarie to Lieutenant-Colonel Cliffe, Adjutant-General, Calcutta, Letterbooks, 15 March 1799, Vol. Z A790, State Library of New South Wales.

75 *Ibid.*

76 *Ibid.*

77 John Montresor, born New York, 11 November 1768; died Penang, East Indies; buried there 9 September 1805. From Bernard Burke, *A Genealogical and Heraldic History of the Landed Gentry of Great Britain & Ireland, Vol. II,* Harrison & Sons, 1898.

78 Macquarie to Lieutenant-Colonel Cliffe, Letterbooks, 15 March 1799, Vol. Z A790, State Library of New South Wales.

79 Macquarie to Lieut. Colonel Cliffe, Adjt. Genl. H. M. Forces, Calcutta., Letterbooks, 15 March 1799, Vol. Z A790, State Library of New South Wales.

80 Macquarie, Journals, 16 April 1799, Vol. Z A769-2, State Library of New South Wales.

81 Macquarie, Journals, 18 April 1799, *ibid.*

82 Macquarie, Journals, 2 May 1799, *ibid.*

83 Alexander Beatson, *A View of the Origin and Conduct of the War with Tippoo Sultaun; Comprising a Narrative of the Operations of the Army Under the Command of Lieutenant-General George Harris, and of the Siege of Seringapatam,* G. & W. Nichol, 1800, Appendix XLII, pp. cxxvii–cxxxi.

84 Later General Sir David Baird, 1st Baronet, born 6 December 1757; died 18 August 1829.

85 Major Alexander Allan (1764–1820).

86 Alexander Beatson, *A View of the Origin and Conduct of the War with Tippoo Sultaun: Comprising a Narrative of the Operations of the Army Under the Command of Lieutenant-General George Harris, and of the Siege of Seringapatam,* G. & W. Nichol, 1800, Appendix No. XLII, pp. cxxvii–cxxxi.

87 Charles Forbes (1773–1849).

88 Macquarie, Journals, 4 May 1799, Vol. Z A769-2, State Library of New South Wales.

89 Macquarie to Dorothea Morley, Letterbooks, 25 June 1799, Vol. Z A790, State Library of New South Wales.

90 Macquarie to Charles Macquarie, Letterbooks, 12 October 1800, *ibid.*

91 Macquarie, Journals, 18 July 1799, Vol. Z A769-1, Item 1, State Library of New South Wales.

92 Field Marshal Sir Alured Clarke, born 24 November 1744; died 16 September 1832.

93 Lachlan Macquarie, 'Journal – No. 4 Kept by L. Macquarie Commencing 28th Septr. 1799; & Ending 11th of Septr. 1801', 2 October 1799, Vol. Z A769-1, Item 2, Lachlan Macquarie and Macquarie Family Papers, State Library of New South Wales, pp. 398–405.

94 Edward Clive, (7 March 1754 – 16 May 1839), known as the Lord Clive.

95 Macquarie to Charles Macquarie, Letterbooks, 12 October 1800, Vol. Z A790, State Library of New South Wales.

96 *Ibid.*

97 Nancy Gardner Cassels, *Social Legislation of the East India Company,* SAGE Publications India, 2010, pp. 114–115.

98 Macquarie, Journals, 5 May 1800, Vol. Z A769-1, Item 2, State Library of New South Wales.

99 *Ibid.*

100 Macquarie, Journals, 13 May 1800, Vol. Z A769-1, Item 2, State Library of New South Wales.

101 Macquarie, Journals, 21 July 1800, *ibid.*

102 Macquarie, Journals, 18 September 1800, *ibid.*

103 Macquarie, Journals, 6 November 1800, *ibid.*

104 Macquarie, Journals, 30 March 1801, *ibid.*

105 Macquarie, Journals, 31 March 1801, *ibid.*

106 John William Cole, *Memoirs of British Generals Distinguished During the Peninsular War,* R. Bentley, 1856, p. 68.

107 Arthur Wellesley to Lieutenant-Colonel Campbell, 10 May 1801, Duke of Wellington (ed.), *Supplementary Dispatches and Memoranda of Field Marshal Arthur Duke of Wellington, K.G., India, 1797–1805, Volume the Second (June 6, 1800 – Dec. 11, 1804),* John Murray, 1858, p. 381.

Chapter 13

1   Macquarie, Journals, 1 September 1801, Vol. Z A769-1, Item 2, State Library of New South Wales.

2   General Sir Ralph Abercromby, born 7 October 1734; died 28 March 1801.

3   Macquarie, Journals, Vol. Z A769-1, Item 2, State Library of New South Wales.

4   Macquarie to Lestock Wilson, Letterbooks, 24 January 1802, Vol. Z A790, State Library of New South Wales.

5   Now called Abu Qir.

6   Lieutenant-General Sir John Moore, born 13 November 1761; died 16 January 1809.

7   Lachlan Macquarie, 'Journal – No. 5 Kept by L. Macquarie Commencing 12 Sept. 1801; & Ending the 14th July 1804', 5 October 1801, Vol. Z A770, Item 1, Lachlan Macquarie and Macquarie Family Papers, State Library of New South Wales, pp. 73–84.

8   Lieutenant-General Sir Hildebrand Oakes, 1st Baronet, born 19 January 1754; died 9 September 1822.

9   At his country estate in Bath, England, on 22 February 1798, aged fifty-five.

10   Macquarie to Dorothea Morley, Letterbooks, 28 February 1802, Vol. Z A790, State Library of New South Wales.

11   Prince Frederick Augustus, Duke of York and Albany, born 16 August 1763; died 5 January 1827.

12   Sir James McGrigor, 1st Baronet, born 9 April 1771; died 2 April 1858.

13   James McGrigor, *Medical Sketches of the Expedition to Egypt from India*, J. Murray, 1804, p. 37.

14   *Ibid*, p. 52.

15   *Ibid*, p. 179.

16   Macquarie to Charles Macquarie, Letterbooks, 10 August 1802, Vol. Z A790, State Library of New South Wales.

17   Macquarie to Dorothea Morley, Letterbooks, *ibid*.

18   Macquarie, Journals, Vol. Z A769-1, Item 2, State Library of New South Wales.

19   Macquarie, Journals, 21 March 1802, Vol. Z A770, Item 1, State Library of New South Wales.

20   Macquarie, Journals, 20 July 1802, Vol. Z A770, Item 1, State Library of New South Wales.

21   Lachlan Macquarie to Josef von Wredé, 'Letterbook 13 September to 4 December 1802', 24 September 1802, Vol. Z A791, Lachlan Macquarie and Macquarie Family Papers, State Library of New South Wales.

22   Macquarie, Journals, 1 January 1803, *ibid*.

23   Macquarie, Journals, 30 December 1802, *ibid*.

24   Macquarie, Journals, 6 January 1803, *ibid*.

25   Macquarie, Journals, 5 March 1803, *ibid*.

26   On 21 February 1803.

27   Macquarie, Journals, 7 March 1803, *ibid*.

28   Macquarie, Journals, 24 March 1803, *ibid*.

29   Robert Patton (1743–1812).

30   Sarah Torrens, née Patton (1781–1863).

31   Later Major-General Sir Henry Torrens (1779–1828).

32   Macquarie, Journals, 4 May 1803, *ibid*.

33   Macquarie, Journals, 13 April 1803, *ibid*.

34   *Ibid*.

35   *Ibid*.

36   Tom Taylor, *Leicester Square: Its Associations and Its Worthies*, Bickers and Son, 1874, p. 339.

37   Macquarie, Journals, 8 May 1803, Vol. Z A770, Item 1, State Library of New South Wales.

38   Macquarie to Murdoch Maclaine, Letterbooks, 5 May 1803, Vol. Z A792, State Library of New South Wales.

39   Macquarie to Dorothea Morley, Letterbooks, 5 May 1803, *ibid*.

40 Macquarie, Journals, 18 May 1803, Vol. Z A770, Item 1, State Library of New South Wales.
41 Macquarie, Journals, 26 May 1803, *ibid.*
42 Macquarie to Charlotte, Queen Consort of King George III, 8 September 1803, Letterbooks, Vol. Z A792, State Library of New South Wales.
43 Robert Hobart, 4th Earl of Buckinghamshire, born 6 May 1760; died 4 February 1816.
44 Macquarie, Journals, 13 July 1803, Vol. Z A770, Item 1, State Library of New South Wales.
45 General Charles Stanhope, 3rd Earl of Harrington (17 March 1753 – 5 September 1829).
46 Macquarie, Journals, 24 July 1803, *ibid.*
47 Macquarie, Journals, 25 July 1803, *ibid.*
48 Macquarie, Journals, 22 July and 3 August 1803, *ibid.*
49 Macquarie to Charles Reeve, Letterbooks, 17 December 1803, Vol. Z A792, State Library of New South Wales.
50 Lachlan Macquarie, 'Journal 15 July 1804 to 16 March 1807', 10 April 1805, Vol. Z A770, Item 2, Lachlan Macquarie and Macquarie Family Papers, State Library of New South Wales, pp. 198–233. The painting is at the State Library of NSW.
51 Macquarie, Journals, 22 December 1803, Vol. Z A770, Item 1, State Library of New South Wales.
52 Macquarie, Journals, 1 January 1804, *ibid.*

Chapter 14
1 Macquarie, Journals, 20 August 1804, Vol. Z A770, Item 2, State Library of New South Wales.
2 Macquarie, Journals, 21 May 1804, Vol. Z A770, Item 1, State Library of New South Wales.
3 Macquarie, Journals, 28 May 1804, *ibid.*
4 Macquarie, Journals, 31 May 1804, *ibid.*
5 Macquarie, Journals, 1 June 1804, *ibid.*
6 Macquarie, Journals, 7 June 1804, *ibid.*
7 Christiana Scott, née Jarvis (1765–1842).
8 Lieutenant-Colonel John Campbell, 6th Baronet of Airds and Ardnamuchan, born 15 March 1767; died 7 November 1834.
9 Macquarie, Journals, 22 June 1804, Vol. Z A770, Item 1, State Library of New South Wales.
10 Macquarie described Elizabeth as 'the youngest daughter of my late second cousin John Campbell Esqr. of Airds in Argyleshire'. Macquarie, Journals, 26 March 1805, Vol. Z A770, Item 2, State Library of New South Wales.
11 John Maclaine (1792–1818).
12 Murdoch Maclaine, 19th Laird of Lochbuie, born 1 August 1791; died 20 August 1844.
13 Macquarie, Journals, 22 June 1804, Vol. Z A770, Item 1, State Library of New South Wales.
14 Macquarie, Journals, 24 to 26 June 1804, *ibid.*
15 Macquarie, Journals, 1 July 1804, *ibid.*
16 Macquarie, Journals, 27 June 1804, *ibid.*
17 Macquarie to Murdoch Maclaine, 4 April 1788, MS 772, Item 4, National Library of Australia.
18 Macquarie, Journals, 27 June 1804, Vol. Z A770, Item 1, State Library of New South Wales.
19 Macquarie, Journals, 29 June 1804, *ibid.*
20 Macquarie to Murdoch Maclaine, 4 April 1788, MS 772, Item 4, National Library of Australia.
21 Macquarie, Journals, 22 June 1804, Vol. Z A770, Item 1, State Library of New South Wales.
22 Macquarie, Journals, 3 July 1804, *ibid.*
23 Macquarie, Journals, 5 July 1804, *ibid.*
24 Macquarie, Journals, 6 July 1804, *ibid.*
25 Hector Maclaine (1783–1803).
26 On 23 June 1803.

27 Macquarie, Journals, 22 February 1804, Vol. Z A770, Item 1, State Library of New South Wales.

28 Hugh Maclaine, also known as Murdoch Hugh Maclaine (1781–1828). Not to be confused with his brother Murdoch Maclaine (1774-1822).

29 Macquarie, Journals, 6 July 1804, Vol. Z A770, Item 1, State Library of New South Wales.

30 Macquarie, Journals, 10 July 1804, *ibid.*

31 Macquarie, Journals, 16 July 1804, Vol. Z A770, Item 2, State Library of New South Wales.

32 *Ibid.*

33 *Ibid.*

34 Macquarie, Journals, 27 July 1804, Vol. Z A770, Item 2, State Library of New South Wales.

35 'Further Particulars of the Late Insurrection at Botany Bay', *Manchester Mercury*, 14 August 1804, p. 2.

36 Tom Dunne, *Rebellions: Memoir, Memory and 1798*, Lilliput Press, 2004.

37 'Insurrection', *Sydney Gazette and New South Wales Advertiser*, 11 March 1804, p. 2.

38 Colonel William Paterson, born 17 August 1755; died 21 June 1810.

39 Elizabeth Macarthur to John Piper, 15 April 1804, SAFE/A 254–256, Captain John Piper Papers and Correspondence 1790–1845, State Library of New South Wales.

40 Captain Philip Gidley King, born 23 April 1758; died 3 September 1808.

41 Later Lieutenant-Colonel George Johnston, born 19 March 1764; died 5 January 1823.

42 'The Johnston Family', *Illustrated Sydney News*, 19 December 1891, p. 20.

43 The site is commemorated at Castlebrook Memorial Park, Rouse Hill.

44 Thomas Anlezark (1765–1834).

45 'Insurrection', *Sydney Gazette and New South Wales Advertiser*, 11 March 1804, p. 2.

46 Macquarie, Journals, 30 July 1804, Vol. Z A770, Item 2, State Library of New South Wales.

47 Macquarie, Journals, 7 August 1804, *ibid.*

48 Macquarie, Journals, 25 August 1804, *ibid.*

49 Hector Macquarie (1794–1845).

50 Macquarie, Journals, 25 August 1804, Vol. Z A770, Item 2, State Library of New South Wales.

51 Macquarie, Journals, 23 August 1804, *ibid.*

52 Macquarie, Journals, 10 March 1804, Vol. Z A770, Item 1, State Library of New South Wales.

53 Later General Sir William Henry Clinton, born 23 December 1769; died 15 February 1846.

54 Macquarie to William Clinton, Letterbooks, 5 September 1803, Vol. Z A792, State Library of New South Wales.

55 Macquarie, Journals, 3 March 1804, Vol. Z A770, Item 1, State Library of New South Wales.

56 Macquarie, Journals, 10 March 1804, *ibid.*

57 Macquarie, Journals, 20 August 1804, Vol. Z A770, Item 2, State Library of New South Wales.

58 *Ibid.*

59 Macquarie, Journals, 21 August 1804, Vol. Z A770, Item 2, State Library of New South Wales.

60 *Ibid.*

61 Lachlan Macquarie to Master Murdoch Maclaine, 'Letterbook 1 March 1804 to 15 May 1807', 16 November 1804, Vol. Z A793, Lachlan Macquarie and Macquarie Family Papers, State Library of New South Wales.

62 Macquarie, Journals, 28 August 1804, Vol. Z A770, Item 2, State Library of New South Wales.

63 Macquarie, Journals, 30 August 1804, *ibid.*

64 *Ibid.*

65 Later Lieutenant-General John Campbell, 4th Earl of Breadalbane (30 March 1762 – 29 March 1834). In 1831, he was made 1st Marquess of Breadalbane.

66 Macquarie, Journals, 8 January 1805, Vol. Z A770, Item 2, State Library of New South Wales.

67 Major-General Calvert to Macquarie, Letterbooks, 11 February 1805, Vol. Z A793, State Library of New South Wales.

68 Macquarie, Journals, 15 March 1805, Vol. Z A770, Item 2, State Library of New South Wales.

69 *Ibid.*
70 *Ibid.*
71 *Ibid.*
72 Macquarie, Journals, 26 March 1805, Vol. Z A770, Item 2, State Library of New South Wales.
73 *Ibid.*
74 *Ibid.*
75 *Ibid.*
76 *Ibid.*
77 Macquarie, Journals, 9 March 1805, Vol. Z A770, Item 2, State Library of New South Wales.
78 Macquarie, Journals, 10 March 1805, *ibid.*
79 Macquarie, Journals, 21 April 1805, *ibid.*
80 Macquarie, Journals, 20 April 1805, *ibid.*
81 *Ibid.*

Chapter 15
1   Macquarie to Earl of Breadalbane, Letterbooks, 20 September 1805, Vol. Z A793, State Library of New South Wales.
2   Genesis 2 to 3.
3   Lachlan Macquarie, 'Journal Commencing at Bombay on Wednesday 18th of March 1807 – by Lt. Colonel McQuarie H.M. 73rd Reg.t', 29 April 1807, Vol. Z A771, Lachlan Macquarie and Macquarie Family Papers, State Library of New South Wales, pp. 1–5.
4   Macquarie, Journals, 21 April 1805, Vol. Z A770, Item 2, State Library of New South Wales.
5   Macquarie to Earl of Breadalbane, Letterbooks, 20 September 1805, Vol. Z A793, State Library of New South Wales.
6   *Ibid.*
7   Macquarie, Journals, 8 April 1805, Vol. Z A770, Item 2, State Library of New South Wales.
8   Macquarie, Journals, 24 April 1805, *ibid.*
9   Macquarie, Journals, 25 April 1805, *ibid.*
10 Macquarie, Journals, 21 June 1805, *ibid.*
11 Later General Sir Ralph Darling, born 1772, Ireland; died 2 April 1858, Brighton, England.
12 Governor of New South Wales from 1825 to 1831.
13 The *Candidate* sank on 28 July 1804.
14 Macquarie, Journals, 11 August 1805, Vol. Z A770, Item 2, State Library of New South Wales.
15 Macquarie, Journals, 12 August 1805, *ibid.*
16 Macquarie, Journals, 16 August 1805, *ibid.*
17 Macquarie, Journals, 18 August 1805, *ibid.*
18 Macquarie, Journals, 25 October 1805, *ibid.*
19 *Ibid.*
20 Yashwantrao Holkar (1776–1811).
21 Macquarie, Journals, 25 October 1805, Vol. Z A770, Item 2, State Library of New South Wales.
22 Macquarie, Journals, 7 November 1805, *ibid.*
23 Now called Varanasi.
24 Macquarie, Journals, 7 November 1805, Vol. Z A770, Item 2, State Library of New South Wales.
25 Now known respectively as the Narmada River, the Fort of Bharuch and the province of Gujarat.
26 Now known as Vadodara.
27 Macquarie, Journals, 30 November 1805, Vol. Z A770, Item 2, State Library of New South Wales. The city is now known as Dahod.
28 Macquarie, Journals, 1 December, *ibid.*

29 Macquarie, Journals, 13 December 1805, *ibid.*

30 Macquarie, Journals, 14 December 1805, *ibid.*

31 Macquarie spelled it 'killedar'.

32 Macquarie, Journals, 11 December 1805, Vol. Z A770, Item 2, State Library of New South Wales.

33 Macquarie to Jonathan Duncan, Letterbooks, 14 July 1806, Vol. Z A793, State Library of New South Wales.

34 Macquarie to Elizabeth Campbell, Letterbooks, 2 November 1805, *ibid.*

35 Macquarie to Elizabeth Campbell, Letterbooks, 28 September 1805, *ibid.*

36 Macquarie, Journals, 9 July 1806, Vol. Z A770, Item 2, State Library of New South Wales.

37 Macquarie to Jane Stewart, 28 September 1805, Vol. Z A793, State Library of New South Wales.

38 Macquarie to C.C. McIntosh, Letterbooks, 22 May 1806, Vol. Z A793, State Library of New South Wales.

39 Following Arthur Phillip (1788–1792), John Hunter (1795–1800) and Philip Gidley King (1800–1806).

40 Rob Mundle, *Bligh: Master Mariner*, Hachette Australia, 2010.

41 Herbert Vere Evatt, *Rum Rebellion: A Study of the Overthrow of Governor Bligh by John Macarthur and the New South Wales Corps*, Angus & Robertson, 1965, p. 140.

42 Macquarie, Journals, 18 October 1806, Vol. Z A770, Item 2, State Library of New South Wales.

43 Macquarie, Journals, 15 January 1807, *ibid.*

44 Macquarie to Samuel Manesty, Letterbooks, 6 October 1806, Vol. Z A793, State Library of New South Wales.

45 Macquarie to Samuel Manesty, Letterbooks, 16 January 1807, *ibid.*

46 Macquarie, Journals, 15 January 1807, Vol. Z A770, Item 2, State Library of New South Wales.

47 Macquarie, Journals, 1 January 1807, *ibid.*

48 Macquarie to Louisa Macquarie, Letterbooks, 26 March 1804, Vol. Z A793, State Library of New South Wales.

49 Macquarie, Journals, 18 February 1807, Vol. Z A770, Item 2, State Library of New South Wales.

50 *Ibid.*

51 Macquarie, Journals, 23 February 1807, Vol. Z A770, Item 2, State Library of New South Wales.

52 Macquarie, Journals, 16 March 1807, *ibid.*

53 Macquarie, Journals, 19 March 1807, Vol. Z A771, State Library of New South Wales.

54 Assistant-Surgeon William Thomas, died 1813.

55 Lieutenant George W. Brande (*c.* 1784–1854).

56 Macquarie, Journals, 18 March 1807, Vol. Z A771, State Library of New South Wales.

57 Now the Iranian city of Bushehr.

58 Macquarie, Journals, 16 April 1807, Vol. Z A771, State Library of New South Wales.

59 Macquarie, Journals, 21 April 1807, *ibid.*

60 *Ibid.*

61 Macquarie, Journals, 22 April 1807, Vol. Z A771, State Library of New South Wales.

62 Macquarie, Journals, 22 to 26 April 1807, *ibid.*

63 Macquarie, Journals, 27 April 1807, *ibid.*

64 Macquarie, Journals, 29 April 1807, *ibid.*

65 Macquarie, Journals, 1 May 1807, *ibid.*

66 Macquarie called it Tauhk Kaissera.

67 Macquarie, Journals, 9 May 1807, Vol. Z A771, State Library of New South Wales.

68   'Imperial Eyes: Lachlan Macquarie in Iraq, Iran, Russia & Denmark, 1807', Lachlan and
      Elizabeth Macquarie Archive, Macquarie University, Sydney, mq.edu.au/macquarie-archive.
69   Macquarie, Journals, 10 May 1807, Vol. Z A771, State Library of New South Wales.
70   Macquarie, Journals, 5 June 1807, *ibid.*
71   *Ibid*: 'Minas Mackeil … a very smart young man'.
72   Macquarie, Journals, 15 May 1807, Vol. Z A771, State Library of New South Wales.
73   *Ibid.*
74   Macquarie, Journals, 17 May 1807, Vol. Z A771, State Library of New South Wales.
75   Macquarie, Journals, 18 May 1807, *ibid.*
76   *Ibid.*
77   Also called the River Halwan.
78   Macquarie, Journals, 20 May 1807, Vol. Z A771, State Library of New South Wales.
79   Macquarie, Journals, 21 May 1807, *ibid.*
80   Macquarie, Journals, 29 May 1807, *ibid.*
81   Macquarie, Journals, 5 June 1807, *ibid.*
82   Macquarie, Journals, 13 June 1807, *ibid.*
83   Macquarie, Journals, 12 June 1807, *ibid.*
84   Macquarie, Journals, 18 June 1807, *ibid.*
85   Macquarie, Journals, 22 June 1807, *ibid.*
86   Macquarie, Journals, 28 June 1807, *ibid.*
87   Macquarie, Journals, 29 June 1807, *ibid.*
88   Macquarie, Journals, 30 June 1807, *ibid.*
89   Macquarie, Journals, 5 July 1807, *ibid.*
90   Macquarie, Journals, 15 July 1807, *ibid.*
91   Macquarie, Journals, 2 August 1807, *ibid.*
92   Macquarie, Journals, 22 August 1807, *ibid.*
93   Macquarie, Journals, 31 August 1807, *ibid.*
94   Macquarie, Journals, 23 August 1807, *ibid.*
95   Macquarie, Journals, 30 August 1807, *ibid.*
96   Macquarie, Journals, 31 August 1807, *ibid.*
97   *Ibid.*
98   Macquarie, Journals, 11 September 1807, Vol. Z A771, State Library of New South Wales.
99   Macquarie, Journals, 13 September 1807, *ibid.*
100   Macquarie, Journals, 6 September 1807, *ibid.*
101   Macquarie, Journals, 8 September 1807, *ibid.*
102   Macquarie, Journals, 6 September 1807, *ibid.*

Chapter 16

1   Lachlan Macquarie to Charles Forbes, 'Papers, 1809 to 1811', 13 February 1809, Vol. Z Safe
      1/51, Lachlan Macquarie and Macquarie Family Papers, State Library of New South Wales.
2   Mary Putland, née Bligh, later O'Connell (1783–1864).
3   Ellis Bent to his mother, 4 March 1810, Letters from Ellis Bent, MS 195/3, National
      Library of Australia, p. 89.
4   Joseph Short (*c.* 1760 – *c.* 1830).
5   William Bligh to Sir Joseph Banks, 1 April 1806, Sir Joseph Banks Papers, State Library of
      New South Wales.
6   William Bligh to Sir Joseph Banks, 15 March 1806, *ibid.*
7   William Windham, born 1750; died 4 June 1810.
8   William *Bligh to William Windham, 7 February 1807,* in Frederick Watson (ed.), *Historical
      Records of Australia, Series I: Governors' Despatches to and from England,* Volume VI: August,
      1806 – December, 1808, Library Committee of the Commonwealth Parliament, 1916, p. 124.

9   *Ibid.*
10 Philip Gidley King to Under-Secretary John King, 8 November 1801, Frederick Watson (ed.), *Historical Records of Australia, Series I: Governors' Despatches to and from England, Volume III: 1801–1802*, Library Committee of the Commonwealth Parliament, 1915, p. 322.
11 Thomas Jamison, born *c.* 1753; died 25 January 1811.
12 William *Bligh to* William *Windham, 31 October 1807,* Watson (ed.), *Historical Records of Australia*, Series I, Volume VI, p. 150.
13 *Ibid.*
14 William *Bligh to* William *Windham, 31 October 1807,* Watson (ed.), *Historical Records of Australia*, Series I, Volume VI, p. 152.
15 Macquarie, Journals, 11 September 1807, Vol. Z A771, State Library of New South Wales.
16 Tim Voelcker, *Admiral Saumarez Versus Napoleon: The Baltic, 1807–12*, Boydell & Brewer, 2008, p. 13.
17 Macquarie, Journals, 24 September 1807, Vol. Z A771, State Library of New South Wales.
18 *Ibid.*
19 Admiral of the Fleet James Gambier, 1st Baron Gambier, born 13 October 1756; died 19 April 1833.
20 Macquarie, Journals, 24 September 1807, Vol. Z A771, State Library of New South Wales.
21 Charles Boswell Norman, *Battle Honours of the British Army: From Tangier, 1662, to the Commencement of the Reign of King Edward VII*, John Murray, 1971, p. 13.
22 Macquarie, Journals, 24 September 1807, Vol. Z A771, State Library of New South Wales.
23 Macquarie, Journals, 25 September 1807, *ibid.*
24 Macquarie, Journals, 28 September 1807, *ibid.*
25 Macquarie, Journals, 29 September 1807, *ibid.*
26 Macquarie, Journals, 12 October 1807, *ibid.*
27 Macquarie, Journals, 17 October 1807, *ibid.*
28 George Canning, born 11 April 1770; died 8 August 1827. Prime Minister from April 1827 until his death.
29 Lachlan Macquarie, memorandum to George Canning, 'Copies of Private Letters written by Colonel L. Macquarie 73rd Regiment Commencing on 15th August 1808; and Ending …', 15 April 1809, Vol. Z A796, Lachlan Macquarie and Macquarie Family Papers, State Library of New South Wales.
30 Owen Lewis Meyrick (1739–1819).
31 Certified copy of marriage certificate of Lachlan Macquarie and Elizabeth Henrietta Campbell, 3 November 1807, AM 17, Item 28(b), Miscellaneous Papers Relating to Lachlan Macquarie, 1799–1941, State Library of New South Wales.
32 Holy Bible, vol. 1 (Edinburgh, 1803), B 1686 vol. 1, and Book of Common Prayer (London, 1812), B 1686 vol. 3, Macquarie Family Bibles 1762–1824, State Library of New South Wales.
33 Genesis 2:24.
34 John 3:3, King James Bible.
35 Macquarie, Memoranda, 20 January 1809, Vol. Z A772, State Library of New South Wales.
36 Jonathan Duncan, the younger (1799–1865).
37 Macquarie to Charles Forbes, Letterbooks, 23 April 1807, Vol. Z A793, State Library of New South Wales; Macquarie to Jonathan Duncan, 15 May 1807, *ibid.*
38 Lachlan Macquarie to Duke of York, 'Copies of Letters etc. From 1st Dec. 1807 to 31st March 1809', 10 March 1808, Vol. Z A795, Lachlan Macquarie and Macquarie Family Papers, State Library of New South Wales.
39 Macquarie to William Harcourt, Letterbooks, 6 September 1808, *ibid.*
40 Macquarie to Dugald McTavish, Letterbooks, 15 August 1808, Vol. Z A796, State Library of New South Wales.

41 *Ibid.*

42 *Ibid.*

43 Macquarie to Dugald McTavish, Letterbooks, 10 January 1809, Vol. Z A796, State Library of New South Wales.

44 'Scotland, Select Births and Baptisms, 1564–1950', Family History Library film no. 1040159, FamilySearch, familysearch.org.

45 John Blaxland (1769–1845).

46 John Blaxland to Earl of Liverpool, 27 November 1809, F.M. Baden (ed.), *Historical Records of New South Wales, Vol. VII – Bligh and Macquarie, 1809, 1810, 1811*, W.A. Gullick, Government Printer, 1901, p. 237.

47 *Ibid.*

48 *Ibid.*

49 William Bligh to Viscount Castlereagh, 30 April 1808, F.M. Baden (ed.), *Historical Records of New South Wales, Vol. VI – King and Bligh, 1806, 1807, 1808*, W.A. Gullick, Government Printer, 1898, p. 608.

50 *Ibid*, p. 610.

51 *Ibid*, p. 611.

52 *Ibid*, p. 613.

53 *Ibid*, p. 615.

54 *Ibid*, p. 617.

55 'Arrest of Governor Bligh, January 26, 1808', New South Wales Government Printer, copy of the original manuscript documents, A 1982, State Library of New South Wales.

56 William Bligh to Viscount Castlereagh, 30 April 1808, Baden (ed.), *Historical Records of New South Wales, Vol. VI*, p. 617.

57 Robert Stewart, 2nd Marquess of Londonderry, Viscount Castlereagh, born Dublin, Ireland, 18 June 1769; died Woollet Hall, Kent, England, 12 August 1822.

58 'Arrest of Governor Bligh', *Clarence and Richmond Examiner and New England Advertiser* (Grafton, New South Wales), 24 January 1888, p. 3.

59 *Ibid*, p. 618.

60 William Bligh to Viscount Castlereagh, 30 April 1808, Baden (ed.), *Historical Records of New South Wales, Vol. VI*, p. 617.

61 Joseph Foveaux (1767–1846).

62 Lachlan Macquarie, Memoranda, 22 December 1808, Vol. Z A772, State Library of New South Wales.

63 Sir Edward Macarthur (1789–1872).

64 A.J. Hill, 'Macarthur, Sir Edward (1789–1872)', *Australian Dictionary of Biography*, National Centre of Biography, Australian National University, adb.anu.edu.au, published first in hard copy 1974.

65 General Sir Miles Nightingall, born 25 December 1768; died 12 September 1829.

66 Sir Lionel Darell (1742–1803).

67 Macquarie, Memoranda, Memoranda, 20 January 1809, Vol. Z A772, State Library of New South Wales.

68 Joseph Bigge, also known as Joseph Bigg (1768–1833). Bigge had previously driven for Stephen Rolleston, Second Chief Clerk (1804–1817) then First Chief Clerk (1817–1824) of the Foreign Office.

69 Macquarie, Memoranda, 6 February 1809, Vol. Z A772, State Library of New South Wales.

70 Macquarie, Memoranda, 28 February 1809, *ibid*.

71 Lachlan Macquarie to Charles Forbes, 'Papers, 1809 to 1821 and *c.* 1824', 22 April 1809, Vol. Z Safe 1/53, Lachlan Macquarie and Macquarie Family Papers, State Library of New South Wales.

72   Macquarie to Charles Forbes, 13 February 1809, Papers, Vol. Z Safe 1/51, State Library of
      New South Wales. Macquarie said it was *twenty-five* years in India and only *two* at home.
73   Henry Colden Antill (1779–1852).
74   J.M. Antill, 'Antill, Henry Colden (1779–1852)', *Australian Dictionary of Biography*,
      National Centre of Biography, Australian National University, adb.anu.edu.au, published
      first in hard copy 1966.
75   Michael Glover, 'The Nightingall Letters', *Journal of the Society for Army Historical Research*,
      Vol. 51, No. 207 (Autumn 1973), p. 129.
76   Later Lieutenant-General Francis Grose (1758–1814).
77   Macquarie to Viscount Castlereagh, Letterbooks, 11 April 1809, Vol. Z A796, State
      Library of New South Wales.
78   Macquarie to Charles Forbes, 22 April 1809, Papers, Vol. Z Safe 1/53, State Library of
      New South Wales.
79   *Ibid*. The *Dromedary* was a teak-built Indian mercantile vessel built in 1799 and originally
      named the *Kaikusroo*. She was bought in 1805 to serve as a forty-gun frigate and renamed
      HMS *Howe*. In 1806, the Admiralty fitted her out as a twenty-four gun store ship and
      renamed her HMS *Dromedary*.
80   Macquarie to Viscount Castlereagh, Letterbooks, 1 May 1809, Vol. Z A796, State Library
      of New South Wales; Macquarie, Memoranda, 27 April 1809, Vol. Z A772, State Library
      of New South Wales, p. 3.

Chapter 17

1   Elizabeth Macquarie, 'Elizabeth Macquarie's Journal, 1809', 3 August 1809, Vol. Z C126,
      Lachlan Macquarie and Macquarie Family Papers, State Library of New South Wales,
      pp. 1–111.
2   Viscount Castlereagh to Macquarie, Dispatches 1 to 4, 13 to 14 May 1809, Frederick
      Watson (ed.), *Historical Records of Australia, Series I: Governors' Despatches to and
      from England, Volume VII: January, 1809 – June, 1813*, Library Committee of the
      Commonwealth Parliament, 1916, pp. 79–85.
3   Macquarie to Edward Cooke, Letterbooks, Vol. Z A796, State Library of New South Wales.
4   Elizabeth Macquarie, Journal, 15 May 1809, Vol. Z C126, State Library of New South Wales.
5   Sir Joseph Banks to Macquarie, 13 May 1809, SAFE/Banks Papers/Series 44.01, Sir
      Joseph Banks Papers, State Library of New South Wales.
6   Field Marshal Henry William Paget, Lord Uxbridge, born 17 May 1768; died 29 April 1854.
7   Nicholas Bayly (1770–1823).
8   Samuel Perkins Pritchard (*c.* 1750–1813).
9   HMS *Hindostan* (also spelled *Hindustan* or *Hindoostan*) was a fifty-gun warship. She was
      originally a teak-built East Indiaman named *Admiral Rainier*, launched at Calcutta in
      1799, and was brought into the service of the Royal Navy in May 1804.
10   Later Rear-Admiral John Pasco (1774–1853).
11   Roy Adkins, *Trafalgar: The Biography of a Battle*, Hachette UK, 2011.
12   Sir Maurice Charles O'Connell (1768–1848).
13   Macquarie, Memoranda, 24 May 1809, Vol. Z A772, State Library of New South Wales.
14   Rebecca Pasco, née Penfold (1785–1841).
15   Henry Colden Antill, *Early History of New South Wales: Two Old Journals – Being the Diaries
      of Major H.C. Antill on the Voyage to New South Wales in 1809, and on a Trip Across the Blue
      Mountains in 1815*, W.A. Gullick, Government Printer, 1914, 29 May 1809.
16   Elizabeth Macquarie, Journal, 12 June 1809, Vol. Z C126, State Library of New South Wales.
17   *Ibid*, 16 June 1809.
18   *Ibid*.
19   Macquarie, Memoranda, 22 June 1809, Vol. Z A772, State Library of New South Wales.

20 Elizabeth Macquarie, Journal, 5 July 1809, Vol. Z C126, State Library of New South Wales.
21 *Ibid.*
22 *Ibid.*
23 Antill, *Early History of New South Wales: Two Old Journals*, 3 August 1809.
24 Elizabeth Macquarie, Journal, 5 July 1809, Vol. Z C126, State Library of New South Wales.
25 *Ibid.*
26 *Ibid.*
27 Elizabeth Macquarie, Journal, 5 August 1809, Vol. Z C126, State Library of New South Wales.
28 Macquarie, Memoranda, 1 September 1809, Vol. Z A772, State Library of New South Wales.
29 Elizabeth Macquarie, Journal, 31 August 1809, Vol. Z C126, State Library of New South Wales.
30 *Ibid*, 7 August 1809.
31 John Macarthur to Elizabeth Macarthur, 3 August 1810, Watson (ed.), *Historical Records of Australia, Series I, Volume VII*, p. 399.
32 John Harris, born 1754, Moneymore, Londonderry, Ireland; died 27 April 1838, New South Wales.
33 Elizabeth Macquarie, Journal, 31 August 1809, Vol. Z C126, State Library of New South Wales.
34 *Ibid.*
35 *Ibid.*
36 *Ibid.*
37 Percy Clinton Sydney Smythe, 6th Viscount Strangford (31 August 1780 – 29 May 1855).
38 Elizabeth Macquarie, Journal, 15 August 1809, Vol. Z A772, State Library of New South Wales.
39 *Ibid.*
40 *Ibid.*
41 Elizabeth Macquarie, Journal, 24 September 1809, Vol. Z C126, State Library of New South Wales.
42 *Ibid.*
43 Elizabeth Macquarie, Journal, 25 September 1809, Vol. Z C126, State Library of New South Wales.
44 *Ibid.*
45 Du Pré Alexander, 2nd Earl of Caledon, born 14 December 1777; died 8 April 1839.
46 Admiral Sir Albemarle Bertie, 1st Baronet, born 20 January 1755; died 24 February 1824.
47 William Sorell, born 1775; died 4 June 1848.
48 Elizabeth Macquarie Journal, 25 September 1809, Vol. Z C126, State Library of New South Wales.
49 *Ibid.*
50 John Thomas Campbell (1770–1830).
51 R.F. Holder, 'Campbell, John Thomas (1770–1830)', *Australian Dictionary of Biography*, National Centre of Biography, Australian National University, adb.anu.edu.au, published first in hard copy 1966.
52 Antill, *Early History of New South Wales: Two Old Journals*, 13 October 1809.
53 *Ibid*, 13 October 1809.
54 *Ibid*, 27 November 1809.
55 *Ibid.*
56 Antill, *Early History of New South Wales: Two Old Journals*, 31 October 1809.
57 David Collins (1756–1810).
58 William Bligh to Viscount Castlereagh, 10 June 1809, Watson (ed.), *Historical Records of Australia, Series I, Volume VII*, p. 128.
59 Macquarie, Memoranda, 15 December 1809, Vol. Z A772, State Library of New South Wales.

60 Elizabeth Macquarie, Journal, 16 December 1809, Vol. Z C126, State Library of New South Wales.

61 Antill, *Early History of New South Wales: Two Old Journals*, 25 December 1809.

62 Elizabeth Macquarie, Journal, 25 December 1809, Vol. Z C126, State Library of New South Wales.

63 Macquarie, Memoranda, 28 December 1809, Vol. Z A772, State Library of New South Wales.

64 Antill, *Early History of New South Wales: Two Old Journals*, 28 December 1809.

Chapter 18

1   Macquarie to Earl Bathurst, 27 July 1822, Frederick Watson (ed.), *Historical Records of Australia, Series I: Governors' Despatches to and from England, Volume X: January, 1819 – December, 1822*, Library Committee of the Commonwealth Parliament, 1917, pp. 671–672.

2   Isaac Nichols (1770–1819).

3   Macquarie, Memoranda, 28 December 1809, Vol. Z A772, State Library of New South Wales.

4   Edward Cooke to William Bligh, 'Letters Received and Copies of Letters Sent, 1809–22', 15 May 1809, Vol. Z A797, Lachlan Macquarie and Macquarie Family Papers, State Library of New South Wales.

5   Ellis Bent to his mother, 4 March 1810, MS 195/3, National Library of Australia, p. 74.

6   Macquarie, Memoranda, 31 December 1809, Vol. Z A772, State Library of New South Wales.

7   *Sydney Gazette and New South Wales Advertiser*, 7 January 1810, pp. 2–3.

8   *Ibid.*

9   Elizabeth Paterson, née Driver (*c*. 1760–1839).

10 Though officially Deputy Judge-Advocate, Bent was usually called Judge-Advocate.

11 *Sydney Gazette and New South Wales Advertiser*, 7 January 1810, pp. 2–3.

12 'Governor Macquarie's Commission', Watson (ed.), *Historical Records of Australia, Series I, Volume VII*, p. 183.

13 *Sydney Gazette and New South Wales Advertiser*, 7 January 1810, pp. 2–3.

14 *Ibid.*

15 *Ibid.*

16 'Proclamation', *Sydney Gazette and New South Wales Advertiser*, 7 January 1810, p. 1.

17 *Ibid.*

18 Macquarie, Memoranda, 1 January 1810, Vol. Z A772, State Library of New South Wales.

19 In a nod to Arthur Phillip, some early descriptions of the church called it St Phillip's.

20 David Collins, *An Account of the English Colony in New South Wales from Its First Settlement, in January 1788, to August 1801*, T. Cadell jun. and W Davies, 1802.

21 'Sydney', *Sydney Gazette and New South Wales Advertiser*, 7 January 1810, p. 3.

22 William Cowper (1778–1858).

23 'Address to His Excellency', *Sydney Gazette and New South Wales Advertiser*, 21 January 1810, p. 1.

24 *Ibid.*

25 Garnham Blaxcell (1778–1817).

26 'Address to His Excellency', *Sydney Gazette and New South Wales Advertiser*, 21 January 1810, p. 1.

27 Joseph Underwood (1779–1833).

28 'Address to His Excellency', *Sydney Gazette and New South Wales Advertiser*, 21 January 1810, p. 1.

29 Macquarie to Viscount Castlereagh, 30 April 1810, Watson (ed.), *Historical Records of Australia, Series I, Volume VII*, pp. 280–281.

30 Macquarie to Viscount Castlereagh, 30 April 1810, *ibid*, p. 285.

31 Macquarie to Christopher Lundin, Letterbooks, 20 March 1795, Vol. Z A788, State Library of New South Wales.

32 Macquarie to Earl Bathurst, 27 July 1822, Watson (ed.), *Historical Records of Australia, Series I, Volume X*, pp. 671–672.

33 Macquarie, Memoranda, 10 January 1810, Vol. Z A772, State Library of New South Wales.

34 Macquarie, Memoranda, 30 April 1810, Vol. Z A772, State Library of New South Wales, pp. 281–283.

35 Macquarie to Viscount Castlereagh, 30 April 1810, Watson (ed.), *Historical Records of Australia, Series I, Volume VII*, p. 321.

36 Macquarie, Memoranda, 15 January 1810, Vol. Z A772, State Library of New South Wales.

37 Macquarie, Memoranda, 8 March 1810, *ibid*, p. 220; Macquarie, Memoranda, 30 April 1810, *ibid*, p. 275.

38 Macquarie, Memoranda, 8 February 1810, *ibid*.

39 'The Female Orphan School: 1813 to 1850', Western Sydney University, westernsydney. edu.au/femaleorphanschool.

40 'Sydney', *Sydney Gazette and New South Wales Advertiser*, 7 January 1810, p. 3.

41 George Howe, born 1769; died 11 May 1821.

42 'Sydney', *Sydney Gazette and New South Wales Advertiser*, 7 January 1810, p. 3.

43 Macquarie, Memoranda, 4 January 1810, Vol. Z A772, State Library of New South Wales.

44 Macquarie to Viscount Castlereagh, 8 March 1810, Watson (ed.), *Historical Records of Australia, Series I, Volume VII*, p. 218.

45 *Ibid*.

46 Macquarie, Memoranda, 10 January 1810, Vol. Z A772, State Library of New South Wales.

47 Macquarie to William Bligh, 6 January 1810, Bladen (ed.), *Historical Records of New South Wales, Vol. VII*, p. 265.

48 Macquarie, Memoranda, 18 January 1810, Vol. Z A772, State Library of New South Wales.

49 Macquarie, Memoranda, 26 January 1810, *ibid*.

50 Macquarie to Viscount Castlereagh, 8 March 1810, Watson (ed.), *Historical Records of Australia, Series I, Volume VII*, p. 219.

51 *Ibid*.

52 Macquarie to Charles Macquarie, 10 March 1810, Bertie, 'Governor Macquarie', p. 27.

53 '73rd Regiment', Journeys in Time 1809–1822, Related Topics, mq.edu.au/macquarie-archive/journeys.

54 William Bligh to Elizabeth Bligh, 8 March 1810, Safe 1/45, William Bligh – Naval and Other Papers 1769–1822, State Library of New South Wales, pp. 267–274.

55 Macquarie to Charles Macquarie, 10 March 1810, Bertie, 'Governor Macquarie', p. 27.

56 Joseph Arnold, 'Letters, 18 March to 10 May 1810', A1849 vol. 2, Joseph Arnold Papers 1808–1817, State Library of New South Wales.

57 *Derwent Star and Van Diemen's Land Intelligencer* (Hobart), 3 April 1810, p. 1.

58 Macquarie to Viscount Castlereagh, 8 March 1810, Watson (ed.), *Historical Records of Australia, Series I, Volume VII*, p. 222.

59 Macquarie to Viscount Castlereagh, 30 March 1810, *ibid*, p. 262.

60 Macquarie, Memoranda, A772, 26 March 1810, Vol. Z A772, State Library of New South Wales..

61 Joseph Arnold, born 28 December 1782; died 26 July 1818.

62 Joseph Arnold, 'Letters, 18 March to 10 May 1810', A1849 vol. 2, State Library of New South Wales.

63 *Ibid*.

64 Joseph Arnold to his brother, 25 February 1810, A1849 vol. 2, State Library of New South Wales, p. 3.

65 Ellis Bent to his mother, 27 March 1810, MS 195/3, National Library of Australia.

66 Macquarie, Memoranda, 8 May 1810, Vol. Z A772, State Library of New South Wales.

67   William Bligh to Elizabeth Bligh, 11 August 1810, Safe 1/45, State Library of New South Wales, pp. 279–286.

68   Michael Massey Robinson (1744–1826).

69   'Epithalamium', *Sydney Gazette and New South Wales Advertiser*, 26 May 1810, p. 2.

70   Ellis Bent to his mother, 4 March 1810, MS 195/3, National Library of Australia, p. 74.

71   Macquarie, Memoranda, 11 May 1810, Vol. Z A772, State Library of New South Wales.

72   Macquarie, Memoranda, 12 May 110, *ibid*.

73   William Bligh to Sir Joseph Banks, 11 August 1810, Bladen (ed.), *Historical Records of New South Wales, Vol. VII*, p. 404.

74   Macquarie to Viscount Castlereagh, 8 March 1810, Watson (ed.), *Historical Records of Australia, Series I, Volume VII*, p. 219.

75   Macquarie, Memoranda, 12 May 1810, Vol. Z A772, State Library of New South Wales.

76   Macquarie to Charles Macquarie, 10 March 1810, Bertie, 'Governor Macquarie', p. 27.

Chapter 19

1   Macquarie to Viscount Castlereagh, 30 April 1810, Watson (ed.), *Historical Records of Australia, Series I, Volume VII*, p. 276.

2   'Sydney', *Sydney Gazette and New South Wales Advertiser*, 5 May 1810, p. 2.

3   'His Majesty's Birthday', *Sydney Gazette and New South Wales Advertiser*, 9 June 1810, p. 2.

4   'Government and General Order', 6 October 1810, Bladen (ed.), *Historical Records of New South Wales, Vol. VII*, pp. 427-428.

5   *Ibid*, p. 427.

6   'Sydney', *Sydney Gazette and New South Wales Advertiser*, 20 October 1810, p. 3.

7   'Sporting Intelligence', *Sydney Gazette and New South Wales Advertiser*, 20 October 1810, p. 2.

8   John Piper (1773–1851).

9   Thomas Sadlier Cleaveland (1785–1812).

10   'Sporting Intelligence', *Sydney Gazette and New South Wales Advertiser*, 20 October 1810, p. 2.

11   William Charles Wentworth (1790–1872).

12   'The Subscribers' Ball', *Sydney Gazette and New South Wales Advertiser*, 20 October 1810, p. 2.

13   Macquarie to Viscount Castlereagh, 8 March 1810, Watson (ed.), *Historical Records of Australia, Series I, Volume VII*, p. 223.

14   'Pistolling Privy-Counsellors', *Cobbett's Weekly Political Register* (London), 7 October 1809, p. 481.

15   *Ibid*, p. 224.

16   Macquarie to Viscount Castlereagh, 30 April 1810, *Historical Records of Australia, Series I, Volume VII*, p. 275.

17   Edward Lord (1781–1859).

18   Macquarie to Viscount Castlereagh, 30 April 1810, Watson (ed.), *Historical Records of Australia, Series I, Volume VII*, p. 290.

19   Edward Lord to Macquarie, 28 March 1810, *ibid*, p. 289.

20   Macquarie to Castlereagh to Viscount Castlereagh, 30 April 1810, *Historical Records of Australia*, Series 1, Vol. 7, p. 261.

21   Macquarie to Viscount Castlereagh, 30 April 1810, Watson (ed.), *Historical Records of Australia, Series I, Volume VII*, p. 274.

22   'Schedule of Printing Materials Required', 24 October 1810, Watson (ed.), *Historical Records of Australia, Series I, Volume VII, Historical Records of Australia*, p. 348.

23   Macquarie to Viscount Castlereagh, *ibid*, 8 March 1810, *Historical Records of Australia, Series 1, Vol. 7*, p. 224.

24   Macquarie, Memoranda, 22 September 1810, Vol. Z A772, State Library of New South Wales.

25   *Ibid*.

26   *Ibid*, p. 266.

27 Macquarie to Viscount Castlereagh, 10 May 1810, Watson (ed.), *Historical Records of Australia, Series I, Volume VII*, p. 332.

28 *Ibid.*

29 'Government and General Order', 6 October 1810, Bladen (ed.), *Historical Records of New South Wales, Vol. VII*, pp. 427–428.

30 *Ibid*, pp. 404–410.

31 Macquarie to Viscount Castlereagh, 30 April 1810, *ibid*, p. 272.

32 'Government and General Order', 23 June 1810, *Historical Records of New South Wales, Vol. VII*, p. 389.

33 'First Post Office', Defining Moments in Australian History, National Museum of Australia, nma.gov.au/defining-moments.

34 Macquarie to Viscount Castlereagh, 30 April 1810, Bladen (ed.), *Historical Records of New South Wales, Vol. VII*, p. 250.

35 'Contract for Rebuilding Bridge Facing Sydney Cove', 24 September 1811, *ibid*, p. 591.

36 Francis Williams (1780–1831). Williams had married Lord's adopted daughter.

37 Macquarie to Viscount Castlereagh, 30 April 1810, Bladen (ed.), *Historical Records of New South Wales, Vol. VII*, p. 275.

38 Alexander Riley (1778–1833).

39 'Hospital Contract', 6 November 1810, Bladen (ed.), *Historical Records of New South Wales, Vol. VII*, pp. 449–453.

40 *Ibid.*

41 Macquarie to Viscount Castlereagh, 30 April 1810, Watson (ed.), *Historical Records of Australia, Series I, Volume VII*, p. 250.

42 'Government and General Order', 27 January 1810, Bladen (ed.), *Historical Records of New South Wales, Vol. VII*, p. 281.

43 'Proclamation', 24 February 1810, Bladen (ed.), *Historical Records of New South Wales, Vol. VII*, p. 292.

44 *Ibid.*

45 *Ibid*, p. 293.

46 *Ibid*, p. 294.

47 Matthew Hughes (*c.* 1770–1845).

48 'Early Schoolmasters', *Sydney Morning Herald*, 6 February 1909, p. 7.

49 *Ibid.*

50 'Government and General Order', 24 February 1810, Bladen (ed.), *Historical Records of New South Wales, Vol. VII*, p. 293.

51 *Ibid.*

52 'Proclamation', 24 February 1810, Bladen (ed.), *Historical Records of New South Wales, Vol. VII*, p. 292.

53 'Government and General Order', 4 October 1810, Bladen (ed.), *Historical Records of New South Wales, Vol. VII*, p. 427.

54 'Government and General Order', 1 October, *ibid*, p. 426.

55 'Proclamation', *Sydney Gazette and New South Wales Advertiser*, 7 January 1810, p. 1.

56 'Official Regulations', 8 January 1810, Bladen (ed.), *Historical Records of New South Wales, Vol. VII*, p. 267.

57 *Ibid.*

58 'Official Regulations', 8 January 1810, Bladen (ed.), *Historical Records of New South Wales, Vol. VII*, pp. 275–276.

59 Lachlan Macquarie, *A Letter to the Right Honourable Viscount Sidmouth, in Refutation of Statements Made by the Hon. Henry Grey Bennet, M.P. in a Pamphlet 'On the Transportation Laws, the State of the Hulks, and of the Colonies in New South Wales'*, Richard Rees, 1921, NK4111, Rex Nan Kivell Collection, National Library of Australia, p. 79.

60 *Ibid.*

61 Macquarie to John Thomas Bigge, 6 November 1819, Watson (ed.), *Historical Records of Australia, Series I, Volume X*, p. 222.

62 Old Bailey Session Papers, 1787 to 1788, pp. 15–20, cited in Kathleen Mary Dermody, 'D'Arcy Wentworth 1762–1827: A Second Chance', Australian National University PhD thesis, April 1990, pp. 23–24, openresearch-repository.anu.edu.au/handle/1885/114504.

63 J.J. Auchmuty, 'Wentworth, D'Arcy (1762–1827)', *Australian Dictionary of Biography*, National Centre of Biography, Australian National University, adb.anu.edu.au, published first in hard copy 1967.

64 William Redfern, born 1774; died 17 July 1833.

65 'Government and General Order', 20 February 1810, Bladen (ed.), *Historical Records of New South Wales, Vol. VII*, p. 291.

66 Macquarie, *A Letter to the Right Honourable Viscount Sidmouth*, p. 38.

67 *Ibid*, p. 39.

68 John Jamieson (*c.* 1766–1850).

69 'Official Regulations', 8 January 1810, Bladen (ed.), *Historical Records of New South Wales, Vol. VII*, p. 267.

70 Esther Johnston, née Abrahams (1767–1846). She came to New South Wales on the First Fleet, then met Johnston; they spent twenty-five years in a de facto relationship before marrying in 1814.

71 James Meehan (1774–1826).

72 Macquarie, memo, 6 January 1821, Frederick Watson (ed.), *Historical Records of Australia, Series IV: Legal Papers, Section A; Volume 1: 1786–1827*, Library Committee of the Commonwealth Parliament, 1922, p. 879.

73 Macquarie, Memoranda, 14 June 1810, Vol. Z A772, State Library of New South Wales.

74 On 26 February 1811, with James Ratty.

75 Macquarie, Memoranda, 7 August 1810, Vol. Z A772, State Library of New South Wales.

76 Macquarie, Memoranda, 19 August 1810, *ibid.*

77 William Macquarie Cowper, known in his youth as Macquarie, born 3 July 1810; died 14 June 1902.

78 Robert Banks Jenkinson, 2nd Earl of Liverpool, born 7 June 1770; died 4 December 1828.

79 Macquarie to Earl of Liverpool, 27 October 1810, Bladen (ed.), *Historical Records of New South Wales, Vol. VII*, p. 346.

80 *Ibid*, p. 343.

81 Macquarie, Memoranda, 6 November 1810, Vol. Z A772, State Library of New South Wales.

82 Thomas Moore (1762–1840). He gave his name to Moore Theological College, Sydney.

83 Thomas Laycock, born *c.* 1786; died 7 November 1823.

84 Macquarie, Memoranda, 7 November 1810, Vol. Z A772, State Library of New South Wales.

85 Macquarie, Memoranda, 22 October 1810, *ibid.*

86 Macquarie, Memoranda, 9 November 1810, *ibid.*

87 Gregory Blaxland (1778–1853).

88 Macquarie, Memoranda, 11 November 1810, Vol. Z A772, State Library of New South Wales.

89 Macquarie, Memoranda, 13 November 1810, *ibid.*

90 Gregory Blaxland to Macquarie, 4 December 1810, Bladen (ed.), *Historical Records of New South Wales, Vol. VII*, p. 430.

91 Macquarie, Memoranda, 16 November 1810, Vol. Z A772, State Library of New South Wales.

92 *Ibid.*

93 Macquarie, Memoranda, 18 November 1810, *ibid.*

94 *Ibid.*

95 Macquarie, Memoranda, 21 November 1810, *ibid.*

96 Macquarie, Memoranda, 22 November 1810, *ibid*.

97 Macquarie, Memoranda, 27 November 1810, *ibid*.

98 Anna Josepha King, née Coombe (1765–1844).

99 Macquarie, Memoranda, 28 November 1810, Vol. Z A772, State Library of New South Wales.

100 George William Evans (1780–1852).

101 Macquarie, Memoranda, 29 November 1810, Vol. Z A772, State Library of New South Wales.

102 *Ibid*, Macquarie noted it as Warragombie.

103 Macquarie, Memoranda, 30 November 1810, Vol. Z A772, State Library of New South Wales.

104 Archibald Bell (1773–1837).

105 Macquarie, Memoranda, 1 December 1810, Vol. Z A772, State Library of New South Wales.

106 *Ibid*.

107 Macquarie, Memoranda, 6 December 1810, *ibid*.

108 Instructions given to James Meehan for the laying out of the Five Townships, 26 December 1810, Copies of Letters Sent: Local and Overseas (Colonial Secretary), NRS 935, 4/3490D, New South Wales State Archives, pp. 55-60, records.nsw.gov.au.

109 Macquarie, Memoranda, 1 January 1811, Vol. Z A772, State Library of New South Wales.

110 Macquarie, Memoranda, 10 January 1811, *ibid*.

111 Macquarie, Memoranda, 12 January 1811, *ibid*.

112 Macquarie, Memoranda, 31 January 1811, *ibid*.

Chapter 20

1 Macquarie, Journal to and from Van Diemen's Land to Sydney in New South Wales. 4 November 1811 – 6 January 1812. Original held in the Mitchell Library, Sydney. ML Ref: A777 pp.1-34. [Microfilm Reel CY302 Frames #347-380], 13 November 1811.

2 *Ibid*.

3 Macquarie, Journals, 29 November 1810, Vol. Z A777, State Library of New South Wales.

4 Macquarie, Memoranda, 29 September 1811, Vol. Z A772, State Library of New South Wales.

5 *Ibid*.

6 William Wilberforce to Macquarie, Letterbooks, 3 December 1810, Vol. Z A797, State Library of New South Wales.

7 Macquarie to Earl of Liverpool, 18 October 1811, Bladen (ed.), *Historical Records of New South Wales, Vol. VII*, p. 600.

8 *Ibid*.

9 'Trial for Murder', *Sydney Gazette and New South Wales Advertiser*, 14 September 1811, p. 1.

10 *Ibid*.

11 *Sydney Gazette and New South Wales Advertiser*, 1 June 1811, p. 1.

12 *Ibid*.

13 Alexander Riley (*c.* 1778–1833).

14 *Sydney Gazette and New South Wales Advertiser*, 23 February 1811, p. 1.

15 *Ibid*, 19 January 1811, p. 2.

16 Macquarie, Memoranda, 4 June 1811, Vol. Z A772, State Library of New South Wales.

17 Macquarie, Memoranda, 5 June 1811, *ibid*.

18 Macquarie, Memoranda, 3 August 1811, *ibid*.

19 Macquarie, Memoranda, 15, July 1811, *ibid*.

20 Macquarie, Memoranda, 2 July 1811, *ibid*.

21 'The Records of the Colonial Secretary – 73rd Regiment', *Garrison Gazette*, Winter 2009, p. 2, quoted in Victoria Schofield, *Highland Furies: The Black Watch 1739–1899*, Quercus, 2012, p. 650.

22 Macquarie, Journals, 11 November 1811, Vol. Z A777, State Library of New South Wales.

23 Macquarie, Journals, 12 November 1811, *ibid*.

24   Macquarie, Journals, 13 November 1811, *ibid*.

25   Macquarie, Journals, 23 November 1811, *ibid*.

26   *Ibid*.

27   Macquarie, Journals, 26 November 1811, *ibid*.   .

28   Macquarie, Journals, 27 November 1811, *ibid*. It was renamed New Norfolk in 1825.

29   Macquarie noted (Journals, 30 November 1811, *ibid*) that he had named Mount Nelson after Viscount Horatio Nelson but, in actual fact, Bligh had beaten him to it, naming the grand peak in 1792 after David Nelson, the botanist on the *Bounty*'s voyage to Tahiti. Nelson had remained loyal to Bligh during the mutiny and was one of the nineteen men who survived the voyage to Timor in an open boat. But he died of fever only a few days after reaching Kupang.

30   'Address', *Sydney Gazette and New South Wales Advertiser*, 11 January 1812, p. 2.

31   Macquarie, Journal to and from Van Diemen's Lands, 3 to 7 December 1811, Vol. Z A777, State Library of New South Wales.

32   Macquarie, Journals, 8 December 1811.

33   *Ibid*.

34   Macquarie, Journals, 18 December 1811, Vol. Z A777, State Library of New South Wales.

35   Macquarie, Journals, 25 December 1811, *ibid*.

36   Macquarie, Journals, 31 December 1811, *ibid*.

37   'Government and General Orders', *Sydney Gazette and New South Wales Advertiser*, 11 January 1812, p. 1.

38   *Ibid*.

39   On 18 January 1812.

40   Macquarie, Memoranda, 27 February 1812, Vol. Z A772, State Library of New South Wales.

41   Sir Maurice Charles O'Connell junior, born 13 January 1812; died 23 March 1879. He became President of the Queensland Legislative Council, the first native-born Australian to hold that position in an Australian government.

42   *Sydney Gazette and New South Wales Advertiser*, 18 January 1812, p. 1.

43   Macquarie, Memoranda, 22 April 1812, Vol. Z A772, State Library of New South Wales.

44   Macquarie, Memoranda, 10 May 1812, *ibid*.

45   Macquarie, Memoranda, 10 and 16 May 1812, *ibid*.

46   Earl of Liverpool to Macquarie, 4 May 1812, *Historical Records of Australia, Series I, Volume VII*, p. 477.

47   *Ibid*.

48   *Ibid*, p. 481.

49   *Ibid*, p. 495.

50   *Ibid*, p. 488.

51   Macquarie to Earl of Liverpool, 9 November 1812, *Historical Records of Australia, Series I, Volume VII*, p. 525.

52   *Ibid*, pp. 595–596.

53   *Ibid*, pp. 597–598.

54   *Ibid*.

55   *Ibid*, pp. 531–532.

Chapter 21

1   Samuel Marsden to William Wilberforce, 27 July 1810, from *The Correspondence of William Wilberforce, Volume 2*, edited by his sons Robert and Samuel Wilberforce, John Murray, 1840, pp 183-84.

2   Spencer Perceval, born 1 November 1762; died 11 May 1812.

3   Perceval was the father of thirteen children, but only twelve of them reached adulthood.

4   *Trial of John Bellingham for the Murder of the Right Hon. S. Perceval, Late Chancellor of the Exchequer, &c., at the Old Bailey, on Friday, the 15th of May, 1812,* J. Morton, 1812, p. 15.

5   'Bellingham', Pathology Museum, Queen Mary University of London, qmul.ac.uk/pathologymuseum.

6   Henry Bathurst, 3rd Earl Bathurst, born 22 May 1762; died 27 July 1834.

7   Macquarie, Memoranda, 25 October 1812, Vol. Z A772, State Library of New South Wales.

8   Macquarie to John Thomas Bigge, 6 November 1819, Watson (ed.), *Historical Records of Australia, Series I, Volume X,* p. 222.

9   Earl Bathurst to Macquarie, 3 February 1814, Watson (ed.), *Historical Records of Australia, Series I, Volume VIII,* p. 135.

10   Macquarie to Earl Bathurst, 7 October 1815, Watson (ed.), *Historical Records of Australia, Series I, Volume VIII,* p. 315.

11   Joseph Arnold to his brother, 25 February 1810, A1849 vol. 2, State Library of New South Wales.

12   Andrew Thompson (1773–1810).

13   J.V. Byrnes, 'Thompson, Andrew (1773–1810)', *Australian Dictionary of Biography,* 1967.

14   Macquarie, Memoranda, 22 October 1810, *ibid.*

15   Macquarie to Castlereagh to Viscount Castlereagh, 30 April 1810, Watson (ed.), *Historical Records of Australia, Series I, Volume VII, Historical Records of Australia,* Series 1, Vol. 7, p. 276.

16   Hainsworth, 'Lord, Simeon (1771–1840)'.

17   D. R. Hainsworth, 'Lord, Simeon (1771–1840)', *Australian Dictionary of Biography,* 1967.

18   *Sydney Gazette and New South Wales Advertiser,* 22 September 1810, p. 2.

19   John Thomas Bigge, 'Report of the Commissioner of Inquiry into the State of the Colony of New South Wales' (Bigge Report), House of Commons, 1822, Appendix, p. 2054.

20   *Ibid,* Box 11, Answer 5.

21   In 1812, he sold 4000 pounds of New South Wales wool to England at 45 pence a pound.

22   Samuel Marsden, *An Answer to Certain Calumnies in the Late Governor Macquarie's Pamphlet,* J. Hatchard, 1826, p. 3.

23   *Ibid,* p. 5.

24   *Ibid,* p. 6.

25   Samuel Marsden to William Wilberforce, 27 July 1810, Robert and Samuel Wilberforce (eds), *The Correspondence of William Wilberforce, Volume 2,* pp. 183–184.

26   Australian Biographical and Genealogical Record of Marsden Female Muster, ca. 1812, Arranged Alphabetically by Name, and by Ship of Arrival, Compiled 1986, MLMSS 4614, State Library of New South Wales.

27   Bigge Report, Convicts, p. 82, State Library of New South Wales.

28   *Ibid; Sydney Gazette and New South Wales Advertiser,* 28 January 1810, p. 2.

29   Barron Field, born 23 October 1786; died 11 April 1846.

30   Bigge Report, Evidence of Mr Justice Field, 1820, Historical Records of Australia, p. 780.

31   Macquarie, *A Letter to the Right Honourable Viscount Sidmouth,* p. 44.

32   *Ibid.*

33   *Ibid,* p. 45.

34   *Ibid,* p. 37.

35   *Ibid.*

36   Bigge Report, 'IV. Nature of the Labour of Convicts in the Service of Settlers', p. 81.

37   *Ibid,* p. 38.

38   Macquarie, Memoranda, 26 October 1810, Vol. Z A772, State Library of New South Wales.

39   At St Matthew's Anglican Church, Windsor.

40   'Reminiscences of a Visit to the Hawkesbury', *Australian Town and Country Journal* (Sydney), 24 January 1874, p. 21.

41 J.V. Byrnes, 'Andrew Thompson, 1773–1810: Part 1 – To the Arrival of Macquarie', *Journal and Proceedings* (Royal Australian Historical Society), Vol. XLVIII (1962), p. 120.

42 John Macarthur to Elizabeth Macarthur, 21 April 1811, Sibella Macarthur Onslow (ed.), *Some Early Records of the Macarthurs of Camden*, Angus & Robertson, 1914, p. 215.

43 Macquarie, Memoranda, 20 November 1810, Vol. Z A772, State Library of New South Wales.

44 John Macarthur to Elizabeth Macarthur, 21 April 1811, Macarthur Onslow (ed.), *Some Early Records of the Macarthurs of Camden*, p. 215.

45 *Ibid*, p. 219.

46 *Ibid*.

47 *Ibid*.

48 'Report from the Select Committee on Transportation', House of Commons, 1812, FRM F543, National Library of Australia, p. 14.

49 *Ibid*, p. 12.

50 *Ibid*.

51 *Ibid*.

52 'Report from the Select Committee on Transportation', House of Commons, 1812, FRM F543, National Library of Australia, p. 14.

53 Macquarie to Earl Bathurst, 28 June 1813, Watson (ed.), *Historical Records of Australia, Series I, Volume VII*, p. 781.

54 *Ibid*, p. 772.

55 *Ibid*, p. 776.

56 *Ibid*.

57 Gregory Blaxland, *A Journal of a Tour of Discovery Across the Blue Mountains, New South Wales, in the Year 1813*, B.J. Holdsworth, 1823, p. 11.

Chapter 22

1 Macquarie, Memoranda, 13 December 1813, A772, State Library of New South Wales.

2 William Lawson (1774-1850).

3 The site of the former farm is on Luddenham Road in the Sydney suburb of Orchard Hills. A monument stands near the corner of Luddenham and Mamre Roads.

4 Blaxland, *A Journal of a Tour of Discovery Across the Blue Mountains, New South Wales, in the Year 1813*, p. 11.

5 Also known as James Byrnes.

6 Wentworth Family Correspondence, Treasury Orders, etc., 1812–1825, SAFE/A763 (Safe 1/345), Series 6, Wentworth Family Papers, 1785–1827, State Library of New South Wales, pp. 51, 73.

7 'Government and General Orders', *Sydney Gazette and New South Wales Advertiser*, 5 December 1818, p. 1.

8 Wilson was convicted in October 1785 at Wigan, Lancashire, of having stolen 'nine yards of cotton cloth called *velveret*, of the value of tenpence', and sentenced to transportation for seven years. He reached Port Jackson with the First Fleet on the *Alexander* in January 1788.

9 A.H. Chisholm, 'Wilson, John (?–1800)', *Australian Dictionary of Biography*, National Centre of Biography, Australian National University, adb.anu.edu.au, published first in hard copy 1967.

10 George Caley (1770–1829).

11 Francis Louis Barrallier (1773–1853).

12 Jill Conway, 'Blaxland, Gregory (1778–1853)', *Australian Dictionary of Biography*, National Centre of Biography, Australian National University, adb.anu.edu.au, published first in hard copy 1966.

13 E.W. Dunlop, 'Lawson, William (1774–1850)', *ibid*, published first in hard copy 1967.

14 Michael Persse, 'Wentworth, William Charles (1790–1872)', *ibid*, published first in hard copy 1967.

15 Macquarie to Earl of Liverpool, 9 November 1812, Watson (ed.), *Historical Records of Australia, Series I, Volume VII*, pp. 558, 598.

16 Macquarie to John Wilson Croker, 3 August 1813, Frederick Watson (ed.), *Historical Records of Australia, Series I: Governors' Despatches to and from England, Volume VIII: July, 1813 – December, 1815*, Library Committee of the Commonwealth Parliament, 1916, p. 32.

17 *Ibid*, p. 35.

18 *Ibid*, p. 36.

19 'Court of Criminal Jurisdiction', *Sydney Gazette and New South Wales Advertiser*, 17 July 1813, p. 2.

20 *Sydney Gazette and New South Wales Advertiser*, 2 January 1813, p. 1.

21 *Ibid*.

22 *Ibid*.

23 Earl Bathurst to Macquarie, 23 November 1812, Watson (ed.), *Historical Records of Australia, Series 1, Volume VII*, p. 671.

24 'Public Notice', *Sydney Gazette and New South Wales Advertiser*, 12 June 1813, p. 1.

25 *Sydney Gazette and New South Wales Advertiser*, 2 January 1813, p. 1.

26 Robert Jenkins (*c*. 1777–1822).

27 Samuel Terry (*c*. 1776–1838).

28 *Sydney Gazette and New South Wales Advertiser*, 2 January 1813, p. 1.

29 *Ibid*.

30 Macquarie, Memoranda, 1 February 1813, Vol. Z A772, State Library of New South Wales.

31 Macquarie to John Wilson Croker, 3 August 1813, Watson (ed.), *Historical Records of Australia, Series I, Volume VIII*, p. 30.

32 John Marshall, *Royal Naval Biography, Vol. IV. – Part I.*, Rees, Orme, Brown Green and Longman, 1833.

33 Robert Watson (1756–1819).

34 Macquarie to William Case, 5 December 1812, Watson (ed.), *Historical Records of Australia, Series I, Volume VIII*, p. 37.

35 *Sydney Gazette and New South Wales Advertiser*, 9 January 1813, p. 2.

36 Macquarie to William Case, 16 February 1813, Watson (ed.), *Historical Records of Australia, Series I, Volume VIII*, p. 45.

37 Macquarie to Earl Bathurst, 3 August 1813, *ibid*, p. 32.

38 Thomas Clarkson (1763–1824).

39 *Ibid*, p. 34.

40 Macquarie to William Case, 22 March 1813, Watson (ed.), *Historical Records of Australia, Series I, Volume VIII*, p. 46.

41 William Case to Macquarie, 22 March 1813, Watson (ed.), *Historical Records of Australia, Series I, Volume VIII*, p. 47.

42 Macquarie to William Case, 23 March 1813, *ibid*, p. 48.

43 William Case to Macquarie, 24 March 1813, *ibid*, p. 48.

44 Macquarie to Lieutenant Butcher, 5 May 1813, *ibid*, p. 53.

45 Macquarie, Memoranda, 11 March 1813, Vol. Z A772, State Library of New South Wales.

46 Macquarie to Earl Bathurst, 28 June 1813, Watson (ed.), *Historical Records of Australia, Series I, Volume VII*, p. 716.

47 George Thomas Palmer (1784–1854).

48 Macquarie to Earl Bathurst, 28 June 1813, Watson (ed.), *Historical Records of Australia, Series I, Volume VII*, p. 717.

49 *Ibid*, p. 716.

50 Matthew Kearns, John Kearns senior and John Kearns junior were all hanged in Sydney on 24 March 1813 for aiding and abetting the murder of Joseph Sutton. On the same day, Pearce Conden and Thomas Mahony were both hanged at the exact site of the crime in George Street, Parramatta.

51 Macquarie, Memoranda, 1 May 1813, Vol. Z A772, State Library of New South Wales.

52 They called it Emu Island, because early explorers thought the land was totally cut off by water. It actually occupies a semi-circular bend of the river.

53 Blaxland, *A Journal of a Tour of Discovery Across the Blue Mountains*, pp. 13-14.

54 George Bass (1771–1803).

55 Henry Hacking (*c*. 1750–1831).

56 Blaxland, *A Journal of a Tour of Discovery Across the Blue Mountains, New South Wales, in the Year 1813*, pp. 24–25.

57 William Lawson, 'Journal of an Expedition Across the Blue Mountains, 11 May – 6 June 1813', 22 May 1813, Safe 1/97, State Library of New South Wales.

58 William Charles Wentworth, 'Journal of an Expedition Across the Blue Mountains, 11 May – 6 June 1813', Safe 1/22a, State Library of New South Wales.

59 Blaxland, *A Journal of a Tour of Discovery Across the Blue Mountains, New South Wales, in the Year 1813, Journal*, p. 32.

60 *Ibid*, pp. 33–34.

61 *Ibid*, p. 36.

62 *Sydney Gazette and New South Wales Advertiser*, 12 June 1813, p. 3.

63 *Ibid*, 18 June 1814, p. 2.

64 *Ibid*.

65 *Ibid*, 3 July 1813, p. 3.

66 'Court of Criminal Jurisdiction', *Sydney Gazette and New South Wales Advertiser*, 17 July 1813, p. 2.

67 Macquarie to Earl Bathurst, 31 July 1813, Watson (ed.), *Historical Records of Australia, Series I, Volume VIII*, p. 17.

68 *Ibid*, p. 26.

69 *Ibid*, p. 2.

70 'Government and General After Orders', *Sydney Gazette and New South Wales Advertiser*, 17 July 1813, p. 4.

71 Macquarie to Earl Bathurst, 31 July 1813, Watson (ed.), *Historical Records of Australia, Series I, Volume VIII*, p. 3.

72 Macquarie to Earl Bathurst, 31 July 1813, Watson (ed.), *Historical Records of Australia, Series I, Volume VIII*, p. 4.

73 Macquarie, Memoranda, 2 February 1813, Vol. Z A772, State Library of New South Wales.

74 Macquarie to Earl Bathurst, 31 August 1813, *ibid*, pp. 83–84.

75 Macquarie, Memoranda, 25 July 1813, Vol. Z A772, State Library of New South Wales.

76 At St John's Church, Parramatta, on 12 November 1814.

77 'Government and General After Orders', *Sydney Gazette and New South Wales Advertiser*, 17 July 1813, p. 4.

78 Macquarie to Earl Bathurst, 31 July 1813, Watson (ed.), *Historical Records of Australia, Series I, Volume VIII*, p. 35.

79 *Ibid*.

80 *Ibid*, p. 36.

81 Blaxcell to Macquarie, 29 July 1813, Watson (ed.), *Historical Records of Australia, Series I, Volume VIII, ibid*, p. 54.

82 Deposition of Robert Campbell, 8 August 1813, *ibid*, p. 62.

83 William Case to Macquarie, 14 August 1813, *ibid*, p. 66.

84 Her father was George Willison, a wealthy Scottish artist.

85 On 15 June 1812.

86 Macquarie, Memoranda, 13 December 1813, Vol. Z A772, State Library of New South Wales.

87 Macquarie, Memoranda, 3 November 1813, *ibid.*

Chapter 23

1 Macquarie, Memoranda, 28 March 1814, Vol. Z A772, State Library of New South Wales..

2 *Ibid.*

3 *Ibid.*

4 Thomas Davey (1758–1823).

5 Davey is said to have invented a rum punch known as 'Blow My Skull'. According to *The English and Australian Cookery Book* by Edward Abbott (Sampson Low, Son, and Marston, 1864), it consists of 2 pints of boiling water, sugarloaf, lime or lemon juice, 1 pint of ale or porter, 1 pint of rum and a half a pint of brandy. An alternative is the drink 'Blow My Skull Off', which mixes rum, cayenne pepper, Turkish opium, water and *Cocculus indicus*, a stupefying drug made from an Indian climbing plant.

6 Michael Howe, born 1787; died 21 October 1818.

7 Macquarie to Henry Goulburn, 30 April 1814, Watson (ed.), *Historical Records of Australia, Series I, Volume VIII*, p. 242.

8 Macquarie, Memoranda, 28 March 1814, Vol. Z A772, State Library of New South Wales.

9 *Ibid.*

10 *Ibid.*

11 George James Molle (1773–1823).

12 Macquarie to Earl Bathurst, 31 August 1813, Watson (ed.), *Historical Records of Australia, Series I, Volume VIII*, pp. 83–84.

13 William Macquarie Molle (1813-1895). The Molle Islands on the Great Barrier Reef were named after him and his wife is remembered through Catherine Field, near Camden.

14 Macquarie, Memoranda, 28 March 1814, Vol. Z A772, State Library of New South Wales. A772.

15 *Ibid.*

16 Baird to Macquarie, 30 March 1813, Letterbooks A797, *ibid.*

17 Macquarie, Memoranda, 29 March 1814, Vol. Z A772, *ibid.*

18 Macquarie, Memoranda, 30 March 1814, *ibid.*

19 *Ibid.*

20 Macquarie, Memoranda, 8 April 1814, Vol. Z A772, State Library of New South Wales.

21 Macquarie, Memoranda, 10 April 1814, Vol. Z A772, State Library of New South Wales.

22 Macquarie, Memoranda, 13 April 1814, *ibid.*

23 Macquarie to Earl Bathurst, 7 August 1813, Watson (ed.), *Historical Records of Australia, Series I, Volume VIII*, p. 58.

24 'Government and General Orders', *Sydney Gazette and New South Wales Advertiser*, 14 August 1813, p. 1.

25 *Ibid.*

26 Macquarie to Earl Bathurst, 19 January 1814, Watson (ed.), *Historical Records of Australia, Series I, Volume VIII*, p. 121.

27 *Sydney Gazette and New South Wales Advertiser*, 28 August 1813, p. 2.

28 *Ibid.*

29 Macquarie to Earl Bathurst, 19 January 1814, Watson (ed.), *Historical Records of Australia, Series I, Volume VIII*, p. 121.

30 Macquarie to Earl Bathurst, 24 May 1814, Watson (ed.), *Historical Records of Australia, Series I, Volume VIII*, p. 255.

31 'Government and General Orders', *Sydney Gazette and New South Wales Advertiser*,
    5 February 1814, p. 1.
32 Macquarie to Earl Bathurst, 28 April 1814, Watson (ed.), *Historical Records of Australia*,
    Series I, Volume VIII, p. 144.
33 Macquarie to Earl Bathurst, 19 January 1814, Watson (ed.), *Historical Records of Australia*,
    Series I, Volume VIII, p. 122.
34 *Ibid*, p. 177, Assistant-Surveyor Evans's Journal 1813-1814.
35 *Ibid*, p. 168.
36 *Ibid*, p. 169.
37 *Ibid*, p. 170.
38 *Ibid*, p. 171.
39 *Ibid*, p. 123.
40 *Sydney Gazette and New South Wales Advertiser*, 8 January 1814, p. 2.
41 Macquarie to Earl Bathurst, 24 May 1814, Watson (ed.), *Historical Records of Australia*,
    Series I, Volume VIII, p. 261.
42 Macquarie to Earl Bathurst, 28 April 1814, *ibid*, p. 150.
43 Macquarie to Earl Bathurst, 14 April 1814, Watson (ed.), *Historical Records of Australia*,
    Series I, Volume VIII, p. 140.
44 Macquarie to Earl Bathurst, 22 March 1815, *ibid*, p. 461.
45 Arthur Wilberforce Jose, Herbert James Carter, *Australian Encyclopedia*, Angus &
    Robertson, 1926, p. 537.
46 On 21 October 1805.
47 Dudley Ryder, 1st Earl of Harrowby (22 December 1762 – 26 December 1847).
48 Henry Goulburn, born 19 March 1784; died 12 January 1856.
49 Frederick Watson (ed.), *Historical Records of Australia, Series III: Despatches and Papers
    Relating to the Settlement of the States, Volume II: Tasmania: July, 1812 – December, 1819*,
    Library Committee of the Commonwealth Parliament, 1921, Introduction, p. xii.
50 Macquarie to Earl Bathurst, 22 March 1815, Watson (ed.), *Historical Records of Australia*,
    Series I, Volume VIII, p. 458.
51 *Ibid*.
52 Macquarie, private memorandum to Thomas Davey, 6 February 1813, Watson (ed.),
    Historical Records of Australia, Series III, Volume II, pp. 23–24.
53 Watson (ed.), *Historical Records of Australia, Series III, Volume II*, Introduction, p. xiv.
54 Macquarie to Earl Bathurst, 22 March 1815, Watson (ed.), *Historical Records of Australia*,
    Series I, Volume VIII, p. 459.
55 *Ibid*, 30 April 1814, p. 240.
56 Broughton to Macquarie, 3 May 1817, Watson (ed.), *Historical Records of Australia, Series III,
    Volume II*, p. 611.
57 'Proclamation, By His Excellency Lachlan Macquarie', *Sydney Gazette and New South
    Wales Advertiser*, 28 May 1814, p. 1.
58 Macquarie to Earl Bathurst, 14 April 1814, Watson (ed.), *Historical Records of Australia*,
    Series I, Volume VIII, pp. 143–144.
59 William Hutchinson (1772–1846).
60 Macquarie, Memoranda, 18 April 1814, *ibid*.
61 Macquarie to Earl Bathurst, 24 May 1814, Watson (ed.), *Historical Records of Australia*,
    Series I, Volume VIII, p. 254.
62 *Sydney Gazette and New South Wales Advertiser*, 21 May 1814, p. 2.
63 *Ibid*.
64 *Ibid*.
65 Macquarie to Earl Bathurst, 24 May 1814, Watson (ed.), *Historical Records of Australia*,
    Series I, Volume VIII, p. 255.

66   On 27 July 1814.

67   Macquarie to Bathurst, 7 October 1814, Watson (ed.), *Historical Records of Australia, Series I, Volume VIII*, p. 295.

68   Jeffery Hart Bent (1781–29 June 1852).

69   Sir John Jamison (1776-1844).

70   Macquarie, Memoranda, 2 June 1814, Vol. Z A772, State Library of New South Wales.

71   Testimony of Private William Merry, 22 August 1814, Davey to Macquarie, March 1815, *Historical Records of Australia*, Series 3, Vol. 2, pp. 77–78.

72   Meeting of Bench of Magistrates, *ibid*, p. 79.

73   'Proclamation Relating to Bushrangers', 28 May 1814, Watson (ed.), *Historical Records of Australia, Series I, Volume VIII*, p. 264.

74   Robert Knopwood (2 June 1763–18 September 1838).

75   Charles Jeffreys (1782-1826).

76   Lt Governor Sorrel to Henry Goulburn, 11 May 1817, Watson (ed.), *Historical Records of Australia, Series III, Volume II*, p. 202.

77   E. R. Pretyman, 'McCarty, Denis (?–1820)', *Australian Dictionary of Biography*, National Centre of Biography, Australian National University, adb.anu.edu.au, published first in hard copy *Australian Dictionary of Biography*, 1967.

78   Deposition of John Whitehouse, Davey to Macquarie, March 1815, Watson (ed.), *Historical Records of Australia, Series III, Volume II*, p. 83.

79   'List of Articles Stolen from the House of Mr Denis McCarty', *ibid*, pp. 84–85.

80   Deposition of William Lucas, Davey to Macquarie, March 1815, *ibid*, p. 84.

81   Thomas E. Wells, *Michael Howe, The Last and Worst of the Bush-Rangers of Van Diemen's Land*, Andrew Bent, 1818.

82   Macquarie to Earl Bathurst, 28 April 1814, Watson (ed.), *Historical Records of Australia, Series I, Volume VIII*, p. 148.

83   Earl Bathurst to Macquarie, 19 August 1813, *ibid*, p. 72.

84   Macquarie to Earl Bathurst, 28 April 1814, *ibid*, p. 148.

85   Macquarie to Earl Bathurst, 19 January 1814, *ibid*, p. 121.

86   Macquarie to Cox, 14 July 1814, from Memoirs of William Cox, J.P., William Brooks, 1901.

87   William Cox, *A narrative of proceedings of William Cox*, p. 2, National Library of Australia, mc N 1475 item 204.

88   Thomas Hobby (1774–1833).

89   *Sydney Gazette and New South Wales Advertiser*, 7 May 1814, p. 2.

90   *Ibid*.

91   Macquarie to Earl Bathurst, 7 October 1814, Watson (ed.), *Historical Records of Australia, Series I, Volume VIII*, p. 315.

92   Macquarie, Memoranda, 18 June 1814, Vol. Z A772, State Library of New South Wales.

93   Macquarie to Earl Bathurst, 7 October 1814, Watson (ed.), *Historical Records of Australia, Series I, Volume VIII*, p. 315.

94   Hamilton Hume (1797–1873).

95   The infection Erysipelas.

96   Macquarie to Henry Goulburn, 15 December 1817, Frederick Watson (ed.), *Historical Records of Australia, Series I: Despatches to and from England, Volume IX: January, 1816 – December, 1818*, Library Committee of the Commonwealth Parliament, 1917, p. 733.

97   *Ibid*, p. 734.

98   Inquest on the body of Charles Thomas, an infant; Macquarie to Henry Goulburn, 15 December 1817, Watson (ed.), *Historical Records of Australia, Series I, Volume IX*, pp. 737–738.

99   Robin Walsh, *In Her Own Words: The Writings of Elizabeth Macquarie*, Exisle, 2011.

Chapter 24

1   Macquarie to Earl Bathurst, 8 October 1814, Watson (ed.), *Historical Records of Australia, Series I, Volume VIII*, p. 368.
2   *Sydney Gazette and New South Wales Advertiser,* 7 January 1810, pp. 2-3.
3   Macquarie *Journal to and from Van Diemen's Land,* 6 November 1811, A777.
4   Macquarie to Earl Bathurst, 8 October 1814, Watson (ed.), *Historical Records of Australia, Series I, Volume IX*, p. 368.
5   *Sydney Gazette and New South Wales Advertiser,* 18 June 1814, p. 1.
6   William Broughton (1768–1821).
7   James Raworth Kennedy (1757-1826).
8   Charles Throsby (1777-1828).
9   Grace Karskens, 'Appin Massacre', dictionaryofsydney.org.
10 *Ibid.*
11 *Sydney Gazette and New South Wales Advertiser,* 14 May 1814, p. 2.
12 *Ibid.*
13 *Ibid.*
14 Grace Karskens, 'Appin Massacre', dictionaryofsydney.org.
15 Sydney Gazette and New South Wales Advertiser, 18 June 1814, p. 1.
16 *Ibid,* 14 May 1814, p. 2.
17 *Ibid,* 4 June 1814, p. 2.
18 Macquarie to Earl Bathurst, 8 October 1814, Watson (ed.), *Historical Records of Australia, Series I, Volume VIII*, p. 368.
19 *Sydney Gazette and New South Wales Advertiser,* 23 July 1814, p. 2.
20 Grace Karskens, 'Appin Massacre', dictionaryofsydney.org.
21 'Government and General Orders', *Sydney Gazette and New South Wales Advertiser,* 2 July 1814, p. 1.
22 *Ibid.*
23 *Sydney Gazette and New South Wales Advertiser,* 24 September 1814, p. 2.
24 *Ibid,* 24 December 1814, p. 2.
25 Macquarie to Earl Bathurst, 8 October 1814, Watson (ed.), *Historical Records of Australia, Series I, Volume VIII*, p. 368.
26 *Ibid.*
27 Macquarie to Earl Bathurst, 8 October 1814, Watson (ed.), *Historical Records of Australia, Series I, Volume VIII*, pp. 368–369.
28 *Ibid.*
29 Macquarie to Earl Bathurst, 8 October 1814, Watson (ed.), *Historical Records of Australia, Series I, Volume VIII*, p. 369.
30 'Plan of the Native Institution', Macquarie to Earl Bathurst, 8 October 1814, Watson (ed.), *Historical Records of Australia, Series I, Volume VIII*, p. 372.
31 'Government and General Order', *Sydney Gazette and New South Wales Advertiser,* 10 December 1814, p. 1.
32 Macquarie to Earl Bathurst, 8 October 1814, Watson (ed.), *Historical Records of Australia, Series I, Volume VIII*, p. 373.
33 William Shelley (1774–1815).
34 Niel Gunson, 'Shelley, William James (1774–1815)', *Australian Dictionary of Biography,* National Centre of Biography, Australian National University, adb.anu.edu.au, published first in hard copy 1967.
35 Macquarie to Earl Bathurst, 8 October 1814, Watson (ed.), *Historical Records of Australia, Series I, Volume VIII*, pp. 369–370.
36 *Ibid,* p. 370.
37 *Ibid,* p. 368.

38   Maria Lock (*c.* 1805–1878) became a prominent Aboriginal landowner.

39   Shelley to Macquarie, 20 August 1814, Watson (ed.), *Historical Records of Australia, Series I, Volume VIII*, p. 371.

40   Macquarie to Earl Bathurst, 24 March 1815, Watson (ed.), *Historical Records of Australia, Series I, Volume VIII*, p. 467.

41   Bungaree, or Boongaree, born 1775; died 24 November 1830.

42   *Sydney Gazette and New South Wales Advertiser,* 4 February 1815, p. 1.

43   J. Brook and J.L. Kohen, *The Parramatta Native Institution and the Black Town: A History,* University of New South Wales Press, 1991, p. 263.

44   Macquarie to Earl Bathurst, 24 March 1815, Watson (ed.), *Historical Records of Australia, Series I, Volume VIII*, p. 467.

45   Ellis Bent to his mother, 27 March 1810, MS 195/3, National Library of Australia.

46   Ellis Bent to J. H. Bent, 2 May 1810, Ellis Bent Letters, National Library of Australia, A141.

47   Deputy Judge Advocate Wylde to Earl Bathurst, 15 August 1821, Watson (ed.), *Historical Records of Australia, Series IV, Volume I*, p. 393.

48   Macquarie to Earl Bathurst, 24 February 1815, Watson (ed.), *Historical Records of Australia, Series I, Volume VIII*, p. 390.

49   *Ibid*, p. 393.

50   Macquarie to Earl Bathurst, 24 February 1815, Watson (ed.), *Historical Records of Australia, Series I, Volume VIII*, p. 390.

51   Macquarie to Earl Bathurst, 28 June 1813, Watson (ed.), *Historical Records of Australia, Series I, Volume VII*, p. 777.

52   *Ibid.*

53   Macquarie to Earl Bathurst, 24 February 1815, Watson (ed.), *Historical Records of Australia, Series I, Volume VII*, p. 391.

54   *Ibid*, p. 393.

55   *Ibid*, p. 394.

56   *Ibid*, pp. 396–397.

57   Macquarie to Earl Bathurst, 24 February 1815, Watson (ed.), *Historical Records of Australia, Series I, Volume VIII*, p. 398.

58   Bent to Under-Secretary Cooke, 7 May 1810, Watson (ed.), *Historical Records of Australia, Series IV, Volume I*, p. 50.

59   C.H. Currey, 'Bent, Jeffery Hart (1781–1852)', *Australian Dictionary of Biography,* National Centre of Biography, Australian National University, adb.anu.edu.au, published first in hard copy 1966.

60   Mr Justice Bent to Earl Bathurst, 21 February 1814, Watson (ed.), *Historical Records of Australia, Series IV, Volume I*, pp. 95–96.

61   William Henry Moore (*c.* 1788–1854).

62   Frederick Garling (1775–1848).

63   Earl Bathurst to Macquarie, 3 February 1814, Watson (ed.), *Historical Records of Australia, Series I, Volume VIII*, p. 125.

64   *Ibid*, p. 130.

65   'Sitting Magistrate', *Sydney Gazette and New South Wales Advertiser*, 4 February 1815, p. 1.

66   J.H. Bent to Earl Bathurst, 5 April 1817, Watson (ed.), *Historical Records of Australia, Series IV, Volume I*, p. 241.

67   J.H. Bent to Earl Bathurst, 1 July 1815, *ibid*, p. 146.

68   J.H. Bent to Henry Goulburn, 25 July 1818, Watson (ed.), *Historical Records of Australia, Series IV, Volume I*, p. 309.

69   Macquarie to Earl Bathurst, 24 June 1815, Watson (ed.), *Historical Records of Australia, Series I, Volume VIII*, p. 554.

70   George Crossley (1749–1823).

71   Edward Eagar (1787–1866).

72   K.G. Allars, 'Crossley, George (1749–1823)', *Australian Dictionary of Biography,* National Centre of Biography, Australian National University, adb.anu.edu.au, published first in hard copy 1966.

73   Bent to Macquarie, 20 April 1815, Watson (ed.), *Historical Records of Australia, Series I, Volume VIII*, p. 495.

74   Macquarie to Earl Bathurst, 24 June 1815, *ibid*, p. 554.

75   *Ibid.*

76   John William Lewin (1770–1819).

77   John Joseph William Molesworth Oxley, born 1784; died 25 May 1828.

78   Lachlan Macquarie, *Journal of a Tour of the Newly Discovered Country West of the Blue Mountains. 25 April 1815–19 May 1815*. Original held in the Mitchell Library, Sydney. ML Ref: A779 1-10 ff. [Microfilm Reel CY303 Frames #4-21], 26 April 1815.

79   *Ibid*, 4 May 1815.

80   *Ibid*, 7 May 1815.

81   *Ibid*, 10 May 1815.

82   Originally called Coura Rocks.

83   Macquarie to Earl Bathurst, 24 June 1815, Watson (ed.), *Historical Records of Australia, Series I, Volume VIII*, p. 576.

84   *Ibid.*

85   Macquarie to Earl Bathurst, 18 March 1816, Watson (ed.), *Historical Records of Australia, Series I, Volume IX*, p. 60.

86   *Ibid*, p. 850.

87   *Sydney Gazette and New South Wales Advertiser*, 6 May 1815, p. 2.

88   Minutes of the Proceedings of the Supreme Court, Watson (ed.), *Historical Records of Australia, Series I, Volume VIII*, p. 510.

89   *Ibid*, p. 511.

90   *Ibid*, p. 515.

91   *Ibid.*

92   *Ibid.*

93   Minutes of the Proceedings of the Supreme Court, Watson (ed.), *Historical Records of Australia, Series I, Volume VIII*, p. 516.

94   Broughton and Riley to Mr Justice Bent, 12 May 1815, *ibid*, p. 516.

95   Mr Justice Bent to Broughton and Riley, *ibid*, p. 517.

96   Statement of Mr Broughton's Opinion, 23 May 1815, *ibid*, pp. 526–527.

97   Proclamation, Macquarie to Earl Bathurst, 24 June 1815, *ibid*, p. 567.

98   Macquarie to Davey, 18 September 1815, Watson (ed.), *Historical Records of Australia, Series III, Volume II*, p. 126.

99   Thomas E. Wells, *Michael Howe*. It was Hunter's Island then.

100 Enclosure No. 12, Watson (ed.), *Historical Records of Australia, Series I, Volume VIII*, p. 528.

101 Memorandum, *ibid*, p. 532.

102 Bent to Macquarie, 31 May 1815, *ibid*, p. 536.

103 Macquarie to Bent, 2 June 1815, *ibid*, p. 540.

104 Macquarie to Earl Bathurst, 'Private and Confidential', *ibid*, p. 621.

105 *Ibid.*

Chapter 25

1   A sermon preached at St. John's [on the death of Ellis Bent, Judge Advocate of New South Wales], 1815 Nov. 19 [manuscript] / by the Reverend Samuel Marsden, Marsden Papers. Mitchell Library C244, p. 3.

2   camdenhistory.org.au.

3 Macquarie, Lachlan. *Journal of a Tour Made by Govr. Macquarie and Suite, into the Interior parts of the Colony of N. S. Wales in Octr. 1815* . [Cowpastures] 3 October 1815 – 12 October 1815. Original held in the Mitchell Library, Sydney. ML Ref: A780 1-41 ff. [Microfilm Reel CY303 Frames #83-123], 4 October 1815.

4 Walter Stevenson Davidson (1785 -1869).

5 The spelling of the village there has now changed to 'Menangle'.

6 James Proctor Harrex (1766 –1825). Sometimes spelled Harrax.

7 Reuben Uther (1791–1880).

8 Andrew Hamilton Hume (1762–1849).

9 David Allan (1780-1852).

10 Macquarie Journal of a Tour, 4 October 1815.

11 *Ibid*, 5 October 1815.

12 *Ibid*.

13 *Ibid*, 8 October 1815.

14 *Ibid*.

15 Rowland Hassall (1768-1820).

16 Michael McGrath a free-man, and Dennis Bryan a convict.

17 Macquarie Journal of a Tour, 7 October 1815.

18 Now a protected nature reserve.

19 Macquarie Journal of a Tour, 9 October 1815.

20 Captain Daniel Woodriff (1756-1842).

21 Mary Birch (1792-1882).

22 George Palmer (1784-1854).

23 Macquarie Journal of a Tour, 12 October 1815.

24 'Proceedings before the Superintendent of Police', Wentworth to Macquarie, 9 September 1815, Watson (ed.), *Historical Records of Australia, Series I, Volume IX, Historical Records of Australia*, Series 1, Vol. 9, p. 17.

25 'Summons issued to Mr Justice Bent', *ibid*, p. 19.

26 'Bent to Wentworth', *ibid*.

27 *Ibid*, p. 20.

28 'Government and General Orders', *Sydney Gazette and New South Wales Advertiser*, 9 September 1815, p. 1.

29 *Ibid*.

30 'Answer to Mr Justice Bent's letter', 2 October 1815, Watson (ed.), *Historical Records of Australia, Series I, Volume IX*, p. 25.

31 Ellis Bent to Earl Bathurst, 14 October 1814, *ibid*, p. 108.

32 Ellis Bent to Earl Bathurst, 1 July 1815, Watson (ed.), *Historical Records of Australia, Series IV, Volume I*, p. 127.

33 'Answer to Mr Justice Bent's letter', 26 October 1815, *ibid*, p. 26.

34 Bent to Macquarie, 9 January 1816, *ibid*, p. 29.

35 Under Henry Secretary Goulburn to Mr Robert Bent, 31 January 1816, Watson (ed.), *Historical Records of Australia, Series IV, Volume I*, Historical Records of Australia, Series 4, Vol. 1, p. 178.

36 Earl Bathurst to Macquarie, 18 April 1816, Watson (ed.), *Historical Records of Australia, Series I, Volume IX*, p. 108.

37 *Ibid*, p. 107.

38 Bathurst to Mr Justice Bent, 12 April 1816, Watson (ed.), *Historical Records of Australia, Series I, Volume IX*, p. 112.

39 *Ibid*.

40 Bathurst to Judge-Advocate Bent, 12 April 1816, Watson (ed.), *Historical Records of Australia, Series I, Volume IX*, pp. 110–111.

41   Macquarie to Earl Bathurst, 20 February 1816, *ibid*, p. 4.

42   Macquarie to Earl Bathurst, 22 February 1820, Watson (ed.), *Historical Records of Australia, Series I, Volume X*, p. 223.

43   Macquarie to Earl Bathurst, 20 February 1816, Watson (ed.), *Historical Records of Australia, Series I, Volume IX*, p. 4.

44   Samuel Marsden to John Hunter, 11 August 1798, F.M. Bladen (ed.), *Historical Records of New South Wales, Vol. III – Hunter, 1796–1799*, Charles Potter, Government Printer, 1895, pp. 439–440.

45   A sermon preached at St. John's [on the death of Ellis Bent, Judge Advocate of New South Wales], 1815 Nov. 19 [manuscript] / by the Reverend Samuel Marsden, Marsden Papers. Mitchell Library C244, pp. 17-40.

46   Bent Sermon p. 10.

47   Paul preached to the Bereans and wrote in Acts 17:11 that they were noble minded because they examined the Scriptures every day to see if what Paul said was true.

48   *Ibid*, pp. 12-13.

49   *Ibid*, p. 14.

50   Handwritten notes on the front of the sermon in the Mitchell Library.

51   J.T. Bigge to Samuel Marsden, 20 January 1821, Marsden Papers, p. 50, Mitchell Library C244.

52   Jeffery Hart Bent to Earl Bathurst, 25 February 1816, Watson (ed.), *Historical Records of Australia, Series IV, Volume I*, pp. 184–185.

53   Macquarie to Earl Bathurst, 20 February 1816, Watson (ed.), *Historical Records of Australia, Series I, Volume IX*, p. 11.

54   *Ibid*, p. 10.

55   Later Sir John Wylde (1781–1859).

56   Ann Hassall, née Marsden (1794–1885).

57   Ann Marsden to Mrs Stokes, 18 June 1813, Hassall Correspondence A1677, State Library of NSW.

58   Wilberforce to Macquarie, 15 March 1814, Letterbooks A797.

59   Wilberforce to Marsden, 21 March 1814, Marsden Papers, C244, State Library of NSW.

60   Macquarie to Earl Bathurst, 22 June 1815, Watson (ed.), *Historical Records of Australia, Series I, Volume VIII*, p. 489.

61   'Government and General Order', 5 February 1814, *ibid*, pp. 257–258.

62   Marsden to Macquarie, 9 April 1814, Bigge Appendix, Box 13, State Library of NSW.

63   'Government and General Orders', *Sydney Gazette and New South Wales Advertiser*, 10 September 1814, p. 1.

64   *Ibid*.

65   Marsden, *An Answer to Certain Calumnies in the Late Governor Macquarie's Pamphlet*, p. 41.

66   Thomas Hill was hanged on 1 March 1816 for cutting and maiming Police Constable Thomas Smith near Parramatta.

67   T. Crofton Croker, *Memoirs of Joseph Holt: General of the Irish rebels, in 1798*, Vol. 2, Henry Coulburn, 1838, pp. 120-122.

68   William Goode, the elder (1762–1816).

69   First published in 1811.

70   Macquarie to Earl Bathurst, 20 February 1816, Watson (ed.), *Historical Records of Australia, Series I, Volume VIII*, p. 337.

71   *Ibid*.

72   *Ibid*.

73   Earl Bathurst to Macquarie, 2 December 1815, Watson (ed.), *Historical Records of Australia, Series I, Volume VIII*, p. 637.

74   Macquarie, Lachlan. *Diary 10 April 1816 – 1 July 1818,* Original held in the Mitchell Library, Sydney. ML Ref: A773 pp.50-59. [Microfilm Reel CY301 Frames #286-295], 14 October 1816.

75   *Sydney Gazette and New South Wales Advertiser,* 9 March 1816, p. 2.

76   *Ibid.*

77   *Ibid.* The *Gazette* reported the warrior as being David Budbury, but corrected that account a week later, 'as we are requested to declare, upon the most undoubted authority, that he was far from the scene, and is perfectly a friendly and well-disposed native towards us. The report, which originated from the mistake of his person, under the circumstances of alarm and terror, we feel it our duty to correct, as a bad name in such a case might be attended with the most unhappy result to an innocent person, and become even doubly fatal, in making an enemy of a friend, and giving him to a condition of extremity that might justify hostility in him, as palpably an act of self-defence.' (*Gazette,* 16 March, p. 2).

78   *Sydney Gazette and New South Wales Advertiser,* 9 March 1816, p. 2.

79   *Ibid,* 16 March 1816, p. 2.

80   Samuel to Thomas Hassall, 16 March 1816, Hassall Family Correspondence, ML A1677/3, 619–22, 627–30, State Library of New South Wales.

81   *Ibid.*

82   *Ibid.*

83   *Sydney Gazette and New South Wales Advertiser,* 30 March 1816, p. 2.

84   Macquarie to Earl Bathurst, 18 March 1816, Watson (ed.), *Historical Records of Australia, Series I, Volume VIII,* pp. 53–54.

85   *Ibid.*

86   *Ibid.*

87   *Ibid,* p. 54.

Chapter 26

1   The Governor's Diary & Memorandum Book Commencing on and from Wednesday the 10th. Day of April 1816. — At Sydney, in N. S. Wales. Entry for Wednesday, 10 April 1816, Macquarie, Lachlan. *Diary 10 April 1816 – 1 July 1818,* Original held in the Mitchell Library, Sydney. ML Ref: A773 pp.1-8. [Microfilm Reel CY301 Frames #237-245].

2   James Wallis (c.1785-1858).

3   Sydney Gazette, *Sydney Gazette and New South Wales Advertiser,* 20 January 1816, p. 2.

4   Macquarie to Earl Bathurst, 22 March 1815, Watson (ed.), *Historical Records of Australia, Series I, Volume VIII,* p. 459.

5   *Ibid.*

6   Marsden to Macquarie, 19 July 1815, from: Henry Grey Bennet, Letter to Viscount Sidmouth, J Ridgeway, 1819, p. 126.

7   *Ibid.*

8   Hannibal Hawkins Macarthur, born 16 January 1788; died 21 October 1861.

9   Bigge Reports, Convicts, p. 68.

10   Macquarie to Earl Bathurst, 17 November 1812, Watson (ed.), *Historical Records of Australia, Series I, Volume VII,* p. 614–615.

11   Benjamin Vale (1788–1863).

12   Macquarie to Earl Bathurst, 7 October 1814, Watson (ed.), *Historical Records of Australia, Series I, Volume VIII,* p. 300.

13   *Ibid.*

14   Macquarie to Earl Bathurst, 8 March 1816, Watson (ed.), *Historical Records of Australia, Series I, Volume IX,* p. 45.

15   Macquarie Diary, 10 April 1816.

16   Charles Throsby to Wentworth, 5 April 1816, Wentworth Papers, A752/CY699 Mitchell Library, pp. 183-6.

17   *Ibid.*

18   Macquarie Diary, 10 April 1816.

19   *Ibid.*

20   Macquarie Diary, 10 April 1816.

21   Journal of the Royal Australian Historical Society, Volume 57, 1971, p. 357.

22   'Instructions to Captain Schaw', Colonial Secretary's Correspondence, 4/1734, 149–68, New South Wales State Records.

23   *Sydney Gazette and New South Wales Advertiser,* 11 May 1816, p. 2.

24   Grace Karskens, 'Appin Massacre', dictionaryofsydney.org.

25   James Wallis diary, Colonial Secretary's Papers, 4/1735.

26   *Ibid.*

27   *Ibid.*

28   *Ibid.*

29   *Ibid.*

30   Also written as 'Kinnahygal'.

31   Carol Liston, *Campbelltown: The Bicentennial History,* Allen & Unwin, 1988, p. 23.

32   Adamson George Parker (1794-1870).

33   William Byrne, *'Old Memories: General Reminiscences of Early Colonists – II'*, Old Times, May 1903, p. 105.

34   Paul Turnbull, 'Outlawed Subjects: The Procurement and Scientific Uses of Australian Aboriginal Heads, ca. 1803-1835', *Eighteenth-Century Life,* Volume 22, Number 1, February 1998, Duke University Press, pp. 156-171.

35   *Joseph L Davis,* The Appin Massacre & Lieutenant Adamson George Parker: The Evidence of the Only Contemporary Written Record Of Travel Through Illawarra in 1816, academia.edu.

36   Mike Pickering, 'Lost in Time?' (paper given at School of Philosophical and Historical Inquiry, University of Sydney, November 2007, 4–7; pers. com. Mike Pickering, Senior Curator, National Museum of Australia, 2008. The heads are still stored in the National Museum of Australia's Canberra repatriation unit, with the remains of up to 700 other Indigenous people, whose bodies were stolen and which can't, for various reasons, be returned to country.

37   James Wallis diary, Colonial Secretary's Papers, 4/1735.

38   George Marriott Woodhouse, born 14 June 1790, Suffolk, England; died 31 May 1869, West Wyalong, NSW.

39   Lt. Adamson George Parker, State Records of NSW, Colonial Secretary Letters, 4/1735, Reel 6045, pp. 60-62.

40   Macquarie Diary, 4 May 1816.

41   Instructions to Captain Schaw', Colonial Secretary's Correspondence, 4/1734, 149–68, New South Wales State Records.

42   'Proclamation', *Sydney Gazette and New South Wales Advertiser,* 4 May 1816, p. 1.

43   *Ibid.*

44   *Ibid.*

45   *Ibid.*

46   Macquarie to Earl Bathurst, 8 June 1816, Watson (ed.), *Historical Records of Australia, Series I, Volume IX,* pp. 139–140.   .

47   Macquarie Diary, 7 May 1816.

48   *Ibid,* 25 May 1816.

49   *Ibid.*

50   *Ibid,* 6 June 1816.

51 Macquarie Diary, 4 June 1816.

52 *Ibid*, 6 June 1816.

53 Macquarie referred to him as 'Dewal' or 'Dual'.

54 'Government and General Orders', *Sydney Gazette and New South Wales Advertiser*, 10 August 1816, p. 1.

55 *Sydney Gazette and New South Wales Advertiser,* 13 July 1816, p. 2.

56 *Ibid*, 31 August 1816.

57 Their names were Murrah, Bunduck, Kongate, Wootan, Rachel, Yelloming, Myles, Wallah alias Warren, Carbone Jack, alias Kurringy, and Narrang Jack.

58 'Proclamation', *Sydney Gazette and New South Wales Advertiser*, 3 August 1816, p. 1.

59 *Ibid*.

60 *Ibid*, 9 November 1816, p. 1.

61 Macquarie Diary, 28 December 1816.

62 Macquarie to Earl Bathurst, 4 April 1817, Watson (ed.), *Historical Records of Australia, Series I, Volume IX*, p. 342.

Chapter 27

1 Macquarie to Henry Goulburn, 21 December 1817, Watson (ed.), *Historical Records of Australia, Series I, Volume IX*, p. 747. From pp. 867–869: 'These were probably the first occasions when the word Australia was used in official correspondence. [Macquarie had also referred to Matthew Flinders' charts of 'Australia']. The origin of the word is involved in obscurity. In the memorial of Fernandez de Quiros, published at Pamplona in 1610, the phrase "*Austrialia* incognita" appeared on the title page, and the word "*Austrialia*" [spelt with an extra i] in the first and seventh paragraphs.'.

2 Macquarie to Castlereagh, 12 March 1810, Watson (ed.), *Historical Records of Australia, Series I, Volume VII*, p. 242.

3 Macquarie to Earl Bathurst, 29 March 1817, Watson (ed.), *Historical Records of Australia, Series I, Volume IX*, p. 219.

4 *Sydney Gazette and New South Wales Advertiser,* 7 January 1810, pp. 2–3.

5 Minute Book for Bank of NSW.

6 Macquarie Diary, 1 and 8 September 1816.

7 *Ibid*, 13 June 1816. The seat is still known as Mrs Macquarie's Chair.

8 Charles Frazer (*c.*1788–1831), also reported as Fraser and Frazier.

9 The central building was for hospital wards (demolished in 1879), a northern wing (now Parliament House) was for the Principal Surgeon D'Arcy Wentworth, a rare visitor, and a southern wing (now The Mint) housed William Redfern, the assistant surgeon who ran the hospital.

10 Wentworth Papers A 752, p. 188, State Library of NSW.

11 On 3 October 1817. From E.W. Dunlop, 'Blaxcell, Garnham (1778–1817)', *Australian Dictionary of Biography,* National Centre of Biography, Australian National University, adb.anu.edu.au, published first in hard copy 1966.

12 Colonial Secretary Letters Sent, SRNSW 4/3494, reel 6004, pp. 412-413.

13 Morton Herman, 'Greenway, Francis (1777–1837)', *Australian Dictionary of Biography,* National Centre of Biography, Australian National University, adb.anu.edu.au, published first in hard copy 1966.

14 Greenway, Bryan and Bradley to Contractors, 15 May 1816, Bigge's Appendix, Volume 133, Bonwick Transcripts 14, CY1454, pp.1392, 1396.

15 Surveyor's Report on Hospital, Bigge's Appendix, Volume 133, Bonwick Transcripts 14, CY1454, pp.1336-8.

16 Greenway, Bryan and Bradley to Contractors, 15 May 1816, Bigge's Appendix, Volume 133, Bonwick Transcripts 14, CY1454, pp.1392, 1396.

17   Greenway, Bryan and Bradley to Contractors, 15 May 1816, Bigge's Appendix, Volume 133, Bonwick Transcripts 14, CY1454, p.1393.

18   Greenway to Macquarie, November 1818, Bigge's Appendix, Bonwick Transcripts 16, CY1553, p.2142.

19   Macquarie, Lachlan. *Diary 1 March 1820 – 8 March 1821.*Original held in the Mitchell Library, Sydney. ML Ref: A774 pp.168-174; [Microfilm Reel: CY301 Frames #574-580], 23 November 1820.

20   Dr Fiona Starr, 'How the "Sidney Slaughter House" Got Its Name', sydneylivingmuseums.com.au.

21   William Redfern notebook, 1797-1825, State Library of NSW, ML MAV_FM3_709, 45.

22   Dr Fiona Starr, 'How the "Sidney Slaughter House" Got Its Name', sydneylivingmuseums.com.au.

23   J. Frederick Watson, *The History of Sydney Hospital from 1811-1911,* W. A. Gullick, Government Printer, 1911, p. 41.

24   Henry Cowper (1800-1849).

25   John Ritchie, *The Evidence to the Bigge Reports,* Volume 1, The Oral Evidence, Heinemann, 1971, p. 142.

26   *Ibid,* p. 126.

27   Macquarie to Earl Bathurst, 24 June 1815, Watson (ed.), *Historical Records of Australia, Series I, Volume VIII,* p. 554.

28   Macquarie Diary, 30 September 1816.

29   Macquarie to Henry Goulburn, 21 December 1817, Watson (ed.), *Historical Records of Australia, Series I, Volume IX,* p. 747.

30   The fort was demolished in 1901 to make way for tramway sheds that remained until the Opera House rose from their rubble.

31   *Australian* (Sydney), 28 April 1825, p. 4.

32   Mary Casey, A Patina of Age: Elizabeth Macquarie (née) Campbell and the Influence of the Buildings and Landscape of Argyll, Scotland, in Colonial New South Wales, *International Journal of Historical Archaeology*, Vol. 14, No. 3 (June 2010), pp. 335-356.

33   Edward Gyfford, *Designs for Elegant Cottages and Small Villas, J. Taylor, 1806.*

34   Macquarie, Lachlan, *Diary 10 April 1816 - 1 July 1818.* Original held in the Mitchell Library, Sydney, ML Ref: A773 pp.50-59. [Microfilm Reel CY301 Frames #286-295], 2 October 1816.

35   Macquarie, Lachlan. *Diary 1 March 1820 – 8 March 1821,* Original held in the Mitchell Library, Sydney, ML Ref: A774 pp.174-194; [Microfilm Reel: CY301 Frames #580-602], 25 December 1820.

36   Manuscript transcription of the complete version of the journal of Rose de Freycinet, kept during her voyage onboard *L'Uranie,* 1817-1820, transcribed by Charles Duplomb, National Library of Australia, MS 10124.

37   Captain John Cliffe Watts (1786-1873).

38   Then called Flagstaff Hill.

39   'St John's Church, Parramatta - manuscript notes describing the origin of the towers, and information regarding Lieutenant John Watts, by M. E. Bagot, 17 January 1895, Papers relating to Parramatta, 1823-1895, Ap 41, State Library of NSW.

40   Earl Bathurst to Macquarie, 24 August 1818, Watson (ed.), *Historical Records of Australia, Series I, Volume IX,* p. 832.

41   Macquarie Diary, 19 September 1816. Built by Edward Cureton for £85.

42   It was built in 1819 by stonemason, Edward Cureton and demolished about 1883 to make way for a statue of Thomas Sutcliffe Mort.

43   Also known as South Head Upper Light.

44 Macquarie Diary, 11 July 1816.

45 The Lighthouse was completed in November 1817, though it was later pulled down and a stronger near-replica built in 1880.

46 *Ibid.*

47 *Sydney Gazette and New South Wales Advertiser*, 12 December 1818, p. 1.

48 Macquarie to Earl Bathurst, 12 December 1817, Watson (ed.), *Historical Records of Australia, Series I, Volume IX*, p. 719.

49 Earl Bathurst to Macquarie, 24 August 1818, Watson (ed.), *Historical Records of Australia, Series I, Volume IX*, p. 833.

50 Macquarie to Earl Bathurst, 20 July 1819, Watson (ed.), *Historical Records of Australia, Series I, Volume X*, pp. 193.

51 The church was completed in 1824 and superseded by the Sydney Town Hall clock tower completed in 1873.

52 Macquarie to Earl Bathurst, 18 March 1816, Watson (ed.), *Historical Records of Australia, Series I, Volume IX*, pp. 70–71.

53 Macquarie to Earl Bathurst, 12 December 1817, *ibid*, p. 719.

54 Macquarie to Earl Bathurst, 24 March May 1819, Watson (ed.), *Historical Records of Australia, Series I, Volume X*, p. 97.

55 Bigge report, Bonwick Transcript, Box 27, pp. 6306-07, State Library of NSW.

56 *Sydney Gazette and New South Wales Advertiser*, 9 November 1816, p. 2.

57 Bigge Appendix, Box 16, pp. 1900-31.

58 *Ibid.*

59 Macquarie to Duke of York, 25 July 1817, Watson (ed.), *Historical Records of Australia, Series I, Volume IX*, p. 445.

60 Macquarie Diary, 28 December 1816.

61 *Ibid*, 12 January 1817.

62 Daniel Moowattin (*c.* 1791–1816), also known as Mow-watty, Moowatting and Dan Mowwatting.

63 *Sydney Gazette & New South Wales Advertiser: Supplement*, 28 September 1816, pp. 1d–2b.

64 Macquarie to Davey, 31 July 1816, Watson (ed.), *Historical Records of Australia, Series III, Volume II*, p. 155.

65 Macquarie to Davey, 27 November 1816, *ibid*, p. 166.

66 *Ibid*, p. 444.

67 *Ibid*, p. 442.

68 *Ibid*, p. 446.

69 *Ibid*, p. 447.

70 Robert William Felton Lathrop Murray (1777–1850).

71 Macquarie to Earl Bathurst, 13 May 1817, Watson (ed.), *Historical Records of Australia, Series I, Volume IX*, pp. 392–393.

72 Watson (ed.), *Historical Records of Australia, Series I, Volume IX*, p. 453.

73 Macquarie Diary, 19 September 1817.

74 Macquarie to Earl Bathurst, 8 March 1816, Watson (ed.), *Historical Records of Australia, Series I, Volume IX*, p. 45.

75 Government and General Orders, 18 March 1816, *ibid*, pp. 100–101.

76 Bigge Appendix, Box 26, pp. 5920-3.

77 Joshua John Moore (1790–1864).

78 Macquarie Diary, 28 June 1816.

79 Macquarie Diary, 11 December 1816.

80 Government and General Orders, Sydney Gazette, *Sydney Gazette and New South Wales Advertiser*, 14 December 1816, p. 1.

81 C.H. Currey, 'Bent, Jeffery Hart (1781–1852)', *Australian Dictionary of Biography*, National Centre of Biography, Australian National University, adb.anu.edu.au, published first in hard copy 1966.

82 Ellis Bent to Henry Goulburn, 25 July 1818, Watson (ed.), *Historical Records of Australia, Series IV, Volume I*, pp. 308–309.

83 Macquarie to Earl Bathurst, 1 December 1817, Watson (ed.), *Historical Records of Australia, Series I, Volume IX*, p. 497.

84 Robert Townson (*c.* 1762–1827).

85 Dr John Horsley (1768–1834).

86 Macquarie to Earl Bathurst, 1 December 1817, Watson (ed.), *Historical Records of Australia, Series I, Volume IX*, p. 501.

87 Allan Cunningham (1791–1839).

88 Macquarie to Earl Bathurst, 13 December 1817, Watson (ed.), *Historical Records of Australia, Series I, Volume IX*, p. 726.

89 'Request for the Building of a Benevolent Society, 1820', NSW State Archives and Records, NRS 897 [4/1744, page 255-256].

90 Edward Smith Hall (28 March 1786 – 18 September 1860).

91 The building was reclaimed in 1901 to build Sydney's Central Railway Station.

92 *Sydney Gazette and New South Wales Advertiser*, 4 January 1817, p. 3.

93 Robert Jenkins (c. 1777-1822).

94 *Sydney Gazette and New South Wales Advertiser*, 4 January 1817, p. 3.

95 *Ibid*, 11 January 1817, p. 2.

96 *Sydney Gazette, Sydney Gazette and New South Wales Advertiser*, 4 March 1814, p. 2.

97 *Ibid*, 18 January 1817, p. 1.

98 Report of the Judge-Advocate of New South Wales, 20 March 1821, Watson (ed.), *Historical Records of Australia, Series I, Volume X*, pp. 447–448.

99 *Ibid*, p. 455.

100 *Ibid*, p. 472.

101 Watson (ed.), *Historical Records of Australia, Series IV, Volume I*, p. 939.

102 Campbell to Macquarie, 31 March 1819, Watson (ed.), *Historical Records of Australia, Series I, Volume X*, p. 140.

103 *Ibid*.

104 Macquarie Diary, 15 October 1817.

Chapter 28

1   Elizabeth Macquarie to James Drummond, 12 December 1817, Letterbooks A797.

2   Earl Bathurst to Macquarie, 6 February 1817, Watson (ed.), *Historical Records of Australia, Series I, Volume IX*, p. 207.

3   Macquarie to Earl Bathurst, 4 November 1817, p. 493.

4   Macquarie to Earl Bathurst, 24 November 1817, Watson (ed.), *Historical Records of Australia, Series I, Volume IX*, p. 491.

5   *Ibid*.

6   *Ibid*.

7   Macquarie to Earl Bathurst, 3 April 1817, *ibid*, p. 330.

8   *Ibid*.

9   Macquarie to Henry Goulburn, 17 May 1817, *ibid*, p. 410.

10 Macquarie to Earl Bathurst, 3 April 1817, Watson (ed.), *Historical Records of Australia, Series I, Volume IX*, p. 330.

11 *Ibid*.

12 Deposition of Daniel Read, 22 April 1816, Watson (ed.), *Historical Records of Australia, Series I, Volume IX*, p. 885.

13 Macquarie to Henry Goulburn, 15 December 1817, *ibid*, p. 735.

14 Watson (ed.), *Historical Records of Australia, Series I, Volume IX*, p. 860.

15 Deposition of Daniel Read, 22 April 1816, *ibid*, p. 885.

16 Macquarie to Henry Goulburn, 15 December 1817, *ibid*, p. 735.

17 Macquarie to Earl Bathurst, 4 December 1817, *ibid*, p. 502.

18 Earl Bathurst to Macquarie, 24 January 1817, Watson (ed.), *Historical Records of Australia, Series I, Volume IX*, p. 197.

19 Bayly to Bunbury, 13 March 1816, *ibid*, p. 858.

20 *Ibid*.

21 Macquarie to Earl Bathurst, 4 December 1817, Watson (ed.), *Historical Records of Australia, Series I, Volume IX*, p. 503.

22 *Ibid*, p. 200.

23 Macquarie to Earl Bathurst, 1 December 1817, *ibid*, p. 503.

24 *Ibid*, p. 495.

25 Macquarie to Earl Bathurst, 4 December 1817, *ibid*, p. 502.

26 Macquarie to Earl Bathurst, *ibid*, p. 503.

27 *Ibid*.

28 Macquarie to Earl Bathurst, 4 December 1817, Watson (ed.), *Historical Records of Australia, Series I, Volume IX*, p. 506.

29 Macquarie to Earl Bathurst, 1 December 1817, *ibid*, p. 498.

30 *Ibid*, p. 499.

31 *Ibid*.

32 Macquarie to Earl Bathurst, 13 December 1817, Watson (ed.), *Historical Records of Australia, Series I, Volume IX*, p. 727.

33 Wells, *Michael Howe*.

34 William Nairn (1767–1853).

35 Macquarie to Sorell, 24 May 1817, Watson (ed.), *Historical Records of Australia, Series III, Volume II*, p. 241.

36 Sorell to Macquarie, 13 September 1817, *ibid*, p. 275–277.

37 Elizabeth Macquarie to James Drummond, 12 December 1817, Letterbooks A797.

38 *Ibid*.

39 *Ibid*.

40 Macquarie Diary, 3 January 1818.

41 Macquarie to Samuel Marsden, 8 January 1818, Letterbooks A797.

42 *A Letter to Earl Bathurst*, p. 123.

43 Macquarie to Samuel Marsden, 8 January 1818, Letterbooks A797.

44 *Ibid*.

45 Marsden to Wilberforce, 5 February 1818, *A Letter to Earl Bathurst*, p. 117.

46 *Ibid*, p. 117-8.

47 Macquarie Diary, 27 January 1818.

48 *Ibid*, 9 July 1818.

49 *Ibid*, 17 July 1818. Maclaine was killed on 13 January 1818.

50 Macquarie recorded the convicts as William Warner, Patrick Byrne, James Blake, George Simpson, James Williams, John Williams, Francis Lloyd, Barnard Butler, Thomas Ellis, John Dwyer, Richard Watts and Henry Shippey. The first five had also been with Oxley on the previous year's 1817 journey up the Lachlan River.

51 'Government and General Orders', *Sydney Gazette and New South Wales Advertiser*, 28 March 1818, p. 1.

52 Macquarie Diary, 11 November 1818.

53 Macquarie to Earl Bathurst, 24 March 1819, Watson (ed.), *Historical Records of Australia, Series I, Volume IX*, pp. 95–96.

54   *Ibid.*
55   Thomas E. Wells, *Michael Howe, The Last and Worst of the Bush-Rangers.*
56   'History of Australian Bushranging', *Sunbury News,* 10 September 1904, p. 4.

Chapter 29

1   Macquarie Diary, 27 December 1819.
2   House of Commons Hansard, Vol. 39, p. 464.
3   Henry Grey Bennet, *A Letter to Earl Bathurst, Secretary of State for the Colonial Department,* J Ridgway, 1820, pp. 56, 71.
4   *Ibid,* p. 4.
5   House of Commons Hansard, Vol. 39, p. 756. api.parliament.uk/historic-hansard/commons.
6   On 16 August 1819, at St Peter's Field, Manchester.
7   House of Commons Hansard, Vol. 39, 471-72.
8   Macquarie Diary, 20 May 1818.
9   Jeremiah Francis O'Flynn (1788–1831).
10   House of Commons Hansard, Vol. 39, p. 475.
11   *Ibid,* p. 473.
12   Macquarie, Journal, 4 June 1819.
13   Macquarie laid the foundation stone on 31 August 1819 on the south side of the burying ground but the plan was abandoned after the Bigge Report.
14   John Ritchie, *Lachlan Macquarie,* Melbourne University Press, 1986, p. 153.
15   Macquarie to Earl Bathurst, 28 February 1820, Watson (ed.), *Historical Records of Australia, Series I, Volume X,* p. 278.
16   Ritchie, *Lachlan Macquarie,* p. 157.
17   House of Commons Hansard, Vol. 39, p. 480.
18   John Thomas Bigge (1780–1843).
19   Thomas Hobbes Scott (1783–1860).
20   James Bowman (1784–1846).
21   Earl Bathurst to Macquarie, 18 October 1818, Watson (ed.), *Historical Records of Australia, Series I, Volume IX,* p. 839.
22   Earl Bathurst to Macquarie, 30 January 1819, Watson (ed.), *Historical Records of Australia, Series I, Volume X,* pp. 2–3.
23   Macquarie Diary, 27 September 1819. Watts returned to England to seek a promotion in the army and in 1823 married Macquarie's niece Jane Campbell.
24   On 27 December 1818.
25   Macquarie Diary, 2 October 1819.
26   'Macquarie, Hector (1794-1845)', mq.edu.au.
27   Lachlan Macquarie to Charles Macquarie, 7 and 19 October 1819, MS 202, National Library of Australia.
28   Macquarie Diary, 7 October 1819.
29   Commission of John Thomas Bigge, Watson (ed.), *Historical Records of Australia, Series I, Volume X,* pp. 3–4.
30   Bathurst to Bigge, 6 January 1819, *ibid,* p. 7.
31   *Ibid,* p. 8.
32   *Ibid,* p. 11.
33   Macarthur to Elizabeth Macarthur, 3 May 1810, from Sibella Macarthur Onslow, *Some Early Records of The Macarthurs of Camden,* Angus & Robertson, 1914, p. 192.
34   Macquarie to Bigge, 6 November 1819, Watson (ed.), *Historical Records of Australia, Series I, Volume X,* p. 221.
35   *Ibid.*

36 *Ibid*, p. 223.
37 Bigge to Macquarie, 10 November 1819, Watson (ed.), *Historical Records of Australia, Series I, Volume X, Ibid*, p. 227.
38 Bigge to Macquarie, 2 November 1819, *ibid*, p. 220.
39 Samuel Marsden to Bigge, 28 December 1819, Bigge Appendix, Vol 130, *Historical Records of New Zealand*, nzetc.victoria.ac.nz.
40 Macarthur to his son John, 20 February 1820, from Sibella Macarthur Onslow, *Some Early Records of The Macarthurs of Camden*, Angus & Robertson, 1914, p. 323.
41 Macquarie Diary, 28 December 1819.
42 Henry Grey Bennet, *Letter to Viscount Sidmouth*, J. Ridgway, 1819, p. 71.
43 Macquarie to Earl Bathurst, 22 February 1820, Watson (ed.), *Historical Records of Australia, Series I, Volume X*, pp. 235–236.
44 *Ibid*, p. 237.
45 *Ibid*, p. 239.
46 Macquarie had threatened to resign once and this was the second time he was submitting a formal resignation.
47 Macquarie to Earl Bathurst, 29 February 1820, Watson (ed.), *Historical Records of Australia, Series I, Volume X*, pp. 291–292.
48 Macquarie Diary, 26 October 1820.
49 Joseph Wild, sentenced on 21 August 1793 in Chester for burglary, together with his brother, George; died 1847.
50 Macquarie Diary, 27 October 1820.
51 Frederick Goulburn (1788–1837).
52 On 25 October 1821, aboard the *Duchess of York*.
53 In July 1823, the British parliament passed the Act 'for the Better Administration of Justice in New South Wales and Van Diemen's Land'.
54 Macquarie Diary, 7 February 1821.
55 *Ibid*, 8 February 1821.
56 Laurence Hynes Halloran (1765–1831).
57 Macquarie to Earl Bathurst, 20 March 1821, Watson (ed.), *Historical Records of Australia, Series I, Volume X*, p. 478.
58 A.G. Austin, 'Halloran, Laurence Hynes (1765–1831)', *Australian Dictionary of Biography*, National Centre of Biography, Australian National University, adb.anu.edu.au, published first in hard copy 1966.
59 Theodore Bryant Bartley (1803-1878).
60 *Ibid*, 25 May 1821.
61 *Ibid*, 25 July 1821.
62 Thomas Reddall (1780-1838).
63 Macquarie, Lachlan. *Journal of a Voyage and Tour of Inspection from Port Jackson to the Settlements of Port Macquarie, and Newcastle. 1 November 1821 – 21 November 1821*. Original held in the Mitchell Library, Sydney, ML Ref: A785 pp.1–54. [Microfilm Reel CY303 Frames #434–#488], 6 November 1821.
64 Macquarie to Earl Bathurst, 27 July 1822, Watson (ed.), *Historical Records of Australia, Series I, Volume X*, p. 675.
65 Macquarie to Mrs Morley, 5 May 1803, Letterbooks, A792, pp. 31-3, Mitchell Library.
66 'His Excellency's Address', *Sydney Gazette and New South Wales Advertiser*, 1 December 1821, p. 2.
67 *Ibid*.
68 *Ibid*.

Chapter 30

1   Elizabeth Macquarie to friends, 3 November 1825, from McGarvie, Rev. J., *Memorandum Book, 1829 – 1832*. Held in the Mitchell Library, Sydney. C254: "Narrative of the Last Days of General Macquarie, by Mrs Macquarie.".

2   HMS *Surry* (1811) Also known as *Surrey*.

3   Macquarie, Lachlan. *Journal of a Voyage to England, 1822* [12 February 1822 – 13 July 1822]. Original held in Mitchell Library, Sydney. ML Ref: A775 1-24 ff. [CY Reel 302 Frames #3-27], 15 February 1822.

4   Macquarie, *Diary 11 March 1821 – 12 February 1822,* Original held in Mitchell Library, Sydney. ML Ref: A774 pp.246-248 [CY Reel 301: Frames 662-664], 20 December 1821.

5   *Ibid*, 23 December 1821.

6   In the possession of the Mitchell Library.

7   Gilbert Elliot-Murray-Kynynmound, 1st Earl of Minto, PC, FRSE (23 April 1751 – 21 June 1814).

8   Macquarie Diary, 15 January 1822.

9   'Classified Advertising', *Sydney Gazette and New South Wales Advertiser,* 4 Jan 1822, p. 1.

10   *Sydney Gazette and New South Wales Advertiser,* 15 February 1822, p. 2.

11   *Ibid.*

12   Macquarie Diary, 15 February 1822.

13   James Wait [Also Waite Or White] (c.1798-1822).

14   Macquarie Diary, 5 July 1822.

15   Macquarie Diary, 6 July 1822.

16   Macquarie to Earl Bathurst, 27 July 1822, Watson (ed.), *Historical Records of Australia, Series I, Volume X*, pp. 671–672.

17   *Ibid*, p. 677.

18   *Ibid*, p. 683.

19   Earl Bathurst to Macquarie, 10 September 1822, Watson (ed.), *Historical Records of Australia, Series I, Volume X*, p. 793.

20   Robert Stewart, Viscount Castlereagh, nndb.com.

21   Macquarie Journal, 2 December 1822.

22   *Ibid*, 4 December 1822.

23   *Ibid*, 12 December 1822.

24   *Ibid*, 1 January 1823.

25   *Ibid*, 11 January 1823.

26   *Ibid*, 12 January 1823.

27   *Ibid*, 25 January 1823.

28   *Ibid*, 15 March 1823.

29   The observatory was closed in 1847. The building became dilapidated and was demolished in 1876.

30   John Dunmore Lang, born 25 August 1799; died 8 August 1878.

31   John Dunmore Lang, *Poems: Sacred and Secular,* Robert Mackay, 1873, pp. 214–215.
The poem is said to have been written by Macquarie's poet laureate Michael Robinson.

32   Macquarie Journal, 28 March 1823.

33   *Ibid*, 29 March 1823.

34   *Ibid*, 4-5 May 1823.

35   *Ibid*, 2 July 1823.

36   *Ibid*, 14 July 1823.

37   W. C. Wentworth, Statistical Account of New South Wales, Geo. B. Whittaker, 1824, pp. 388-9.

38   Elizabeth Macquarie to friends, 3 November 1825.

39   *Ibid.*

40   *Ibid.*

41   Lachlan Macquarie, *Diary of Visit to London, 1824,* [15 April 1824 - 10 June 1824]
     Original held in Mitchell Library, Sydney, ML Ref: A776-2 1-9 ff. [CY Reel 302
     Frames #293-317], 15 May 1824.

42   Elizabeth Macquarie to friends, 3 November 1825.

43   Macquarie Diary, 23 April 1824.

44   *Ibid,* 24 April 1824.

45   Elizabeth Macquarie to friends, 3 November 1825.

46   Macquarie Diary, 6 May 1824.

47   *Ibid,* 25 May 1824.

48   *Ibid,* 15 May 1824.

49   *Ibid,* 9 June 1824.

50   *Ibid,* 11 June 1824.

51   Elizabeth Macquarie to friends, 3 November 1825.

52   *Ibid.*

53   *Ibid.*

54   *Ibid.*

55   *Ibid.*

56   'The Late Governor Macquarie', *Sydney Gazette and New South Wales Advertiser,*
     18 November 1824, p. 2.

57   Proverbs 22:29 King James Bible.

58   'The Late Governor Macquarie', *Sydney Gazette and New South Wales Advertiser,*
     18 November 1824, p. 2.

59   M.H. Ellis, *Lachlan Macquarie; his life, adventures, and times,* Angus & Robertson, 1952, p. 520.

60   Robin Walsh, 'Jarvis, George (1790–1825)', *Australian Dictionary of Biography,* National
     Centre of Biography, Australian National University, adb.anu.edu.au, published first in
     hard copy 2005.

61   Her headstone says she died on 17 March 1835, but this is incorrect.

62   Curious Case - Reduction of a Will'. *Caledonian Mercury* (Edinburgh, Scotland), Monday,
     10 November 1851; Issue 20135.

63   'Bitter Legacy – The Dispute Over the Macquarie Estate', paulineconolly.com.

64   His tomb incorrectly states he was 32.

Index

The abbreviation LM refers to
Lachlan Macquarie.
Many subentries are ordered
chronologically, not alphabetically.
Names beginning with Mac and Mc
are alphabetised as though all begin
with Mac.